Lecture Notes in Computer Science 9169

Commenced Publication in 1973
Founding and Former Series Editors:
Gerhard Goos, Juris Hartmanis, and Jan van Leeuwen

More information about this series at http://www.springer.com/series/7409

Masaaki Kurosu (Ed.)

Human-Computer Interaction

Design and Evaluation

17th International Conference,
HCI International 2015
Los Angeles, CA, USA, August 2–7, 2015
Proceedings, Part I

 Springer

Editor
Masaaki Kurosu
The Open University of Japan
Chiba-shi, Chiba
Japan

ISSN 0302-9743   ISSN 1611-3349 (electronic)
Lecture Notes in Computer Science
ISBN 978-3-319-20900-5   ISBN 978-3-319-20901-2 (eBook)
DOI 10.1007/978-3-319-20901-2

Library of Congress Control Number: 2015942556

LNCS Sublibrary: SL3 – Information Systems and Applications, incl. Internet/Web, and HCI

Springer Cham Heidelberg New York Dordrecht London

Printed on acid-free paper

Springer International Publishing AG Switzerland is part of Springer Science+Business Media
(www.springer.com)

Foreword

The 17th International Conference on Human-Computer Interaction, HCI International 2015, was held in Los Angeles, CA, USA, during 2–7 August 2015. The event incorporated the 15 conferences/thematic areas listed on the following page.

A total of 4843 individuals from academia, research institutes, industry, and governmental agencies from 73 countries submitted contributions, and 1462 papers and 246 posters have been included in the proceedings. These papers address the latest research and development efforts and highlight the human aspects of design and use of computing systems. The papers thoroughly cover the entire field of Human-Computer Interaction, addressing major advances in knowledge and effective use of computers in a variety of application areas. The volumes constituting the full 28-volume set of the conference proceedings are listed on pages VII and VIII.

I would like to thank the Program Board Chairs and the members of the Program Boards of all thematic areas and affiliated conferences for their contribution to the highest scientific quality and the overall success of the HCI International 2015 conference.

This conference could not have been possible without the continuous and unwavering support and advice of the founder, Conference General Chair Emeritus and Conference Scientific Advisor, Prof. Gavriel Salvendy. For their outstanding efforts, I would like to express my appreciation to the Communications Chair and Editor of HCI International News, Dr. Abbas Moallem, and the Student Volunteer Chair, Prof. Kim-Phuong L. Vu. Finally, for their dedicated contribution towards the smooth organization of HCI International 2015, I would like to express my gratitude to Maria Pitsoulaki and George Paparoulis, General Chair Assistants.

May 2015

Constantine Stephanidis
General Chair, HCI International 2015

HCI International 2015 Thematic Areas and Affiliated Conferences

Thematic areas:

- Human-Computer Interaction (HCI 2015)
- Human Interface and the Management of Information (HIMI 2015)

Affiliated conferences:

- 12th International Conference on Engineering Psychology and Cognitive Ergonomics (EPCE 2015)
- 9th International Conference on Universal Access in Human-Computer Interaction (UAHCI 2015)
- 7th International Conference on Virtual, Augmented and Mixed Reality (VAMR 2015)
- 7th International Conference on Cross-Cultural Design (CCD 2015)
- 7th International Conference on Social Computing and Social Media (SCSM 2015)
- 9th International Conference on Augmented Cognition (AC 2015)
- 6th International Conference on Digital Human Modeling and Applications in Health, Safety, Ergonomics and Risk Management (DHM 2015)
- 4th International Conference on Design, User Experience and Usability (DUXU 2015)
- 3rd International Conference on Distributed, Ambient and Pervasive Interactions (DAPI 2015)
- 3rd International Conference on Human Aspects of Information Security, Privacy and Trust (HAS 2015)
- 2nd International Conference on HCI in Business (HCIB 2015)
- 2nd International Conference on Learning and Collaboration Technologies (LCT 2015)
- 1st International Conference on Human Aspects of IT for the Aged Population (ITAP 2015)

Conference Proceedings Volumes Full List

1. LNCS 9169, Human-Computer Interaction: Design and Evaluation (Part I), edited by Masaaki Kurosu
2. LNCS 9170, Human-Computer Interaction: Interaction Technologies (Part II), edited by Masaaki Kurosu
3. LNCS 9171, Human-Computer Interaction: Users and Contexts (Part III), edited by Masaaki Kurosu
4. LNCS 9172, Human Interface and the Management of Information: Information and Knowledge Design (Part I), edited by Sakae Yamamoto
5. LNCS 9173, Human Interface and the Management of Information: Information and Knowledge in Context (Part II), edited by Sakae Yamamoto
6. LNAI 9174, Engineering Psychology and Cognitive Ergonomics, edited by Don Harris
7. LNCS 9175, Universal Access in Human-Computer Interaction: Access to Today's Technologies (Part I), edited by Margherita Antona and Constantine Stephanidis
8. LNCS 9176, Universal Access in Human-Computer Interaction: Access to Interaction (Part II), edited by Margherita Antona and Constantine Stephanidis
9. LNCS 9177, Universal Access in Human-Computer Interaction: Access to Learning, Health and Well-Being (Part III), edited by Margherita Antona and Constantine Stephanidis
10. LNCS 9178, Universal Access in Human-Computer Interaction: Access to the Human Environment and Culture (Part IV), edited by Margherita Antona and Constantine Stephanidis
11. LNCS 9179, Virtual, Augmented and Mixed Reality, edited by Randall Shumaker and Stephanie Lackey
12. LNCS 9180, Cross-Cultural Design: Methods, Practice and Impact (Part I), edited by P.L. Patrick Rau
13. LNCS 9181, Cross-Cultural Design: Applications in Mobile Interaction, Education, Health, Transport and Cultural Heritage (Part II), edited by P.L. Patrick Rau
14. LNCS 9182, Social Computing and Social Media, edited by Gabriele Meiselwitz
15. LNAI 9183, Foundations of Augmented Cognition, edited by Dylan D. Schmorrow and Cali M. Fidopiastis
16. LNCS 9184, Digital Human Modeling and Applications in Health, Safety, Ergonomics and Risk Management: Human Modeling (Part I), edited by Vincent G. Duffy
17. LNCS 9185, Digital Human Modeling and Applications in Health, Safety, Ergonomics and Risk Management: Ergonomics and Health (Part II), edited by Vincent G. Duffy
18. LNCS 9186, Design, User Experience, and Usability: Design Discourse (Part I), edited by Aaron Marcus
19. LNCS 9187, Design, User Experience, and Usability: Users and Interactions (Part II), edited by Aaron Marcus
20. LNCS 9188, Design, User Experience, and Usability: Interactive Experience Design (Part III), edited by Aaron Marcus

Human-Computer Interaction

Program Board Chair: Masaaki Kurosu, Japan

- Jose Abdelnour-Nocera, UK
- Sebastiano Bagnara, Italy
- Simone Barbosa, Brazil
- Kaveh Bazargan, Iran
- Thomas Berns, Sweden
- Adriana Betiol, Brazil
- Simone Borsci, UK
- Apala Lahiri Chavan, India
- Sherry Chen, Taiwan
- Kevin Clark, USA
- Torkil Clemmensen, Denmark
- Michael Craven, UK
- Henry Duh, Australia
- Achim Ebert, Germany
- Xiaowen Fang, USA
- Stefano Federici, Italy
- Sheue-Ling Hwang, Taiwan
- Wonil Hwang, Korea
- Yong Gu Ji, Korea
- Esther Jun Kim, USA
- Mitsuhiko Karashima, Japan
- Heidi Krömker, Germany
- Cecília Sík Lányi, Hungary
- Glyn Lawson, UK
- Cristiano Maciel, Brazil
- Chang S. Nam, USA
- Naoko Okuizumi, Japan
- Philippe Palanque, France
- Alberto Raposo, Brazil
- Ling Rothrock, USA
- Eunice Sari, Indonesia
- Dominique Scapin, France
- Milene Selbach Silveira, Brazil
- Guangfeng Song, USA
- Hiroshi Ujita, Japan
- Anna Wichansky, USA
- Chui Yin Wong, Malaysia
- Toshiki Yamaoka, Japan
- Kazuhiko Yamazaki, Japan
- Alvin W. Yeo, Malaysia

The full list with the Program Board Chairs and the members of the Program Boards of all thematic areas and affiliated conferences is available online at:

http://www.hci.international/2015/

HCI International 2016

The 18th International Conference on Human-Computer Interaction, HCI International 2016, will be held jointly with the affiliated conferences in Toronto, Canada, at the Westin Harbour Castle Hotel, 17–22 July 2016. It will cover a broad spectrum of themes related to Human-Computer Interaction, including theoretical issues, methods, tools, processes, and case studies in HCI design, as well as novel interaction techniques, interfaces, and applications. The proceedings will be published by Springer. More information will be available on the conference website: http://2016.hci.international/.

General Chair
Prof. Constantine Stephanidis
University of Crete and ICS-FORTH
Heraklion, Crete, Greece
Email: general_chair@hcii2016.org

http://2016.hci.international/

Contents – Part I

HCI Design and Evaluation Methods and Tools

Interaction Design

Contents – Part II

Touch-Based and Haptic Interaction

Natural User Interfaces

Adaptive and Personalized Interfaces

Contents – Part III

HCI in Business, Industry and Innovation

Societal and Cultural Impact of Technology

User Studies

HCI Theory and Practice

An Activity Theory Approach to Intuitiveness: From Artefact to Process

Sturla Bakke[✉]

Department of Technology, Westerdals - Oslo School of Arts,
Communication and Technology, Oslo, Norway
sb@westerdals.no

Abstract. Intuition is a widely employed term when describing or evaluating user interfaces in an HCI context. It is used in by most people in their daily life, regardless of technology use; it is applied by users in various socio-technical contexts; it is even utilized by developers themselves. While Susanne Bødker and others brought activity theory into the HCI discourse, in much of the literature, *intuition* has largely remained within the cognitive science discourse. In an activity theoretical approach, this paper attempts to connect intuitiveness to activity and pointing out the changing perception of the concept of intuitiveness in relation to skill levels; changing from being connected primarily to artifacts at an unskilled level, to being linked exclusively to tasks and processes at expert level.

Keywords: Intuitive use · User interfaces · Activity theory · Experience

1 Introduction

This paper discusses an activity theoretical approach to intuitive use in user interfaces, an approach based on a human activity perspective rather than the cognitive science perspective we have seen in much of the previous literature within the HCI discourse [1–3]. The paper contributes to the field by specifically link this much-utilized term to *human practice*, placing it within the current activity theoretical HCI–discourse [4–12].

The paper presents and discusses some of the related literature, starting with a brief introduction to activity theory, which in its asymmetry focuses on the range of human activities in a human-computer relationship rather than the computer artefact, followed by a description of flow and breakdowns as aspects of intuitiveness. Based on the literature the paper discusses how an absence of breakdowns, and a maintained sense of flow are both connected to human activity, and as such inflicts upon the user's perceived intuitiveness in an activity theoretical approach.

Among non-HCI practitioners, there exists a kind of vague understanding of the concept of intuitiveness [13], and what it means when talking about people's intuitive understanding of, and approach to technology, i.e. human-computer interactivity through a user interface. This term is, according to the literature, one of the most common ones when describing user interfaces, especially among non-practitioners and otherwise colloquially [3, 13]. This is not so strange in times where human agency is increasingly dependent on being able to interact with computers through various types of user interfaces.

© Springer International Publishing Switzerland 2015
M. Kurosu (Ed.): Human-Computer Interaction, Part I, HCII 2015, LNCS 9169, pp. 3–13, 2015.
DOI: 10.1007/978-3-319-20901-2_1

2 Literature

First a brief introduction to the parts of activity theory relevant to this paper will be presented, followed by a description of the relationship between flow and intuitiveness in a user-interface context.

2.1 Activity Theory

Activity theory «focuses on practice, which obviates the need to distinguish 'applied' from 'pure' science—understanding everyday practice in the real world is the very objective of scientific practice. [...] The object of activity theory is to understand the unity of consciousness and activity» [12].

Activity-theoretical HCI, mainly conceptualized by Bødker [8], Kuutti [10], Bannon [4], Grudin [14], Kaptelinin [15] and Nardi [12], and others, distances itself from the traditional cognitive science perspective on HCI. Instead, it is focusing on an analysis (and design) in a specific work/activity practice in a multi-user setting. This also includes user participation in the development process, and addresses *actual use* as a part of the design and development phase, in addition to seeing the importance of an interface artefact as a mediator for human action.

In i.e. Kuutti [10] and Engeström [16] we see that human activity, being contextual or social or both, has a certain direction and is mediated by artefacts, or tools. E.g. Kaptelinin and Nardi describe these artefacts as mediated affordances [17] (Fig. 1).

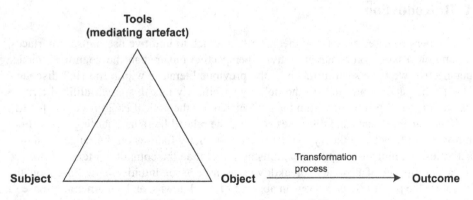

Fig. 1. The structure of activity [10]

Kuuti focuses on the structure of activity. "An activity is a form of doing directed to an object, and activities are distinguished from each other according to their objects. Transforming the object into an outcome motivates the existence of an activity. An object can be a material thing, but it can also be less tangible" [10]. Engeström [18] states that the unit of analysis when studying human-mediated activity, is the community of actors/subjects who shares the goal of the activity.

These are key elements in the discussion about the activity theoretical structure, since the theory's ability to absorb various aspects or strengthening of human agency is formalized through this conceptual framework that must be made strong enough to encompass both humans and technology within the same conceptual models [15].

Also, Kaptelinin et al. argues that activity theory in itself is "built upon the concept of mediation", which makes it particularly suitable for HCI "exploration" [19], meaning it is especially suitable as an analytical tool in a human-artefact interaction context since this relation is, by definition, always mediated.

Activity theory «focuses on practice, which obviates the need to distinguish 'applied' from 'pure' science—understanding everyday practice in the real world is the very objective of scientific practice. [...] The object of activity theory is to understand the unity of consciousness and activity» [12].

The perspective in this paper is that the character of abstraction through mediation should provide for an intuitive understanding of the possible features of activity.

Contradictions. Human activities are part in an overall interacting context, where related activities might change the conditions in such a way that users, during a working process, may experience problems that may cause downtime or a stop in ongoing activities. A case of 'misaligned' activities resembles what are labeled as *contradictions* within Activity Theory, i.e. events that manifest themselves as complications, mismatches, breakdowns, and so on. Misalignment could be represented by e.g. not sufficiently trained users or inadequate design of interfaces that fail to support the processes of skilled workers intuitive use. Activity Theory regards contradictions as options for learning [20].

2.2 Intuitiveness and Flow

Intuitive is an often used term when describing human-technology relations; be it either regular software, information systems, web-based systems that have some socio-technological connection or relevance or tangible user interfaces. There are situations in daily life, where we often employ this term as 'quick and easy understanding', or 'immediate apprehension or cognition'. In everyday life, then, *intuition* is encompassed by the sense of 'just knowing' without a rationale or previous experience, like some non-rational gut feeling; something along the lines of the definition found in i.e. Merriam-Webster,[1] where the meaning of the term intuition is described as:

- «a natural ability or power that makes it possible to know something without any proof or evidence
- a feeling that guides a person to act a certain way without fully understanding why
- something that is known or understood without proof or evidence»

which may be perceived as somewhat contradictory of what researchers in the field possibly would recognize as intuitive. This is not necessarily perceived as a problem

---

[1] http://www.merriam-webster.com/dictionary/intuition. Accessed October 17, 2014.

among ordinary people in their daily life; it might, however, be regarded as rather imprecise for the practitioners within the HCI community.

The scientific literature on intuitiveness is somewhat limited within the HCI discourse, not unlikely because of its vagueness and rather loose definition [13, 21].

Raskin [3] explains the term "intuitive interface" as normal human "intuition" would be enough to use a technological appliance. He claims that interfaces being perceived as intuitive will depend on whether a person recognizes the user interface elements as familiar. He does, however, state that it is the experience that leads to something being recognized as an opportunity to act, which is the basis for an intuitive approach to activity [3]. This is also concurred in more recent research, by e.g. Blackler et al., who, in focusing on intuitive use, state that "using familiar labels and icons and possibly positions for buttons helps people to use a product quickly and intuitively the first time they encounter it" [22].

In much of the literature that do describe intuitive interfaces, the term is, to a great extent, linked to people's cognitive understanding in a setting of human-technology relations. [1, 23–27]. Also, In 'Subconscious and Conscious Systems of Cognition', Norman goes further and relates an intuitive approach to problem-solving to the subconscious [28].

In addition, much of the literature that discusses the term, do so from an approach comprising physicality, embodiment or tangible user interfaces, while some researchers claim that intuition is a matter of experience [3, 29–31].

Leaning on Raskin's and Blackler's notion of sameness and familiarity, which are grounded on experience, we turn to Dreyfus and Dreyfus' Skill Acquisition framework. According to Dreyfus and Dreyfus, the *novice* user is identified by a strict following of rules and regulations, with a rather rudimentary situational perception, and without the capability to relate to situational adjustments. The *competent* user is able to handle tension and complexity, and is capable of evaluating actions as part of or appropriate within a larger context while adhering to a set of standards or routines regarding processes. The *expert* practitioner, no longer relies on regulations and guidelines, and maintains an intuitive approach to work processes based on experience and tacit knowledge, only employing an analytic approach in extraordinary or problematic situations.

Dreyfus and Dreyfus' framework was developed as an argumentative element in the discussions of the limits of artificial intelligence. It was not constructed as a general learning model as such. However, since this framework was based on "the dynamic processes of human skill acquisition" [30], we recognize its benefits to our argument of activity-based comprehension of what constitutes intuitive use of user interface elements. Therefore, we argue that their skill development matrix, in itself, can be made to use in describing the various degrees of intuitive use of user interfaces.

Blackler et al. [29] argue that an understanding of technology must also include recognition of similar technology. They claim that the knowledge and experience that a person acquires through using a different technology could be the basis for intuitive interaction in a similar context. They claim that recollection or recognition takes priority over expertise, i.e. an ordinary user who remembers a similar task will be capable of working in a way that resembles intuitive task solution in the similar way as an expert user would. Their three principles of familiarity that developers can rely on the work of creating user-interface that are intuitive to use:

1. Use familiar symbols/words in expected positions for functions that are the same or similar features that the users already know.
2. Metaphors for something that is already known should be linked to new functionality in the process of creating familiarity with something that is unknown.
3. Knowledge and metaphorical content and meaning should be coherent in all parts of an interface.

This is described by Israel et al. [21], who also emphasize mental efficiency by leaning on Mohs' discussion of mental focus on problem solving. Here we can see how attention shifts from the 'interface' by non-intuitive use to be 'task oriented' by intuitive use (Mohs in [21]).

Naumann et al. also focus on intuitive use rather than the UIs themselves should be intuitive [32]. In addition to discussing whether, or possibly how, intuitive use relates to the visual part of the user interface design, which is outside the scope of this paper, also intuitive use that is contextually related to tangible user interfaces is discussed.

Flow. In order to say something about breakdowns, or rather the importance of the *absence* of breakdowns, we ought first, perhaps, to say something about the concept of flow. According to Mihaly Csikszentmihalyi, flow is to be in a state of focused motivation, by being completely focused on a task in such a way that the ability and the task at hand is completely aligned, and that the work process feels natural and unobstructed, not unlike what we might consider as the intuitive acts of skilled workers. According Csikszentmihalyi, a user will, through a state of flow, be able to experience the absence of concern for losing the control or overview of how a task should be solved [33].

Csikszentmihalyi et al. [34] state that flow theory propose three conditions for achieving a state of flow:

- One must engage in an activity contains a *clear set of goals*, that adds direction and purpose for the activity.
- There must be a good balance between perceived challenges and perceived skill.
- Flow is dependent on clear and immediate feedback in order for the individual to adjust work processes to maintain the sense of flow.

Following the second condition, we argue that such a state of flow is also often associated with the joy of mastery. Csikszentmihalyi [34] states:

«As people master challenges in an activity, they develop greater levels of skill, and the activity ceases to be as involving as before. In order to continue experiencing flow, they must identify and engage progressively more complex challenges. [...] A flow activity not only provides a set of challenges or opportunities for action but it typically also provides a system of graded challenges, able to accommodate a person's continued and deepening enjoyment as skills grow.»

3   Discussion

In this section, a discussion of how contradictions, and a maintained sense of flow are related to human activity, and as such inflicts upon the user's perceived intuitiveness in an activity theoretical approach.

Intuition based on experience and skills resembles what Csikszentmihalyi describes as a state of flow. Since the experience of flow occurs when something perceived as possible actions corresponds with the person's perception of abilities, we might say that the senses of both intuition and flow stem from the perception of knowledge and experiences.

According to Csikszentmihalyi, a user will, through a state of flow be able to experience the absence of concern for losing control or overview of a task [33]. By linking this to tasks solved via user interface, we will be able to get a perception that it is through the prerequisites for a state of flow that we might see intuitive actions undertaken by a skilled user via a screen based interface tool.

By grounding the sense of experience on recollection, we might regard experience as a partly cognitive quality. However, Dreyfus and Dreyfus [30] claim that intuition comes from «[...]deep situational involvement and recognition of similarity» and not «wild guessing nor supernatural inspiration...]». Recognition of similarity requires previously acquired skills, to such an extent that it coincides with the descriptions of a proficient or, preferably, an expert user.

The choice of including Dreyfus and Dreyfus is due to their Skill Acquisition framework, revealing the attributes of the five Skill levels, from 'novice' to 'expertise' [30]. In Table 1, we see the possible requirements of a user-interface that is to support work processes initiated by users in a similar setting, but on different skill levels.

Table 1. The five stages of skill acquisition framework by Dreyfus and Dreyfus [30].

Skill level	Components	Perspective	Decision	Commitment
1. Novice	Context-free	None	Analytical	Detached
2. Advanced beginner	Context-free and situational	None	Analytical	Detached
3. Competent	Context-free and situational	Chosen	Analytical	Detached under-standing and deciding. Involved in outcome
4. Proficient	Context-free and situational	Experienced	Analytical	Involved under-standing. Detached deciding
5. Expert	Context-free and situational	Experienced	Intuitive	Involved

In this table 'totally dependent' is used to explain that users on this level are dependent, as in 'can not do without', on affordances in the user-interface. A user on this level would, probably, encounter more contradictions than a more experienced one. 'Occasionally' is employed to explain that users on this level have reached a certain degree of expertise and competence to a level at which they only occasionally will need the help of a mediated affordance in the user-interface, and by that experience less contradictions and possibly a state of flow and a sense of intuitiveness in working through the interface.

By adding a column for the varying need of mediated affordances to Dreyfus and Dreyfus' matrix of skill levels [30], Table 2 shows how a novice user must rely almost solely on mediated affordances provided by the user-interface. Observing the expert- or super-users revealed that they just occasionally lean on affordances in the user-interface in order to maintain a fluent task-flow. Also, the notion of a balancing 'agent' is needed when looking at the often experienced tension between interface design and the 'real world' work tasks in user-interface design as this is formulated by e.g. Gaver [35]. On those grounds it is possible to discuss user-interface requirements meeting the users' skill levels, recognizing the need for a collection of mediated affordances which support the need for work task support through the mediated affordances in the interface, while supporting the need for work task efficiency that will occur when users move downwards the skill level matrix by Dreyfus and Dreyfus.

Table 2. The UI-mediated affordances linked to the five stages of skill acquisition framework by Dreyfus and Dreyfus.

Human activity			Artefact
Skill level	Decision	Commitment	Relying on UI affordances
1. Novice	Analytical	Detached	Totally dependent
2. Advanced beginner	Analytical	Detached	Dependent
3. Competent	Analytical	Detached under-standing and deciding. Involved in outcome	Some to occasionally
4. Proficient	Analytical	Involved under-standing. Detached deciding	Occasionally
5. Expert	Intuitive	Involved	Occasionally to never

A central aspect of user interface elements is *use*. If an affordance represents an instruction for use, it must also be an element in facilitating intuitive use of user interfaces. This must be situated in a goal directed, human activity centered, vocational context. This is also supported by Bødker, who states, «The user interface cannot be seen independently of the goal or object, or of the other conditions of the use activity» [8]. This supports our argument of task or activity based understanding of what constitutes intuitive use of user interface elements.

A screen based user interface can, then, be regarded as a framework for mediation; a mediated whole, in which to situate functional elements and the adhering affordances that might linked to them in order to give the user the possibility, or sense, of immediate action pointing towards immediacy as the activity theoretical approach to intuitiveness in user interfaces.

Just as our world evolves, the terms we use to describe it, should evolve equally. In the networked and digital modernity that most of us live in, screen based user-interfaces are ubiquitous. By regarding all interfaces, analogue and physical as well as digital, as some kind of mediating tool through which people might perform work or communicative activity, interfaces have become a natural and obvious part of both our private and professional life.

Much research work within the HCI field in later years has placed the so-called second wave HCI firmly within the activity theoretical tradition, while the much-used term of intuition has somewhat remained within the cognitive science discourse.

This paper's perspective supports an understanding of intuitiveness in user interfaces should be derived from human activity – of what a user tries to achieve – referring to the 'object' dependency on the structure of an activity system [10, 18] (Kuutti 1991). We will never really gain general access to a user's or a group of users', mental model (s), but their tools and objectives are accessible. One person's cognitive abilities and processes might be different from another while the same two persons might perform the same task, and through the same UI. In addition, actions and goals could be quantifiable and as such offer possibilities for establishing a framework for measuring intuitiveness with some degree of precision (Fig. 2).

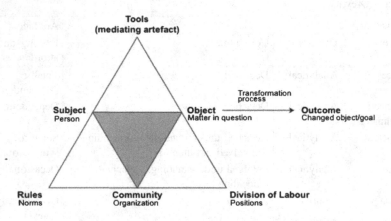

Fig. 2. The structure of an activity system. Based on Engeström [18]

We argue that intuitiveness is a contextual and dynamic term that should be related to human practice, and the additional aspects of the task at hand, i.e. 'Object' in the activity system, and the transformation process that follows it. Then, the character of intuitiveness would be a matter of evolvement, from affordance dependency to experiential tacit processing.

While opting to maintain the second argument in this paper, I also lean on e.g. Kaptelinin and Nardi [17], in grounding the argument that also screen representations like buttons, sliders, metaphors or abstractions of real world objects, represent affordances as well. A button affords clicking. A slider affords sliding. Even as elements on a screen, mediated as they are, they afford goal directed activity - actions. They are what Kaptelinin and Nardi, and others coin as mediated affordances [17]. This is also supported by McGrenere and Ho, who claim that a screen element that affords acting upon is "an affordance that is built into the software" [36]. This is in line with what Bærentsen and Trettvik [7] describe as "operational affordances", i.e. affordances that imply which activities can be undertaken with the tools that are available.

By obseiving intuitiveness through the lens of activity theory, that shifted the focus of analysis from technology to user activity, this will support our claim that intuitiveness, through skill acquisition, will change in nature, from being tied to the cognitive understanding of familiar artefacts among new and untrained workers to being connected to the action-oriented process and task flow among skilled workers and super-users. In short, we see this as the transition from the inexperienced user's dependence of *intuitiveness of things* to the skilled immediate action by experts; from familiarity with objects to familiarity with process.

4   Concluding Remarks

In this paper we have situated the attempts to understand intuitive use in user interfaces within an activity theoretical discourse, by linking the notion of familiarity and flow to:

1. *Experience* as previously acquired skills and habitual practice, and further describing the transition of the character of intuitiveness from, a beginners point of view, being dependent on
2. *Affordances,* as mediated artifacts in the user-interface that, in addition to facilitate actions, also clearly explain *how* the user-interface artifacts are to be used or operated, resembling the notion of a, per-element, user guide as an inherent or 'inscribed' part of the user-interface, and by acquiring skills and expertise through the gaining of expertise skill to familiarity of
3. *Activity,* as a transforming action, with the use of tools, towards an object to achieve a certain result, leaning on Kuuti who argues that "The tool is at the same time both enabling and limiting: it empowers the subject in the transformation process with the historically collected experience and skill 'crystalised' to it, but it also restricts the interaction to be from the perspective of that particular tool or instrument; other potential features of an object remain invisible to the subject..." following the Skill acquirement matrix by Dreyfus and Dreyfus.

4.1   Limitations

This conceptual paper is presented as a literary discussion and serves as a starting point for a wider discussion on activity theoretical intuitiveness in user interfaces, and how this might be interconnected to agile participatory design.

References

1. Card, S.K., Moran, T.P., Newell, A.: The Psychology of Human-Computer Interaction. Taylor & Francis, New York (1983)
2. Norman, D.A.: Perspectives on Cognitive Science. Ablex Publishing Corporation, New York (1981)
3. Raskin, J.: Viewpoint: intuitive equals familiar. Commun. ACM **37**(9), 17–18 (1994)

4. Bannon, L.: From human factors to human actors: the role of psychology and human computer interaction studies in system design. In: Greenbaum, J., Kyng, M. (eds.) Design at Work: Cooperative Design of Computer Systems. Lawrence Erlbaum, Hillsdale (1991)
5. Bardram, J.E.: Plans as situated action: an activity theory approach to workflow systems. In: Proceedings of the Fifth European Conference on Computer Supported Cooperative Work. Springer, The Netherlands (1997)
6. Bertelsen, O.W., Bødker, S.: Activity theory. In: Carroll, J.M. (ed.) HCI Models Theories, and Frameworks: Toward a Multidisciplinary Science. Morgan Kaufmann, San Francisco (2003)
7. Bærentsen, K.B., Trettvik, J.: An activity theory approach to affordance. In: Proceedings of the Second Nordic Conference on Human-Computer Interaction, pp. 51–60. ACM (2002)
8. Bødker, S.: Through the Interface. CRC Press, Boca Raton (1990)
9. Kaptelinin, V., Nardi, B.: Activity theory in HCI: fundamentals and reflections. Synth. Lect. Hum. Centered Inform. 5(1), 1–105 (2012)
10. Kuutti, K.: Activity theory as a potential framework for human-computer interaction research. In: Nardi, B.A. (ed.) Context and Consciousness: Activity Theory and Human-Computer Interaction. MIT Press, Cambridge (1995)
11. Nardi, B.A.: Activity Theory and Human-Computer Interaction. MIT Press, Cambridge (1996)
12. Nardi, B.A.: Context and Consciousness: Activity Theory and Human-Computer Interaction. MIT Press, Cambridge (1996)
13. Naumann, A.B., Hurtienne, J., Israel, J.H., Mohs, C., Kindsmüller, M.C., Meyer, H.A., Hußlein, S.: Intuitive use of user interfaces: defining a vague concept. In: Harris, D. (ed.) HCII 2007 and EPCE 2007. LNCS (LNAI), vol. 4562, pp. 128–136. Springer, Heidelberg (2007)
14. Grudin, J.: Interactive systems: bridging the gaps between developers and users. Computer 24(4), 59–69 (1991)
15. Kaptelinin, V.: Computer-mediated activity: functional organs in social and developmental contexts. In: Nardi, B.A. (ed.) Context and Consciousness: Activity Theory and Human-Computer Interaction. MIT Press, Cambridge (1996)
16. Engeström, Y.: Expansive learning at work: toward an activity theoretical reconceptualization. J. Educ. Work 14(1), 133–156 (2001). doi:10.1080/1363908 0020028747
17. Kaptelinin, V., Nardi, B.: Affordances in HCI: toward a mediated action perspective. In: Proceedings of the 2012 ACM Annual Conference on Human Factors in Computing Systems, pp. 967–976. ACM (2012)
18. Engeström, Y.: Learning by Expanding: An Activity-Theoretical Approach to Developmental Research. Orienta-Konsultit, Helsinki (1987)
19. Kaptelinin, V., Kuutti, K., Bannon, L.: Activity theory: basic concepts and applications. In: Blumenthal, B., Gornostaev, J., Unger, C. (eds.) Human-Computer Interaction. LNCS, vol. 1015, pp. 189–201. Springer, Heidelberg (1995)
20. Kaptelinin, V., Nardi, B.A.: Acting with Technology: Activity Theory and Interaction Design. MIT Press, Cambridge (2009)
21. Israel, J.H., Hurtienne, J., Pohlmeyer, A.E., Mohs, C., Kindsmuller, M., Naumann, A.: On intuitive use, physicality and tangible user interfaces. Int. J. Arts Technol. 2(4), 348–366 (2009)
22. Blackler, A., Popovic, V., Mahar, D.: Investigating users' intuitive interaction with complex artefacts. Appl. Ergon. 41(1), 72–92 (2010)

23. Barnard, P.J.: Cognitive resources and the learning of human-computer dialogs. In: Carroll, J.M. (ed.) Interfacing Thought: Cognitive Aspects of Human-Computer Interaction, pp. 112–158. MIT Press, Cambridge (1987)
24. Green, T.R.G., Davies, S.P., Gilmore, D.J.: Delivering cognitive psychology to HCI: the problems of common language and of knowledge transfer. Interact. Comput. 8(1), 89–111 (1996)
25. Newell, A., Card, S.K.: The prospects for psychological science in human-computer interaction. Hum. Comput. Interact. 1(3), 209–242 (1985)
26. Norman, D.A.: Cognitive engineering–cognitive science. In: Caroll, J.M. (ed.) Interfacing Thought: Cognitive Aspects of Human-Computer Interaction, pp. 325–336. MIT Press, Cambridge (1987)
27. Payne, S.J.: Users' mental models: the very ideas. In: Caroll, J.M. (ed.) HCI Models, Theories, and Frameworks: Toward a Multidisciplinary Science, pp. 135–156. Morgan Kaufmann, Amsterdam (2003)
28. Norman, D.: The Design of Everyday Things. Revised and Expanded Edition. Basic Books, New York (2013)
29. Blackler, A.L., Popovic, V., Mahar, D.P.: Intuitive interaction applied to interface design. In: International Design Congress - IASDR 2005, Douliou, Taiwan (2005)
30. Dreyfus, H.L., Dreyfus, S.E.: Mind Over Machine: The Power of Human Intuition and Expertise in the Era of the Computer. Free Press, New York (1986)
31. Hurtienne, J., Weber, K., Blessing, L.: Prior experience and intuitive use: image schemas in user centred design. In: Langdon, P., Clarkson, J., Robinson, P. (eds.) Designing Inclusive Futures. Springer, London (2008)
32. Naumann, A.B., Pohlmeyer, A.E., Husslein, S., Kindsmüller, M.C., Mohs, C., Israel, J.H.: Design for intuitive use: beyond usability. In: CHI 2008 Extended Abstracts on Human Factors in Computing Systems, pp. 2375–2378. ACM, New York (2008)
33. Csikszentmihalyi, M.: Flow and the Foundations of Positive Psychology. Springer, Amsterdam (2014)
34. Csikszentmihalyi, M., Abuhamdeh, S., Nakamura, J.: Flow. In: Elliot, A.J., Dweck,C.S. (eds.) Handbook of Competence and Motivation, pp. 598–608. The Guildford Press (2005)
35. Gaver, W.W.: Technology affordances. In: Proceedings of the SIGCHI Conference on Human Factors in Computing Systems, pp. 79–84. ACM (1991)
36. McGrenere, J., Ho, W.: Affordances: clarifying and evolving a concept. In: Graphics Interface, pp. 179–186 (2000)

The Closer the Better: Effects of Developer-User Proximity for Mutual Learning

Sturla Bakke[1][(✉)] and Tone Bratteteig[2]

[1] Department of Technology, Westerdals - Oslo School of Arts,
Communication and Technology, Oslo, Norway
sb@westerdals.no
[2] Department of Informatics, University of Oslo, Oslo, Norway
tone@ifi.uio.no

Abstract. In this paper we report from a software development project, where much attention was given to the users – so much, in fact, that the developers moved in with them and stayed. Our aim has been to understand the effects of this level of proximity in the cooperation between developers and users. We discuss the impact on continuous knowledge exchange, organisational structure and accountability when the developers move in. How do the participants experience the mutual learning process? Based on the findings, we offer the two suggestions: (1) that the mutual learning necessary for establishing a common understanding of the character of a user-centred software system and its intuitive operation has a greater possibility of succeeding when developers and participating users are located in the immediate vicinity of each other, and (2) the impact on user interface design is visible through early user participation, leading to the sense of user interfaces facilitating an immediate user interaction.

Keywords: Participation · Reciprocal learning · Organisational structure

1 Introduction

"Mutual learning" is one of the fundamental characteristics of participatory design, denoting the ways in which developers and users work to share enough knowledge to understand each other's perspectives on the future IT system [1]. In this paper, we discuss the character of and prerequisites for mutual learning between users and developers in a software development project in a shipping company. We pay particular attention to the level and character of the physical proximity between users and developers, and analyse the project as it unfolded for patterns in organisational structure and looked at the formal and informal knowledge exchange of the mutual learning process.

We have followed the process of developing a new software system in a shipping company. The company is regarded as a world leading shipping company, and is among the biggest entities in the business of transportation and storing chemicals and bulk liquids. The company owns and operates a large fleet of chemical tankers, both globally and regionally.

© Springer International Publishing Switzerland 2015
M. Kurosu (Ed.): Human-Computer Interaction, Part I, HCII 2015, LNCS 9169, pp. 14–26, 2015.
DOI: 10.1007/978-3-319-20901-2_2

A secure software solution for stowage planning of chemical tankers is important for the business as well as for security. A secure system supporting these operations might ultimately prove to be the difference between life and death, since stowing, potential, hazardous liquids on board chemical tankers might be, well – hazardous. Getting it right is vital.

A motivation for creating the new system was that the old one had become slow and outdated. Also, they were about to replace their business system, which would render the stowage system they already had, obsolete. When they decided to build a new system, the question was whether they should change and adapt what they already had (an old, slow and a bit dull system) or buy something new. Searching for an off-the-shelf solution, they realized that there was no off-the-shelf software fitting their requirements. The field of stowage planning on chemical tankers is rather specialized, and instead of tailoring a SAP or ORACLE system, as one might have done when developing large information systems in recent times [2], the company chose to develop the new software from scratch.

The paper is based on fieldwork on the development process in the shipping company HQ. The new system turned out to be immediately useful for both expert and novice users, hence we wanted to understand what was done right in the development of this successful system:

- What did they do well – does the proximity of developers and users explain the success?
- How close together should developers and users co-locate in order to experience positive effects? Same address? Same floor? Sharing the coffee machine?
- Our main research question is: how can we understand the prerequisites for and mechanisms of co-location in a developer/user relationship with regards to organisational structure and mutual learning?

The paper is structured as follows. We start with a literature review of mutual learning and proximity from the participatory design (PD) and computer-supported cooperative work (CSCW) fields, respectively, followed by research method in Sect. 3. We discuss our empirical data with reference to specific themes in four sections: (1) goals and visions, (2) organisational and procedural structure, (3) proximity, and (4) Accountability. Section 5 concludes the paper.

2 Literature

In this paper we lean on the participatory design (PD) discourse that was pioneered in Europe, and especially in Scandinavia, in the 1970s social, political and, subsequently, technological transformation of work conditions [2–10]. The ambition of PD was increased influence and participation by the workers towards the computerisation of the workplace. PD emphasized that workers should have a voice and have a say [10] and a lot of methods has been developed to facilitate cooperation between developers and users in the design of a future system or artefact [1, 4, 7]. Mutual learning is a key aspect in PD: developers should learn from users about their needs and wishes for a new solution, but users should also learn about technical possibilities so that they can participate in generating design ideas. The point is that both developers and users learn from each other during the process, hence the discussion about the new solution develops as their knowledge develops. This also means that users need to be present all through the process since a static description of needs developed before the process cannot replace the learning users who get new ideas as their knowledge about the possibilities and problems grow [1].

Traditionally, mutual learning happens all through the development process, collapsing the traditional division between analysis and design [1]. Prototyping or concretizing bits of the solution acts as a way to learn more [3]. Analysis of the work practices looks for trouble and problems to be solved, hence contributes to both solving and setting the problem [11]. Using Schön [11–13] we see design as sequences of 'see-move-see': the designer 'sees': understands and evaluates the situation, s/he makes a 'move': selects a way to change it and tries it out, and 'sees' the new situation: evaluates if the move seemed productive towards the end (the final system/artefact) [5]. Users and developers both can participate in seeing and making moves, however, users normally participate more in making the choices to select from when making a move, and in the seeing parts (before and after the move) [5]. Mutual learning hence needs to support the 'see-move-see' sequences so that all participants get the possibility to participate and collaborate as much as possible.

Bratteteig et al. [1] discuss the preconditions for mutual learning to happen, emphasizing repeated contact over time. The activities scheduled to encourage learning from each other represent a shared experience for the participants and act to build a common ground for design. The learning that takes place ideally enables the participants to understand each other better – and build mutual trust [14]. A rule of thumb is that the participants should understand the logic of a design idea and they should recognize how the argumentation is grounded in the professional logic of the other participants [1, 3]. Throughout the mutual learning process, the participants develop their understanding of the use context and the technical possibilities enabling new ideas to emerge as the understanding deepens. When repeated contact over time with the same people is not possible, the mutual learning process has to be designed differently [1].

Repeated contact over time with the same people presupposes some organizational and physical conditions, e.g., a formal organization of the communication that enables the participants to take the time to collaborate and being located close enough for them to meet regularly. This is, however, not always possible [1], e.g., in cases of large, distributed organizations or in designing for the public.

Proximity is, of course, a topic in CSCW: much of CSCW is about supporting collaboration over distance. Thus, the characteristics of proximity are key to understand and develop such support. The focus in CSCW is mainly on the awareness of co-workers' activities as a prerequisite for one's own (part of the) work [15–20], and not on how proximity affects the mutual learning or trust.

3   Case and Research Approach

We have conducted a longitudinal study following the development and implementation phases, ranging from late 2011, until summer 2013. The empirical material consists of observations of the cooperative process, namely the communication between the development team, project owners and participant super-users, in addition to interviews with members of the developer team, management, and super-users.

During this period, we have followed the development of the system development process from the very beginning, following SCRUM teams, project management, and participant (super users) and regular users during this development period.

3.1 Data Collection

Data collection consists of semi-structured interviews with stakeholders, developers, project management, expert- and super-users:

- [MR] - Management representative. Member of the governing group for the ORCA development process. He was involved in the development of the previous system, as a project manager. He has participated as an advisor, and as a member of the steering committee. Interviewed two times; once, early in the project, and once after the system had been in use for about a year.
- [HD] - Head of the Development team, Programmer and SCRUM master in the project. Interviewed two times; once, early in the project, and once towards the end.
- [PO] – Project owner. Involved in the project from mid-2011. Project manager for the development of the new stowage system, ORCA. Interviewed three times; once, early in the project, once towards the end of the development period, and finally after the system had been in use for about a year.
- [dev] – Developer and co-located member of the SCRUM team. Interviewed once, mid-way through the development process.
- [SU] - Super-User, who acted as a premise provider in terms of which functionality that should be included in the software, and as a participating user representative. He was what we in actor-network theory would have called an Obligatory Passage Point; the one person that all involved participants had to go to with wishes, ideas and suggestions for how the new software should function and be operated. Educated as Captain; 25 years of naval experience, 11 of them as Chief Officer or Captain at Odfjell Tankers. The super-user has worked as an operator and having had the role as super-user at the company headquarters for the last 12 years. Interviewed three times; once, early in the project, once towards the end of the development period, and finally after the system had been in use for about a year.

The interviews lasted about 45–90 min. Observation sessions of regular users lasted for approx. 2–3 h. This involved observing the employee's work tasks. Un-targeted observations have been continuous while the researcher has been present in the field.

3.2 Case Overview

The company decided early in 2011 to develop a new ICT platform in order to provide one common software solution to support Odfjell's commercial shipping activities onshore as well as on board the vessels. The new stowage software, named ORCA (Odfjell Resource Control Application), which is described in this paper, is part of that platform. The new system was meant to support a new workflow, allowing the operator on land and the shipboard officer to work on the same stowage plan with the same software. This development period lasted from late 2011 to early 2013. From the very beginning, the company vision was to facilitate a high degree of user-centeredness, and the key personnel within the company discussed what would be the most important requirements for the new software they were about to develop, such as support for 'intuitive' workflow for skilled users, and allowing operators on land and officers at sea to work on the same stowage plan with the same software.

A main characteristic of the software development process is that the software developers and the users moved in and stayed together from the conceptual model phase until the end of the implementation period almost two years later. Bringing users and developers together is not a new or revolutionizing move within software engineering or development processes related to technical innovation. There are, however, aspects of this kind of co-location, related to the level of the proximity and cooperation that are interesting to discuss. The replaced system was developed in a traditional user-developer setting, very different from the dynamics experienced by the co-location of the developer team in this project.

In the following, we discuss our findings thematically, with emphasis on *goals and visions, organisational and procedural structure, proximity,* and *accountability.*

4   Findings and Discussion

4.1   Theme 1: Common Goals and Visions

In this project, the primary goal focused on developing what they called «a user's system», meaning that their main focus was a heightened user-experience. The users were included from the very beginning through both formal and informal communication. A group of people was formally picked to contribute to the development, but the initial brainstorming session had the rather informal character of a mountain leisure trip. Other techniques for collaboration included mail, from officers at sea, and mail correspondence between regular users and the super-user, and face-to-face meetings between super-user and the developer team about functionality and interface issues.

There had been some signs of discontent with the previous system, and it was important for the company that input from the users were taken care of in a different manner than their development project of the previous stowage software. During the last eleven years they have based their daily stowage operations on one specific application: Othello, that, although sophisticated, contained features that were rarely used, and in principle just made it more complex and slow to work with. The character of co-location experienced in the ORCA project is contrasted with the development of the Othello system, in which the software company did not co-locate. The Othello Project met a great deal of resistance, with heated discussions among the group of people involved in the development of the software, and the cargo brokers that were going to use it. During the Othello development period, the management struggled to convince people to accept what they were about to design.

This time, both the management and the users wished to develop a software system that would support the natural task flow of how humans would stow a ship.

[PO:] -The intention with the use of the software is, if you know how to stow a chemical tanker, you should, intuitively, understand how the system works. If you do not know how to stow a chemical tanker, then you don't have the experiential knowledge of using the system. Experienced personnel should not need long training. The system should be intuitive. It's a bit like an experienced operator thinking «If I'm doing THIS, then THAT should happen», and then THAT will happen.

Thus, they had an early focus on what meets the user: the user interface, to such an extent that the very first digital sketches on how the screen elements would actually look like, largely survived the entire development process (see also [5]).

[PO] -Focusing on the user interface, was the very first thing on our list when we started the project. This means that the screen elements in the first mock-up are more or less identical to the way they are now. We have changed some details here and there, and changed a bit of the information that is in there, but the main principle, of making the system as user-friendly as possible, is the same. And I, as project manager, was very concerned that we should end up with the users having a good user experience.

The transfer of vocational experience within the user group that are experienced cargo brokers, to the developers of the software, was important in two regards: 1. to ensure that the correct design choices were made and 2. to ensure that the design choices were grounded within the user group. This was achieved by co-location. The first central decisions were made by a group of hand-picked, particularly skilled, employees and the project management, already in the pre-study period. This decision-making helped establish a common goal that remained unchanged throughout the process with just minor changes [5].

[SU] -Quite early, just to get a bit away, we went to my cottage in the mountains. There, we spent three days, five guys of us. We discussed from 8-9 o'clock in the morning until 3-4 o'clock in the morning the next day. We were so enthusiastic and managed to keep our concentration and focus. Many complex problems got disentangled up there. Many decisions were made during these discussions. Most of them were mainly focused on the user interface. Who is the user? How will the system be used? What should we try to make it look like?»

The new system turned out to be immediately useful for both expert and novice users; hence we wanted to understand what was done right in the development of this successful system. Being what the project owner describes as a «user's system» , the intention with the use of the system was that, if you know how to stow a chemical tanker, you should, intuitively, be able to understand how the system works. If you do not know how to stow a chemical tanker, then you don't have the experiential knowledge of using the system. Experienced personnel should not need much training: the vision for the system was to make it intuitive to use. The following quotes from users confirm that they evaluated the system as simple to use:

"ORCA is easier, in a way, because you get all the data from another system, OTIS.[1] That didn't happen in SuperCargo, where you had to type everything manually."
"It's is very easy to use. Even without having that much computer knowledge."

---

[1] OTIS: Odfjell Tankers Information System. The system has, since January 1. 2015, been replaced by IMOS (Integrated Maritime Operations System, by Veson Nautical).

"Hold the mouse there. Drag there. It runs by itself. If you have done it once, you'll understand the workings."
"I don't feel that I spend that much energy. I maintain the flow."
"It's a puzzle, and a great fun puzzle, which makes it really fun to work with."

This is in line with Dreyfus and Dreyfus, who describe intuition as a method of problem-solving that distinguishes between experts and beginners; acknowledging the indistinct nature of the intuitive method, and state that:

«Experienced intuitive [practitioners] do not attempt to understand familiar problems and opportunities using calculative rationality [...] When things are proceeding normally, experts don't solve problems and don't make decisions: they do what normally works» [21].

Experienced users themselves can hardly ever give a rational explanation for their behaviour in a particular way [21].

4.2   Theme 2: Organisational and Procedural Structure of Participation

During the first phase, the users were very much involved. However, another aspect of early involvement of users was discovered; too many participants could cause the development process to become messy and unclear. This was resolved by running user surveys and conduct so-called 'back-on-track' workshops, employing a greater group of people than would be practical for regular developing work.

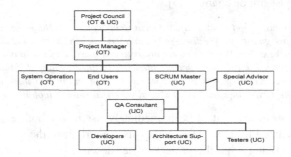

Fig. 1. The project organisation chart.

Figure 1 shows the project's formal organisation in three main levels, with a project council, consisting of employees from the company (OT) and the developers (UC[2]) directly connecting with end users and system operation (super-user). We also see the SCRUM Master/Head of the developer team working as an entry point for user participants' access to the developers. However, since all from the developer team were located in the same room, the communication between the project manager and system operation ([SU]) was informal, continuous and direct.

---

[2] Umoe Consulting.

The blend of formal organisational structure and informal knowledge exchange and creation seemed well suited for employing an agile development method. Also, in a development process where such emphasis has been put on the users, we saw that SCRUM as an agile development method was rather well suited for encompassing the informal liaison between developers and users. The feedback that the developers received from the users during a Sprint could take on a rather informal character. This was not the case regarding all information exchange, however. After the iterations, there would be a sprint review, a sprint retrospective, and a sprint planning. Also, the workshops, where the theme would be certain specifics, would, to some extent, have a formal character.

After the system was released and implemented in the organization, and during implementation on the ships, the development process was described as extremely agile. So agile in that fact, that some of the Sprint reviews were considered unnecessary, since everyone, through the continuous presence of the developer team, already knew what was in the release. The developer team got continuous feedback, from the users through the super user, during the process.

By running these surveys and workshops, they engaged a large group of people in a controlled manner. The surveys provided brief clarifications while the workshops would bring out the engagement within the user group. It also provided the users with an outlet where they could present ideas and suggestions for different functions or menus; the way it could possibly look; what they would need on board or at company headquarters, and so on.

During the first phase, the users were very much involved. The early involvement of users engaged many participants and could result in a messy and unclear development process [22], but by running user surveys and conduct back-on-track workshops, employing a greater group of people than would be practical during regular developing work, this problem was addressed.

The formal structure provided an opportunity for the informal structure to evolve, by first getting to know each other in formal settings, like meetings and workshops, and conversely, that the close and informal organization made the formal easier or even superfluous, as e.g. making Sprint reviews unnecessary. The formal influenced the informal and vice versa. A strong focus on mutual learning was salient in the project, knowing that its outcome would be dependent on a shared easy access to the discourse of the field [3, 23] through being *close* together, side by side, meeting each other several times a day by the coffee machine, or for lunch, or simply by being in the same place – mutual learning by walking around – which provided the opportunity to exchange knowledge both formally and informally.

4.3   Theme 3: Proximity for Mutual Learning

Locating developers close to the users was a joint decision. According to the management representative and project leader on the previous system development, user involvement was rather similar to the last time they developed a stowage system. One notable difference between these two projects lies in the actual location of the developers. During the ORCA development period they have been situated on the same floor (see Fig. 2), which is in contrast to the previous stowage system, Othello, where the developers did not co-locate but were remotely situated.

One of the findings in the study was that communication got a bit less formal. When they encountered a problem, they could pop in and ask whether to try this or that, getting instantaneous, informal, feedback. This development pattern turned out to be so agile with such efficiency that they could, in fact, skip some of the weekly project update meetings.

In an interview with one of the developers about the possible impact of sitting so close to the future users, he underscored the convenience in being able to just walk into the room next door, to the users. With an expressed proximity like this, a developer can receive immediate answers on the questions he might have, without having to wait for any significant amount of time. In an interview with one of the developers, he said:

> [dev] -If we had been sitting in a secluded room in the basement, the question is, how many times one had managed to muster enough energy to leave the desk and to go up four floors and down again, with some unfinished business. We would have ended up using the phone anyway, and then there's no point in sitting together, is there?
> [researcher] - In what way has the fact that you have been sitting among the users influenced your work?
> [dev] -That we have focused on making it easy to use. We were told that there are two different user groups in the company. One of them, the naval personnel, is not so good with computers

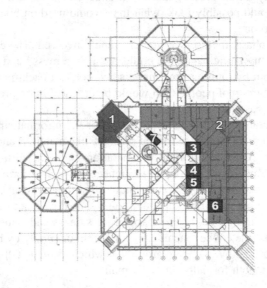

Fig. 2. Proximity: developers and users located on the same floor. The development team (1). The operators (2), project owner, PO (3), management representative, MR (4), super-user, SU (5), expert-user (6), and coffee machine (7).

The required level of proximity in the developer/user relationship proved to be right next door; anything other than the immediate vicinity, i.e. when walking distance exceeding «a few floors» would have led the participants to switch to telephone communication, which would have eliminated the effect of co-location altogether.

The co-location has also made it easier for the *project owner* to work very closely with the developers, and come by often, i.e. several times a day. For the developers this way of co-operating seemed rather unlike previous projects they had been involved in, where they might have to write a list of questions or suggestions and send it to the developers sitting somewhere else and get the answer days later.

[HM]: -The project owner drops by several times a day. We work very closely together. When we have a question, I don't have to wait for a response. I just talk to him and get an answer immediately."

[researcher] - In what way do you think it affects your work, that many of the users are working right next door?

[HM]: -It gets a bit less formal. When they encounter a problem, they can just pop in and ask whether we can try this or that. We get rapid, informal, feedback. Normally we would've held meetings every week, with project updates, but we don't need that here.

[researcher] - Is all communication informal?

[HM] -When we receive feedback from a user during a Sprint, that's pretty informal, but after an iteration, where we have a sprint review, sprint retrospective and sprint planning, I send a report from the sprint review and sprint retrospective to all who were present on the presentation plus copies to other interested parties. We also do workshops, with specific things to be done.

In this project, tremendous attention has been given to the users. The developers knew nothing about the vocational specifics of the tasks their system had to resolve, which is an interesting aspect of the choice to co-locate. This led to a situation where the developers, during the development process, got to know the users exceptionally well, since they are located in the same place. This gave them the opportunity to identify expertise among the users. This meant to have immediate access to the users' repository of extensive vocational knowledge and experience; their vast knowledge on how to stow a ship but it also meant that they had to relate to strong opinions from the users on how to do their work, and how *not* to do it; on what they want from a task flow supporting software. This sense of being in the immediate vicinity could, potentially, be double-edged. Co-location is all about being available.

According to one of the developers, there would be no point of co-location if they could not be immediately available to each other. However, the developers become equally accessible to the users, and thus vulnerable to being interrupted at work. The company solved this potentially counterproductive aspect of user participation, by channeling user input through the super-user, who became a kind of 'user proxy'. We argue that this level of proximity facilitated the mutual learning necessary for developing a system that supported the work tasks in a manner that was perceived as intuitive by its skilled workers, and that one of the possible explanations of the successful user acceptance and work-flow support was the continuous mutual learning between skilled users, and developers. The users could get a sense of the possible complexity of programming seemingly simple functionality, while the developers got direct and continuous access to the vast knowledge base of the chemical tanker trade, i.e. the importance of tank coating, or the precision of Trim & List.[3]

---

[3] The boat's position in the water.

4.4   Theme 4: Accountability and Task Distribution

In this project, the task of giving the developers a certain direction were split between the project owner and super-user. In addition to the project owner providing regular requests and input for software functionality, the super user was instrumental in giving the developers a certain direction, determining what vocational specifics that needed be included in the (next) release. In addition, there were three naval officers involved from day one. From them, the developers received some initial comments. They were also involved in the preliminary project, when they ran the initial workshop, discussing user interfaces and which features were adamant to include. The group of naval personnel was actively involved in the pilot phase, but not to the same extent in the implementation phase.

We use the term 'accountability' in an ethnomethodological sense [24–26], referring to the fact that by collaborating so closely, both users and developers of the ORCA software became mutually responsible for its clarity and user-friendliness. In an interview, the project manager for the development of the previous system, who is the present management representative, said:

> [MR]: -The fact that the developers are sitting here, on this floor, makes the operators aware that the guys in the room next door develop the new stowage planning system. Instead of the rather abstract «somebody out there is working on a program for us», it becomes much more concrete.»

During the development of the ORCA software, the users were aware that the developers were sitting right nextdoor, working on 'their' new stowage system. It seems like this awareness made the project more immediate and real, rather than the kind of an abstract notion that "someone out there" is making a new program. Both developers and users expressed that this reciprocal accountability made an impact on the exchange of knowledge that took place during the development process and made it possible for them to not develop a clear requirement specification and relay on communication for clarifying the expectations. The ship management and the personnel from the ships and 'nautical personnel' at company headquarters made their expectations clear from the start. The base of user representatives was quite extensive, in its inception it was more extensive in ORCA project than the Othello project. During the Othello process, the company based the development on a requirement specification that was developed by a management consulting firm, not on workshops and dialogue between the involved parties as in the case of ORCA.

This kind of proximity also made the software developing team aware of being regarded as colleagues, and the fact that they could bump into regular users on their way to the coffee machine, or at lunch, contributed to the sense of being accountable for developing choices, and for the contribution in the process of empowering the user with a good tool.

5   Concluding Remarks

In this paper we have reported on a software development project, where much attention was given to the users: the developers moved in and stayed with the users throughout the project. Our aim has been to understand the effects of this level of proximity on the cooperation between developers and users. We found that the proximity had an impact on the continuous knowledge exchange, the organisational structure and the experience of being accountable in the software development process. Moreover, we think these elements of the software development process influenced the quality of the end-result and, in particular, how it facilitated immediate activity.

Based on the findings, we suggest that the mutual learning necessary for establishing a common understanding of a user-centered software system and its intuitive operation is more likely to succeed if developers and users can build up a common knowledge base over time facilitated by being located in the immediate vicinity of each-other. Our data analysis demonstrates that one impact from this level of proximity in a user-developer relationship is a resulting system that is immediately usable by skilled users and easily learnt by novice users.

References

1. Bratteteig, T., Bødker, K., Dittrich, Y., Mogensen, P., Simonsen, J.: Methods: organizing principles and general guidelines for participatory design projects. In: Simonsen, J., Robertson, T. (eds.) Routledge International Handbook of Participatory Design. Routledge, New York (2013)
2. Bansler, J.P., Havn, E.C.: Information systems development with generic systems. In: ECIS, pp. 707–715 (1994)
3. Bjerknes, G., Bratteteig, T.: Florence in wonderland. In: Bjerknes, G., Ehn, P., Kyng, M. (eds.) Computers and Democracy - a Scandinavian Challenge. Avebury, Wiltshire (1987)
4. Bjerknes, G., Bratteteig, T.: User Participation and democracy: a discussion of scandinavian research on system development. Scand. J. Inf. Syst. 7(1), 73–98 (1995)
5. Bratteteig, T., Wagner, I.: Disentangling Participation: Power and Decision-making in Participatory Design. Springer, Cham (2014)
6. Ehn, P.: Scandinavian design: on participation and skill. In: Schuler, D., Namioka, A. (eds.) Hillsdale Participatory Design: Principles and Practices, pp. 41–77. Lawrence Erlbaum Associates, Hillsdale (1993)
7. Greenbaum, J.M., Kyng, M.: Design at Work: Cooperative Design of Computer Systems. L. Erlbaum Associates Inc., Hillsdale (1991)
8. Nygaard, K.: The iron and metal project: trade union participation. Computers dividing man and work - Recent Scandinavian research on planning and computers from a trade union perspective Demos project report 13, pp. 94–107 (1979)
9. Schuler, D., Namioka, A.: Participatory Design: Principles and practices. L. Erlbaum Associates Inc., Hillsdale (1993)
10. Simonsen, J., Robertson, T.: Routledge International Handbook of Participatory Design. Routledge, New York (2013)
11. Schön, D.A.: The Reflective Practitioner: How Professionals Think in Action. Basic books, New York (1983)
12. Schön, D.A., Wiggins, G.: Kinds of seeing and their functions in designing. Des. Stud. 13(2), 135–156 (1992)
13. Schön, D.A.: Knowing-in-action: the new scholarship requires a new epistemology. Change: Mag. High. Learn. 27(6), 27–34 (1995)

14. Bjerknes, G., Bratteteig, T.: The memoirs of two survivors: or the evaluation of a computer system for cooperative work. In: Proceedings of the 1988 ACM Conference on Computer-Supported Cooperative Work, pp. 167–177. ACM (1988)
15. Bellotti, V., Bly, S.: Walking away from the desktop computer: distributed collaboration and mobility in a product design team. In: Proceedings of the 1996 ACM Conference on Computer Supported Cooperative Work, pp. 209–218. ACM (1996)
16. Dourish, P., Bellotti, V.: Awareness and coordination in shared workspaces. In: Proceedings of the 1992 ACM Conference on Computer-Supported Cooperative Work, pp. 107–114. ACM (1992)
17. Heath, C., Svensson, M.S., Hindmarsh, J., Luff, P., Vom Lehn, D.: Configuring awareness. Comput. Support. Coop. Work (CSCW) 11(3–4), 317–347 (2002)
18. Luff, P., Heath, C.: Mobility in collaboration. In: Proceedings of the 1998 ACM Conference on Computer Supported Cooperative Work, pp. 305–314. ACM (1998)
19. Schmidt, K.: The problem with awareness: Introductory remarks on awareness in CSCW. Comput. Support. Coop. Work (CSCW) 11(3–4), 285–298 (2002)
20. Schmidt, K., Bannon, L.: Taking CSCW seriously. Comput. Support. Coop. Work (CSCW) 1(1), 7–40 (1992)
21. Dreyfus, H.L., Dreyfus, S.E.: Mind Over Machine: The Power of Human Intuition and Expertise in the Era of the Computer. Free Press, New York (1986)
22. Brooks, F.P.: The Mythical Man-Month. Addison-Wesley, Reading (1975)
23. Bødker, S., Ehn, P., Kammersgaard, J., Kyng, M., Sundblad, Y.: A UTOPIAN experience: on design of powerful computer-based tools for skilled graphic workers. In: Bjerknes, G., Ehn, P., Kyng, M. (eds.) Computers and Democracy: A Scandinavian Challenge. Avebury, Wiltshire (1987)
24. Garfinkel, H.: Ethnomethodological Studies of Work. Routledge, New York (2005)
25. Heath, C., Luff, P.: Technology in Action. Cambridge University Press, Cambridge (2000)
26. Suchman, L., Trigg, R., Blomberg, J.: Working artefacts: ethnomethods of the prototype. Br. J. Sociol. 53(2), 163–179 (2002). doi:10.1080/00071310220133287

How to Join Theoretical Concepts, Industry Needs and Innovative Technologies in HCI Courses? The Big Challenge of Teaching HCI

Clodis Boscarioli[1(✉)], Sílvia Amélia Bim[2], Milene S. Silveira[3],
and Simone D.J. Barbosa[4]

[1] Colegiado de Ciência da Computação, UNIOESTE, Cascavel, PR, Brazil
clodis.boscarioli@unioeste.br
[2] Departamento Acadêmico de Informática, UTFPR, Curitiba, PR, Brazil
sabim@utfpr.edu.br
[3] Faculdade de Informática, PUCRS, Porto Alegre, RS, Brazil
milene.silveira@pucrs.br
[4] Departamento de Informática, PUC-Rio, Rio de Janeiro, RJ, Brazil
simone@inf.puc-rio.br

Abstract. The relation between HCI Education and the Industry needs is a challenge to the HCI community. HCI professors should be aware of their role to persuade students that user experience and experience design are cross-cutting concepts, which therefore influence all other areas involved in innovative product and service development, from conceptual design to implementation and testing. In this paper we present a revised HCI Brazilian syllabus for undergraduate Computer Science courses, discussing HCI requirements for UX professional and academic formation of the students. We also describe some research questions that have been raised in this context.

Keywords: HCI education and industry needs · Syllabi recommendations · HCI in Brazil

1 Introduction

The Brazilian HCI community has made several efforts to discuss the relationship between academia and industry and the challenge to include innovative technologies in HCI graduate and undergraduate courses. In 2006, the first working group related to HCI Education has recommended a list of topics that should be taught in an HCI course within Computer Science (CS) departments [6]. Since 2010, an annual HCI Education workshop has taken place alongside the Brazilian HCI conference, where HCI professors have taken part in face-to-face meetings to discuss the syllabi of HCI courses, teaching strategies, and other subjects related to HCI education.

In order to understand how HCI has been taught in Brazil, three surveys have been applied in recent years. In 2009, the questionnaire aimed to uncover the HCI courses being taught countrywide [5]. In 2012, another survey was conducted in response to an

© Springer International Publishing Switzerland 2015
M. Kurosu (Ed.): Human-Computer Interaction, Part I, HCII 2015, LNCS 9169, pp. 27–36, 2015.
DOI: 10.1007/978-3-319-20901-2_3

opportunity to collaborate with SIGCHI efforts on HCI Education [2], which targeted a broader audience, not taking into account specificities of the Brazilian context. Finally, in 2013, aiming to gather richer data while taking into consideration the specificities of the Brazilian context, a new survey was designed and applied [3]. It was distributed in Computer Science mailing lists and to researchers in other areas such as Psychology and Design, through the social networks of the survey creators. As the survey was quite extensive, although 114 respondents started to answer it, only 75 completed the survey. Considering the results of this recent survey, it was possible to deepen the analysis about undergraduate, graduate and ad hoc or standalone HCI courses taught in Brazil. Data were collected about their curricula, syllabi, recommended bibliography, as well as the professors'/lecturers' profiles.

In 2011 and 2013 the São Paulo chapter of UxPA[1] (User Experience Professionals Association) conducted online surveys to investigate the profile of UX professionals in Brazil. The survey was distributed in several online communities, such as Information Architecture, User Experience, Human-Computer Interaction (HCI), trying to reach a wider audience, reflecting the multidisciplinary nature of the area. In 2011 [5], 247 answers were collected, and in 2013 [8], the survey achieved a wider public with 367 respondents. The surveys aimed to identify the profile of UX professionals concerning their background, their activities during the workday, how they have learned UX or HCI, how they work, and where they work.

In this paper, we present the HCI Education developments achieved by the Brazilian community, with an emphasis on:

- Topic recommendations for different courses related to Computer Science (i.e., Computer Engineering, Computer Science, Information Systems, Software Engineering), according to the profile of each course and based on successive refinements from the 2006 list of suggested topics [4].
- Elicitation of the software industry needs (e.g., concepts and techniques HCI professionals must master), highlighting the topics that they consider essential to an HCI professional, and reflections on the integration of these contents within the context of our core HCI concepts.

This paper is organized as follows: Sect. 2 presents the syllabi of HCI courses for Brazilian CS-related majors; Sect. 3 presents HCI and Industry Requirements, discussing these needs with respect to what is taught in Brazilian CS-related courses. Finally, Sect. 4 presents our conclusions, discussing questions raised and future work.

2   HCI Brazilian Curricula Recommendations

Figure 1 demonstrates how topics addressed in HCI disciplines are comprehensive and diversified, mostly when it comes to introductory disciplines. This gives a hint as to the lecturers' difficulty to handle such topics adequately in a single HCI discipline.

---

[1] http://www.uxpasaopaulo.com.br/perfil-do-profissional-de-ux/.

INTRODUCTION TO HUMAN-COMPUTER INTERACTION
Evolution (history) – Contexts, Influence on Society
Areas and disciplines
Interface and interaction
Quality of use: usability, communicability and accessibility
~~Return on Investment~~
Basic concepts: Affordances; Users; User frustration; ISO 9241; System-user communication; Designer-user communication
Devices / Software and Hardware Components

THEORETICAL FOUNDATIONS
Cognitive Engineering
Semiotics Engineering
Human Factors; Cognitive Psychology; Human Cognition; Ergonomics; Computer Semiotics; Semiotics; Communication; Collaboration; Aspects of affection;

HCI EVALUATION
Overview: what, why and when to evaluate;
Observation and monitoring of use – Empirical methods; User tests; Usability tests; Ethical aspects; Verbal protocols; Communicability Evaluation Method (CEM)
Gathering of users opinion
~~Experiments and performance tests (benchmarking)~~
Interpretative evaluation – Inspection; heuristic evaluation; ergonomic evaluation; Semiotic Inspection Method (SIM); Cognitive walkthrough
Predictive Evaluation – theoretical methods; GOMS

USER INTERACTION DESIGN
Interaction styles – Interaction paradigms; multitouch interfaces; GUI; Window manager and controller; Virtual reality; 3D interfaces; Advanced interfaces and new tendencies; Expressive interfaces;
Style guides and Interaction – Graphic design
Guidelines and Interaction Design Standards -- ergonomic criteria

HCI DESIGNING PROCESS
User-centered design; Usability Engineering; Participatory practices; Ethnographic methods; Design / Universal usability; Redesigning;
Vision of Software Engineering and of HCI
Elicitation and Analysis – Modeling Techniques; Metaphors; Conceptual models; Information architecture; User modeling; Scenarios;
Task modeling
Interaction modeling – Dialogue model
Storyboarding and Prototyping – Interface design/modeling; Construction; Interface construction tools;
Designing Online Help systems

DOMAINS/PLATFORMS
Games; web; multimedia; collaborative systems; mobile devices; social applications;

Fig. 1. 2006 syllabus revised to include topics informed in the 2013 survey

We thus analyzed the results of the questionnaire on HCI education in Brazil with respect to two other sets of data:

- The recommendations made in 2013 in the revised curriculum for Computer Science majors,[2] a joint effort by ACM and IEEE Computer Society;
- The latest revision of the Information Systems (IS) curriculum,[3] made in 2010 in partnership with the Association for Information Systems (AIS).

In our analysis, we did not consider the recommendations for either the Computer Engineering course, since the available version dates back to 2004, or Software Engineering. By solely observing the analysis of topics, it is possible to claim that the HCI education in Brazil includes the topics described as mandatory in CS courses and recommended for IS courses.

2.1 Results of the 4th WEIHC on Proposals for HCI Syllabi

During the Workshop on HCI Education (WEIHC), in its fourth edition in 2013, whose main theme was "HCI curricula", members were organized into four groups to discuss and recommend topics for HCI courses in the following bachelor courses in the Computing field: Information Systems, Computer Science, Computer Engineering and Software Engineering.

The group which discussed the topics for an HCI course in the context of **Computer Engineering** program suggested the inclusion, under the topic *Introduction to HCI*, the following subtopics: User Experience, Human-factors and Process of Interaction Design. They also suggested the inclusion of Ergonomics under *Theoretical Foundations*.

Under *Evaluation*, suggested topics were Objectives, Applicability, Methods and Techniques for Observation of Use and Extraction of User Opinion in the lab, in the field or remotely), as well as Inspection Methods. The topics related to *Design* were set in the categories of Problem and Solution, and in turn Solution was subdivided into Concept Solution and Construction Solution.

Hence, under *Problem* the proposed subtopics are: Personas, Problem Scenarios and Problem Task Model. Under *Solution*, proposed subtopics were: in the Conceptual part – User Model, Solution Scenario, Solution Task Model and Interaction Model; in the Construction part – Help Model, Interface Model, Prototyping and Implementation.

The group which discussed the topics for the **Computer Science** program emphasized *Introduction to HCI*, *HCI Design* and *Theoretical Foundations*. However, it did not detail the subtopics under *HCI Evaluation*. Under *HCI Design*, it joined together the topics of *User Interaction Design* with *HCI Design Process*, with slightly different subtopics, as Fig. 2 demonstrates.

---

[2] http://www.acm.org/education/CS2013-final-report.pdf.

[3] http://www.acm.org/education/curricula/IS%202010%20ACM%20final.pdf.

```
┌──────────────────────────────────────────────────────────────────────────┐
│ INTRODUCTION TO HUMAN-COMPUTER INTERACTION                                 │
│ HCI in Context (webpage, mobile, new technologies, etc)                    │
│ Evolution and Multidisciplinarity (Psychology, Sociology, Anthropology, Ergonomics) │
│ THEORETICAL FOUNDATIONS                                                    │
│ Interface and Interaction                                                  │
│ Quality of Use: user experience, usability, communicability and accessibility. │
│ Affordance.                                                                │
│ Mental models, conceptual models, cognitive models (attention, perception and recognition) │
│ and social models (culture, communication and organization).              │
│ Design Process (focused on user and grounded on communication)            │
│ HCI DESIGN                                                                 │
│   Design Principles                                                        │
│    - Interaction styles                                                    │
│    - Interaction guides                                                    │
│    - Guidelines                                                            │
│   Elicitation and Analysis                                                 │
│   Task modeling                                                            │
│   Interaction Modeling                                                     │
│   Storyboarding and Prototyping                                            │
│   Help and Documentation                                                   │
└──────────────────────────────────────────────────────────────────────────┘
```

Fig. 2. HCI syllabus proposed at the 4th WEIHC for CS-related courses

The group which discussed the **Information Systems** program proposed few changes in relation to the 2007 Syllabus. It suggested replacing Interaction and Interface for "key concepts" and including the expression "and so on" in Quality of Use in *Introduction to HCI*. It also brought topics that belonged to *User Interaction Design* to the *Introduction*. It is worth to emphasize that this was the only group which hinted at keeping *Return to Investment* as a topic. As for *HCI Evaluation*, it only brought a few subjects together into two items and offered a *Special Topics* item in order to approach emerging themes in the area.

The proposal of the group which discussed the **Software Engineering** program was to offer a single "Introduction to HCI" course (or "Software Use Experience" or "HCI Foundations"), encompassing broad themes such as: why it is important to take the user into consideration; interaction and interface; quality of use; ways to interpret use; what HCI is and how to evaluate it. The remaining HCI subjects should be included in various of the program courses, which would allow for a detailed study of the software development process, in a way to foster an interdisciplinary perspective.

3   HCI in Practice

UxPA [7] defines a User Experience (UX) professional broadly as a person who conducts research, designs, and evaluates the user experience of products and services. It also presents the vectors of user experience and usability (Fig. 3). Looking at the labels on the vectors it is possible to see many different kinds of skills that are expected from a user experience professional. These skills are frequently required in UX job openings.

Fig. 3. The vectors of user experience and usability [7]

Companies have increasingly expressed concerns related to human factors, design and evaluation (including HCI) of their products, aiming to forward, through the perspective of interaction, the development of intuitive products that enhance their customers' productivity. Moreover, as claimed in [1], the HCI field is very likely to increase user productivity, to reduce the number and severity of problems, to reduce the cost of training and technical support, and to increase sales and customer loyalty.

In line with findings from the 2012 survey, academia and industry ought to establish closer ties, to articulate better their common interests.

Jobs in the fields of HCI/Interaction Design present different designations, for instance: information architect, interaction designer, user experience designer, interface designer, just to name a few. Currently, the most usual one is *User Experience Specialist*.

Diversity also appears in the degrees such professionals have. A survey conducted by UxPA São Paulo [8], comprising 367 survey takers, reveals the following degrees obtained by UX professionals: Graphic Design (23 %), Advertising and Marketing (20 %), Design (19 %) and Industrial Design (13 %). Computer Science was mentioned by 5.1 % of participants (the fifth most frequently mentioned major), while Information Systems had 4.7 % of the mentions (in the sixth place). In the previous survey, conducted in 2011 [9], Information Systems was in fourth place in the top-mentioned courses (6 % of respondents) and Computer Science was in eighth (4.5 % of respondents).

Such survey also aimed to map the knowledge, jobs, salary and profile of UX professionals in Brazil. When asked about activities they perform at work, UX professionals mentioned: Wireframes (89 %); Presentations to (external or internal) clients (82 %); Flowcharts (80 %); Navigable prototypes (80 %); Benchmarking (79 %); Sitemaps (77 %); Validation and inspection of development (73 %); Requirement surveys (71 %); Paper prototypes (70 %) and usability tests (planning and analysis) (63 %).

When inquired into things they knew but had never done throughout their professional lives, the following activities were mentioned: Diary Studies (62 %); Ethnographic studies (55 %); Online attendance management (54 %); Discussion groups (mediation) (52 %); Thorough interviews (40 %); Discussion groups (planning and analysis) (37 %); Programming (interface and/or system development) (37 %); Accessibility testing (36 %); Workshops and UX trainings (external or internal) (35 %) and Quantitative research (34 %).

When questioned about the tools they used in their daily practice, answers pointed to different tools. Figure 4 illustrates the main tools cited by respondents in [8]. In addition to these, the following tools were mentioned infrequently: Visio, InDesign, Camtasia, Morae, MindManager, Omnigraffe, CrazyEgg, Wufoo, Mockflow, Clicktale, Ethnio e Webnographer.

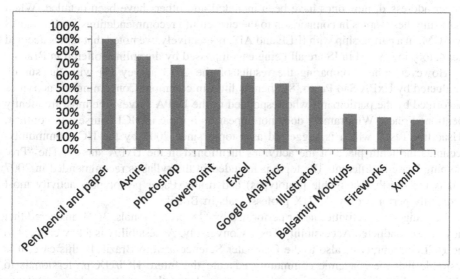

Fig. 4. Main tools used for UX professionals in Brazil (source: [8])

The relation between performed the activities and the tools used is important to understand the market needs for a UX professional. It can help revise the topics and the tools addressed in HCI courses (or the emphasis given to them), qualifying students to become professionals in this area.

The research by UxPA São Paulo in 2013 [8] also found that the number of people who learn UX at work has increased to 38 %, and to 30 % in classroom environments. The number of self-learners has decreased 31 % in comparison to the other research conducted in 2011 [9]. Such data reveals the need to expand the qualification in HCI in CS-related courses and graduate programs.

Human-computer interaction is a mandatory discipline in many bachelor's degrees in CS-related programs in Brazil, as was shown by the survey responded the academic community in 2013 [3]. However, it is no surprise that professionals who got a degree in such majors are currently not working in UX/HCI, because not long ago HCI was not included in the CS programs syllabi and, consequently, previously advertised openings would not explicitly include a degree in CS as a mandatory prerequisite.

We understand that, quite often, job openings in Computing are distributed among peers, in search of professional references and recommendations. Such openings are eventually disclosed in electronic mailing lists related to the opening itself, or even in specific channels used by organizations, but recently graduated professionals hardly ever reach them.

4   Conclusions and Future Work

By contrasting data collected by the HCI community survey conducted in 2013 [3], which refers to topics addressed in HCI courses, with the ones from the syllabus proposed by the first working group on HCI Education in Brazil, we noticed that a few topics are no longer addressed, new ones have been included and others have been detailed. When analyzing these topics in comparison to the curriculum recommendations for CS and IS by ACM, in a partnership with IEEE and AIS, respectively, we noted that topics deemed mandatory in CS and in IS are all being encompassed by disciplines offered in Brazil.

However, when comparing the results of the 2013 survey [3] with the survey conducted by UxPA São Paulo [8], there is little in common. Concerning the activities performed by the participants who responded to the UxPA survey, the most frequently mentioned one ("Wireframe") does not appear as a topic in HCI courses. In contrast, "Usability Test," which is suggested as a topic since 2007 by the HCI community, occupies the tenth place of the activities mentioned in the UxPA survey. The "Prototyping" case is different. The topic is included in the syllabus recommended in 2007 and is the fourth (Navigable prototypes) and ninth (Paper prototypes) activity most frequently performed by the UX professionals in Brazil.

Looking at the activities never performed by UX professionals, 36 % answered that they never conducted Accessibility Tests. Conversely, Accessibility is a key concept to the HCI community as also to the Computer Science area in Brazil. In this case, it is desirable that the academic community educate the future HCI/UX professionals to address such an important topic to the society at large, thus reducing the mismatches with industry practices.

Concerning the relationship between other areas, the Computer Engineering group included Ergonomics as a topic in HCI undergraduate courses. This topic is significant for Design courses, although it does not appear explicitly in the UxPA survey, possibly because it does not consist of an activity per se.

Tools were not detailed in the HCI survey results because it was not explicitly asked. Conversely, it is a significant item in the UxPA survey. It is important to discuss whether and how the tools used by the industry could be used in undergraduate HCI courses. Most of them are proprietary tools which have a high cost, which many Brazilian universities cannot afford.

The results of the surveys conducted in 2013 [3, 8] cannot be considered statistically significant. However, they are very relevant and provided important insights about the relationship between HCI Education and practice in Brazil. They reveal that more research needs to be carried out in order to identify strategies to bring the teaching of HCI and the current market needs and challenges closer together. Bringing the market closer can mean using strategies such as: real-life case studies, internship practicum offers, and expanded forums in local colleges.

Several issues emerged for which both the HCI community and the UX community need to seek answers, as follows:

- What should we teach in undergraduate HCI courses? Should undergraduate HCI courses taught within different computer science curricula have different focus, some more towards academia and others towards industry?
- What should we teach in graduate HCI courses? How should we deal with the fact that the graduate students' degrees of previous knowledge of HCI vary widely?
- How can we extend the dialogue about HCI education to related areas, such as Design, Psychology, Sociology, Communications, among other areas that are important for a broad view of HCI?
- How can we educate HCI students to meet the current needs and challenges of the software industry? How feasible is it to approach the industry in search of real cases to address in the classrooms?
- How can we enhance the effects of HCI education in other undergraduate courses? Would it be possible to include HCI content in other courses that also deal with the conception and development of interactive computational systems and new technologies?
- What do we need to rethink in the way we teach HCI? How can we look for or create new teaching strategies to face the challenges of the area?

Finally, a reflection on these initiatives reveals the need to increase the visibility and to ensure room for HCI courses in CS-related programs. HCI lecturers should be aware of their role in persuading students that HCI, user experience and experience design are cross-cutting concepts, which influence all other areas involved in innovative product and service development, from conceptual design to implementation and testing. Therefore, they need to bring the knowledge acquired in HCI courses to the other courses in their bachelor's program.

Acknowledgements. The authors thank the São Paulo chapter of UxPA (User Experience Professionals Association) for the survey data available on the web. Simone DJ Barbosa thanks CNPq for her research grant (#313031/2009-6).

References

1. Barbosa, S.D.J., Silva, B.S.: Interação Humano-Computador. Editora Campus-Elsevier, Rio de Janeiro (2010)
2. Boscarioli, C., Bim, S.A., Silveira, M.S., Prates, R.O., Barbosa, S.D.J.: HCI education in brazil: challenges and opportunities. In: Proceedings of HCI International, pp. 3–12 (2013)

3. Boscarioli, C., Silveira, M.S., Prates, R.O., Bim, S.A., Barbosa, S.D.J.: Charting the landscape of HCI education in brazil. In: Kurosu, M. (ed.) HCI 2014, Part I. LNCS, vol. 8510, pp. 177–186. Springer, Heidelberg (2014)
4. Boscarioli, C., Silveira, M.S., Prates, R., Bim, S.A., Barbosa, S.D.J.: Currículos de IHC no brasil: panorama atual e perspectivas. In: WEI - XXII Workshop sobre Educação em Computação, 2014, Brasília, DF. Anais do XXXIV Congresso da Sociedade Brasileira de Computação, CSBC 2014, pp. 1294–1303 (2014)
5. Prates, R.O., Filgueiras, L.: Usability in brazil. In: Douglas, I., Zhengjie, L. (eds.) Global Usability, vol. 1, 1st edn, pp. 91–110. Springer, London (2011)
6. Silveira, M.S., Prates, R.O.: Uma proposta da comunidade para o ensino de IHC no brasil. In: Proceedings of XIV Workshop sobre Educação em Computação, Sociedade Brasileira de Computação, vol. 1, pp. 76–84 (2007)
7. UxPA. About UX. User Experience Professionals Association Oficial Site. https://uxpa.org/resources/about-ux. Accessed 6 March 2015
8. Vieira, A., Martins, S.: Perfil do Profissional de UX no Brasil - 2ª Edição (2013). http://pt.slideshare.net/slideshow/embed_code/30197445. Accessed 6 Mar 2015
9. Vieira, A., Martins, S., Volpato, E., Niide, E.: Pesquisa sobre o perfil do Profissional de UX no Brasil (2011). http://pt.slideshare.net/upasaopaulo/perfil-do-profissional-de-ux-no-brasil. Accessed 6 Mar 2015

Challenges for Human-Data Interaction – A Semiotic Perspective

Heiko Hornung[1(✉)], Roberto Pereira[1,2], M. Cecilia C. Baranauskas[1], and Kecheng Liu[2]

[1] Institute of Computing, University of Campinas (UNICAMP),
Campinas, Brazil
{heiko,rpereira,cecilia}@ic.unicamp.br
[2] Informatics Research Centre, University of Reading, Reading, UK
k.liu@henley.ac.uk

Abstract. Data has become ubiquitous and pervasive influencing our perceptions and actions in ever more areas of individual and social life. Data production, collection and editing are complex actions motivated by data use. In this paper we present and characterize the field of study of Human-Data Interaction by discussing the challenges of how to enable understanding of data and information in this complex context, and how to facilitate acting on this understanding considering the social impact. By understanding interaction with data as a sign process, and identifying the goal of designing human-data interaction as enabling stakeholders to promote desired and to avoid undesired consequences of data use, we employ a semiotic perspective and define research challenges for the field.

Keywords: Human-data interaction · Semiotics · Digital display

1 Introduction

Due to informatization and computerization, we have today an unprecedented access to data about all aspects of life. This data includes data about individuals, groups of people or even societies, as well as data about things, events, and so on. Examples include personal diet or exercise data, metadata related to email or web site traffic, data about economic or environmental indicators, or real-time traffic data.

The ecosystem within which data is produced, collected, edited (e.g. analyzed and synthesized) and used is complex and ranges from simple scenarios where data producer, collector, editor and consumer are the same person (e.g. nutrition diaries in paper form) to complex scenarios where many stakeholders are involved (e.g. a population census). Furthermore, the methods and purposes of how and why data is produced, collected, edited, and used vary greatly.

Data production, collection and editing are actions motivated by data use. While the abstract goal of data use commonly is to "extract" information or even "gain" knowledge, concrete goals vary and might be related to several domains e.g. entertainment, commerce, security, politics, arts, or science. These actions have given rise to

© Springer International Publishing Switzerland 2015
M. Kurosu (Ed.): Human-Computer Interaction, Part I, HCII 2015, LNCS 9169, pp. 37–48, 2015.
DOI: 10.1007/978-3-319-20901-2_4

questions such as: how to facilitate understanding of data and information, and how to facilitate acting on this understanding considering its potential social impact.

Scientific fields of study related to the interaction of people with data include but are not limited to the multi-disciplinary fields of data visualization or sonification, information visualization, and big data. While these areas are concerned with facilitating understanding and reasoning, big data focuses on the amount of data, visualization and sonification on representation.

More recently, different authors have begun to investigate challenges under the perspective of "Human-Data Interaction" (HDI; [3, 5, 14]), proposing to investigate how people interact with data in analogy to how HCI investigates the relation between people and computers. The common ground of these works seems to be the assumption that, in order to gain information or knowledge from data, people (or "end users of data") need to interact with data instead of only passively consuming them. This interaction goes beyond data analysis and includes interactive exploration of data sets. HDI should investigate interaction with data and questions related to understanding, but also technical, social and ethical issues such as privacy, transparency, commerce, as well as the question of how knowledge gained from data might benefit society.

We agree with Elmquist, Cafaro and Mortier et al. that HDI poses relevant and scientifically interesting challenges. We believe that these challenges can and should be addressed by the HCI community and also involve other disciplines. Furthermore, we believe that the challenges are more ample than presented by the cited authors. We argue that data production, collection, editing and use need to be investigated systematically, focusing on social impact they might provoke. This means an approach is required that goes beyond the challenges of representation and sense-making, and that is capable of conceptualizing pragmatic and social issues, i.e. issues related to meaning in context, intentions, negotiations and the effects and impact of decisions and other manifestations of data or information use.

In this paper, we define our view of Human-Data Interaction and adopt a perspective informed by (Organizational) Semiotics [12] in order to systematically describe challenges and outline a research agenda for Human-Data Interaction that considers the complex processes of data production, collection, editing and use. This paper extends previous HDI work by presenting a more systematic and comprising view of HDI research challenges, and builds upon Liu's [13] semiotic perspective on digital visualization by investigating HCI-related issues of data production, collection and editing, besides use.

The paper is structured as follows: Sect. 2 provides a brief motivation for investigating HDI, and characterizes HDI considering HCI and previous work; Sect. 3 presents a semiotic perspective on HDI; Sect. 4 outlines research challenges for HDI; Sect. 5 concludes.

2   Characterizing the Human-Data Interaction Problem

People using digital artifacts come into contact with data on many occasions. They produce data both intentionally, e.g., when using fitness trackers, and unintentionally, e.g., when leaving digital traces in browser search histories or being tracked by cookies.

People analyze data using methods of varying complexity, e.g., when reading an infographic or when trying to find an affordable flight from London to Tokyo during two weeks of May. They use data with different intentions, e.g. when sharing fitness data it might be to elicit encouraging feedback from peers ("I ran the mile faster than last week") or brag about their lifestyle ("I ran the mile at Rio de Janeiro's Ipanema Beach"). Accordingly, data use might have different consequences.

The way data is captured and analyzed influences data use and its consequences. People are often not aware of how the digital traces they leave are used by third parties, e.g. advertisers, credit-scoring companies, or data brokers (e.g. [1]). This has given rise to questions about privacy and other ethics-related issues, and how Interaction Design might or should address these (e.g. [8]).

People with no statistical background are often not able to analyze certain data. This might lead to them drawing false conclusions based on flawed analysis or to being dependent on data analysts. In complex data sets it is often not straightforward to extract relevant and significant information, and different analysts might thus focus on different aspects of the data and present different results. People using these results might not be aware that in order to get a more complete picture, one needs to look at data from different perspectives and might need to consider additional data sets.

Data, and specifically seemingly quantitative data, are often equated with objective facts. However, data is often subjective since methods for data collection carry subjectivity. Examples include medical, political or economical data, e.g. patients' self-reports or data collected according to ideologically charged collection methods (e.g. regarding crime statistics, is an assault on a person of different skin color an act of random violence, politically motivated or an act of racism or terrorism?). Data analysts bring their own beliefs and values into the analysis and act within complex contexts of organizational norms and values. Different analysts might interpret data and present analyses differently, influencing people's behaviors differently.

Without further context, the term "Human-Data Interaction" is not very specific. "Humans" have "interacted" with "data" for thousands of years, e.g. using astronomic or calendar data for planning hunting or agricultural activities. In scientific literature, particularly in the area of Computing, but later also in other areas, the expression is known at least since the 1990s (e.g. [10]).

Regarding the context of HCI, we found three independent lines of inquiry about Human-Data Interaction [3, 5, 14, 15]. While Cafaro [3] and Elmqvist [5] seem to focus on embodied aspects of data analysis (building on the work of Johnson [9], Dourish [4], and Lakoff and Johnson [11]), Mortier et al. seem to focus less on HCI-related aspects and more on the interaction between humans, datasets and analytics (e.g. algorithms). Furthermore, they seem to concentrate on personal data [14, 15].

Elmqvist [5] defines HDI as "*the human manipulation, analysis, and sensemaking of large, unstructured, and complex datasets*". Cafaro [3] defines HDI as "*the problem of delivering personalized, context-aware, and understandable data from big datasets*" and HDI systems "*as technologies that use embodied interaction to facilitate the users' exploration of rich datasets*". Mortier et al. [14] state that "*HDI concerns interaction generally between humans, datasets and analytics [...]. HDI refers to the analysis of the individual and collective decisions we make and the actions we take [...]. The term makes explicit the link between individuals and the signals they emit as data [...]*".

The least common denominator of these three definitions is that people need to make sense of large and complex data sets. Furthermore, according to the three authors, the area overlaps multiple disciplines including HCI. Apart from that, the proposals of Elmqvist and Cafaro seem to be individual research endeavors that focus on the embodiment of interaction and try to prescribe a method to solve the respective research challenges: Elmqvist proposes tangible interaction, Cafaro gestural interaction as possible solutions. Mortier et al. frame the problem as a more general research challenge. Acknowledging the works of Elmqvist and Cafaro, we build upon the work of Mortier et al. [14, 15] to define our perspective on HDI and the related challenges.

"Data" plays an important role in many disciplines. In order to define a research challenge that is distinct from existing ones and that does not simply hijack topics from other areas, we need to investigate and try to define important core concepts such as "data", "interaction" and "humans". Furthermore, we need some conceptual framework that supports the organization of research challenges and a research agenda. Without this framework, we run the risk to simply create an unordered bag of topics and to omit important aspects.

Mortier et al. [15] started from the dictionary definition of "data", which they did not find very helpful, and then compounded "data" with seemingly arbitrary nouns, some of which appear in scientific literature, arriving at "data trail", "data smog", "big data", "small data" (potentially complex data sets about a single person [6]), participatory personal data ("any representation recorded by an individual, about an individual, using a mediating technology" [19]), or "open data"[1].

In the next step, Mortier et al. [15] look at "interacting" and at the "humans", i.e. at who is interacting with data. They contrast their proposal to the ones of Elmqvist and Cafaro and state, among others, that HDI does not only refer to embodied interaction, but to all kinds of interaction, especially not only to data exploration but also to other activities. Furthermore, they emphasize that data is "under constant revision and extension", and that "data" does not only concern the individual who provided the data or about who the data is, but also other stakeholders that might have different interpretations of the data. They then describe a data flow in which personal data (data by or about a person) is subject to analytics, which results in inferences, which in turn results in actions influencing people's behavior or in feedback to further analytics.

We think "personal data" as described by Mortier et al. [15] needs clarification. "Data about a person" could refer to personally identifiable information in the sense of privacy law or information security, but it could also refer to personally unidentifiable information such as anonymized or aggregated data, e.g. the unemployment rate or average creditworthiness of the neighborhood a person is living in. "Data by a person" might refer to data recorded or authored by a person or simply to data provided by a person, e.g. after this person conducted some data processing or acquired the data from a third person. To clarify the subject we propose that HDI should investigate "data that affects people". This includes stakeholders in the data lifecycle as well as data provenance, i.e. investigating previous stages in the data lifecycle such as data generation, collection, processing, etc. Moreover, the data lifecycle has not necessarily a simple

---

[1] https://okfn.org/opendata/.

sequential or circular form but might take the form of an arbitrary graph, e.g. when data sets are split or merged and used in other HDI processes.

The aforementioned authors tried to characterize "data" by citing a range of properties (e.g. "unstructured", "complex" or "large scale"). In fact, there exist numerous definitions of the term "data" that all have their strengths and weaknesses.

Merriam-Webster's definition of "data"[2] seems unnecessarily limited. "Factual information" for example excludes information that is uncertain, "numerical form" excludes qualitative data. "Information output by a sensing device or organ" seems to indicate that there is an agent actively providing data, which is questionable. Despite these limitations, these definitions show that "data" is something that has to be used, and indicate what can be done with data: data can be measured, collected, given meaning, analyzed or used for reasoning, discussion, interpretation, etc. The definitions also show that the term is somewhat problematic. The general Wikipedia definition[3] first conflates data and information ("pieces of data are individual pieces of information"), only to put them into a hierarchical relationship one sentence later ("Data as an abstract concept can be viewed as the lowest level of abstraction, from which information and then knowledge are derived."). This hierarchical relationship seems to be compatible with the "knowledge pyramid" [18], a model used in Information Science that, however, is controversial [7].

Since we are proposing HDI as a research challenge for HCI, we think it is unwise to subscribe to a definition from a specific scientific area since this might restrict approaches and methods to tackle the challenge and consequently restrict the number of interested researchers. For now, we preliminarily define "data" in the context of HDI as artifact-mediated representations of phenomena that need to be given meaning by people and that serve some purpose.

After characterizing the term "data", Mortier et al. [15] subsequently arrive at three themes (legibility, agency, and negotiability) which they use to structure further discussion. Legibility is concerned with processes of understanding, which requires making transparent data processing. Agency is concerned with the power of acting upon data and within systems that process data. Negotiability seems to be related to legibility and agency. It stresses contextual and dynamic factors such as changes over time or different social, legal contexts. As Mortier et al. [15] state, organizations of the HDI landscape other than legibility-agency-negotiability are possible. Legibility, agency and negotiability can be interpreted as requirements for interacting meaningfully with data or based on data. There might be other requirements, and from the point of view of HCI research or design, it is also pertinent to consider contexts where these requirements have not been met. We thus propose to employ the more general "understanding data" and the consequences thereof as top-level concerns of HDI. A main goal of HDI then should be to design human-data interaction that enables stakeholders to promote desired and avoid undesired consequences of data use.

"The consequences of understanding data" are actions that are or are not taken based on the actual understanding. For example, "data" might refer to private pictures

---

[2] http://www.m-w.com/dictionary/data.

[3] http://en.wikipedia.org/wiki/Data.

a person publishes in online social network services, "understanding" might refer to the interpretation of these pictures by an employee in a human-resources department, and "consequence" might refer to influencing a hiring decision by the interpretation of said pictures. Another simple example is credit scoring based on generalized data of a person (e.g. gender, race, or neighborhood). "Understanding" and "consequences" then cover the "interaction" part of HDI, and the two examples above show that this also encompasses legibility, agency and negotiability according to Mortier et al.

On the other hand, if we open the context from Mortier et al.'s "personal data" to "data that affects people", then legibility, agency and negotiability are not sufficient. Even if we completely understood issues related to legibility, agency and negotiability, we would still not know much about consequences of data interpretation in the social world.

Consider for example the 2014/2015 water crisis in the Brazilian state of São Paulo, which at the time of writing this paper is still ongoing[4]. News media started printing or posting water levels of the principal reservoirs that supply water to the region. This data is legible to a certain degree: it is known where the data comes from and people understand a part of its meaning ("drinking water supply is on a critical level" and "if the current data trend continues we will run out of water soon"). People have some agency and there exists some degree of negotiability, e.g. exerting public pressure or suggesting to news outlets to collect data more frequently and to also include secondary water reservoirs, weather forecasts, or other prognoses.

Based on the water level data, only a small part of the problem is understood, and this limited understanding might lead to short- or mid-term consequences such as reducing water consumption, denunciating water squanderers, complaining against the government, or moving to another region of the country. In order to understand a larger part of the problem and be able to take different actions, one has to ask questions such as what is the ratio of water consumption between private households and industry; has the water supply infrastructure kept up with population and industry growth; is the draught a singular phenomenon, or is it related to climate change or deforestation in other regions, etc. Answering these questions might result in a broader understanding and different consequences.

To give an example closer to Mortier et al.'s personal data [15], consider a person keeping a food log and monitoring body weight and related figures using a smartphone app. Even if legibility, agency and negotiability regarding collected data were guaranteed, we would not know whether this self-monitoring would lead to a higher degree of well-being or to an eating disorder, and how the latter behavior might be avoided or mitigated.

In order to be able to understand consequences or even design "data interaction" that promotes or inhibits certain consequences, we need to consider complex contextual factors including the systems of beliefs, values and norms of the involved people. Instead of proposing additional topics to legibility, agency and negotiability, that might need to be amended as our knowledge of the problem grows, we thus propose to stay at the more general level of understanding data and the consequences thereof.

---

[4] E.g. http://www.bbc.com/news/world-latin-america-29947965, last access on Feb 25th, 2015.

As a consequence of the need to consider people's norms, values and beliefs, regarding the "human" part of HDI, we subscribe to Bannon's "more human-centered perspective", i.e. we give "primacy to human actors, their values, and their activities" and understand HCI as "human activities mediated by computing" [2]. This human-centered perspective should not be confounded with flavors of human-centered design that are too narrowly focused on users and atomistic interactions with artifacts [16]. Furthermore, the "humans" in HDI do not only include those who directly access and use data but also those who affect and are affected by the consequences of this use.

3   A Semiotic Perspective on HDI

Semiotics is the doctrine of signs, and in Peircean Semiotics, "a sign is something [...] which denotes some fact or object [...] to some interpretant thought" ([17], vol. 1, par. 346), or paraphrased, "a sign is something which stands to somebody for something in some respect or capacity" [20]. Framing data as "artifact-mediated representations of phenomena that need to be given meaning by people and that serve some purpose" means we can understand data as signs that are subject to processes of interpretation. The three main branches of Semiotics—Syntax, Semantics and Pragmatics—are concerned with the structure, meaning and use of sign.

To give some examples of areas related to HDI, Data Visualization is mostly focused on Syntax, trying to reveal the structure of data (e.g. local or global maxima or minima, trends, distribution) by choosing adequate visualizations (e.g. bar charts, box plots, scatter plots). Information Visualization is focused on Semantics, trying to reveal the meaning of data (e.g. how the gross domestic product per person is related to life expectancy in different countries). Pragmatics is always present since any visualization or other representation of data or information is created with a purpose or intention. In fact, Pragmatics is already relevant when choosing data sources, deciding how to select which data from these sources, how to cleanse and process data, etc. From an HCI and HDI perspective, these are all design decisions that need to be taken deliberately and consciously, considering users and other relevant stakeholders.

Apart from Syntax, Semantics and Pragmatics, additional aspects are relevant for HDI as conceptualized in this paper, in particular the effects that intentional and purposeful actions have in the social world. Examples include privacy, trust, health or personal well-being. Organizational Semiotics [12] understands organizations of people as complex systems of sign processing and extends the traditional semiotic framework by including the Physical World, Empirics, and the Social World [20]. The physical layer is concerned with the media in which signs appear and the hardware with which they are transmitted or processed. The empirical layer is concerned with statistical properties and the coding of signs across different media. The social layer is concerned with the effects of the use of signs in the social world, i.e. with beliefs, expectations, or commitments. HDI-related topics on this layer include privacy, trust or security.

We can use the six layers of the extended semiotic framework and cross them with the different stages of the data lifecycle, e.g. data origin, selection, cleansing, mapping, display or interaction. As a third dimension we can introduce the different stakeholders that appear at each stage in the data lifecycle. For each triple [layer in the Semiotic Framework, stage in the data lifecycle, stakeholder] we can now map design issues or questions (Fig. 1) that make the data lifecycle more explicit, clarify how data might be understood, and help to understand possible consequences of data use.

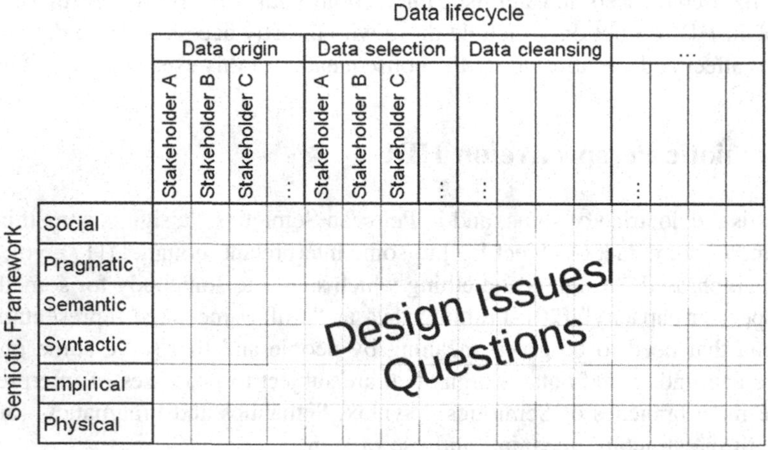

Fig. 1. Mapping design issues in the data lifecycle using the extended semiotic framework

As an example of how to use Fig. 1, consider data in the context of Quantified Self applications. In this case, the origin of data are sensor outputs of different devices (e.g. for tracking hear rate, insulin level, weight), as well as the actual self-quantifying person (e.g. keeping a manual food log). Stakeholders include the self-quantifying person, the manufacturers of hardware devices, software developers, as well as possibly a spouse, family and other relatives or friends, physicians, nutritionists, etc.

A design issue on the physical level that is of interest to varying degrees to the self-quantifier, the hardware manufacturer, and people in the self-quantifiers social environment is whether the used hardware devices can be fit into the physical context of the daily routine. Related issues on this layer include the hardware specification, e.g. memory capacity, processing power, or battery life. These issues might have ramifications in other layers of the semiotic framework or other stages of the data lifecycle.

An example issue on the empirical level related to "noise on the data channel" is whether the used devices allow accurate and precise observation of data, for instance when keeping a food log to track calorie intake "one apple" is not very precise since the weight of an apple might vary. A related issue is the choice of data encodings and formats, e.g. paper annotation or digital, standard or proprietary format. Again—and this can be generalized to all semiotic layers and the complete data lifecycle—these issues might affect other semiotic layers and later stages in the data lifecycle.

The syntactic layer is concerned with structure, e.g. in the case of self-quantification and data origin the procedures required for making data observable. Issues here are related to the correct use of capturing devices, as well as to questions such as whether it

Is possible to cross-reference food intake with insulin levels or heart rate with type of physical activity.

Regarding semantics, an example question is whether it is meaningful to register food intake without registering physical activity, or even mental activity or psychological states. For a nutritionist it might be sufficient to simply monitor body weight in order to assess the success of a diet plan, while for a person who has a low self-awareness of food intake it might be more meaningful to observe more detailed data.

Issues in the pragmatic layer are related to people's intentions. The intentions of a self-quantifying person might include self-improvement, curious exploration, staying in control, increasing performance or mitigating health problems. The intentions of device manufacturers might be of a commercial nature with sub-goals such as providing reliable and pleasant means for observing data, or be related to altruistic motives such as improving people's well-being.

In the social layer, i.e. regarding effects or consequences, the self-quantifier might gain a higher self-awareness when recording data. Friends or family members might become amused, annoyed, interested or inspired to also start self-quantifying.

We can make similar investigations for the data lifecycle stages posterior to "data origin". Data use by the self-quantifying person or other stakeholders depends on the tools provided by software manufactures. On the syntactic level, if these tools provide limited functionality (e.g. only provide static graphs or tables of aggregated data) or have poor usability, some aspects of the data might remain unexplored. If the tools use poorly implemented gamification mechanisms ("new personal record!" after an insignificant change) data might be misinterpreted. This might influence stakeholders' understanding on the semantic level (e.g. a change of body weight within a short time span might not be significant while a trend during a longer period might be). The understanding shapes how stakeholder intentions are materialized, e.g. if weight loss or gain is interpreted as significant, data might be shared with friends or a nutritionist. On the social level, understanding of data and materialization of intentions might lead to a change of the self-quantifiers attitudes and behaviors. Device manufacturers on the other hand might be perceived as facilitators of personal well-being or exhibitionism, and public expectation regarding the quality of their products might change.

This superficial and very incomplete investigation of HDI-related issues of self-quantification, an arbitrarily chosen topic, demonstrates that HDI encompasses more than the interaction of an end-user with the product of some data processing. It also shows that for understanding this complex context, not only semantics, but all layers of the extended Semiotic Framework are required. Furthermore, consequences of data understanding and use appear in the social layer, and are shaped by all stages of the data lifecycle.

4   Research Challenges for HDI

Data lifecycles might vary among problem domains, but generally at least four major stages are present: data production and collection; data transformation and filtering; data presentation; and data display and interaction. The example of the previous section served to argument that if we want to design for purposeful interaction with data, i.e. for data understanding and actions based on this understanding, we need to consider all stages of the data lifecycle and the relevant stakeholders.

The following questions might help to clarify an HDI problem. What does the data lifecycle look like? Who are the respective stakeholders and what are their responsibilities and competences? Who has access to which data at which stage? Who provides the hardware and software tools at each stage, and is it possible or necessary to design or redesign them? How to anticipate social implications of HDI design? These questions are relatively easy to answer—although they might require some effort as in the case of stakeholder identification—and do not depend on the domain and design problem, nor on the adopted conceptual framework.

The chosen conceptual framework enables a systemic view of processes related to the data lifecycle. We proposed to employ Organizational Semiotics, outlining the use of the extended semiotic framework as a tool for mapping design issues in the data lifecycle, but this does not preclude the use of alternative or additional frameworks.

We stated that one of the main goals of HDI should be to design human-data interaction that enables stakeholders to promote desired and avoid undesired consequences of data use. Since it is impossible to know any potentially conflicting consequences of data use beforehand, this is not a goal for design, but a desired outcome of the use of designed artifacts. A goal is to enable stakeholders to understand data on different levels, and in particular on the semantic, pragmatic and social level. Possible actionable objectives include making users aware of and understanding the intentions of different stakeholders involved in the data lifecycle, as well as enabling users to access different data sources and interacting with data representations that match their preferences and capabilities.

We identify two overarching research questions regarding these objectives: (1) how do the different stages of the data lifecycle affect each other; and (2) how do different representations of different data and different mechanisms to use these representations (e.g. explore, manipulate, share) affect people's ability to understand and act upon this understanding?

A first step to answering question (1) would be to investigate existing examples of human-data interaction such as those given in this paper, to reconstruct the data lifecycle as well as involved stakeholders and to try to identify patterns and invariants. A subsequent step might be to conduct different case studies in order to validate and refine knowledge about the impact of different data lifecycle stages and in order to create and test different data representations and interaction mechanisms.

In order to answer both questions, we can build upon already existing work in various areas. Regarding question 1, e.g. Software Engineering, HCI or Organizational Semiotics provide us with methods for identifying stakeholders and their concerns. HCI and Organizational Semiotics also allow investigating pragmatic aspects from different perspectives. Regarding question 2, we can build on concepts and use methods from—to name but a few—HCI, Semiotics, and Data or Information Visualization or Sonification, Theories of Human Perception and Cognition.

Despite this rich base of concepts and methods, many questions remain.

The semiotic concept of abduction, i.e. the process of generating, verifying and refuting hypotheses, allows us to reason about how people gain an understanding of data. How can we leverage the concept of abduction during design and evaluation, e.g. how can we support users with little or no statistical knowledge to generate sensible hypotheses regarding quantitative data?

Data and Information Visualization and Sonification provide us with knowledge about good representations of data, albeit focused on the syntactic or semantic level. What are good representations that consider the pragmatic and social level? Are visual and auditory displays and interaction mechanisms enough or should we also explore haptic displays or, more general, embodied interaction?

HCI knows various frameworks that consider stakeholder concerns and the social impact of design and use, e.g., Participatory Design or Value Sensitive Design. How can these be employed in HDI? How can we conduct a participatory design of the data lifecycle? Does it make sense and is it possible to conduct a participatory data analysis? How can we apply principles of Value Sensitive Design to HDI?

5 Conclusion

The production, collection, processing and use of data have taken new dimensions in terms of complexity and possible social impacts. In this paper, we have presented problems related to Human-Data Interaction, and identified HDI as a research field for HCI and related areas. We have characterized HDI and outlined research challenges, adopting a semiotic perspective to ground future investigations.

Our discussion adds to the existing literature by offering an alternative view HDI and its challenges. We argue that the goal of designing Human-Data Interaction should be to enable stakeholders to promote desired and to avoid undesired consequences of data use. Therefore, data production, collection, processing and use need to be investigated systematically, focusing on the social impact they provoke. Understanding interaction with data as a sign process, we draw attention to an approach that goes beyond the challenges of representation and sense-making, also considering pragmatic and social issues related to meaning in context, intentions, negotiations and the effects of data use.

Acknowledgements. This work received financial support by CAPES, CNPq (#308618/2014-9), and FAPESP (#2014/01382-7).

References

1. Anthes, G.: Data brokers are watching you. Commun. ACM **58**(1), 28–30 (2014)
2. Bannon, L.: Reimagining HCI: toward a more human-centered perspective. Interactions **18**(4), 50–57 (2011)
3. Cafaro, F.: Using embodied allegories to design gesture suites for human-data interaction. In: Proceedings of the 2012 ACM Conference on Ubiquitous Computing, UbiComp 2012, pp. 560–563. ACM, New York, NY, USA (2012)
4. Dourish, P.: Where the Action Is: The Foundations of Embodied Interaction. MIT Press, Cambridge (2001)

5. Elmqvist, N.: Embodied human-data interaction. In: ACM CHI 2011 Workshop "Embodied Interaction: Theory and Practice in HCI", pp. 104–107 (2011)

6. Estrin, D.: Small data, where n = me. Commun. ACM **57**(4), 32–34 (2014)

7. Frické, M.: The knowledge pyramid: a critique of the DIKW hierarchy. J. Inf. Sci. **35**(2), 131–142 (2009)

8. Goodman, E.: Design and ethics in the era of big data. Interactions **21**(3), 22–24 (2014)

9. Johnson, M.: The Body in the Mind. The University of Chicago Press, Chicago (1987)

10. Kennedy, J.B., Mitchell, K.J., Barclay, P.J.: A framework for information visualisation. SIGMOD Rec. **25**(4), 30–34 (1996)

11. Lakoff, G., Johnson, M.: Metaphors We Live By. University of Chicago Press, Chicago (2003)

12. Liu, K.: Semiotics in Information Systems Engineering. Cambridge University Press, New York, NY (2000)

13. Liu, K.: Semiotics in digital visualization. In: Keynote Lecture at the 16th International Conference on Enterprise Information Systems, ICEIS 2014. http://vimeo.com/95737955. Accessed 10 Nov 2014

14. Mortier, R., Haddadi, H., Henderson, T., McAuley, D., Crowcroft, J.: Challenges and opportunities in human-data interaction. In: The Fourth Digital Economy All-hands Meeting: Open Digital (DE), Salford (2013)

15. Mortier, R., Haddadi, H., Henderson, T., McAuley, D., Crowcroft, J.: Human-data interaction: the human face of the data-driven society. Available at SSRN: http://ssrn.com/abstract=2508051 or http://dx.doi.org/10.2139/ssrn.2508051 (2014)

16. Norman, D.A.: Human-centered design considered harmful. Interactions **12**(4), 14–19 (2005)

17. Peirce, C.S.: Collected Papers of Charles Sanders Peirce, vols. 1–6. Harvard University Press, Cambridge (1931–1935)

18. Rowley, J.: The wisdom hierarchy: representations of the DIKW hierarchy. J. Inf. Sci. **33**(2), 163–180 (2007)

19. Shilton, K.: Participatory personal data: an emerging research challenge for the information sciences. J. Am. Soc. Inf. Sci. Technol. **63**(10), 1905–1915 (2012)

20. Stamper, R.K.: A semiotic theory of information and information systems/applied semiotics. In: Invited Papers for the ICL/University of Newcastle Seminar on "Information", 6–10 Sept 1993

Relationship Between Trust and Usability in Virtual Environments: An Ongoing Study

Davide Salanitri[1(✉)], Chrisminder Hare[1], Simone Borsci[1],
Glyn Lawson[1], Sarah Sharples[1], and Brian Waterfield[2]

[1] Human Factors Research Group, Faculty of Engineering,
The University of Nottingham, Nottingham, UK
{ezxds2,Chrisminder.Hare,simone.borsci,Glyn.Lawson,
Sharples.Sarah}@nottingham.ac.uk
[2] Jaguar Land Rover, Virtual Innovation Centre (VIC), Coventry, UK
bwaterfl@jaguarlandrover.com

Abstract. Usability and trust have been observed to be related in several domains including web retail, information systems, and e-health. Trust in technology reflects beliefs about the attributes of a technology. Research has shown that trust is a key factor for the success of different systems – e.g., e-market, e-commerce, and social networks. Trust in technology can be supported or prevented by the perceived usability. Therefore, a low level of usability could compromise an individual's trust in their use of a technology, resulting in a negative attitude towards a product. Even if this relationship has been seen as important in the fields listed above, there is limited research which empirically assesses trust and usability in virtual reality (VR). This work will present the first set of data on the relationship between usability and trust in VR. To gather this data, three different VR systems (Desktop 3D tool, CAVE, and a flight simulator) were tested. The findings show that (i) the best-known questionnaire to measure usability and trust could be applied to VR, (ii) there is a strong relationship between people's satisfaction and trust in the use of VR, (iii) the relationship between usability and trust exists for different systems.

Keywords: System usability scale · Trust · Trust in technology measures · Virtual reality · Usability

1 Introduction

Can you treat Virtual Reality (VR) as a coworker? What does it mean to trust VR?

Trust is a fundamental concept in everyday life, being a factor influencing several types of interaction, from interpersonal to group behavior, from economic to politic [1]. It can be assumed that for every situation where an interaction is provided, trust is indispensable. Thus, many researchers in the past decades studied the concept of trust applied in several domains such as inter-organizational trust [2], or trust in leadership [3].

Nowadays, the nature of interaction has changed with the introduction of technologies. Thus, other than with people, many interactions occur between people and technologies and, also for this type of relationship, trust is an essential part. It is clear that trusting people and trusting technologies is different [4]. As suggested by [5],

© Springer International Publishing Switzerland 2015
M. Kurosu (Ed.): Human-Computer Interaction, Part I, HCII 2015, LNCS 9169, pp. 49–59, 2015.
DOI: 10.1007/978-3-319-20901-2_5

person-person trust is "a psychological state comprising the intention to accept vulnerability based upon positive expectations of the intention of the behavior of another" (p. 395). This definition cannot be applied to trust in technology, since the technology does not have any "intention". This assumption led some authors to state that only people can be trusted [6]. Conversely, several authors (including the authors of this paper) suggest that some characteristics of person-person trust are extendable to the trust in the use of technology [7, 8]. Reference [4] specified that when referring to the relationship with technologies, "trust situations arise when one has to make oneself vulnerable by relying on another person or object, regardless of the trust object's will or volition" (p. 3). In literature, trust in technology is considered a more problematic form of relationship to the one between person-person [4], mostly because technologies may not guarantee to people the same level of assurance and support to reach their goals (e.g. pay for a service, fill a form) that another human being can guarantee [6]. However, in each interactive situation, trust in technology, intended as a set of beliefs in the use of a product (i.e., belief in the functioning, reliability, safety, etc.) is a key factor for a satisfactory relationship between user and product [4]. A clear example of the importance of trust in technologies is the use of personal data to buy goods on websites [9]. Moreover, research has shown that trust is a key factor for the success of technologies in several domains such as decision to purchase a product online [10], in the business-to-consumer field trust has a direct effect on the vendor opinion and an indirect effect on consumer intention to purchase [11]. Concurrently, in social networks, [12] found that technological factors of trust are as important as interpersonal trust.

Regarding the definition of trust in technology, [4, 8] claim that trust in technology reflects at least three main beliefs about the attributes of a technology: (i) belief about the functionality of the product, which refers to the capability of a technology to perform specific tasks; (ii) belief that the technology is helpful. Thus to the fact that the technology will help the user to perform a specific task; (iii) Belief that the technology is reliable, hence, the perception that a technology works properly.

Even though the studies on trust in technology are growing, currently there is not a clear framework on the factors affecting users' trust before and during the interaction with different technologies. However, some theoretical and empirical studies have suggested that trust in technology can be supported or prevented by the perceived usability of the system [13]. Concurrently a relationship between trust in technology and usability was underlined in several domains, such as web retail [13], information systems [7] and e-health [14].

Usability is defined as the extent to which a product can be used by specified users to achieve specified goals with effectiveness, efficiency and satisfaction in a specified context of use [15]. A low level of usability could compromise the users' interaction with a product, thus affecting the individual's trust in the technology functionality, reliability and helpfulness.

Although the relationship between trust in technology and usability is known in HCI, currently there are no empirical studies that analyzed the relationship between trust and usability during the interaction with virtual reality (VR) environments. VR is defined as an experience where an individual is placed in a 3D environment generated by a technology, and is able to interact inside this environment [16]. VR systems are today commonly applied in several situations – such as phobia treatment [17–19], pain reduction [20–23], training [24] etc. Nevertheless, as [24] suggested these systems are, still today, quite expensive, and often researchers and practitioners are so focused on testing the functionalities of their systems that they missed to explore, with standardized tools, aspects such as the perceived usability and trust.

Present work aims to discuss the initial results of ongoing research on trust in VR.

The objective of the research is to identify the main factors of trust, and validate a model to assess trust in the use of VR. The initial framework hypothesizes that trust in VR is influenced by at least three main factors: (i) Usability, (ii) Presence [25], and (iii) Acceptance [26] (see Fig. 1).

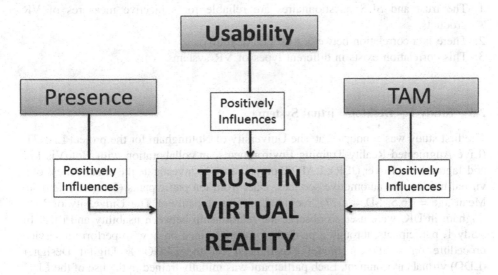

Fig. 1. The framework of trust in virtual reality

An ongoing set of data on the relationship between usability and trust[1] of different VR environments will be presented and discussed in this paper. To gather data, three VR systems - a Desktop 3D tool, a Cave Automatic Virtual Environment (CAVE), and a flight simulator - were tested using twenty five participants – ten participants for the 3D Desktop, ten for CAVE, and five for the simulator. Whilst three different virtual environments were experienced for different experimental aims, the same methodology was used after each interaction to assess both trust and usability. This methodology is described below.

2 Experimental Design

2.1 Materials

Three experiments were organized from October 2014 to December 2014. Each study used a common set of standardized evaluation tools (i.e., questionnaires) to gather data about perceived usability and trust.

---

[1] From now on, the term "trust" is referred to "trust in technology" as defined before.

- System Usability Scale (SUS). The SUS has been built by [27]. SUS is composed by two factors: Usability and Learnability [28–30].
- Trust in Technology Measures (TTM) questionnaire, developed by [4] has been built to investigate trust in technology.

2.2 Hypotheses

The hypotheses of the study were:

1. The trust and SUS questionnaires are reliable for subjective measures of VR products.
2. There is a correlation between trust and usability.
3. This correlation exists in different types of VR systems.

2.3 Study 1 – Desktop Virtual System

The first study was conducted at The University of Nottingham for the project LARTE (Live Augmented Reality Training Environments, in collaboration with HoloVis Ltd and Jaguar Land Rover (JLR). LARTE project aims to investigate the effectiveness of a virtual training for automotive services. Data from ten participants (5 male, 5 female; Mean age = 26.5, SD = 4.77), recruited among students of The University of Nottingham in UK, were used to observe the relationship between usability and trust. In study 1, participants, through a pc desktop, were trained on how to perform a service procedure on a 3D car model experienced on the LEGO ® Digital Designer (LDD) virtual environment. Each participant was initially trained in the use of the LDD for 15 min by an expert. After that, participants received a video training on the service procedure and were asked to perform the procedure on the LDD and on a real model of a car. After the performance, participants were asked to assess the usability (SUS) and the trust in the use (TTM) of LDD application as a virtual training tool.

2.4 Study 2 – CAVE Environment

The second study, conducted at JLR Virtual Innovation Centre (VIC), was designed with a twofold objective, as follows: (i) to investigate the applicability of the trust questionnaire to VR environments experienced in a CAVE; (ii) to have a first set of data on the relationship between trust and usability in CAVE. The participants were 10 all were JLR employees (7 Male, 3 Female; Mean age = 33.21, SD = 15.01). Participants of this study received an initial training (15 min) to learn how to use a CAVE system and become familiar with the manipulation of the objects in the 3D immersive environment. After that, participants were asked to interact with the technology to perform a set of assembly and reassembly tasks with a limited amount of time. After the performance participants were asked to assess the usability and the trust in the use of a CAVE application to perform object manipulation and assembly and reassembly tasks.

2.5 Study 3 – Flight Simulator

Study 3 aimed to investigate the reaction of pilots of Airbus Group to a new interface for a jet commercial aircraft. A part-task simulator was used to allow pilots to interact with the new interface. Moreover, the simulation experience also used flight gear for a short haul flight.

Study 3, as well as the above studies, is ongoing research. For the aim of this work, we discuss here only the outcomes collected by five male pilots (Mean age = 50.2, SD = 8.23). Pilots have both military and commercial licenses and are based at Airbus Group. Each participant experienced the interface of fly simulator to achieve three emergency activity tasks given to the participants. The emergencies given to the participant include; engine fire, fuel leak and a combination of the two. Each task starts during cruise phase; consequently the participants do not have to take-off or land.

The procedure for experiment three requires two experimenters in the assessment. The first experimenter is the lead experimenter, who looks after the participant, explains the tasks and delivers the questionnaires. The second experimenter's role is to handle the simulator, explain the cockpit philosophy to the pilot and act as Air Traffic Control (ACT).

Firstly, the lead experimenter briefs the participants regarding the flight including the route, what they would be required to do i.e. to manually fly the aircraft, the weather, etc. This can be considered similar to what would occur during a briefing session before a flight was to take place. The participants are then introduced to the system and asked to have a trial run using the interfaces. Pilots were instructed to freely interact with the system until they were comfortable and ready to start the task. The order of the tasks is controlled to reduce the learning effect. During the task they need to maintain aircraft control, attend to the emergency using the relevant checklists and comply with the ATC instructions (delivered by the second experimenter). After the performance of the three tasks, pilots are asked to complete the SUS and Trust questionnaire about the use of the fly simulator application to learn how to react in emergency situations.

2.6 Data Analysis

Pearson's correlation coefficient analysis was used to assess the correlation between SUS and Trust questionnaires. Moreover, Cronbach alpha index is used to check the scales reliability. Finally a linear regression with stepwise method was performed to observe the effect of usability on trust. The results of the TTM are converted in percentage.

All the data were processed by IBM SPSS ® 22.

3 Results

The three VR applications tested in the studies were perceived by participants as usable – average SUS overall score equaled 78.9 % - and trustworthy – average TTM score equaled 77.9 %. Nevertheless the three applications have different levels of usability and trust, in particular the flight simulator resulted in the most usable and trustable VR environment among the studies (see Fig. 2).

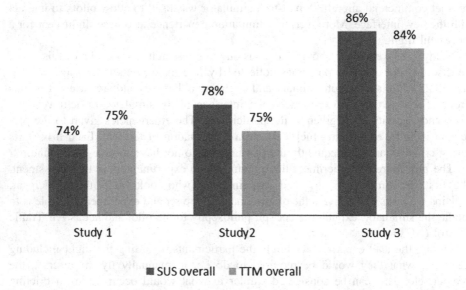

Fig. 2. Overall scores (in percentage) of SUS and TTM scales for each study. Study 1 LDD application experienced through a Desktop pc. Study 2 a VR environment experienced through a CAVE. Study 3 a VR application experienced in a fly simulator.

Independently from the hardware experienced by participants (Desktop, CAVE and simulator), SUS and TTM questionnaires resulted reliable tools when applied to measure usability and trust in the use of VR environments. As Table 1 shows SUS reliability ranges from .65 to .92, while TTM ranges from .792 to .884.

Table 1. Cronbach's alpha (α) of SUS and TTM scale estimated in each study

	SUS	TTM
	α	α
Study 1	.65	.792
Study 2	.92	.884
Study 3	.903	.831

Table 2. Correlation between the overall scale of TTM and the usability factor of SUS. Correlation was measure through the Pearson's correlation coefficient (r).

	Overall TTM					
	Study 1		Study 2		Study 3	
	r	p	r	p	r	P
Usability SUS	.645	.044	.693	.026	.895	.04

Table 3. Outcomes of linear regression to observe the effect (F, β and p) of the usability factor of SUS on the overall level of trust, and to analyze the percentage of explained variance (AdjR²).

			Overall SUS	Usability SUS
Overall TTM	Study 1	F	6.35	5.69
		β	0.665	0.645
		p	0.036	0.04
		AdjR²	0.373	0.343
	Study 2	F	6.56	7.39
		β	0.762	0.693
		p	0.04	0.026
		AdjR²	0.382	0.415
	Study 3	F	-	12.11
		β	-	0.809
		p	-	0.04
		AdjR²	-	0.735

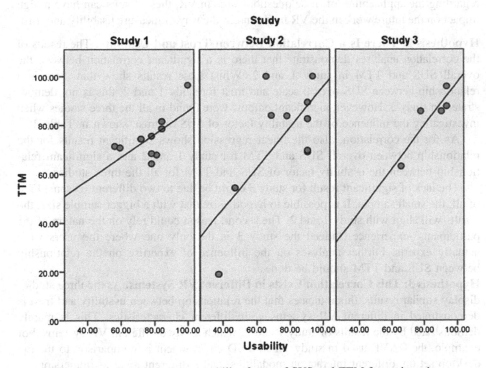

Fig. 3. Relationship between usability factor of SUS and TTM for each study

The overall scale of TTM and SUS questionnaires correlated in study 1 (r = .665, p = .036) and 2(r = .672, p = .033). Concurrently, as Table 2 shows, TTM overall scale correlate with the usability factor of SUS in all the three studies.

Linear regression, as showed in Table 3, revealed that overall scores of SUS predict TMM overall scores only for participants of study 1 and 2. Nevertheless, the usability factor of SUS resulted as a good predictor of TTM scores for the participants of all the three studies. Figure 3 shows the relationship between the usability factor and TTM in the three studies.

4   Discussion

The relationship between usability and trust has usually been studied in web and software domains. These three studied aimed to investigate if this relationship is applied also to VR systems. This section will discuss the results of the three studies in light of the hypotheses explained above in the paper.

Hypothesis 1: TTM and SUS are Reliable for Subjective Measures of VR Products. The results of the Cronbach's alphas indicate that the two questionnaires are reliable for VR domain, mainly in study 2 and 3. Since there is lack of literature regarding the applicability of these questionnaires in VR, these results can have a high impact on the future work in the VR fields and in the way of measure usability and trust.

Hypothesis 2: There Is a Correlation Between Trust and Usability. The results of the correlation analyses demonstrate that there is a significant correlation between the overall SUS and TTM in study 1 and 2. Whist these results show that there is a relationship between SUS overall scale and trust for study 1 and 2, this is not demonstrated in study 3. However, significant outputs were found in all the three studies when investigating the influence of the usability factor of SUS on trust, shown in Table 2.

As for the correlation, also the linear regression shows significant results for the relationship between overall SUS and TTM for study 1 and 2 and a significant relationship between the usability factor of SUS and TTM for all the three studies.

The lack of significant result for study 3 could be due to two different reasons. First of all, the small sample. It is possible to hypothesize that with a bigger sample size, the results will align with study 1 and 2. The second reason could rely on the nature of the participants' experience. Indeed the study 3 is the only one where the users were actually experts. Further analyses on the influence of expertise on the relationship between SUS and TTM should be done.

Hypothesis 3: This Correlation Exists in Different VR Systems. As the three studies display similar results, this indicates that the relationship between usability and trust is demonstrated in different VR systems with different characteristics. This is mainly demonstrated by the results of study 1 and 2, which use two different VR systems. For example, the CAVE used in study 1 had a 3D environment in comparison to the 2D desktop set up, different interaction modalities, and a different level of immersion.

5 Conclusion

As stated in the introduction, VR is a growing technology and it is applied in several domains. Investigating the factors influencing the trust that users have in the technology could change the way people interact with VR and the way VR is developed. This study aimed to have a first set of data on the relationship between one of the most known factor of HCI, usability, and trust. It is important to address that this is one of the first studies where trust is applied to VR systems.

Generally, it can be said that the results of the three experiments fulfill the hypotheses of the study, demonstrating (i) that standardized tools largely applied in HCI studies may be reliably used to test the user experience of different VR systems (ii) that a strong relationship between usability and trust in VR systems exists, thus usability could be a predictor of users' trust in VR systems and (iii) that the relationship between usability and trust is present in different VR technologies.

Further data will be collected in the next months, to add more users to our evaluation cohorts. Nevertheless, current results support the idea that the designers who want to deliver a successful VR application have to carefully define the functioning of the system by proving usable tools. As said above, trust is a wide and multi factorial concept, therefore understanding the usability role is just one step toward the full comprehension of the trust in technology concept applied to VR application. In tune with that, future works are needed to investigate the role of usability in the development of people beliefs and attitudes (such as trust) toward a technology, but also to understand the effect of other factors (such as Presence and Technology Acceptance) on trust in VR.

Acknowledgments. The authors of this paper would like to thank the technology strategic board (in alphabetic order: HoloVis ltd., Jaguar Land Rover, The University of Nottingham) of the Live Augmented Reality Training Environments (LARTE)– 101509 project for study one, Jaguar Land Rover in the person of Brian Waterfield for study 2 and, for study 3, the Horizon centre for Doctoral Training at the University of Nottingham (RCUK Grant No. EP/G037574/1). Study 3 has been part funded by the RCUK's Horizon Digital Economy Research Hub grant, EP/G065802/1 and part funded by Airbus Group.

References

1. Hosmer, L.T.: Trust: The connecting link between organizational theory and philosophical ethics. Acad. Manag. Rev. **20**, 379–403 (1995)
2. Seppänen, R., Blomqvist, K., Sundqvist, S.: Measuring inter-organizational trust—a critical review of the empirical research in 1990–2003. Ind. Mark. Manage. **36**, 249–265 (2007)
3. Burke, C.S., Sims, D.E., Lazzara, E.H., Salas, E.: Trust in leadership: a multi-level review and integration. Leadersh. Q. **18**, 606–632 (2007)
4. Mcknight, D.H., Carter, M., Thatcher, J.B., Clay, P.F.: Trust in a specific technology: an investigation of its components and measures. ACM Trans. Manage. Inf. Syst. (TMIS) **2**, 12 (2011)

5. Rousseau, D.M., Sitkin, S.B., Burt, R.S., Camerer, C.: Not so different after all: a cross-discipline view of trust. Acad. Manag. Rev. **23**, 393–404 (1998)
6. Friedman, B., Khan Jr., P.H., Howe, D.C.: Trust online. Commun. ACM **43**, 34–40 (2000)
7. Lippert, S.K., Swiercz, P.M.: Human resource information systems (HRIS) and technology trust. J. Inf. Sci. **31**, 340–353 (2005)
8. McKnight, D.H., Choudhury, V., Kacmar, C.: Developing and validating trust measures for e-commerce: an integrative typology. Inf. Syst. Res. **13**, 334–359 (2002)
9. Gefen, D., Karahanna, E., Straub, D.W.: Trust and TAM in online shopping: an integrated model. MIS Q. **27**, 51–90 (2003)
10. Gefen, D.: E-commerce: the role of familiarity and trust. Omega **28**, 725–737 (2000)
11. Pennington, R., Wilcox, H.D., Grover, V.: The role of system trust in business-to-consumer transactions. J. Manage. Inf. Syst. **20**, 197–226 (2003)
12. Lankton, N.K., McKnight, D.H.: What does it mean to trust Facebook?: examining technology and interpersonal trust beliefs. ACM SIGMIS Database **42**, 32–54 (2011)
13. Roy, M.C., Dewit, O., Aubert, B.A.: The impact of interface usability on trust in web retailers. Internet Res. **11**, 388–398 (2001)
14. Fruhling, A.L., Lee, S.M.: The influence of user interface usability on rural consumers' trust of e-health services. Int. J. Electron. Healthc. **2**, 305–321 (2006)
15. ISO: ISO 9241-11:1998 Ergonomic requirements for office work with visual display terminals – Part 11: Guidance on usability. CEN, Brussels, BE (1998)
16. Rheingold, H.: Virtual Reality: Exploring the Brave New Technologies. Simon & Schuster Adult Publishing Group, New York (1991)
17. Anderson, P.L., Zimand, E., Hodges, L.F., Rothbaum, B.O.: Cognitive behavioral therapy for public-speaking anxiety using virtual reality for exposure. Depress. Anxiety **22**, 156–158 (2005)
18. Bouchard, S., Côté, S., St-Jacques, J., Robillard, G., Renaud, P.: Effectiveness of virtual reality exposure in the treatment of arachnophobia using 3D games. Technol. Health Care **14**, 19–27 (2006)
19. Rothbaum, B.O., Hodges, L.F., Ready, D., Graap, K., Alarcon, R.D.: Virtual reality exposure therapy for Vietnam veterans with posttraumatic stress disorder. J. Clin. Psychiatry **62**, 617–622 (2001)
20. Gershon, J., Zimand, E., Lemos, R., Rothbaum, B.O., Hodges, L.: Use of virtual reality as a distractor for painful procedures in a patient with pediatric cancer: a case study. Cyberpsychol. Behav. **6**, 657–661 (2003)
21. Hoffman, H.G., Patterson, D.R., Magula, J., Carrougher, G.J., Zeltzer, K., Dagadakis, S., Sharar, S.R.: Water-friendly virtual reality pain control during wound care. J. Clin. Psychol. **60**, 189–195 (2004)
22. Steele, E., Grimmer, K., Thomas, B., Mulley, B., Fulton, I., Hoffman, H.: Virtual reality as a pediatric pain modulation technique: a case study. Cyberpsychol. Behav. **6**, 633–638 (2003)
23. Wismeijer, A.A., Vingerhoets, A.J.: The use of virtual reality and audiovisual eyeglass systems as adjunct analgesic techniques: a review of the literature. Ann. Behav. Med. **30**, 268–278 (2005)
24. Borsci, S., Lawson, G., Broome, S.: Empirical evidence, evaluation criteria and challenges for the effectiveness of virtual and mixed reality tools for training operators of car service maintenance. Comput. Ind. **67**, 17–26 (2015)
25. Slater, M., Wilbur, S.: A framework for immersive virtual environments (FIVE): speculations on the role of presence in virtual environments. Presence Teleoperators Virtual Environ. **6**, 603–616 (1997)
26. Davis, F.D.: Perceived usefulness, perceived ease of use, and user acceptance of information technology. MIS Q. **13**, 319–340 (1989)

27. Brooke, J.: SUS-a quick and dirty usability scale. Usability Eval. Ind. **189**, 194 (1996)
28. Borsci, S., Federici, S., Lauriola, M.: On the dimensionality of the system usability scale: a test of alternative measurement models. Cogn. Process. **10**, 193–197 (2009)
29. Lewis, James R., Sauro, Jeff: The factor structure of the system usability scale. In: Kurosu, Masaaki (ed.) HCD 2009. LNCS, vol. 5619, pp. 94–103. Springer, Heidelberg (2009)
30. Lewis, J.R.: Usability: lessons learned … and yet to be learned. Int. J. Hum. Comput. Inter. **30**, 663–684 (2014)

Cultural Issues in HCI: Challenges and Opportunities

Luciana Salgado[1](✉), Roberto Pereira[2], and Isabela Gasparini[3]

[1] Department of Computer Science, Fluminense Federal University (UFF),
Niterói, Brazil
luciana@ic.uff.br
[2] Institute of Computing, University of Campinas (UNICAMP),
Campinas, Brazil
rpereira@ic.unicamp.br
[3] Department of Computer Science, Santa Catarina State University (UDESC),
Joinville, Brazil
isabela.gasparini@udesc.br

Abstract. Culture strongly influences people's values, expectations, behavior, and even perceptions and cognitive reasoning. Although HCI researchers recognize culture as an important factor, the research about cultural issues and HCI needs to go further. This paper discusses why culture should not be viewed as a threat or something that is better to relegated to minor importance in Human-Computer Interaction, but that has a key role in the investigations and development of new theories, methods and techniques. In the light of the grand challenges prospected in GranDIHC-BR by the Brazilian HCI community, we explore some of the opportunities and challenges culture brought to HCI as a research area.

Keywords: HCI and culture · Cultural aspects of HCI · Research challenges in HCI

1 Introduction

In 1959, Hall [16] argued that technology is the most efficient way to introduce changes in culture and to redefine a society. Today, we live in a society mediated by information and communication technologies (ICTs). The changes introduced by this scenario are not only visible but have defined the way we work, study, eat, interact to each other, understand time and space, and live.

Among the main disciplines of Computer Science, Human-Computer Interaction (HCI) is the one that should deal with issues that are universal and transversal to the other areas of computing and, at the same time, should consider specific and situated aspects (e.g., cultural, social, economic, political, geographical) of the environment in which it is applied. It means that HCI has a fundamental (and complex) role in technology development and innovation, as well as a strong responsibility and ethics in the design, evaluation and implementation of interactive computing systems for human use.

© Springer International Publishing Switzerland 2015
M. Kurosu (Ed.): Human-Computer Interaction, Part I, HCII 2015, LNCS 9169, pp. 60–70, 2015.
DOI: 10.1007/978-3-319-20901-2_6

In fact, as we live in an increasingly globalized world and we frequently interact with ubiquitous technology in many places and contexts (e.g., work, school, leisure, relationships, etc.), the HCI research should explore the cultural issues that permeate and influence the design, development, evaluation and use of interactive technologies. However, considering and dealing with cultural issues have become an even complex and critical challenge when thinking in terms of a culture mediated by ICTs. The very idea of culture, in its broadest sense, has suffered transformations that require us to revisit our theoretical and methodological grounds and practices.

Different initiatives have been conducted to identify and inspire future directions in HCI for the next years. In 2007, for instance, researchers from academy and industry, from several countries and with different backgrounds, joined efforts for discussing the HCI in 2020 [28]. The participants were unanimous when pointing out to the need for placing human values in the core of HCI area. In 2012, the HCI Brazilian community, in turn, presented an initiative to prospect 5 (five) Grand research challenges for HCI in the Brazilian context for the next 10 years [3, 7]: (1) Future, smart cities and sustainability; (2) Accessibility and digital inclusion; (3) Ubiquity, multiple devices and tangibility; (4) Human values; and (5) HCI education and industry. "Human values" is one of them. Values cannot be understood outside their cultural context, and the same is true for other social issues such as human needs, preferences, habits and behavioural patterns. While these issues reveals important aspects that should be considered when designing a technology, the cultural context will explain why they are important and indicate how to address them.

We have recently started a discussion about the 5 grand challenges identified by the Brazilian HCI community through the lenses of culture, arguing that culture is transversal to them and cannot be ignored if we desire to advance in these challenges [24]. In this paper, we analyze more deeply the cultural issues related to each 5 grand challenges. Although there are influential literature about culture in technology, recent literature regarding culture and HCI claims that the treatments given to culture in HCI research has been often fragmentary and guided by practical and specific problems [27]. So, in this paper, we extend the discussions presented in [24], approaching culture as an important subject that is transversal to some HCI challenges and hot topics (e.g., information visualization, wearable computing, big data, etc.). Additionally, we show that culture itself is a challenge for HCI, once it requires that our traditional HCI theories, methods and practices to be jointly rethought and redefined.

The paper is structured in five sections. Section 2 presents a brief literature review on the theme, from the definition for culture to some of the main works developed around the subject. Section 3 presents some challenges and hot topics in HCI discussed through the lenses of culture; in this section we highlight critical factors that are related to/dependent on culture for each challenge, and discusses on the general relation between culture and usability. Finally, Sect. 4 presents our final remarks and conclusions.

2 Background

Anthropological scientific research on culture started about 150 years ago [10]. Although there is not a single definition for culture, there is a consensus that the term emerged in 1871 as a synthesis of the "Kultur" and "Civilization" terms. Kultur was used to refer to all the spiritual aspects of a community; and Civilization referred to the material achievements of a people. Edward Tylor synthesized both terms in the term "Culture". Culture, or civilization, in its wide and ethnographic sense, is that complex whole which includes knowledge, belief, art, morals, law, custom and any other capabilities and habits acquired by man as a member of society [29].

Culture can have a serious effect on the way people interact with, react to, and feel about symbols, terms and situations [5]. In HCI literature dealing with culture, Hofstede's perspective [19] is among the most known and cited [8, 13]. According to the author, culture is the sharing of beliefs, values and practices of a group of people; the collective programming of mind that distinguishes the members of one culture from the members of another. On the one hand, this approach has been advantageous for those interested in predicting the behavior of cultural groups, because it assumes the existence of generalized cultural traits [27]. On the other hand, Hofstede's approach does not favor the ones interested in identifying relevant cultural aspects that may emerge from, and be relevant for, a particular cultural context.

Hall [17] and Geertz [15] views of culture has also been adopted in research about practical and methodological culture and HCI. From a broader perspective, Hall understands culture as the way of life of people, their learned behavior patterns, attitudes, values and material goods. Hall analyzes culture as a form of communication giving emphasis on the non-verbal one (behaviors, values, intentions, needs, expectations, etc.). According to Hall, culture is related to the different ways of organizing life, thinking and understanding basic assumptions about the family, the state, the economic system, and even the human being, acting as a link between humans and the mean to interact with each other [16].

When talking about culture, Hall [17] believes that it is more important to look at the way things are put together than at specific theories. In this sense, the author proposed 10 (ten) primary messages systems (PMS), or areas, he named the basic building blocks of culture (interaction, association, learning, play, protection, exploitation, temporality, territoriality, classification, and subsistence), arguing that any culture could be characterized, analyzed and compared through a combination between these areas.

Geertz in his interpretive or symbolic anthropology, in turn, believes that man is suspended in webs of significance he himself has spun and take culture to be those webs. This view is in line with the third HCI paradigm discussed by Harrison and co-authors, in 2007 [18], which views interaction as a form of meaning making, and also with the view of Salgado [27] and colleagues about culture-sensitive meanings, as a large portion of the content communicated in cross-cultural systems.

The interest in culture in HCI research dates back to the 1980s, as explained by Marcus in [21]. Some authors have considered cultural issues in the creation of interactive technologies, particularly investigating its influence on usability evaluation

[4, 11, 30, 32, 35], and proposing (or revisiting) design methods from a cultural perspective [1, 13, 25, 26, 34]. Culture is also on the core of researches related to internationalization and globalization [21]. However, recommendations for the interface design for international users are often based on collective knowledge, personal experiences and few case studies [22].

In this sense, some authors [22, 25] argue that although HCI researchers recognize culture as an important factor, studies that explicitly consider cultural issues are still scarce. In fact, the treatments given to culture in HCI research have been mostly fragmentary and guided by practical and specific problems [27]. Therefore, it is necessary to discuss and generate new knowledge that will help HCI professionals to recognize the importance of cultural factors in the design and evaluation of interactive technologies. The very understanding of culture, its role in technology design, and existing theories and methods for dealing with cultural issues, are topics that need to be discussed, disseminated and revisited.

3 Challenges in Culture and HCI

Winograd and Flores [32] argued that the role of an interactive system designer goes beyond the construction of an interface to encompass all the interspace in which people live. The author advocates that it is necessary a shift from understanding the machinery to understand people life's while using it. In fact, the very definition of HCI provided by ACM (Association for Computing Machinery) indicates that this shift is not only necessary, but should be an already well-established concern and practice: *"a discipline concerned with the design, evaluation and implementation of interactive computing systems for human use and with the study of major phenomena surrounding them"*[1]. This definition represents the complexity and comprehensiveness of the area, and attributes to HCI the responsibility to consider not only technical issues, but also the ones related to the cultural context in which interactions occurs.

There are relevant works on the literature intended to identify, discuss and inspire current and future HCI research. Harrison and co-authors [18] discuss a new paradigm in HCI that must deal with the establishment and multiplicity of meaning in situated interactions. Bødker [6], in turn, speaks in terms of a new wave in HCI where new elements of human life are included, such as culture, emotion, and experience; and where the focus is on the cultural level and on an expansion of the cognitive to the emotional. Bannon [2] claims for a "re-imagination" of the HCI area, and Sellen and co-authors [28] and Baranauskas and co-authors [3] prospect challenges and opportunities for HCI in the near future.

The Five Grand Research Challenges proposed by the Brazilian community [3, 7] is a good starting point to show the challenge of dealing with culture in HCI. Brazil is a country of continental dimensions, with a heterogeneous population in terms of ethnicity, behaviors, geographic, etc., and marked by inequalities (in its widest) and chronic deficiencies (e.g., infrastructure, education, health, safety). We believe that

---

[1] http://old.sigchi.org/cdg/cdg2.html#2_1, last access on February 10th, 2015.

although these challenges have been proposed specially for the Brazilian context, they may be considered relevant for the HCI field as a worldwide research area, and for a globalized society.

Following, we draw the 5 Grand Challenges and discuss them through the lenses of culture. Each topic requires research and advances in different perspectives that are equally challenging, covering technical, theoretical and methodological, and social issues. Our discussion is guided by these three perspectives and shows that all professionals in the HCI community have more than a direct or indirect relation with culture (regardless the adopted focus or topic investigated).

3.1   Future, Sustainability and Smart Cities

Discussed as a Grand Challenge, Future, Sustainability and Smart Cities bring into consideration that issues related to renewal, reuse and disposal of software and hardware should be considered as part of design requirements. Smart Cities is a hot topic for technology design, being both an additional challenge for sustainability and an ideal context to investigate solutions and solve critical problems.

There are several points that need to be considered when talking about sustainability and the future. Some of them require deep cultural changes in society. To promote sustainability, there must be a change in people's behavior. There are studies being carried out in the context of persuasive technologies that aim to promote people's sustainable behavior (e.g., saving water and electricity, recycling). Besides ethical issues (and values) involved in the design of technologies that want to promote a certain type of behavior, if there is not a deep understanding of how people organize themselves, survive and operate in society, then, it will be impossible this promotion to occur in the correct (desired?) direction.

A key step in designing a solution for promoting or inhibiting a sustainable action is to understand the needs and the behavior patterns of a social group and to know their origin. For example, if a given community does not separate the garbage for recycling, there maybe several possible reasons that explain this behavior, such as: (i) people are not aware of it, (ii) people are not motivated, (iii) they do not agree with the idea, (iv) they do not have resources to support garbage collection, etc.

Every possible reason has different explanations and leads to different understandings that influence the type of action for encouraging behavior change: social training and awareness activities/publicity; an incentive and reward program; providing the equipment and structures that enable the collection and recycling, etc. Each group of people develop their social organization strategy and is placed in a physical environment with opportunities and weaknesses. Understanding this situated context is central to analyze what is important (and necessary) to people and how to design something that can add to their life, well-being and dignity; and for this, we should consider the specificities of their culture.

From this first "Grand Challenge", thus, we argue that besides usability, adaptability and so on, HCI design and evaluation should deal with cultural sustainability, i.e., the quality of support sustainable behavior. HCI as a research area should advance the quality criteria concepts currently disseminated to include world's urgent needs.

3.2   Accessibility and Digital Inclusion

This topic makes it explicit the concern with accessibility issues and their role to promote digital inclusion, highlighting the need to build systems that can be used both on different devices and specialized for different users and their needs. Promoting accessibility is a basic requirement for supporting people's and a democratic society, guaranteeing that people will find no barriers for living and acting regardless their limitations and specificities.

In this sense, it is essential to consider cultural issues when thinking about accessibility. The way accessibility is understood and treated, the importance given to universal access of citizens to existing resources, and the strategies to ensure such access are closely linked with cultural issues. Economic resources, educational background, gender and age, the environment and the physical infrastructure, the need for information, etc., are examples of issues that vary greatly according to the group analyzed. These issues directly influence the accessibility, the type of strategy and technology to be adopted and results.

In [23, 25], the authors argue that accessibility should be discussed as a cultural value related to the exploitation of the world, and with different levels of formality. For instance, it is necessary to recognize that people have different needs, views, understandings and expectations regarding accessibility; different stakeholders value and react to accessibility in a different way. There are also social rules, laws and norms related to accessibility that must be understood and followed; there are accessibility standards and certifications, formal training and education, etc. Finally, there are physical structures, tools and technical devices for providing accessibility (e.g., assistive technologies), or that require accessibility; there are public and private services related to accessibility, technical procedures, frameworks, and so on.

For this challenge, it is important a mutual understanding in HCI between technology and users. In this context, designers and researchers cannot impose their points of view, for example, they should support to local culture to develop, and thereafter pass it in the technology. This mean approaching people to the technology without trample, because we need to know the different users' facets. Besides, there are often political and cultural decisions within technology, even when we think we are neutral, because we carry our personal believes and understanding about the world.

Nowadays, interactive systems can be anywhere and anytime. Therefore, today it is important to know how to deal with cultural issues, especially when developing or evaluating wide-access applications and interactive systems. Interactive systems for the web need to provide support for an ever increasing amount of material and make it available for local-language populations across the world. One of the main challenges for designers is to build/evaluate systems that aim explicitly at acknowledging the diversity of their users' cultural background and attending to a wider variety of needs and expectations [14, 27].

3.3   Ubiquity, Multiple Devices and Tangibility

This topic draws attention to a new range of interactive technologies and interactions possibilities, encompassing immersive and engagement aspects in interactions. Ubiquitous systems, simultaneous interaction with multiple devices, brain-computer interfaces, tangible interfaces and gesture-based interfaces are examples of new forms of interaction.

Besides the issue of accessibility and other considerations presented previously, this challenge makes it explicit the need to understand how to design new forms of interaction that make sense to people and contribute to make their life easier. Identifying the kind of physical artifact to be designed, the feasibility of designing it, people's interesting using it, and the benefits that can be offered, are issues that need a cultural understanding to be clarified.

There are several cultural factors that influence this challenge, ranging from more known issues, such as gestures that are recognized by a group of people and the preferred types of devices to use, to more subtle issues, such as the knowledge to use them, the time and the location where the devices are available and how the interaction occurs, the possible impacts on emotional, affective and physical aspects of users, etc.

The security and privacy are one of the main burdens ways to accepting ubiquitous computing. They are dynamic and contextual, e.g. privacy laws and regulations vary widely all over the world, and individual participation (and his/her consent) is an important issue. In this way, the cultural needs are different, the access to the technology and to the cities are different, and a new perspective emerge - the human now interacts with all environment, not only with the computer. This is a new perspective that must be understood.

3.4 Human Values

The link between culture and human values is inseparable. A value cannot be understood outside its cultural context [25]: while a value indicates something that is important and needs to be taken into account, the cultural context explains why such value is important. What people like, consider importance and value is closely connected with the environment in which they live and their social relations. Therefore, the most important point here is the need to approach values and culture in an integrated and articulated way, including the concern for both concepts in the methods, practices and artifacts used to support the design of interactive technologies.

The explicitly consideration of values and culture is not only a challenge in theoretical, methodological and technical issues, but also a cultural challenge for the HCI community in its posture and practices. There is a tendency to leave these issues to the margins of the developed works, underestimating their importance or even neglecting them altogether. Therefore, we must make an explicit commitment to understanding and respecting values and culture in our research and practices.

Many open issues emerge when we discuss human values and culture itself in interaction design, and HCI, including:

- How can we understand and represent human values and use them appropriately in the interaction design?
- How do we obtain relevant cultural information about a specific community and how do you determine each is relevant?
- How do we generate design ideas from this cultural information?

- How important is culture among all other aspects being considered in an interaction design?
- How Brazilian HCI community, and other communities, can address cultural issues in their research?

This paper obviously has not an answer to these questions, it just tries to provide some directions of how culture in HCI still an open issue. Therefore, it is yet a limited journey into a territory that includes many other possible perspectives and paths to be explored.

3.5 HCI Education and Industry

HCI Education and Industry have a two-way relationship with cultural issues: on the one hand, cultural issues influence on what need to be taught, how it should be taught, what kinds of skills need to be developed, what strategies should be adopted, etc. On the other hand, the HCI education is usually the only opportunity that students of technology and computing courses have to be able to deal with social issues, such as culture and values. Therefore, the HCI education plays a key role in capacitating students to conduct a socially responsible work in academy as well as in industry.

As claimed by HCI researchers [28], computer technologies are not neutral – they are laden with human, cultural and social values. So, HCI disciplines should emphasize the interdisciplinary aspect of the field, involving different perspectives and people, creating something new by crossing boundaries.

Additionally, we should understand that the companies and organizations are not looking only for technical skills, but they are looking for creativity and talent. In Computerworld last research about the hottest IT skills for 2015, for instance, talent was explicitly included by John Reed: "The leaders who realize that IT talent trumps technology put hiring at the top of their priority list and create the urgency and enforce the message that bringing on top talent is of the utmost importance." [9].

Another challenge is to bridge the gap between what and the way we teach and the practice of computing. As claimed by Matt Leighton, director of recruitment at Mondo, a tech staffing agency, "there is a gap in terms of what the companies want to do and the talent that is out there to execute these initiatives" [9]. HCI education should motivate, therefore, initiatives to bring industry experts and academy (teachers and students) closer together. Strengthening the links between the two parts is an important way of ensuring mutual understanding.

3.6 Culture and Usability

Usability is a relative concept rather than an absolute one. You cannot say, for instance, that some design is usable or has good usability. You can say, however, that design 'X' is relatively more usable than design 'Y' based on some measure of effectiveness, efficiency, satisfaction, and learn ability [12]. Numerous usability evaluation techniques have emerged to measure these factors, and, nowadays, different researches have been studying these techniques and how they are adapted for different cultures [12, 30, 35].

Some researchers have gone beyond these more mechanical measures to focus on the emotional impacts of design, and many practitioners would now prefer to focus on what is the user experience (UX), rather than just usability. This recognizes that while usability is important and an often neglected part of design, the holistic nature of design is such that a successful design requires a balancing of all the different aspects of that design (usability, functionality, aesthetics, and why not culture?, etc) and not just concentrating on one to the neglect of the others. It recognizes that a finished design is a gestalt – the whole is greater than the sum of its parts [12]. Such view brings a new perspective about how to deal with cultural issues (e.g. in the design and the evaluation process, and analyzing all stakeholders cultures – i.e., designer, user, programmers, and so on). All people involved in the design or evaluation process have their particular cultural characteristics, and these could bias the interpretation of a design concept or an understanding on the evaluation.

Cultural awareness become central when we have to interact with people from other cultures. The quality of user experience is intricately related to the users' cultural characteristics [20]. System features appropriated for one culture may not be suitable for others; as well as system's design needs to be adapted for different cultures [20].

The influences of culture can be seen in products, by choices concerning use of colors, symbols, language set, and so on, and in the design process, e.g., culture influences higher level design issues, the design methods employed in building interfaces and in usability methods [11]. The cultural influence, if ignored, can compromise usability evaluations, therefore giving information that is inaccurate [31].

Although culture issues is becoming increasingly important to HCI, many of its concepts, techniques and approaches are not known by the designers. Besides this, culture is in a constant movement, and must be preserved and respected. It is not our goal to point out what is the best approach (if this answer is possible), but to make a stand in communicate to HCI practitioners and researchers to be aware of cultural issues involved in their design and solutions.

4 Conclusion

How can we turn HCI cross and/or intercultural issues into opportunities? UNESCO argues that cultural diversity needs to be addressed as an asset and not a threat, a source of renewal for public policies in service to development, social cohesion and peace [30]. The challenges cultural diversity may represent to ICT should be tamed in favor of a sustainable world.

Today, in the context of discussions about the future of HCI research area and the need to rethink the theories, methods and practices adopted to support the design of interactive and more innovative technologies, the concern with aspects related to cultural diversity is a trend and a challenge by itself. In fact, we must understand and acknowledge that these aspects directly influence the way an interactive technology is created, perceived, understood and used. Research on the impacts of cultural differences on HCI [4, 31, 33, 35] has led professionals to the creation of products that do not meet the demands of its users, does not make sense to them, and often cause unwanted effects on the environment in which they are introduced.

Therefore, we, as HCI designers, have an ethical responsibility to ensure that the solutions we design do not trigger unwanted effects on the environment in which they are inserted and on the different stakeholders involved. While researchers, in turn, we must assume a compromise to investigate and create solutions to support designers in industrial and academic contexts in this task. We hope this paper to promote discussions about the complexity in designing interactive technologies, and the need to direct efforts to solve fundamental problems that still affects society.

Acknowledgements. This research is partially funded by FAPESP (#2013/02821-1; #2014/01382-7), CAPES and CNPq.

References

1. Abou-Zeid, E.-S.: A culturally aware model of inter-organizational knowledge transfer. Knowl. Manag. Res. Pract. **3**, 146–155 (2005)
2. Bannon, L.: Reimagining HCI: toward a more human-centered perspective. Interactions **18**(4), 50–57 (2011)
3. Baranauskas, M.C.C., de Souza, C.S., Pereira, R. (orgs.). I GranDIHC-BR — Grandes Desafios de Pesquisa em Interação Humano-Computador no Brasil. Relatório Técnico. Comissão Especial de Interação Humano-Computador da Sociedade Brasileira de Computação (2014)
4. Barber, W., Badre, A.: Culturability: the merging of culture and usability. In: Proceedings of the 4th Conference on Human Factors and the Web, pp. 1–14 (1998)
5. Blanchard, E.G.: Adaptation-oriented culturally-aware tutoring systems: when adaptive instructional technologies meet intercultural education. In: Song, H., Kidd, T. (eds.) Handbook of Research on Human Performance and Instructional Technology. Information Science Reference, Hershey (2009)
6. Bødker, S.: When second wave HCI meets third wave challenges. In: Proceedings of 4th Nordic Conference on Human-Computer Interaction: Changing Roles, pp. 1–8. ACM Press, Oslo (2006)
7. Carvalho, A.C.P.L., et al.: Grandes Desafios da Pesquisa em Computação no Brasil–2006–2016. Sociedade Brasileira de Computação, São Paulo (2006)
8. Clemmensen, T., Roese, K.: An overview of a decade of journal publications about culture and human-computer interaction (HCI). Working paper nr. 03-2009. http://openarchive.cbs.dk/bitstream/handle/10398/7948/WP_2009_003.pdf
9. ComputerWorld magazine. http://www.computerworld.com/article/2844020/10-hottest-it-skills-for-2015.html. Accessed March 2015
10. Danesi, M., Perron, P.: Analysing Cultures. Indiana University Press, Bloomington (1999)
11. Del Gado, E., Nielsen, J.: International Users Interface. Wiley, New York (1996)
12. Douglas, I., Liu, Z.: Global Usability. Human-Computer Interaction Series. Springer, London (2011)
13. Gasparini, I., Pimenta, M.S., Palazzo M. de Oliveira, J.: Vive la différence!: a survey of cultural-aware issues in HCI. In: X Brazilian Symposium on Human Factors in Computer Systems (IHC 2011), pp. 13–22 (2011)
14. Gasparini, I, Kimura, M.H., Moraes Junior, S.L., Pimenta, M.S., Palazzo M. de Oliveira, J.: Is the Brazilian HCI community researching cultural issues? An analysis of 15 years of the Brazilian HCI conference. In: The Fourth International Workshop on Culturally-Aware Tutoring Systems (CATS 2013). Proceedings of the Workshops at the 16th International Conference on Artificial Intelligence in Education (AIED 2013), pp. 11–19. Memphis (2013)

15. Geertz, C.: The Interpretation of Cultures: Selected Essays. Basic Books, New York (1973)
16. Hall, E.T.: The Silent Language. Anchor Books, New York (1959)
17. Hall, E.T.: Beyond Culture. Doubleday, New York (1976)
18. Harrison, S., Tatar D., Sengers, P.: The three paradigms of HCI. In: Proceedings of ACM AltCHI 2007, pp. 1–21 (2007)
19. Hofstede, G.: Cultures and Organizations: Software of the Mind, 2nd edn. McGraw-Hill, New York (2005)
20. Lee, I., Choi, G.W., Kim, J., Kim, S., Lee, K., Kim, D.: Cultural dimensions for user experience: cross-country and cross-product analysis of users' cultural characteristics. In: Proceeding of the 22nd British HCI Group Annual Conference on People and Computers: Culture, Creativity, Interaction, BCS-HCI 2008, vol. 1, pp. 3–12 (2008)
21. Marcus, A.: International and intercultural user interfaces. In: Stephanidis, C. (ed.) Users Interfaces for All: Concepts Methods and Tools, pp. 47–63. Lawrence Erlbaum, Hillsdale (2001)
22. Noiwan, J., Norcio, A.F.: Cultural differences on attention and perceived usability: investigating color combinations of animated graphics. Int. J. Hum Comput Stud. **64**, 103–122 (2006)
23. Pereira, R., Baranauskas, M.C.C., Silva, S.R.P.: Social software and educational technology: informal, formal and technical values. Educ. Technol. Soc. **16**(1), 4–14 (2013)
24. Pereira, R., Gasparini, I., Salgado L.: Cultura Importa e faz Diferença: uma Discussão sobre os Grandes Desafios de Pesquisa em IHC no Brasil. In: Proceedings of the XIII Simpósio Brasileiro Sobre Fatores Humanos em Sistemas Computacionais (2014)
25. Pereira, R., Baranauskas, M.C.C.: Value pie: a culturally informed conceptual scheme for understanding values in design. In: Kurosu, M. (ed.) HCI 2014, Part I. LNCS, vol. 8510, pp. 122–133. Springer, Heidelberg (2014)
26. Salgado, L.C.C., Souza, C.S., Leitão, C.F.: On the epistemic nature of cultural viewpoint metaphors. In: X Brazilian Symposium on Human Factors in Computer Systems (IHC 2011), pp. 23–32 (2011)
27. Salgado, L.C.C., de Souza, C.S., Leitão, C.F.: A Journey Through Cultures: Metaphors for Guiding the Design of Cross-cultural Interactive Systems. Springer, Berlin (2013)
28. Sellen, A., Rogers, Y., Harper, R., Rodden, T.: Reflecting human values in the digital age. Commun. ACM **52**, 58–66 (2009)
29. Tylor, E.B.: Primitive Culture: Researches into the Development of Mythology, Philosophy, Religion, Art, and Custom. Cambridge University Press, Cambridge (2010)
30. UNESCO. Investing in Cultural Diversity and Intercultural Dialogue (2009). http://www.unesco.org/new/en/culture/resources/report/the-unesco-world-report-on-cultural-diversity. Accessed Feb 2015
31. Vatrapu, R., Pérez-Quiñones, M.A.: Culture and usability evaluation: the effects of culture in structure interviews. J. Usability Stud. **1**(4), 156–170 (2006)
32. Winograd, T., Flores, F.: Understanding Computers and Cognition: A New Foundation for Design. Addison-Wesley, Reading (1986)
33. Winschiers H., Fendler, J.: Assumptions considered harmful: the need to redefine usability. In: 2nd International Conference on Usability and Internationalization, pp. 22–27 (2007)
34. Xinyuan, C.: Culture-based user interface design. In: IADIS International Conference on Applied Computing, pp. 127–132 (2005)
35. Yeo, A.W.: Are usability assessment techniques reliable in non-western cultures? Electron. J. Inf. Syst. Dev. Countries (EJISDC) **3**(1), 1–21 (2000)

Biologically Inspired Artificial Endocrine System for Human Computer Interaction

Hooman Samani[1](✉), Elham Saadatian[2], and Brian Jalaeian[3]

[1] Department of Electrical Engineering, National Taipei University,
Taipei, Taiwan
hooman@mail.ntpu.edu.tw
[2] Department of Electrical and Computer Engineering, National University
of Singapore, Singapore, Singapore
[3] Bradley Department of Electrical and Computer Engineering, Virginia Tech
University, Blacksburg, USA

Abstract. The aim of this paper is to illustrate the design process and development of a novel model for cause - effect artificial intelligence system, which is based on the digital endocrine model in human computer interaction. The model is inspired by the architecture of the endocrine system, which is the system of glands that each of them secretes different type of hormones directly into the bloodstream. The digital hormonal model can provide a new methodology in order to model various advanced artificial intelligence models for predictive analysis, knowledge representation, planning, learning, perception and intelligent analysis. Artificial glands are the resource of the causes in the proposed model where the effects can be modeled in the data stream. In this paper such system is employed in order to develop a robotic system for the purpose of language translation.

Keywords: Artificial endocrine system · HCI · Translation robot

1 Introduction

State of the art in computer science allows users to use various software and applications for the purpose of language translation; however the availability of hardware for this usage is very limited. Apart from computer and smart phone applications only limited systems such as wearable devices in the form of glasses have been developed in the domain of language translation [1]. With the aim of combining hardware and software and as an application of our proposed AI model, in this work, we have equipped the smart phone translation APP with robotic platform by adding touch and voice sensors, improving the audio output quality via a speaker and designing wheels for the robot movement.

In the age of digital technology, smart phones became an essential tool for everyone. Moreover, several software and APPs have been developed for the purpose

© Springer International Publishing Switzerland 2015
M. Kurosu (Ed.): Human-Computer Interaction, Part I, HCII 2015, LNCS 9169, pp. 71–81, 2015.
DOI: 10.1007/978-3-319-20901-2_7

of language translation. These several APPs for translation enable us to benefit from basic translation between languages. Even though the accuracy is not perfect yet, but the current technology can help us to understand the basic meaning of statements in a different language. Our motivation in this research was to equip the available APPs on smart phones with embodiment and navigation facility in order to develop a mobile translator robot. We have developed artificial intelligent systems which can process the user input for smooth and correct functionality of the robot.

Our ultimate goal is that the translation robot can function fully autonomous and that's why AI modules such as artificial endocrine system and state flow are employed in our system. In this way the robot would acts intelligently based on the situation during interaction.

In our research we have focused on the robotic interaction design and development and for the translation module. We decided to simply use available translation modules such as Google translator. Hence our contribution is to extend the available translator APPs into embodied robot with intelligent behavior. We believe that empowering the APPs with robot navigation and interaction capabilities could improve the quality of communication and furthermore makes it more convenient and efficient. Despite various APPs, translation application has been very limited in robotic systems. The wearable translation robot is basically intelligent glasses, which can automatically translate multiple languages in real-time [1]. Such kind of technology could be promoted with applications such as Google's glass. Our aim was to change the wearable nature to a robot shape.

Various advanced robots are equipped with basic translation capabilities. However, that is still limited to expensive robots, which are currently in the research phase. Our goal was to make the robotic system low cost, functional and available for public use. We have considered various modes for the functionality of the translation robot. The main function is to have voice as the medium of communication. Furthermore, users can use text for data entry. Additionally, the robot can use the camera of the smart phone in order to scan, identify and translate any written text in the environment which is shown to the robot. This paper is extension of our work for this research [2, 9].

2   Background

2.1   Artificial Endocrine System

Homeostasis is the property of a system in which variables are regulated so that internal conditions remain stable and relatively constant [3]. The endocrine system include pituitary gland, thyroid gland, adrenal gland, gonads, insulin, parathyroid glands etc. They can secrete a variety of hormones. Hormone delivery to the desired effect with the blood cells, take to change a chemical change in the body, to coordinate physiological function. The basic flowchart of hormones functionality is presented in Fig. 1.

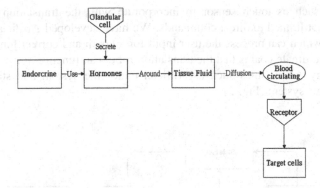

Fig. 1. Flowchart of the hormonal reactions functionality

We have employed Artificial Endocrine System (AES) on top layer of our robot navigation system. Artificial endocrine system concept is inspired from the biological system which empowers the robot to behave smoothly like the way hormones help biological system to behave smoothly with collaboration with the emotional system. AES is the calculation of the biological role of the endocrine system containing the basic model and the endocrine system by biological principles, models inspired by the wisdom of generic methods [4]. With such system, we will be able to make a response to external stimuli, and has control of the system using artificial hormones.

AES system has been used in various robotics applications such as Lovotics [5]. Physiological unit of the Lovotics artificial intelligence employs artificial endocrine system consisting of artificial emotional and biological hormones. Artificial emotional hormones include Dopamine, Serotonin, Endorphin, and Oxytocin. For biological hormones Melatonin, Norepinephrine, Epinephrine, Origin, Ghrelin, and Leptin hormones are employed which modulate biological parameters such as blood glucose, body temperature and appetite [6]. By using the artificial endocrine system in the robot's AI, the robot can operate smoothly in an unstable environment. Another advantage of AES system is to make it possible to express "slow" relation between causes and effects as it takes time for an artificial hormone to be effective. Such property generates smooth and realistic behaviors by the robot.

Another advantage of AES system is to make it possible to express "slow" relation between causes and effects (as presented in Fig. 3) as it takes time for an artificial hormone to be effective. Such property generates smooth and realistic behaviors by the robot.

2.2 Translation

We have considered various modes for the functionality of the translation robot. The main function is to have voice as the medium of communication. Furthermore, users can use text for data entry. Additionally, the robot can use the camera of the smart phone in order to scan, identify and translate any written text in the environment which is shown to the robot. In order to give an appropriate command, we have employed extra sensors such as touch sensor to incorporate with the translation APP. Such interaction is not limited to direct commands. We have developed Artificial Intelligent (AI) systems, which can process the user input for smooth and correct functionality of the robot. Our ultimate goal is that the translation robot can function fully autonomous, and that is why AI modules such as artificial endocrine system and state flow are employed in our system (Fig. 2).

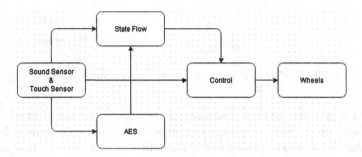

Fig. 2. Software architecture of the system

Considering the limited functionality of available translation software, we tried to keep our design simple and believable where the user does not expect perfect translation but enjoys the help of the robot of conveying the message in different language.

Data from touch and sound sensors are transmitted to the processor unit which includes three modules. The State Flow module handles state transitions of the robot. Artificial Endocrine System (AES) is highest level of AI for smooth behavior generation. Finally, the Control unit includes a PID controller for navigation of two motors, which are connected to wheel.

3   Interaction Channels

In the time that almost everyone has a smartphone, the use of telephone is beyond traditional way of merely audio communication. Our communication in enriched with various capability and possibilities were phones have been changed to media device with multimodalities. Language is still a barrier in international communications and smartphones are getting equipped with different tools to provide easier understanding. We see the change from traditional phones to smartphones and believe that future communication tools require robotics structure where output would be beyond simple display. We believe that robotics can change the way of current communication during interactions. In our developed translator robot three channels of communication are still via current smart phones.

3.1   Audio

Our robot is using two audio sensors, one is the one on the smart phone and the extra one is integrate in the robotic body. The microphone on the smart phone is directly employed for using the capabilities of the smart phone to use available APPs such as Google Translate. The other sound sensor is used beyond natural language processing (NLP) were sound parameters are input of robot AI system for controlling the behavior of the robot. In this case robot has two processors: One on the smart phone and the other on the microcontroller of the robot which run parallel software. The reason for separating these two channels was to use independent channel for two different tasks of NLP and control considering the heavy computation cost.

3.2   Video

Using the camera on the smartphone to scan the environment, interpret and understand the text translated into the other person, translation results will be presented on the screen as well. Such application is useful for example when user is in a restaurant and would like to read a menu in a foreign language. We also consider more development when robot can help the user to read various letters and translate with smart notification. For example a person who lives in another country can put all his utility bills in front of the robot and robot can send notification to pay bills in appropriate time.

3.3   Text

Using the screen and text entry capability of the smart phone, the users can also input the text by simply typing. In our user studies such functionality was especially useful when it was mistake in NLP and users wanted to enter a statement with exact words. These three modes are to facilitate the needs of users in different conditions to select the appropriate translation mode.

4   Robot

Our proposed robot design is beyond basic functionality of translation in this version of the robot. Current robot is especially useful in application like restaurants and coffee shops where the role of robot can combine translation and entertainment interaction. Our experiences in the lab where we have members from various countries were also pleasant when the robot became a medium between lab members as entertaining way of communication. One of our success achievements was to change the way people are disconnected these days by focusing on their own smart phones. By using the robot, smart phone is moved from hands of individuals to between people.

5 Method

The simple schematic of the proposed AI model is presented in Fig. 3. It is expressed that our proposed AES can relate causes and effects by taking into account the time factor.

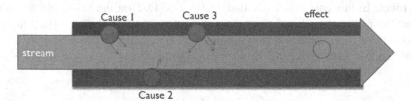

Fig. 3. The schematic of the proposed cause-effect system

For the purpose of implementation we have employed hydraulic system (Using physical modeling module of Simulink) in our AI engine in order to develop as system according to Fig. 4.

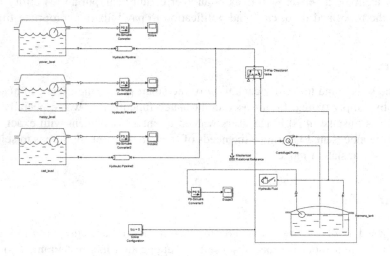

Fig. 4. The structure of the one unit of AES system

When the system receives external signal information, which in our translator robot is touch and sound, the system behaves naturally to use that cause to define two artificial hormones. One relates to sound and one to touch. For example, if the input sound signal is active for long duration, it increases the level of artificial sound hormone which leads that robot navigates slower to hear all the conversation. We defined various commands for the touch sensors for changing mode. For example if touch sensor is activated multiple times, the level of relevant hormone increases, which makes the robot to change between modes frequently.

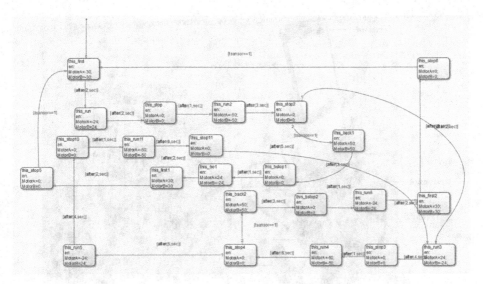

Fig. 5. Translate robot state flow

The output of AES is related to the State Flow module where several states are defined and managed in the robot. The detail of state flow is illustrated in Fig. 5. In the state flow module, we let the robot translate back and forth between two people. Based on our experiments, we adjusted the timing. The default value for changes of navigation between two people is 5 s. Users can commend the robot via voice or more directly via touch sensor. We explain the way of handling the robot for the user before experiment. In many cases, users also like to use the smartphone interface which can simply interrupt the robot movement using the touch sensor.

6 Result

Figure 6 is the prototype of the robot hardware architecture including a touch sensor and a sound sensor which is responsible for receiving and transmitting signals to the central controller, and two outputs to control the motor, which makes the robot users can easily back and forth, Speak is to make use of who can more clearly hear the contents of the translation, but the top of the translation of the robot we have prepared an upright physical infrastructure to carry a Smartphone.

As presented in Fig. 7 the robot prototype is covered to improve the believability of the robot. An example of changes in these two hormones is illustrated in Fig. 8 when we tested it for sinusoid input signals.

An instant of robot performance is illustrated in Fig. 9. In this experiment the robot is placed between two people where they can communicate in two different languages with the assistance of the translator robot.

Another example of using the translator robot is presented in Fig. 10 where the user is employing the translator robot in a restaurant which the menu is in another language

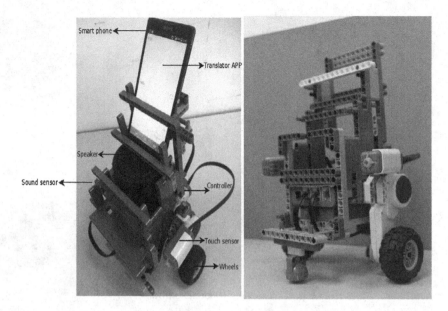

Fig. 6. The hardware structure of the translator robot

Fig. 7. Appearance of the robot

and the camera sensor is used to read the menu. Our experiment shows that such facility could be provided directly by the restaurant which engages the customer and facilitates the ordering process.

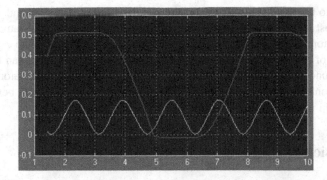

Fig. 8. AES hydraulic translate simulation with touch sensor and sound sensor

Fig. 9. Translate robot between two users

Fig. 10. One user is using the translator robot to read the menu in a foreign language

Compare to using a human translator the robotic translator has several advantages. Apart from cost benefit, the robot is able to translate between several languages were human translators often only know couple of languages. Some users also expressed the positive issue of privacy when using the robot compare to having a human to translate. Users also found the robot entertaining during interaction. The translator robot acts beyond functionality when users enjoy having a smart robot navigating between them and assist them in conversation.

7 Conclusion

We have presented a robotic system which is used for the purpose of translation between different humans using various modes of interaction such as audio and text. The proposed system empowers available APPs with embodiment which enables the translation system to navigate in the environment and facilitate multilingual communication between users. We have tested this system in the country were English is not the main language and communication between foreigners is often troublesome because of the language barriers. Our robotic design also triggers positive interaction between users due to curiosity about the developed robot. This system can be used in various applications such as meetings, ordering foods in restaurants, shops, museums and tourist attractions. In future, we aim to further develop this robot with more extra performance and behavior such as adaptive movements. We also plan to perform formal user studies to improve the design and behavior of the robot.

Apart from the mobile robot platform for hardware we have also presented a comprehensive software structure for controlling the behavior of the robot. Apart from low level PID control system, the state flow architecture could manage the transition between various states and in highest level of software the artificial endocrine system manages the main behavior of the robot based on touch and audio sensory data.

In future we aim to focus on user experience analysis [7] and also we hope to be able to design a variety of different shapes and patterns of the shell, through the concept of user experience with mobile devices [8] collected for different user groups with different preferences.

References

1. Shi, X., Xu, Y.: A wearable translation robot. In: Proceedings of the 2005 IEEE International Conference on Robotics and Automation, 2005. ICRA 2005. pp. 4400–4405. IEEE, Apr 2005
2. Ren, W.J., Samani, H.: Artificial endocrine system for language translation robot. In: Proceedings of the Second International Conference on Human-Agent Interaction, pp. 177–180. ACM, Oct 2014
3. Timmis, J., Neal, M., Thorniley, J.: An adaptive neuro-endocrine system for robotic systems. In: Robotic Intelligence in Informationally Structured Space, 2009. RIISS 2009. IEEE Workshop on, pp. 129–136. IEEE, Mar 2009
4. Timmis, J., Neal, M.: Timidity: a useful emotional mechanism for robot control? Informatica 27, 197–204 (2003)

5. Samani, H.A., Cheok, A.D.: Probability of love between robots and humans. In: 2010 IEEE/RSJ International Conference on Intelligent Robots and Systems (IROS), pp. 5288–5293). IEEE, Oct 2010
6. Samani, H.: Lovotics, Loving Robots. LAP LAMBERT Academic Publishing, Saarbrücken (2012). ISBN 3659155411
7. Tokkonen, H., Saariluoma, P.: How user experience is understood? In: Science and Information Conference (SAI), 2013, pp. 791–795. IEEE, Oct 2013
8. Yong, L.T.: User experience evaluation methods for mobile devices. In: 2013 Third International Conference on Innovative Computing Technology (INTECH), pp. 281–286. IEEE, Aug 2013
9. Ren, W.J., Samani, H.:Designing an interactive translator robot. In: SIGGRAPH Asia 2014 Designing Tools for Crafting Interactive Artifacts, p. 6. ACM, Dec 2014

Improving IT Security Through Security Measures: Using Our Game-Theory-Based Model of IT Security Implementation

Masashi Sugiura[1(✉)], Hirohiko Suwa[2], and Toshizumi Ohta[3]

[1] NEC Corporation, Tokyo, Japan
m-sugiura@fine.biglobe.ne.jp
[2] Nara Institute of Science and Technology, Nara, Japan
h-suwa@is.naist.jp
[3] The Institute of Administrative Information Systems, Tokyo, Japan
tohta@aqua.ocn.ne.jp

Abstract. We developed a quantitative model based on game theory related to IT security promotion and implementation in an organization. This model clarified the kinds of organizational conditions in which an employee does or does not carry out security measures. We also clarified the desired and undesired conditions for security implementation in an organization. In addition, we showed that an extremely undesirable dilemma that hitherto has not attracted attention might occur. Then we applied this model to an incident that occurred at a certain school. Using public information and survey data, we calculated the parameters of the model quantitatively. Then we found what kinds of changes to the parameters would be effective for making security improvements. Furthermore, we used the model to show the appropriate order of promoting security measures.

Keywords: Security · Incident · Game theory · Model · Dilemma · Organization

1 Introduction

Serious security incidents are likely to occur when security measures that have been decided upon in an organization are not carried out. To prevent the occurrence of such incidents, it is necessary to analyze the mechanisms for promoting the security measures within the organization. To meet this requirement, we apply an IT security implementation model to an actual Information Technology (IT) security incident and analyze the results obtained in applying it.

2 IT Security Implementation Game

The subject of IT security has been studied from the viewpoint of economics and social psychology [1–3]. On the basis of these studies, we have previously developed a game-theory-based model for implementing IT security in organizations [4].

© Springer International Publishing Switzerland 2015
M. Kurosu (Ed.): Human-Computer Interaction, Part I, HCII 2015, LNCS 9169, pp. 82–95, 2015.
DOI: 10.1007/978-3-319-20901-2_8

This model consists of two players: one is an IT security promotion section, which promotes the implementation of IT security, and the other is an employee who implements IT security in his or her section. In this study, we applied the model to an actual IT security incident and investigated the effect of the model parameters on the promotion of security implementation and the effectiveness of varying the parameters.

This model is a security measures promotion and implementation game in which security measures are promoted and implemented on the basis of a strategy of non-cooperativity that does not consider repetition or a mixed strategy. The IT security promotion section selects security measures and promotes their implementation. The employee is sometimes instructed by the promotion section to implement security measures while carrying out his or her duties.

The strategy of the IT security promotion section regarding security measures is either "promotion" or "non-promotion". The employee thinks about how the measures will affect his or her duties and the efforts that will be necessary to carry them out. As a result, the employee uses his or her judgment in deciding whether to implement a given measure. That is to say, the strategy of the employee is either "implementation" or "non-implementation" of the measure in question. Table 1 shows the payoff matrix of this game.

In the matrix, P_1 is the probability that the promotion section recognizes a security incident, S_p is the post-measure expense incurred after the incident occurs, M is the gain to the IT security promotion section obtained by promoting the security measure, P_2 is the probability that the employee recognizes the incident, Y_d is the loss of duties that the employee cannot perform due to time limitations and a decline in the efficiency of carrying out the security measure, Y_2 is the quantity of losses of money an employee incurs when an incident occurs, C_a is the cost that an employee expends when he or she carries out the security measure requested by the promotion section, and V is the penalty that the promotion section gives the employee when the incident occurs.

Moreover, x and y are defined as the difference between the payoff of "implementation" and the payoff of "non-implementation" when the IT security promotion section selects "non-promotion" and "promotion", respectively. {The strategy of the IT security promotion section: the strategy of the employee} denotes the combination of the strategy of the IT security promotion section and the strategy of the employee. G_2 (The strategy of the IT security promotion section: the strategy of the employee) denotes the payoff for the employee.

Table 1. Game between promotion section and employee. (Source: IPSJ Journal, vol. 52, no. 6, p. 2024).

		Employee	
		Implementation	Non-implementation
Promotion section	Promotion	$0, -Y_d$	$-P_1 S_p, -P_2 Y_2$
	Non-promotion	$M, -Y_d - C_a$	$M - P_1 S_p, -P_2 Y_2 - P_2 V$

Payoff of the promotion section appears as the first expression of each pair, payoff of the employee as the second

x and y are given as follows:

$$x = G_2(\text{non-promotion: implementation})$$
$$- G_2(\text{non-promotion: non-implementation}) \tag{1}$$
$$= -Y_d + P_2 Y_2;$$

$$y = G_2(\text{promotion: implementation})$$
$$- G_2(\text{promotion: non - implementation}) \tag{2}$$
$$= -Y_d - C_a + P_2(Y_2 + V),$$

respectively.

From expressions (1) and (2),

$$y = x - C_a + P_2 V. \tag{3}$$

Based on the x and y values, five types of the game exist. Figure 1 shows x, y, and the five games.

(1) Regular implementation game (x ≥ 0, y ≥ 0)

In this case, the Nash equilibrium and the Pareto optimum are {promotion: implementation}. Regardless of the strategy of the promotion section, the dominant strategy of the employee is "implementation". With or without the promotion of the

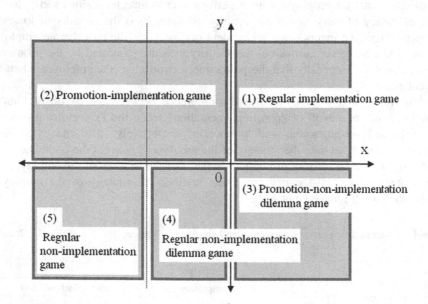

Fig. 1. Five games between the IT security promotion section and the employee. (Source: IPSJ Journal, vol. 53, no. 9, p. 2163).

promotion section, the employee always carries out a security measure. This game is therefore the most desirable state for implementing security measures.

(2) Promotion-implementation game ($x < 0$, $y \geq 0$)

The Nash equilibrium and the Pareto optimum are {promotion: implementation}. The dominant strategy of the employee is "implementation" when the strategy of the promotion section is "promotion" and "non-implementation" when the strategy of the promotion section is "non-promotion". With the promotion of the promotion section, the employee carries out a security measure. This game is therefore a desirable state for implementing security measures.

(3) Promotion-non-implementation dilemma game ($x \geq 0$, $y < 0$)

The Nash equilibrium is {promotion: non implementation}, and this combination of the strategy is not the Pareto optimum. This game is in a dilemma state. The dominant strategy of the employee is "implementation" when the strategy of the promotion section is "non-promotion" and "non-implementation" when the strategy of the promotion section is "promotion". That is to say, the dominant strategy of the employee is to always take the opposite action to the strategy of the promotion section. This game is therefore the most undesirable state for implementing security measures.

(4) Regular non-implementation dilemma game ($-P_2V \leq x < 0$, $y < 0$)

The Nash equilibrium is {promotion: non-implementation}, and it is not the Pareto optimum. This game is in a dilemma state. All strategies except {promotion: non-implementation} are the Pareto optimum. Regardless of the strategy of the promotion section, the dominant strategy of the employee is "non-implementation". With or without the promotion of the promotion section, the employee does not ever carry out a security measure. This game is therefore in an undesirable state for implementing security measures.

(5) Regular non-implementation game ($x < 0$, $x < -P_2V$, $y < 0$)

The Nash equilibrium is {promotion: non-implementation}. All strategies are the Pareto optimums. Regardless of the strategy of the promotion section, the dominant strategy of the employee is "non-implementation". With or without the promotion of the promotion section, the employee always does not carry out security measure. This game is therefore in an undesirable state in which to implement security measures.

3 Analysis of Actual IT Security Incident

3.1 Analysis Method

The model described in Sect. 2 was applied to an actual IT security incident. To enable the same standard to be used in comparing and analyzing the model parameters, the parameter values are considered in monetary terms.

3.2 Actual IT Security Incident

The proposed model was applied to an actual IT security incident that happened with a PC used by teachers at a school [5]. In this case, the PC was set so that its password had to be changed every week by the manager of the system, who belonged to the security promotion section. However, one of the teachers wrote down the password, and stored it in his desk drawer because he was not able to remember it. Some students found the password and, consequently, information stored in the PC was leaked out. It was therefore necessary to re-examine the achievement test in place. The teacher remembered the password at first, but when he forgot it, he asked the IT security promotion section to cancel it and reissue a new password, which he then wrote down and saved.

In this case, the security measure implemented by the promotion section was "change the password every week". That is to say, the strategy of the IT security promotion section was "change the password every week" or "do not change the password every week". When the promotion section chooses the strategy "do not change the password every week," changing the password is left to the judgment of the employee (in this example, a teacher).

When the promotion section chooses a strategy of "changing," the system forces the employee to change the password every week. The strategy of most employees is therefore to either "remember the password (or do not write it down)" or "do not remember the password (and write it down)".

The payoff for an employee regarding security measures is examined as follows.

(1) The cost per time of the employee

According to a survey by the Ministry of Internal Affairs and Communications, the (monthly basis) average salary of a high-school education job teacher is 430,111 yen [9]. On the basis of this value, cost per time is calculated as the employee works for 20 days in a month for 8 h a day. The cost per time of the employee is 2,688 yen.

(2) The loss of duties of employee when carrying out the security measure

The time necessary for an employee to make a password and memorize it is equivalent to Y_d, that is, the loss of duties that the employee cannot perform owing to time taken carrying out the security measure and to a decline in his or her efficiency. It is thought that this work is completed in several minutes, including the work to make a so-called "good password" and memorize it. In this case, that time is estimated to be 3 min. In terms of cost per time, this time is equivalent to 134.4 yen.

(3) The cost that an employee expends when carrying out the security measure

When the security promotion section chooses the strategy "change the password every week," it is necessary for the employee to make a new password and memorize it 51 times a year (in addition to setting the first password). For the employee, this work for 51 times a year is given as cost Ca. From the cost per time, this work is calculated as 6,854 yen in monetary terms.

(4) The quantity of losses that employee incurs when an incident occurs

On the other hand, a security incident and a business loss occur with a certain probability when a promotion section does not order a password change every week and when the employee does not perform it. In this case, a leak really occurred, and the achievement test was necessary. Therefore, trouble such as re-making, re-enforcement, and re-marking the achievement test incurs loss Y_2, that is, the quantity of losses an employee incurs when an incident occurs. In this case, it is estimated that the quantity of losses takes two days. From the cost per time, this is calculated as 43,008 yen.

(5) Penalty

In addition, when an employee takes a strategy to write down a password on paper, even though that employee was instructed to change the password every week by the promotion section, without obeying the instructions, the work involved is only writing a random character string on paper; it hardly incurs a necessary cost at all. However, a penalty is imposed on the employee when a security incident thereby occurs.

According to an investigation performed for a personnel manager of a private enterprise, when an employee did not have malice, the most common penalty was a reprimand (submit an apology) issued to the employee in question [6].

When an employee writes down a password on paper, and it becomes a case security incident, it is therefore assumed that penalty V is to write a written apology and apologize to the person concerned within half a day. From the cost per time, V is calculated as 10,752 yen.

(6) The probability that the employee recognizes the incident

We considered a rate of the number of information leakages reported in an investigation to be the probability of the incident that the employee recognized. This investigation was carried out for 206 randomly selected elementary schools, junior high schools, and high schools throughout the country [7]. A total of 99 answers to the questionnaire were received (48 % of recoveries) from 105 schools. According to this, the investigation revealed that eight schools had information leakage problems. Because there were 105 schools, probability P_2 (that an employee of the school recognizes the incident) is 7.62 %. Table 2 lists the values of the employee parameters for this case.

Table 2. Employee parameters. (Source: IPSJ Journal, vol. 53, no. 9, p. 2165)

Parameter	Value	Unit	
Y_d	134.4	Yen	The loss of duties that the employee cannot perform
Y_2	43,008	Yen	The quantity of losses an employee incurs when an incident occurs
C_a	6,854	Yen	The cost that an employee expends when he/she carries out the security measure
V	10,752	Yen	The penalty that the promotion section gives the employee when the incident occurs
P_2	7.62	%	The probability that the employee recognizes the incident

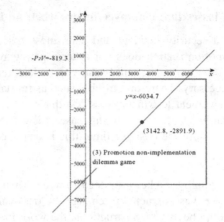

Fig. 2. State of actual incident. (Source: IPSJ Journal, vol. 53, no. 9, p. 2165)

The x and y values are calculated from these parameter values. From an expression (1) and an expression (3), the x and y values are calculated as 3142.8 and −2891.9. Because x ≥ 0 and y < 0, the state of this actual IT security incident is "(3) Promotion-non-implementation dilemma game" (Fig. 2).

In this incident, the teacher remembered the password at first but forgot it later. This case shows that if the promotion section had not required a password change, the teacher would probably have remembered it and not written it down. That is to say, it is understood that a "(3) Promotion-non-implementation dilemma game" occurs in this case. It was estimated that the employee considered probability P_2 of a security incident as from 0.31 % to 13 %.

Figure 3 shows a game position that was calculated by changing the value of P_2 every 1 %. If the value becomes big, the game position moves towards the direction of the "(1) Regular implementation game" domain.

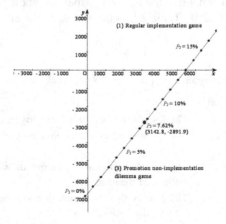

Fig. 3. Value of P_2 and state of the incident. (Created based on: IPSJ Journal, vol. 53, no. 9, p. 2165)

4 Examination on Improving IT Security Implementation in an Organization

We examined a number of methods to improve security. We changed parameter values where appropriate and analyzed game states by calculating the values of x and y at that time.

4.1 Extending Password Change Period

In the actual IT security incident, the PC had been set so that the password had to be changed by the system manager every week. We examined the measure of extending the password change period to once a month.[1] This means eleven changes (the first one made in the second month) per year are necessary, and the corresponding cost (C_a) incurred by the employee decreases to 1,478 yen. Table 3 lists the employee parameter values obtained in implementing this measure.

Table 3. Employee parameter values (C_a is improved) (Source: IPSJ Journal, vol. 53, no. 9, p. 2166).

parameter	value
Y_d	134.4
C_a	1,478
Y_2	43,008
V	10,752
P_2	7.62

The calculated x and y values are respectively 3142.8 and 2484.1. Figure 4 shows the position of this game, which is a "(1) Regular implementation game". Since the original game state was a "(3) Promotion-non-implementation dilemma game", this means extending the password change period is a desirable security measure.

4.2 Increasing Penalty

The measure of increasing penalty V was investigated next. A representative penalty is a salary reduction (that is, a disciplinary measure). Article 91 of the Japanese Labor Standards Law stipulates that the amount of salary reduction must not exceed half the average wage for a day. It also stipulates that the total sum of the amount of salary reduction must not exceed one tenth of the total sum of wages in one wage-payment

---

[1] Note that, theoretically, a change period of password should be decided on the basis of the decoding time. This problem, however, is not addressed in this study.

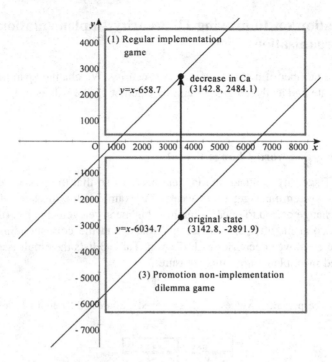

Fig. 4. Decrease in *Ca* obtained by extending password change period. (Created based on: IPSJ Journal, vol. 53, no. 9, p. 2166).

period [8]. In cost per time terms, this penalty comes to 21, 504 yen. Table 4 lists the employee parameter values for this measure.

The calculated x and y values are respectively 3142.8 and −2072.6. This is a "(3) Promotion-non-implementation dilemma game". Figure 5 shows the game position, which is improved over the original state. However, increasing penalty *V* has little effect as a security measure because the game state remains a "(3) Promotion-non-implementation dilemma game".

Table 4. Employee parameter values obtained by increasing penalty V. (Source: IPSJ Journal, vol. 53, no. 9, p. 2167)

parameter	value
Y_d	134.4
C_a	6,854
Y_2	43,008
V	21,504
P_2	7.62

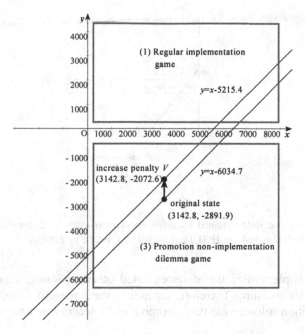

Fig. 5. Change in game state obtained by increasing penalty V. (Created based on: IPSJ Journal, vol. 53, no. 9, p. 2167).

4.3 Extending Password Change Period and Using Encryption Software

Encryption software can be used to reduce security damage even if a third party illegally accesses PC files. We therefore investigated the measures of further extending the password change period and applying encryption software to PC files. The password change period was changed to half a year and the Y2 value was reduced by one-tenth by using encryption software. Table 5 lists the employee parameter values obtained in implementing these measures.

The calculated x and y values are respectively 193.3 and 878.6. Figure 6 shows the position of this game, which is a "(1) Regular implementation game". Furthermore, the "(3) Promotion-non-implementation dilemma game" state, which was the original state

Table 5. Employeee parameter values obtained by using encryption software and extending password change period. (Source: IPSJ Journal, vol. 53, no. 9, p. 2168)

parameter	value
Y_d	134.4
C_a	134
Y_2	4,301
V	10,752
P_2	7.62

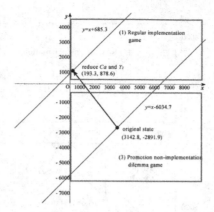

Fig. 6. Change in game state obtained by using encryption software and extending password change period. (Created based on: IPSJ Journal, vol. 53, no. 9, p. 2168).

and existed in implementing the aforementioned other measures, does not exist in implementing this measure. Therefore, extending the password change period and applying encryption software are very desirable as IT security measures.

5   Order of Security Measures

Using the game-theory-based model, we examined the order of several security measures.

5.1   Changing Organization State by Changing Parameters

We examined the case in which the state of the organization is at point P in Fig. 7.

From expressions (1)–(3), the state changes as follows when each parameter increases.

(a) **Increase Y_d.** The state moves in the direction of arrow A to point Q.
(b) **Increase P_2.** The state moves in the direction of arrow B to point R.

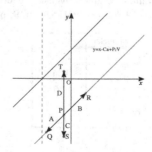

Fig. 7.   Increase in parameters and change of state

(c) **Increase** y_2. The state moves in the direction of arrow B to point R.

(d) **Increase Ca.** The state moves along the Y-axis in the direction of arrow C to point S.

(e) **Increase V.** The state moves along the Y-axis in the direction of arrow D to point T.

5.2   Promotion Order of Two Security Measures

Here we assume that there are two security measures, 1 and 2. Measure 1 is effective in reducing the value of Y_d and measure 2 is effective in reducing the value of Ca. As shown in Fig. 8, we assume that the organization is at point P in "(4) Regular non-implementation dilemma game".

Let us examine the order of promoting these two security measures.

(a) Measure 1 is promoted first

Because measure 1 makes the value of Y_d small, the state moves from point P to point Q in the direction of arrow A. Since point Q is in "(3) Promotion-non-implementation dilemma game," this state is undesirable.

(b) Measure 2 is promoted first

Because measure 2 makes the value of Ca small, the state moves from point P to point R in the direction of arrow B. Since point R is in "(2) Promotion-implementation game," this state is desirable.

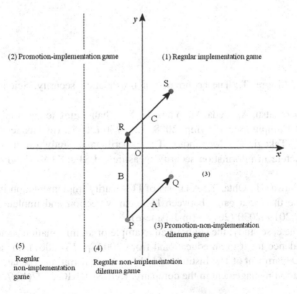

Fig. 8. Order of promoting two security measures

The state moves from point R to point S along the direction of arrow C if we promote security measure 1 in this state. Since point S is in "(1) Regular implementation game," this state is most desirable.

Thus, even when the same combination of security measures is applied, the result becomes undesirable or desirable depending on the order in which they are promoted. In other words, our model makes it possible to determine the appropriate order of promoting security measures.

6 Summary

We applied the IT security implementation model of an organization to an actual security incident, calculated the model parameters, and clarified in which state of the model the incident is. We also used the model to examine the effects obtained in implementing a number of security measures by using this model. The results clarified the security measures that were the most effective.

We conclude from the results that this model has the potential to be a useful means for promoting security measures in an organization.

7 Limitations and Future Work

In this study, we made a number of assumptions when we calculated the model parameters. In future, it will be necessary to determine more accurate model parameters by giving questionnaires to general employees and performing several types of experiments.

References

1. Anderson, R., Moore, T.: The economics of information security. Science **314**, 610–613 (2006)
2. Sugiura, M., Komatsu, A., Ueda, M., Yamada, Y.: Challenging to economics of information security. IPSJ Comput. Secur. Symp. **2008**, 725–730 (2008). (in Japanese)
3. Komatsu, A., Takagi, D., Matumoto, T.: Experimental study on individual gain and cognitive structure in information security measures. IPSJ J. **51**(9), 1711–1725 (2010). (in Japanese)
4. Sugiura, M., Suwa, H., Ohta, T.: Analysis of IT security implementation in an organization by using game theory: a game between IT security section and implementing employee. IPSJ J. **52**(6), 2019–2030 (2011). (in Japanese)
5. NPO ISEF: The case study: the study of an example of an information security incident and the correspondence for it in an educational front 2007, p. 13 (2007) (in Japanese)
6. An Editorial Department of The Institute of Labour Administration: The latest actual situation of the information management in the company. ROUSEIJIHO **3777**(10.7.9), 51–77 (2010). (in Japanese)
7. Ministry of Economy, Trade and Industry: Present conditions working papers to affect the information security in the elementary and secondary education spot (2003) (in Japanese)

8. Watanabe, T., Kato, J.: A step of the correspondence from the outbreak of the disgraceful affair to a disciplinary measure and a legal point to keep in mind. ROUSEIJIHO **3774** (10.5.28), 60–82 (2010). (in Japanese)
9. Ministry of Internal Affairs and Communications: The investigation into about the actual situation salary of local government official (2009) (in Japanese)
10. Sugiura, M., Suwa, H., Ohta, T.: Analysis of an Actual IT-security incident occurred with a PC used by teachers: using IT-security implementation model in an organization. IPSJ J. **53** (9), 2160–2170 (2012). (in Japanese)

A Psychological Approach to Information Security

Some Ideas for Establishing Information Security Psychology

Katsuya Uchida[✉]

Institute of Information Security, Yokohama, Japan
uchidak@gol.com

Abstract. Information Systems are composed in four main portions, people, information, appliance and facilities. These four portions are called information assets. Information security protects information assets and keeps safe them from the view point of Confidentiality, Integrity and Availability (CIA).

Recently, cyber-attacks to people in specific organizations are called advanced persistent threat (APT) or targeted attacks. APT attacks are attacks using psychological and behavioral science weakness of people, are not technical attacks.

Kevin Mitnick, the most competent and the most famous attacker for people says "Security is not a technology problem. It is a human and management problems" in his book.

By using the knowledge of psychology, behavioral science and criminology, the attackers attack people, and achieve the purposes. Targets of the attacks are not only the direct objects that are theft or destruction of information, but also the indirect objects that obtain the information necessary to achieve the goal.

Sun Tzu, a Chinese military general, strategist and philosopher said "If you know your enemies and know yourself, you can win a hundred battles without a single loss".

Attackers and victims are classified into people, appliance (hardware and software) and hybrid (people and appliance).

The methods of attackers for each attack and cases of attacks are classified in this paper.

Some organizations are beginning to use the elements of games and competitions to motivate employees, and customers. This is known as gamification which is the application of game elements and digital game design techniques to non-game problems, such as business and social impact challenges.

Gamification is very useful for awareness training of information security, I believe.

© Springer International Publishing Switzerland 2015
M. Kurosu (Ed.): Human-Computer Interaction, Part I, HCII 2015, LNCS 9169, pp. 96–104, 2015.
DOI: 10.1007/978-3-319-20901-2_9

This paper attempts to classify and systematize attackers, victims and the methods of attacks, as by psychology, behavioral science, criminal psychology, and cognitive psychology I have proposed some ideas for education, training and awareness for information security using the findings of psychology and behavioral science.

Keywords: Information security psychology · Social engineering · Deception

1 Introduction

Information security psychology is to research the information security from the human aspects or psychology.

Information security is to protect information and information systems from unauthorized access, use, disclosure, disruption, modification, or destruction in order to provide confidentiality, integrity and availability.

The attacker is to attack victims by using the findings of psychology, behavioral science and criminology. The objective of attack is to be a theft or destruction of information assets, and to obtain information to achieve the final goal.

Defenders acquire the knowledge that the attackers use, and must think about the defense systems. By performing the education and training, etc. for the user of the information assets, it is necessary to consider measures to protect the information assets from the attacker. By using the knowledge of psychology, behavioral science, and criminology, effective education and training are performed.

In education and training, we have two areas:

– One is that the course contents include knowledge of psychology, behavioral science and criminology.
– The other one is that the design of education and training include psychological concepts, especially regarding motivation, behavior, and personality.

2 Information Assets

2.1 Definition of Information Assets

The following are definition of the information assets which are classified with the four groups [1].

• **People** are those who are vital to the expected operation and performance of the service. People may be internal or external to the organization.
• **Information** is any information or data, on any media including paper or electronic form.
• **Technology** describes any technology component or asset that supports or automates a service and facilitates its ability to accomplish its mission. Some technology are specific to a service (such as an application system) and others are shared by the organization (such as the enterprise-wide network infrastructure).

- **Facilities** are the places where services are executed and can be owned and controlled by the organization or by external business partners. In general, any of the information assets are targeted attackers and many of the cyber-attacks use the findings of psychology and behavioral science as well as the technical knowledge.

2.2   Attacks of Deception Against Information Assets

In general, any of the information assets are targeted attackers and many of the cyber-attacks use the findings of psychology and behavioral science as well as the technical knowledge.

The following are the psychological and behavioral scientific attacks for each group.

- **People:** Attacker makes a call by pretending to be someone else and gets the necessary information.
- **Information:** One example is a targeted attack which has been aimed at a specific user, company or organization using e-mail of attached file or embedded url.
- **Technology:** A SYN flood attack is intended to deceive the three-way handshake of TCP, that is, this attack works by not responding to the server with the expected ACK code.
- **Facilities:** Attacker enters premises by pretending to people of a delivery company or an electrical work company, and often looks for information discarded by a company employees.

3   Basic Model of the Deception

From time immemorial, human beings have been deceived others. Recently, some people begin to deceive new field, computer systems. Directly, some people deceive other people related to the computer systems instead of deceiving the computer systems.

In the information security, we call this social engineering.

1. **Definition of Social Engineering**

    Some definitions for social engineering are as follow;

- Social engineering refers to psychological manipulation of people into performing actions or divulging confidential information. A type of confidence trick for the purpose of information gathering, fraud, or system access, it differs from a traditional "con" in that it is often one of many steps in a more complex fraud scheme [2].
- Social engineering is the act of manipulating a person to take an action that may or may not be in the "target" best interest. This may include obtaining information, gaining access, or getting the target to take certain action [3].

I would like to take a further more wide definition, that is, social engineering or the art of the deception is the act of manipulating person and/or things to take an action that may or may not be in the target best interest.

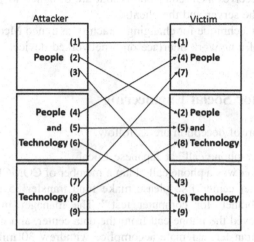

Fig. 1. Basic model of deception

2. Basic model of deception

Figure 1 shows the relationship between attacker and victim. Attacker and victim are classified three group, People, Technology, and People and technology.

Each group of attackers deceives each group of victims by social engineering techniques

(1) "People" attacks "People"
   This is mainstream part in social engineering. There are phone call with victim, URL embedded e-mail, and targeted email attack induced by message exchange.
(2) "People" attacks "People and Technology"
   Shoulder hacking and site intrusion are famous in this attack.
(3) "People'" attacks "Technology"
   Biometrics system authenticates the fake biometric, such as fingerprint.
(4) "People and technology" attacks "People"
   Vishing (Voice phishing) uses telephone system for automatic call and attacker's voice.
(5) "People and technology" attacks "People"
   Nothing special.
(6) "People and technology" attacks "People and technology"
   The e-mail attached with malware is this area.
(7) "Technology" attacks "People"
   Caller ID spoofing is the practice of causing the telephone network to indicate to the receiver of a call that the originator of the call is a station other than the true originating station.
(8) "Technology" attacks "People and technology"

Malware is malicious code that includes viruses, worms, and Trojan horses.
(9) "Technology" attacks "Technology"

- SYN Flooding deceives TCP connections that are designed to perform the 3-way handshake with the server and the client.
- Mac spoofing is a technique for changing a factory-assigned Media Access Control (MAC) address of a network interface on a networked device.

4   Some Cases for Social Engineering

Some cases for the art of deception are as follow.

(1) Oct. 1981, "Fake phone call" at Japanese Local
bank1The attacker was a phone call "I am a member of COMCEN (the local bank jargon, "computer center") so please make fund transfer 35 million yen to the account of S branch for computer test." The manager in Savings account department believed the phone call from the data center, and made fund transfer. After the fund transfer, a female accomplice withdrew 30 million yen from the account in S branch.

(2) Dec. 1987, Forged sender address (Mail spoofing) CHRISTMAS.exe worm
A user would receive an e-mail Christmas card that included executable code. If executed the program claimed to draw a Xmas tree on the display. It also sent a copy to everyone on the user's address lists.

(3) Nov. 2011, "DARPA Shredder challenge" for Dumpster diving [4]
Dumpster diving is the most exciting thing for attackers, they can find a lot of valuables, CD-ROM, USB memory, and user manual, etc., in dumpsters.
Straight cut of documents by a shredder was restored by Iranian students about 35 years ago. Cross cut documents by recent shredder was also restored at DARPA's Shredder challenge in Dec. 2011.

(4) Shoulder hacking
From some results of the simple experimental, shoulder hacking is very difficult without the recording of the video or photo.
Therefore, you can see ATM skimming instead of shoulder hacking. ATM skimming is when someone illegally copies your account details from the magnetic strip on your credit or debit card when you use an ATM. Card skimming can also happen when you use ATM.2.

(5) Pretexting
At the request of a private detective hired by the stalker, the executive of a research company who pretended to be the housewife husband, telephoned some city hall in Japan on the day before the murder occurred and got the information of the housewife.
In leakage of personal information from the city hall, the stalker killed a housewife, and also killed himself [5].

(6) Microexpressions

A microexpression is a brief, involuntary facial expression shown on the face of humans.

They express the six universal emotions: disgust, anger, fear, sadness, happiness, and surprise. They are very brief in duration, lasting only 1/25 to 1/15 of a second. A social engineer understands the true feelings from microexpression of the victim.

Example of microexpression, I know only in the movie series, "Lie to me".

5 Psychological Findings Used in Social Engineering

It most important response to social engineering is to understand how social engineers to use what kind of psychological findings.

5.1 Six Weapons of Influence

Cialdini has been written compliance techniques into six categories based on psychological findings that direct human behavior [6].

(1) Reciprocation recognizes that people feel indebted to those who do something for them or give them a gift.
(2) Commitment and Consistency
   (a) Low-ball technique is a technique used in sales and other styles of persuasion to offer products or services at a bargain price in order to first attract a buyer, but then adds on additional expenses to make the purchase less of a bargain than originally thought.
   (b) Door-in-the-face technique is to make a costly large first request that the recipient will probably refuse, and then is to make less costly and more realistic request.
   (c) Foot-in-the-door technique is the tendency for people to comply with some large request after first agreeing to a small request.
(3) Social Proof: When people are uncertain about a course of action, they tend to look to those around them to guide their decisions and actions.
(4) Liking: People prefer to say 'yes' to people who are attractive, similar to themselves, or who give them compliments.
(5) Authority: People want to follow the lead of real experts.
(6) Scarcity: The more rare and uncommon a thing, the more people want it.

5.2 Elicitation

The following is the definition of elicitation by FBI [7]

Elicitation is a technique used to discreetly gather information.
Elicitation is to extract information from people without giving them the feeling they are being interrogated.

A trained elicitor understands certain human or cultural predispositions and uses techniques to exploit those.

An elicitor is an excellent communicator.

Mentioned before at 4.(5) pretexting, the executive of a research company was good elicitor.

5.3   Environmental Criminology

A criminal is a normal ordinary people who is a weak presence in the temptation of crime opportunity. Many people have weak characteristic that would not resist temptation and suffering.

6   Education and Training

6.1   Education, Training, and Awareness

(1) Against Pretexting

As personal information leakage countermeasures, we hold an awareness training as follow.

As actually an example that occurred, an awareness training introduces a telephone deception technique by the attacker, and the characteristics of the victims. From the introduced contents, at the awareness training, we discuss what the victims should be done in this situation with taking into account the characteristics of the attacker and the victims.

An example of characteristics of an attacker and a victim are as follow;

- Attacker
  - Posting as a housewife husband or a fellow employee
  - Using insider lingo and terminology to gain trust
  - Refuse to give call back number, and ask to call mobile phone number
  - Stress urgency
- Victims
  - believe kindness and politeness are good for his or her customers
  - tend to trust others
  - do not want to involve with the problem
  - become a feeling that perpetrators want going well.

(2) Training a targeted attack

A targeted attack is designed to test employees' level of user awareness or their detection and response capabilities.

First step: from the address of address spoofing, the email that attached a file is sent to employees. After the mail was sent, we count the number of employees who opened the attached file, and calculate the percentage of employees who opened it.

Second step: from the address of address spoofing, email of the embedded URL is sent to employees. After the mail was sent, we count the number of employees who clicked the URL, and calculate the percentage of employees who clicked it.

6.2 Gamification

Werbach says that;

> Gamification is the use of game elements and game design techniques in non-game contexts [8].
> Gamification is about learning, learning from game design but also learning from fields like psychology and management and marketing and economics.
> It's a way in to understand things about motivation.

The best usage of gamification is security awareness training, so we are planning to the information security contents for business area.

7 Conclusion

As Sun Tzu said "If you know your enemies and know yourself, you can win a hundred battles without a single loss", basically, learning techniques of attackers is to be the best protection of social engineering.

In addition, Gamification become an effective tools to education, training, and awareness to improve the security level of the user.

Attack defense methods and education and training, properly I do well-known classification.

In addition, there is a need to crime characteristics of the crime, etc. both research from the side of criminal psychology deepen.

In this research, it is not able to sufficiently classification deceptive, if it is possible to consider dealing appropriate classification of new attacks method utilizing psychological or behavioral science, and lead to the establishment of information security Psychology

Acknowledgements. This research of the Information Security Psychology study group has been granted by the Japanese Psychological Association from 2011.

References

1. Caralli, R.A. et al.: CERT Resilience Management Model, version 1.0, pp. 4–5. Software Engineering Institute, Carnegie Mellon University, Pittsburgh (2010)
2. Wikipedia: Social engineering (security). http://en.wikipedia.org/wiki/Social_engineering_(security)
3. Hadnagy, R.: Social Engineering: The Art of Human Hacking. Wiley, New York (2010)
4. DARPA: DARPA's shredder challenge (2011). http://archive.darpa.mil/shredderchallenge/

5. Japan Times: Stalking victim info leak laid to tax man (2013). http://www.japantimes.co.jp/news/2013/11/08/national/crime-legal/stalking-victim-info-leak-laid-to-tax-man/#.VOC3g-_9n9Q
6. Cialdini, R.: Influence: Science and Practice. Prentice Hall, Needham (2008)
7. FBI: Elicitation techniques (2011). http://www.fbi.gov/about-us/investigate/counterintelligence/elicitation-techniques
8. Werbach, K., et al.: For the Win: How Game Thinking Can Revolutionize Your Business. Wharton Digital Press, Philadelphia (2012)
9. Thornton, D., et al.: Gamification of information systems and security training: issues and case studies. Inf. Secur. Educ. J. 1(1), 16–24 (2014)

Cross-Over Study of Time Perception and Interface Design

Huizhong Zhang[2](✉), Guanzhong Liu, and Hai Fang[2]

[1] B464 Academy of Art and Design, Tsinghua University,
Haidian, Beijing, China
[2] School of Art and Design, Guangdong University of Technology,
Guangdong, Guangzhou, China
zhanghuizhong05@126.com

Abstract. Pace of life is getting faster today, and it even affects the quality of people's life. Time is so important to human while it also troubles us a lot. Sometimes time seems so valuable that we take everything to earn more seconds. However, during a vacation, we ignore the passing of time. We are willing to consider what kind of pace of life can bring us more happiness. Time sense becomes an important experience in our daily life. This research is trying to improve our time experiences of interaction with interface design. As we know, people without specialized training cannot count time precisely without a clock, while they surely have an individual habit of perceiving time. Psychology of time is a psychology about human's time perception. Therefore, the research is a cross-over study of interaction and time psychology in terms of knowing how design can improve people's time experiences.

This study takes some time psychology theories as a foundation to know about the principles of human's perception of time. With the purpose of elevating the time experiences of people, three aspects are considered having effects on it: signal stimulus, time information processing and personal psychological condition.

Signal stimulus—human's perception of time always depends on some time signals, which are necessary materials of the brain processing. They could be numbers, visual dimensions, colors, temperatures, sound volumes, frequency of motion and so on.

Time information processing: several time processing models and calculative strategies of the time duration explain basic rules of processing time information in a human brain.

Personal psychological conditions: different time perceptions can trigger different emotions. And people in different moods can have different feelings about the same time interval.

In the study, the author summarized four possibilities to bring people better time experiences.

Following that, some assumptions in accordance with the research were made. Based on these assumptions, several experimental products, which are calendar design and traffic lights design, are designed. Finally, some experiments were conducted to test if the new designs can indeed create better time experiences. And one of the experiments would be reported in this article.

© Springer International Publishing Switzerland 2015
M. Kurosu (Ed.): Human-Computer Interaction, Part I, HCII 2015, LNCS 9169, pp. 105–116, 2015.
DOI: 10.1007/978-3-319-20901-2_10

Keywords: Interactive design · Psychology of time · Time experiences of users · Experiments

1 Program Illustration

1.1 Study Context

People have their own feelings about time. Philosopher Guyan (1980) said time was just a systematic disposition, a mental representation organization of the description on the variation in universe [1]. People can feel the temporal moments and the duration of time. Beyond doubt, those estimations are usually not accurate, and they deviate from the clock time more or less. Moreover, those illusions also cause emotional reactions to the duration of an event. For example, a person, who is blow-drying hair in 1 min, usually has a better mood than the one who is waiting at a red traffic light in 1 min. The former person is relaxed and the 1 min goes without an attention. By contrast, the other one is eager to cross a street so that the 1 min is suffering. Seizing seconds and killing time are very contradictory while common in our daily lives as well. We can be affected by the positive and the negative aspects of time. In brief, time perception has significant influences on our experiences in life.

1.2 Research Objectives

Emotions make our experiences colorful. Products with both functions and emotions complete our lives better [2]. With the pace of life is speeding up, people have a more critical requirement of life quality. Time experiences become an important part of our happiness. As Steve Taylor said in Making Time, human's perception of time was variable and he proposed an idea of controlling the time perception. Thereby, according to the study and references, there are four possibilities for designers to improve the interaction of time experiences:

- To release the anxiety of waiting.

   Anxiety of waiting is the most common human feeling of time. During a waiting process we cannot decide the end time and we hope time passes faster, especially when we are in a bad mood, time seems pass slower. This research needs to find several ways to release the anxiety.

- To improve people's efficiency of reaction.

   Time has several subjective attributes. Because of the attributes, people particularly for those who have procrastination, usually cannot notice the time fleeing and have a low utilization of time. Nevertheless, they could use time better if they are reminded.

- To help people to recreate.

   In the world, especially in China, a job occupies most of a person's life and many people are in sub-health status. Timekeeping devices can help people to catch every second while also make them forget to have a necessary rest. Helping people to recreate and release pressure is an important responsibility of this research.

– To eliminate or correct people's time cognition bias in order to avoid misoperation.

Some timekeeping devices deliver unreasonable time information leading to a wrong action by users. To find those mistakes and correct them will eliminate people's misoperations.

Time perception has already been found having effects on interaction experience. Some designs, such as the countdown of advertisement during shows, the appealing loading bars and so on, have already involved people's time experiences. These ideas improved the time experiences by reducing the anxiety of waiting. But we do not know if there will be better ideas and if the time perception be controlled as required. The research objective is to improve the time perception in a product-human interaction with the cross-over study of time psychology and design. Interaction design is a new field of design, and it changes the relationship of human and products from "use" to "interact". It starts to focus on the interaction of both sides (human and products). Inevitably, human-centered and user-friendly criterions become significant to product design. In order to understand the deeper and more complex human behaviors, designers have to find helps form other subjects. This research is based on the inter-active design and the time psychology. Using design methodologies to apply the time psychology theories in cases, designers can understand the users' specific time sense and design products well, so that to create better time experiences in interaction. On the other hand, as a big branch of psychology, the time psychology has lots of achieve-ments while many of them still stay in theory. Blending with design, the time psy-chology theories can be transferred into products and it can improve the interaction experience.

2 Psychological Mechanism of Time Experience

2.1 Generation and Operation of Time Perception

Time psychology is a science studying of the reaction of an individual brain to the duration and the succession of time [3]. In terms of the time psychology, it has three attributes: succession, duration and focus of events. Temporal duration means the length of time between two successive events. Human can estimate the temporal duration. Temporal duration is more comprehensive than the succession and the focus of event. Duration estimation is a very common behavior in time perception study [4]. The perception of time succession is very important to interaction experience.

Tools for Measuring Time: Physical Time and Human Internal Clock. The reason of human even animals can have the time perception and estimation is the inter-reaction between the physical time and the human internal clock.

– Physical time covers artificial timekeeping devices: clock, calendar, as well as inartificial ones: sun rise and down, lunar cycle, day-night cycle, season changing etc.

– Inner clock: the biological model of time perception explains human body has an internal clock, which is consist of rhythmic physiological activities and mental activities inside of the body, like hart beating, breath, digestion and memory representation lapse. Even certain status of nervous system can be temporal signals. All of these are the premise of organism and the basic time perception [5].

Processing of Temporal Duration Information. Several mental models have been developed to explain how human process temporal stimulation and they mainly reveal the types of the temporal duration estimations. The most famous ones are storage size model (SS model), processing-time model (PT model), change/segmentation model (CS model) and range-synthetic model [6]. Each of them is trying to explain time perception behaviors. In PT model, there is a cognitive timer in human brain being responsible for processing the non-time information. And there is also a stimulation processor for the stimulation of the event. As human's attention resource in brain is limited, putting more attention resources on the cognitive timer inevitably will lead to less resources put on the stimulation processor, and a longer temporal duration will be perceived vice versa.*(vroon,1970; hicks 1977, burnsides, 1971, zakay 1983 macar).* This model explains that when we are doing nothing but waiting, time passes very slowly to us. But when we are playing cell phones or reading a funny book, the temporal duration can be shortened obviously. The range-synthetic model advocates different duration length, days-weeks-months-years, involves the particular cognitive strategies and different representations *(Huang Xi ting, Xu Guang guo 1999).*

Estimation Strategy of Temporal Duration. Temporal duration estimation strategy means people can infer the duration of an event according to the processing speed and content of it. And even if the processing speed is changed, people still can speculate the rest progresses and judge the ending time based on the present speed [7].

Hecht said people could estimate the rest of time with arithmetic and operational perception. This strategy explains the principles of people inferring the future temporal duration. Stephken K. Reed and Bob Hoffman proposed 4 advanced strategies for the temporal estimation [8].

Influential Variables in the Estimation Strategy of Temporal Duration. If the environmental variables and the individual variables are changed in an event, people's estimation strategy will be changed accordingly as well as the estimation. Usually, the individual variables are difficult to control. But we can put more concentrations on the environmental variables which can be easily perceived and designed. The environmental variables can be into many forms: numbers, shapes [9], frequencies of act, colors, and so on. E.g., the size of digits is in the direct proportion to the length of the estimation of temporal duration.

Comparing to the values of number, people all tend to compare the temporal durations by the scales of number. As the Fig. 1 shows, although the value of 3 in left is equal to the right one, the right one is considered having a longer duration [10].

Summary. In this research, the time psychology theories mainly are estimation models and strategies of temporal duration. According to the PT model, designers can simply set some attractions for users in waiting process to reduce their anxiety. It is a very simple and effective method. The estimation strategy is the main method for an event

Fig. 1. Two '3' with different scales

temporal prediction. By controlling the environmental variables, it can impact people's estimation strategy and then change the time perception.

2.2 The Interacting of Time Perception and Emotion

Time experience is complicated. It is not only depends on time perception, but also the users' psychological conditions. Comparing to the time perception, people's initial psychological conditions are fickle factors, which can affect people's time perception while also be affected by time perception [11]. Thereby, the time experience improvements in interaction can be achieved with the user's time perception and the psychological condition.

1. **Impacts of psychological conditions on the temporal perceptions**

– Anticipation [12]

Generally, people's anticipate is opposite to the temporal actual changes. In other words, when you are wishing the events to go faster, time seems to get slower. What is more; the harder your wish is, the slower time is.

– Psychological conditions

Generally, the positive emotions will make time pass faster while the negative emotions make it slower.

– Attentions

Highly concentrated attentions can shorten and lengthen the estimated durations.

2.3 Impacts of Time Perception on Emotions

Emotions can affect people's time perception. Moreover, the time perception can affect the emotions vice versa. And that is the key of this research. The emotions are a big part of the interaction experience. The time perception can have effects on emotions because time has several subjective attributes in human brain [4].

- Time has variations—time senses of human are different in one day. Time could be flash or very slow.
- Irreversible and loose—time can be irreversible and free that is very appreciable to people having different careers.
- Fragility of time—helps people to be punctual.
- Invariability—time stays in one pace to people leading to inefficiency.

These subjective attributes are the connections between the emotions and the time perception, as well as the premise of the time experiences. They can affect people's emotions and cause the experiences changed during an interaction procedure. The time sense and the user's emotional status are the evaluation criteria for the time experiences.

3 Product Carriers

Not all human-product interactions need the time experience design. Products directly correlating to time sense decides this interaction to have a requirement of a time experience design. Basically, they contain two types as below.

3.1 Timekeeping Devices

As the timekeeping devices, clocks and timers are directly associated with time experiences, e.g., watches, clocks, timers, calendars, sundials, sand timers as Fig. 2 indicates. This category shows the objective time is trusted by people. When people's time estimations have bias with the indication of a timekeeping device, they adjust their inner clock. The objectivity of time information is essential to those kinds of devices so that they are avoided delivering the false time information.

3.2 Indirectly Time Indicators

Loading bars, traffic lights, display panels of elevators are the devices delivering the developing progresses which are the indirect time information. These kinds of products

Fig. 2. Timekeeping devices

Fig. 3. Indirectly time indicators

as Fig. 3 presents, cannot offer the accurate time information even their designs are more flexible comparing to the clocks. There are more capacities and potentials provided to the designers.

4 Experimental Research

The experiments were based on two product designs and they will be described in this paper. The experimentations of traffic lights will be demonstrated as well. It is helpful in understanding how to explore more opportunities and methodologies for the designs of the time experience improvements.

4.1 Red Traffic Light Experiments

Research Context. There are many people running red traffic lights because of the loss of patience. Actually, the duration of a red traffic light is two minutes maximum. The two minutes procedure is very short comparing to other activities. But people run the red light for skipping over the short waiting. This behavior is not only because of the anxiety of the pedestrians, but also the red light form which is not good enough for people with a good patience. So this experiment focus on the red light designs to improve the interaction experiences.

There is one thing need to be noticed, the red light interaction is very complex. As well the light forms, the pedestrians' individual variables are also varying a lot. The research and experiments cannot cover all variables as only the ones very closed to the time perception will be studied. In saying so, the general practicability of traffic lights cannot be the test criteria of the experiments.

The constrained temporal duration of the red lights cannot be shortened. So the only way to improve experiences is to decrease the anxiety and enhance the degree of pleasure. There are three methods to enhance the pleasure degree. The first one is to shorten the temporal duration of pedestrians. The second method is to distract attentions from the time signals. The last one is to lower their expectations. The distraction is the easiest and most common method. For example, enjoying with a cell phone when people are waiting is a very useful way of distracting them. It takes up lots of attention resources and the pedestrians can feel little of temporal duration. But as this method is not a design of traffic lights, there will be no further discussion in this article. Lowering the expectations is also hardly achieved by the traffic light designs. To shorten the temporal duration estimations is a method to be pleased to use the interaction between time signals and pedestrians.

Objectives. According to the reaction of the participants to different temporal signals, the experiments can find how and why the samples affect the time perception.

Research Methods.

– Participants: 10 males and 10 females with ages between 23 and 28 from Tsinghua University. All of them are Chinese and have no experience with a similar experiment before.
– Materials: A laptop with flash animations. The flash content 6 red light designs which are illustrated in Fig. 4. The interfaces of the samples are designed as fading lattices and each sample's combinations of shape and speed appear once in one time. All durations of the samples are 30 s.
– Experiment design: the experiment is a 2*3 within-subjects design. The independent variables are presenting as the A-shapes and the B-fading speeds. The dependent variables are the temporal estimation durations and the pleasure degrees of users. The shapes have 2 conditions: The A1-rectangle and the A2-reverse trapezium. The speeds have 3 conditions: the B1-constant speed, the B2-acceleration and the B3- deceleration.

Procedures.

– Experiments take oral reports and comparative methods. Each of 20 participants randomly accepts 6 sample tests for 10 times.
– Without the use of any timekeeping devices, participants need to watch the animations and they are required to estimate the temporal duration of each sample. Then they write down an estimated number of different durations and give a score (the maximum number is 10) of the pleasure degrees about each sample. The participants must mentally simulate they are waiting at the red lights.
– Conducting the experiment when the participants are free and calm. During the tests, the participants cannot talk, move, count in their head, while have to focus on the animations. That is to unify the psychological contexts or control manipulated variables.

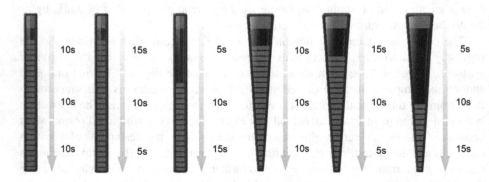

Fig. 4. Red traffic light samples

Hypotheses.

- Different combinations of various shapes and speeds cause people's different time perceptions and interactive experiences.
- Affecting temporal duration estimation strategy can influence the temporal estimations.
- The lengths of the temporal estimation durations and the experience qualities are in positive correlation. It means the shorter estimation durations cause better emotions than the longer estimated durations.

Result. All data were submitted to SPSS 15.0 for analysis.

- Estimated durations.

The means of the estimated duration in different conditions are shown in Fig. 5. The results of the two-way repeated measure analysis of variance show there are no significant shapes & speeds interaction, $F (2, 38) = 1.117$, $p > .05$. However, it reveals the significant main effects of shapes, $F (1, 19) = 7.214$, $p < .05$, and the speeds, $F (2, 38) = 2.978$, $p < .05$, indicates that the estimated durations are indeed influenced by the shapes and the speeds. Post hoc analysis demonstrates that the participants in the A2 condition presenting a significantly longer duration as compared to A1 condition (23.2 vs 22.4, $p < .05$), and it has a similar situation in B1 condition as compared to the B2 condition (23.3 vs 22.2, $p < .05$).

- Degrees of pleasure

Degrees of pleasure in different conditions are shown in Fig. 6, and the same process of the two-way repeated measures analysis of variance is performed. In the same way, the results demonstrate there are no significant shapes & speeds interactions, $p > .05$ and both the main effects of the shapes and the speeds are significant. Post hoc analysis shows that the participants in A2 condition has a significantly positive experience compared to the A1 condition (7.21 vs 6.78, $p < .05$), and significantly, more positive experiences are presented in B2 condition compared to the B3 condition (7.32 vs 6.31, $p < .05$).

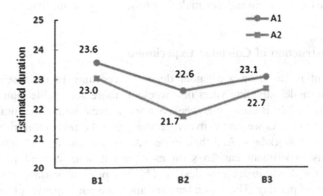

Fig. 5. The means of estimated duration in different conditions

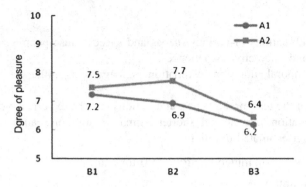

Fig. 6. The means of pleasure degrees in different conditions

Discussion.

- Different shapes can affect the estimated durations and the pleasure degrees during the interactions. In details, the duration of shape A1 (rectangle) is longer than shape A2 (Inverted trapezoidal); while the pleasure degree is lower than shape A2.
- Different speeds also cause distinct changes of the durations and the pleasure. The speed B2 (acceleration) catches a longer estimated duration a higher degree than the speed B3 (deceleration).
- The effects of Variable A on the duration and the pleasure degree cannot be influenced by variable B.

Conclusion. Synthesizing the experiment data and the interviews, we found the sample A2B2 brought the shortest estimated duration and the highest pleasure degree. A2B2 was so popular because its tapering shape and accelerated diminishing catered to most of the participants' expectation—crossing the road as soon as possible. The rectangle, the constant speeds and the deceleration did not meet the expectation. Both visual dimensions of time signals showed in a diminishing change and an accelerated development would reduce the estimating temporal durations and delight the moods. We also found that the participants had different reactions to one sample in different sections. It is because they have both prospective and retrospective estimations in one sample. But this experiment did not make a further study about that.

4.2   Brief Instruction of Calendar Experiment

This experiment is based on a calendar design. According to the research and the range-synthetic model, dividing years into weeks is more acceptable than into months to people having a job. Because one week is a work cycle while one month is only a regular calendar unit. As we know, many people enjoy the relaxation in weekend and hate the tension in workdays. And their expectations and moods are changing during one week. This experiment has 16 samples of a calendar showed in Fig. 7. The experiment is a 4*4 within-subjects design. The independent variables are font sizes and paper areas of per day. The dependent variables are participants' pleasure degrees

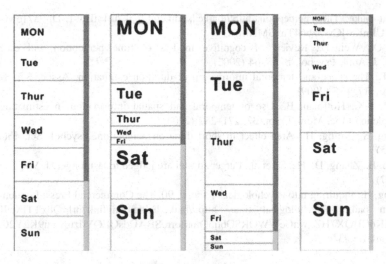

Fig. 7. Calendar sample

of different sections in per week. Each of samples has different combinations of the font sizes and areas. This experiment assumes different combinations have different effects to the users' time perception. The experiment report will not be displayed here.

5   Conclusion

This research used psychological theories and design methods. It is a new angle for time psychology study and design study. In one product, to improve the time experiences is very complicated and difficult. A psychological theory is only a basic premise and there is a long way of context study, sample design and experiment to go. This research's intention is not to forward the psychology theories but to test the theories in the practical cases and find practicable solutions. The four main steps of the time experiences design are problem finding, psychological defining, samples design and experiments. Besides, being different to the psychological research, the qualitative data collection takes a great part in this research. At last, this cross-over study of time psychology and design is far from the end, and it has a great potential.

References

1. Gu yau, J.M.: The origin of the idea of time. In: Michon, JA., Pou Thas, V., Jackson, JL (eds.) Guyao and the Idea of Time. Amsterdam, North Holland (1988)
2. Norman, D.A.: Living with Complexity, p. 195. The MIT Press, Cambridge (2010)
3. Song, Q.Z., Huang, X.T.: Thinking about the Orical model of time cognition. J. Southwest China Norm. Univ. **30**(1)25–28 (2004)
4. Tan Jia, L.: Study on time cognition and feeling in time perspective. D. China: Southwest Univ. 7–8 (2004)

5. Baidu baike: Time perception. http://baike.baidu.com/link?url=lBw-LsDi-9a71ewC8NGm Y1KUEnK8-ICy-5zb64ThJGMNMRL
6. Xu, Q., Wei, L.: Review of cognitive models of time perception and estimation. Chin. J. Appl. Psychol. **8**, 58–64 (2002)
7. Xu T.: The space and temporal information of duration estimation. Assoc. Sci. Technol. Forum. **17**, 185 (2009)
8. Reed, S.K., Hoffman, B.: Use of temporal and spatial information in estimating event completion time. Mem. Cogn. **32**, 271–282 (2004)
9. Zhang, S., Xiting, H.: Area effect in short duration perception. Psychol. Sci. **18**(1), 6–9 (1995)
10. Xuan, B., Zhang, D., He, S., et al.: Larger stimuli are judged to last longer. J. Vis. **7**(10), 1–5 (2007)
11. Xiting, H.: Inquiring into Psychological Time, p. 90. The Commercial Press, London (2014)
12. Baidu baike: Psychological time. http://baike.baidu.com/link?url=QbxTTiXc9I8A7c_ cBPIKdGHQX7HZgwnGeWWORSObqbQmnIorreSBAUdsQEOVdzuXwu9K2Y2CzGn6 pIIyopJeUK#3

HCI Design and Evaluation Methods and Tools

Guidelines to Integrate Professional, Personal and Social Context in Interaction Design Process: Studies in Healthcare Environment

Janaina Abib[1,2(✉)] and Junia Anacleto[2]

[1] Federal Institute of São Paulo, Araraquara, SP, Brazil
janaina@ifsp.edu.br
[2] Federal University of São Carlos, São Carlos, SP, Brazil
junia@dc.ufscar.br,
{janaina.abib,junia.anacleto}@gmail.com

Abstract. In this paper we're presenting the formalization of a set of guidelines to support interaction designers in their activities during the processes to design applications. We are using these guidelines in the construction phase of the design process and these strategies are being applied to support the interaction design of user's workflow, integrating professional, personal and social contexts. These strategies were used in a hospital for treatment of chronic mental illness in Brazil. During this study we observed healthcare professionals in their daily activities and with these data we developed information and communication solutions to bring new technologies into their day-by-day activities, in the way not to interrupt their routines. After some data collection and analysis we evaluated the results of our research. These analyses helped us to understand some weak points in the design process that do not simplify the integration of the different contexts in which users are naturally inserted. Thus, we proposed a set of guidelines to an interaction design process with the objective of supporting interaction designers in their work of developing natural solutions, integrating the different contexts of the users. Also, with the integration of contexts, we promote the extending of user's abilities.

Keywords: Design process · User interface · Interaction design · Non ICT user

1 Introduction

It is a difficult task to monitor the evolution and the advances of concepts, methods and applications related to information and communication technologies (ICT), which are always changing or improving. Such transformations are mainly related with user interaction with computer applications, and according to [14], the professionals who work with interaction design need continuous updating models and design approaches, especially for applications that uses new interactions technologies, such as technologies for gestures, touches, sounds, movements and others. So, the technological resources for social interaction, resources for communication and exchange

© Springer International Publishing Switzerland 2015
M. Kurosu (Ed.): Human-Computer Interaction, Part I, HCII 2015, LNCS 9169, pp. 119–131, 2015.
DOI: 10.1007/978-3-319-20901-2_11

of information should be connecting seamlessly with the non-technical traditional forms [14]. In [12], the authors point out that given the technological developments it is not possible to have models of complete and stable design, because everything is in a transitional stage and that, from time to time, the models need to be adapted and created for the new reality. According to [17], this new reality needs to focus some efforts in solutions that take into account the human ability - good tools addresses human needs as they extend their abilities - is the transformation of what can be made for what you want to do.

The paper is organized as follow: Contextualization is presented in Sect. 2. Section 3 presents the observations and analysis of experiments related with the interaction design process used in healthcare environments. The guidelines and discussion are showed at Sect. 4. Section 5 presents the conclusions.

2   Contextualization

To create good interaction designs, those that allow to access characteristics and functionalities in a pleasant way [11], and to allow the adoption and appropriation process of a new technology be effective and can extend the users abilities, it is important to consider the appropriation process of technological innovation. Appropriation is the term used by [3, 4, 6] in situations where the user creates new uses for technology solutions, thereby creating new requirements that must be considered by designers. During the appropriating process, users perceive more clearly their abilities, the best way to interact with technology solutions, how to adapt them to new uses and contexts and how the users performs that in a better way.

Systems with natural interaction that support the professional's work within the dynamics of this professional, to facilitate their activities of communication and interaction with their colleagues and with the environment, leads the professional to the perception and awareness of its procedures and its working group, allowing that the professional craves for efficiency and effectiveness in their work practices. But how to account for the fact that ICT solutions permeate among professionals, integrating the contexts of personal, social and professional lives of these professionals? And how this integration of the contexts affects the interaction design process? These questions exposed gaps in the research on design processes for systems with natural interaction that integrate personal, social and professional contexts, considering worker's experiences in using ICT to promote the abilities of these professionals.

The proposal to create guidelines that support interaction designs assisting and guiding designers during the design process, development and validation of systems with natural interaction is relevant, because the guidelines uses the personal, social and professional experiences with technological resources, it uses what the user already knows to make the interaction more natural and close and may thus stimulate the development of user's abilities. For reach this goal it is necessary to integrate the different contexts in which the user is in, looking for their experience and abilities, by encouraging the use of personal devices that the user is already familiar and bringing his experience to use during the interaction design process.

3 Interaction Design Process and the Experiments in Healthcare

This project relies on a partnership between a research group of designers from Advanced Interaction Laboratory (LIA) Department of Computer Science at UFSCar (Federal University of São Carlos – São Paulo State) in Brazil and the healthcare professionals from CAIS Hospital Clemente Ferreira, a mental care hospital located at Lins (countryside of São Paulo State – Brazil). This research intended to determine how information technology can facilitate and improve healthcare professional's work, improving the communication process among them, considering the nomadic nature of their work, with long working shifts, without cause a disruption in their work routines. The groups of healthcare professionals have long periods of work time and it's very usual some small absences forced by their needs to contact family and/or friends or solve personal and social situations during work shift. So, for during the time they are looking after patients who spend long periods in hospital (and most of the patients live in the hospital while they pass through rehabilitation process/treatments), these healthcare professionals must deal with patient's situations, assisting and supporting in the day-by-day activities' routines.

The development of this project was executed using observations processes, interviews procedures, building functional scenarios, creating prototypes and doing experiments for the study of the environment and activities of healthcare professionals within the hospital: requirements were collected and analyzed, the solutions for application of ICT were proposed in the this environment and some proposed solutions were validated. A group of LIA's designers were monitored during the preparation and development of several prototypes with human and professional interactions. We observed and make some remarks of the procedures adopted by these researches during their studies for interaction design process.

Annotations and experiments were conducted and an initial scheme of interaction design was modeled during the development of various applications and technology solutions to help and support the activities of healthcare professionals in the hospital. These observations lead to organize and lay out all activities of designers during the collection of data, requirements analysis, development, implementation and evaluation of prototypes. Design activities were grouped into three cycles: Cycle 1 – Recognition; Cycle 2 – Prototyping; and Cycle 3 – Evaluation (see Fig. 1).

In the first cycle the designers defined the objects of their research, identifying the user's groups. They also created some ideas to prototype and collected all requirements. These activities were performed with techniques of participatory design and scenario-based design. Reports with interviews and observations, photos, movies, stories shading and creating scenarios were generated as artifacts by the end of this cycle. The second cycle of activities involved analysis of the collected requirements and their validation through interviews. Several prototypes were developed, refined and validated. During the validation, some solutions of interaction design were proposed and the prototypes were reevaluated. In the third cycle the designers have proposed some evaluations and usability tests, thus, several improvements were incorporated into

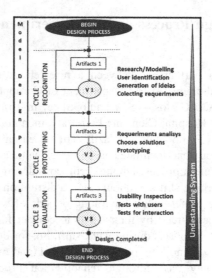

Fig. 1. Activities of interaction design

the prototypes or new prototypes were developed, considering user's skills and the technology innovations.

The first cycle of the design was lead through the following actions: (1) participatory design, actions in which researchers and users conducted brainstorming sessions, interviews and dynamic with drawings of scenarios so that researchers could define the object of study, the profile of users and their work activities; (2) formalization of requirements, actions in which researchers discussed the scenarios with user and analyzed the collected materials to create similar scenarios with the addition of technological innovations; and (3) evaluation (acceptance) by users, actions in which researchers and users validated the proposed scenarios. The following artifacts were generated in the first cycle: meeting minutes; drawings/diagrams on cardboard; schemes digitally represented; scenarios with technologies; textual description of scenarios; responses to questionnaires; photos and videos, description/interpretation of photos and videos (see Fig. 2). The research team involved in this first cycle reported their experiments and materials generated in dissertations and articles [1, 3–10, 15, 18, 19].

The second cycle was conducted through the following actions: (1) continuation of the activities of participatory design, grouping activities of User Centered Design (UCD), where researchers and users were in brainstorming sections performed to further data collections of scenarios defined in the previous cycle; (2) prototyping, actions in which the researchers created prototypes for the areas of Education [7, 18, 19], Nursing Care [1, 2] and Physiotherapy [5]; and (3) evaluation by users, actions in which researchers and users evaluated the developed prototypes. The following artifacts were generated in this second cycle: meeting documents; prototypes on paper; prototypes in computational tools for middle and high fidelity; textual documents, photos and videos, description/interpretation of photos and videos. (see Fig. 3). At the end of Cycle 2, the research team produced the materials: (1) the definition of shapes

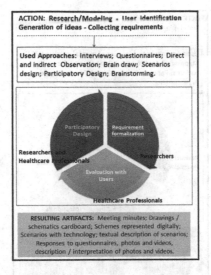

Fig. 2. Activities of Cycle 1

and objects to interact; (2) the definition of the features; and (3) the prototypes (paper and executable models).

The third cycle was conducted through the following actions: (1) enhancement of prototypes - performed from the analysis of the evaluations with users of the previous cycle to develop enhancements and new features in the creation of new prototypes; (2) preparation of assessments – the research team who developed evaluations, through questionnaires, interviews and observations to check how technological innovations and interactions were being adopted and appropriated by users in hospital; (3) user testing - where users participated in usability tests monitored and guided by the research team; (4) analysis of results - where researchers analyze the data collected during testing with users. Figure 4, presents the actions and artifacts generated and the result at the end of the cycle. Validations were made by researchers through discussions and improvements were proposed on the developed prototypes. User tests were executed and some data have been collected and analyzed and they are reported in published articles [1, 2, 5, 10, 18, 19].

This entire process was documented, the applications and technological resources were adopted and validated by users - it is important to note that the group of users, the healthcare professionals from the partner hospital, are not familiar with ICT in their professional activities, which makes the study most interesting in observing and understanding how applications with technological innovations are placed in the context of this work, and how the process of appropriation happens. Our observations indicated that introducing new technology cannot stop or change the workflow of healthcare professionals involved in the study, and that the proposed technology can also be used in other contexts [3, 6].

These studies involved the developing improvements at prototyping, and the evaluation and observation of these studies resulted in a new proposal in interaction design, encouraging the appropriation of technologies resources. In [3, 6], the authors

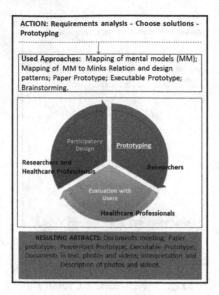

Fig. 3. Activities of Cycle 2

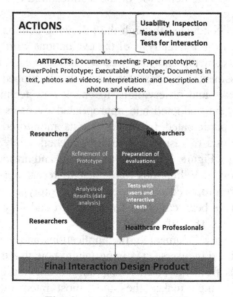

Fig. 4. Activities of Cycle 3

created an interaction design process by modifying the traditional design process: design - prototype - to assess [16]. They proposed to add iteration in the process of adoption and appropriation of technologies designed during design. They also created two new criteria for maintaining the workflow of professionals using ICT.

Based on authors [3, 6], the level of appropriation determines how the design is the natural measure that allows users to create new uses for the expected design, as well as use it in different contexts. The criteria proposed by [3] determine that the adoption of new technologies should not interrupt or interfere with the professional's tasks and the technology should be chooser to allow its appropriation in other contexts.

After all observations and studies, we have proposed a model and a prototype were developed in accordance with the activities of the three mapped and described cycles. This helped us to percept the concepts of appropriation of technologies in the work-place. The prototype, called Collab, was developed, in its first version, by [15] as part of his master degree. After initial utilization of the tool, the prototype was re-designed and a new version was deployed to use in the same partner hospital, because we noticed that professionals were using Collab mostly to exchange personal messages (messages related to patient's personal life) and to share congratulation messages (see Fig. 5 – Interacting with Collab using smartphone).

The Collab is an application to support the activities of communication and socialization among healthcare professionals, who spend long periods at work and they have, in most of the time, to help patients in their daily activities. The prototype has three features: (a) sending public messages to all or to a specific person, (b) public notification of tasks that must be performed by others and (c) notify when and who finish a task. For this, the application has been installed on a server in the hospital, to which the devices that were connected over Wi-Fi network and all healthcare professionals could access the application via any web browser, allowing professionals to use their own devices to access the application or any available tablets in the hospital. For sending messages and sending public tasks feature, we considered the existing uses of tables and whiteboards for messages that were there in the corridor of the ward a TV of 46 in. functioning as an information panel, which shows the last messages sent to all persons and pending tasks - sorted from oldest to newest. Previously, it was identified the benefits of public demonstrations to promote cooperation in health, described in [13]. They argued that public notifications, such as job boards, which are naturally used to provide task management, increase sharing of awareness, leading to a more efficient solution of the problem.

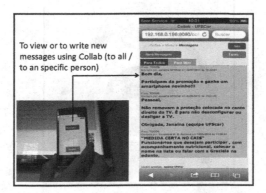

Fig. 5. Interacting with Collab using smartphone

In this work we used the public TV display to promote greater sharing of responsiveness among professionals, integrating the personal, social and professional contexts, since the data collected initially show all messages being aware and attentive to the events in the workplace. In the first two interactions with the use of Collab, many data were collected and analyzed. The results are published in [7, 17].

We realized, during the implementation of this project and through studies conducted by the LIA designers, that users need to integrate different contexts in which they live: professional, personal and social. This observation allowed us comprehend two gaps in existing models of interaction design: (1) the models do not facilitate the integration of professional, personal and social contexts in which users are included, which is essential for long term care professionals; (2) and the models do not make use or do not extend the abilities of these users regarding the use and adoption of technologies, leaving faster the appropriation of technologies.

These observations inspired us to propose a set of guidelines which will assist designers during the design process of interaction, to promote interaction of the different contexts in which users are included and to extend their abilities.

4   Guidelines and Discussion

From the analysis of Collab experiment we managed to extract 12 guidelines related to designing interactive applications to help designers integrate professional, personal and social context, and extends the user's abilities. We considered two main aspects for designing: extends user's abilities and support the integration of contexts. The guidelines were grouped in these two domains and when an interaction design process achieves these domains, technological adoption happens naturally (see Fig. 6 – Integration – Expansion – Appropriation).

These domains presents common goals of facilitating the appropriation: as the integration of contexts happens, users discover, or become aware, of the use of various technological resources and applications on the same and other contexts; and the

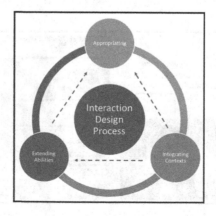

Fig. 6. Integration – Expansion – Appropriation

expansion of user abilities facilitates the use of technological resources and applications, extending the use of these. The set of 12 guidelines were formalized, grouped and classified according of two defined domains.

4.1 Guidelines to Integrating User's Context Domain

The INTEGRATING CONTEXTS domain guidelines highlight actions that guide designers on how consider all aspects of the user's context and that should be considered during the design.

GIC1. Make clear the purpose of sections design

Before starting the process of interaction design it is important to chat with the user group and explain what and how the sections will be executed. Explain how valuable the integration of personal and social context is to the choice of applications and technological resources to be adopted. Before each section of the design, you may explain which activities will be held, the duration of each and what you want to achieve at the end.

GIC2. Promote a fast socialization before the design sessions

Start the sections with an activity of socialization and encourage each participant to expose what he/she are waiting as a result of the day/week/month or to tell something new, about work or not. This socialization should be fast, 1 min for each participant may be enough. It helps to know and discover other abilities of the user or what he/she expects, not only related with technological resources. You can also use some games or dynamics.

GIC3. Ask which of the social networking (or e-communication services) user participates

Designers must know how the user interacts and communicates outside the work environment, and it can help choosing forms of interaction to be adopted. The use of communication mechanisms that user already use can be incorporated into the design, making it easier to use and motivating its use.

GIC4. Use group dynamics techniques to understand what kind of messages users usually share

It is interesting to know what kinds of messages are exchanged between users inside and/or outside work. During our experiments in [2], we realized that 75 % of messages were related to the personal or social context. The perception of this situation indicated us the requirement to incorporate personal and social contexts in the work routine of the users.

GIC5. Provide fast rest breaks between sessions of design with the user

Intervals during the sections assist to provide a moment of relaxation between the activities of the design section, but also should be used to observe user behavior. In our experiments [2, 4, 8], during the intervals between design activities, some participants used their mobile phones to check messages or calls, to make professional and personal connections and to talk about subjects not related to work with colleagues. These observations allowed us to understand the requirement to propose a way and/or a time for social interactions among participants. And, whenever possible, offer something to eat (coffee break intervals) - it makes intervals more relaxed and affable.

GIC6. Design for appropriation

During the experiments, in brainstorm sessions and during the user testing [1, 2, 4, 5, 8–10, 19], we realized that users can appropriate the technological resources or applications if they tried new uses or have used them in other context. One case that was interested to us was the story of the physiotherapist which using your own camera in her sessions of physiotherapy took some photos, printed these photos and wrote comments about the therapy session. In the course of our experiments, she realized she could take the photos with a tablet and make notes to send to her colleagues and each could add other comments, so they could discuss a specific case. This perception provide us highlight the importance of proposing designs flexible enough to appropriation.

4.2   Guidelines to Extending User's Abilities Domain

The EXPANDING ABILITIES domain guidelines highlight actions that guide designers on how explore user's abilities in different context of uses and that should be considered during the design.

GEA1. Don't waste the user's time

The duration of design sections should be short and be prepared in advance. The goals of each design section must be clear and defined previously. When the objectives and activities are not defined, the designers are lost during the section and this can make the participants annoyed, hindering their participation.

GEA2. Ask user what technological resource he/she knows

The cell phone or smart phone model, tablet, automatic machines (ATM), TV at home – every resource that user knows how to use can help the designers and can be used in new applications. So, it is important to ask how resources are handled and in what situations.

GEA3. Ask user which application he/she uses in everyday activities

The use of applications such as task managers, electronic calendars, app to support diets or sports, can illustrate the user's abilities that he/she did not expose. Other important observation that should be noted is the readiness of the user to receive notifications and/or hints of these applications. Also the designers have to notice if the user separates or links the personal, social and professional notes when using these applications. The user's expertise with some applications can help in the acceptance and practice of new applications that use similar forms of interaction.

GEA4. Encourage communication among users and designers through new technological resources

Designers can use environments and communication applications that the user does not know, just knows a little or frequently uses. Thus, users may have the opportunity to know or learn new technologies and communications methods. And designers can notice some common practices and specific characteristics of users to incorporate them in design process.

GEA5. Observe the things user have with them

During our experiments some participants said they had no account in social networks, but when we asked about Facebook, they said they had a profile on "Face." They did not know the term "social network", only knew it by Facebook. Users can say they do not know a technological resource or application, but it's very common he/she uses them without knowing, or knowing them by another name, or, also, he/she uses them in another context and another purpose. Design must use popular names, marks and try different forms to refer a technological resource or application, when they are interviewing the users.

GEA6. Program the sections of design to be done in the user's environment of work, but do not disturb the user environment

Designers must take in consideration the working environment, in which users are included, the locations where each one performs their activities. However, the designers must not disturb other employees and their activities. In addition, designers should ensure that the design sections do not disturb the routine of the participants, not to cause embarrassment or bothered.

5 Conclusion

It this paper we presented a set of guidelines to support the interaction design process that integrate professional, personal and social context of the user, using and extending the user abilities. With Collab experiment we learned that professionals working with long term care and have long shift of work, trend to mix the professional, personal and social contexts. This warned us during the process of interaction with user's participation, so these contexts must be taken into consideration and the abilities that users have in other contexts can be used and extended their work environment. These aspects drove the appropriation's design and allowed greater user's awareness in relation to its potential in the use of technological resources.

Based on these feelings and the ones we collected while the researchers of LIA were creating application at the hospital, we were able to formalize our lessons learned as a set of guidelines that are applicable to designers who want to incentive the appropriation, through the integration of professional, personal and social context and are trying to extends the abilities of the user. As future work we want to make others experiments changing the group of users of the experiment and the way to design to confirm if these guidelines can be generalized.

Acknowledgments. We thank all team from LIA/UFSCar by collected data, with observations, interviews and design meetings in the hospital. We also thank the Federal Institute of São Paulo for the financial support.

References

1. Abib, J.C., Bueno, A., Anacleto, J.: Understanding and facilitating the communication process among healthcare professionals. In: Duffy, V.G. (ed.) DHM 2014. LNCS, vol. 8529, pp. 313–324. Springer, Heidelberg (2014)
2. Abib, J.C., Anacleto, J.C.: Improving communication in healthcare: a case study. In: Proceedings of IEEE International Conference on Systems, Man, and Cybernetics – SMC (2014)
3. Anacleto, J., Fels, S.: Adoption and appropriation: a design process from HCI research at a Brazilian neurological hospital. In: Kotzé, P., Marsden, G., Lindgaard, G., Wesson, J., Winckler, M. (eds.) INTERACT 2013, Part II. LNCS, vol. 8118, pp. 356–363. Springer, Heidelberg (2013)
4. Anacleto, J.C., Fels, S., Silvestre, R.: Transforming a paper based process to a natural user interfaces process in a chronic care hospital. Proc. Comput. Sci. J. **14**, 173–180 (2012)
5. Anacleto, J., Fels, S., Silvestre, R., Souza Filho, C.E., Santana, B: Therapist-centered design of NUI based therapies in a neurological care hospital. In: Proceedings of the IEEE International Conference on System, Man, and Cybernetics, pp. 2318–2323, Korea (2012)
6. Anacleto, J.C., Fels, S.: Lessons from ICT design of a healthcare worker-centered system for a chronic mental care hospital. In: Proceedings of the ACM Conference on Human Factors in Computing Systems (CHI 2014), Canada (2014)
7. Anacleto, J.C., Silva, M.A.R., Hernandes, E.C.M: Co-authoring proto-patterns to support on designing systems to be adequate for users' diversity. In: Proceedings of the 15th International Conference on Enterprise Information Systems, vol. 1, pp. 84–89. SCITEPRESS Science and Technology Publications, Portugal (2013)
8. Britto, T., Abib, J.C., Camargo, L.S.A., Anacleto, J.C.: A participatory design approach to use natural user interface for e-health. In: Proceedings of 5th Workshop on Software and Usability Engineering Cross-Pollination: Patters, Usability and User Experience, pp. 35–42 (2011)
9. Calderon, R., Fels, S., Oliveira, J.L., Anacleto, J.: Understanding NUI-supported nomadic social places in a Brazilian health care facility. In: Proceedings of the 11th Brazilian Symposium on Human Factors in Computing Systems, pp. 76–84, Brazil (2012)
10. Calderon, R., Fels, S., Anacleto, J., Oliveira, J.L.: Towards supporting informal information and communication practices within a Brazilian healthcare environment. In: Proceedings of the ACM CHI Conference on Human Factors in Computing Systems - Extended Abstracts (CHI EA 2013), pp. 517–522. ACM 978-1-4503-1952-2/13/04, France (2013)
11. Hassenzahl, M.: User experience and experience design. In: Soegaard M., Dam R.F. (eds.) The Encyclopedia of Human-Computer Interaction, 2nd edn. The Interaction Design Foundation, Aarhus, Denmark (2014). https://www.interaction design.org/encyclopedia/user_experience_and_experience_design.html
12. Koskinen, I., Zimmerman, J., Binder, T., Redstrom, J., Wensveen, S.: Constructive design research. In: Koskinen, I., Zimmerman, J., Binder, T., Redstrom, J., Wensveen, S. (eds.) Design Research Through Practice: From the Lab, Field, and Showroom, pp. 1–14. Elsevier, Waltham (2011)

13. Lasome, C., Xiao, Y.: Large public display boards: a case study of an OR board and design implications. In: Proceedings of the American Medical Informatics Association pp. 349–352 (2001)
14. Milne, A.J.: Entering the interaction age: implementing a future vision for campus learning spaces…today. EDUCAUSE Rev. **42**(1), 12–31 (2011)
15. Oliveira, J.L.: Recommendation system for promotion of homophile networks based in cultural values: observing the impact of homophile on reciprocity relations supported by technology, p. 76. Master degree dissertation, Federal University of São Carlos/Brazil (2013). (In Portuguese)
16. Preece, J., Rogers, Y., Sharp, H.: Interaction design, 1st edn. Wiley, New York (2002)
17. Rogers, Y., Sharp, H., Preece, J.: Interaction Design: Beyond Human-Computer Interaction, 3rd edn, p. 585. Wiley, New York (2011)
18. Silva, M.A.R., Anacleto, J.C.: Adding semantic relations among design patterns. In: Proceedings of the 15th International Conference on Enterprise Information Systems, vol. 1, pp. 1–11. SCITEPRESS Science and Technology Publications, Portugal (2014)
19. Silva, M.A.R., Anacleto, J.C.: Patterns to support designing of co-authoring web educational systems. In: Proceedings of IADIS WWW/Internet 2013 Conference, pp. 117–124. International Association for Development of the Information Society (IADIS Press), Fort Worth (2013)

Practices, Technologies, and Challenges of Constructing and Programming Physical Interactive Prototypes

Andrea Alessandrini[✉]

College of Art, Science and Engineering, University of Dundee,
Perth Road 13, Dundee DD1 4HT, UK
a.alessandrini@dundee.ac.uk

Abstract. The prototyping process is a key phase in the design of interactive systems. Designing connections and communications for computational elements is a challenging part of constructing physical interactive prototypes. The goal of this study is to explore and describe the practices and technologies used in the construction of physical interactive prototypes in a university course on interaction design. This study reviews constructed physical interactive prototypes, presents excerpts of interviews with students, and analyses students' blogs. In particular, the study describes and analyzes how connections and communications were made and which components and technologies were used in a course on interaction design. Finally, the implications of the findings of this study are discussed.

Keywords: Interaction design · Prototyping · Design

1 Introduction

Prototypes are key artifacts used in the design of interactive systems [1]. In the last decade, new paradigms of interaction have challenged the prototyping process. Ubiquitous computing [2], tangible interfaces [3], augmented reality [4], and ambient intelligence [5] have challenged existing prototyping tools and techniques. Prototypes have become mobile, physical, embedded, connected, portable, and intelligent. Prototyping tools are essential to support interaction designers in exploring and programing the design space. In recent years, many platforms have become available for designers to construct physical interactive prototypes rapidly in a way that was unimaginable a few years ago. Readily available sets of compatible microcontrollers, sensors, actuators, and other components now support designers in constructing interactive physical prototypes. *Raspberry Pi*, *LittleBits*, *.NET Gadgeteer*, *Arduino*, and *Phidgets* are a few examples of these platforms [6–10]. These new technologies have helped the process of prototyping interactive products. However, designing the connections and communications between computational elements remains a challenge in the construction of these physical interactive prototypes.

In this paper, I present the results of a study that investigated how design students constructed physical interactive prototypes in an interaction design class. This work

© Springer International Publishing Switzerland 2015
M. Kurosu (Ed.): Human-Computer Interaction, Part I, HCII 2015, LNCS 9169, pp. 132–142, 2015.
DOI: 10.1007/978-3-319-20901-2_12

examined 15 physical interactive prototypes, conducted fieldwork observations, and interviewed seven design students who participated in the construction of physical interactive prototypes. This research aimed to yield detailed insights into how design students construct prototypes in practice. The study examined physical interactive prototypes, the technologies used, and student practices with the objective of understanding how designers connect hardware and software components. The study also aimed to describe and analyze how connections were made and which components and technologies were used. The research was driven by three specific questions: (1) How do design students construct communication between components? (2) What types of connections do they use? (3) What issues do they encounter and how do they overcome them? From the design perspective, there is a need for the simple design, construction, installation, and configuration of components. This work focuses on the important area of the design of tools used in the design and construction of interactive systems.

2   Background

There is little previous research on prototyping tools and design practices and challenges in physical interactive prototyping. Nevertheless, in recent years, eminent researchers have highlighted the importance of this area. For example, Shneiderman [11] reported that the literature on the topic is scarce, pointing out that more studies on the field are needed. From the same perspective, Stolterman stressed that by expanding the amount of research on this underexplored area, researchers could contribute to the development of better design tools [12].

The study presented in this paper is grounded in the theories of distributed cognition [13], communities of practice [14], and activity [15]. It builds on two bodies of related work: (1) studies of how designers design and construct prototypes; and (2) the design of systems that help designers construct better prototypes. The importance of this research is evident in the challenges and issues that have been reported in studies that have described the process of designing interactive prototypes. For example, Myers et al. [16] discussed the difficulties inherent in designing prototypes that contain complex interactions. Alessandrini et al. [17] describes the limits of prototyping tools used to design tangible technologies for children. Boucher and Gaver reported the challenges in designing the drift table [18]. Hazlewood et al. [19] described the challenges faced in designing a large-scale installation. The design process of the Wironi Project clearly showed the limitations and challenges of using existing prototyping tools to design gestural interfaces for browsing audible internet content [20–22]. From a learning and educational perspective, in an unpublished work, Mellis [23] reported the challenges encountered by students of interaction design in developing physical interaction prototypes. Alessandrini [24] also highlighted the importance of developing simpler prototyping tools for interaction design students.

Further studies were based on the results of field studies aimed at supporting designers through the design of novel design tools for prototyping. For example, in their study on opportunistic design, Hartmann et al. [25, 26] identified common strategies adopted by practitioners to build physical interactive systems. Alessandrini [27] explored the design challenges and limitations for researchers and designers in constructing Internet of Things systems using existing prototyping tools. In a fieldwork study based on interviews and observations, Carter et al. [28] investigated the challenges and issues encountered by researchers and practitioners of ubiquitous computing to create physical interactive prototypes. Another recent study [29, 30] used interviews to determine the process involved in the design of novel prototyping tool-kits, the findings of which were important for our research.

This study is intended to extend the literature by focusing on designers with little or no programming experience, such as design students, who usually do not have strong programming skills. Most previous studies are based on brief, narrow field studies, which aimed to determine the process of constructing novel design tools. This research intends to extend this literature by providing an extensive dedicated, longer, and wider study with the specific aims to understand physical interactive prototyping.

3 Methodology

Fieldwork observations, semi-structured interviews, and project blog analyses were used to gather data that were used to answer the research questions. The fieldwork observations and semi-structured interviews were conducted using students in a third-year course on interaction design in the social digital Program in the Design Department at the University of Dundee (United Kingdom). The aims of the projects in the course were to create interactive objects that conveyed information in an audible form. The design brief focused on the following: *building and crafting an "audible information object," which was defined as a dedicated, physical product that sits/hangs/lives in someone's home and conveys some meaningful information to them, existing data/content found on the internet—through sound.* The class was part of the four-year social digital program. Fifty-five students worked in groups of three on a 10-week project. The class was composed of product design (PD) and interaction design (IxD) students. Emphasis was placed on building working electronic prototypes. The students were forbidden to use screens in their projects. Arduino was specified as the prototyping platform used by the students. During the first half of the course, the students developed concepts and defined their own design directions. In the second half of the course, the students designed and implemented their projects, which was supported by the tutors and technicians. The classroom was organized as a design studio space. The students had accessibility to a workshop, electronic lab, and other related facilities.

This study presented here analyzed the physical interactive prototypes constructed by the students, which provided an opportunity to describe the challenges and issues that emerged during the ideation, development, and testing of the prototypes, as well as the prototypes' behavior. I focused on analyzing the different types of connections established between diverse devices and components in order to describe the challenges encountered and the solutions developed to overcome them. I also conducted semi-structured interviews with seven students with the specific aim of understanding how the interviewees constructed their physical interactive prototypes.

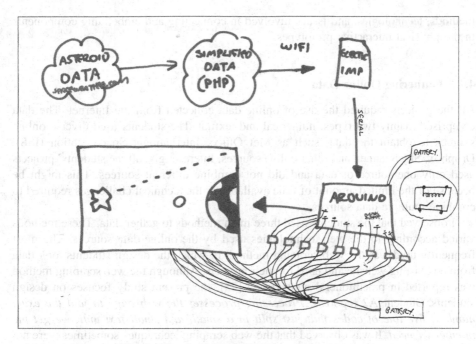

Fig. 1. Sketch of the architecture of a prototype

The participants were chosen randomly from the design class. I contacted 55 students via e-mail, seven of whom agreed to be interviewed. The participants ranged in age from 18 to 22 years; five were male, and two were female. They had an average of one to two years of experience in building physical interactive prototypes. The same procedure and interview schedule was adopted in all interviews. A single face-to-face interview ranging from 40 min to 2 h was conducted with each interviewee. All interviews were video-recorded with the participants' permission, and written notes were taken by the researcher. The semi-structured interviews were conducted in the design studio. After briefly introducing the scope of the study, I asked a series of open-ended questions designed to gather data about one recent project completed by each interviewee, such as the construction of the system, the purpose of the system, whether there had been any problems in connecting the components, and how they solved such issues. I also asked each interviewee to sketch a functional representation of the system on paper, highlighting the methods used to connect the different components (Fig. 1). The transcribed interviews, the interview notes, and the interviewees' sketches were later analyzed and coded. All the data found in the analysis were mapped and clustered according to each discussion topic.

4   Results

The next section describes the methods and technologies used and the issues encountered by students in designing their physical interactive prototypes, all of which were connected to Internet data sources. The following section will present the methods, technologies, and issues involved in connecting and embedding components in the physical interactive prototypes.

4.1 Gathering Online Data

All the projects required the use of online data collected from the Internet. The data comprised mainly two types: numerical and textual. The students used diverse online sources to obtain the data, such as Met Office, International Space Station (ISS), Dropbox, Sky Scanner, and other online sources. Interestingly, all the students' projects used only one source of data and did not combine different sources. This might be because of the limited amount of time available or the technical challenges required to combine multiple data sources.

I observed that the students used three main methods to gather data. These methods varied according to the web technologies used by the online data sources. The most frequently used was the web scraping method, in which the design students took data from an existing website and used for their projects. Although the web scraping method was reported in practitioners' contexts by [25], the present study focuses on design students. Student A2 reported: *Processing processes the web page to find the exact number, five line of codes that just split in a small, and small text until we get the number we need.* It was observed that the web scraping techniques sometimes were not facilitated by the particular web technology used to build the websites. Student A3 reported: *The web site was in Java script, and I couldn't get the data. I used cURL with PHP to set the timetable bus information.* In several projects, the interviewees reported that the web scraping methods required several steps to shape the data. For example, Student A1 reported: *So to get those numbers there are other step sites. It goes through three .... It goes from this site to a PHP site, and then from there it goes into ... two other steps. It goes to an XML file. It tidies it up, and it makes it searchable. So it labeled date, distance, magnitude, name. And then, now this file eliminated all the thing we don't want. 3, 4 are the numbers we are looking today.*

Another widely used method was the data feed, in which the prototypes received updated data from online data sources. These types of data were aggregations of public data, such as news, weather, and traffic. The BBC, the Met Office, and Hong Kong's department of city traffic provided the web-feed data that the students used to construct their prototypes.

Few students used web application programing interfaces (API) because they are challenging. The students interrogated a web service (e.g. Twitter) through a web request-response message system. Compared to the other data sources, these comprised mostly personal data that were linked with the use of an online service. Student A5 reported: *The computer runs Processing. Processing is going to a PHP scripts. The script goes to Twitter API looks for hashtag requested. When it has tweets with a hashtag it sends back to Processing. Than Processing goes back to PHP it calls the text-to-speech web site. It downloads an mp3 file, which is the spoken tweet.* Student A4 reported the challenging issue in overcoming the security requirements necessary to obtain the data: *For security reasons Dropbox API require https, also you can use http running on the local machine.*

Although the students had not taken classes in processing (processing.org) they used it as a tool to scrape data from websites or to connect to a local server that ran PHP scripts. The students considered that processing was the unique tool available for obtaining Internet data. The data sources were chosen because they provided quality data, which were both free of cost and relatively easy to use. It was also interesting that many projects embedded a button, a potentiometer, or other input parts as methods to simulate online data. This was done for two main reasons: First, it enabled the students to test more easily interactive behaviors or the hardware prototype when they were working offline, and it permitted the development of hardware parallel to the data-gathering system. Second, because the methods and the tools used to gather data were unreliable, these simulation inputs helped in the case that something went wrong during the demonstration. The students usually implemented these inputs first in testing their hardware design, especially when the data gathering systems were neither ready nor reliable (Fig. 2).

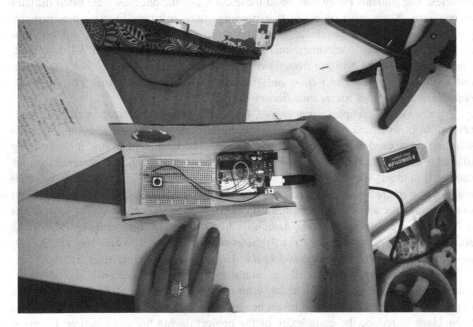

Fig. 2. Early working prototype

4.2 Making Components Communicate

All the physical interactive prototypes required communication between diverse embedded components. All the prototypes used input and output components. The most commonly used input components were photo-resistors, potentiometers, conductive threads, and RFID readers. Speakers, solenoids, servos, or water pumps were the most frequently used output components. The students collected Arduinos, sensors, actuators, and other electronic components from the technical departments of the university. The required components were given to students only after they consulted technicians about the requirements and functionalities of the prototypes. Hazlewood et al. [19] noted the importance of consultation.

The students used four main approaches to create communication between the components. These techniques varied according to the complexity of the technologies used by the components. The most frequently used components were solenoids, buttons, and LEDs, which communicate through simple digital protocols (0 or 1 values). It was observed that the students connected these components easily and rapidly. Other sets of components, such as photo-resistors and potentiometers, were also used by the students, which provided rich analog values (0–1023). Although the students implemented the connections of these values easily and quickly, programming the software required to use the rich value sets required more attention and understanding than the less complex technologies did.

A small number of components, such as conductive threads or servos, required more complex programming techniques that were based on dedicated software libraries. The students easily connected these components, but they were often difficult to program. It was also observed that running more software libraries concurrently generated unresolvable problems. Based on multiple software libraries, this communication strategy was sometimes impossible to implement, as Student A2 described: *You can listen to the Arduino trough processing, but this was the first thing we tried, but unfortunately you can't have an Arduino library in Processing. This with the capacitive sensor that use is own library.*

Another set of complex components, Radio-frequency identification (RFID) readers, audio boards, and computers, which communicate via the serial communication standard, were used in some interactive prototypes. Most students found it challenging to make communication between these components via the serial communications standard. Student A6 stated: *Connecting Processing and Arduino was the most challenging part of the project; we don't know how to do it.* Many students found it difficult to understand the serial communication standard. Student A7 reported: *The system has a RFID reader connected to the Arduino via serial to the Mac running Processing code. When you have to upload the Arduino sketch, you need to take this [Rx RFID] wire out. RFID's Rx connection blocks the Arduino programming* (Fig. 3).

It was very interesting that all the interactive prototypes used only one advanced communication connection (e.g. serial) with the other components. This might be due to the lack of time available, or it might be due to the simplification process done by the technicians to reduce the complexity of the project during the consultation. Communication protocols, communication units and frequency rate, where complex concepts to grasp and use by the students. The study observed that they often used libraries, which facilitate the communication between serial components, as A3 reported: *Arduino has FIRMATA library and communicate via serial, which it does, trough FIRMATA.* Interviewees reported that to facilitate the serial communication between components, data was appropriately elaborated and formatted. As A4 reported: *Processing is used to clean and shape the data. From 4,004 % to 4 %. Processing converts the data to an integer.* A2 also stated: *We have 0.05, each time we multiply the have a whole number like 500 and we store as an integer instead of a float, and float doesn't go across the serial.* Further strategies were used to simplify the communication between two components, for example as A7 reported: *The RFID reader is sending in BYTES. Arduino translate this in HEX value that I think has 10 characters. I'm always sending the last two [characters] to Processing. This is because if I tried to send the whole string the data get lost and it won't differentiate between RFID Tags.*

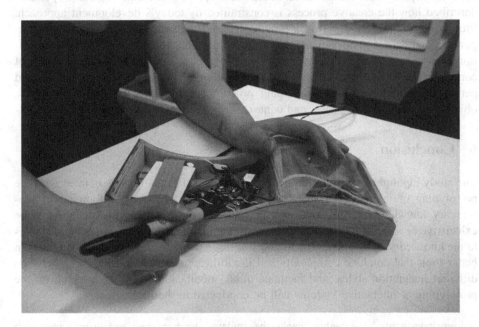

Fig. 3. Arduino with the RFID reader

The students used Arduino (arduino.cc) as the physical tool used to power, control, and communicate with all components. The students learned how to use Arduino in the social digital program. Although the class was composed of IxD and PD students, I observed that only the IxD students were actively involved in embedding the technology in their physical interactive prototypes.

5 Discussion

This research investigated the technologies, techniques, and challenges encountered by students in constructing physical interactive prototypes. The findings contributed to the general understanding of prototyping, provided suggestions for the design of novel prototyping tools, and yielded information about education in this field.

The findings showed that communication between hardware and software components is complex. In certain situations, data and information are necessary to activate and establish a communication session. The findings revealed a fluid and dynamic communication model in which data and information could be conveyed from both hardware and software. In their study on opportunistic design, Hartmann et al. [25, 26] identified similar strategies used to build interactive systems.

Although prototyping is a creative activity that requires experimentation and design-thinking skills, most tools used today do not fully support these processes. Prototyping tools require an approach that is different from that used in engineering. In design it is fundamental to soften technology to make it quick, imaginative, and easy in order to shape the user's experience. In the "Triumph of Tinkering," Turkle [31] clearly described how the creative process is constrained by today's development approach. Prototyping tools should permit a progressive and dynamic transition between components and behavioral arrangements. Prototyping tools should permit smooth transitions between different solutions, thus enabling easy and fluid rearrangements of components and behaviors according to the system's requirements. Such tools would permit fluid control of the prototyping process according to the designer's skills, objectives, development phase, and context.

6 Conclusion

The study highlights the opportunities, challenges, and limitations associated with the prototyping of interactive systems. As an initial effort in the development of preliminary knowledge in this area, the analysis presented here is not intended to be exhaustive or complete. Instead, it focuses on the qualities that each project contributes to the knowledge of this area. The findings of this study indicate that we need to design better tools that combine complexity and flexibility, support fluid transitions between different integration styles, and facilitate quick modification. Further research on the prototyping of interactive systems will be conducted in the near future.

Acknowledgements. The author thanks the students, teachers, and technicians who were involved in the study.

References

1. Ehn, P., Kyng, M.: Cardboard computers: mocking-it-up or hands-on the future. In: Design at Work, pp. 169–196. Lawrence Erlbaum Associates Inc, Hillsdale (1992)
2. Weiser, M.: The computer for the 21st century, 1991. Sci. Am. **256**, 66–75 (1991)
3. Ishii, H., Ullmer, B.: Tangible bits: towards seamless interfaces between people, bits and atoms. In: Proceedings of the SIGCHI Conference on Human Factors in Computing Systems, p. 241. ACM (1997)
4. Azuma, R.T.: A survey of augmented reality. Presence **6**, 355–385 (1997)
5. Aarts, E.H.L., Marzano, S.: The New Everyday: Views on Ambient Intelligence. 010 Publishers, Rotterdam (2003)
6. Bdeir, A.: Electronics as material: littlebits. In: Proceedings of the 3rd International Conference on Tangible and Embedded Interaction, pp. 397–400. ACM, Cambridge (2009)
7. Greenberg, S., Fitchett, C.: Phidgets: easy development of physical interfaces through physical widgets. In: Proceedings of the 14th Annual ACM Symposium on User Interface Software and Technology, pp. 209–218. ACM, New York (2001)
8. Mellis, D., Banzi, M., Cuartielles, D., Igoe, T.: Arduino: an open electronic prototyping platform. In: CHI: ACM Conference on Human Factors in Computing Systems (2007)

9. Villar, N., Scott, J., Hodges, S., Hammil, K., Miller, C.:NET gadgeteer: a platform for custom devices. In: Kay, J., Lukowicz, P., Tokuda, H., Olivier, P., Krüger, A. (eds.) Pervasive 2012. LNCS, vol. 7319, pp. 216–233. Springer, Heidelberg (2012)
10. Raspberry Pi. http://www.raspberrypi.org/
11. Shneiderman, B.: Creativity support tools: a grand challenge for HCI researchers. In: Redono, M., Bravo, C., Ortega, M. (eds.) Engineering the User Interface, pp. 1–9. Springer, London (2009)
12. Stolterman, E., McAtee, J., Royer, D., Thandapani, S.: Designerly Tools. Sheffield Hallam University, Sheffield (2009)
13. Hollan, J., Hutchins, E., Kirsh, D.: Distributed cognition: toward a new foundation for human-computer interaction research. ACM Trans. Comput. Hum. Interact. (TOCHI) 7, 196 (2000)
14. Wenger, E.: Communities of Practice: Learning, Meaning, and Identity. Cambridge University Press, Cambridge (1998)
15. Engeström, Y.: Learning by Expanding: An Activity-Theoretical Approach to Developmental Research. Orienta-Konsultit, Helsinki (1987)
16. Myers, B., Park, S.Y., Nakano, Y., Mueller, G., Ko, A.: How designers design and program interactive behaviors. In: IEEE Symposium on Visual Languages and Human-Centric Computing, 2008. VL/HCC 2008, pp. 177–184. IEEE (2008)
17. Alessandrini, A., Cappelletti, A., Zancanaro, M.: Audio-augmented paper for therapy and educational intervention for children with autistic spectrum disorder. Int. J. Hum. Comput. Stud. 72, 422–430 (2014)
18. Boucher, A., Gaver, W.: Developing the drift table. Interactions 13, 24–27 (2006)
19. Hazlewood, W.R., Dalton, N., Marshall, P., Rogers, Y., Hertrich, S.: Bricolage and consultation: addressing new design challenges when building large-scale installations. In: Proceedings of the 8th ACM Conference on Designing Interactive Systems, pp. 380–389. ACM (2010)
20. Rizzo, A., Rubegni, E., Grönval, E., Caporali, M., Alessandrini, A.: The net in the park. Knowl. Technol. Policy 22, 51–59 (2009)
21. Rubegni, E., Brunk, J., Caporali, M., Gronvall, E., Alessandrini, A., Rizzo, A.: Wi-Wave: urban furniture for browsing internet contents in public spaces. In: Proceedings of the 15th European Conference on Cognitive Ergonomics: The Ergonomics of Cool Interaction, p. 10. ACM (2008)
22. Alessandrini, A., Rizzo, A., Rubegni, E.: Drama prototyping for the design of urban interactive systems for children. In: Proceedings of the 8th International Conference on Interaction Design and Children, pp. 198–201. ACM (2009)
23. Mellis, D.A.: Making Prototypes Work: Reflections from a Course in Tangible User Interfaces
24. Alessandrini, A.: Digital Bricolage: Hands-on Experiences with Digital Interaction Construction. FabLearn Europe, Aahrus (2014)
25. Hartmann, B., Doorley, S., Dontcheva, M.: Hacking, mashing, gluing: understanding opportunistic design. IEEE Pervasive Comput. 7, 46–54 (2008)
26. Hartmann, B., Doorley, S., Klemmer, S.R.: Hacking, mashing, gluing: a study of opportunistic design and development. Pervasive Comput. 7, 46–54 (2006)
27. Alessandrini, A.: End-user construction mechanisms for the internet of things. In: Proceedings of the 27th International BCS Human Computer Interaction Conference, pp. 1–6. British Computer Society, London (2013)
28. Carter, S., Mankoff, J., Klemmer, S.R., Matthews, T.: Exiting the cleanroom: on ecological validity and ubiquitous computing. Hum. Comput. Interact. 23, 47–99 (2008)

29. Klemmer, S.R., Landay, J.A.: Toolkit support for integrating physical and digital interactions. Hum. Comput. Interact. **24**, 315–366 (2009)
30. Klemmer, S.R., Li, J., Lin, J., Landay, J.A.: Papier-Mache: toolkit support for tangible input. In: Proceedings of the SIGCHI Conference on Human Factors in Computing Systems, pp. 399–406. ACM (2004)
31. Turkle, S.: Life on the Screen. Simon and Schuster, New York (2011)

ISO 9241-11 Revised: What Have We Learnt About Usability Since 1998?

Nigel Bevan[1(✉)], James Carter[2], and Susan Harker[3]

[1] Professional UX Services, 12 King Edwards Gardens, London W3 9RG, UK
nigel@nigelbevan.com
[2] Computer Science Department, University of Saskatchewan, Saskatoon,
Canada
carter@cs.usask.ca
[3] Loughborough Design School, Loughborough University, Loughborough
LE11 3TU, UK
S.D.Harker@lboro.ac.uk

Abstract. A revision is currently being undertaken of ISO 9241-11, published in 1998 to provide guidance on usability. ISO-9241-11 defines usability in terms of effectiveness, efficiency and satisfaction in a particular context of use. The intention was to emphasise that usability is an outcome of interaction rather than a property of a product. This is now widely accepted. However, the standard also places emphasis on usability measurement and it is now appreciated that there is more to usability evaluation than measurement. Other developments include an increasing awareness of the importance of the individual user's emotional experience as discretionary usage of complex consumer products and use of the World Wide Web have became more widespread. From an organisational perspective, it is now appreciated that usability plays an important role in managing the potentials risks that can arise from inappropriate outcomes of interaction. The revision of ISO 9241-11 takes account of these issues and other feedback.

Keywords: Standards · Usability · User experience

1 Origins of ISO 9241-11

What is usability?[1] In the English language, usability is typically defined as the "capability of being used", implicitly the capability of an entity to be used. In the 1980s and 1990s a considerable amount of material was published describing the attributes that would make a product usable (e.g. Smith and Mosier [20], and the early parts of the ISO 9241 series [9]). From this perspective, usability could be designed into the product, and evaluated by assessing consistency with these design guidelines, or by heuristic evaluation. This was the perspective taken in ISO 9126:1992: "Software engineering—Product quality", which defined usability as "a set of attributes of

---

[1] This is a problem that has been troubling the first author since work started on developing the original ISO 9241-11 in 1988 [1–3].

© Springer International Publishing Switzerland 2015
M. Kurosu (Ed.): Human-Computer Interaction, Part I, HCII 2015, LNCS 9169, pp. 143–151, 2015.
DOI: 10.1007/978-3-319-20901-2_13

software which bear on the effort needed for use and on the individual assessment of such use by a stated or implied set of users".

However an alternative approach recognised that the same product could have significantly different levels of usability depending on who was using it with what goals. In order to achieve usability for the intended users it would be necessary to address the actual outcomes of their use of the product. This was the approach advocated by Whiteside, Bennett and Holzblatt in 1988, based on an operational view of usability in terms of user performance and satisfaction [22].

The approach taken to usability in ISO 9241-11 (1998) was similar, defining usability as: "The extent to which a product can be used by specified users to achieve specified goals with effectiveness, efficiency and satisfaction in a specified context of use."

This approach has the benefit that it directly relates to user and business require-ments: effectiveness means success in achieving goals, efficiency means not wasting time and satisfaction means willingness to use the system.

ISO 9241-11:1998 explains that in order to specify or measure usability it is necessary to identify the goals and to decompose effectiveness, efficiency and satis-faction and the components of the context of use into sub-components with measurable and verifiable attributes. The standard identifies the benefits of this approach:

- The framework can be used to identify the usability measures and the components of the context of use to be taken into account when specifying, designing or evaluating the usability of a product.
- The performance (effectiveness and efficiency) and satisfaction of the users can be used to measure the extent to which a product is usable in a particular context.
- Measures of the performance and satisfaction of the users can provide a basis for the comparison of the relative usability of products with different technical character-istics which are used in the same context
- The level of usability needed for a product can be defined, documented and verified (e.g. as part of a quality plan).

2   What Have We Learnt About Usability Since 1998?

ISO 9241-11:1998 has been highly successful in providing an internationally accepted basis for understanding and applying usability. Its definition of usability is widely referenced in research, industry, and other international standards. This widespread use has been accompanied by a greater level of understanding of usability than was available when this first version of ISO 9241-11 was developed. As a result, work was started in 2011 to revise this standard to provide enhanced guidance based on over a decade of experience with the concepts that it introduces. This revision is intended to retain the basic concept of usability and to provide users of the concept with further levels of understanding about usability taking account of what we have learnt about usability since 1998, including the issues identified below.

2.1   It Is Important to Understand the User's Experience

In much early work in industry, usability was operationalised primarily in terms of the user's performance (effectiveness and efficiency), which was regarded as the prime issue given the many problems that were experienced by users of commercial systems. But as use of complex consumer products and of the World Wide Web became widespread, there was an increasing awareness of the importance of the user's sub-jective reactions and emotional experience. This has led some authors to regard usability as being restricted to "ease-of-use", and relegate it to the role of a "hygiene factor", e.g. [5] usability "…is a thermometer that sets the 'hygiene' level of a product. Users today take the 'ease of use' part of product concepts for granted and will not praise the fact that a product or service has good usability." Similarly, Hassenzahl et al. [4] differentiate between ease of use as a "pragmatic quality being a 'hygiene factor', enabling the fulfilment of needs through removing barriers but not being a source of positive experience in itself", and "hedonic quality being a 'motivator', capturing the product's perceived ability to create positive experiences through need fulfilment". ISO 9241-210:2010 "Human-centred design for interactive systems" defines user experi-ence as a "person's perceptions and responses resulting from the use and/or anticipated use of a product, system or service". User experience focuses on the experience of an individual in contrast with the view of effectiveness, efficiency and satisfaction as representing the collective responses of a group of users.

One objective of the revision of ISO 9241-11 is to clarify that the satisfaction component of usability includes aspects of user experience.

2.2   There Is More to Usability Evaluation Than Usability Measurement

ISO 9241-11:1998 focussed on the evaluation of usability by user based measurement of effectiveness, efficiency and satisfaction, as this was a convincing way of demon-strating the existence of usability problems to system developers. ISO/IEC DIS 25066:2015 "Common Industry Format (CIF) for usability: Evaluation report" pro-vides a broader view explaining that usability evaluation can be based on inspection to identify potential usability problems, in addition to observation of user behaviour and the collection of user-reported data. The revision of ISO 9241-11 needs to make it clear that effectiveness, efficiency and satisfaction represent the intended outcomes of interaction, but that their measurement does not represent the only way of evaluating usability.

Another issue is that many authors have emphasised the importance of more spe-cific aspects of usability. For example Nielsen's definition of usability [19] includes, in addition to efficiency in normal use and satisfaction with use:

- Learnability in early use.
- Memorability after a period of non-use.
- That errors during use can be corrected, and do not lead to undesirable consequences.

2.3   Avoidance of Negative Outcomes

In the existing ISO 9241-11 effectiveness focuses on the accuracy and completeness with which goals are achieved. But an unintended outcome can have significant undesirable negative consequences for the individual or the organisation (such as inconvenience, wasted time, or financial loss). The ISO/IEC 25010:2010 "System and software quality models" standard takes account of both positive and negative outcomes by defining "quality in use" as a combination of the positive outcomes of usability in the existing ISO 9241-11 combined with freedom from risk of negative outcomes. The revised ISO 9241-11 also needs to explain how to take account of the risk of any negative outcomes that could arise from inadequate usability.

3   The New Version of ISO 9241-11

3.1   Requests for Changes and Feedback

The revision of ISO 9241-11 was preceded by consultation with the countries that participate in the ISO TC159/SC4 Ergonomics standards committee and the related ISO working groups. The feedback (which identified many of the issues above) provided a starting point for the changes listed below that have been made in the first draft that has been circulated for national voting and comment. The text will be revised based on these comments, and will be circulated for further voting and comment later in 2015.

3.2   Changes Made in the New Draft

Systems, Products, Services and Environments. ISO 9241-11 currently applies to the usability of "products". In line with changes in standards such as ISO 9241-210 this has been extended in the new draft to "products, systems and services", as the concept of usability applies equally well to all these categories. The new draft also explains that although environments are considered as part of the context of use, user interactions with a specific environment or component of the environment can be considered in terms of the usability of an environment (e.g. the smoothness of a path used by a wheelchair).

Goals. The current standard only mentions goals that achieve well-defined outputs. In reality, people may have other reasons for interacting with a product, system or service, so the new draft takes account of a much wider range of goals that include aspects of user experience:

(a) output related outcome(s) that could either be assigned (in an organisational context) and/or personally chosen;
(b) personal outcomes such as entertainment or personal development;
(c) usability outcomes in terms of levels of specific (sub)dimensions of usability, such as the desired level of accuracy;
(d) other outcomes (e.g. related to safety, security or privacy) to be satisfied in the course of achieving output-related or personal outcomes.

Effectiveness. The effectiveness with which a goal is achieved was previously defined in terms of accuracy and completeness. Appropriateness has been added as an additional consideration that can include: a) the form and needed degree of precision of the output (e.g. is information displayed appropriately on a web page?) and b) avoidance of errors and minimization of the risk of any unacceptable consequences that could arise from lack of accuracy and completeness. Adding appropriateness to the other components of effectiveness goes some way towards taking account of both the potential positive outcomes (accuracy and completeness) and the risk of negative outcomes.

Efficiency. Efficiency was previously defined as the ratio of effectiveness divided by the resources consumed. While this is scientifically correct as a productivity measure, it is only meaningful for continuous output, which is not a common situation. So, efficiency has been redefined in the revised standard as the resources (time, human effort, costs and material resources) that are expended when achieving a specific goal (e.g. the time to complete a specific task).

Satisfaction. In the current ISO 9241-11, satisfaction is defined as "freedom from discomfort, and positive attitudes towards the use of the product". The new draft identifies a much wider range of personal responses, including those that have been highlighted in research on user experience: "the extent to which attitudes related to the use of a system, product or service and the emotional and physiological effects arising from use are positive or negative".

Context of use. The current ISO 9241-11 does not say anything about how wide a range of users, tasks and environments should be included in the context of use. The revised standard explains that usability can be related to: (a) All potentially relevant contexts of use (when considering overall usability), (b) Specified contexts of use (the users, goals and environments of particular interest), (c) A single instance of the context of use, or (d) The context of use for a single individual (for individual usability when considering a user's experience).

The current ISO 9241-11 provides detailed information on how to specify the context of use. This has been removed from the new standard as it is now included in ISO/IEC 25063:2014 "Common Industry Format (CIF) for usability: Context of use description".

Scope of "Usability". The revision explains the relationships between the approach to usability in ISO 9241-11, and other interpretations. By defining usability in terms of the measurable outcomes of effectiveness, efficiency and satisfaction, ISO 9241-11 takes an approach to usability that:

(a) *Focuses on the outcomes of interaction rather than the user interface design activities and resulting product attributes that make a product usable.*

The new draft explains that the term "usability" can also be used as a qualifier to refer to design related activities and product attributes. Thus it may be used refer to the knowledge, competencies, activities and design attributes that contribute to usability (such as usability expertise, usability professional, usability issue, usability method, usability evaluation, usability problem, and usability guidance).

(b) *Defines usability a high-level concept rather than referring to normal use of a product in contrast to learning to use or reuse a product.*

The new draft makes it clear that usability applies to all aspects of use, including:

- Learnability, to enable new users to be effective, efficient and satisfied when learning to use a new system.
- Regular use, to enable users to achieve their goals effectively, efficiently and with satisfaction.
- Error protection, to minimise the possibility that users can make errors that could lead to undesirable consequences.
- Accessibility, so that the system if effective, efficient and satisfying for users with the widest range of capabilities.
- Maintainability, to enable maintenance tasks to be completed effectively, efficiently and with satisfaction.

Usability Measures. The current ISO 9241-11 focuses on specification and measurement of usability, and includes detailed information on usability measures and specification of usability. This information has not been included in the new draft. It is possible that it might be included in a new related standard on usability measurement.

3.3   Additional Proposed Changes

Some of the other aspects of usability that have been proposed as relevant, but that have not yet been included are explained below.

System and User Outcomes. One of the issues raised in the feedback was that it is sometimes necessary to take account of both the objective system outcome (e.g. whether an ecommerce transaction has been completed) and the subjective user outcome (e.g. whether the user believes that the transaction is complete). Both types of goals may need to be achieved for a successful outcome that can be regarded as effective.

An additional distinction could be made in the standard between goals for system outcomes resulting from interaction (such as information provided to the user, completing a purchase or casting a vote), and the outcomes for the user such as acquiring knowledge or making a decision based on the output of a system, product or service.

Evolving Goals. The user's goals can evolve during interaction, particularly when the user is exploring use of a product. So a product may have low usability for the initially intended outcomes, but be quite usable for the final outcomes achieved. Conversely, with new goals the user may find that the level of usability is lower for these goals. Usability can be considered in relation to the user's goals at any stage during the time that the user interacts with the product, system or service.

Social Responsibility. One critique of ISO 9241-11 is that it ignores social responsibility (for which there is now a standard: ISO 26000). A clear distinction needs to be made between considering usability for the user's intended outcomes and for another stakeholder's intended outcomes. Taking account of the user's goals satisfies fundamental human needs and produces designs that respects human dignity.

The new draft defines accessibility as usability for people with the widest range of capabilities. To respect social responsibility, systems, products and services should be designed to be usable by people with the widest range of capabilities who could potentially use the system, product or service.

3.4   Related Concepts

In addition to elaborating on the understanding of usability, the revised version of ISO 9241-11 provides an explanation of the relationship between usability and some associated concepts including:

Human-Centred Quality. The objectives of human-centred design are identified in ISO CD 9241-220:2015 "Processes for enabling, executing and assessing human-centred design within organizations" as achievement of human-centred quality, which is composed of usability, accessibility, user experience and risk reduction. While usability as described in the revised ISO 9241-11 takes account of aspects of accessibility, user experience and the risks that could arise from poor usability, use of the concept human-centred quality makes each of these explicit and independent objectives.

Accessibility. ISO 26800 emphasises the importance of widening the target population to take account of the range and diversity of human characteristics, thus making products, systems, services, environments and facilities more accessible to more people. ISO 9241-11 interprets accessibility as usability for people with the widest range of capabilities, which is applied in the same way as usability. This provides a basis for specifying and evaluating accessibility in terms of effectiveness, efficiency and satisfaction for a wider range of user capabilities.

User Experience. User experience focuses on the user's preferences, perceptions, emotions and physical and psychological responses that occur before, during and after use, rather than the observed effectiveness and efficiency. While usability typically deals with goals shared by a user group, user experience is concerned with individual goals, which can include personal motivations including needs to acquire new knowledge and skills, to communicate personal identity and to provoke pleasant memories. User experience also puts emphasis on how the experience changes with repeated use.

One source of potential confusion is the increasingly widespread use of the term user experience to refer to an overall view of all aspects of the user's interaction with a system, product or service, rather than the original meaning that emphasized the importance of emotional experience. This use of the term user experience is closer to the concept of usability in the revised version of 9241-11, which explicitly includes the personal factors for individuals.

4   Contributing to the Development of ISO 9241-11

If you would like to contribute to the development of ISO 9241-11, or to comment on drafts, you can either do this via your national standards body [6], or if you are a member of one of the ISO TC159/SC4 liaison organisations [7] such as UXPA [21] you can participate through the liaison organisation.

Acknowledgements. ISO 9241-11 is being developed by the ISO working group TC159/SC4/WG6 and the new draft was produced by the authors of this paper. Particular thanks are due to Karsten Nebe for his feedback on the paper, and to the other members of the working group that include: S. Fukuzumi, C. Hoback, J. Earthy, K. Enflo, T. Geis, T. Jokela, C. Lutsch, S. Turner, A. Walldius, and J. Williams.

References

1. Bevan, N.: Usability is quality of use. In: Anzai, Y., Ogawa, K., Hirohiko, M. (eds.) Symbiosis of Human and Artifact: Proceedings 6th International Conference on Human Computer Interaction, vol. 2. Elsevier, Amsterdam, July 1995
2. Bevan, N.: Extending the concept of satisfaction in ISO standards. In: Proceedings of KEER2010, Paris, 2–4 Mar 2010
3. Bevan, N., Kirakowski, J., Maissel, J.: What is usability? In: Bullinger, H.J. (eds.) Proceedings of the 4th International Conference on Human Computer Interaction, Stuttgart. Elsevier, Sept 1991
4. Hassenzahl, M., Diefenbach, S., Göritz, A.: Needs, affect, interactive products - facets of user experience. Interact. Comput. **22**, 353–362 (2010)
5. Hellman, M., Rönkkö, K.: Controlling user experience through policing in the software development process. In: Proceedings of I-USED 2008, Pisa, Sept 2008
6. ISO: Members. www.iso.org/iso/home/about/iso_members.htm
7. ISO: TC159/SC4 Ergonomics of human-system interaction. www.iso.org/iso/home/standards_development/list_of_iso_technical_committees/iso_technical_committee.htm?commid=53372
8. ISO/IEC 9126: Software engineering—product quality (1991)
9. ISO 9241: Ergonomic requirements for office work with visual display terminals (VDTs)
10. ISO 9241-11: Ergonomic requirements for office work with visual display terminals (VDTs) - Part 11 Guidance on usability (1998)
11. ISO CD 9241-11: Ergonomics of human-system interaction – Part 11: Usability: definitions and concepts (2015)
12. ISO 9241-210: Ergonomics of human-system interaction – Part 210: Human-centred design for interactive systems (2010)
13. ISO CD 9241-220: Ergonomics of human-system interaction - Part 220: Processes for enabling, executing and assessing human-centred design within organizations (2015)
14. ISO/IEC 25010: Systems and software engineering – systems and software product quality requirements and evaluation (SQuaRE) – system and software quality models (2011)
15. ISO/IEC 25063: Systems and software engineering – systems and software product quality requirements and evaluation (SQuaRE) – common industry format (CIF) for usability: Context of use description (2014)

16. ISO/IEC DIS 25066: Systems and software engineering – software product quality requirements and evaluation (SQuaRE) – common industry format (CIF) for usability: Evaluation report (2015)
17. ISO DIS 26800: Ergonomics – general approach, principles and concepts (2011)
18. ISO 26000: Social responsibility (2010)
19. Nielsen, J.: Usability Engineering. Academic Press, Waltham (1993)
20. Smith, S.L., Mosier, J.N.: Guidelines for Designing User Interface Software. MITRE Corporation, Bedford, Mass. ESD-TR-86-278 (1986)
21. UXPA: User experience professionals association liaison with ISO. www.uxpa.org/standards
22. Whiteside, J., Bennett, J., Holzblatt, K.: Usability engineering: our experience and evolution. In: Helander, M. (ed.) Handbook of Human-Computer Interaction. Elsevier, New York (1988)

Incorporating Marketing Strategies to Improve Usability Assurance in User-Centered Design Processes

Iunia C. Borza and José A. Macías(✉)

Escuela Politécnica Superior, Universidad Autónoma de Madrid,
Tomás y Valiente 11, Madrid 28049, Spain
iunia-cristina.borza@estudiante.uam.es,
j.macias@uam.es

Abstract. Nowadays, international companies have been using different strategies in order to obtain more attractive products and get a higher impact on the market. But when referring to software products, it is necessary to keep in mind that such strategies are affected by specific quality criteria as usability. Usability and marketing can be combined to offer more attractive products. In fact, specific instances of marketing technics have been gradually adopted by software engineers to improve usability. All in all, there is a lack of systematic approaches dealing with the integration of both marketing and usability through activities in a user-centered development process. To face such challenge, in this paper we have selected the most important marketing strategies to be integrated as activities in a user-centered process model. Activities were classified into Pre-Development, Development and Post-Development, and they have been sorted out depending on the marketing processes taking place before, during and after the development of a software product, respectively.

Keywords: Usability · User-centered process · ISO 9241-210 · Marketing

1 Introduction

In the last years, even the biggest companies have come using different strategies oriented to offering more attractive products and make them easier to sell. In this process, strategies related to marketing management and sales play an important role. But, when referring to software products we need to keep in mind that these strategies need to be accompanied by quality criteria. More specifically, and mostly for products oriented to the final user, usability, as a quality characteristic of the software product, is an essential criteria that such products need to include when being released on a specific market.

In general, there is a great deal of technics used to improve usability in software products, not only from the *Human-Computer Interaction* (HCI) point of view, but also from the perspective of the marketing strategies being used. Some well-known strategies of this kind are related to *Digital Marketing* for software applications, *Search Engine Optimization* [1], *E-mail Marketing* [2] and *On-line advertising* [3]. Also, some new technics can be mentioned, such as *Holistic Marketing* [4], a term related to

© Springer International Publishing Switzerland 2015
M. Kurosu (Ed.): Human-Computer Interaction, Part I, HCII 2015, LNCS 9169, pp. 152–162, 2015.
DOI: 10.1007/978-3-319-20901-2_14

software products and personalized solutions, and the *Customer Relationship Management* [5], which is a strategy based on *Relational Marketing* [6] where the largest beneficiary is the final user, and not the product itself.

However, when thinking of obtaining usable and attractive products for the final user, the development process is as essential as the product itself. In fact, one of the standards highly used for the construction of usable applications is the ISO 9241-210 [7]. This standard provides a framework for usability assurance by stating planning and analysis phases that can be meaningful to integrate usability and marketing strategies. Those are: planning of the human centered design process, specification of the context of use, and specification of user requirements. In order to accomplish this goal, it is necessary to identify what marketing technics can be integrated in specific activities of the ISO 9241-210 standard, with the goal of obtaining more usable and attractive software products.

In the state of the art, there are some specific examples of marketing technics that have already been adopted by the usability engineering paradigm. This is the case for the *Competitive Analysis* [8], a technic that allows to analyze the market competitor's strengths and weaknesses. However, marketing technics adapted from the usability field are only a few, and there is not a systematic approach when dealing with specific activities and tasks to be considered in a development process model according to the software engineering's criteria.

This way, the main aim of this paper is focused on establishing relationships between the marketing field and the development of user-centered software to improve usability overall. In order to do so, after a conscientious analysis, the most important marketing strategies were selected in form of activities, in order to be integrated in a user-centered process model. These activities were classified in the following categories: Pre-development, Development and Post-development, and they were sorted out depending on the marketing processes taking place before, during and after the development of the software product. The objective pursued is to ensure the usability of a software product throughout the development process.

The paper is structured as follows. Section 2 presents research context and related work. Section 3 provides the main contributions to this paper, that is, the detailed description of Pre-development, Development and Post-development marketing activities to ensure usability. Finally, Sect. 4 presents conclusions and future work.

2 Related Work

In this section, a thorough analysis of the current literature has been made. First, an informal bibliographical research was carried out but, at first sight, it did not show any relevant results related to the research objective pursued, so that a more focused research method needed to be applied. To carry out this task, a *Mapping Study* [9] was achieved. The main goal of the Mapping Study is to discover academic works that can combine the main fields of research, which are marketing and HCI. After concluding the Mapping Study, there were no academic papers found embodying relevant information about marketing and HCI, or others that could describe an existing and explicit relationship between the two domains either. Studies between areas of software engineering and usability were found separately, but with no reference to the marketing field. This results back up our initial hypothesis concerning the inexistence of previous works combining marketing activities in a user-centered process to ensure usability.

On the other hand, in order to relate marketing and usability, it is necessary to obtain a common understanding of each field by describing usability engineering and marketing paradigms.

Usability engineering is a discipline that involves user participation during the development of software and it facilitates effectiveness, efficiency and satisfaction of a product through the use of usability specifications and metrics [10]. Also, it is important to get an understanding of the marketing field.

Marketing, more than any other business paradigm, handles customer issues. The general definition that can be given to this process is: "marketing is about managing profitable customer relationships" [11]. In this way, marketing can pursue the goal of attracting new customers by promising superior value and, also, keeping and growing current customers by increasing satisfaction. In addition, marketing can be meant as the process by which companies create value for customers and build strong customer relationships in order to capture value from customers in return. It is also a well-known fact that marketing needs to be viewed as a sense of *satisfying customer needs* [11]. In addition, one of the main goals of marketing is to sell products easily. This step can be easily achieved by understanding the consumer's needs, developing products that provide superior customer value and prices, and distributing and promoting products effectively. Furthermore, a marketing strategy represents the marketing logic by which a company expects to create customer value and achieve profitable relationships. It is very important to decide which customer the strategy will serve (by applying methods of segmentation and targeting) and by which manner it will serve the customer (by differentiation and positioning). From a general point of view, marketing strategies have the role of identifying the total market and, after that, dividing the market into smaller segments.

Integrating marketing in the development of products provides an interesting challenge. In fact, in [9] authors present points of integration where marketing might enrich the overall development process. The integration points related to the marketing field were offered by analyzing the image from a general point of view. Thus, some examples of synchronization tasks are presented, such as the identification of the user's characteristics (from usability engineering), the analysis of the consumer behavior (from marketing), and the identification of the environment (from marketing); all can influence the description of the context of use. Furthermore, one of the principal point of connection between marketing and software development is the consumer behavior. As stated in [12], there are lots of commercial websites that have the goal of inducing users to take part in an idea or encouraging decision-making for a purchase by using marketing strategies. Whereas market research is interested in demographics, usability is more interested in a qualitative understanding of people as individuals with a history, goals, interests and a relationships for the website or product.

Another issue is to select a right development model to create usable software products. After having revised the different user-centered process models, it can be concluded that none of them is completely adequate for a marketing environment, because there are no specific activities such as those for the identification of marketing experts and others concerning marketing environment strategies. However the ISO 9241-210 standard [7] is a good alternative to be used as a starting point for a user-centered process, as it can integrate the description of the marketing activities and allows the integration of the marketing process model. In addition, the IEEE Standard [13] has proven to be very useful, especially concerning activities categorization according to their main role and moment of realization in the lifecycle.

ISO 9241-210 comprises a multi-part standard covering aspects of HCI. Concretely, the 210 part studies the ergonomics of the human-computer interaction and it also provides some guidance on human-system interaction throughout the lifecycle of an interactive systems. In order to integrate the marketing activities in the user-centered model, first we need to design activity groupings for the proposed process model, which involves structuring and ordering activities creating also specific tasks, as it will be described down below.

3 Proposal of Marketing Activities and Integration in a User-Centered Process Model

3.1 Integration Framework

The major contribution to this work is the definition of different marketing activities that can be integrated in the development of software products through a user-centered approach.

The activities proposed in this model, described in Fig. 1, have been structured using the following categories [13]:

- Pre-development: Initial activities that are carried out before starting the development of a software product. Those include team building, marketing research and market analysis (IntA.1, IntA.2 and IntA.3).
- Development: Activities that take place during the development of a software product. These activities are grouped inspired by ISO 9241-210 [7] iterative process, in which the design solution is always evaluated and validated by the user after implementing the final system (IntB.1, IntB.2, IntB.3).
- Post-development: Activities that belong to the marketing mix, mostly related to price and promotion strategy. These two categories of activities are explained at the end of the development of the software product, because of the importance that they can bring to the software development (IntC.1, IntC.2).

In addition, there is also some integral activities that need to be addressed in pre-development, development and post-development stages, respectively. This is the case for activities concerning the marketing strategy, the marketing mix, and the product strategy (IntA.4 and IntB.4, and also the aforementioned IntC.1, IntC.2).

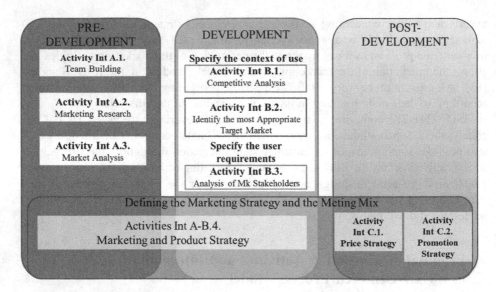

Fig. 1. Proposal of marketing and user centered model process

3.2 Process Model

We propose a model including three kinds of process elements: Activity Groupings, Activities and Tasks (see Fig. 1):

- Activity Grouping: Are categories of activities grouped according to a same development stage, according to the IEEE 1074-2006 Standard [13] and, also, fitting the definition of marketing strategy and the marketing mix [11].
- Activity: They represent main actions to carry out during the process.
- Task: They correspond to a subdivision of activities into smaller ones in order to split workload and sharing.

3.3 Activity Groupings

As commented before, in order for marketing activities to be integrated in a user-centered process model, activities were classified into Pre-development, Development and Post-development groupings. Groupings and activities will be described down below.

Pre-development Activities (IntA). These activities are depicted in Table 1. It is a common fact that there are different aspects that need to be taken into account before starting the development of a software product, such as processes and workflow, authorization and assignment control, when and where change happens across the lifecycle and who is in charge of communicating such changes to all involved, and so on. This way, at the beginning of the software development the work team needs to be built (IntA.1.). As it can be shown in Table 1, the most important aspect that needs to be taken into account here is that, not only usability engineers, requirements engineers, developers, analysts, but also marketing experts need to be included in the team (IntA.1.1). Furthermore, after having identified the exact marketing experts that will be included in the product development, an analysis of their main goals and interests is also needed (IntA.1.2.).

After having accomplished the team building, it is necessary to represent the systematic design, collection, analysis and reporting of data relevant to a specific marketing situation involving an organization. In order to achieve a good research plan, there are some steps that need to be accomplished (IntA.2): the definition of the problem and main research objectives (IntA.2.1.) and the gathering of all the research information and its analysis (IntA.2.2.).

The process continues with the identification of a target market in which the product will be further developed and then launched (IntA.3.), thus identifying the size of the market (IntA.3.1.), the market segmentation (IntA.3.2.) and also targeting the most important segments of the chosen market (IntA.3.3.) and the market differentiation (IntA.3.4.)

The product strategy activity represents the beginning of the marketing mix description, which is the main phase regarding the marketing process model. Products are considered a key element in the overall market offering. Marketing mix planning begins with building an offer that brings value to target customers (IntA.4.). This activity grouping is focused on detailing the initiation of the product development (IntA.4.1.).

Development Activities (IntB). These activities are depicted in Table 2. In this case, as development activities imply technical task concerning product development, the activities have been designed taking into consideration the ISO 9241-210 user-centered development process, in which the design solution is always evaluated and validated by the user after implementing the final system. This way, as shown in Fig. 1, activity groupings IntB.1 and IntB.2 have been integrated in the ISO 9241-210 stage "Specify the context of use", whereas activity grouping IntB.3 has been integrated into the ISO 9241-210 stage "Specify the user requirements". Also, activity groupings concerning marketing and the marketing mix strategy has been added.

The main point here is to gather and analyze information on the current context in order to understand and then specify the context for the future system. For this reason, a thorough Competitive Analysis and the identification of the most appropriate target market need to be done (IntB.1.). Also, marketers need to identify the competitor's goals (IntB.1.1.), and carefully assess strengths and weaknesses (IntB.1.2.). This process is usually achieved by analyzing secondary data, personal experience and word of mouth, or by conducting primary marketing research with customers, suppliers and dealers (IntB.1.3.). After having identified its main competitors, a company needs to design some broad marketing strategies by which it can gain competitive advantage. The problem in this situation represents what broad competitive marketing strategies might the company use and, from these, which are best suited for a company or for the company's different visions and products. After having realized a marketing research and also an analysis of the most important competitors that exist nowadays on the market, there is a high demand on determining the most important target market (IntB.2.). In order to realize this activity, there are two main steps that need to be

Table 1. Pre-development activities

Activity groupings	Main activities	Main tasks
IntA.1. Team building	IntA.1.1. Incorporation of marketing experts in the software development project	—
	IntA.1.2. Analysis of the main goals and interests of every marketing expert	—
IntA.2. Marketing research	IntA.2.1. Defining the problem and research objectives	IntA.2.1.1. Exploratory research
		IntA.2.1.2. Descriptive research
		IntA.2.1.3 Causal research
	IntA.2.2. Developing the research plan for collecting information	IntA.2.2.1 Analysis of primary data
		IntA.2.2.2 Analysis of secondary data
IntA.3. Market analysis	IntA.3.1. Determining market size	IntA.3.1.1 Analysis of market volume and the market potential
		IntA.3.1.2 Analysis of competitive sales (bottom-up approach)
		IntA.3.1.3 Analysis of competitive sales (top-down approach)
	IntA.3.2. Market segmentation	IntA.3.2.1 Geographic segmentation
		IntA.3.2.2 Demographic segmentation
		IntA.3.2.3 Behavioral segmentation
		IntA.3.2.4 Psychographic segmentation
	IntA.3.3. Market targeting	IntA.3.3.1. Selection of two important market targets
	IntA.3.4. Market differentiation	IntA.3.4.1. Undifferentiated targeting
		IntA.3.4.2. Concentrated targeting
		IntA.3.4.3. Multi-segment targeting

(Continued)

Table 1. *(Continued)*

Activity groupings	Main activities	Main tasks
IntA.4. Defining the marketing strategy and the marketing mix	IntA.4.1. Product strategy – the new product development process	IntA.4.1.1 Idea generation
		IntA.4.1.2 Idea screening concept
		IntA.4.1.3 Concept development and testing

Table 2. Development activities

Activity groupings	Main activities	Main tasks
IntB.1. Competitive analysis	IntB.1.1. Identify the competitor's goals	—
	IntB.1.2. Selecting the most or least dangerous competitors	—
	IntB.1.3. Competitive strategies	IntB.1.3.1 Adopting overall cost-leadership
		IntB.1.3.2. Differentiation
		IntB.1.3.3. Focus
IntB.2. Identifying the most appropriate target market	IntB.2.1 Analysis of the internal factors of the usability company	–
	IntB.2.2. Analysis of the external factors of the usability company	
IntB.3. Analysis of the marketing stakeholders	IntB.3.1. Identifying the stakeholders	–
	IntB.3.2. Analysis of the goals, interests and conflicts of the stakeholders	IntB.3.2.1. Identifying and characterizing the necessities and the interests of each stakeholder
IntB.4. Product strategy	IntB.4.1.Managing the new product development	IntB.4.1.1.Customer centered new product development
		IntB.4.1.2.Team-based new product development
		IntB.4.1.3. Systematic new product development
	IntB.4.2. Marketing test	—

accomplished: the analysis of the internal factors of the company (IntB.2.1.) and also the analysis of the external factors (IntB.2.2.). Furthermore, an analysis of the most important marketing stakeholders (IntB.3.), referred to different users that will work with the software application in the future, needs to be realized (IntB.3.1.). Also, after the product has passed the business test, it goes to the next stage, which is the product development. In this stage, the research and development department or the engineering department will be in charge of transforming the concept of product into a physical one. It represents an important step to show whether the product idea can be turned into a workable product or not (IntB.4.1.). Finally, a marketing test should be carried out in order to expose the product to a sample population for deciding whether to reject it before launch or not (IntB.4.2.).

Table 3. Post-development activities

Activity groupings	Main activities	Main tasks
IntC.1. Pricing strategy	IntC.1.1. Market skimming pricing	—
	IntC.1.2. Market penetration pricing	—
	IntC.1.3. Product mix pricing	IntC.1.3.1. Product-line pricing
		IntC.1.3.2. Captive product pricing
		IntC.1.3.3. By-product pricing
		IntC.1.3.4. Product bundle pricing
	IntC.1.4. Pricing adjustment strategies	IntC.1.4.1. Discount allowance pricing
		IntC.1.4.2. Segmented pricing
		IntC.1.4.3. Psychological pricing
		IntC.1.4.4. Promotional pricing
		IntC.1.4.5. Geographical pricing
		IntC.1.4.6. International pricing
IntC.2. Promotion Strategy	IntC.2.1. Identifying the promotion strategies	

Post-development Activities (IntC). These activities are depicted in Table 3. After having accomplished the pre-development and development of the software product, the post-development activities take place. In this situation, the activities that belong to the marketing mix enter into discussion: price strategy (IntC.1.) and promotion strategy (IntC.2.). These two categories of activities have been addressed at the end of the development of a software product because of the importance that they can bring to the software development, especially from the marketing point of view, in order for the software/usability company to obtain a certain amount of benefits after finishing the software product. Actually, one of the most difficult and important elements is the decision on money and how much to charge the customer (IntC1.1., IntC1.2., IntC1.3. and IntC1.4.). Finally, current promotion strategies need to be identified (IntC2.1.) in order to correctly advertise the brand image of the product. Some of the tactics that are applied here are advertising, sales promotion, public relations and direct marketing.

3.4 Methods and Technics

In order to accomplish the presented activities, some of the existing methods and technics appearing in the current literature can be used, such as *focus groups*, *questionnaires*, *Delphi method*, *ethnography field research*, *unstructured interviews*, *conceptual maps*, to cite a few [1, 10]. For instance, unstructured interviews, where questions are not prearranged, allow flexibility as questions are developed during the interview. Another important technic is focus groups in order for the user to present spontaneous reactions and ideas, allowing the expert to observe group dynamics and organizational issues.

4 Conclusions

The main goal of this paper was to analyze the development of user-centered software through the use of marketing strategies, with the aim of increasing usability assurance [14]. In particular, the main contribution presented is the proposal of specific activities in a user-centered process model, establishing a relationship between marketing and usability, and addressing the lack of specific approaches in the state of the art so far. Standard ISO 9241-210 has been considered as a user-centered process model that recognizes important aspects of planning the human centered process or the specification of user requirements, highlighting appropriate aspects useful to be considered for integrating the marketing activities in the proposed model. Therefore, marketing activities were gathered in three development groupings: pre-development, development and post-development. This classification has been achieved according to the IEEE 1074:2006 standard. In general, we propose the integration of specific activities such as team building, marketing research, and market analysis. Also, other proposed activities identify the importance of knowing the competitors that the specific product might be facing before released, as well as a better knowing of the market in which the product will be further launched. Finally, other late activities are also presented including promotion and price strategies.

As future work, we expect to refine the development activities and create others. Also, we plan to carry out a validation of the proposed process model with a real application construction, and propose an evaluation criteria based on a quality model.

Acknowledgements. This work has been supported by the funding project S2013/ICE-2715 granted by the Madrid Research Council.

References

1. Guzzo, T., D'Andrea, A., Ferri, F., Grifoni, P.: Evolution of marketing strategies: from internet marketing to m-marketing. In: Herrero, P., Panetto, H., Meersman, R., Dillon, T. (eds.) OTM-WS 2012. LNCS, vol. 7567, pp. 627–636. Springer, Heidelberg (2012)
2. Lewis, H.G.: Effective E-mail Marketing. The Complete Guide to Creating Successful Campaigns. American Management Association (AMACOM), New York (2002)
3. Guha, S., Cheng, B., Francis, P.: Challenges in measuring online advertising systems. In: IMC, pp. 81–87. ACM, New York (2010)
4. Ashutosh, N.: Holistic marketing of software products: the new paradigm. IJCSMS Int. J. Comput. Sci. Manag. Stud. 11(01), 1–7 (2011)
5. Verhoef, P.C.: Understanding the effect of customer relationship management efforts on customer retention and customer share development. J. Mark. 67, 30–45 (2003)
6. Stephen, V.L., Lusch, R.F.: Evolving to a new dominant logic for marketing. J. Mark. 68, 1–17 (2004)
7. ISO International Standard: Ergonomics of human-system interaction – Part 210: Human-centered design for interactive systems (ISO 9241-210:2010), www.iso.org (2010)
8. Nielsen, J.: Usability Engineering. Academic Press, Boston (1993)
9. Kitchenham, B.A.: Procedures for Performing Systematic Reviews. Keele University, Technical report TR/SE-0401 and NICTA Technical report 0400011T.1 (2004)
10. Fischer, H., Nebe, K., Klompmaker, F.: A holistic model for integrating usability engineering and software engineering enriched with marketing activities. In: Kurosu, M. (ed.) HCD 2011. LNCS, vol. 6776, pp. 28–37. Springer, Heidelberg (2011)
11. Kotler, P., Armstrong, G.: Principles of Marketing, 15th edn. Pearson, New York (2014)
12. Benini, M.J., Batista, L.L., Zuffo, M.K.: When marketing meets usability: the consumer behaviour in heuristic evaluation for web. In: CLIHC 2005, pp. 307–312. Cuernavaca, México, 23–26 Oct 2005
13. IEEE Standard 1074-2006: IEEE standard for developing a software project life cycle process (2006)
14. Macías, J.A.: Integrating internationalization in the user-centered software development process. In: Patrick Rau, P.L. (ed.) HCII 2013 and CCD 2013, Part I. LNCS, vol. 8023, pp. 243–252. Springer, Heidelberg (2013)

Communication of Design Decisions and Usability Issues: A Protocol Based on Personas and Nielsen's Heuristics

Joelma Choma[1(✉)], Luciana A.M. Zaina[1], and Daniela Beraldo[1,2]

[1] Federal University of São Carlos – Campus Sorocaba, São Carlos, SP, Brazil
{jchoma,lzaina}@ufscar.br,
[2] Indiana State University, Terre Haute, IN, USA
danielaberaldol2@gmail.com

Abstract. Although both agile developers and UX designers have a common concern regarding to build software with quality, they usually have different viewpoint of the user experience and usability. We have proposed a protocol in which personas and Nielsen's heuristics were used as a common vocabulary between designers and developers (SCRUM team) for the communication of recommendations and/or design solutions. We have adopted action research to conduct our research, performing a workshop and interviews to study the feasibility of the proposal; and later two case studies to compare and evaluate the use and non-use the protocol. In the final, adding to the case study comparison, we interviewed the SCRUM team who revealed that the protocol improved the understanding of recommendations and the Nielsen's heuristics contributed to objectively communicate the main problems of interaction.

Keywords: Action research · User experience · Interaction design · SCRUM · ERP

1 Introduction

The integration of interaction design into the practice of software development may improve the process to support the development of products, which could be more adherent to user needs and expectations. The main concern of professionals who work in the field of User Experience (UX) is on drawing interactive products, which properly supply user-software communication and interaction [19]. Although the issues of UX and interaction design have been discussed by the software development area, few results have been achieved from the inclusion of interaction design practices within the phases of the main agile processes [20].

Boivie et al. [4] point out that the incorporation of interaction design in the software development process is not the simple addition of some UX activities. It requires new approaches and assets, such as guidelines of planning and practical methods. It also achieves cultural aspects in the organization triggering changes in the relationship among project managers, development team and UX designers. Wolkerstorfer et al. [23] spotlight that the difference between the mindset of software engineers and experts

M. Kurosu (Ed.): Human-Computer Interaction, Part I, HCII 2015, LNCS 9169, pp. 163–174, 2015.
DOI: 10.1007/978-3-319-20901-2_15

in human-computer interaction area (HCI) - who use different practices and ways of expressing from their knowledge areas - may complicate the integration of design artifacts into the phases of agile processes. Moreover, developers are not familiar, as the usability experts, to give attention to the cognitive aspects of the end-user. Despite common concern of the agile developers and UX designers - they aim at building software with quality - each one addresses the development activities from a different perspective [11, 22], especially on the aspects of user experience and usability issues.

Considering the statements, this paper presents a protocol composed by decisions and recommendations of interaction design which aims to improve the communication of the agile development team and support the integration of user interaction design into the phases of SCRUM process [21]. The protocol for communication is based on concepts of personas and usability Nielsen's heuristics. The motivation for the adoption of personas and Nielsen's heuristics emerged from the hypothesis that these concepts can aid the developers and the UX designers to level out their interpretation on the usability fundamentals. Furthermore, the protocol can enhance the understanding of interaction design decisions for guiding the efforts of developers during the coding and testing activities. In the protocol the personas and the usability heuristics are used as a common vocabulary for the communication between both teams SCRUM and UX.

2   Research Approach

The protocol proposed is a partial result of a research project that has been developed in partnership with a producer company of ERP (Enterprise Resource Planning) systems. The objective of the research project is to propose methods and artifacts, suitable to the domain of ERP systems, for which can be incorporated into the SCRUM process, recently adopted by the company. To achieve the project goal, our strategy has been to work the mindset of the employees on the importance of the UX in the software development. Some workshops to introduce, promote user experience practices and evangelize the usability [18] have been developed during the last two years.

The research project is naturally incremental which partial findings applied directly to the company's processes, so the Action Research (AR) [1] has been the most appropriate methodology to conduct our research. According to Hayes [13], Action Research offers HCI researchers theoretical lenses, methodological approaches, and pragmatic guidance for conducting socially relevant, collaborative, and engaged research. Particularly, in the work reported in this paper, we used a qualitative approach of AR called Cooperative Method Development (CMD), which combines qualitative empirical research, with problem-oriented method, technique and process improvement [9]. In this approach the researchers, who are motivated to understand how the software developers face the daily challenges in software development, can combine both technical innovation, and method and process improvement within one CMD cycle. We adopted the interview and ethnography as supported techniques. The three stages of the CMD cycle are (1) Understanding Practice, (2) Deliberate Improvements, and (3) Implement and Observe Improvements.

In the following sections we describe the procedures used to mastermind, develop and validate one of the artifacts created to be used in the development process model proposed in the research project: a protocol based on personas and Nielsen's heuristics for communication of design decisions and usability issues.

3 Understanding Practice

Both concepts of personas and Nielsen's heuristics are largely used in industry of software development. They are recognized by the experts as good practices to keep the focus on the end-user and on the software usability [3, 10].

Persona is a concept frequently used to create fictional characters, hypothetical archetypes of a group of real users, thus defining the typical users and their relevant features within a context of interaction. The personas are artifacts guiding the development of interaction scenarios and/or used to describe the typical tasks in usability testing [7]. The research presented by Billestrup et al. [3] reveals that the companies' developers recognize and understand the potential and advantages of using personas. The application of the persona technique has proved that designing for a small set of personas can meet a significant number of users by their similar goals and features. However, the construction of personas should be grounded in the research on target users, which requires a longer time spent on this work and that often the development companies cannot adopt [12]. Miller and Williams [15] present a simplified structure proposal for personas specification, thus allowing greater flexibility in the creation process and in the use of personas.

Nielsen's heuristics are usability guidelines commonly used to drive the design of interactive interfaces [17]. Heuristic is defined as a general principle or rule used to forward a decision in the process of designing an interactive system, support the critical analysis of a design decision already performed, or confirm problems identified in usability testing [12]. The ten Nielsen's heuristics are: Visibility of system status (H1); Match between system and the real world (H2); Control and freedom for user (H3); Consistency and standards (H4); Error prevention (H5); Recognition rather than recall (H6); Flexibility and efficiency of use (H7); Aesthetic and minimalist design (H8); Help users recognize, diagnose, and recover from errors (H9); Help and documentation (H10).

Nielsen's heuristics are known as general rules rather than specific usability guidelines, since they are not entirely suitable to address for particular use's characteristics of different interactive systems [16]. For this reason we have proposed Nielsen's heuristics to ERP systems by perspectives of presentation and task support. According to the impact of each orientation to usability inspection some heuristics were mapped to perspective of presentation; others to perspective of tasks support; and others to both perspectives. The perspectives may be used to guide the inspection in ERP software and lead properly the inspectors during the inspection of ERP systems. Results of empirical studies detailed in [6] have pointed that the perspective-based ERP heuristics can be efficient and effective to detect usability issues, especially in medium-fidelity prototypes.

On the assumption that the personas and Nielsen's heuristics concepts can be used as artifacts which cross the whole development process to support the different development phases, we decided to apply them to ensure that a minimum set of usability aspects would be implemented. We supposed that the artifacts that cross in the process should provide tools to the developer to work in final products, which supply the target audience with a good interaction experience. Aiming at putting in practice the assumption in the ERP software area, we try to address the following questions:

- RQ1 – Can the concepts of personas and Nielsen's heuristics level out the awareness and concerns on usability aspects of UX designers and developers (programmers and testers)?
- RQ2 – How could personas and Nielsen's heuristics concepts be used as a common vocabulary for the communication between the UX and SCRUM teams?

In order to answer the questions, we planned and carried out a workshop (to evangelizing the usability issues) and interviews with the UX and SCRUM teams (who participated of the workshop). In the next subsections, we report the activities and the analysis of the data collected.

3.1 Evangelizing Usability

First, we work with the workshop entitled "Usability Heuristics for ERP system" which had the goal of spreading the concepts and practices of application of personas and Nielsen's heuristics by perspectives (presentation and task support) in the ERP systems development.

A UX specialist (from the company) and two UX researchers organized and drove – in 2 days – the workshop. The 59 employees who participated in the event were professionals of the development area: developers (36), testers (12), analysts (5), technical leaders (4) and software architects (2). The workshop was divided into (i) explanation of the concepts of personas, heuristic inspection and Nielsen's heuristics to ERP systems by perspectives; and (ii) a heuristic inspection activity – in groups of up to 5 individuals – in two modules of ERP systems that were developed by the company – the Material Receiving module and the Sales Order module – both are modules of the Business Management System. The participants were clustered by the UX designer in order to prevent that one participant could perform the inspection in a module that s/he had interacted previously in the developing process. Before starting the inspection groups should observe the description – goals, difficulties and knowledge – of 2 hypotheses of personas by module. The hypotheses of personas are supposition of personas that are built based on the previous knowledge of the end-users that the company can have.

In the end of the workshop, we applied one based questionnaire on TAM model [8] to collect data of the perception of the participants on the usability evaluation technique using Nielsen's heuristics to ERP systems by perspectives and personas, focusing in three points: the perception of ease of use, the ease of understanding, and the usefulness of the heuristics. In this moment, the participants not answered question regarding the personas technique.

Although the main approach of this study is qualitative, we analyzed data collected from the questionnaire using the quantitative approach. Most participants had less than five years of experience in software development, and 56 % had less than five years of experience in developing ERP systems. Only 11 participants (18.64 %) had more than ten years of experience in software development and 9 participants (15.25 %) had experience in the development of ERP systems. The issues of perception of the ease of use and understanding in the application of usability evaluation technique with Nielsen's heuristics to ERP systems by perspectives and personas revealed that most participants broadly agree that the technique was easy to use and easy to understand, and 55 participants agree – completely (10) or largely (25) or partially (20) – that was easy to obtain skills for use the technique. Regarding the utility of technique, 28 participants (47.45 %) strongly agree that the technique is useful for usability inspections, 57 participants (96.61 %) agree (at some level) that the use of the technique has improved awareness on good interaction development practices, and 54 participants (91.52 %) believe that all heuristics are applicable to ERP systems.

3.2   Interviewing Participants of the Workshop

In order to investigate the impact of the workshop in daily practice of the employees who attended it, we conducted an interview to observe: (i) the expertise and skills obtained from the workshop; and (ii) the contribution of the workshop in changing the participants' viewpoint on the usability aspects in the software development, especially in ERP systems. We led the interview thirty days after workshop for the purpose of pointing out the real changes that the event caused in the employees' work. The interviews were audio recorded with the prior permission of the interviewees, and later transcription to a report. During 1 day, we performed a semi-structured interview with ten individuals with different features (roles and experience), including questions that summarize three aspects: (i) their viewpoint of usability aspects, (ii) their perception for practical application of the Nielsen's heuristics and personas in ERP system, and (iii) their evaluation regarding the improvements on ERP systems brought by the application of usability issues. We analyzed qualitatively the participants' answers, categorizing them in the three points listed above. We include some participant's comments and our observations that are shown in Table 1.

3.3   Findings

Based on the interviews outcomes, we found evidences to answer our first question (RQ1). We confirmed that the subjects and activities of the workshop had been enough to influence the participants' mindset. The participants considered that personas and Nielsen's heuristics can guide the product development and also can be used as a common vocabulary among the developers, testers and UX designers.

Taking into account the need of using a common vocabulary between designers and developers, we answered the second question (RQ2) masterminding a protocol to support the communication between the teams that consists of three items:

recommendations and/or design solutions, personas and Nielsen's usability heuristics. The starting point is the research, ideation and prototyping activities performed by UX designers, generating indications about the end-user needs. After the UX designer has validated (using inspection or user tests techniques) the interaction design, s/he lists the usability issues and/or solutions, in accordance with the hypothesis of personas, mapping the issues/solutions to Nielsen's heuristics. The Nielsen's heuristics work as a classifier of the listed item (usability issues and/or solutions), allowing the teams to achieve the same interpretation of the items.

Table 1. Overview of participants comments in the three aspects

Aspect observed	Participants' comments	Findings
(i) viewpoint of usability aspects	"(...) I pay more attention and recognize that simple points are important improvements which we should do (...) the workshop opens my mind of user interaction." "(...), now when we look at a new screen we try to simulate the persona's interaction, we are able to identify usability problems." "(...) we are working on changes of error messages of a project because we noted the messages had no significance to the user (...)"	The majority of the respondents say that they are more careful and pay attention the simple details, which can improve the system. They are concerned about the needs and perceptions of the users (the personas).
(ii) perception for practical application of the Nielsen's heuristics and personas in ERP system	"(...) The heuristics and personas facilitated my work (...) We developed a new user interface applying the concepts of colors in a caption. We had not decided to use them randomly; we had looked for color patterns." "(...) In my opinion, the heuristics showed to me that my concerns should not be only about the functional aspects, I also have to consider the screen, the content arrangement, pattern, etc. (...) After seeing the personas, I become more critical about the user interaction issues." "(...) The heuristics could be used as a checklist during the software tests."	All respondents agree with the useful of the heuristics and personas in the practice of ERP development. They believe that heuristics can guide the usability verification and aid the developer in finding alternatives to solve usability issues. The personas have a psychological influence, because they have a concrete person that represents the users.
(iii) evaluation regarding the improvements on ERP systems brought by the application of usability issues	"Some people and some professionals believe that in big and complex systems, like ERP systems, the usability is not necessary. They think the user is familiar with the idea of a difficult system. On the contrary, I do not agree. Even though ERP systems are complex and require complicated processes, I think our job, as developers, is to facilitate the user interaction, through the usability heuristics application, for example." "The ERP system is really complex, I have no doubt about it, but it is always possible to improve the user interaction."	Although the ERP system complexity, the respondents believe that it is possible to make the user experience more enjoyable.

Formalizing, the protocol can be represented in Eq. (1). In next section, we describe in details the protocol.

$$\text{Protocol} = \{\text{item}: \text{item} \equiv \text{description}, NH_{subset}, HP_{subset}\} \qquad (1)$$

where:

- description $\in$ {recommendation, solution}   (1a)
- $NH_{subset} = \{nh : nh \in NH\}$ (1b)
- $NH = \{H_1, H_2, ..., H_{10}\}$ (1c)
- $HP_{subset} = \{hp : hp \in HP\}$ (1d)
- $HP = \{hypPersona_1, ..., hypPersona_j\}$ (1e)

NH = Nielsen's Heuristics   HP = Hypotheses of Personas

4 Deliberate Improvements: The Protocol Elaboration

The activities and their outcomes were reported to the employees, UX designers and SCRUM (developers and testers), who keep the bridge between the company and the academic researchers. Up to the meetings, the company has never performed user tests formally, so we have suggested some improvements in the planning/execution/analysis of usability tests. The idea of using the protocol as an artifact to communicate and report results of evaluations and design solutions in usability testing was shared with the meetings' participants. In order to fulfill the agile principals we proposed to plan and perform the usability testing in a single day as proposed by Kjeldskov et al. [14]. Another important issue pointed out by the meetings' participants was the effort to identify and model the personas. Aiming to meet the company demand for producing artifacts quickly, we suggested them to follow the model proposed by Miller and Williams [15], named hypothesis of personas, whose the proposal is the description of personas in briefly way using a few fictitious data: name; skills and abilities; goals, motives and concerns; and usage patterns.

Adding the usability test proposal to the protocol we draw the process that the teams should follow. Figure 1 shows the approach to conduct user tests, implementing the improvements proposed in the meetings, and the generation of the usability solutions/recommendations from evaluation outcomes based on the communication protocol.

In the planning phase (Fig. 1a); the UX team selects the artifacts (low/media/high prototypes) and hypotheses of personas - relevant to the tests. The steps are performed to produce the test plan (phase output): (i) to list the critical tasks usually played by the users and match them to the hypothesis of personas; (ii) determine the quantitative and/or qualitative metrics that matched to the test goal (the task, time spent on task, difficulties to find resources, use of appropriate messages, etc.); and (iii) recruit at least 5 users that correspond to the hypothesis of personas, balancing the distribution of user into the personas. The number of users of a test followed the suggestion of the Borsci et al. [5] study.

In the execution phase (Fig. 1b) the UX designer carries out the test in a prepared computer, or even in the user's computer for convenience. Software suites - to capture images or for online observation - may be used to improve the data caught during the tests and the further analysis.

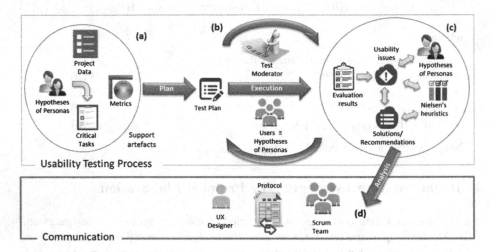

Fig. 1. Approach to conduct the user tests and report the usability solutions/recommendations

In the analysis phase (Fig. 1c), the test moderator and/or UX designers review and analyze the notes and eventually the images recorded during the test, performing the four steps: (i) list the issues caught, removing the duplicate issues (same issues pointed out by more than one persona) and false positives (issues that were not considered real); (ii) analyze each pointed issues, and propose their respective solutions/ recommendations; (iii) pinpoint the personas that can be affected by the issues; and finally (iv) map each issue to Nielsen's heuristics.

Following the protocol, the UX designer reports the outcomes of analysis phase to communicate to the SCRUM teams the solutions and recommendation that should be followed in the Sprint (Fig. 1d). The outcomes can be discussed between designer and developers during a Planning Meeting or in Daily Meetings according to the needs. The team evaluates the reported items, seeing the effects of them, and the personas and the Nielsen's heuristics that would be achieved. After the report evaluation, the SCRUM team writes the user stories (basic SCRUM artifact), considering the protocol items.

5   Implement and Observe Improvements: Usability Testing and Protocol

Based on a principle of CMD, in a collaboratively agreement between the academic researchers and the company employees – UX designers and project managers – we carried out the validation of the protocol through two case studies performed in a real redesign project. In addition, we checked the guidelines to plan and conduct the usability tests as we proposed (Fig. 1). The UX designer and SCRUM team, who attended of the validation, had participated of the workshop and interviews, so they had previously knowledge of the Nielsen's heuristics, and personas. The same redesign project was used in both case studies: a new design for a high fidelity prototype to Registration of Employees that is a sub module of a Web-based Human Resources module. In order to compare the viability of the use of protocol and the guidelines to the usability test, we chose to implement the protocol only in the second case study.

5.1   First Case Study

In the first case study, we did not interfere in the planning and conduction (for 5 days) of the usability test. We observed the UX designer actions who outlined as relevant to user test on the high fidelity prototype the following issues: (i) navigability and overall usability; (ii) the adherence of the terminologies and languages to the domain and users; (iii) number of steps performed by the user in the execution of the tasks; and (iv) new design recommendations from the identified usability issues.

Considering the features of the sub module and without using the personas conception, the UX designers recruited for the test five participants who were company' employees from different departments; the participants had different educational backgrounds, and no one has never used the sub module which would be tested. The tests were run on a computer prepared for this purpose and the UX designer played the role of test moderator; the sessions of each participant were recorded by a simple camera with the consent of the participants. Afterwards, the recordings would aid the UX designer on the analysis phase to calculate task execution time, and to pick the user difficulties up.

An important outcome observation was that none of the users was able to complete the proposed tasks in the number of steps previously estimated by the UX designers. The most efforts of users were on performing more steps caused by their mistakes, as required fields that were not filled, and four users had tried to login on the sub module before their registration. After the test analysis, the UX designer listed ten identified issues (without duplications) and reported them in natural language without any kind of pattern, in writing and orally, to the SCRUM team during an informal meeting. In sequence, the SCRUM team implemented some adjustments in accordance with their understood of the usability issues reported.

5.2   Second Case Study

Differently from the first case study, in the second, we participated in the usability test and in the protocol implementation, working in collaboration with the UX designer. The usability testing was planned following the guidelines proposed in Fig. 1a during 1 day, keeping up the same test goals of the first case study. For this test, we considered a new version of the same high fidelity prototype delivered after the SCRUM team had implemented the changes based on the user test report of the first case study.

Nonetheless, on this occasion, before the recruitment of the users, the UX designer built the three personas – using the format that we proposed in Sect. 4 – by mining information from the company's database about the target audience. Considering the features of the sub module, the personas were created to represent three different levels of expertise regarding the use of technology: basic, intermediate and advanced.

After the steps of planning, six participants for the test – none of them had participated in the first case study – were recruited, distributed two of them by persona. We played the role of observer and the UX designer of test moderator, and the tests were performed (Fig. 1b) in the same conditions of the previous study: in a computer for the test, and recording the user interaction with their consent.

We followed step by step – (i) to (iv) of analysis phase (Fig. 1c) to compose the information of the protocol to communicate recommendations and solutions, taking into account the protocol structure (Eq. 1), and the notes and video snippets collected in the test. Aiming to create an easier format for reporting the protocol items to the SCRUM team, we decided to build a table in which a row is equivalent to an item of the protocol. Figure 2 shows an example of the components of an item based on the Eq. (1).

(1a)   description = All users needed help to relate the acronyms of their identity card to the interface labels. We do not recommend using the acronyms adopted by identity card, adding to them a hint with brief non-technical information.

(1b) $NH_{subset} = \{H_6\}$

(1c) $NH = \{H_1, H_2, \ldots, H_{10}\}$

(1d) $HP_{subset} = \{Basic, Intermediate, and\ Advanced\}$

(1e) $HP = \{Basic, Intermediate, and\ Advanced\}$

Fig. 2. Item to communicate recommendation and usability issues

5.3   Lessons Learned

In the first case study, the report was composed by the tasks performed by the user, and the correlated issues found in the test described in natural language. The UX designer stated to us that the SCRUM team asked his/her, a couple of times, the clarification of some description, arguing in a contrary view of the recommendation. We noticed that from the ten issues pointed out by the UX designer in the report only six issues had been fixed and four had triggered doubts of their need of fixing. In the second case study, the test revealed three new issues, and the four issues, which had not been fixed, were confirmed once again. The SCRUM team - who had no doubts regarding the results and recommendations - fixed all the items reported through the protocol.

Days later of the second case study, we have interviewed the SCRUM team in order to collect their opinion of the use of the protocol aiming to reassert or not the research questions (RQ1 and RQ2) described in Sect. 3. Two developers who implemented the improvements commented *"(…) it was clear to understand the need of the adjustments, because I could see the equivalent heuristic and the consequence of the fix in the software"*. Regarding the personas one of them said: *"we could understand that the problem was really serious and was affecting more than one kind of user"*.

According to Bak et al. [2], although the software companies have stated to apply usability testing, many have mentioned that software developers (analyst, programmer, testers) have difficulties to understand the test results, and in some cases they do not accept the results. Based on this assertion, and adding our findings during the two case study, we can answer in the affirmative the research questions and confirm that the proposed protocol, in its formally structure, is an good alternative to promote the communication between the UX and developer teams. Moreover, the UX designers perform the test observing the usability issues by the standpoint of Nielsen's heuristics that is the same viewpoint of the developers.

6 Conclusion and Further Work

The contribution of this work was to propose a protocol based on the concepts of personas and Nielsen's heuristics that improves the communication of usability aspects between the UX team and SCRUM team. The outcomes of this work are part of a set of actions - technological and cultural - which have aimed to promote the inclusion of HCI techniques into the software development process of ERP system company.

Our proposal has been conducted by action research approach allowing us to deal with particularities on practices of software development; and also to facilitate the deliberation of improvements and the validation of proposals collaboratively with the industry. The protocol has enhanced the common understanding between UX team and SCRUM team from a unique code language and observing the features of personas. Moreover the SCRUM team felt more comfortable to fix the modifications outlined where the Nielsen's heuristics communicate, in their opinion, objectively the main problems of the interaction. In further work we will refine the protocol, and test it again on other projects. Currently we have discussed with the representatives of both teams SCRUM and UX to find out what is the best site to deliver the protocol and thus facilitate the team's access.

References

1. Avison, D.E., Lau, F., Myers, M.D., Nielsen, P.A.: Action research. Commun. ACM **42**(1), 94–97 (1999)
2. Bak, J.O., Nguyen, K., Risgaard, P.S.: Obstacles to usability evaluation in practice: a survey of software development organizations. In: Proceedings of the 5th Nordic Conference on Human-Computer Interaction: Building Bridges. ACM (2008)
3. Billestrup, J., Stage, J., Nielsen, L., Hansen, K.S.: Persona usage in software development: advantages and obstacles. In: ACHI 2014, The Seventh International Conference on Advances in Computer-Human Interactions, pp. 359–364 (2014)
4. Boivie, I., Gulliksen, J., Göransson, B.: The lonesome cowboy: a study of the usability designer role in systems development. Interact. Comput. **18**, 601–634 (2006)
5. Borsci, S., Macredie, R.D., Barnett, J., Martin, J., Kuljis, J., Young, T.: Reviewing and extending the five-user assumption: a grounded procedure for interaction evaluation. ACM Trans. Comput.-Hum. Interact. **20**, 29 (2013)

6. Choma, J., Quintale, D.H., Zaina, L.A., Beraldo, D.: A perspective-based usability inspection for ERP systems. In: Proceedings of the 17th International Conference on Enterprise Information Systems (ICEIS), Barcelona (2015)
7. Cooper, A., Reimann, R., Cronin, D.: About Face 3: The Essentials of Interaction Design. Wiley, New York (2007)
8. Davis, F.D.: Perceived usefulness, perceived ease of use, and user acceptance of information technology. MIS Q. **3**, 319–339 (1989)
9. Dittrich, Y., Rönkkö, K., Eriksson, J., Hansson, C., Lindeberg, O.: Cooperative method development. Empirical Softw. Eng. **13**(3), 231–260 (2008)
10. Fernandez, A., Insfran, E., Abrahão, S.: Usability evaluation methods for the web: a systematic mapping study. Inf. Softw. Technol. **53**(8), 789–817 (2011)
11. Ferreira, J.: Agile development and UX design: towards understanding work cultures to support integration. In: Bajec, M., Eder, J. (eds.) CAiSE Workshops 2012. LNBIP, vol. 112, pp. 608–615. Springer, Heidelberg (2012)
12. Følstad, A., Law, E.L., Hornbæk, K.: Outliers in usability testing: how to treat usability problems found for only one test participant? In: Proceedings of the 7th Nordic Conference on Human-Computer Interaction: Making Sense Through, pp. 257–260 (2012)
13. Hayes, G.R.: The relationship of action research to human-computer interaction. ACM Trans. Comput.-Hum. Interact. (TOCHI) **18**(3), 15 (2011)
14. Kjeldskov, J., Skov, M.B., Stage, J.: Instant data analysis: conducting usability evaluations in a day. In: Proceedings of the third Nordic conference on Human-computer interaction, pp. 233–240. ACM (2004)
15. Miller, G., Williams, L.: Personas: Moving Beyond Role-Based Requirements Engineering. Microsoft and North Carolina State University, Raleigh (2006)
16. Mirel, B., Wright, Z.: Heuristic evaluations of bioinformatics tools: a development case. In: Jacko, J.A. (ed.) HCI International 2009, Part I. LNCS, vol. 5610, pp. 329–338. Springer, Heidelberg (2009)
17. Nielsen, J.: 10 Usability heuristics for user interface design (1995). http://www.nngroup.com/articles/ten-usability-heuristics/. Accessed July 2013
18. Nielsen, J.: Evangelizing usability: change your strategy at the halfway point (2005). http://www.nngroup.com/articles/evangelizing-usability/. Accessed Sept 2014
19. Nielsen, J., Norman, D.: The definition of user experience (2013). http://www.nngroup.com/articles/definition-user-experience/. Accessed May 2014
20. Salah, D., Paige, R.F., Cairns, P.: A systematic literature review for agile development processes and user centred design integration. In: Proceedings of the 18th International Conference on Evaluation and Assessment in Software Engineering (EASE 2014). ACM, New York (2014)
21. Schwaber, K.: Agile Project Management with SCRUM, vol. 7. Microsoft Press, Redmond (2004)
22. da Silva, T.S., Silveira, M.S., de O. Melo, C., Parzianello, L.C.: Understanding the UX designer's role within agile teams. In: Marcus, A. (ed.) DUXU 2013, Part I. LNCS, vol. 8012, pp. 599–609. Springer, Heidelberg (2013)
23. Wolkerstorfer, P., Tscheligi, M., Sefelin, R., Milchrahm, H., Hussain, Z., Lechner, M., Shahzad, S.: Probing an agile usability process. In: CHI'08 Extended Abstracts on Human Factors in Computing Systems, pp. 2151–2158. ACM (2008)

Web-Systems Remote Usability Tests and Their Participant Recruitment

Piotr Chynał[(⊠)] and Janusz Sobecki

Department of Informatics, Wroclaw University of Technology,
Wyb.Wyspianskiego 27, 50-370 Wroclaw, Poland
{piotr.chynal,janusz.sobecki}@pwr.edu.pl

Abstract. In this paper we present a description of a proposed hybrid, remote usability testing method and a comparison of different approaches to participant recruitment for the test conducted according to this usability evaluation method. Moreover this paper contains a description of the implemented hybrid method and its characteristic. One of the main features of this method is that it allows to perform remote online tests. These tests are an alternative to traditional laboratory tests. They don't require a special laboratory space, gathering participants in one place, a moderator or other equipment to perform the tests. However we have to face a challenge – how to recruit participants for remote usability test, which is more complicated because we must motivate our users to participate in such test without having a direct contact with them.

This paper presents a comparison of a few selected methods that we used to encourage users of website HotelGo24.com to take part in usability evaluation test of that site. We present how many users were ready to participate in our study depending on the applied method of encouragement and their reward for participating in the study.

Keywords: Usability evaluation · Remote testing · Participant recruitment methods

1 Introduction

Since the emerging of web-systems usability evaluation field, many various testing methods have been proposed. They have been changing and adopting according to the used technologies and trends in web-system development. Currently there are almost one hundred usability methods that can be used for such evaluation [1] that have been developed in the last four decades. They evolved from the laboratory end-user testing [2], through inspection methods [3], to remote testing [4]. They also utilize very different equipment from video recorders, eye trackers [5] or EEG devices. Having so many various usability testing methods we can combine few of them, during one evaluation, to perform a full usability audit of a given system. However doing so can be time and effort consuming. The solution to this problem is to create one method, which would combine particular elements of other methods – hybrid method.

The main assumptions for the hybrid method are following: it should have an ability to perform complex usability tests much quicker than using other methods and

© Springer International Publishing Switzerland 2015
M. Kurosu (Ed.): Human-Computer Interaction, Part I, HCII 2015, LNCS 9169, pp. 175–183, 2015.
DOI: 10.1007/978-3-319-20901-2_16

ability to gather all sorts of data regarding user's interaction with the web-based system being evaluated. Moreover it should be low cost, without the requirement of moderation, and it should allow to test a large group of users at once. The detailed description of hybrid method assumptions can be found in [4].

One of the main features of this method is that it allows to perform remote online tests. These tests are an alternative to traditional laboratory tests. They don't require a special laboratory space, gathering participants in one place, a moderator or other equipment to perform the tests. Main goal of such evaluation is to test the usability of a given system by users working in their natural environment, so they behave more naturally, like they would normally do while using the given web-based system. Another advantage of such tests is that they do not require to gather all the users at one time, they can take part in the evaluation when they want. Moreover it is possible to test participants from all over the world and not only those who can physically visit our laboratory. Also some studies have been performed that show that the same usability problems have been found using traditional laboratory testing and remote tests [6–8]. In the end, in the hybrid method we have used elements of the following methods:

- Questionnaires - survey regarding experience with the system
- Individual User Testing - tasks for users in the evaluated system, task success rate and task completion time
- Clicktracking - clicks and path on the website for each user
- Unmoderated Testing - frame on the top of the evaluated system with tasks for participants
- Automatic Testing - automatic usability calculation from obtained data
- Remote Testing - online application for testing

After our hybrid method was developed we have faced another serious challenge - how to recruit participants for usability tests to be carried out with the proposed method? This problem has already been addressed by at least several works. In the remote usability tests described in [6] the participants were recruited by email message that was sent to randomly selected employees of a company for which usability tests have been made. In [9] and [10] from the other hand, authors describe utilization of crowdsourcing platforms such as Amazon Mechanical Turk and CrowdFlower for conducting remote usability tests. Crowdsourcing is defined in [11] as 'the act of taking a job traditionally performed by a designated agent and outsourcing it to an undefined, generally large group of people in the form of an open call'.

The following chapters present the description of implementation of hybrid usability evaluation method, the experiment with participants using this method and different ways to encourage users to take part in this experiment, results of this experiment, summary and future works.

2   Hybrid Method Implementation

After designing the hybrid method, the next step was to implement an application that would allow to perform usability tests according to this method. According to the method assumptions this method works as an application that allows to perform remote

Fig. 1. The usability application is open in a small frame on the top of the screen and displays task for users, questionnaires etc.

unmoderated online tests. With this method participants perform predefined tasks in the system and the application records their progress. At the end the application displays this data and some calculated metrics that allow the evaluator to assess the usability of the evaluated system.

This part of research has been completed with help of the company Fragria Systems as a part of the Grant Plus Scholarship (Human Capital Operational Programme, Priority VIII Regional Human Resources Management, Measure 8.2 Transfer of Knowledge, Sub-measure 8.2.2 Regional Innovation Strategies) from the Faculty of Economy Lower Silesian Marshal Office.[1] After testing various ideas and technologies, finally the system was implemented in JavaScript and PHP languages and works as a script that is added to the evaluated web-system. Working application is presented in Fig. 1.

The usage of this application is simple, the evaluator creates tasks and questionnaires for users, inserts the JavaScript code into each of subpages and after those participants complete the tasks, during which the data is recorded. The process of evaluation with hybrid method is presented on the following schema (Fig. 2).

After the evaluation, the recorded data for each participant can be viewed in the administrator panel (Fig. 3).

This data allows to perform detailed analysis of each participant's performance. We can view the task success rate and completion times, answers to the questionnaire and we are able to check the progress for each task (visited subpages and clicked elements). This way we can look for some usability issues that participant may have encountered, for example, while completing a task, participants spend a lot of time on a particular

---

[1] http://www.grantplus.dolnyslask.pl/.

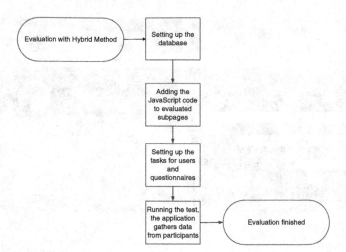

Fig. 2. Evaluation with the hybrid method

subpage, before they clicked on proper element – that means that this element is not visible to users and it is a usability problem regarding design of information presentation.

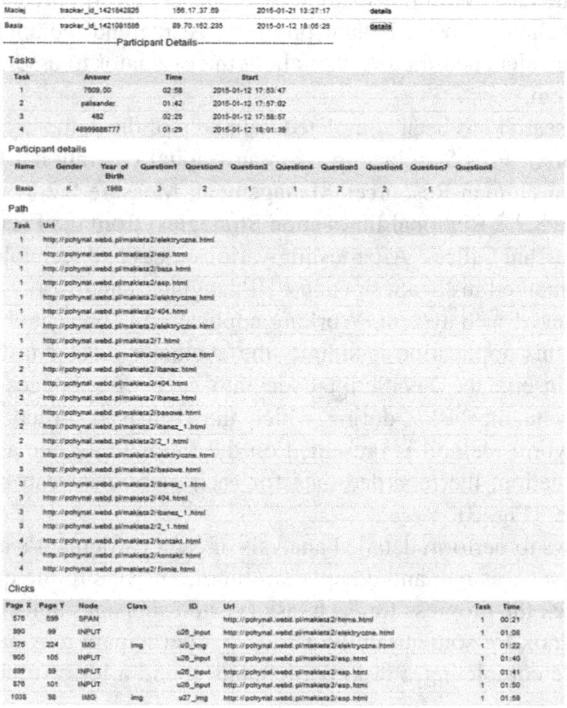

Fig. 3. Data gathered during the test – task completion times with answers to those tasks, questionnaire scores, path for each task and click for each task.

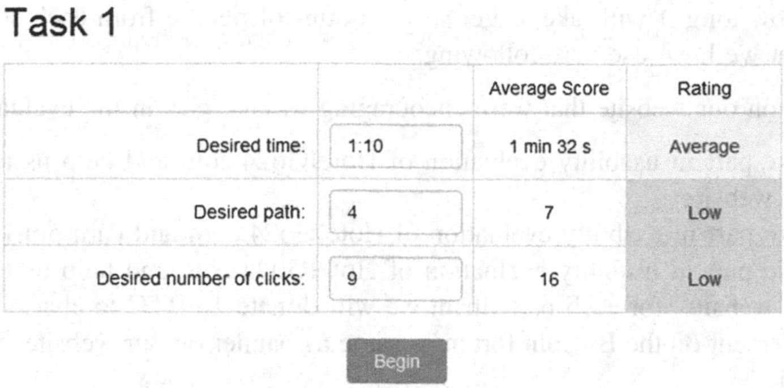

Task 1

		Average Score	Rating
Desired time:	1:10	1 min 32 s	Average
Desired path:	4	7	Low
Desired number of clicks:	9	16	Low

Begin

Fig. 4. Automatic usability assessment based on optimal parameters and data recorded from participants.

Moreover the evaluator can view the usability of the website that was calculated based on implemented rules that assess usability taking into account provided optimal parameters and data gathered from the participants, for each task, as shown in Fig. 4.

3   The Experiment

The experiment was part of the evaluation of the hybrid method. We wanted to check how it compares to other methods by performing usability evaluation of a website www.hotelgo24.com. It is a typical hotel booking website that allows its users to search and book hotel rooms all around the world. For the purpose of the evaluation with the hybrid method we have created four tasks for the participants:

- Enter the name of the three star hotel, which is available to book from 1st to 7th April 2015 - in London, UK, and has the highest guest rating.
- Check if you can indicate special room requests or preferences, such as connecting rooms, bed type, smoking type, or early check-in?
- Enter the address of the cheapest hotel that is available to book from 3rd to 8th May 2015 - in New York, USA.
- Enter the telephone number to HotelGo24.

The next step was to recruit participants for the tests. Our target was to recruit 100 users to participate in our test. We wanted to check the effectiveness of various recruitment methods. We have divided them into two groups – banners on the evaluated website and advertisements on other websites. For the first group the effectiveness would be calculated by comparing the total visits on the website with the number of people that participated in the evaluation, during the time that advertisement was on the website. For the second group we would set a goal of 20 participants and we measured how long it will take to get such amount of people from each source. The methods that we have used are following:

a. Banners on our website that were encouraging to take part in the evaluation:
  (i) Take part in usability evaluation of HotelGo24.com and help us to improve our website
  (ii) Take part in usability evaluation of HotelGo24.com and earn 5mBTC
  (iii) Take part in usability evaluation of HotelGo24.com and help us to improve our website, for each participant we will donate 1mBTC to charity[2]
b. Advertisement on the BitCoin forum[3] – same as banner on our website, 5mBTC as a reward
c. Advertisement on HotelGo24.com profile page and hotel/travel related groups on Google+ - same information as banner on our website, 5mBTC as a reward
d. Advertisement among friends on Facebook – encouragement to help a friend with the research and to share the post on own Facebook Timeline.

Duration of visibility of banners on the website was 10 days. We used BitCoin (BTC) currency because it is the easiest way to make payments on the Internet. 5mBTC was worth around $1 during the evaluation. More on BTC can be found in [12]. For those methods that included payment we have used verification with vouchers – after the evaluation was completed, participants were presented with generated voucher that they were supposed to enter on HotelGo24.com Google+ profile, along with the Bit-Coin account number (in case of charity only voucher).

We also wanted to place an advertisement on charity website – encouraging users and Facebook fans of this website to take part in the evaluation, for each participant 1mBTC would be donated to that organization. However after sending e-mail to about 15 different charity organizations that accept BTC with a proposal of such cooperation, none of those organizations expressed willingness or even replied to our e-mail. There are also other methods that we have considered such as payment for the recommendation of other users – after the evaluation participants enter the voucher that they have received from the recommending user, who gets paid for each of those participants. We will try to check this method in the future research. Moreover there are some obvious ways to recruit participants such as asking students to take part in the evaluation or simply asking friends and family, but they results may not be entirely credible as they will have some predefined attitude towards the evaluation (friends will look more favorably on the product and students probably the opposite). Another possible ways of participants' recruitment is application of platforms such as Amazon Mechanical Turk, CrowdFlower MTurk or other crowdsourcing platform.

---

[2] http://thewaterproject.org/.
[3] https://bitcointalk.org/.

4 Results of the Experiment

Till the moment of writing of this article, we were able to evaluate 73 patricians. The results of the experiment in terms of effectiveness of hybrid method will be published in future works. Here we present results from participant recruitment methods that we have used (Tables 1 and 2).

First table presents how many people completed the evaluation depending on the encouragement method on the displayed banner. Percentage of participants was the highest for the method with reward for each participant. For other two methods percentage was about the same, people were not tempted to support charity organization. However even though users were encouraged by payment in BTC, only few more than without any reward were inspired to complete the evaluation. It might be caused by a fact that BitCoin awareness is still small and people do not use this currency. However for the second table, we can clearly see that people who were encouraged by payment and were familiar with BTC were eager to participate in the evaluation. As for the ads on Google+, the response was much slower, probably also because of people being not familiar with the BTC. Maybe a good idea would be to promote such ad on some groups related to BitCoin instead of groups related to traveling and hotels. From Facebook friends it was relatively easy to find 20 people willing to help, without any financial benefits. However as mentioned earlier, evaluation by such people might not be fully objective, as friends have some predetermined attitude towards the person posting for help.

Table 1. Results for encouragement with banners on the HotelGo24.com website

Banner	No reward	5mBTC	1mBTC to charity
Number of unique visits on the website during evaluation	278	309	284
Number of participants of the evaluation (visited link)	11	25	14
Number of successful participants of the evaluation (completed)	3	7	3
Percentage of successful participants	1.08 %	2.26 %	1.06 %
Cost	0	35mBTC	3mBTC

Table 2. Results for the advertisements on other websites

Advertisement	B-forum	C-Google+	D-Facebook
Time for 20 people to complete the evaluation	2 days	7 days	9 days
Range	1238 views of the ad	Around 1100 People might view the ad	Around 700 people might view the ad
Cost	100mBTC	100mBTC	0

5 Summary and Future Work

To sum up, our experiment has shown that encouraging participants to take part in the remote usability tests is not an easy task. If we try to evaluate a website with a statistically significant number of users, without giving them any reward for completing the evaluation, it would take a very long time to do so. On the other hand, rewarding the participants makes them much more eager to take part in such evaluation as we found out from the advertisement on BitCoin forum. It was the fastest way to gather 20 participants. Bit Coins prove to be an easy way to reward users for their participation, however many people that visited HotelGo24.com website did not know what BTC is and they were afraid that it is some kind of hoax. Experiment results show also that people are not eager to perform some tasks without any reward, even if they work would correspond to some donation to charity organization.

Moreover the direct advertisements on some websites, where people are looking for ways to earn money are definitely more efficient then trying to encourage the hard users of our website. This however has some drawbacks, because the test participants might not be the target group of our website and might never use it without this reward. The best way is to try to encourage users of our website and simultaneously hire some other people to complete the evaluation, to get the best diversity of user profiles and most valuable usability testing results.

Regarding future work, we would like to test other methods of participant encouragement, for example by rewarding user for recommending the evaluation to other participants, application of crowdsourcing platforms or other forms of rewarding the participants, i.e. mobile phone top-up, which could encourage especially young people to participate in our tests. We would also like to try rewarding users differently than using BTC. Moreover the proposed hybrid method is going to be thoroughly evaluated and further developed.

Acknowledgements. The work was supported by The European Commission under the 7th Framework Programme, Coordination and Support Action, Grant Agreement Number 316097 [ENGINE].

References

1. Rajeshkumar, S., Omar, R., Mahmud, M.: Taxonomies of user experience (UX) evaluation methods. In: 2013 International Conference on Research and Innovation in Information Systems (ICRIIS), pp. 533–538, 27–28 Nov 2013
2. Rubin, J., Chisnell, D.: Handbook of Usability Testing: How to Plan, Design and Conduct Effective Tests. Wiley, New York (2008)
3. Nielsen, J.: Usability inspection methods. In: Conference Companion on Human Factors in Computing Systems, pp. 413–414. ACM, Apr 1994
4. Chynał, P.: Hybrid approach to web based systems usability evaluation. In: Nguyen, N.T., Attachoo, B., Trawiński, B., Somboonviwat, K. (eds.) ACIIDS 2014, Part I. LNCS, vol. 8397, pp. 384–391. Springer, Heidelberg (2014)

5. Holmqvist, K., Nyström, M., Andersson, R., Dewhurst, R., Jarodzka, H., Van de Weijer, J.: Eye Tracking: a Comprehensive Guide to Methods And Measures. Oxford University Press, Oxford (2011)
6. Tullis, T., Fleischman, S., McNulty, M., Cianchette, C., Bergel, M.: An empirical comparison of lab and remote usability testing of web sites. In: Usability Professionals Association Conference, July 2002
7. Brush B., Ames M., Davis J.: A Comparison of Synchronous Remote and Local Usability Studies for an Expert Interface. In CHI 2004 Extended Abstracts on Human Factors in Computing Systems, ACM, New York, USA, pp. 1179–1182 (2004)
8. Oztoprak A., Erbug C.: Field versus Laboratory Usability Testing: a First Comparison. Technical report, Department of Industrail Design - Middle East Technical University, Faculty of Architercture, Inonu Bulvari, 06531 Ankara, Turkey (2008)
9. Liu, D., Bias, R.G., Lease, M., Kuipers, R.: Crowdsourcing for usability testing. Proc. Am. Soc. Inf. Sci. Technol. **49**(1), 1–10 (2012)
10. Kittur, A., Chi, E.H., Suh, B.: Crowdsourcing user studies with Mechanical Turk. In: Proceedings of the SIGCHI Conference on Human Factors in Computing Systems, pp. 453–456. ACM, Apr 2008
11. Howe, J.: Crowdsourcing: A Definition. http://crowdsourcing.typepad.com/cs//06/crowdsourcing_a.html. Accessed Jan 2015
12. Nakamoto, S.: Bitcoin: a peer-to-peer electronic cash system. Consulted **1**(2012), 28 (2008)

User Experience Evaluation Towards Cooperative Brain-Robot Interaction

Chris S. Crawford[1(✉)], Marvin Andujar[1], France Jackson[1],
Sekou Remy[2], and Juan E. Gilbert[1]

[1] Computer and Information Science and Engineering Department,
University of Florida, Gainesville, FL, USA
{chrisscrawford,manduja,france.jackson,juan}@ufl.edu
[2] School of Computing, Clemson University, Clemson, SC, USA
sremy@clemson.edu

Abstract. Brain-Robot Interaction (BRI) research has mainly focused on analyzing system's performance through objective data. Recently research on Brain-Computer Interfaces (BCI) has begun moving towards applications that go beyond the lab and medical settings. To create successful BRI applications in the future for healthy users User Experience (UX) should be evaluated throughout the development process. This paper discusses single and cooperative BRI systems and analyzes affective and objective task performance data collected while cognitively controlling a robot. Also this paper discusses how this approach can benefit future research on the usability of BRI applications.

Keywords: Cooperative brain-robot interaction · Brain-computer interface · User experience · Human-computer interaction

1 Introduction

A Brain-Computer Interface (BCI) measures the central nervous system (CNS) activity, which translates into an artificial output that replaces, restores, enhances, supplements or improves the natural CNS output [1]. Traditionally BCI has been primarily for clinical research in which focus on the development of applications on assistive technologies for people with disabilities. In recent years, there has been an increase of interest in BCI research in the HCI community. The main focus is to design, develop, and evaluate BCI applications for healthy users to assist them with their daily life. Therefore, there has been discussions on the importance on the use of User Experience evaluations towards BCI research. By utilizing UX evaluation, these applications can be improved and adapted to the users needs and preferences. Cooperative Brain-Robot Interaction (cBRI) can benefit from UX user's data. BRI consists of studying how humans interact with robots (physical and simulated) via cognitive (non-muscular) communications. cBRI is the study of how two users or more can collaborate to control machines cognitively. Similar to entertainment applications UX evaluation is needed for cBRI to investigate how users feel while controlling robots. Previous cBRI work focuses mainly on objective data collected during studies. Although this approach assists with understanding a system's functionality, it may exclude important

M. Kurosu (Ed.): Human-Computer Interaction, Part I, HCII 2015, LNCS 9169, pp. 184–193, 2015.
DOI: 10.1007/978-3-319-20901-2_17

information on how users perceive the system's performance. In addition, UX evaluation could have an impact on the system's performance [2].

This paper explores how UX evaluation and Affective measurement can be beneficial towards BRI research. It explains how concepts such as interviews and questionnaires can contribute towards the enhancement of BRI systems. However, Interviews and questionnaires could fail to report useful information at times because sometimes participants may be unaware of how they truly feel. Therefore, neurophysiological measurements (affective analysis) may be useful to assist with interpreting how users feel while performing BRI tasks. Neurophysiological measurements provide physiological objective data that can be used to gage user's emotional state. This paper focuses on interpreting engagement data to support both the robot and UX provided data. Engagement information has shown to be beneficial in recent BCI studies [3, 4]. Users that are more engaged could be more focused on BRI tasks. In result engagement levels could relate to situational awareness. Analyzing engagement data along side other measurements could provide insight into how affective data can be used to supplement research similar to this work in the future. Furthermore, this paper discusses how robotic objective, subjective, and affective data may be used together to provide a more holistic evaluation of the UX of cBRI. An example of evaluating single versus cooperative BRI is included in this paper to show the usefulness of using affective, subjective and objective data together. The last sections of this paper provide recommendations for evaluating UX of BRI applications in the future.

2   Related Works

Recently there have been efforts to investigate how multiple users interact and/or perform when using BCI devices together. Much of this work is aimed towards healthy users. Although no UX evaluation for BRI has been done to date, previous research suggest that cooperative brain control could cause less fatigue and cognitive load in comparison to solo brain control [5]. Much of the work in this area has been done in the area of gaming. Nijholt and Gürkök surveyed research on multi-user brain-computer applications [6]. In particular they looked into gaming applications that incorporated a multi-brain setup. After investigating various existing multi-brain applications the authors concluded that even though there is still much work to be done in this research area, multiparty brain gaming has potential to provide challenging, engaging and enjoyable experience for players. This work also goes on to mention some cooperative control research that took place recently. Although they mentioned a system similar to full cooperative control of a robot, there is no evidence that this topic has been thoroughly investigated. Hjelm et al. provided an early example of multi-brain interaction [7]. In their work two players controlled the ball through their state of relaxation. The objective of the game was to place the ball in the opponent goalmouth. This research showed an example of how one can compete and relax at the same time. Gürkök et al. researched muti-player BCI UX [8]. In this work, UX was reported via observational analysis of social interaction. This information was gathered while a pair of players played a collaborative BCI game. To get more information on how users viewed BCI control, participants compared BCI with using a mouse to complete the same tasks. According to the article users collaborated less when using the BCI in efforts to try to keep control of the robot. It was concluded that the UX of games that use BCI for direct input is dependent on advances in classical BCI. Bonnet et al. evaluated a multi-player BCI game both in a collaborative and competitive mode [9]. In this study users attempted to move a ball to either the left or right side of the screen. This literature provides a comparison of solo and multiplayer motor imagery based BCI gaming. Eckstein et al. worked on research that investigated whether a collection of brain signals cold together make better decisions [10]. In this work a collection of twenty humans made perceptual decisions together via brain signals. Obbink et al. looked into the social interaction aspect of multi-brain BCI gaming [11]. According to their report, though users felt they collaborated better using a point and click device, there was also some promising results for the use of multi-brain BCI. Nijholt et al. investigated multi-party social interaction [12]. This literature discusses how it is important to research the ways healthy BCI users can use BCI technology collaboratively. Poli et al. discusses how cooperative BCI can be used to assist with space navigation [13]. They reported that results from cooperative control were statistically significantly better than solo control.

There is multiple work on using BCI to control robots. Although existent in other areas of BCI there has been little investigation of the user's overall experience while performing BRI tasks. Most of the previous work mentioned above relied only on task performance data when evaluating BRI systems. This paper discusses a novel concept of using subjective UX data, neurophysiological measurements, and objective data as a metric of success.

3   UX Impact on BRI

Currently there is a limited amount of research on BRI systems with a focus on HCI. There is even less work or none on the study of implementing UX evaluations to BRI systems. There are multiple factors contributing to this issue. One factor is that these types of systems are still mostly in a proof of concept phase [15]. As a result, the research has taken place mainly in labs that concentrate mostly on optimizing system performance. These projects mostly focus on detection, performance and speed. This research has assisted with progressing BCI, but as the fields of BCI and HCI begin to merge new findings about the impact of UX on BRI are being discovered. An example of this was shown in recent studies that suggest there is a relation between motivation and task performance [16]. This finding was a result of only a few studies. More focus on evaluating UX of BRI could lead to even more discoveries that could enhance future BRI applications. Additionally, BCI for control has been a key topic in the medical domain form the beginning. With these implementations, system performance weighs very heavily on practitioners, which often results in UX evaluation being overlooked or ignored. One possible reason causing this issue is that participants in the target population may not have the capacity to provide efficient subjective data. A possible solution to this problem is to utilize methods used in other areas to assess UX for non-healthy users. The introduction of off-the-shelf non-invasive BCI devices has enabled researchers and developers outside of the medical domain to work in the field. This has resulted in more applications targeting healthy users. The UX of these new applications matters greatly to the target population. BCI studies that have investigated

UX, mention user acceptance, system performance, and user enjoyment as the main reasons evaluating UX is vital [2]. User acceptance can play a key role in BRI systems. Users who are frustrated with a system's design could perform cognitive task poorly due to system level issues. One BCI study reported that users performed worse both with positive bias and negative bias when giving inaccurate feedback [17]. To address this issue a user-centered design process that involves users iteratively throughout the process should be used. This in result could increase user-acceptance and reduce factors that could hinder UX. To assess user-acceptance, tools such as the System Usability Scale (SUS) and NASA Task Load Index (TLX) can be used. More specifically, these tools can be used to assess usability and cognitive workload respectively.

Many current BCI systems for healthy users are marketed as entertainment applications. User enjoyment is crucial for these applications to be successful. UX evaluation provides an opportunity to assess this through various methods. One method of doing this is through surveys. The Game Experience Questionnaire (GEQ) is an example of a tool that has been used previously to gain insight on users' level of enjoyment with BCI applications [18]. Based off the trends with-in BCI, BRI could become popular for entertainment purposes. Considering this possibility, addressing issues regarding UX impact on BRI will be important for future applications. Currently there are many limitations of using BCI for control, but investigating the impact of UX could provide clues to ways to addresses some of these limitations. Although UX is not commonly assessed during BRI studies, previous research suggest that UX can influence objective performance measures in these kinds of system [2].

For example, by collecting subjective can one can gain insights about possible confounding factors, such as the BCI device being uncomfortable, therefore distracting the user. Other possible distraction could have occurred such as the user being unclear about directions or uncomfortable with the experimenter mounting the device. These are just some examples of latent issues that might come out only if researchers investigate the more subjective side of their experiment.

Collecting UX data is important to determine user acceptance, system performance, and user enjoyment, but it can also be used to help further validate the objective data.

4   Approach

To investigate the use of affective data and objective data with BRI task evaluation, a simulation environment was developed. Both solo and cooperative control was tested using this environment. While the robot was being cognitively controlled, affective data was collected to measure engagement levels. This data was then used to gain insights on the relationship between neurophysiological measurements and objective performance measures.

4.1   Non-invasive Emotiv BCI Apparatus

The Emotiv EPOC non-invasive device (Fig. 1) is a wireless EEG data acquisition and processing device. It connects via Bluetooth to a computer. This device consists of

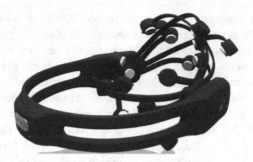

Fig. 1. EEG Emotiv EPOC device

14 electrodes (AF3, AF4, F7, F3, FC5, T7, P7, O1, O2, P8, T8, FC8, F4, F8) and 2 references (P3/P4 locations) to obtain the EEG signals. These channels are based on the international 10–20 locations, which is the standard naming and positioning for EEG devices. The sampling method of the device is based on the sequential sampling with a sampling rate of 2048 Hz. This device was chosen among others for its portability and its adaptability as a wearable computing system. This device was selected for the infrastructure as it has been widely used by other HCI researchers as an input and to study the user's state, which shows its adaptability and accuracy among different task assignments.

Using the BCI begins with mounting the device. Once mounted the Emotiv Control Panel can be used to get visual feedback of the signal quality of electrodes. Green, yellow, red, and black colored electrodes represents good, fair, bad, and no signal respectively. Prior to cognitively controlling a robot in the simulation training must be complete. Training is managed in the control panel. The training phase consists of visualizing movement over a time period. In this work, push and right were the two trained commands. The push command translated into a move the forward command. The right command updated the current angle of the robot causing it to rotate clockwise. Once training is complete the robot can be moved cognitively based on the trained commands. EmoKey, another component from the Emotiv software suite was used to map cognitive commands to keystrokes. In this implementation forward commands were mapped with the 'w' keystroke. Right was mapped to the 'd' keystroke. When the simulation application in the detected these keystrokes the robot performed the corresponding action.

4.2 Simulation Design

The simulation was developed using HTML5 and JavaScript. The yellow canvas served as the main stage as shown in Fig. 2. The red block represents a top down view of the simulated robot. The black bars are obstacles in the environment. The green square in the simulation is the target. Cognitive commands sent to the robot from the BCI device moved it up or rotated it clockwise. The position of the robot is determined by the equations shown in Fig. 3. The first equation calculates the robot's next position. The x in the equation holds the current position of the robot and the y represents the

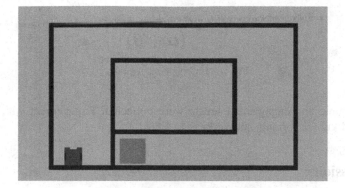

Fig. 2. Simulation environment

$$\begin{pmatrix} x = x + f * \sin(angle) \\ y = y - f * \cos(angle) \end{pmatrix}$$

Fig. 3. Equation to determine robot's position

current location of the robot in the y-axis. The new x and y variables are located on the left side of the equation. The equation also includes a variable f, which controls how far the robot will travel. To maintain the same speed throughout a session this variable is set to a constant. For the x equation f is multiplied by the sin of the current angle of the robot. In the y equation f is multiplied by the cosine of the robot's current angle. The current angle is converted to radians to retrieve the 2D coordinates. This is a well known formula commonly used in 2D simulations. When the robot receives a move forward command the x and y coordinates are updated. When the robot receives a rotate command the current angle is updated. Due to the current limitations of BCI the setup was kept simple so that the robot could be navigated throughout the simulation environment successfully.

5   Results

Two tests were performed to collect affective and objective data while cognitively controlling a robot. The first test consisted of a solo BRI task. During this test the user was responsible for the push and rotate commands. The second test consisted of two users cooperatively controlling a robot. The two commands were divided between the users in this case. One user was responsible for the forward command and the second user controlled the robot's rotation. In both cases the goal of the task was to move the robot to the green square shown in Fig. 2. Once a command was sent, the robot moved and afterwards stopped to wait for further commands. When the robot ran into a wall it was logged as an error. The task ended once the robot reached the green square. Task

$$E = \frac{\beta}{(\alpha + \theta)}$$

Fig. 4. Engagement formula

completion time and engagement levels were collected. Engagement was computed using a well-known formula shown in Fig. 4 [14].

6 Discussion

Prior to completing the solo task the user trained the push and right commands. Engagement and objective data collection was synced so that user state, robot position, and commands could be analyzed together. During solo control, it took 351 s to navigate the robot to the target. The average engagement level during this task was 0.15213. As shown in Fig. 6 the amount of time for this task was greater than the cooperative task as expected. The average time the robot stayed idle during this task was 2.92 s. Figure 5 shows engagement levels for the solo task during the initial 133 s. Shown by the green line there were a few drops in engagement during this task. Although at times the engagement increased, the graph shows that engagement for the solo task on average remained less than cooperative control during the initial seconds of the task. There could be multiple reasons why this was the case. One reason may be that the user only needed to focus on self-motivated movements. During the solo tasks there was no need to collaborate, which could have also influenced the engagement levels.

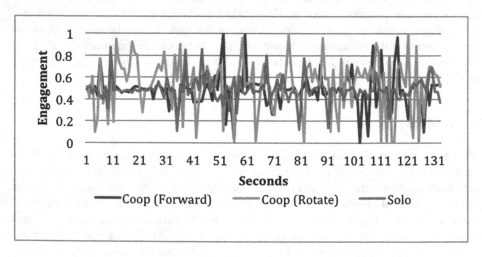

Fig. 5. Solo and cooperative engagement levels

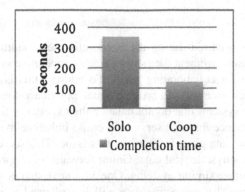

Fig. 6. Tasks completion times

The two users for the cooperative task trained one command each. The cooperative task took 133 s to complete. The average engagement for the user controlling the forward command was 0.043891. The average engagement for the user controlling the rotate command was 0.137043. The robot stayed idle on average 1.012 s which is less than it did during the solo task. This was probably due to the fact that each user only had to worry about one command. This resulted in users being able to move the robot more often. There was a cost associated with this ability to move the robot more frequently. Robots that stay idle for long periods could have slower completion times. As shown in Fig. 7, the cooperative tasks had more errors. Errors were classified as anytime the robot collided with the black walls shown in Fig. 3. These errors probably occurred because users were unsure of each other intentions at time. Feedback in the form of a dynamic cognitive gage could be used to communicate users desired intentions. This would help avoid collisions with walls. Figure 5 shows that the cooperative forward user and solo users had similar levels of engagement. This would be expected due to the constant need for the forward command.

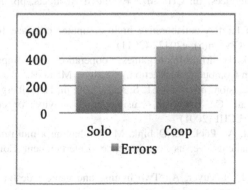

Fig. 7. Tasks errors

7 Conclusion

Although more errors occurred during the cooperative test, additional training could have reduced this. The engagement data shows that a cooperative system could result in a different experience for collaborating users. To address this issue further research should be done to investigate ways to provide equal experience for collaborating users. Cooperative cognitive systems that do not balance the experience for users could result in a degrading performance for one user, which could influence the system as a whole. Analyzing the affective data gives insight into this issue. This serves as an example of the usefulness of neurophysiological data. Going forward this approach could uncover further details about other similar systems. One key next step is to extend this work with more participants. Also subjective data will be collected to investigate the relationship between neurophysiological, subjective, and objective data. Further investigation could give more insights into how UX evaluation can benefit BRI research.

References

1. Wolpaw, J.R., Wolpaw, E.W.: Brain-computer interfaces: something new under the sun. In: Brain-Computer Interfaces Principles and Practice, pp. 3–12. Oxford University Press, New York, New York (2012)
2. van de Laar, B., Gürkök, H., Plass-Oude Bos, D., Nijboer, F., Nijholt, A.: Perspectives on user experience evaluation of brain-computer interfaces. In: Stephanidis, C. (ed.) Universal Access in HCI, Part II, HCII 2011. LNCS, vol. 6766, pp. 600–609. Springer, Heidelberg (2011)
3. Szafir, D., Mutlu, B.: Pay attention! designing adaptive agents that monitor and improve user engagement. In: CHI 2012 Proceedings of the 2012 ACM Annual Conference on Human Factors in Computing Systems, Austin, Texas, USA, pp. 11–20. New York, NY, 5–10 May 2012
4. Andujar, M., Gilbert, J.E.: Let's learn! enhancing user's engagement levels through passive brain- computer interfaces. In: CHI 2013 Extended Abstracts, pp. 703–708. ACM Press (2013)
5. Wang, Y., Jung, T.P.: BA collaborative brain-computer interface for improving human performance. PLoS ONE 6(5), e20422 (2011)
6. Nijholt, A., Gürkök, H.: Multi-brain games: cooperation and competition. In: Universal Access in Human-Computer Interaction. Design Methods, Tools, and Interaction Techniques for eInclusion, pp. 652–661. Springer, Berlin, Heidelberg (2013)
7. Hjelm, S.I., Browall, C.: Brainball – using brain activity for cool competition. In: Proceedings of NordiCHI (2001)
8. Gürkök, H., Nijholt, A., Poel, M., Obbink, M.: Evaluating a multi-player brain–computer interface game: challenge versus co-experience. Entertainment Comput. 4(3), 195–203 (2013)
9. Bonnet, L., Lotte, F., Lécuyer, A.: Two brains, one game : design and evaluation of a multiuser BCI video game based on motor imagery. IEEE Trans. Comput. Intell. AI Games 5(2), 185–198 (2013)

10. Eckstein, M.P., Das, K., Pham, B.T., Peterson, M.F., Abbey, C.K., Sy, J.L., Giesbrecht, B.: Neural decoding of collective wisdom with multi-brain computing. NeuroImage **59**(1), 94–108 (2012). doi:10.1016/j.neuroimage.2011.07.009

11. Obbink, M., Gürkök, H., Bos, D.P.O., Hakvoort, G., Poel, M., Nijholt, A.: Social interaction in a cooperative brain-computer interface game. In: Proceedings of 4th International ICST Conference on Intelligent Technologies for Interactive Entertainment, 2012, pp. 183–192. Genoa, Italy (2012)

12. Nijholt, A.: Towards multimodal, multi-party, and social brain-computer interfacing. In: Camurri, A., Costa, C. (eds.) INTETAIN 2011. LNICST, vol. 78, pp. 12–17. Springer, Heidelberg (2012)

13. Poli, R., Cinel, C., Matran-Femandez, A., Sepulveda, F., Stoica, A.: Towards cooperative brain-computer interfaces for space navigation. In: Proceedings of the International Conference on Intelligent User Inteljaces (IUI), pp. 19–22, Santa Monica, CA, USA (2013)

14. Pope, A.T., Bogart, E.H., Bartolome, D.S.: Biocybernetic system evaluates indices of operator engagement in automated task. Biol. Psychol. **40**(1–2), 187–195 (1995)

15. Moore Jackson, M., Mappus, R.: Applications for brain-computer interfaces. In: Nijholt, A., Tan, D. (eds.) Brain-Computer Interfaces: Applying our Minds to Human-Computer Interaction, pp. 89–103. Springer-Verlag London Ltd., London (2010)

16. Leeb, R., Lee, F., Keinrath, C., Scherer, R., Bischof, H., Pfurtscheller, G.: Brain– computer communication: motivation, aim, and impact of exploring a virtual apartment. IEEE Trans. Neural Syst. Rehab. Eng. **15**, 473–482 (2007)

17. Barbero, A., Grosse-Wentrup, M.: Biased feedback in brain–computer interfaces. J. Neuroeng. Rehabil. **7**(1), 34 (2010)

18. Plass-Oude Bos, D., Poel, M., Nijholt, A.: A study in user-centered design and evaluation of mental tasks for BCI. In: Lee, K.-T., Tsai, W.-H., Liao, H.-Y.M., Chen, T., Hsieh, J.-W., Tseng, C.-C. (eds.) MMM 2011 Part II. LNCS, vol. 6524, pp. 122–134. Springer, Heidelberg (2011)

Analysis of Factors Influencing the Satisfaction of the Usability Evaluations in Smartphone Applications

Ayako Hashizume[1(✉)] and Shuwa Kido[2]

[1] Faculty of System Design, Tokyo Metropolitan University, Hachioji, Japan
hashiaya@tmu.ac.jp
[2] Graduate School of System Design, Tokyo Metropolitan University,
Hachioji, Japan
shuwa.tmu@gmail.com

Abstract. It is often said that there is an age difference in the use of ICT devices such as cell phones and smartphones, but the empirical evidences are rare regarding the details of the literacy and the use of such devices. The usability and satisfaction of such devices and applications are important for users. In this paper, authors focus on the factors influencing satisfaction with smartphone application use.

Keywords: User experience · Usability · Smartphone · Elderly people · Satisfaction

1 Introduction

With the progress and the diffusion of Information and Communication Technology (ICT), many devices, such as computers, cell phones, smartphones and tablets, have become more convenient and are used in a variety of ways in our everyday life. At the same time, in Japan, the progress of aging is very rapid and since 2005 Japan has become the most aged society in the world. The percentage of elderly people (percentage of total population aged 65 and over) in Japan has risen up from 5 % in 1950, 10 % in 1985, and 20 % in 2005, to 25 % in 2013, and is expected to rise to 30.3 % in 2025 and 39.9 % in 2060 [1]. Against these factors, manufacturers in electronics have developed cell phones, smartphones and computers for elderly users [2, 3], but there still exists a gap between high-skilled end users and low-skilled end users depending on theie demographic traits. One of the marked differences is related to differences within the age group [4].

In previous studies [5, 6], we conducted a questionnaire survey based on a quantitative approach to grasp the overall trend of using cell phones. Answers to the questionnaire showed some variation, such as how elderly people are using afewer number of functions and how they cannot operate functions that are widely known and used among other age groups. Compared to young people, elderly people do not use cell phones actively and do not use as many functions effectively. It was also found that there are differences in the relative importance of the value criteria regarding age and

M. Kurosu (Ed.): Human-Computer Interaction, Part I, HCII 2015, LNCS 9169, pp. 194–201, 2015.
DOI: 10.1007/978-3-319-20901-2_18

sex. Younger people, ages 20s, tend to emphasize performance, functionality and design, though there is a slight disparity between male users who emphasize performance and female users who emphasize design. On the other hand, elderly people emphasize the ease of operation and the display size. Elderly people do not simply neglect the design of devices (Kansei aspect) but put more emphasis on the usability and will regard the design as important if there are no usability problems. There is a generation gap between those people in regards to the value criteria, how the design (appearance) and the usability are affecting the purchase of cell phones by adopting the research results. The usability of the device is significant to the elderly, so the usability of software such as smartphone applications should also be considered through the spread of smartphones.

ISO9241-11's definition of usability is the "Extent to which a product can be used by specified users to achieve specified goals with effectiveness, efficiency and satisfaction in a specified context of use [7]." Regarding this definition, Kurosu argued that the concept of usability consists of just effectiveness and efficiency. They should be considered objective quality characteristics in the same way that reliability, cost, safety, compatibility and maintenance are. However, satisfaction is related to subjective quality characteristics such as pleasure, joy, beauty, attachment, motivation and value, as well as objective quality characteristics [8].

In this paper, satisfaction was regarded as one of the key criteria for the evaluation of artifact quality. We focused on the following points, and conducted the usability evaluation of smartphone applications as follows:

(1) What is the most important factor affecting the satisfaction when using artifacts?
(2) Whether the strongest determinant of satisfaction differs depending on age groups?

2 Usability Evaluation of Smartphone Application

We conducted a usability evaluation for the purpose of getting detailed information regarding the users' subjective impressions and feelings while using a new application we developed. The application focuses on the connection between satisfaction and other items used the evaluation.

2.1 The Stress Measurement Application Overview

We developed an application that can estimate mental stress levels more easily than the conventional method of using an electrocardiograph (ECG). Figure 1 is the flow diagram of calculations for the heart rate variation (HRV) in the conventional method, ECG measurement using many devices, and from the proposed application to measure the pulse wave using only the smartphone.

We confirmed the accuracy of HRV detected by our application with a verification experiment. According to the verification experiment, HRV measurement using our application was found to be valid for assessing mental stress at the same precision as the ECG method [9].

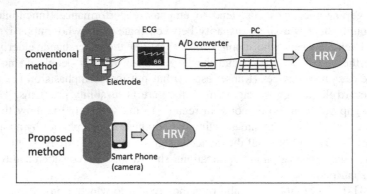

Fig. 1. HRV calculation flow

Figure 2 shows how to hold the smartphone during the HRV measurement using our application. The first step is to place a fingertip over the lens of the smartphone camera and the light-emitting diode (LED). The left index finger is preferable. The camera acquires images of blood vessels in the finger, and obtains the pulse wave data by measuring the timing of the blood flow. Using this algorithm, we can calculate the HRV from the pulse wave data using a smartphone.

2.2 Method of Usability Evaluation

Participants were 17 young people in their 20s and 12 elderly people in their 60–70s, all living in Tokyo. The average age of the young people was 20.9 years with a standard deviation (SD) of 0.5, and the average age of the elderly users was 66.2 years with an SD of 1.9. All 17 young participants had their own smartphones and all 12 elderly people had cell phones.

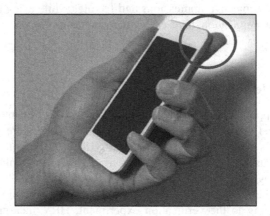

Fig. 2. Measurement of the pulse wave with the smartphone application

We defined elderly people as those who are over 65 years of age, based on the World Health Organization (WHO) definition.

First we explained the research it is for the academic purposes and does not have anything to do with the sales or marketing. We then told the participants the expected duration of the experiment and that they were free to quit at anytime during the experiment should they feel uncomfortable with our questions or our treatment of any information gathered.

After obtaining their consent, we explained the evaluation procedure and how to use the application to each participant. Then the participants performed a trial to measure their mental stress level using the application. After the measurement, subjects answered the following questions and commented on the application.

2.3   Contents of Usability Evaluation

The usability evaluation included the following questions (Table 1): demographic characteristics (name, sex, age, experience with using ECG, etc.), number of errors

Table 1. Contents of usability evaluation

	Question items			Components of usability
1	Age			-
2	Sex			-
3	Experience with using ECG			-
4	Errors in the use of App	a	Number of operation errors	efficiency
		b	Number of measurement errors	efficiency
5	Achievements after the use of App	a	Success of measurement until the end	effectiveness
		b	Success of using the App until the end	effectiveness
6	Description on basic characteristic of the App (5-point scale)	a	Ease of understanding on the contents	
		b	Ease of understanding on the operational procedure	
		c	Ease of understanding on the screen structure	
		d	Ease of understanding on displayed charts	
		e	Readability of displayed characters	
		f	Ease of use	
		g	Responsiveness	
		h	Reliability of data	
		i	Length of measurement time	
7	Comprehensive evaluation of the App (5-point scale)	a	Safety	
		b	Usefulness	
		c	Likability	
		d	Repetitive use of the App	
		e	**Satisfaction**	**satisfaction**
8	Free coments			-

during the use of the application, whether or not the measurement was successful, and their impressions after using the application.

Description on basic characteristic of the application and comprehensive evaluation of the application were evaluated by 5 point rating scale. Only the results of the usability evaluation are described in terms of the association with satisfaction and other evaluation items in this paper.

2.4   Results

The evaluation first quantified the degree of subjective belief in the questions and then analyzed by Kendall's rank correlation coefficient. The rank correlation coefficients were calculated using a software excel statistics: Ekuseru-Toukei 2012 (Social survey research information Co., Ltd., Tokyo, Japan). In the results of the rank correlation coefficients analysis, we found some differences in the use of the ICT devices between young people and elderly people (Table 2).

It was shown that elderly people made more positive evaluations than the youth on the following 5 items. Among the 5 items that the elderly rated positively, these 3 items showed a significant difference with a value of .001; "(6-a) Ease of understanding on the contents", "(6-g) Responsiveness" and "(6-i) Length of measurement". Items "(6-f) Ease of use" and "(7-e) Satisfaction" also showed a significant difference with a value of .005.

Table 2. Rank correlation coefficients between age/sex and items

Kendall's rank correlation coefficient

	Age		Sex	
(4-a) Number of operation errors	0.008		0.164	
(4-b) Number of measurement errors	-0.266		-0.306	
(5-a) Success of measurement until the end	-0.008		-0.164	
(5-b) Success of using the App until the end	-0.008		-0.164	
(6-a) Ease of understanding on the contents	-0.430	**	-0.030	
(6-b) Ease of understanding on the operational procedure	-0.185		-0.253	
(6-c) Ease of understanding on the screen structure	-0.149		0.268	
(6-d) Ease of understanding on displayed charts	-0.121		-0.011	
(6-e) Readability of displayed characters	0.315		-0.154	
(6-f) Ease of use	-0.334	*	-0.401	*
(6-g) Responsiveness	-0.518	**	-0.294	
(6-h) Reliability of data	-0.201		-0.033	
(6-i) Length of measurement time	-0.509	**	-0.202	
(7-a) Safety	-0.284		0.010	
(7-b) Usefulness	-0.225		0.260	
(7-c) Likability	-0.103		0.166	
(7-d) Repetitive use of the App	-0.199		-0.031	
(7-e) Satisfaction	-0.375	*	-0.046	

$*p<.005, **p<.001.$

Table 3. Rank correlation coefficients between satisfaction of 2 age-groups and items

Kendall's rank correlation coefficient

	Youth' Satisfaction	Elderly' Satisfaction
(4-a) Number of operation errors	0.077	0.426
(4-b) Number of measurement errors	0.347	0.250
(5-a) Success of measurement until the end	-0.077	-0.426
(5-b) Success of using the App until the end	-0.077	-0.426
(6-a) Ease of understanding on the contents	0.778 **	0.426
(6-b) Ease of understanding on the operational procedure	0.280	0.632 *
(6-c) Ease of understanding on the screen structure	0.155	0.632 *
(6-d) Ease of understanding on displayed charts	0.168	0.250
(6-e) Readability of displayed characters	0.167	0.500
(6-f) Ease of use	0.146	0.250
(6-g) Responsiveness	0.538 *	0.632 *
(6-h) Reliability of data	0.561 *	0.853 **
(6-i) Length of measurement time	0.277	-0.316
(7-a) Safety	0.435	0.707 *
(7-b) Usefulness	0.369	0.632 *
(7-c) Likability	0.530 *	0.943 **
(7-d) Repetitive use of the App	0.663 **	0.943 **
(7-e) Satisfaction	1.000	1.000

*p<.005, **p<.001.

The association between evaluation of satisfaction and other items are shown in Table 3. 4 items were commonly linked to satisfaction for both age groups: "(6-g) Responsiveness", "(6-h) Reliability of data", "(7-c) Likability" and "(7-d) Repetitive use of the App". On the other hand, "(6-a) Ease of understanding on the contents" had a statistically significant association with satisfaction from only young people. Additionally, 4 items: "(6-b) Ease of understanding on the operational procedure", "(6-c) Ease of understanding on the screen structure", "(7-a) Safety" and "(7-b) Usefulness" were statistically significant linked to the satisfaction among elderly people only.

2 of the 5 items suggested the association with satisfaction from the youth, were linked to satisfaction at the significance level of .001: "(6-a) Ease of understanding on the contents" and "(7-d) Repetitive use of the App". 8 items indicated the significant association with satisfaction among elderly people. 3 of the 8 items were related to satisfaction at the significant level of .001: "(6-h) Reliability of data", "(7-c) Likability" and "(7-d) Repetitive use of the App".

3   Discussion

This study focused on factors that influence satisfaction with the usability evaluation. The evaluation of satisfaction with the application was more positive among elderly people. Factors affecting satisfaction were different depending on the age groups.

All young participants were using smartphones in their daily lives, hence they are accustomed to using such applications. Because the application does not require any special operation, they reported boredom while staring at the screen during the use of the application. On the other hand, all member in the group of elderly users who had never used smartphones but had experienced ECG measurements in hospitals, felt that the measurement time was short and was content with the application.

The results showed that understandability of the application contents and whether to use the application repetitively were strongly linked to satisfaction among young people. Whether to use the application repetitively, in addition to reliability and likeability, had deep connections with satisfaction from the elderly. It was also found that understandability of the application contents had association with satisfaction from only the youth, and that the understandability of the application procedure and screen structure, safety and usefulness of the application were linked to satisfaction among the elderly only. It can be interpreted that only the elderly were strong satisfied with the safety and usefulness of the application based on their prior experiences of with standard ECG measurement practices.

Early in the application development process, we conducted a product test using a prototype for another paticipants and extracted the requirements from young and elderly groups [10]. Requests obtained from the youth included a demand to make application contents easy to understand, and requests from elderly people were also embraced demands to make the application procedure and the screen structure more understandable. In order to get high level of satisfaction with the quality of artifacts, it is important to ensure conformance to the requirements from each user.

4 Conclusion

In this paper, we focused on the factors influencing satisfaction with the usability evaluation of smartphone application. We conducted the usability evaluation of the application for obtaining information regarding the relationship between satisfaction and other evaluation items.

It was found that the evaluation of the application was more positive among elderly people, and the youth and elderly evaluated satisfaction of the application use by different criteria. The result showed that factors influencing to satisfaction could be determined by the conformance to requirements of each user group.

References

1. Cabinet Office Japan: Annual Report on the Aging Society (2014)
2. Ministry of Internal Affairs and Communications: A Report on the Use of Communication System in 2013 (2014)
3. Irie, R., et al.: The Challenge to the universal design in the development of the cell phone easy phone (Raku-Raku Phone). FUJITSU 56(2), 146–152 (2005). (in Japanese)
4. Furuki, K., et al.: Approach to commercialization of RakuRaku smartphone. FUJITSU 63 (5), 548–554 (2012). (in Japanese)

5. Hashizume, A., Yamanaka, T., Kurosu, M.: Real user experience of ICT devices among elderly people. In: Kurosu, M. (ed.) HCD 2011. LNCS, vol. 6776, pp. 227–234. Springer, Heidelberg (2011)
6. Hashizume, A., Kurosu, M., Kaneko, T.: The choice of communication media and the use of mobile phone among senior users and young users. In: Lee, S., Choo, H., Ha, S., Shin, I.C. (eds.) APCHI 2008. LNCS, vol. 5068, pp. 427–436. Springer, Heidelberg (2008)
7. ISO 9241-11:1998: Ergonomic Requirements for Office Work with Visual Display Terminals (VDTs) – Part 11: Guidance on usability (1998)
8. Kurosu, M.: New horizon of user engineering and HCD. HCD-Net J. 2(1), 22–29 (2006)
9. Kido S., et al.: Development and evaluation of a smartphone application for self-estimation of mental stress level. In: International Symposium on Affective Science and Engineering 2015 Proceedings (2015)
10. Kido S., et al.: Development of an application for measuring the mental stress level using the heart rate variability based on human-centered design. HCD-Net Journal (2015)

The Definition and Use of Personas in the Design of Technologies for Informal Caregivers

Susanne Hensely-Schinkinger[(⊠)], Aparecido Fabiano Pinatti de Carvalho, Michael Glanznig, and Hilda Tellioğlu

Multidisciplinary Design Group, Vienna University of Technology,
Vienna, Austria
{susanne.hensely-schinkinger, fabiano.pinatti, michael.
glanznig, hilda.tellioglu}@tuwien.ac.at

Abstract. This paper refers to the significance of defining and using personas for the design and development of technological solutions for informal care. It not only argues for the importance of carefully defining personas, but also discusses the influence that personas exert in the design decisions made throughout the process. We illustrate these two aspects with empirical results gathered in the project TOPIC – The Online Platform for Informal Caregivers – in which a series of online technological solutions are being designed and developed to integrate a *CarePortfolio* to provide caregivers with emotional, informational and tangible support, as they go on to handle their care responsibilities.

Keywords: Personas · User-centered design · Informal care · Ethnographic study

1 Introduction

The past number of years has witnessed an increase in the demand for care work, which in the European Union is primarily provided by informal caregivers [1]. Such work is often associated with high psychological pressure, which subjects caregivers to a great deal of emotional stress, usually evolving to some sort of emotional burden [2, 3]. Furthermore, informal caregivers can sometimes be exposed to severe physical loads stemming from the care procedures they perform, which can potentially lead to the development of a physical burden as well [4]. Such physical and psychological burdens can increase the risk for both psychical and physical morbidity and mortality among caregivers [5]. Therefore, it can be argued that informal caregivers are our society's "hidden patients", who deserve especial attention and need support [6, 7].

One possibility of support refers to providing technological solutions to help informal caregivers to deal with their care work and be in contact with people in similar situations, with whom they could share their burden [8]. This is the main goal of TOPIC,[1] a European project funded by the AAL Joint Program, aiming at designing

---

[1] For more information, visit the project website at: http://topic-aal.eu.

© Springer International Publishing Switzerland 2015
M. Kurosu (Ed.): Human-Computer Interaction, Part I, HCII 2015, LNCS 9169, pp. 202–213, 2015.
DOI: 10.1007/978-3-319-20901-2_19

and implementing technological solutions to support informal caregivers to reduce the impacts of the potential burden stemming from the care work that they carry out.

In order to design systems that support informal caregivers' daily lives and potentially reduce their burdens, it is crucial to understand their needs, problems, and expectations. Hence, the project has been using a user-centered design approach and applying qualitative ethnographic methods [9]. One of the main tools being used in the project to keep the users' needs in focus is personas [10, 11], which have been created based on the empirical data collected for the project. This paper reports on the approach that we used to define our personas and discusses how the defined personas have impacted on our design decisions.

The paper is organized as follows: Sect. 2 introduces the notion of personas and discusses literature on the relevance of using it in user-centered design efforts; Sect. 3 provides an overview on the personas devised for TOPIC; Sect. 4 discusses how the empirical data collected for the project informed the elaboration of the project personas and introduces the impacts that our personas had in our design decisions; finally, we conclude with a further reflection on how personas have shaped our design.

2 Related Research

Personas are a useful methodological tool in defining and assessing system requirements for challenging user groups, like older persons, with regard to their diversity [11, 12]: they are crucial to find accurate representations of the target group and are a valuable approach in capturing the conceptual model of the users, so that usable and useful technologies can be designed and developed to meet their needs, capabilities and expectations [10]. For instance, the Center for Usability Research and Engineering (CURE) in Vienna have demonstrated how important it is to use personas to identify and describe certain type of users – like older persons – for a better estimation of the European population [13].

Furthermore personas are valuable in providing a shared basis for communication between all relevant groups of stakeholders and make design decisions more transparent [14]. However, personas are not a self-sufficient tool: although Bredies [15] defends that the relevance of a persona approach to design is more relevant than using interviews for eliciting requirements, authors like Pruitt & Grudin [14] argue that personas should complement and not replace other quantitative and qualitative methods; according to them, personas can amplify the effectiveness of the other methods used for the requirements elicitation. Combined with scenarios in which personas' context and main activities are described a thorough picture can be provided to help understand the circumstances under which a certain group of people (as potential users of systems in development) live and what their habits and expectations are, especially in relation to technology support for everyday life.

Personas can be defined according to Moser et al. [12] by three different approaches: purely qualitative, purely quantitative and mixed qualitative and quantitative. Although these three approaches exist, there is no framework to inform the decision about which approach should be used. In an attempt to close this gap, Moser et al. propose the use of decision diagrams to support choosing the appropriate approach for the creation of personas [12].

Notwithstanding the existence three approaches for defining personas, we argue that it is not clear what each of these approaches entails and what is the process to be followed for their definition. Therefore, we set out to clarify the process for defining personas through the mixed qualitative and quantitative approach, which according to our finding is the best approach for elaborating and choosing personas that can be indeed representative of the target group.

3 Methodology

In TOPIC, we base our research work on a user-centered design approach supported by ethnographically informed studies. We started our project with a pre-study to understand the daily lives of our informal caregivers and to identify their problems, needs and burdens. The pre-study was conducted with 10 informal caregivers – 1 male and 9 female. They were facing different care situations: 5 were caring for their spouse, 3 for their parent and 2 for their child. 2 out of the 10 users were not living in the same household as their care receiver. The age of the informal caregiver participating in the pre-study ranged from 55 to 80 years – the average was 64 years. 2 out of the 10 informal caregivers were still working – the rest retired or unemployed.

The pre-study began with a *first contact interview* at the homes of the informal caregivers: We talked about their situation, their care receiver and themselves. Furthermore we gave them a short overview about the project and what they have to expect. Then we started with the *participatory observations*: For this part of the pre-study we defined 3 to 4 appointments with the informal caregivers where we visited them again in their homes and observed their daily life – at each appointment for approximately half a day. Before and after each appointment we conducted *informal interviews* through which we engaged in deep conversations with our participants about their situation, the status of the care receiver and also about news that happened since the last appointment. Always when possible, we also tried to involve the care receiver in the conversations.

At the beginning of the participatory observation phase we also distributed a *cultural probes* kit for collecting additional data about the care situation and the caregivers' everyday lives. The kits contained a diary (for caregivers to write down daily activities, feelings and thoughts), an *actimoClock* (for them to register the different kinds of work and activities during a day), polaroid camera (to capture situations of the daily life), smiley stickers (to underline emotions in the diary and/or *actimoClock*), a social map (to visualize the frequency and amount of social contacts) and picture cards (to describe feelings and thoughts related to pictures showing different care situations). Furthermore we included two questionnaires: A care questionnaire to gather (socio-demographic) information about the care receiver, the care situation and also the informal caregiver itself, and the Zarit Burden questionnaire to stage the level of burden from that the informal caregiver is suffering at the moment.

Once finished the participatory observation phase, we carried out an *in-depth interview* with the care receivers to clarify what we saw during the participatory observations and what we read from the filled items of the cultural probes. Based on all data resulted from the pre-study, we tried to identify and define personas from different perspectives to be used for the TOPIC project. We basically focused on *person-related characteristics*, but also included all necessary aspects of *care-* and *context-related characteristics* to understand and better identify the personas we need. We elaborate on our approach to define our project personas in the following sections.

4 Personas Definition and Its Impacts upon Design Decisions

In preparation for the definition of our project personas, we created an overview table with the different characteristics of our participants (Table 1), so to visualize the variety of profiles we had. Knowing that personas must be representative of the users of the system being designed and the activities that they will perform on it, we focused on typical characteristics used for defining personas (e.g., age, gender, social environment, etc.) [16] and added some new ones that fitted to the context of informal care (e.g., care situation, care receiver, relationship with care receiver, etc.), as suggested by CURE [13].

After careful consideration of the profiles of the participants in our sample, we started working on the characteristic of our project personas. As a result, we elaborated two personas, namely Anna and Otto, whose characteristics are listed in Table 2. Besides Otto and Anna, we also created a non-persona called Carola (Table 3). Carola represents people that are not potential users of our future TOPIC platform. Defining a non-persona has been proven to be a good design practice, since it reminds the designers of the types of people whom they are not designing for [14]. The personas and non-personas work together in opening and restricting the design possibilities, so to achieve an appropriate list of requirements accurately addressing the user needs. Drawing on the results of our pre-study data analysis, we were confident that by addressing the *person-related, care-related* and *context-related* aspects, we would create precise representations of the different types, or archetypes, of people for whom we are designing in the TOPIC project.

In the following section, we will discuss how our findings from the pre-study have informed the definition of the characteristics and therefore for the personas and non-persona. In doing so, we aim to illustrate the relevance of empirical data for the definition of personas.

4.1   Person-Related Characteristics

Person-related characteristics mainly refer to demographic information concerning the profiles of the types of users targeted by the system – for TOPIC, the informal care-givers. The three characteristics that we decided to represent were *age, gender* and *mobility*. These allow inferring quite a few things in terms of functional and non-functional requirements for the representatives of the target group. For instance, it is known that the older the people are, the bigger the possibility for them to suffer from some types of sensory impairment that comes with the age [17], e.g., visual impairments, which have a stronger impact on the activities of daily living than hearing impairments [18]. This means that the interfaces should be prepared to require less effort to read, which can be done with the use of larger fonts, the presentation of less

Table 1. Summary of the pre-study participants characteristics

	Reisende[a]	Netzwerk[a]	Kreativ[a]	Yoga[a]	Wandern[a]	Sorgsam[a]	Pünktlich[a]	Adrett[a]	Liebe[a]	Ehrenamt[a]
Age	76	58	56	59	72	67	80	59	60	55
Gender	Female	Female	Female	Female	Female	Male	Female	Female	Female	Female
Care situation	> 2 yrs.	> 2 yrs.	> 2 yrs.	> 2 yrs.	> 2 yrs.	2 yrs.	> 2 yrs.	> 2 yrs.	> 2 yrs.	> 2 yrs.
Care receiver	Partly mobile husband	Partly mobile mother	Fully mobile mother	Partly mobile mother	Partly mobile husband	Partly mobile wife	Partly mobile husband	Partly mobile husband	Non-mobile daughter	Partly mobile daughter
Mobility	Full mobile	Full mobile	Full mobile	Full mobile	Full mobile	Full mobile	Full mobile	Full mobile	Full mobile	Full mobile
Social environment	Children, nieces, neighbors, friends	Friends	Daughter, nephew, friends	Friends	Friends	Friends, but no contact to sons	Sons, few friends	Colleagues, sons, friends	Husband, 2. Child, friends, colleagues	No contact to family, no friends
Isolated	No	No	No	No	No	No	Yes	No	No	Yes
Living situation	Live together	Live separated (58 km)	Live together	Live together	Live together	Live separated (4 km)	Live together	Live together	Live together	Live together
Relation with CR	Lovely but stressed	Tensed	Annoying	Lovely	Lovely	Attentive	Lovely	Distanced	Lovely	Lovely
Financial dependency	No	No	Yes	Yes	No	No	No	No	Yes	Yes
Technical skills	Average	Average	Average	Average	Average	High	Low	High	Average	High
Internet access	Yes	Yes	Yes	Yes	Yes	Yes	No	Yes	Yes	Yes

[a]Pseudonyms are used to assure confidentiality to the participants and imprint one of the strong characteristics of the person in question.

Table 2. Overview of the characteristics of personas Anna and Otto

	Anna	Otto
Age	60 years old	70 years old
Gender	Female	Male
Living situation	Live separated	Live together
Care situation	Starting (inexperienced with care procedures, takes care of some chores at the care receiver's house, share the care responsibility with her daughters)	3 years (experienced with care procedures, takes care of all chores at the house, does not share the care responsibilities)
Care receiver	Partially mobile mother	Non-mobile wife
Mobility	Very good	Not very good anymore
Social environment	Husband, children	No contact to children
Isolated	No	Yes
Relation with CR	Non-aggressive	Aggressive
Financial dependency	Exists (Anna depends on her mother)	Does not exist.
Technical skills	High	Low
Internet access	Yes	Yes

Table 3. Overview of the characteristics of the non-persona Carola

	Carole (non-persona)
Age	50 years old
Gender	Female
Care situation	2 years (visits the CR twice a week, manages the paperwork)
Care receiver	Partly-mobile father, live in a retirement home
Mobility	Not very good anymore
Social environment	Existing, has own family and work
Isolated	No
Living situation	Does not live with the father in the same house
Relation with CR	Lovely and non-aggressive
Financial dependency	Exists
Technical skills	Average (she uses computer at work)
Internet access	Yes for her children

information in each interface and careful positioning of the interface elements [19].
Also, taking account of people's ages, it is perfectly possible to assess the types of
technologies they grew up with, which can be a source of inspiration for the design

of interaction mechanisms with which the users are familiar. In the following, we discuss how the attributes assigned to our personas and non-persona connects with the pre-study data analysis.

Age. The age in our sample was in average 64 years. This is similar to the general situation in Vienna, where the average is 63 years, and the age ranged 55 to 72 years for persons taking care for people older than 60 years [4]. Therefore, we decided to assign Anna and Otto an age within this age range. Anna was given 60 years and Otto 70 years. The gap of 10 years was chosen deliberately because we judge that 10 years of age would impact considerably on the skills and health situation of people, especially when it comes to older adults. It is widely accepted that 10 years entail considerable changes in the types of technology available. Therefore, considering that Anna and Otto are separated by a 10-year time frame means that they have been born in times where the technological apparatus available to them was considerably different. In terms of design implications, this would mean that the solutions should be flexible enough to be used by people with different technological backgrounds. Concerning Carola, our non-persona, she was aged 50 because this lies under the TOPIC participant inclusion criteria of 55 + years of age.

Gender. The general situation in Vienna shows that more than two-thirds of all informal caregivers are female [4]. Compared to our sample, male caregivers were underrepresented – for the pre-study, only 1 male informal caregiver has accepted to partake in the data collection activities of the project. Nonetheless, we have decided that it would be important to have both genders represented in our personas. Past and current research has demonstrated that gender plays a very important role in informal care: there are many differences in caregiving related to gender. For instance, there is evidence of a generalized culture assuming that women should take over the role of caregiving: they are often likely to shoulder the bulk of caregiving responsibilities compared with their male counterparts [20]. This does not come without a cost. Since female caregivers usually do not seek support with the care responsibilities in which they should engage, they have a higher prevalence of chronic health disorders, stress, anxiety, depression, and social isolation. Also female caregivers are more restricted in their mobility and life activities and have a worse self-care compared to male caregivers [21]. This information is important for designing different types of supports for caregivers with different gender.

Mobility. The mobility of both the informal caregivers and the care receivers is a very important issue for the design of technological solutions for informal care. Knowing whether (i) the caregivers can freely move and engage in short distance mobility, (ii) the care receiver can accompany them or (iii) stay alone at home for short periods of time when the caregivers need to be absent leads to different types of requirement to be fulfilled. Although we observed homogeneity in our sample, we decided to have one of our personas, Anna, as fully mobile, the other, Otto, as partially mobile due to limited physical ability. This actually reflects the results from some other studies pointing out to possible degeneration of physical movements with the passage of the years – also showing an obvious worsening from the age group 50-69 years to the age group older than 70 years [22]. We found out relevant to represent such a variety in order to prepare our system accordingly.

4.2   Care-Related Characteristics

In addition to demographic information, personas must voice the users' goals and aspirations. Designers should be reminded of what the users want to achieve through the system and understand what types of activities are meaningful for them [16]. Providing TOPIC is thought for informal caregivers, it is important to make it clear the types of care situations with which the users of the system are involved. The care-related characteristics focus on this. It mainly describes the care context in which persona is situated and, consequently, it provides information about the care receivers and their health condition. In the following, we present the rationale behind choosing the specific care related characteristics for our personas.

Care Situation. Most of the caregivers in our sample are caring for an ailing relative for more than two years. However, the needs of informal caregivers who are starting caring for somebody and the ones of those caring for someone for a longer period of time are considerably different. For instance, many participants told us about the difficulties they faced at the beginning with all the bureaucracy regarding social welfare benefits, for which they are eligible, the lack of information about the proce-dure to apply for it. On the other hand, participants also mentioned that once you get the gist of it, you do not need this type of information. Instead, for caregivers who have been caring for somebody for a longer period of time, the need for support with the emotional burden they experience is definitely more important than information about the procedures to apply for financial benefits or the care procedures. Not only that, according to the participants, more experienced caregiver could in fact provide the aforementioned types of information to caregivers starting with the care work. From our observations, it was clear that some of our participants, like Mrs. Liebe, were very experienced with the care procedures that they had to perform. Hence, we decided to make one of our personas – Anna – as a beginner caregiver and the other – Otto – as a more experienced one. Regarding Carola, we decided to assign her a care situation that is not the focus of our project, i.e., one in which the caregiver is not really engaged in the care work. In Carola's case, the father lives in a retirement home and she visits him just twice a week in order to check upon him and sort out any paper work that is necessary for his permanency and for the treatments that he must receive.

Care Receiver. Information about the family relationship of the caregiver and the care receiver as well as about the mobility capabilities of the care receiver is very important to better define the care context with which the caregiver deals with. Most of our participants were taking care for their spouses, their parents or their children. Following these observations, we decided to have one of our personas – Anna – caring for her mother, whilst the other – Otto – is caring for his wife. To have these different family relationships reflected in the personas is important, because it exposes some differences in the pattern of caregiving depending on who are you caring for [23]. In addition to that, we described Anna's mother as partly mobile whilst Otto's wife is non-mobile. By partially mobile we mean that the person can walk short distances, even though with difficulties. Non-mobile means that the person cannot walk and can have some other types of motor impairment – e.g., parts of the body can be paralyzed. This differentiation is rather relevant in terms of system requirements and allows for the description of different scenarios.

Living Situation. This attribute provides information telling whether caregivers and care receivers live in the same household. We found it important to account for it, as our data suggested that it is directly connected with feeling of security. From the data analysis it became noticeable that informal caregivers who do not live together with the care receivers experience certain emotional burden stemming from the uncertainty about how the care receivers are doing when they are not around. Although situations in which informal caregivers and care receivers live together in the same household is commoner in our sample, Robison et al. [24] show that almost three quarters of all care situations correspond to caregivers and care receivers living in different households. Providing these distinct residential situations (i) may contribute to increased social isolation, decreased preventive care, greater activity restriction and less relationship strain in shared households [21, 24] and (ii) can lead to different technical requirements, we decided to represent this diversity in our personas.

Relation with Care Receiver. Empirical evidence collected through fieldwork suggested us that the quality of the relation between the caregiver and the care receiver can be a source of emotional and psychological burdens. Although, we observed that in one half of our sample the relationship between the informal caregivers and their ailing relatives was good, the relationship in the other half of the sample showed that sometimes the caregivers have to deal with difficult situations. Since one of our aims is to provide informal caregivers emotional support so that the impacts of any burden stemming from the care work can be relieved, it is important to have this issue represented in one of our personas, so to provide the necessary tools for this. However, we should also account for good relationships, as these leads us to different user needs.

Financial Dependency. Another characteristics that we judge relevant to represent are financial dependency, as we observed that it impacts most of the times upon the relationship between the caregiver and the care receiver. Financial dependencies in both ways were observed in our sample. For instance, Ms. Yoga is financially dependent on her mother, who seemed to play a dominant role in the relationship. On the other hand, Mrs. Liebe's and Ms. Ehrenamt's daughters depend financially on their mothers, who happen to be their caregivers. Except four cases, no financial dependency has been found between the caregivers and their care receivers. However it is worth pointing out that this does not guarantee the rise of some issues in the relationship between the caregivers and the care receivers. Mr. Sorgsam, for instance, told us about the extra work that required from him to keep his and his partner's expenses separated. He explained that they decided to keep their expenses totally separated. They have separate incomes and bank accounts, but Mr. Sorgsam is the one responsible to sort all the financial issues out. In terms of work, this requires half an hour everyday from him to log into the spreadsheets he uses to control their monthly expenses what he has spent and what she has spent during the day.

4.3 Context-Related Characteristics

This cluster includes characteristics describing the social context as well as technologies in use or under consideration. The social context of a future user of the TOPIC platform is a very important point in defining personas: both the social environment, meaning how does the family circle and the circle of friends and acquaintances look like, and the isolation, indicating how intense the contact is to members of these circles, describes the social context. The social context of a persona implies how big the need of social contacts over digital media could be. Defining Internet access and technical skills for a persona on the TOPIC project is necessary to identify the users' technological skills and allow the designers to focus on these different needs in aspects like usability, user interaction and user experience.

Social Environment. In terms of social environment, we observed very different situations in our pre-study regarding this characteristic about family and friends. In general, it can be said that the social surrounding from informal caregivers starts shrinking as soon as they engage in handling a care situation. Because some informal caregivers of our sample have no regular or any contact at all to their family especially their children, friends are very important although often rare. But if the family is available, they are an important help. Our data also shows that (former) colleagues and neighbors are an important part of their social life. These issues have been addressed by having Anna with a loving family and lots of friends around her, and Otto without contacts with his friends and his children.

Isolation. Although in most cases, people have to accept the fact of being isolated due to external reasons, we also observed informal caregivers who choose to be in such situations. Despite the fact that just two participants from our sample seem to be socially isolated, we judged relevant to represent both manifestations of this characteristic in our personas: Anna and Otto shows different needs and requirements to the platform, due to their different isolation levels.

Technical Skills. More than half of our sample considers having average technical skills, whilst one third of them consider being highly skilled with technology. As observable in Table 1, only one user low skills about technology. In order not to forget to take into consideration the needs of these three groups we defined Anna as being experienced with technologies and Otto as the newbie with it. Although only one participant from our sample considered having low technical skills, past research shows that for the age group we target, it is very common to find people with low or no technical skills [25]. In terms of design implications, this means that the platform must show high usability levels, being simple to understand and use and accommodating also the needs of more skilled people with technologies.

Internet Access. Concerning Internet access, all, but one participant has it. Therefore both Anna and Otto have been defined as having access to it. This also goes towards the fact that the final product of the project will be an online platform. Carola, our non-persona, has no Internet access, highlighting the fact that we are designing for people who can go online.

5   Conclusion

Meaningful personas like Otto and Anna and the non-persona Carola are a very helpful tool for the design of systems, especially in terms of their functionality, interfaces and interaction mechanisms. Personas' age is connected to their technical skills and the level of technical skills itself influence the design of the user interfaces. One of the biggest challenges in TOPIC is to define simple and usable user interfaces to support not only experienced users but also the newbies. However, we do not lose sight of configurability and personalization, so to accommodate more advanced users.

Furthermore, the different time periods of caring for someone reflects on the different needs and expectations from the platform: people who are new to a care situation seek for information from experienced users and the experienced informal caregivers want to help by providing tips and advices. Mobility is a very important aspect we have to support both from the caregivers' and care receivers' point of view. In order to support mobility of caregivers, we have to think of wearable technologies equipped with GPS for the care receiver in the future work.

To conclude, social support provided by a community of peers or care professionals, different ways of communicating by using messages, notes, video and audio transmissions, information about legal, medical or care-related procedures and measures are some examples that call for a care-related protected multi-level platform like TOPIC *CarePortfolio*.

Acknowledgements. We would like to thank the AAL Joint Program for financial support, our participants for all the useful information they have been giving us, and our project partners for insightful ideas and productive discussions.

References

1. UNFPA.: Ageing in the Twenty-First Century: A celebration and A challenge. United Nations Population Fund (UNFPA), New York (2012)
2. Brouwer, W.B.F., van Exel, N.J.A., van de Berg, B., Dinant, H.J., Koopmanschap, M.A., van den Bos, G.A.M.: Burden of caregiving: evidence of objective burden, subjective burden, and quality of life impacts on informal caregivers of patients with rheumatoid arthritis. Arthritis Care Res. **51**(4), 570–577 (2004)
3. Chwalisz, K., Kisler, V.: Perceive stress: a better measure of carer burden. Measur. Eval. Couns. Dev. **28**, 88–98 (1995)
4. Schneider, U., Trukeschitz, B., Mühlmann, R., Jung, R., Ponocny, I., Katzlinger, M., Österle, A.: Wiener Studie zur informellen Pflege und Betreuung älterer Menschen 2008 (Vienna Informal Carer Study - VIC2008) Wirtschaftsuniversität Wien, Forschungsinstitut für Altersökonomie, p. 98 (2009)
5. Coon, D., Evans, B.: Empirically based treatments for family carers distress: what works and where do we go from hear. Geriatr. Nurs. **30**(6), 426–436 (2009)
6. Emlet, C.A.: Assessing the informal caregiver: Team member or hidden patient? Home Care Provid. **1**(5), 8 (1996)
7. Chen, Y., Ngo, V., Park, S.Y.: Caring for caregivers: designing for integrality. In: Proceedings of the 2013 conference on Computer supported cooperative work, San Antonio, Texas, USA, pp. 91–102. ACM
8. Breskovic, I., de Carvalho, A.F.P., Schinkinger, S, Tellioğlu, H.: Social awareness support for meeting informal carers' needs: early development in TOPIC. In: Adjunct Proceedings of the 13th European Conference on Computer Supported Cooperative Work (ECSCW 2013), Paphos, Cyprus. Department of Computer Science Aarhus University, Aarhus, Denmark, pp. 3–8 (2013)

9. Schinkinger, S., de Carvalho, A.F.P., Breskovic, I., Tellioğlu, H.: Exploring social support needs of informal caregivers. In: CSCW 2014 Workshop on Collaboration and Coordination in the Context of Informal Care (CCCiC 2014), Baltimore, MD, USA, February 15, 2014. TU-Wien, pp. 29–37 (2014)
10. LeRouge, C., Ma, J., Sneha, S., Tolle, K.: User profiles and personas in the design and development of consumer health technologies. Int. J. Med. Inform. 82(11), 18 (2013)
11. Cooper, A., Reimann, R., Cronin, D.: About Face 3: The Essentials of Interaction Design, 3rd edn. Wiley, USA (2007)
12. Moser, C., Fuchsberger, V., Neureiter, K., Sellner, W., Tscheligi, M.: Revisiting personas: the making-of for special user groups. In: CHI 2012 Extended Abstracts on Human Factors in Computing Systems Austin, Texas, USA, pp.453–468. ACM (2012)
13. CURE 2011: Results of Multivariate Analysis and CURE-Elderly-persona. Project Deliverable
14. Pruitt, J., Grudin, J.: Personas: practice and theory. In: DUX 2003 - Designing for User Experiences, p. 1–15. ACM (2003)
15. Bredies, K.: Using system analysis and personas for e-Health interaction design. In: Undisciplined Design Research Society Conference 2008, Sheffield Hallam University, Sheffield, UK (2009)
16. Benyon, D.: Designing Interactive Systems: A Comprehensive Guide to HCI and Interaction Design, 2nd edn, p. 712. Addison Wesley, USA (2010)
17. Klaver, C.C.W., Wolfs, R.C.W., Vingerling, J.R., Hofman, A., de Jong, P.T.V.M.: Age-specific prevalence and causes of blindness and visual impairment in an older population. Arch. Ophthalmol. 116(5), 6 (1998)
18. Burmedi, D., Becker, S., Heyl, V., Wahl, H.-W., Himmelsbach, I.: Behavioral consequences of age-related low vision. Vis. Impair. Res. 4(1), 30 (2002)
19. Picking, R., Robinet, A., Grout, V., McGinn, J., Roy, A., Ellis, S., Oram, D.: A case study using a methodological approach to developing user interfaces for elderly and disabled people. Comput. J. 53(6), 842–859 (2010)
20. del Río-Lozano, M., del Mar García-Calvente, M., Marcos-Marcos, J., Entrena-Durán, F., Maroto-Navarro, G.: Gender identity in informal care impact on health in spannish caregivers. Qual. Health Res. 23(11), 1506–1520 (2013)
21. Chepngeno-Langat, G., Madise, N., Evandrou, M., Falkingham, J.: Gender differentials on the health consequences of caregiving people with AIDS-related illness among older informal carers in two slums in Nairobi, Kenya. AIDS Care 23(12), 1586–1594 (2011)
22. Iezzoni, L.I., McCarthy, E.P., Davis, R.B., Siebens, H.: Mobility difficulties are not only a problem of old age. J. Gen. Intern. Med. 16(4), 9 (2001)
23. Neal, M.B., Ingersoll-Dayton, B., Starrels, M.E.: Gender and relationship differences in caregiving patterns and consequences among employed caregivers. Gerontol. 37(6), 13 (1997)
24. Robison, J., Fortinsky, R., Kleppinger, A., Shugrue, N., Porter, M.: A broader view of family caregiving: effects of caregiving and caregiver conditions on depressive symptoms, health, work, and social isolation. J. Gerontol.: Soc. Sci. 64B(6), 788–798 (2009)
25. White, H., McConnell, E., Clipp, E., Bynum, L., Teague, C., Navas, L., Craven, S., Halbrecht, H.: Surfing the net in later life: a review of the literature and pilot study of computer use and quality of life. J. Appl. Gerontol. 18, 21 (1999)

An Interaction Design Method to Support the Expression of User Intentions in Collaborative Systems

Cristiane Josely Jensen[1,3]([⊠]), Julio Cesar Dos Reis[1],
and Rodrigo Bonacin[1,2]

[1] FACCAMP, Rua Guatemala, 167, 13231-230
Campo Limpo Paulista, SP, Brazil
cris_jensen3@hotmail.com, julio.reis@faccamp.br,
rodrigo.bonacin@cti.gov.br
[2] Center for Information Technology Renato Archer, Rodovia Dom Pedro I,
km 143, 6, 13069-901 Campinas, SP, Brazil
[3] FAH, Rua Pr. Hugo Gegembauer, 265, Pq. Ortolândia, 13184-010
Hortolândia, SP, Brazil

Abstract. The communication and interpretation of users' intentions play a key role in collaborative web discussions. However, existing mechanisms fail to support the users' expression of their intentions during collaborations. In this article, we propose an original interaction design method based on semiotics to guide the construction of interactive mechanisms, which allow users to explicitly express and share intentions. We apply the method in a case study in the context of collaborative forums for software developers. The obtained results reveal preliminary evidences regarding the effectiveness of the method for the definition of interface components, enabling more meaningful and successful communications.

Keywords: Collaborative web · Intentions · Pragmatics · Collaboration · Interaction design · Organizational semiotics

1 Introduction

Collaborative web-based systems provide opportunities for lifelong learning and are no longer restricted to specific contexts of use [1]. The diversity and comprehensiveness of the web encompasses people with different physical constraints and from various cultural and social backgrounds, allowing them to share both professional and personal problems as well as solutions. This diversified context makes web-mediated communications increasingly complex, and requires advanced computational solutions to support more meaningful collaborations among users.

Various factors underlying collaborative discussions influence the interpretation of exchanged messages, which may prevent participants from easily sharing, managing, retrieving and exploring available content. In this context, pragmatic aspects of human communication, such as intentions, play a central role in enabling adequate

© Springer International Publishing Switzerland 2015
M. Kurosu (Ed.): Human-Computer Interaction, Part I, HCII 2015, LNCS 9169, pp. 214–226, 2015.
DOI: 10.1007/978-3-319-20901-2_20

collaboration support. During face-to-face communication, people explore a variety of mechanisms, such as facial expressions, gestures, inflection, etc. Nevertheless, people predominantly use written language when interacting via collaborative systems, which does not favor the clear expression of intentions, and other pragmatic aspects, in a way that participants can obtain successful communication.

The literature presents limited interactive solutions to support user expression and perception of intentions. For example, some approaches aim at analyzing audio feedback in controlled environments, while other studies focus on natural language text analysis to make user intentions more explicit through techniques of keyword tagging and metadata descriptions. However, existing approaches still demand a lot of user effort and are dependent on continuous monitoring of user activities. The complexity of the web requires more precise and effective approaches.

This research investigates the conception of an original Interaction Design (IxD) method that can lead to interactive solutions allowing users to efficiently communicate intentions with little effort. This article makes the following contributions: (1) we define and describe the Interaction Design for Intention Expression method (InDIE) demonstrating the phases and elements involved in the solution; and (2) we present a case study illustrating the application of the method in the design of prototypes. A total of 22 users participated in the activities in this study.

The InDIE method relies on empirical research studies of our previous work [1–3] aligned with techniques and concepts from Organizational Semiotics [4] (OS) and Speech Acts Theory [5] (SAT). The method is composed of five phases in an iterative (*i.e.,* phases occurring in small cycles) and interactive process, where design solutions are produced and analyzed with end-users.

The obtained results highlight the major advantages and limitations of the approach through an assessment of the proposed method via the case study. This study shows the potential benefits of the solution for supporting designers and users in their creation of meaningful interfaces for expressing the users' declared intentions.

We structure the remainder of this article as follows: Sect. 2 presents the related work as well as the methodological foundations; Sect. 3 details the proposed method; Sect. 4 describes the application of the method in a case study; Sect. 5 wraps up with concluding remarks and outlines future research.

2 Background

We present the related work followed by the methodological framework.

2.1 Pragmatic Web and Users' Intention Expression

The Semantic Web (SemWeb) stands for an extension of the current web [6] comprising meaning representation, sharing, and interpretation by artificial agents and humans. The Pragmatic Web (PragWeb) concept emerged to cope with several critical issues of the SemWeb [7]. PragWeb aims at investigating and capturing the complexity of social and human behavioral interaction via web-based technologies, which includes people's intentions, interests, and participation [7]. PragWeb includes less objective observable facts such as beliefs, norms, people's social and cultural background, as well as intentions.

Our systematic literature review emphasized the issues of detection and influence of intentions, as well as the design and communication of intentions, and explored indexed documents from ISI, IEEE, ACM and Scopus. The analysis revealed three categories closely related to our work. Category 1 refers to empirical examinations focused on understanding human behaviors, and points out a view of the users' behavior that must be considered. Category 2 presents methods for the recognition of user's intentions via an interface that maps onto alternatives that can be employed in design solutions. Category 3 encompasses investigations of pragmatic factors in the design and construction of interactive web systems. Table 1 summarizes the objectives and results of each study and denotes their category.

The existing studies highlight multidisciplinary research issues, including the need to deeply investigate communication on the Web, as well as to apply these studies to design methods and complex computational mechanism. Although the explored literature indicates various relevant aspects to be included in the design of systems that consider intentions and other pragmatic aspects, the related work lacks a proposal of design process that explicitly guides the construction of interfaces to communicate intentions, which is addressed in this research.

2.2 Methodological and Theoretical Framework

Organizational Semiotics and Pragmatics Communication Analysis. OS studies organizations and information systems using the Peirce theory of signs [16]. In OS, the organization concept is not only restricted to enterprises. It refers to a social system in which people behave in an organized manner. MEASUR (*Methods for Eliciting, Analyzing and Specifying Users' Requirements*) stands for a set of methods employed by the OS researchers [17]. In this work, we considered and adapted some of the methods from MEASUR, described as follows:

- *Stakeholder analysis (Organizational Onion).* The stakeholders are analyzed according to their involvement in the given problem. This includes an informal level where the intentions are understood and the beliefs are formed; a formal level where meanings and intentions are replaced by forms and rules; and a technical level where the formal system is automated by computers;
- *Semiotic framework (Semiotic diagnosis).* This method is used to examine the organization based on Stamper's six semiotic layers [17]. In addition to Morris' syntactic, semantic, and pragmatic Semiotic layers (*i.e.,* structures, meanings, and usage of signs), Stamper [17] proposed three additional layers: physical, empirical, and social world. While the *pragmatic layer* deals with the purposeful use of signs, intention, negotiation, and the behavior of agents, etc.; the *social layer* deals with the social consequences of using signs in human affairs, including beliefs, expectations, commitments, law, and culture.

In addition to these methods, we adopted the Liu [4] perspective of pragmatics, which is based on OS and Speech Act theory (SAT) [5]. In the *Pragmatics*

Table 1. Summary of the existing approaches

Cat	Objectives	Results	Ref
1	Examined the effects of distinct interface styles on users' perceptions and behavioral intention to accept/use computer systems	Interface styles indicated direct effects on the utility and perceived usability by users, which affected the intentional behavior of system usage	[8]
1	Identified the motivational behavioral factors influencing students' intention to participate in online discussion forums	The students' intentions to participate were positively influenced by hedonic outcome, utilitarian outcome, and peer pressure	[9]
2	Investigated the recognition of users' intentions in virtual environments, more specifically in a fight simulation	Highlighted the possibility of recognition of intentions by using virtual interfaces that monitor the users' behavior and compare with predefined actions models	[10]
2	Explored natural language interfaces, such as dialogue systems, in ambient assisted living. Their aim was to incorporate conversational agents that consider the external context of interaction and predict the user's state	A context-aware system, which adapts to the context of patients with chronic pulmonary diseases	[11]
2	Captured and interpreted users' search intentions to improve image based search engines	Use of visual information as a search parameter was described as positive, but dependent on extra user actions. The work also highlighted limitations on the use of a single image to express intentions	[12]
2	Proposed observation of users' behavior using pattern recognition of linguistic features via data mining techniques to gather user intentions	Data mining techniques can support the recognition of users' intentions	[13]
3	Automatic synthesis of user interfaces based on intentions captured by communication acts	The automatically generated interfaces showed good usability levels	[14]
3	Proposed a conceptual framework for interaction design based on the WebPrag concept	Contributions of the interaction design for the realization of WebPrag, such as the design of mechanisms for the materialization of intentions in user actions	[15]
3	Investigated the dynamic aspects of pragmatics in messages exchanged during collaborative problem solving	Presents the influences of intentions on Web collaboration and proposes an entire research framework	[1]

(Continued)

Table 1. (*Continued*)

Cat	Objectives	Results	Ref
3	Identified recurring situations of use that might require the design of solutions to facilitate or avoid the manifestation of a wrong interpretation in collaborative systems	A set of recurrent patterns detailing problems, examples and abstract design solutions	[3]

Communication Analysis, a communication act refers to the minimal unit of analysis. A communication act consists of a structure with three components: the speaker, the listeners, and the message. A message has two parts: the content manifests the meaning, while the function specifies the illocution, which reflects the intention of the speaker. The illocutions has three dimensions: *time* (*i.e.,* whether the effect is on the future or the present/past), *invention* (*i.e.,* if the illocution used in a communication act is inventive or instructive, it is called prescriptive, otherwise descriptive), and *mode* (*i.e.,* if it is related to expressing the personal modal state mood, such as feeling and judgment, then it is called affective, otherwise denotative).

Emotions and Meta-Communication. Emotions can affect the interpretation and meaning of a communication. According to [18] people express their emotions to establish a more sociable and friendly conversation. To minimize communication problems in online conversations, users explore various alternatives to express their emotions, including graphical tricks, pictures with text symbols, and emoticons.

Several studies show the benefits of using emoticons in communication. Emoticons are highly disseminated on *Instant Messaging* (IM) tools. They can produce positive effects on personal interaction, perceived usefulness, user satisfaction, among other benefits [19]. Hayashi [20] employed OS methods in participatory activities to identify requirements for tools with expressive components (*i.e.,* that express emotions) to support users via meta-communication mechanisms on inclusive social networks.

Based on these studies, we propose that emotions can be an alternative to express intentions in collaborative systems, which is originally explored in the method presented in the next section.

3   The InDIE Method

The InDIE method relies on preliminary studies [1] based on OS and SAT. These studies were important to elucidate how the theoretical framework would adequately support the method. InDIE is composed of five phases in which the design solutions are produced and validated with end-users in an interactive and iterative process. In each phase, we pay special attention to how to elucidate the pragmatic aspects so that they can be incorporated into the requirements for design interactive mechanisms. Dashed rectangles in Fig. 1 represent the five phases. Each phase is composed of specific activities. We detail the method as follows:

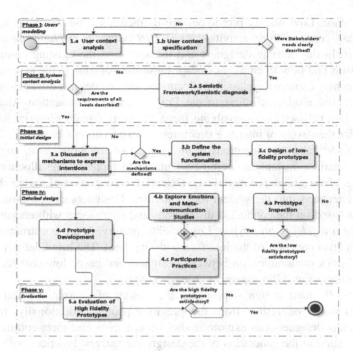

Fig. 1. Overview of the InDIE method

1. Phase I: *User modeling* – focuses on how end-users explore and make sense of information systems to communicate on a daily basis, and how they express intentions in collaborative tasks. This phase contains two activities: (1.a) *User context analysis*. It studies the users' context, their discussions in the collaborative systems and their location. Various activities can be used to elicit and understand the users' context, such as: interview techniques, focus groups, and participatory activities. The results should be formalized and summarized in order to be used in further activities. Designers may inquire about specific aspects of intentions via questions elaborated for this purpose. The questionnaire results are evaluated using statistical tools. (1.b) *User context specification*. This activity proposes the use of the organizational onion artifact [4], as well as the detailing of problems and stakeholders' needs. This is relevant in order to understand the way that stakeholders can communicate with each other and the types of intention elements they explore;

2. Phase II: *System context analysis* – emphasizes the analysis of the context where the systems will be used. This phase contains one activity: (2.a) *Semiotic Framework*. The requirements, problems, and possible solutions are grouped according to the semiotics levels. For each level, problems are elicited from the users and discussed collaboratively. The analysis of the pragmatic and social levels focuses on the investigation of problems due to misunderstanding of the users' intentions;

3. Phase III: *Initial design* – elicits from users the system functionalities where the pragmatics communication aspects are critical. Both users and designers discuss the benefits of having mechanisms to directly express intentions in each case of specific

user interface. Low fidelity prototypes are defined and constructed in this phase. This phase contains three activities: (3.a) *Discussion of mechanisms to express intentions*. In this activity designers and users discuss the existing computational mechanisms and how to employ or adapt these mechanisms to the system context. Designers may explore the classified illocutions and the defined dimensions of *time, invention,* and *mode* according to the Pragmatics Communication Analysis (*cf.* Section 2.2.1). Discussions involving these elements remain essential in order to materialize the design of interface structures for expression of intentions. End-users need to understand the illocutions in the context of collaboration to suggest how possible interface metaphors would be suitable to represent the illocutions. (3.b) *Definition of the system functionalities*. Discuss the integration of the mechanism to express intentions into the system functionalities. Designers can propose potential solutions based on the conducted discussions and share them with end-users. (3.c) *Design of low-fidelity prototypes*. Low-fidelity prototypes are constructed to evaluate high level concepts of the interface with the users. The low-fidelity prototypes enable a quick communication between designers and users, low-cost refinements, and detection of usability issues in an early stage.

4. Phase IV: *Detailed design* – proposes the design of alternatives and interface structures based on results from the previous phases. Additionally, this phase suggests that designers can explore studies on emotions and meta-communication, aiming to support the generation of the design alternatives. Practices with the users to discuss the design alternatives are also recommended. This phase contains four activities: (4.a) *Prototype Inspection*. The prototypes are deeply analyzed and examined with the users. Participatory evaluation, focal groups, interviews, among other techniques, can be used in this activity. Users can already detect whether their expectations regarding the mechanisms are materialized in the prototypes. (4.b) *Explore Emotions and Meta-communication Studies*. Determine possible design alternatives by exploring studies on emotions and meta-communication (*cf.* Sect. 2.2.2). For example, this activity includes the discussion of how to adapt interfaces and icons representing emotions for transmitting intentions. The illocutions can have representative emoticons that might make sense to users. (4.c) *Participatory Practices*. At this stage, the design decisions are more fine-grained and the design choices are duly documented. This action aims to define the adequate mechanisms discussed with end-users that would enable them to easily express intentions. (4.d) *Prototype Development*. Development of a high fidelity prototype and functional prototyping based on the previous decisions. Fast prototyping techniques and low incremental cycles should be used interactively;

5. Phase V: *Evaluation* –evaluates practices and proposes improvements for a next design cycle. This phase contains one activity: (5.a) *Evaluation of High Fidelity Prototypes*. This evaluation can be guided by key issues such as, if the design solutions enable users to explicitly express their intentions, and if users will make real use of these solutions. This evaluation may lead to the decision to take the mechanisms to the phase of implementation. Otherwise, designers would go back to Phase III.

4   A Case Study on Software Development Forums

This section presents the application of the InDIE method in a case study.

4.1   Context, Subjects, and Methodology

The case study examines the experimental evaluation of the InDIE method, and includes the identification of open issues in the design of mechanisms for intention sharing. The following questions guided the study: (1) To which extent can InDIE support the design of mechanisms to express intentions? and (2) What are the central strengths and deficiencies of InDIE?

First, we informally invited developers from the following programming forums: Clube do Hardware,[1] Clube da Programação,[2] Script Brasil[3] and GUJ.[4] Additional developers were personally invited according to their previous experiences and availability for face-to-face activities. We presented the participants a summary of the study, objectives, and subsequent activities. Afterwards, the participants answered an initial questionnaire with their profile.

Table 2 summarizes the key features from the participants' profile. A total of 22 developers participated in the study. These participants are from various parts of Brazil, have different experiences with using collaborative forums, and have different levels of programming skills. As shown in Table 2, the majority of the developers participated in the phases 1–2 of InDIE due to time restrictions.

Initially the designers interacted with the participants using distance communication technologies. We adopted the *Google Form*[5] tool for the questionnaires. A smaller group with users 1, 12, and 19 participated in face-to-face meetings according to the activity (*cf.* Table 2). In addition to face-to-face evaluation, designers constructed and digitalized the low fidelity prototypes (on paper) for distance evaluation. Supplementary tools including emails and online/video communication tools were also applied during the study.

4.2   Results and Discussion

The users' modeling analysis started with the application of two online questionnaires and interviews collecting information for the Organizational Onion (first phase). These activities contributed to the elicitation of stakeholders' needs as follows. The *informal level* presented a set of topics typically related to how users communicate using informal conventions, such as: What are the conditions for the community to accept the inclusion of a new topic on the forum?; and What is the commitment of a user to give a

---

[1] www.clubedohardware.com.br.

[2] www.clubedaprogramacao.com/.

[3] www.scriptbrasil.com.br.

[4] www.guj.com.br.

[5] www.google.com/Forms.

Table 2. Basic profile of the participants

N#	Age	Programming languages	Experience	Academic level	Employment position	Participation (Phases)
1	24	Java, C#, Delphi	1–5 year	MSc. Stud.	Scholarship	3–5
2	23	C#, VB, VB.net	5–10 year	Graduate	Director	1–2
3	30	Cobol, Abap	1–5 year	Graduate	System Analyst	1–2
4	27	C ++,C#, javascript	5–10 year	Graduate	System Analyst	1–2
5	32	Abap e Java	1–5 year	Graduate	Unemployed	1–2
6	25	Visual Basic	5–10 year	Specialist	System Analyst	1–2
7	21	php, Java, js	1–5 year	Undergra.	Web Develop.	1–2
8	22	C#,Delphi,Java	5–10 year	Graduate	Developer	1–2
9	27	C#,ActScr,Delphi	10+ year	Master	Proj. Manager	1–2
10	21	Html,Php,Python	5–10 year	Graduate	Developer	1–2
11	42	Python, Java	10+ year	Specialist	System Analyst	1–2
12	50	Java,Delphi,C ++	10+ year	Graduate	IT Manager	3–5
13	12	C, Python	1–5 year	Sec. School	Student	1–2
14	24	C,Pascal,Java	5–10 year	Undergra.	IT Technician	1–2
15	32	PHP, jQuery, Html	1–5 year	Graduate	Chief Develop.	1–2
16	30	Java,C#,VFoxPro	10+ year	Graduate	System Analyst	1–2
17	26	Java,C ++,Phyton	5–10 year	Graduate	System Analyst	1–2
18	34	Java	1–5 year	Specialist	Scholarship	1–2
19	35	Java, C, C#	10+ year	Master	Lecturer	3–5
20	19	.Net	less 1 year	Undergra.	Trainee	1–2
21	29	C#, Java, PHP	10+ year	Graduate	Owner	1–2
22	35	JS, C#, Java	10+ year	Graduate	IT Coordinator	1–2

solution? The *formal level* presented a set of topics on how the participants are aware of, and interpret the description of, the programming language problems, and how they formalize (express in a formal language) their intentions in the text. Finally, the *technical level* included questions about the software applications used to recover, share, and transmit questions and solutions.

The answers obtained during the first phase contributed to the identification of how stakeholders informally and formally interact with the collaborative system to transmit their intentions. These are key aspects to support subsequent steps, and the definition of the new mechanisms. For example, when we asked about the commitment of a user to present a solution, we are examining the strength of a prescriptive communication act (question) before determining a design solution to represent it. Similarly, at the formal level, we can analyze the way users express the prescriptive communication acts in writing language. The level of formalization can indicate, for example, whether or not it is acceptable to use icons embedded in the text (a design solution).

During the second phase, the semiotic framework guided the elicitation of requirements on all OS levels. The responses used to support structured interviews and discussions with users. The key topics addressed were:

1. Physical level. We analyzed the infrastructure necessary to access and host collaborative systems with solutions that support intention sharing. We verified if the design alternatives are feasible in terms of the existing computational resources, *e.g.*, the computational requirements for solutions with text interpretation algorisms;
2. Empirical level. We investigated the data transmission availability and throughput requirements to share intentions. This includes, for instance, the viability of sharing multimedia artifacts;
3. Syntactic level. We took into account the protocols, syntactic conventions, codes, and language structures used to transmit intentions in collaborative systems. This level includes, for example, the analysis of codification/programming limitations for implementing a proposed design solution, as well as syntactic conventions for expressing intentions in a formal language;
4. Semantic level. We examined the meanings of signs in the interfaces to represent and share intentions. A key aspect is whether the meanings of the interface components in the design candidates are correctly interpreted by the users or not;
5. Pragmatic level. We investigated if the participants' intentions are effectively shared in the collaborative systems. This level includes the analysis of how users share intentions in the existing systems, and the identification of limitations and misunderstandings. With respect to the initial design alternatives we were also interested in how the participants could share intentions;
6. Social level. We analyzed the consequences on the agents' social behavior as a function of whether or not they shared their intentions in the existing systems. At this level, designers examined the potential social consequences of a prospective design.

In general, the semiotic framework contributed with the elicitation of issues such as: (1) many existing systems are basically restricted by the use of textual language; (2) many novice users do not understand the technical language used by expert users; and (3) programming codes shared by users are frequent causes of misunderstanding among the participants.

During the third phase, the participants were informed about the importance of sharing intentions in collaborative work, and then we discussed design alternatives. Low fidelity prototypes materialized the initial proposals. These prototypes included basic elements using emoticons (adapted to represent intentions) and meta-communication, which clarified how to express intentions in the proposed interface.

Figure 2a presents a low fidelity prototype of a Web form to post questions on a "generic" collaborative forum. The prototype included boxes to represent the writer's mood and a meta-communication area.

In the fourth phase, the designer defined a high fidelity prototype based on the low fidelity prototypes and design alternatives established as a result of participatory practices. During the prototype inspection (4.a), the participants proposed to move the emotions from the "format bar" to the right side as shown in Fig. 2b. The users

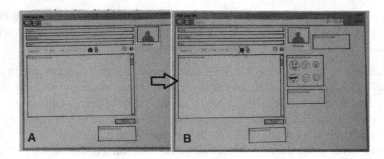

Fig. 2. Evolution of the low fidelity prototypes during the phases of InDIE

suggested additional meta-communication boxes to accommodate information close to the mechanism.

Figure 3 presents a prototype containing three mechanisms, in which users can optionally express intentions, as follows. (1) Associate a phase with a color according to a predefined palette. In this palette "cool colors" are denotative and "warm colors" are affective illocutions. (2) Use icons (named *intenticons*) in the text. Users can choose these icons from a predefined set. (3) Associate a selected illocution (from the text) with dimensions using "range sliders". In the proposal, these dimensions are also displayed to the readers when the mouse hovers over the given mechanism.

We started the fifth phase with a preliminary evaluation in which the prototype was informally presented to users and other designers. Although the participants agreed on the general structure of the interface, they pointed out the need to advance the design of the proposed mechanisms. For example, they suggested the definition of a more representative set of icons. Consequently, we have to go back to the third phase.

This case study remains limited in the following major aspects: (1) it does not evaluate the effectiveness of the produced interface in real cases, and (2) it fails to directly compare the InDIE with other methods. Despite these limitations, the study was able to present how each InDIE phase contributed to the design of an interface mechanism, as well as how we considered users' opinions and participation in the

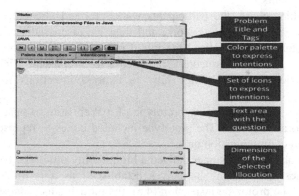

Fig. 3. High fidelity prototype proposed in the fourth phase

design decisions. The case study also pointed out the need for further research, including the study of (semi-)automatic methods that could suggest the positions of the proposed "range sliders".

5 Conclusion

The expression of intentions plays a central role in human communication. Collaborative systems (*e.g.*, programming forums) are typically restricted to textual communication, which leads to misunderstandings and difficulties in the collaborative process. We proposed the InDIE method aiming to guide designers in the construction of interactive mechanisms that support users' expression of their intentions in collaborative systems. The InDIE method was instantiated in the context of programming forums, and this research achieved a high fidelity prototype with the participation of 22 users. The results highlighted the potential of the mechanisms.

As next steps, the goal is to carry out detailed studies to determine a set of representative icons to express intentions, and to conduct a controlled experiment to verify the effectiveness of the proposed interface by comparing it to interfaces without the mechanisms. We also aim to improve InDIE by conducting new case studies with other collaborative contexts and users.

References

1. Bonacin, R., Hornung, H., Reis, J.C., Pereira, R., Baranauskas, M.C.C.: Pragmatic aspects of collaborative problem solving: towards a framework for conceptualizing dynamic knowledge. In: Cordeiro, J., Maciaszek, L.A., Filipe, J. (eds.) ICEIS 2012. LNBIP, vol. 141, pp. 410–426. Springer, Heidelberg (2013)
2. Bonacin, R., Reis, J.C., Hornung, H., Baranauskas, M.C.C.: An ontological model for supporting intention-based information sharing on collaborative problem solving. Int. J. Collaborative Enterp. 3(2–3), 130–150 (2013)
3. Hornung, H.H., Pereira, R., Baranauskas, M.C.C., Bonacin, R., Reis, J.C.: Identifying pragmatic patterns of collaborative problem solving. In: Proceedings of IADIS International Conference WWW/Internet 2012, pp. 379–387 (2012)
4. Liu, K.: Semiotics in Information Systems Engineering. Cambridge University Press, Cambridge (2000)
5. Searle, J.R.: A classification of illocutionary acts. Lang. Soc. 5(1), 1–23 (1976)
6. Berners-Lee, T., Hendler, J., Lassila, O.: The semantic web. Sci. Am. 284(5), 34–43 (2001)
7. Singh, M.P.: The pragmatic web. IEEE Internet Comput. 6(3), 4–5 (2002)
8. Hasan, B., Ahmed, M.U.: Effects of interface style on user perceptions and behavioral intention to use computer systems. Comput. Hum. Behav. 23(6), 3025–3037 (2007)
9. Yang, X., Li, Y., Tan, C., Teo, H., et al.: Students' participation intention in an online discussion forum: why is computer-mediated interaction attractive? Inf. Manag. 44(5), 456–466 (2007)
10. Goss, S., Heinze, C.A., Pearce, A.: Recognising user intentions in a virtual environment. In: Proceedings of the Simulation Technology and Training Conference, pp. 247–254 (1999)

11. Griol, D., Molina, J., Callejas, Z.: Modeling the user state for context-aware spoken interaction in ambient assisted living. Appl. Intell. **40**(4), 749–771 (2014)
12. Tang, X., Liu, K., Cui, J., Wen, F., Wang, X.: IntentSearch: capturing user intention for one-click internet image search. IEEE Trans. Pattern Anal. Mach. Intell. **34**(7), 1342–1353 (2012)
13. Chen, Z., Lin, F., Liu, H., Liu, Y., Ma, H., Wenyin, L.: User intention modeling in web applications using data mining. World Wide Web **5**(3), 181–191 (2002)
14. Falb, J., et al.: Using communicative acts in interaction design specifications for automated synthesis of user interfaces. In: 21st IEEE/ACM International Conference on Automated Software Engineering (2006)
15. Hornung, H., Baranauskas, M.C.C.: Towards a conceptual framework for interaction design for the pragmatic web. In: Jacko, J.A. (ed.) Human-Computer Interaction, Part I, HCII 2011. LNCS, vol. 6761, pp. 72–81. Springer, Heidelberg (2011)
16. Peirce, C.S.: Collected Papers. Harvard University Press, Cambridge, USA (1931–1958)
17. Stamper, R.K.: Information in Business and Administrative Systems. Wiley, New York (1973)
18. Neviarouskaya, A., Prendinger, H., Ishizuka, M.: EmoHeart: Conveying Emotions in Second Life Based on Affect Sensing from Text, pp. 1–13. Hindawi Publishing Corporation, Cairo (2010)
19. Huang, A.H., Yen, D.C., Zhang, X.: Exploring the potential effects of emoticons. Inf. Manage. **45**(7), 466–473 (2008)
20. Hayashi, E.C.S., Baranauskas, M.C.C.: Understanding meta-communication in an inclusive scenario. In: Proceedings of the 2010 ACM Symposium on Applied Computing, pp. 1213–2328 (2010)

Usability, Quality in Use and the Model of Quality Characteristics

Masaaki Kurosu[✉]

The Open University of Japan, Chiba, Japan
masaakikurosu@spa.nifty.com

Abstract. In this paper, a history of usability concept is reviewed including Shackel and Richardson, Nielsen, and ISO standards to show how the usability is located among relevant quality characteristics. Secondly, the importance of subjective quality is emphasized in relation to the usability. Thirdly, the concept of quality in use is considered in relation to the usability. Finally, a new scheme on quality characteristics is presented.

Keywords: Usability · Quality in use · Quality characteristics · ISO standards

1 Introduction

The UX is now a buzzword. But the concept of usability is still very important even though the connotation of UX is much wider than usability. In this paper, the author presents the historical review of usability concept, the emphasis on subjective quality, the difference between the usability and the quality in use are discussed and finally a new scheme on quality characteristics is presented.

2 Historical Review of Usability

One of the important characteristics of artifacts that constitute the everyday experience of the user is the usability. Artifacts are made to be used. All the hardware, the software and the humanware (i.e. services) are used to expand the range of our experience, thus the ability for use, i.e. the usability is very much important. Artifacts that are difficult to use will have a little meaning and will lead to the dissatisfaction.

2.1 Shackel and Richardson

In academia, the concept of usability was first systematically defined by Shackel and Richardson (1991). They listed up three positive aspects of artifacts; utility, usability and likeability, to be important. The utility means that the artifact will do what is needed functionally. In other words, it is the functionality that matches to the users' need. The usability means the degree of the success that the user can work with the artifact. The success can be regarded as the same with the goal achievement. The likeability, a coinage by authors, is similar to the subjective feeling of suitability, thus

© Springer International Publishing Switzerland 2015
M. Kurosu (Ed.): Human-Computer Interaction, Part I, HCII 2015, LNCS 9169, pp. 227–237, 2015.
DOI: 10.1007/978-3-319-20901-2_21

will lead to the satisfaction. On the other hand, there is a negative aspect, the cost, including the initial cost and the running cost. The balance between the sum of utility, usability and likeability and the cost will affect the degree of acceptance, or the acceptability. If the former is equal to or larger than the latter, the artifact will be accepted and be purchased and used.

The significance of their model lies in that the usability is regarded as one of the important aspects of the artifact. But they didn't specify the relative importance among utility, usability and likeability. In other words, if an artifact may have a high degree of utility and likeability and the sum of the two will exceed the cost, there is a question if the artifact will be accepted even though it has a low level of usability. There must be a kind of absolute threshold for each of utility, usability, likeability and cost. Furthermore, not such other characteristics as performance, safety, reliability, compatibility, etc. than utility, usability, likeability and cost are not included. There is a question whether utility, usability, likeability and cost are more important than performance, safety, reliability, compatibility, etc. or not.

2.2   Nielsen

Following Shackel and Richardson, Nielsen (1993) proposed a hierarchical model of acceptability including the usability. In his model, the influence of Shackel and Richardson can be seen. At the top, the system acceptability is located that is split into the social acceptability and the practical acceptability. The latter consists of cost, compatibility, maintenance, reliability, safety and usefulness. The usefulness is composed of the utility and the usability where the latter is further divided into the sub-characteristics such as learnability, efficiency, memorability, errors and satisfaction.

His model is more acceptable than the one proposed by Shackel and Richardson because the structure of quality characteristics are more systematically described and the location of usability is clearly specified. But we'll have to take care that Nielsen is also the one who proposed the heuristic evaluation method. In other words, learnability and other sub-characteristics below the usability are focal points when that method is applied for evaluating the usability of artifacts. In other words, the learnability, for example, means having less problems regarding the learning. Likewise, with the exception of satisfaction, all sub-characteristics under the usability are proposed for detecting the usability problems. That is, these sub-characteristics are directing towards the zero level from the negative (minus) level. On the contrary, the utility that can be presumed as consisting of the functionality and the performance is directing towards the plus zone from the zero level because having some functionalities or higher performance can be accepted by users positively.

This reflects the situation of the usability engineering in 80 s and 90 s when managers and engineers were directed more to the utility than to the usability. Furthermore, there is another problem that the components of usability are not systematically chosen and do not cover all relevant characteristics. For example, the ease of cognition including the visual size of the target, the contrast of the target against the background, etc. is not included.

2.3   ISO9241-11

In 1998, ISO9241-11 was standardized. In this standard, the definition of usability is the "Extent to which a product can be used by specified users to achieve specified goals with effectiveness, efficiency and satisfaction in a specified context of use" where the effectiveness is defined as "Accuracy and completeness with which users achieve specified goals", the efficiency is defined as "Resources expended in relation to the accuracy and completeness with which users achieve goals" and the satisfaction is defined as "Freedom from discomfort, and positive attitudes towards the use of the product". This definition was quite influential in TC159 (Ergonomics) and was referred later in such standards as ISO13407:1999, ISO18529:2000, ISO16982:2002, ISO18152:2003, ISO9241-210:2010 and ISO20282 series with minor changes in some cases.

In the Annex B of ISO9241-11, there is a list of measures for overall usability, desired properties of the product, and some others, with the measures of effectiveness that is mostly the number or the percentage, measures of efficiency as the time and measures of satisfaction as the rating scale. This list shows that the effectiveness and the efficiency as usability components can be objectively measured while the satisfaction can be subjectively measured.

According to Bevan (2001), the origin of the concept of usability in this standard was defined at ISO TC159/SC4/WG5 meeting in 1988 as "the degree to which specified users can achieve specified goals in a particular environment effectively, efficiently, comfortably and in an acceptable manner" and "the word satisfaction was introduced for simplifying the definition as 'freedom from discomfort and positive attitudes towards the use of the product' to have essentially the same meaning as the phrase 'comfortably and in an acceptable manner'". But the author cannot understand the reason why the satisfaction was included as a part of usability even though it is a very important aspect. It could have been included in the model as an independent characteristic as in the case of Shackel and Richadson's likeability.

The model describes the dynamic process on how the usability and its measures can be located. But we will have to be careful that usability measures are not mutually exclusive and collectively exhaustive (MECE) with each other. Especially, they are not independent with each other. Firstly, the efficiency cannot be measured when the goal was not achieved, hence the efficiency is dependent on the effectiveness. Secondly, the satisfaction will be experienced when the effectiveness and the efficiency are satisfactory and furthermore, it will be influenced by other such characteristics as reliability, safety, beauty, etc. hence the satisfaction is dependent on all these characteristics. Thus the author has been using only the effectiveness and the efficiency as the measures of usability.

2.4   Kurosu-1

Within the scope of ISO9241-11, Kurosu (2005) proposed the model of goal achievement as in Fig. 1. This model describes the effectiveness and the efficiency in the context of the goal achievement.

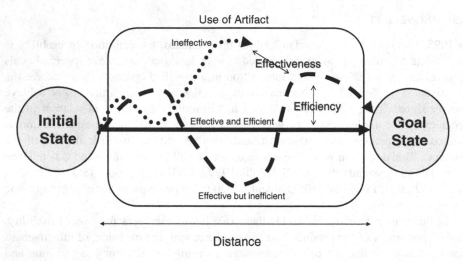

Fig. 1. Model of goal achievement by Kurosu (2005)

The dotted line ends up on the way to the goal and this suggests the occurrence of the error or the user being puzzled. It means that the use of an artifact is ineffective in this case. The dashed line reaches the goal and represents the effectiveness, but it took a winding path thus is inefficient. It suggests that there was a trial and error. The straight line that reaches the goal in the shortest path means it is effective and efficient.

Anyway, this figural representation only describes the usability concept proposed in ISO9241-11. No other such quality characteristics as reliability, safety, compatibility are not included here.

2.5   ISO9241-210

ISO13407 that adopted the definition of usability of ISO9241-11 was standardized in 1999 and focused on the human centered design. It was then revised into ISO9241-210 in 2010. The definition of usability in ISO9241-210 (2010) is expanded to include the "system, product or service" from that of ISO9241-11 that was applied only to the product. In other words, ISO9241-210 covers almost all kinds of the artifact.

3   Subjective Quality Characteristics

Although the usability is very important for the artifact, some researchers also pointed out the importance of subjective quality. As an example, we saw that the likeability was juxtaposed with the usability by Shackel and Richardson in a similar sense to the satisfaction. We also found that the satisfaction was located as a component of usability in the concept structure of Nielsen and ISO9241-11. The question here is whether such subjective quality as the satisfaction be independent to the usability or be included in the usability.

3.1   Jordan

Jordan (1998, 2000) proposed a three-layered hierarchical model composed of functionality, usability and pleasure. According to Jordan, the functionality is the fundamental characteristics for a product. But the usability is also important in order for the function to be used (effectively and efficiently). His idea is more than that. He put the pleasure atop of functionality and usability, because it makes the product attractive. Then he differentiated four types of pleasure, namely, physio-pleasure, socio-pleasure, psycho-pleasure and ideo-pleasure.

The pleasure as the subjective quality characteristics is similar to the notion of satisfaction in the ideas of Nielsen and ISO9241-11, but is different from them in the sense that it is differentiated from the usability and is an independent concept. In this sense, his idea is more similar to that of likeability by Shackel and Richardson, but is more marked as being positioned at the top of other quality characteristics.

3.2   Hassenzahl

A clear differentiation between the objective quality characteristics and the subjective quality characteristics was done by Hassenzahl (2003). Using his terminology, he distinguished pragmatic attributes from hedonic attributes. Hedonic attributes is his unique terminology but has something common to the subjective quality characteristics.

3.3   Kurosu-2

For the purpose of integrating the concept of Nielsen and ISO9241-11 and clarifying the conceptual location of satisfaction, Kurosu (2006) proposed a model in Fig. 2. There are several ideas embedded in this figure.

(a) The small usability consisting of the ease of cognition and the ease of operation is a part of the big usability.
(b) The big usability includes the utility as well as the small usability.
(c) The concept of (big) usability has two sub-concepts: effectiveness and efficiency.
(d) Unlike ISO9241-11, the satisfaction is located far above of all relevant quality characteristics.
(e) There are objective quality characteristics such as reliability, cost, safety, compatibility and maintenance as well as the usability.
(f) On the other hand, there are subjective quality characteristics such as pleasure, joy, beauty, attachment, (matching for) motivation, and (matching for) value.
(g) All these quality characteristics are put together to the satisfaction.

3.4   Satisfaction

According to OED (third edition), the satisfaction is defined as "The action of gratifying (an appetite or desire) to the full, or of contenting (a person) by the fulfilment of a desire or the supply of a want. The fact of having been thus gratified or contented". The important

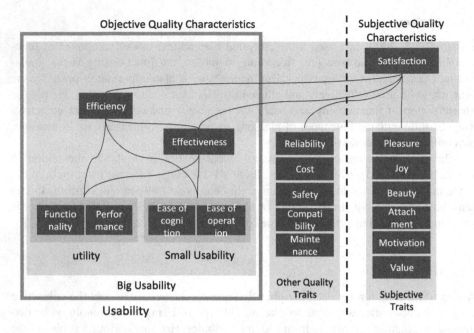

Fig. 2. A model of quality characteristics proposed by Kurosu (2006)

keyword here is "full". In other words, there is a certain mental space to be filled in the human need or want. People recognize something as attractive when it seems to fill their need of want. And they tend to try to do something to get it so that the space will be filled. That is the motivation mechanism of the human being. The room to be filled could be in terms of many quality characteristics including both of objective and subjective ones, i.e. usability, reliability etc. and novelty, scarcity and beauty and cuteness.

The mechanism of need-fulfillment is rather the multiplication than the addition. Take an example of objective quality characteristics and subjective quality characteristics. In the additive model, the lack on one side can be filled by other side so that the sum of the two will exceed the threshold for acceptance. But the fact is not just so. Because the lack of subjective quality characteristics, for example, cannot be filled by the high level of objective quality characteristics. Instead, the mechanism is more of the multiplication. The low level (e.g. 0.3 where $0<=level<=1$) on one side cannot be supplement by the high level (e.g. 0.8) on the other side, thus $0.3 \times 0.8 = 0.24$. Even if it is not the simple multiplication, the minimum rule can be applied instead to give the result of $0.3 = minimum (0.3, 0.8)$. This kind of logic can be viewed in Kano's theory of attractive quality.

3.5 Kano's Theory of Attractive Quality

Taking the satisfaction as a dependent variable, Kano et al. (1984) distinguished the attractive quality and must-be quality in relation to the needs fulfillment as an independent variable. Must-be quality will give the dissatisfaction to users when it is not fulfilled. Even when it is fulfilled, it doesn't give users a high level of satisfaction. On the contrary, the attractive quality will be accepted even when it is not fulfilling the user needs, but when its degree of fulfillment grows it will give the user an excitement and satisfaction.

A typical example is that usability, reliability and safety as well as ordinary functionalities are must-be qualities while new functionality and good design can be perceived as attractive.

For this reason, managers, planners, engineers and designers tend to focus more on the attractive quality than on the must-be quality. But the important point is that the attractive quality can be attractive only when must-be quality as a fundamental is fulfilled. The attractive quality without any considerations on the must-be quality is a quasi-attractiveness.

3.6 Usability and Utility

A similar relationship between attractive quality and must-be quality can be found between utility and usability. The relation between utility and usability is not an addition but a multiplication. That is, the lack of usability cannot be compensated by the utility. Thus, we will have to build up a stable usability when we are developing a new functionality and improving the performance.

4 Quality in Use

Although Kurosu (2006) dealt with many quality characteristics, the artifact's quality and the quality in use were not clearly separated in his model. The artifact's quality is the quality characteristics of the artifact itself and can be measured without consider-ations on the user's specific traits and the contextual information of the actual use of the artifact. In terms of the quality of software, ISO/IEC9126-1:1991 made a distinction between the internal quality and the external quality. The Internal quality is defined as "the totality of characteristics of the software product from an internal view and is measured and evaluated against the internal quality requirements". And the external quality is "the quality when the software is executed, which is typically measured and evaluated while testing in a simulated environment with simulated data using external metrics". This notion of the quality of software can be expanded to all kinds of artifact.

On the other hand, the quality in use is "the user's view of the quality of the software product when it is used in a specific environment and a specific context of use" according to the standard.

The key difference between the artifact's quality and the quality in use is that the former is the quality of the artifact TO BE used while the quality in use is the quality of the artifact DURING the use. Conceptually this relationship can be described as

Quality in Use = f (Quality of the Artifact, User, Context)

where the Quality of the Artifact is the sum of the internal quality and the external quality, and the Context includes the environment and the situation. And this relationship is important when we think of the UX.

4.1   ISO/IEC9126-1

ISO/IEC9126-1 was first standardized in 1991 based on the thorough study of (objective) quality characteristics. While ISO9241-11 was standardized by TC159 of ISO on the ergonomics, ISO/IEC9126-1 was standardized by JTC1 (Joint Technical Committee 1) of ISO on the information technology to "develop worldwide Information and Communication Technology (ICT) standards for business and consumer applications". Because of this reason, ISO/IEC9126-1 was standardized in terms of the software and was not intended to be applied to the hardware and the humanware. But the author thinks that the fundamental idea of this standard can be applied to all kinds of artifacts.

In this standard, there are functionality, reliability usability, efficiency, maintainability and portability included as quality characteristics each of which has a list of sub-quality characteristics on the side of the internal and external quality (left) and there are effectiveness, productivity, safety and satisfaction on the side of the quality in use (right).

An interesting point in comparison with ISO9241-11 is that the sub-concepts of usability in ISO9241-11, i.e. the effectiveness, the efficiency and the satisfaction are split into the left side and the right side. Furthermore, the productivity on the right side is a generic concept and will be affected by the effectiveness (and possibly by the efficiency too).

4.2   ISO/IEC25010

ISO/IEC9126-1 was abolished and was renewed into ISO/IEC25010 in 2011. The quality model was changed. There are many changes from ISO/IEC9126-1 among which major ones are that the title of the left side was changed from "internal and external quality" to "system/software product quality" and that all the sub quality characteristics of usability in ISO9241-11 were moved to the right (quality in use). But it's quite confusing that the sub quality characteristics of usability, i.e. effectiveness, efficiency and satisfaction, were all moved to the side of the quality in use even though the usability is still located on the left side, i.e. the product quality.

5   A Model of Quality Characteristics

5.1   Kurosu-3

Kurosu (2014) proposed his latest model as in Fig. 3 based on his previous model in Fig. 2 and the some concepts of ISO/IEC25010. This figure contains such ideas as follows:

(a) There are the artifact quality (the product quality in ISO/IEC25010) and the quality in use. Hence the usability is different from the quality in use.
(b) There are objective quality characteristics and subjective quality characteristics.
(c) As a result, there are objective artifact quality and subjective artifact quality on the left side and objective quality in use and subjective quality in use on the right side.

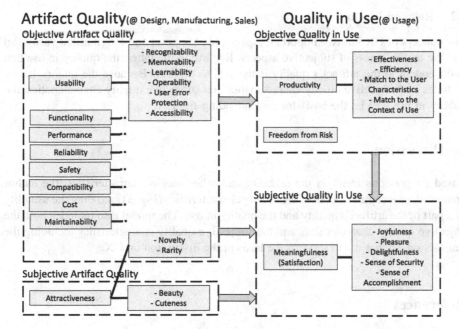

Fig. 3. Quality model of Kurosu (2014)

(d) Objective artifact quality includes those quality characteristics that were included in the list of ISO/IEC25010. In Fig. 3, all the sub-characteristics are suppressed for the purpose of simplicity regarding functionality, performance, reliability, safety, compatibility, cost, and maintainability. For the sub-characteristics on these quality characteristics, ISO/IEC25010 can be referred.

(e) Novelty and scarcity were added because they are objective but can be categorized as the part of attractiveness.

(f) Subjective artifact quality is the attractiveness that includes beauty and cuteness as well as novelty and scarcity.

(g) Objective quality in use consists of the productivity and the freedom from risk where the former includes effectiveness and efficiency. In terms of the position of productivity, the author thinks it is more reasonable to summarize all relevant sub-quality characteristics into it.

(h) Subjective quality in use is the satisfaction and also is the meaningfulness. These two characteristics are almost identical because something meaningful will bring the satisfaction and the artifact that satisfies users will be regarded as meaningful.

(i) Under the subjective quality in use, such Kansei quality characteristics as joyfulness, pleasure, and delightfulness and some more are included.

(j) Objective artifact quality will influence the objective quality in use and the subjective quality in use.

(k) Subjective artifact quality will influence the subjective quality in use.

(l) Furthermore, objective quality in use will influence subjective quality in use. Thus the satisfaction (meaningfulness) can be regarded as the utmost quality characteristic.

5.2   Relationship to the UX

The concept of UX has two important aspects; the temporal and longitudinal viewpoint and the inclusiveness of subjective aspects. Regarding the latter, the quality in use that is dependent to the artifact's quality is the key to the UX. Because the quality in use includes both objective quality characteristics and subjective quality characteristics, the quality in use will be the basis for understanding the UX.

6   Discussion

Based on previous ideas on the usability and other quality characteristics, the author presented a conceptual model of the quality characteristics (Fig. 3) including the usability as a part of the artifact's quality and the quality in use. The model also includes both the objective quality characteristics and the subjective quality characteristics including the satisfaction, so that it will serve as the basis of the discussion on UX.

References

Bevan, N.: Personal Communication (2001)

Hassenzahl, M.: The thing and I: understanding the relationship between user and product. In: Blythe, M., Overbeeke, C., Monk, A.F., Wright, P.C. (eds.) Funology: From Usability to Enjoyment, pp. 31–42. Kluwer, Dordrecht (2003)

ISO/IEC 13407:1999. Human-Centred Design Processes for Interactive Systems (1999)

ISO/TR 16982:2002. Ergonomics of Human-System Interaction – Usability Methods Supporting Human Centred Design (2002)

ISO/PAS 18152:2003. Ergonomics of Human-System Interaction – Specification for the Process Assessment of Human-System Issues (2003)

ISO/TR 18529:2000. Ergonomics of Human-System Interaction – Human Centred Lifecycle Process Descriptions (2000)

ISO 20282-1:2006. Ease of Operation of Everyday Products – Part 1: Design Requirements for Context of Use and User Characteristics (2006)

ISO/IEC 25010:2011. Systems and Software Engineering – Systems and Software Product Quality Requirements and Evaluation (SQuaRE) – System and Software Quality Models (2011)

ISO/IEC 9126-1:2001. Software Engineering – Product Quality – Part 1: Quality Model (2001)

ISO 9241-11:1998. Ergonomic Requirements for Office Work with Visual Display Terminals (VDTs) – Part 11: Guidance on Usability ISO TC159/SC4/WG5. WG5 Usability Assurance Sub Group, London Meeting Report (1998)

ISO 9241-210:2010. Ergonomics of Human-System Interaction - Human-Centred Design for Interactive Systems (2010)

Jordan, P.W.: An Introduction to Usability. Taylor & Francis, London (1998)

Jordan, P.W.: Designing Pleasurable Products – An Introduction to the New Human Factors. Taylor & Francis, London (2000)

Kano, N., Sera, N., Takahashi, F., Tsuji, S.: Attractive Q. Must-be Qual. Hinshitsu 14(2), 39–48 (1984). (in Japanese)

Kurosu, M.: How cultural diversity be treated in the interface design? A case study of e-learning system. In: HCI International 2005 (2005)

Kurosu, M.: Human centered design – understanding of user and evaluation of usability. In: HQL Seminar (2005) (in Japanese)

Kurosu, M.: New horizon of user engineering and HCD. HCD-Net J (2006)

Kurosu, M.: A tentative model for kansei processing – a projection model of kansei quality. In: KEER 2010 Conference Proceedings (2010)

Kurosu, M.: Re-considering the concept of usability. In: Keynote speech at APCHI2014 conference (2014)

Kurosu, M., Hashizume, A.: Concept of Satisfaction. In: KEER 2014 Conference Proceedings (2014)

Nielsen, J.: Usability Engineering. Academic Press, Waltham (1993)

Shackel, B., Richardson, S.J. (eds.): Human Factors for Informatics Usability. Cambridge University Press, Cambridge (1991)

Creating Personas to Reuse on Diversified Projects

Andrey Araujo Masiero[1,2](✉) and Plinio Thomaz Aquino Jr.[1]

[1] Centro Universitário da FEI - Fundação Educacional Inaciana Pe. Sabóia de Medeiros, São Paulo, Brazil
{amasiero,plinio.aquino}@fei.edu.br
[2] Universidade Metodista de São Paulo, São Paulo, Brazil

Abstract. This paper presents an automatized creation process for Personas user modeling focus on minimize stereotyping and to increase Persona's reuse on many different projects. This creation process has focus on similarity and automation which, are some main issues of variation from project to project. We discuss this process applying it on two different projects. First is a medical web system (HCI-M) and the second one is a human-robot interaction project with Sony AIBO pet robot (HRI-P). Results show that the process makes possible to minimize the stereotyping and also we reuse Personas from project HCI-M to help us on planning phase of project HRI-P which, turns it practicable.

Keywords: QSIM · Clustering · User modeling · Personas

1 Introduction

Worries about users during product development are more frequent on design and software teams nowadays [10]. To become possible to develop products focus on users is necessary, first, to comprehend them. For understanding users is required to identify their needs, motivations, objectives, skills, and among others features which, will help us to define the target audience profile [1,4,10].

Jung discuss on his work [9] that a person can adopt different personalities according to a certain scenario. This capability Jung calls as Personas. Cooper describes Personas as hypothetical archetypes once it proves that a Persona really represents real users of a launching product [3].

However, user modeling with Personas has as objective to increase communication between project teams. Exchange information is favored due to Persona is like a fictitious character who has name, biographic description and even a picture to illustrate it. In that way, designers and developers can focus on user's features only and saving efforts to create user models using thoughts about how they think that final users are going to be. This is important because avoid bias user models from project team [1].

When designer creates some product and pay attention on needs and behavior of a certain Persona, he will be attending a biggest number of real product users.

M. Kurosu (Ed.): Human-Computer Interaction, Part I, HCII 2015, LNCS 9169, pp. 238–247, 2015.
DOI: 10.1007/978-3-319-20901-2_22

Thus, many works present methods to create Personas [7,12,15]. Nevertheless, biggest part of these works are manual and can lead this process with bias or stereotyped according to specialist experience. One way to minimize the bias on Personas creation process is to use clustering algorithms and then to perform statistical data analysis for finding relevant information and most similar users between each other. This paper presents a whole process for creating Personas using a clustering algorithm as a support tool and how to reuse the Personas created on diversified projects.

Clustering algorithm brings some benefits for reuse process and it is main focus of this paper. Some benefits which, can be mentioned here is the automation process and high speed during data mining from project HCI-M to project HRI-P. Another important thing to consider is that on some project the difference between one project to another is the similarity between them. It influences directly the number of personas created on the project.

This paper goes first with the explanation of the whole process for creating Personas and each step of the process explains particularities of two real projects that we applied it. First project was a web system developed for a hospital (Project HCI-M) and the second one is applied for human-robot interaction proposals (Project HRI-P). After that, we discuss some ideas presented during the description of process. In the end, we present conclusions and future works about creation and reuse of Personas.

2 Creating Personas

Many projects present methods for creating Personas [7,12,15]. However, the biggest part of these projects present a manual process that can lead to create bias Personas or stereotyped ones, in other words, according to specialist experience. One way to minimize the bias on creation process is the use of clustering algorithms and after this to perform statistical data analysis to find most relevant information and subjects with biggest similarity between each other. That way, a process for creating Personas with six basics steps presented on Fig. 1.

2.1 Step 1 - User Information Collection

Many methods are used to collect data from users. Some examples are questionnaires, system event logs, observation, focus groups, and brainstorms, among others [14–16]. Questionnaires are an easy way of declared data collection, using online tools. Users can answer in a comfortable place and pay more attention during the process. However, questionnaire creation process is not easy to execute. Specialist needs to be careful for elaborating questions and answer options to not generate doubts. Another way to collect user data information is to use event log collection. This kind of data collector helps specialist to look through user behavior during system's use and it helps to follow the evolution of user profile over time. In that way, information about user profile are reused on other projects. These two manner to collect user information are the focus on this paper, and it will be detailed as following.

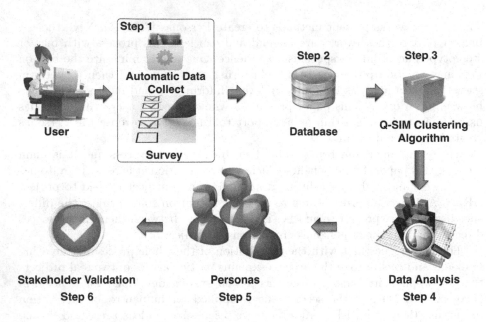

Fig. 1. Personas Creation Process

Questionnaires. With questionnaires it is easy to collect information declared by subjects using an online tool. Thus, subjects can answer in places that they think it is better to make this task and they pay more attention on it. Beyond that, it is easy to diversify the population of target audience. This concept can be applied at two different moments of the project. First one is on conception idea, before project begins. The second one is after build the project which, can be used to improve final product or even during developing time to fix designer issues.

To build questionnaires isn't an easy task and it requires attention to elaborate questions and answers once each of those items cannot be ambiguous. Furthermore, it is needed to identify the population who will answer the questionnaire to maximize results.

At project HRI-P we used questionnaires pre-defined by technique Big-Five [6]. As a project on human-robot interaction (HRI) we are interesting on psychological behavior of subject. After some related works studies we realize that Big-Five produces the result needed to create Personas with interaction characteristics. It will help us to develop HRI components for our robots.

System Event Logs. The automatic data collection through system's log helps to trace user behavior during the use. Beyond that, it is easy to measure the computational skills of users. An important thing to work with automatic data collection is to determine what kind of system the information will be collected, i.e., desktop system, web system, mobile system, among other ones. It will help to determine what component can be used.

D'Angelo [5] presents a list of variables that could help to capture user skills, scenario complexity and so on for web systems. Burzacca and Paternò [2] present variables applied to mobile systems. Even though work focus on usability tests, these variables can identify users profile. Furthermore, this information is closer to real profile of users than questionnaire answer. The capture automation decrease the subjectivity of user behavioral information and user preferences and it turns possible to follow user computational experience evolution.

Decision of how to collect information depends on project. At project HCI-M we decided to adapt the component presented by D'Angelo [5] using seven variables focus on user skill. It was a web system and we need to trace the evolution of learning of the users. The chosen variables are: (I) Interval of time to fill the fields on a form; (II) Typing speed; (III) Percentage of "backspace" key press; (IV) Amount of errors in form filling; (V) Amount of recurrent errors in form filling; (VI) Usage of double clicks when a single click is expected; and (VII) Unexpected click (or clicking on a not clickable component).

2.2 Step 2 - Preparing Information

Algorithms always perform your process based on numerical information. Even if the problem presents categorical or textual information. Categorical or textual information are transformed, in some way, on numerical information during the process to be an input for algorithms. Because of this, it is preferable that such information is stored or captured directly on numerical format. On way to perform it is through human interpretation. Human will translate textual values into numerical codes making possible to keep the fidelity on analyzed data. When the algorithm makes this translation, instead of a specialist, some mistakes can occur on a semantic classification or syntactic of attributes values significance.

With translation executed and it implemented on data collect mechanism, it is necessary to define how it will be stored. First option is the use of a Comma-Separated Values (CSV) file. This file separate each attribute by comma storing them at columns. A second option to store information is to use a database system. To store this kind of information is preferable to use only one table without any normal form, because it will make easy for the read processing of the algorithm.

There are many other kinds of store information like XML and JSON file. For the projects studied here we use CSV file and database system. At project HCI-M we choose database due to integration with the web system was easier than use another way to store this information.

As we use Google Forms for questionnaires on project HRI-P, we decided to use CSV file due to is how the tool store information already. It make easy to adapt QSIM algorithm to receive this kind of entrance for processing.

2.3 Step 3 - Performing QSIM

At this moment data collected can be processed by clustering algorithm. The algorithm used to perform is QSIM [13]. A clustering algorithm which, finds the number of existing classes based on data similarity. By using QSIM on grouping process is interesting to diversify Q value (minimum similarity) to observe group behavior. At both projects were executed this variation of Q value. During the experiments, we noted that some similarity values reproduce a minimal group element exchange. Because of it, we determined a similarity classification to turn communication easier between specialists then to use numerical values. Table 1 presents the classification determined.

Table 1. Similarity Intervals

Intervals	Classification
$Q > 0.69$	High Similarity
$0.49 < Q < 0.7$	Moderate Similarity
$Q < 0.5$	Low Similarity

QSIM presents some advantages in grouping process, mainly on user profile information. First one is the quality for keeping similarity inside group. At this point QSIM was the best algorithm [13]. It doesn't need of preview information about how many groups exists, as the classical algorithm k-means [8]. It is necessary to inform only the desire similarity that QSIM finds exactly how many groups exist for this Q value. Results of grouping compared to k-means are similar, however when exists a dense information QSIM makes softer boundaries than k-means [13]. All in all, QSIM spends a higher computational time of processing than k-means if it has a big number of elements on his Related Sets. At this point, k-means has a better performance than QSIM. A version of QSIM is implement in Java Programming Language and available on-line through the link http://amasiero.github.io/qsim/.

With creation of groups complete it is important to perform two analysis procedures to obtain a better use of Personas. First step is verify what group has the biggest density. Those groups can help specialist to determine the most significant Personas of the project. Second step is verify the existence of groups that represent the same Persona. In that case, those groups have to become one avoiding duplicity. The second step explanation has more sense after the execution of step 4 of whole process, due to attribute values of each group are defined and we can identify if there are two or more groups with the same attribute values.

2.4 Step 4 - Data Analysis

After step 3, groups are determined and the number of generated groups represents how many Personas exist on the project. However, the information that will compose Personas is not ready yet. For each attribute it should finds the measure of central tendency to determine the value for that group. The most common measures are mean, median and mode [12]. Although it is important to attempt for a rule present by Masiero et al. [11], where the mean is only validate for attributes that has no bias problems. It can be checked through Eq. 1.

$$CV < 0.3 \tag{1}$$

where CV is data coefficient of variation. If condition of Eq. 1 is true then data mean can be used as measure of central tendency, else it is recommended to use median or mode. Through this procedure is possible stipulate a common value that will compose each attribute of group. At this moment, it is good to translate the categorical or textual variable for its original state. Finishing it, Personas should be create on presentation format for the best team communication.

2.5   Step 5 - Personas Creation

To finally create Personas in your final state methods from interaction scenarios and problem scenarios are necessary [1]. With these methods, we can add description for all users needs, skills, motivations and objectives that was quantified on earlier steps. Now with Personas ready to use, it is necessary to validate them with project's stakeholders.

2.6   Step 6 - Validating Personas Significance

All Personas created during this entering process are presented to project's stakeholders. They will validate if presented Personas are corresponding to the target audience of the project. At this validation process, it could occurs some small adjusts to increase the Persona's description quality. After that, the set of Personas is presented to all team, developers and designers, so they can always focus on these profiles during the project's life-cycle.

3   Results and Discussions

This process was applied on two different projects. First one is a medical web system and second one is a human-robot interaction project. As presented at Sect. 2, first step of the process is to determine what variables will be capture by data collect mechanism (manual or automatic one). For the first project, we adapted 7 from 28 variables presented by D'Angelo [5], as discuss on Sect. 2.1. The focus on these variables is user computational skills.

After variables definition and implementation of collect component at the web system, data was collected during test with users. It was recorded 200 records during the tests. Then some similarities variations, homogeneous group was noted with Q value equals to 0.6 in other words 60 % of similarity between the subjects. It generate of five Personas. Applying step 4 of the process, it obtained results present on Table 2.

During the process of step 4 we validate that there is no bias for anyone of the variables. Thus, we applied for each variable the data mean to obtain common

Table 2. Common information obtained through step 4 of the process.

# Persona	Typing speed (touch/sec)	Interval to fill the fields on a form (sec)	% Backspace	Amount of errors in form filling	Amount of recurrent errors in form filling	Usage of double clicks when a single click is expected
1	1.21	4.17	8.33%	16	2	0
2	1.31	5.49	1.47%	3	1	1
3	1.46	6.41	48.52%	5	1	0
4	0.92	5.94	75%	7	1	0
5	1.11	11.46	23.22%	2	1	0

value of the group, once the rule of Eq. 1 has been attempted, presented on cells of Table 2. The sequence of common values generation for each group, it was necessary to create Personas formatted for team presentation. Table 3 presents one of five Personas obtained during the process.

Dr. John (Persona of Table 3) was created based on information of row 2 from Table 2. It was the only Persona with a value different of zero for attribute "Usage of double clicks when a single click is expected". It surprised the team because he has satisfy values for the others attributes which, indicates high computational skills. Analyzing all the set of information about this Persona, we realize that

Table 3. Persona 2: Dr. John

Picture:	
Name:	Dr. John
Description:	Doctor, 43 yld, he is responsible for hospital's innovation department. He is a technologic enthusiast and he likes to spend his time in creation of automatize systems for his researches. He looks for technology updates which can bring improvements to the team workflow. He is worried about information security and control access to its information. He spends lots of time developing simple applications with tools like Access and e-mail to keep contact with people. His errors rates are lower than other users.

despite high computational skills people that compose it has experience only on desktop systems which, is necessary to interact with double click frequently.

Following the validation with stakeholders' projects was done and as expected some users were recognized among Personas created. In that way, it is possible to affirm that the application of the process was successful.

The main objective of second project is to identify the Personas behavior to serve as a guideline for developing new social robots mechanism. Although, Personas created for project HRI-P are behavioral and we use then to create the reception robots interaction for the hospital of project HCI-M. These robots will substitute the team of public service support which, gives out passwords and information to the public. The data collection was made with pre and post questionnaires created focus on information of Personas created on the first project. The answers were quantified from process of identification of people behavior profile called Big Five (see Sect. 2.1). This process quantifies user answers into a numerical degree of intensity for each Big Five attribute. Thus, it is intuitive to identify behavior profile of the user. Table 4 presents the common values for Big Five attributes after step 4 analysis process.

Table 4. Common information obtained through step 4 of the process for project HRI-P.

#	Age	Gender	Extroversion	Agreeableness	Conscientiousness	Neuroticism	Openness
1	7	Female	5.0	4.5	5.0	4.5	6.0
2	11	Male	5.0	4.5	4.0	4.5	4.5
3	18	Male	4.5	5.0	5.5	4.0	5.5
4	23	Female	5.0	5.0	5.5	5.0	5.0
5	41	Male	5.0	4.5	6.0	3.5	6.5

The values presented on Table 4 help us to create the description of Personas. How it contains psychological information, the description can be detailed with behavioral data, like openness for new experience as row 5. This information will help us to identify better information for interact with this kind of Persona. To create Personas based on the kind of Table 4 helps to minimize Persona's stereotyping once team project has real data to support description creation and they do not need to think how is target audience of the project.

This human-robot interaction project used a Q value equals to 0.8 which means 80 % of similarity desired. High similarity can best split groups with small samples or data record. In that case, validation process occurs a little bit different, because the team is your own client. After creation of Personas were analyzed videos of each test and so it was possible to realize that, some subjects are similar to some Personas, as earlier project.

In that way, that the proposed process by this work supports an automatize creation of Personas for any kind of project and that Personas created through this process can be reused in another projects decreasing the cost and analyses time of users at a first step. Also, Personas create in future projects can help to improve older projects like happen on project HCI-M and project HRI-P. Beyond that, the process tends to minimize the Persona's stereotyping which, before are only based on information acquired by team experience.

4   Conclusion and Future Works

The process presented at this work allows that Personas can be created in an automatized way and it minimize stereotyping of Personas. This is an important point because it formalize that user-centered projects effectively attempt objectives and needs of target audience.

Another important point that may be highlighted here is that QSIM algorithm makes it easy due to it finds the number of existent groups in database keeping the similarity quality inside each group, proved on [13]. The proposed cycle implementation in many projects of the same company or even the same market segment allow knowing the users of new products or service before to start the project. All of it through the user modeling based on Personas.

It is also possible to follow Personas evolution all time long. It can determine a cycle of life as the user they represent. Some preliminary tests show that is possible to realize some intersection between Personas and projects which, makes reuse of Personas and also to create a Personas repository practicable. However, more tests are necessary to complete this task fully. This extra works are developing and we will publish it soon.

Acknowledgment. To CAPES PROSUP Scholarship and to FAPESP (Fundação de Amparo à Pesquisa do Estado de São Paulo) for financial support.

References

1. Aquino Junior, P.T., Filgueiras, L.V.L.: A expressão da diversidade de usuários no projeto de interação com padrões e personas. In: Proceedings of the VIII Brazilian Symposium on Human Factors in Computing Systems. IHC 2008, Sociedade Brasileira de Computação, pp. pp. 1–10, Porto Alegre, Brazil (2008). http://dl.acm.org/citation.cfm?id=1497470.1497472
2. Burzacca, P., Paternò, F.: Remote usability evaluation of mobile web applications. In: Kurosu, M. (ed.) HCII/HCI 2013, Part I. LNCS, vol. 8004, pp. 241–248. Springer, Heidelberg (2013)
3. Cooper, A., Reimann, R., Cronin, D.: About face 3: the essentials of interaction design. Wiley, India (2007)
4. Cooper, A.: The Inmates are Running the Asylum. Macmillan Publishing Co., Indianapolis, IN, USA (1999)
5. D'Angelo, F.d.M.: Identificação automática de perfis de grupos de usuários de interfaces web (2012). biblioteca Digital de Teses e Dissertações da FEI. Disponível em: http://tede.fei.edu.br/tede/tde-busca/arquivo.php?codArquivo=231/
6. Gosling, S.D., Rentfrow, P.J., Swann, W.B.: A very brief measure of the big-five personality domains. J. Res. Pers. **37**, 504–528 (2003)

7. Guimarães, D.B., Carvalho, C.R.M., Furtado, E.S.: Panorama, oportunidades e recomendações para o contexto brasileiro de interação humano-computador e design centrado no usuário a partir do uso de personas. In: Proceedings of the 10th Brazilian Symposium on on Human Factors in Computing Systems and the 5th Latin American Conference on Human-Computer Interaction. IHC+CLIHC 2011, pp. 167–176. Brazilian Computer Society, Porto Alegre, Brazil (2011). http://dl. acm.org/citation.cfm?id=2254436.2254467
8. Jain, A.K.: Data clustering: 50 years beyond k-means. Pattern Recogn. Lett. **31**(8), 651–666 (2010)
9. Jung, C.: The archetypes and the collective unconscious, vol. 2. Bollingen (1975)
10. Masiero, A.A.: Algoritmo de agrupamento por similaridade aplicado a criação de personas (2013). biblioteca Digital de Teses e Dissertações da FEI
11. Masiero, A.A., de Carvalho Destro, R., Curioni, O.A., Junior, P.T.A.: Automa-persona: a process to extract knowledge automatic for improving personas. In: Stephanidis, C. (ed.) HCI International 2013 - Posters' Extended Abstracts, pp. 61–64. Springer, Heidelberg (2013)
12. Masiero, A.A., Leite, M.G., Filgueiras, L.V.L., Aquino, Junior, P.T.: Multidirec-tional knowledge extraction process for creating behavioral personas. In: Proceed-ings of the 10th Brazilian Symposium on on Human Factors in Computing Sys-tems and the 5th Latin American Conference on Human-Computer Interaction, IHC+CLIHC 2011, pp. 91–99. Brazilian Computer Society, Porto Alegre, Brazil (2011). http://dl.acm.org/citation.cfm?id=2254436.2254454
13. Masiero, A.A., Tonidandel, F., Aquino Junior, P.T.: Similar or not similar: this is a parameter question. In: Yamamoto, S. (ed.) HCI 2013, Part I. LNCS, vol. 8016, pp. 484–493. Springer, Heidelberg (2013)
14. Preece, J., Rogers, Y., Sharp, H., Benyon, D., Holland, S., Carey, T.: Human-computer interaction. Addison-Wesley Longman Ltd., Boston, MA (1994)
15. Pruitt, J., Adlin, T.: The Persona Lifecycle: Keeping People in Mind Throughout Product Design. Morgan Kaufmann Publishers, San Francisco (2005)
16. Rogers, Y., Sharp, H., Preece, J.: Interaction design: beyond human-computer interaction. Wiley & Sons, New York (2011)

Using Diary Studies to Evaluate Railway Dispatching Software

Isabel Schütz[✉], Anselmo Stelzer, and Andreas Oetting

Railway Engineering, Technische Universität Darmstadt, Darmstadt, Germany
{schuetz,stelzer,oetting}@verkehr.tu-darmstadt.de

Abstract. In this paper, we present the application of User Diaries in the context of connection dispatching. Connection dispatching is a field with quickly rising requirements which also affect the used dispatching support software. The usage of User Diaries will be motivated for this specific domain. The diary will briefly be presented as well as the results of the study. We will point out the advantages and disadvantages using User Diaries in the given context.

1 Introduction

In the field of connection dispatching currently no specifically adapted software is used. Since connection dispatching has an impact on the quality of service for the customers and thus has a high visibility for them, its importance rises. Also, traffic contracts contain rules for connection assurance which are often linked to penalties in case of not achieving them. This increases the importance of connection dispatching and therefore also the requirements for the connection dispatcher. That is why a new prototype software was developed to better support dispatchers in the field of connection dispatching.

Before integrating the prototype software in the daily working environment of the dispatchers, a field study should be conducted to prove its suitability, to further improve and better adapt it to the users' needs. During this field study, the dispatchers should be involved in evaluating this prototype software. They should test it during their work and state their opinion and improvement proposals, if any.

To get detailed and diversified information about the usage of the prototype, three evaluation methods were carried out in a row: First, Diary Studies were conducted. Then an Observation followed before ending the evaluation process with a Focus Group. In this paper, we will concentrate on the Diary Studies in the context of a field study with a prototype software for connection dispatching.

The focus of this paper will be on describing the evaluation method of Diary Studies and the reflection of its suitability for use in the field of connection dispatching rather than on the prototype software as such.

So, first an overview over related work in the field of connection dispatching will be given in Sect. 2. In Sect. 3, current problems and our motivation for conducting a field test using Diary Studies will be presented. A description of

© Springer International Publishing Switzerland 2015
M. Kurosu (Ed.): Human-Computer Interaction, Part I, HCII 2015, LNCS 9169, pp. 248–258, 2015.
DOI: 10.1007/978-3-319-20901-2_23

the methodology can be found in Sect. 4. The results are presented in Sect. 5 and discussed in Sect. 6. In Sect. 7, a conclusion will be drawn.

2 Related Work

Connection dispatching is a well-studied field of research where several focuses can be distinguished. Particularly, two of them are interesting for this research paper. The first involves software engineering and usability engineering. Many studies exist which concentrate mainly on software evaluations. The methods used are the following:

- Event Logging [1]
- Screen Capturing Software [1]
- Semi-Structured Interviews [2]
- Observation [2,3]
- Questionnaires [2–4]
- Observations [2,3]
- Unstructured Interviews [3]
- Collegial Verbalisation [2]
- Interactive Diary [2]

Only the studies of [2] are real field studies, meaning that dispatchers used the software during their everyday work. All other references mentioned are rather laboratory studies. Although the study was conducted at their work place, the dispatchers had to handle a specific scenario created for the test. Only the methods Questionnaires, Interviews and Observations are dealt with in detail in these papers. Reference [2] only mentions the methods Collegial Verbalisation and Interactive Diary, but no further details about method, procedure or results. That is why, in this paper, we will further concentrate on Questionnaires, Interviews and Observations when comparing and discussing User Diaries in Sect. 3.2.

The second focus is past and ongoing research concerning the detection and solution of connection conflicts. Here, the focus is often on the optimization of (traveler) delays as in [5–7]. Reference [8] developed a system for connection dispatching which is also based on customer delay, but interacts with an infrastructural counterpart. Reference [9] present a system which focused on the traveler's side of connection dispatching including a smart phone prototype application. In [10,11], a modular dispatching support system for connection dispatching including an evaluation for connection conflicts and solutions exceeding classical waiting strategies is presented.

Little attention has been paid to the design and evaluation of dispatching software in this field, but has been addressed in [12,13].

3 Problem Description

For a (railway) transportation company, connection dispatching is one of the dispatching tasks with the most influence on their customers and thus has a high visibility. Apart from travelers expecting more sophisticated solutions in traffic management, also, traffic contracts contain rules for connection assurance. This makes connection dispatching an important task with increasing requirements for the connection dispatcher.

Historically, connection dispatching in the German railway environment was performed by the infrastructure company, but has been assigned to the transportation company as fulfilling contractor of the traveler. First, the task was performed by staff also responsible for personnel and vehicle dispatching whereas today dedicated positions for connection dispatching and traveler information are being created.

The task of connection dispatching comprises the surveillance of connections, conflict detection, conflict resolution and customer information. As the requirements grow, the dispatcher needs to find better solutions for more connection conflicts on a dense schedule in shorter periods of time. For this, he increasingly relies on software systems that should on one hand provide the necessary information and on the other hand need to be user friendly and easy to use such that the connection dispatcher can easily gather information about the connection conflicts which currently require dedicated attention.

3.1 Connection Dispatching Software

Dispatching software needs to support the dispatcher in the aforementioned tasks. This is done on different levels such as conflict detection [12], conflict resolutions [11] and visualization [12]. While the first two are background processes which produce data to be displayed, the latter implies direct interaction with the user and is also used to present results from conflict detection and resolution.

To address the problem described in Sect. 3, a prototype software to visualize relevant information in connection dispatching has been developed in cooperation with a German railway company [12]. An example screen shot is given in Fig. 1. The software has been designed such that the dispatcher is able to gather information about many connections at a glance. For this, a matrix interface is used on which the feeders are arranged vertically and the distributors horizontally. Whenever an interchange between a feeder and a distributor exists, the corresponding cell in the matrix contains information regarding the connection status, otherwise it is left blank. Lines or columns without any connection relation are hidden.

The standard view shows current and future connections. As soon as a dispatching action is applied to a connection, it will be hidden in the standard view. To be able to keep track on her/his decisions, the dispatcher can switch the view to see dispatched connections.

Another interface, shown in Fig. 2, enables the user to reduce the displayed information providing a greater (time-wise and regional) overview of the current situation.

The software first has been developed for a simulation environment, the Eisenbahnbetriebsfeld Darmstadt (EBD) [14], to be tested by dispatchers [13].

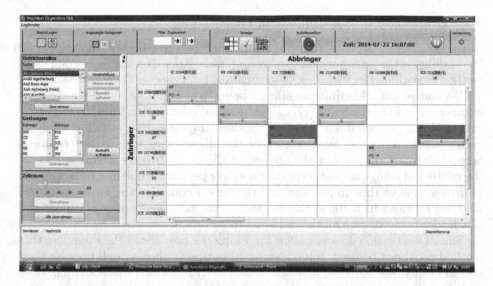

Fig. 1. Matrix view of the connection dispatching software

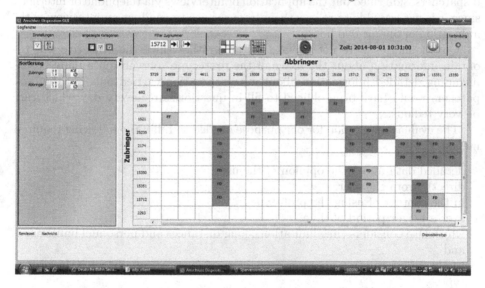

Fig. 2. Compacted matrix view of the connection dispatching software

Considering the results of the evaluation in the EBD [13] and an expert evaluation using the IsoMetrics Questionnaire [15] and Cogintive Walkthrough [16], the user interface of the existing software was adapted and improved such that a first test in the field could be performed. The aim was to obtain information about the usability of the software interface in the field.

3.2 Evaluation in the Context of Dispatching

When deciding on an appropriate evaluation method to gain information about the usability of the software interface, we first concentrated on the three evaluation methods mentioned in Sect. 2 – Questionnaires, Interviews and Observations.

We started with describing significant boundary conditions and defined evaluation criteria of the study (cf. [17]). First, detailed information from the dispatchers to learn more about how to further improve the software and to better adapt it to the requirements of the dispatchers had to be obtained. Second, detailed data about the opinion of the users directly from the user in the context of using the prototype over a longer period of time had to be gained. Moreover, due to time limitations and the long distance to the locations of the field test, a way which allows the dispatchers to state their opinion without the test leader being on-site all the time had to be found.

Since Observation does not allow for asking the user about their opinion, this method could not be used. Interviews could not be applied as well because they should ideally be conducted in a face-to-face situation which was not compatible with the above-mentioned time limitations. Also, personnel restrictions on the dispatchers' side ruled out the application of interviews via telephone or internet, since it is not possible to relieve them from service to conduct an interview with a duration of one or two hours.

Questionnaires were not deemed suitable either since the objective was to obtain information about the usage of the prototype software on a daily basis, including detailed information about every operation carried out. So, the dispatchers would have been obliged to fill in questionnaires every day which can be very tedious.

The evaluation method for our purpose needed to fulfill the following requirements:

- detailed data about the opinion of the user,
- directly from the user,
- in the context of using the prototype,
- over a longer period of time,
- which also considers time limitations, long distances and personnel limitations and
- to obtain information about every operation they carried out with the prototype.

Only User Diaries met all these requirements and were therefore chosen for this field test.

4 Methodology

In this section, we will first present general aspects of Diary Studies. Then, we will concentrate on the structure and the layout of the User Diaries for the aforementioned prototype software. Finally, we continue with the procedure of conducting this method.

4.1   Introduction to User Diaries

The evaluation method of Diary Studies aims at gaining information about

- context/situation of use,
- frequency of use,
- operations,
- work,
- dates,
- duration,
- problems and
- opinions.

over a longer period of time with the help of a diary, either handwritten or electronical [18–20].

A huge disadvantage is the dependency on the compliance of the user to fill in the User Diary. The initiative and motivation of the users are decisive for the amount of entries and the degree of detail. Furthermore, entries are very subjective, exaggerations are possible and the data cannot be verified by the test leader. Moreover, the users are on their own during the evaluation. A functioning prototype is needed [18,20].

Advantages of this method are its applicability during a longer period of time and at different, distant locations. No special resources or equipment are needed, so it is cost-efficient to use [18,19].

4.2   Structure and Layout

The design and the degree of standardization of the User Diary depends on the specific context. The objective is to allow the user to fill it in rather quickly and easily. For the presented purpose, half checkboxes and half text fields are used.

The structure of the diaries is as follows: First, a general introduction to using the diary and about the procedure of conducting the evaluation is presented. Then, a general introduction into the prototype software follows. Subsequently, a short demographic questionnaire gathering age, working place, working function and professional experience is interposed. Then, the actual diary starts with an example on how to fill in the columns and rows of the diary followed by about 20 pages of diary. Every page contains three rows for describing one operation each. At the end of the diary, there are two pages for stating general remarks about the prototype software and one page with contact data of the test leader.

On the actual diary page, we asked for time, current workload, delay of entry (if any), dispatching actions, reasons for dispatching actions, how many and which dispatching decisions were made and the functions, program views and auxiliaries used.

4.3   Procedure

The procedure of conducting the User Diaries consisted of six steps:

1. training power users in using the prototype (one per working place)
2. training power users in using the User Diaries (one per working place)
3. introduction to the prototype software for all participating dispatchers
4. introduction to the User Diaries for all participating dispatchers
5. free exploration
6. filling in the User Diaries

At first, power users were trained on the software and on the User Diaries to cope with one major disadvantage of the diary studies, in particular that users are dependent on themselves (step 1 and 2). Moreover, training power users was helpful to find last bugs in the software and to specifically adapt the User Diary and especially the examples used to the needs of the dispatchers.

Then, an introductory event for the dispatchers participating in the evaluation was organized to train them in using the software and the diary (step 3 and 4). All functions and program views were introduced and the structure and layout of the User Diary were explained to them. Moreover, the example for filling in the User Diary was discussed in detail.

Then, the dispatchers had about two weeks for freely exploring the prototype software, to try all the functions and program views and to get used to it. This aimed at allowing the dispatchers to establish a work process with the software (step 5).

In the following three weeks, the dispatchers filled in the user diary (step 6) before sending them back to the test leader for evaluation. The dispatchers were asked to use the User Diary for at least three times, if possible in a row.

5   Results

In this section, results of the User Diaries will be presented briefly. The focus will be on general results relevant to the usage and the situation of usage which are important for the discussion in Sect. 6, to reflect the suitability of the prototype.

In total, 91 entries were handwritten by the nine participating dispatchers. These document 471 dispatching decisions, such as dispatching connections or finding alternative trains. In 63.95 %, the current situation was described as calm, 27.91 % as medium – in-between calm and stressful – and in 8.14 % as stressful. 61.54 % of the entries were registered directly after the operation, whereas 38.46 % were delayed by about 12 min in average. The time shifted entries consisted of all entries in stressful situations and half of the entries in medium situations.

Since going into detail about operations or improvement proposals requires a detailed knowledge of the prototype software, only a few examples according to operations and program views will be given.

The most frequently used function (35.8 %) is the filter adjustment function which can be seen on the left hand side in Fig. 1. The train number search function which can be seen in both figures, once without a number (cf. Fig. 1) and once with a number (cf. Fig. 2) in the upper area of the program, was used in 13.0 % of cases. The least used function was the sorting function which can be seen in Fig. 2 and which was only used in 3.25 % of cases. Concerning the program views, in 85.44 % of cases they used the standard matrix view which can be seen in Fig. 1. The program view with reduced displayed information as shown in Fig. 2 was used only in 9.70 % of cases. The third program view which shows the already dispatched trains was the least used one (4.85 %).

Summarizing, dispatching actions and the reasons for conducting them were comparable or even identical to the ones foreseen when designing the prototype. So, the use cases which aided in maintaining a clear focus during the design process are identical to the usage patterns of the dispatchers in their everyday work.

6   Discussion

Unfortunately, different problems arose during the field test. As stated in Sect. 5, the 9 dispatchers participating in the study wrote 91 entries in total which were often redundant. So, the variance of the data was rather small.

Moreover, only 8.14 % of the entries were done in stressful situations, all of them later on with a certain delay. The problem is that during normal operations, dispatchers do not face a high workload. It increases dramatically when disturbances occur which is also when the dispatcher starts to heavily use dispatching support software. It can be stated that stressful situations are the most important and interesting ones, but in these situations, dispatchers do not seem to be able to fill in the User Diary. Thus, data from stressful situations will be reported in the User Diary with a certain delay as stated in Sect. 5. These are the most revealing and insightful situations for improving the prototype and to better adapt it to the dispatchers' operational requirements. As we get only delayed entries in these situations, the question arises if the provided data is still complete, and thus, whether we can rely on the time-shifted entries. The dispatchers might not remember every operation they carried out with the prototype software as well as every detail. The reliability and the working environment for stressful situations are issues for further research using User Diaries in dispatching contexts.

Nonetheless, we gained a lot of useful and valuable information for improving the software, especially regarding the most used functions and views. It could be shown that, e.g., the sorting function which can be seen in Fig. 2 and which was explicitly required by an expert panel during the design process was not intensely used. The same is valid for the program view with reduced displayed information as shown in Fig. 2. This view was later implemented because it seemed to be necessary to provide the dispatchers a view which allows to have a better overview over the current situation by reducing information, but it was not intensively used either. It could be clearly proven that dispatchers prefer the standard matrix view which can be seen in Fig. 1. Moreover, it became obvious that we had to concentrate on improving the filter adjustment function which can be seen on the left hand side in Fig. 1 because of the frequent use to better support dispatchers and also to save time during operations.

Also, valuable hints for the Observation we conducted after the User Diaries were gained. It was much easier to decide on a specific focus for the Observation since we could identify the most used functions and program view with the help of the User Diaries. Moreover, the entries and especially the remarks gave us hints about problems that arose while using the prototype which we could concentrate on during the Observation.

The process of conducting Diary Studies and also the structure and the layout of the User Diary has proven of value. There were no further inquiries regarding the use of the diary and the users filled it in a correct manner. When having a closer look at the remarks given by the dispatchers, we can conclude that the dispatchers seem to feel quite comfortable about using the diary and the prototype.

User Diaries are useful to obtain meaningful information about a prototype software in the described context. Nevertheless, weaknesses of the method, especially regarding stressful situations, could be discovered during our study. To overcome these weaknesses, a carefully considered combination with other methods needs to be developed. Further investigation how Diary Studies can be adapted better to the specific situation of dispatchers and how to combine them with other methods is necessary.

7   Conclusion

We successfully used the evaluation method of Diary Studies in a field study with connection dispatchers. A lot of insightful data could be gathered which provided helpful input for further improving and better adapting the prototype software to the needs of the users, but also to decide on a specific focus for the following evaluation methods. Thus, User Diaries have proven to be useful in the context of evaluating dispatching software regarding the standard working environment.

Nevertheless, further field tests using the evaluation method of Diary Studies need to be conducted to prove its suitability for use in similar working environments and to further investigate the problematic stressful working times. This method can either specifically be adapted to the specific environments. Otherwise, an alternative evaluation method fulfilling all the criteria we were looking for in this field study with dispatchers needs to be developed.

Using the results of the User Diaries presented in this paper, our prototype software will be developed further and improved to better support dispatchers in doing their work.

References

1. Kauppi, A., Wiktström, J., Sandblad, B., Andersson, A.W.: Future train traffic control: control by replanning. Spec. Issue Int. J. Cogn. Technol. Work (IC-CTW) **8**, 50–56 (2006)

2. Isaksson-Luttemann, G., Kauppi, A., Andersson, A.W., Sandblad, B., Erlandsson, M.: Operative tests of a new system for train traffic control. Rail Human Factors around the World: Impacts on and of People for Successful Rail Operations, pp. 424–433 (2009)
3. Isaksson-Luttemann, G.: Future Train Traffic Control: Development and deployment of new principles and systems in train traffic control. Licentiate thesis, Uppsala University, Uppsala (2012)
4. Wikström, J., Kauppi, A., Hellström, P., Andersson, A.W., Sandblad, B.: Train traffic control by re-planning in real-time. In: Allan, J., Brebbia, C., Hill, R., Sciutto, G., Sone, S. (eds.) Computers in Railways IX. Computers in Railways IX, vol. 74, pp. 733–742. WIT Press, Wessex (2004)
5. Schöbel, A.: Integer programming approaches for solving the delay management problem. In: Geraets, F., Kroon, L.G., Schoebel, A., Wagner, D., Zaroliagis, C.D. (eds.) Railway Optimization 2004. LNCS, vol. 4359, pp. 145–170. Springer, Heidelberg (2007)
6. Kliewer, N.: Mathematische optimierung zur unterstützung kundenorientierter disposition im schienenverkehr. In: Chamoni, P. (ed.) Selected Papers of the International Conference on Operations Research. Operations research proceedings, vol. 2001, pp. 473–480. Springer, Heidelberg (2002)
7. Suhl, L., Biederbick, C., Kliewer, N.: Design of customer-oriented dispatching support for railways. In: Voss, S., Daduna, J.R. (eds.) Computer-aided scheduling of public transport. Lecture Notes in Economics and Mathematical Systems, vol. 505, pp. 365–386. Springer, Berlin (2001)
8. Kurby, S.: Makroskopisches Echtzeitdispositionsmodell zur Lösung von Anschlusskonflikten im Eisenbahnbetrieb. Zugl. Dissertation an der TU Dresden, Technische Universität Dresden, Dresden (2012)
9. Scheier, B., Schöne, S., Dietsch, S.: Assistenz zur anschlusssicherung im intermodalen verkehr mittels echtzeitdaten. ZEV rail Glasers Annalen 138(6–7), 224–230 (2014)
10. Stelzer, A., Oetting, A.: Konzeption einer Konfliktlösung einschließlich einer Bewertungsmethode für die Anschlussdisposition. In: Fakultä Verkehrswissenschaften Friedrich List, (ed.): 24. Verkehrswissenschaftlichen Tage 2014, Fakultät Verkehrswissenschaften Friedrich List (2014)
11. Oetting, A., Stelzer, A.: Conflict resolution in connection dispatching. In: Hansen, I.A., Tomii, N., Hirai, C. (eds.) 6th International Conference on Railway Operations Modelling and Analysis (2015) (accepted for presentation)
12. Stelzer, A., Oetting, A., Chu, F.: Connection dispatching - an algorithmic and visual support for the dispatcher. In: WCTRS (ed.) Selected Proceedings WCTR 2013, Rio de Janeiro, WCTRS (2013)
13. Stelzer, A., Schütz, I., Oetting, A.: Evaluating novel user interfaces in (safety critical) railway environments. In: Kurosu, M. (ed.) HCI 2014, Part III. LNCS, vol. 8512, pp. 502–512. Springer, Heidelberg (2014)
14. Streitzig, C., Stelzer, A., Schön, S., Chu, F.: TU darmstadt - research training and more besides. EURAILmag 26(26), 152–159 (2012)
15. Willumeit, H., Gediga, G., Hamborg, K.C.: IsoMetrics: ein verfahren zur formativen evaluation von software nach ISO 9241/10. Ergonomie und Informatik 27, 5–12 (1996)
16. Polson, P.G., Lewis, C., Rieman, J., Wharton, C.: Cognitive walkthroughs: a method for theory-based evaluation of user interfaces. Int. J. Man. Mach. Stud. 36(5), 741–773 (1992)

17. Stelzer, A., Schütz, I.: Field evaluation of a new railway dispatching software. In: The Eighth International Conference on Advances in Computer-Human Interactions, Lisbon, Portugal, Feb 2015 (accepted for presentation)
18. Sharp, H., Rogers, Y., Preece, J.: Interaction Design: Beyond Human-Computer Interaction. John Wiley & Sons Ltd, Chichester (2007)
19. Schlick, C., Bruder, R., Luczak, H.: Arbeitswissenschaft. Springer-Verlag, Heidelberg (2010)
20. Rubin, J., Chisnell, D.: Handbook of Usability Testing: How to Plan, Design, and Conduct Effective Tests. John Wiley & Sons, Indianapolis (2008)

Heuristic Evaluation in Information Visualization Using Three Sets of Heuristics: An Exploratory Study

Beatriz Sousa Santos[1,2(✉)], Beatriz Quintino Ferreira[2],
and Paulo Dias[1,2]

[1] Department of Electronics Telecommunications and Informatics,
University of Aveiro, Aveiro, Portugal
[2] Institute of Electronics Engineering and Telematics of Aveiro/IEETA,
Aveiro, Portugal
{bss,mbeatriz,paulo.dias}@ua.pt

Abstract. Evaluation in Information Visualization is inherently complex, and it is still a challenge. Whereas it is possible to adapt evaluation methods from other fields, as Human-Computer Interaction, this adaptation may not be straightforward since visualization applications are very specific interactive systems.

This paper addresses issues in using heuristic evaluation to evaluate visualizations and visualization applications, and presents an exploratory study in two phases and involving 25 evaluators aimed at assessing the understandability and effectiveness of three sets of heuristics that have been used in Information Visualization.

Keywords: InfoVis evaluation · Usability, cognitive and visual heuristics · Heuristic evaluation

1 Introduction

Throughout the last decades numerous information visualization techniques and applications have appeared. These are generally highly interactive visual exploratory tools or methods aimed at allowing users to formulate better hypothesis and develop a deeper understanding of the underlying phenomena. Yet, these techniques tend to be complex and thus adequate development methods for them to effectively support users are pivotal. In this scope, a proper evaluation of the tools, including the visualization techniques they provide is crucial. Though, how to evaluate visualization applications, or techniques has been (and still is) a challenge in several ways [1–6], and numerous publications as well as several workshops have been devoted to discuss this topic (e.g. the beliv workshop series).

A natural approach to this problem, although not without risks, was to adapt evaluation methods developed and applied in other fields. Indeed, this was the case of several usability evaluation methods widely used in Human-Computer Interaction (HCI), each fostering the detection of different types of problems and having different

© Springer International Publishing Switzerland 2015
M. Kurosu (Ed.): Human-Computer Interaction, Part I, HCII 2015, LNCS 9169, pp. 259–270, 2015.
DOI: 10.1007/978-3-319-20901-2_24

limitations, implying that evaluators should select and use various appropriate techniques that best fit the situation [7].

Using the taxonomy of usability evaluation methods by Dix et al. [8], we may divide them in analytical and empirical; while the latter involve users, tend to be more complex and onerous, there are low-cost analytical evaluation methods widely used, capable of producing useful results with a low investment. Heuristic evaluation is such a method, possibly the most popular discount usability evaluation method [9], and has been adapted to evaluate Information Visualization tools, and techniques by several authors [10–14]. We have previously used the method and believe that it may provide useful results with an interesting cost-benefit [15]; still, some heuristics may be difficult to understand hindering their applicability by not very experienced evaluators, which suggests the need for a study on the comprehensibility and applicability of visualization-specific heuristics. This paper describes a first step towards this goal: a study involving 25 evaluators aimed at assessing how easy to understand and apply are the Nielsen's heuristics in Information Visualization evaluation, as well as two sets of visualization-specific heuristics, the ones proposed by Zuk and Carpendale [10] and by Forsell and Johanson [11].

The remainder of the paper is organized as follows: Sect. 2 presents the method of heuristic evaluation and the three sets of heuristics used, Sect. 3 presents the example selected to be evaluated and the methodology used in the study, Sect. 4 presents and discusses the results, and some conclusions are drawn in Sect. 5.

2 Heuristic Evaluation

Heuristic evaluation is a widely used discount usability evaluation method that allows finding potential problems in a user interface [9]. As it is subjective, it should involve several evaluators who inspect the interface concerning its compliance with a set of established usability principles (the "heuristics"). Non-compliant aspects should be compiled in a list of usability problems rated according to their severity, including possible suggestions of how to fix them. This list is supposed to help the development team to prioritize the problems to tackle.

According to Munzner [16], heuristic evaluation is an "immediate validation approach" that can be used at the visual encoding and interaction design level, the third level of the nested model for visualization design and validation proposed by this author. At this level the threat is that the design does not convey the desired abstraction to the user. We believe heuristic evaluation can be most useful in the scope of a (iterative) user centered development process of visualization applications and techniques as it is a pragmatic way to obtain quickly, inexpensively, and effectively valuable formative information if adequately employed, however, several issues must be carefully considered when applying this method [17], namely:

- what heuristic set to use;
- how well does it represent the relevant aspects of the type of user interface under evaluation;
- how to train evaluators to use correctly the set of heuristics;

- if they will be able to use it effectively to find problems;
- and how many evaluators should be involved.

It is possible to use specific heuristics to evaluate specific types of products (e.g. groupware [18] or mobile applications [19]), or considering a particular class of target users (as seniors or children). Nonetheless, selecting a set of heuristics adequate to an actual situation is not easy and a poor choice will influence the problems found, and consequently how many evaluators are needed and the quality of the obtained evaluation. Hence, a careful consideration of the heuristic set to use concerning the above mentioned aspects is essential before applying heuristic evaluation. Moreover, the evaluators' experience in using the method and their understanding of the set of heuristics used are also relevant factors.

Tory and Moller [20, 21] considered heuristic evaluation as a useful expert review method to evaluate visualization systems, outlined how to conduct a heuristic evaluation, and advised the usage of visualization heuristics.

However, while a number of rules have been used for that purpose (e.g. in the works by Shneiderman; Ware; Amar and Stasko; Zuk and Carpendale; Forsell et al.; [10, 11, 22–24]), their understandability and scope is not yet fully assessed and selecting a set of heuristics may not be a trivial task for a development team.

In this work we used the well-known Nielsen's Ten Usability heuristics [9] and two other sets developed specifically for Information Visualization, namely the ones proposed by Zuk and Carpendale [10] and Forsell and Johanson [11], and then tried to assess how easy they might be to understand and use by evaluators having some but not much experience in evaluating visualization applications, a scenario we deem rather realistic, for instance in a company.

Nielsen's heuristics are general enough to be applicable to any kind of interactive product; yet, whereas they may have value in finding problems also in Information Visualization, as usability issues are often associated to visualization problems, developing heuristics sets that comprise the most common problems in this type of applications (namely encompassing issues related to visual representation, presentation, and interaction and manipulation of the parameters) is important in order to fine tune the method and reduce the risk of assuming too much in reusing the process of heuristic evaluation from usability [25]. This goal has been pursued by several authors, and the sets of heuristics selected for this study seem two interesting candidates for practical use.

2.1 Nielsen's Heuristics

As mentioned, this set of heuristics is very general, which makes it interesting for the developer's evaluation toolkit; nevertheless, that might be a disadvantage, as it may not be completely adjusted to a specific situation. We decided to use it as baseline to compare the understandability and number of problems found with the other heuristics, as our evaluators were familiarized with this set and had previous experience in using it to evaluate interactive systems. Even though it is widely known, we include the list of 10 heuristics [9], for the sake of clarity and completeness:

1. Visibility of system status
2. Match between system and the real world

3. User control and freedom
4. Consistency and standards
5. Error prevention
6. Recognition rather than recall
7. Flexibility and efficiency of use
8. Aesthetic and minimalist design
9. Help users recognize, diagnose, and recover from errors
10. Help and documentation

As mentioned, these heuristics are general enough to be useful to evaluate any kind of interactive product; however, we expect them to help finding problems mainly related to the interaction mechanisms provided and not so much related with visual representation and presentation aspects that should also be assessed in any Information Visualization technique or application [26].

2.2 Zuk and Carpendale's Heuristics

This set was compiled specifically to evaluate the visual and cognitive aspects of visualization solutions from the works of Bertin, Tufte [27], and Ware [23]:

1. Ensure visual variable has sufficient length
2. Don't expect reading order from color
3. Color perception varies with size of items
4. Local contrast affects color and gray perception
5. Consider people with color blindness
6. Pre-attentive benefits increase with field of view
7. Quantitative assessment requires position or size variation
8. Preserve data to graphic dimensionality
9. Put the most data in the least space
10. Remove the extraneous (ink)
11. Consider Gestalt Laws
12. Provide multiple levels of detail
13. Integrate text wherever relevant

Detailed descriptions of all heuristics are available in the original paper [10], which also provides an analysis of eight examples of uncertainty visualization using this set. In another work Zuk et al. [25] performed a meta-analysis aimed at understanding the issues involving the selection and organization of the heuristics based on a case study.

2.3 Forsell and Johanson's Heuristics

This set was compiled empirically by Forsell and Johanson [11] to find common and important problems in Information Visualization techniques through heuristic evaluation. The method used by the authors was based on Nielsen's approach to develop the widely known Ten Usability Heuristics [9]. The heuristics of six previously published sets ranging from very specific low-level heuristics to very high-level ones (Nielsen [9];

Shneiderman [22]; Freitas et al. [26]; Amar and Stasko [24]; Zuk and Carpendale [10]) were used to analyze a number of problems derived from earlier evaluations and the 10 heuristics that provided the highest explanatory coverage were selected to integrate the following new set:

1. Information coding
2. Minimal actions
3. Flexibility
4. Orientation and help
5. Spatial organization
6. Consistency
7. Recognition rather than recall
8. Prompting
9. Remove the extraneous
10. Data set reduction

According to the authors, the six heuristic sets considered cover important aspects, yet none seemed general enough to be used on its own for the evaluation of any Information Visualization technique. On the contrary, this new empirically determined set, comprising the highest ranked heuristics (according to the method used) from the considered sets was considered by the authors to have significantly wider coverage than any of the previous.

Detailed descriptions of all heuristics can be found in the original paper [11], as well as the method used, and suggestions on how to improve and validate the reliability, usefulness and applicability of the derived set.

3 Experimental Data Set and Method

The exploratory study described in this paper aimed at better understanding how to use heuristic evaluation in the context of Information Visualization and encompassed two main phases both performed with the collaboration of Information Visualization students of the MSc in Information Systems (University of Aveiro) during two academic years (2012-14).

In the first phase we asked 15 students to analyze a simple InfoVis example of their choice in a non-structured way (we dubbed "naïve critique") using only their judgment based on the common sense and experience acquired in their previous use of applications, web-sites, etc., and list the potential problems they had found. We provided an example and explained it in a lecture. Later in the semester, after having practiced the heuristic evaluation method with other visualization applications, the students evaluated the first example using heuristic evaluation with two of the three selected sets. Results of this exploratory phase suggested that on one hand, heuristic evaluation (irrespective the heuristic set used) does help evaluators to consider issues that they would have otherwise missed as it fosters a more systematic inspection of the user interface relevant aspects. On the other hand, evaluators generally found that Nielsen's heuristics are less finely tuned to Information Visualization examples, as expected. Concerning the heuristics specifically developed for Information Visualization evaluation, participants felt some difficulties in interpreting and applying some of them, (e.g. number 1, 2, 6 and 10 by Zuk and Carpendale).

In the second phase, we selected a simple example (http://spotfire.tibco.com/en/demos/spotfire-soccer-2014) from the Spotfire gallery that includes interactive and coordinated visualizations of data from the soccer world cups going back to Uruguai 1930. This example was chosen due to the concrete and easy to understand data set visualized; moreover the experiment was performed in 2014 at a time when the fifa World Cup Brazil had high media coverage. Thus, we anticipated this example would motivate our evaluators fostering the discovery of a higher number of problems.

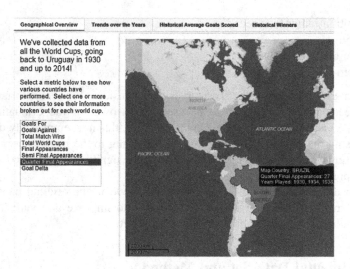

Fig. 1. World cup soccer analysis (spotfire demo gallery) - aspect of the geographical overview of the application.

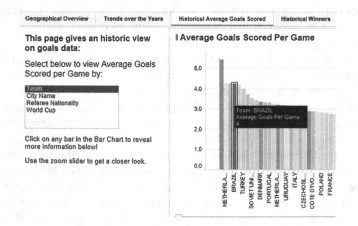

Fig. 2. World cup soccer analysis (spotfire demo gallery) - aspect of the historical view of the goals data.

Figures 1 and 2 show main aspects of the selected example allowing access to:

1- Data corresponding to the selected country on a map concerning a specific metric (goals for, goals against, etc.) (Fig. 1 – geographical overview)

2- Data corresponding to average goals scored filtered by team, city, etc. (Fig. 2 – historical view).

Ten students of the Information Visualization course participated in the experiment as evaluators. They all had some previous experience with heuristic evaluation using Nielsen's heuristics to evaluate interactive systems, had attended the majority of the course classes, performed and presented to the class a naïve critique of an example of their choice, attended a session on the two other heuristics sets and performed an heuristic evaluation using the Nielsen's heuristics and one of the visualization specific sets. Therefore, we deem that while not being experienced evaluators, the students had already a significant experience allowing them to obtain useful results using the method and provide valuable insight regarding understandability of the heuristics.

The experiment consisted in evaluating the Soccer example using heuristic evaluation with the Nielsen's heuristics and one of the two other sets of heuristics (at their discretion), and answering two simple questionnaires.

The protocol involved the following steps:

1- Answer a questionnaire to collect data concerning the participants' experience in using heuristic evaluation, as well as their background in Information Visualization and familiarity with heuristics and guidelines used in Information Visualization (e.g. the Bertin's principles, or the Shneiderman's Information Sseeking Mantra);

2- Carefully analyze the three heuristics sets and rate the understandability of each heuristic in Likert-like scale (1- not at all … 5- very much understandable);

3- Perform a partial heuristic evaluation of the example using the Nielsen's heuristics; find 6 interaction problems, and classify each problem recording the heuristic (or heuristics) not complied with.

4- Select one of the two other heuristic sets and perform a partial heuristic evaluation; find 6 problems related to visual aspects, and record the heuristic (or heuristics) not complied with.

The complete session had a maximum duration of 90 min and time of completion of each step was recorded.

Throughout the experiment participants had access to the Internet and were allowed to search for any information they needed. The entire process took one hour and a half. At the end of the experiment, there was an informal discussion with the participants concerning what was more difficult or simpler in applying the method and the various heuristics to the example, among other issues.

4   Results and Discussion of the Experiment

This section presents the main results regarding heuristics understandability obtained through the questionnaire and the number of problems found by the 10 evaluators using each list of heuristics as well as a discussion of the most relevant findings.

4.1   Understandability of Heuristics

Figure 3 depicts median values of understandability as rated by the 10 students concerning the Nielsen's heuristics. All heuristics were considered highly understandable (at least 4/5). Probably this is due to the fact that all students were familiarized with these heuristics (as confirmed by the answers to the first questionnaire); yet, heuristics 9 (Help users recognize, diagnose, and recover from errors) and 10 (Help and documentation) obtained the maximum value (5), which suggests that participants consider these particularly clear and easy to understand and apply. We took these results as a baseline for understandability of the other heuristics sets, for this group of participants.

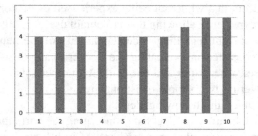

Fig. 3. Nielsen's heuristics - median values of understandability (1-not at all understandable; 5 – very much understandable).

The median values of understandability concerning the Zuk and Carpendale's heuristics are shown in Fig. 4. Most heuristics were considered very understandable; however, two heuristics were rated 3: 1- Ensure visual variable has sufficient length, and 7- Quantitative assessment requires position or size variation. Moreover, the understandability of heuristic number 1 was rated 1 by one evaluator, meaning that its meaning was completely incomprehensible to him. Confronted with this, the evaluator explained that the heuristic should be more specific to what is sufficient length, since it is too vague and no clue is given on how to assess compliance with this rule. The same evaluator also rated 1 another heuristic, and did not rate 5 any heuristic, which suggest he might have been less familiarized with this set of heuristics.

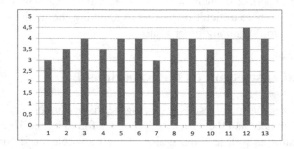

Fig. 4. Zuk and Carpendale's heuristics - median values of understandability (1-not at all understandable; 5 –very much understandable).

4.2   Problems Found

Tables 1 and 2 show the results concerning the potential problems found by each evaluator using the Nielsen's heuristics, and the visualization specific heuristics. They also show the number of problems that were considered as correctly classified, and the time each evaluator spent to find all problems.

Table 1. Problems found with Nielsen's heuristics by 10 evaluators: time spent, number of problems found, and number of problems correctly classified.

Evaluator	Using Nielsen's heuristics		
#	t (min)	N prob	N prob OK
1	19	6	6
2	20	6	6
3	27	5	5
4	19	6	6
5	28	6	6
6	31	3	3
7	20	6	6
8	28	3	3
9	35	3	3
10	21	6	6

Analyzing Table 1 we observe that the evaluators altogether found 50 potential problems (not all different; some problems were identified by several evaluators), and that all the problems were considered as correctly classified regarding the heuristic not complied with. This most probably is due to that fact that all evaluators had previous experience in using heuristic evaluation with Nielsen's heuristics to evaluate interactive systems. We notice also that seven evaluators were able to detect 5 or 6 problems in a relatively short time (19 to 27 min) and that the evaluators taking more time were the ones reporting less potential problems suggesting that these were the less experienced evaluators (this fact was confirmed analyzing their background and performance in the course).

Analyzing Table 2 we observe that eight evaluators chose to use the heuristics by Zuk and Carpendale and only two used the heuristics by Forsell and Johanson. Moreover, one evaluator (#6) was not able to apply the heuristics he had selected to use. Inspecting his answers to the questionnaire we noticed that unlikely all other evaluators he decided to use the heuristic set he had not previously used. The other nine evaluators found altogether 35 potential problems (not all different; some problems were found by several evaluators). In contrast to what happened with the Nielsen's heuristics, some of the problems (20 %) were considered as incorrectly classified regarding the heuristic not complied with. The heuristics misused to classify these latter problems were Zuk's number 2 (Don't expect reading order from color); 3 (Color perception varies with size of item); 6 (pre-attentive benefits increase with field of view); 10 (Remove the extraneous). Analyzing the rates given by the evaluators who misused these heuristics we noticed that most had rated the misused heuristic less than 4 (in a scale 1 to 5, meaning much understandable).

This suggests that, while all but one evaluator were capable of finding relevant potential problems using visualization specific heuristics, they needed more practice in order to attain the same performance they had with Nielsen's heuristics.

Similarly to what happened in the first phase of the study, evaluators generally agreed that Nielsen's heuristics are adequate to find interactive problems, even in InfoVis, however the other two sets are preferable to evaluate visual aspects.

Table 2. Problems found with Visualization specific heuristics by 10 evaluators: heuristics, time spent, number of problems found, and number of problems correctly classified.

Evaluator	Visualization specific heuristics			
#	Set	t (min)	N prob	N prob OK
1	Zuk	18	6	6
2	Zuk	18	4	2
3	Zuk	----	2	2
4	Zuk	25	5	4
5	Zuk	16	6	5
6	Zuk	Was not able to apply heuristics		
7	Zuk	20	6	4
8	Forsell	30	4	4
9	Forsell	20	4	3
10	Zuk	27	6	4

5 Conclusions and Future Work

We reviewed relevant issues involved in using heuristic evaluation in Information Visualization and performed an exploratory study to assess how understandable are the heuristics of three sets that have been used to evaluate interaction and visual aspects in InforVis, and how difficult it is to find potential problems using heuristic evaluation with those sets. The first phase of this study, involving 15 evaluators with some experience in using this method, suggested that, irrespective of the heuristics set used, heuristic evaluation is useful as it fosters a more systematic inspection of the user interface relevant aspects.

In the second phase of the study 10 evaluators, with some experience in using heuristic evaluation in InfoVis, rated the understandability of each heuristic and applied the method to an example. The obtained results suggest that heuristic evaluation is indeed suitable and produces useful results with a low investment even when performed by analysts not very experienced and hence it should be included in the developer's evaluation toolkit. We found also that some of the heuristics are easier to understand than others and confirmed that the heuristics by Nielsen seem adequate to evaluate the interaction aspects even in InfoVis applications and the Zuk and Carpendale's heuristics are useful to detect potential problems related to the visual aspects.

Even though this study has involved 25 evaluators and provided insights concerning the applicability of heuristic evaluation in Information Visualization further research is needed to compare and validate the use of these heuristics, namely involving more InfoVis examples, and evaluators with different degrees of experience.

Acknowledgments. The authors are grateful to the participants. This work was partially funded by FEDER through the Operational Program Competitiveness Factors – COMPETE – by National Funds through Foundation for Science and Technology – FCT (references FCOMP-01-0124-FEDER-022682 and PEst-C/EEI/UI0127/2011).

References

1. Plaisant, C.: The challenge of information visualization evaluation. In: Proceedings of the International Conference on Advanced Visual Interfaces (AVI2004), pp. 109–116. ACM, New York (2004)
2. Chen, C.: Top 10 unsolved information visualization problems. IEEE Comput. Graph. Appl. 25(4), 12–16 (2005)
3. Carpendale, S.: Evaluating information visualizations. In: Kerren, A., Stasko, J.T., Fekete, J.-D., North, C. (eds.) Information Visualization. LNCS, vol. 4950, pp. 19–45. Springer, Heidelberg (2008)
4. Sedlmair, M., Isemberg, P., Baur, D., Butz, A.: Information visualization evaluation in large companies : challenges, experiences and recommendations. Inf. Vis. J. 10(3), 248–266 (2011)
5. Lam, H., Bertini, E., Isenberg, P., Plaisant, C., Carpendale, S.: Empirical studies in information visualization: seven scenarios. IEEE Trans. Vis. Comput. Graph. 18(9), 1520–1536 (2012)
6. Aigner, W., Hoffmann, S., Rind, A.: EvalBench: a software library for visualization evaluation. Comput. Graph. Forum 32(3pt1), 41–50 (2013)
7. McGrath, J.E.: Methodology matters: doing research in the social and behavioural sciences. In: Baecker, R., Grudin, J., Buxton, W., Greenberg, S. (eds.) Readings in Human-Computer Interaction: Toward the Year 2000, 2nd edn, pp. 152–169. Morgan Kaufmann Publishers, San Francisco (1995)
8. Dix, A., Finlay, J., Abowd, G., Beale, R.: Human-Computer Interaction, 3rd edn. Prentice Hall, Harlow (2004)
9. Nielsen, J.: Usability Engineering. Morgan Kaufmann Publishers, San Francisco (1993)
10. Zuk, T., Carpendale, S.: Theoretical analysis of uncertainty visualizations. In: SPIE & IS&T Conference Electronic Imaging, Visualization and Data Analysis 2006, vol. 6060, pp. 606007. SPIE (2006)
11. Forsell, C., Johanson, J.: An heuristic set for evaluation in information visualization. In: Proceedings of AVI 2010, pp. 199–206. ACM, New York (2010)
12. Trainer, E., Quirk, S., Souza, C., Redmiles, D.: Analyzing a socio-technical visualization tool using usability inspection methods. In: 2008 IEEE Symposium on Visual Languages and Human-Centric Computing, pp. 78–81. IEEE (2008)
13. Trainer, E., Quirk, S., Souza, C., Redmiles, D.: Usability Inspection Method-based Analysis of a Socio-Technical Visualization Tool. Tech. report, ISR, University of California, Irvine (2012)

14. Andrews, K.: Evaluation comes in many guises. In: Proceedings of the 2008 AVI workshop on BEyond time and errors: novel evaluation methods for information visualization, (BELIV 2008). ACM, New York (2008)
15. Sousa Santos, B., Dias, P.: Evaluation in visualization: some issues and best practices. In: SPIE Conference Electronic Imaging, Visualization and Data Analysis 2014, vol. 9017, pp. 90170O-1–8. SPIE, San Francisco (2014)
16. Munzner, T.: A nested model for visualization design and validation. IEEE Trans. Vis. Comput. Graph. 15(6), 921–928 (2009)
17. Gutwin, C., Greenberg, S.: The mechanics of collaboration: developing low cost usability evaluation methods for shared workspaces. In: Proceedings of the IEEE 9th International Workshops on Enabling Technologies: Infrastructure for Collaborative Enterprises (WET ICE 2000), pp. 98–103. IEEE Computer Society, Washington (2000)
18. Baker, K., Greenberg, S., Gutwin, C.: Empirical development of a heuristic evaluation methodology for shared workspace groupware. In: Proceedings of the 2002 ACM Conference Computer Supported Cooperative Work (CSCW 2002), pp. 96–105. ACM, New York (2002)
19. Kuparinen, L., Silvennoinen, J., Isomäki, H.: Introducing usability heuristics for mobile map applications. In: Proceedings of the 26th International Cartographic Conference (ICC 2013) (2013)
20. Tory, M., Möller, T.: Human factors in visualization research. IEEE Trans. Vis. Comput. Graph. 10(1), 72–84 (2004)
21. Tory, M., Möller, T.: Evaluating visualizations: do expert reviews work? IEEE Comput. Graph. Appl. 25(5), 8–11 (2005)
22. Shneiderman, B.: The eyes have it: a task by data type taxonomy for information visualizations. In: Proceedings of the IEEE Symposium on Visual Language, pp. 336–343. IEEE (1996)
23. Ware, C.: Information Visualization: Perception for Design, 2nd edn. Morgan Kaufmann Publishers, Waltham (2004)
24. Amar, R., Stasko, J.: A knowledge task-based framework for design and evaluation of information visualizations. In: IEEE Symposium Info Vis, pp. 143–150. IEEE (2004)
25. Zuk, T., Schlesier, L., Neumann, P., Hancock, M.S., Carpendale, S.: Heuristics for information visualization evaluation. In: BELIV 2006, pp. 1–6. ACM, New York (2006)
26. Freitas, C.M., Luzzardi, P.R.G., Cava, R.A., Winckler, M.A.A., Pimenta, M.S., Nedel, L.P.: Evaluating usability of information visualization techniques. In: Proceedings of the 5th Symposium on Human Factors in Computer Systems (IHC 2002), pp. 40 − 51 (2002)
27. Tufte, E.: The Visual Display of Quantitative Information, 2nd edn. Graphics Press, Anaheim (2001)

Extending MoLIC for Collaborative Systems Design

Luiz Gustavo de Souza(⊠) and Simone Diniz Junqueira Barbosa

Department of Informatics, PUC-Rio, Rio de Janeiro, Brazil
{lgsouza, simone}@inf.puc-rio.br

Abstract. Much interaction design research has been devoted to collaborative systems, resulting in diverse design methodologies. Despite these efforts, we still lack a widely adopted interaction model for collaborative systems design. In this paper, we present a study on model-based design approaches, focusing on their limitations with respect to the 3C Model of Collaboration. Based on the 3C Model, we propose an extension to MoLIC, an interaction design language grounded in semiotic engineering but with no support for collaboration. We then illustrate the expressiveness of the extended MoLIC in the interaction design representation of a collaborative document editor.

Keywords: Interaction design · Semiotic engineering · MoLIC

1 Introduction

Collaborative systems allow users to interact with each other, collaborating, coordinating and communicating, as defined by the 3C Model of Collaboration [1], [2]. This kind of system brought about new problems and challenges for different fields, especially for interaction design. The field of Computer Supported Collaborative Work (CSCW) studies the development of collaborative systems, in which the interactions between users and between user and the system occur in a distributed and synchronized way [3, 4]. Some examples of collaborative systems include e-mail services, chat, social networks, and collaborative document editing [4–6]. Different works propose ways to ease and improve the design process for collaboration [5, 7–10], as well as present studies about design practice [4, 6, 11, 12]. In this paper, we identify problems and gaps that motivate the improvement of MoLIC, a design language grounded in Semiotic Engineering, to represent collaborative interaction.

Semiotic Engineering (SemEng) [13] considers the human-computer interaction to be a conversation between designer and user, and as such all computational artifacts are viewed as a kind of computer-mediated communication. According to SemEng, the user interface is the designer's deputy, conveying a one-shot message from designer to user, called a metacommunication message, or simply metamessage, allowing the user to interact with it to achieve his goals. This metamessage represents the solution proposed by the designer about his understanding of the users' problems, needs and preferences, and how they may interact with the system to achieve a range of anticipated (or unanticipated) goals. When it comes to collaborative systems, users also want

M. Kurosu (Ed.): Human-Computer Interaction, Part I, HCII 2015, LNCS 9169, pp. 271–282, 2015.
DOI: 10.1007/978-3-319-20901-2_25

or need to cooperate, coordinate, and communicate with other users. According to SemEng, the content of the metamessage for collaborative systems includes support for the user to see who is talking, what they are saying, whether they are listening, and how they respond.

Based on SemEng, different researchers proposed modelling languages to represent user and system interaction, such as MoLIC, a design language that allows designers to conceive and represent the interaction between the user and the designer's deputy. On multi-user interaction, there are two proposed modelling languages, MetaCom-G*, a tool that provides a design language to create interaction models, based on the collaborative work of the users and their objectives in the communication process; and Manas, another design language to create interaction models, based on the collaborative section of the metamessage and on social aspects of the interaction.

The MoLIC language has improved over the years in various researches, and can be used in a design process with different artifacts, such as interaction scenarios, task models, and user interface mockups. The main research on MoLIC points to improvement opportunities to be able to design a broader set of systems, which is the case of collaborative systems. The state of the art of MoLIC regarding collaboration provides elements for a simplified representation of the contact between users, not considering synchronization issues or any other collaboration concepts defined by collaboration models (such as the 3C Model).

Based on the SemEng and the 3C Model of Collaboration, in this paper we address the following research question: *How can we extend MoLIC in order to represent the design of collaborative systems based on the 3C Model, grounded in Semiotic Engineering?*

To answer this question, we have investigated related interaction models and the 3C Model, which allow us to list a set of concepts expected for an extension and propose new elements for the language. The next section presents briefly the SemEng and the 3C Model, as well as the related model: Manas, ConcurTaskTrees (CTT) and a variation of CTT in a methodology called CIAM (Collaborative Interactive Application Methodology) [14], and the MoLIC language. Following, we present the concepts that an interactive model must represent in order to include the 3C Model, showing in the studied interactive models gaps related to these concepts. We conclude by proposing the extension and showing a design example, followed by some concluding remarks.

2 Background

In this section, we briefly present Semiotic Engineering concepts, in which MoLIC is rooted, and the 3C model of collaboration, followed by the background works based on interaction models for collaboration.

2.1 Semiotic Engineering

As we presented in the introduction section, SemEng considers that the designer, through signs codified in the interface of interactive systems, communicates with the user, including both in the role of interlocutors in the communicative process. The user interface reflects the designer's deputy, who represents the designer at interaction time. Through the user interface, the designer must inform the user about the meaning of the constructed artifact, and the user is expected to understand and respond to it by interacting with the designer's deputy [13].

The metacommunication from designer to user can be as the following template:

"Here is my understanding of who you are, what I've learned you want or need to do, in which preferred ways, and why. This is the system that I have therefore designed for you, and this is the way you can or should use it in order to fulfill a range of purposes that fall within this vision" [13, p. 84].

Considering not only the user-system interaction, but also the collaborative interaction among users, the metacommunication artifact template is extended, including the following:

"You can communicate and interact with other users through the system. During communication, the system will help you check:

1. Who is speaking? To whom?
2. What is the speaker saying? Using which code and medium? Are code and medium appropriate for the situation? Are there alternatives?
3. Is (are) the listener(s) receiving the message? What for?
4. How can the listener(s) respond to the speaker?
5. Is there recourse if the speaker realizes the listener(s) misunderstood the message? What is it?" [13, p. 210].

This way, the user can understand whether he can collaborate with other users, and how he can do it, based on the tools provided.

The MoLIC language, as we present in Sect. 2.6, describes the metamessage, supporting the designer to reflect on it. Our study presents the intention to represent the extended metamessage, allowing MoLIC to support collaborative interaction design.

2.2 3C Model of Collaboration

The 3C Model envisioned by Fuks [1] and based on the work of Ellis, Gibs and Reins [2] defined that the collaboration process can be described by three elements: communication, coordination, and cooperation. During collaboration it is necessary to provide ways for *communication* among users, synchronized or not, allowing for sharing of ideas, information and data. The *coordination* is achieved as a task organizer, improving the collaboration process as a whole while preventing conflicts and task rework. The *cooperation* is the process of joint work, sharing one task with members aiming at the overall goal.

These three elements work in a circular dynamic, where the communication is intended for preparing the coordination. While coordinating, the group acts and cooperates, creating demands again for communication in diverse situations like decision making and task renegotiation, restarting the cycle.

As a representation of the collaboration, we use the 3C Model as basis to understand what an interaction model should provide in order to represent collaborative interaction. Along with the study of other design models, we present the concepts based on 3C to be represented in the MoLIC language on Sect. 3.

2.3 Design Scenario

The following sections present background works for interaction models, illustrating their main concepts through an example: the design of a collaborative text editor. The design intention is as follows:

> A user can create a document and edit it. At any moment, he can share this document with other users, so they can all edit it at the same time, keeping the synchronization and the awareness of each user's actions. It is also possible to chat with the group.

2.4 SemEng Collaborative Model: Manas

Barbosa [5] proposed Manas, a tool that considers social factors and focuses on the metacommunication artifact of SemEng, instead of considering the users' work, understanding that users might want to interact with no work-related, predetermined tasks.

Manas aims to support the designer's reflection on the users' problems, providing qualitative information about the communication. It provides the L-ComUSU language, which creates a m-ComUSU model, to be interpreted by a design logic interpreter.

The interpreter returns two types of information: the interpretation of the model exposing decisions both made and disregarded in the design process; and a set of the possible social impacts on the communication process and on the experience of the users.

Example. The design process of Manas involves defining the user roles and, for each possible user task, a speech is created, indicating who is talking, the purpose, topic and who the listeners are. When there is interaction among users, all the speeches involved are encapsulated as a conversation process. This way the designer can structure when there is user collaboration, and the role of each user in the collaboration.

For the design using Manas, we achieve the complete application design, specifying the sharing, editing and communication processes. After creating the model, the tool generates a report, indicating all the decisions made during design, also pointing to situations not considered, giving feedback about the possible problems and how they can be avoided.

Different from other models, Manas does not present a visual schema, and does not support a more tactical level of interaction, that is, Manas does not support the definition of how the interaction can occur, as it allows the definition of the users, what each one can do and how what they do will affect others.

Manas also does not indicate explicitly the cooperation objects, nor the expression elements to interact with them. The tool also does not support reactions based on another user action, that is, something that occurs to a user when another user performs some other action. For example, when some user A removes a user B from a shared document while B is editing it, B not only needs to be notified, but also prevented from reading and editing the new document, by closing it automatically or disabling the interface. For Manas, in this situation, the user would only be notified as a listener of the "remove share" speech, but what happens beyond that is not considered.

2.5   Collaborative Task Model: ConcurTaskTrees

ConcurTaskTrees (CTT) was proposed by Paternò [15], and reflects the interaction design aiming to support the users and their tasks. CTT leads the designer to reflect on the users' tasks, decomposing them to the desired level of abstraction, modeling their representation in a temporal sequence.

The model takes the form of a tree, where the root represents the general task, and each level represents a more specific detail of the task. Each level of the tree uses temporal associations among tasks from left to right depending on their relationships. This means that each task can be executed at the same time, in a given order or based on some condition.

To support the design of cooperation, Paternò created the idea of multiple user roles, where one task to be performed by more than one user can be described in a cooperative CTT model, and then that task is shared among each user role, having an indication that the task belongs to the cooperative model.

Example. CTT gives support only for cooperation, with the concepts that the act of cooperation is to allow members to perform tasks sequentially and synchronized among each other. From the 3C Model's point of view, the cooperation aims to support the task performed in a shared environment, that is, there is task synchronization, but this synchronization is made on demand, not necessarily needing a logical sequence, allowing members to perform their tasks at any time, not just when another user reaches a desired state.

This way, it is possible to affirm that the support for cooperation given by CTT is limited, considering the full specification of the collaboration as defined by the 3C Model.

The figures above present a possible design solution for the collaborative text editor. The model in Fig. 1 shows the tasks to be performed by the user interacting with the system, including the emission of an asynchronous message. In the model presented in Fig. 2 it is possible to see that there is not a description of the shared environment, and also there is no description of the cooperation objects that the users are manipulating, which include the message log and the document itself. Besides, The document editing and the message exchange by other users do not create notifications, that is, there is no awareness about what the other users are doing and, as such, there is no coordination. The use of the CTT's cooperation was not the right solution for this case, giving a model that can be read as single or multi user. These issues and ambiguities show that the model:

- Does not represent the synchronous message exchange
- Does not define cooperation objects

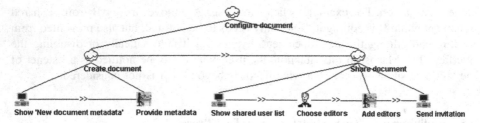

Fig. 1. CTT model to create and share the collaborative document

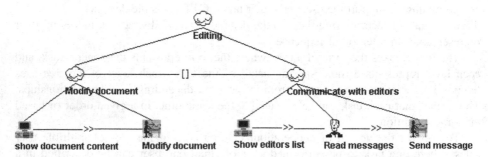

Fig. 2. Collaborative document editing

- Does not offer awareness mechanisms
- Does not allow the notification emission
- Does not explicitly shows which users are participating in the collaborative environment

CTT extension: CIAM. Using CTT as the base interaction model, and defining a complete method and notation to represent collaboration as a set of artifacts, Molina, Redondo and Ortega [14] proposed the Collaborative Interactive Application Method (CIAM). To use CTT, they argued that CTT does not have everything needed to represent collaboration, proposing new types of tasks pursuing the gaps found. This new notation allows to indicate collaborative/cooperative tasks and shared context tasks.

In this method, as the new notation indicates only collaborative tasks, the model is still not capable to solve the first, second and fourth limitations listed for CTT. The Fig. 1 would stay the same, and the Fig. 2 can be is enhanced resulting in Fig. 3.

2.6 SemEng Interaction Model: MoLIC

MoLIC (Modeling Language for Interaction as Conversation) is an interaction design language proposed by Barbosa and Paula [16] based on SemEng. As the theory perceives the interaction as a conversation between the designer's deputy and the user, MoLIC allows the representation of the interaction as a set of conversations that the user can have with the designer's deputy, expecting that the designer present clearly the metamessage. The language also serves as an epistemic tool, leading designers to improve their understanding about the problem to be solved and the artifact to be created.

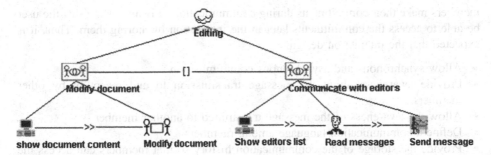

Fig. 3. CIAM extension CTT collaborative document edition

The design project starts with the definition of the user roles, their goals, analysis and interaction scenarios and the signs used in these scenarios. The model is then created to represent how the scenarios may occur, leading the users to achieve their goals during the interaction. In the process, the designer is led to reflect on the met-amessage, creating better ways to solve communication breakdowns and, exploring alternatives before creating the final user interface. Figure 4 presents the traditional MoLIC elements.

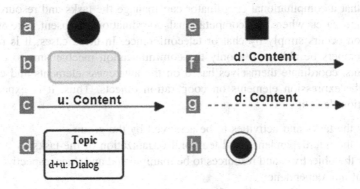

Fig. 4. Elements of the MoLIC language where: **a** is the opening point; **b** is a ubiquitous access; **c** is a user utterance; **d** is a conversation scene; **e** is a system processing; **f** is a designer utterance; **g** is a breakdown utterance; and **h** is a closing point.

3 Collaboration Concepts

Based on the 3C Model, we studied the meaning of each element and how interaction design models can incorporate its underlying concepts.

3.1 Communication

Communication involves the direct (sync or async) message exchange, that is, the ability to talk to another user or member of the collaborative process. Also, as the members make their commitments during communication, it is interesting that the user be able to access the commitments later in the interaction by storing them. Thus, it is expected that the interaction design:

- Allow synchronous and asynchronous communication
- Provide awareness about the message transmission to and reception by other members
- Allow the awareness of the message transmitted to another member
- Define a communication language among members
- Provide the storage of the communication history so that members can access the commitments

3.2   Coordination

Coordination can be defined as the joint work, promoting the collaboration through the sum of the individual works. This process involves preparing the objectives and their division between the members, managing the collaboration, and continuously rene-gotiating the commitments and tasks, ending by analyzing the collaboration.

In order to support cooperation, the members organize the tasks temporally, including their interdependencies, identifying also the resources to be jointly manip-ulated, so that a computational coordinator can manage the tasks and resources.

There are cases where the computational coordination is absent, like when the collaboration occurs simply by chat or teleconference. In these cases, it is necessary that the members be able to use only the communication mechanisms to create the commitments, coordinate themselves based on the awareness elements and cooperate based on the expression elements on cooperation objects. Thus, it is expected that the interaction design:

- Identify the tasks and activities to be achieved by the group
- Identify the interdependency and temporal organization of the tasks
- Identify the objectives and resources to be manipulated and their respective types of temporal interdependency
- Allow the organization and coordination of the members based on communication

3.3   Cooperation

Cooperation is the joint effort in the shared environment, where the group perform the tasks, creating or modifying cooperation objects by using expression elements, so that awareness elements can track each user's work and inform the group, creating a shared environment. Thus, it is expected that the interaction design:

- Provide expression elements
- Provide cooperation objects
- Control the concurrent access to the cooperation objects through the expression elements
- Provide balanced information using the awareness elements

3.4   MoLIC Extension

The second version of MoLIC proposed an alternative to represent the contact between users using a contact point, where a user could reach another user's conversation topic to inform him. This led to some problems based on the user to designer communication process, seeing that a user speaks directly to another. This idea was to be the basis for collaboration, but further studies and with the use of the 3C Model of collaboration showed how collaboration must include other elements and dynamics.

To extend MoLIC allowing the representation of the collaboration based on the 3C Model, we propose the use of three new elements, the Incoming Message Indicator (IMI), Outgoing Message Indicator (OMI), and the Shared Space Indicator (SSI). Figure 5 presents the new elements.

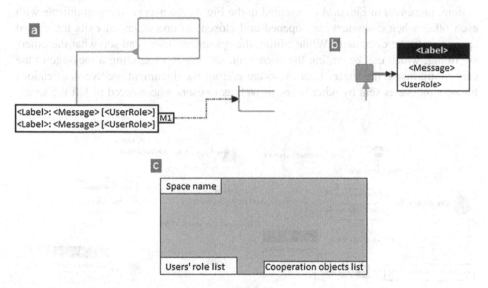

Fig. 5. New proposed elements, where: **a** is the incoming message indicator; **b** is the outgoing message indicator; and **c** is the shared space indicator.

The IMI indicates which message the user can receive during his conversation on the attached scene, and transitions from IMI indicate that when the user receives some message, he can or must change his current conversation topic to attend to the message. The OMI indicates that when the user make a request, the system will send some message to other users, to be received using the IMI.

The OMI is mandatorily attached to a system processing, indicating that the message to be sent is to be performed by the system, being either synchronous or asynchronous. The IMI is mandatorily attached to a scene, indicating that the user will receive a notification for some message only when an IMI attached to the scene has that message defined.

The SSI element represents one space area instance that all users share, and are able to seeing which topic the others are during their communication with the designer's deputy. The top left text describes the name of the space, the bottom left lists the user roles that can participate in that space, and the bottom right lists the cooperation objects that the users share inside the space. Modifications on a cooperation object are seen by all users inside the space, not specifying the type of synchronized access when modifying it. We understand that concurrency to access these objects might change based on different implementations, and the interaction model does not need to specify it at the interaction design phase. The expression elements to interact with the cooperation objects are defined by the SSI space itself and the conversations the user can have with the designer's deputy inside the space, allowing the extension to express the main components of each of the 3C's elements.

Based on the proposed extension, we designed the collaborative document editor system, presented in Fig. 6. As presented in the Fig. 6, the users can communicate with each other when documents are opened and closed, as one enters of exits the shared space to edit the document. While editing the document, users can see what the others are doing, which can be editing the document, sharing it, or sending a message to the user group inside the space. Users who are editing the document receive notifications for new messages sent by other users, as well as to users who entered of left the space.

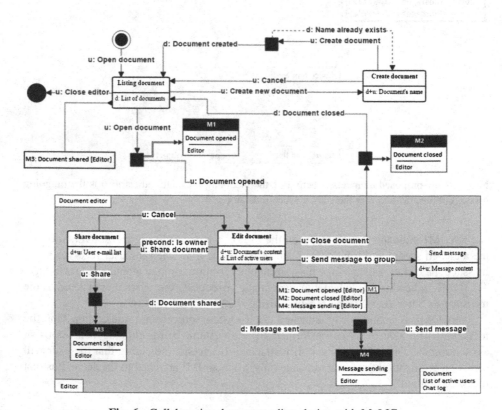

Fig. 6. Collaborative document editor design with MoLIC

The cooperation objects are referenced by name using plain text on the scenes, as well as other objects that can be defined using simply the original MoLIC language.

3.5   Concluding Remarks

Using the 3C Model of collaboration as the foundation theory for collaboration, we created a set of resources that an interaction model should provide to fully represent the collaboration. Based on these concepts, we analyzed related models, designing an example to verify their efficiency on representing such concepts. This study motivated our intention to extend the MoLIC language to represent the collaboration as defined by the 3C Model.

Based on the concepts and the related works, we defined new elements to represent the collaboration along with the complete MoLIC language, designing the proposed example to verify its expressiveness.

We see that using the elements can cause the diagram to be too large depending on the problem, by the number of IMI and OMI needed, as well as the size that the SSI might need to take. It shows that further studies on our solution are needed to evaluate this other kinds of problems, as well as to use it in a real design environment to evaluate its ease of use and its epistemic capacity when thinking of collaboration.

For future works we intend to test this extension with students in an academic setting and in professional settings.

References

1. Fuks, H., Raposo, A.B., Gerosa, M.A., Lucena, C.J.P.: Applying the 3C model to groupware engineering. In: Monografias em Ciência da Computação. PUC-Rio, Rio de Janeiro (2004)
2. Ellis, C.A., Gibbs, S.J., Rein, G.L.: Groupware - some issues and experiences. Commun. ACM **34**(1), 38–58 (1991)
3. Grudin, J.C.S.C.W.: History and focus. IEEE Comput. **27**, 19–26 (1994)
4. Rama, J., Bishop, J.: Survey and comparison of CSCW groupware applications. In: Proceedings of SAICSIT, pp. 1–12 (2006)
5. Barbosa, C.M.A.: Manas: Uma Ferramenta Epistêmica de Apoio ao Projeto da Comunicação em Sistemas Colaborativos. Doctoral thesis. Department of Informatics IIn (In Portuguese), PUC-Rio, Rio de Janeiro (2007)
6. Iacob, C. Using Design Patterns in Collaborative Interaction Design Processes. In: Proceedings of the ACM 2012 conference on Computer Supported Collaborative Work Companion, pp. 107–110. New York, (2012)
7. Alarcon, R., Guerrero, L.A., Ochoa, S.F., Pino, J.A.: Analysis and design of mobile collaborative applications using contextual elements. Comput. Inform. **25**, 469–496 (2006)
8. Barbosa, C.M.A.: MetaCom-G*: Especificação da Comunicação entre Membros de um Grupo. Master thesis. Depatment of Informatics (In Portuguese), PUC-Rio, Rio de Janeiro (2002)
9. Molina, A.I., Redondo, M.A., Ortega, M.: A methodological approach for user interaface development of collaborative applications: a case study. Sci. Comput. Program. **74**, 754–776 (2009)

10. Prates, R.O.A: Engenharia Semiótica de Linguagens de Interface Multi-usuário. Doctoral thesis. Department of Informatics (In Portuguese), PUC-Rio, Rio de Janeiro (1998)
11. Iacob, C.: Identifying, relating and evaluating design patterns for the design of software for synchronous collaboration. In: Proceedings of the 3rd ACM SIGCHI Symposium on Engineering Interactive Systems, pp. 323–326, New York (2011)
12. Schadewitz, N.: Design patterns for cross-cultural collaboration. Int. J. Design 3(3), 37–53 (2009)
13. De Souza, C.S.: The Semiotic Engineering of Human-Computer Interaction. The MIT Press, Cambridge (2005)
14. Molina, A.I., Redondo, M.A., Ortega, M.: A methodological approach for user interface development of collaborative applications: a case study. Sci. Comput. Program. 74(9), 754–776 (2009)
15. Paternò, F.: ConcurTaskTrees: an engineering notation for task models. In: The Handbook of Task Analysis for Human-Computer Interaction, pp. 483–503 (2004)
16. Barbosa, S.D.J., de Paula, M.G.: Designing and evaluating interaction as conversation: a modeling language based on semiotic engineering. In: Jorge, J.A., Jardim Nunes, N., Falcão e Cunha, J. (eds.) DSV-IS 2003. LNCS, vol. 2844, pp. 16–33. Springer, Heidelberg (2003)

Using Readers' and Organizations' Goals to Guide Assessment of Success in Information Websites

Robert B. Watson[✉] and Jan Spyridakis

Department of Human Centered Design & Engineering,
University of Washington, Seattle, WA, USA
{rbwatson,jansp}@uw.edu

Abstract. Informational and reference websites benefit readers without providing their publishing organizations with any direct or immediate financial benefit; however, organizations do expect return on their investment. We propose two website stakeholder taxonomies: one about the goals of readers when they use informational websites and the other about the goals of organizations when they produce sites. These taxonomies should help organizations measure readers' success with their sites and understand how well their sites support the organizations' goals, and in turn help them author and design better web content to meet their readers' goals.

Keywords: Reader goals · Organization goals · User goals · Usability · Measurement · Metrics · Effectiveness · Efficiency · User satisfaction · User-Centered Design (UCD)

1 Introduction

Informational and reference websites help readers accomplish their goals without the publishing organizations realizing any immediate financial benefits. While the cost of producing and supporting these sites is often easy to track, the value they provide can be much more difficult to measure. Schaupp et al. [1] recognized that measuring the success of such sites is difficult "because the definition of success changes depending on the perspective that the stakeholder adopts." The stakeholders in an informational site include, at a minimum, the site's readers and its sponsoring organization, who have different, yet ideally related, goals and definitions of success. As the definition of success varies with the stakeholder perspective, it becomes difficult to know what to measure, let alone how to measure it. The taxonomies we propose in this paper seek to clarify the goals of these stakeholders. As a result, strategies for measuring success towards meeting those goals can then be identified, and organizations can chose how to measure reader performance more accurately and obtain a better indication about their return on investment.

This paper reviews the theory and previous literature from which we propose two taxonomies that delineate reader and organization goals with informational websites. Within the framework of these taxonomies, we discuss how and when organizations

© Springer International Publishing Switzerland 2015
M. Kurosu (Ed.): Human-Computer Interaction, Part I, HCII 2015, LNCS 9169, pp. 283–294, 2015.
DOI: 10.1007/978-3-319-20901-2_26

should collect data about the readers' experiences in order to track how well they relate to the readers' and organizations' goals, and help organizations author and design effective content to meet their readers' goals.

2   Background and Literature Review

The lack of an expectation of generating revenue is the key factor that differentiates informational sites (e.g., government, medical, library, and reference sites) from commercial websites. This paper focuses on informational sites that do not have any immediate commercial goals. An example of such an informational site is the United States National Aeronautics and Space Administration (NASA), www.nasa.gov. An example of an informational/commercial site is the W3Schools site (www.w3schools. com) because the site contains advertisements, making its real motive commercial. While such commercial/informational sites might be able to apply some of the concepts in this paper, their hybrid goals are not the focus of this paper.

The following sections describe published work that helped us develop an improved taxonomy of stakeholder goals. We build on Rouet's TRACE model [2] of document processing and then review usability properties and website measurement metrics in order to characterize readers' experiences as readers interact with the content they encounter on the web. Finally, we describe reader and organization goals to explore appropriate measures for meeting differing stakeholder goals.

2.1   Document Research Task Models

Rouet [2] describes how people research information on the web in a 9-step Task-based Relevance Assessment and Content Extraction (TRACE) model that starts with readers formulating the information-seeking task and constructing a task model to use to accomplish the task. If external information is required, the TRACE model says that readers will iteratively evaluate documents to collect and process the information necessary to accomplish the task, until they feel that they need no additional information to complete the task. This model is consistent with Redish's observation that readers will read until the think they have the answer [3].

2.2   Website Usability and Measurement Metrics

Website usability has been characterized in many ways and assessed with many metrics and tools. Watson [4] summarizes usability properties from ISO-9241 [5], Nielsen [6], and Quesenbery [7]. Nielsen and Loranger [8] reiterated the same usability properties that Nielsen [6] listed. Many have noted that an understanding of usability involves appreciating its purpose and use [9–11]. To assess the reader (user) experience, many have suggested the use of usability measures such as effectiveness, efficiency, satisfaction, memorability, engagement, ease of learning, error rates, and error tolerance [6–8].

Organizations use many metrics to assess website activity and effectiveness [1, 12–14]. Web servers provide activity logs; services such as Google Analytics provide rich data from instrumented websites [15]; and online and offline questionnaires can solicit feedback from web-site visitors [16]. However, because many of these metrics were originally designed to support the specific goals of revenue-producing sites, they can present challenges when they are used to monitor and assess the effectiveness of informational sites. If the tools' goals align with the goals of an informational site, the tools can provide valuable information. However, when they misalign, the data provided can range from not useful to confusing. By characterizing the goals of informational sites more precisely than earlier taxonomies have afforded, measurement metrics and tools aligned with these goals can be identified and developed.

3   Goal-Oriented Taxonomies of Informational Sites

We propose two stakeholder taxonomies that identify goals for using and posting informational content on a website: one that identifies the readers' goals for visiting informational websites and one that identifies the organizations' goals for producing informational websites. Categorizing readers' goals in this way should help organizations analyze where and how readers accomplish their goals and in turn identify suitable metrics to measure how well the site helps readers accomplish their goals.

3.1   Reader Goal Taxonomy

Redish [17] extended the reader's goals tested by Sticht et al. [18] to describe three reading goals: reading to do, reading to learn, and reading to learn to do. These reading goals still apply to web readers today, but they do not help identify where the content fits within the reader's task(s) to accomplish his or her goals. We therefore propose five goals that readers can have when they visit informational websites:

- Reading to be reminded (Reading to do lite)
- Reading to accomplish a task in a website (Reading to do here)
- Reading to accomplish a task outside a website now (Reading to do now)
- Reading to accomplish a task outside a website later (Reading to learn to do later)
- Reading to learn (Reading to learn to use later or to apply with other information)

Reading to be Reminded. Reading to be reminded, or Reading to Do Lite, occurs when readers visit an informational site with the confidence that they know most of what they need to know about a topic and just need a refresher. Readers use the website as a form of offline information storage that they may use either online or elsewhere. Brandt et al. [19] noticed this pattern while observing software developers who "delegated their memory to the Web, spending tens of seconds to remind themselves of syntactic details of a concept they new [sic] well." By knowing the information is available online, readers do not need to remember the details, just where they can find them. An example of such a website might be an online help website that reminds one how to get the ribbon to reappear in Microsoft Office.

Because readers will read "until they've met their need" [3], readers will spend as little time in the site as they need accessing the site shortly before or after they start a task. Once readers have been reminded of the information they need, they will finish their original task when convenient. Figure 1 illustrates an example of readers' interactions with the content when reading to be reminded. In Fig. 1, the reader referred to the content once before starting the task and twice while performing the task to accomplish his or her goal.

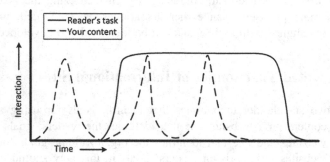

Fig. 1. Task and content interaction with a reading to be reminded goal

Topic design principles needed to serve this reader goal include making content easy to find, navigate, and read. Visible headings and short "bites" and "snacks" of information [3] are well suited to such a goal. Because such content access is typically very short and highly focused, the readers' success in using a search engine is critical; however, it is often successful because readers already know the terms and context they are seeking and may have already bookmarked the page in their browser.

One success metric that can be measured in the background is the search term relevance to the topics sought by the reader. Asking about the reader's satisfaction should be done soon after the interaction with a brief satisfaction questionnaire— perhaps just one question, such as "Did this topic help you?" Otherwise, the survey could impose on the readers' overall task flow.

Those who assess a reader's success with informational websites should be aware that traditional, commerce-oriented web metrics could allow for misinterpretation of the reader's short interaction with the site. Google Analytics [20] describes Bounce Rate as "the percentage of sessions…in which the person left your site from the entrance page without interacting with the page." In a commerce-oriented site, the goal is to attract customers, have them engage with the site, and then go through the purchase funnel. In that context, a high bounce rate is a bad outcome because it suggests that people are not interacting with the site and not finding what they are looking for. In a Reading to Be Reminded interaction, however, a high bounce rate could be a sign of success, with readers finding what they need quickly and leaving the website.

Short average time-on-page values [21] could also be misleading. If the page is well designed and needed information is found quickly, readers who come to the page for a reminder will leave quickly and spend little time reading the page. An understanding of the readers' satisfaction is required in order to interpret whether a high bounce rate or a short average time-on-page is good or bad. Otherwise, these page visit values could easily be misinterpreted in the context of informational websites.

Reading to Accomplish a Task in the Website (Reading to Do *Here*). Reading to accomplish a task in the website, or Reading to Do Here, is characterized by readers interacting with a page in a website to accomplish a specific task through the site. The readers' goal is to complete the desired task, such as register for a library account, subscribe to an online newsletter, or renew a business license.

The readers' interaction with the content begins shortly after they decide to accomplish the task and ends just after they complete it. Figure 2 illustrates such a task. Readers want to find the page to help them accomplish the task as quickly as possible and complete the task in the least number of steps and amount of time possible. They want to know if they have successfully completed the task before they leave the website. After they leave the website, they generally will not remember much about the experience unless it was especially negative or positive.

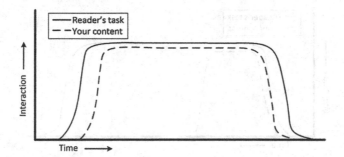

Fig. 2. Task and content interaction with a reading to do here goal

Figure 2 shows a very common type of web interaction. Web usability guidelines describe the design implications that depend on the site, context, and audience in many texts [3, 22]. Because the task is performed almost entirely in the context of the web interaction, measuring the success of the interaction is easily accomplished without imposing on the reader. The web server can collect data concerning the time spent in the interaction; the rate of successful operations (e.g., registrations, applications, or whatever the interaction is designed to accomplish); and the path through the interaction (e.g., back tracks, sidetracks, and early exits). Requests for qualitative feedback should occur soon after the interaction so readers' remember the interaction.

Reading to Accomplish a Task *Outside* the Website Now (Reading to Do *Now*). Readers interacting with a website to accomplish a specific task outside the website now, or Reading to Do Now, seek to complete the desired task at the same time that the website provides the information necessary to achieve their goal. Examples of such websites include sites that describe how to repair a household appliance or how to cook a meal.

The readers' interaction with the content begins after they decide to perform the task. Depending on the nature and duration of the task, the reader might return to the content several times during the task; however, the readers' interaction with the content ends when they feel confident to complete the task without additional information—which may or may not coincide with task completion. Figure 3 shows the task and content interaction of a task in which the reader refers to the content for only the first half of the task and feels confident enough to continue without further reading the content.

This interaction can influence several aspects of the design. For example, if readers would be likely to print the web content to save or take with them, it might be inconvenient to have the web content spread over several web pages. However, because readers might stop interacting with the content at any point, the content could be divided into individual pages of logical steps with natural breaks. Such a design could provide the sponsoring organization with information about the readers' interactions without inconveniencing readers. Breaking a task into steps or subtasks could be modeled as a sequence of reading to do now tasks.

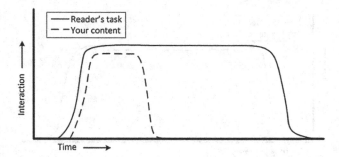

Fig. 3. Task and content interaction with a reading to do *now* goal for accomplishing a task outside the website

Because time can elapse between when readers stop interacting with the content and when they actually complete the task, asking for satisfaction or successful task completion might require creativity. For example, one could use social media to indicate the task was completed with a "post your finished project to Facebook" link, which could trigger a short satisfaction survey or a "rate this recipe" dialog.

Tracking progress, success, and satisfaction for this type of interaction requires coordination with the content design. The task and subtask flows must be modeled in the content's design so that the instrumentation used to collect data about the interaction coordinates with the readers' interaction. Because readers can leave the content without reading all of it and still complete their task successfully, metrics such as average time-on-page and path are less relevant to the readers' experiences than satisfaction and success. It is impossible to know if it is bad or good that readers exit a procedure on the first step without knowing whether they are also dissatisfied or unsuccessful. Perhaps the instructions were confusing and they left with a negative experience. Alternatively, the instructions on the first page might have provided the information and the confidence the readers needed to proceed and be successful without further reading. In either case, without assessing the readers' experience, most of the web metrics collected by the server and web analytics modules may provide only ambiguous data.

Reading to Accomplish a Task *Outside* **the Website Later (Reading to Learn to Do** *Later***).** When a reader is Reading to Accomplish a Task outside the Website (Reading to Learn to Do Later), the task and the content that provides the prerequisite learning to accomplish the task later are separated in time, to the point where they may become separate but related tasks. An example of a website that facilitates this type of reader's goals—where the ultimate task is accomplished outside the website—is the United States Internal Revenue Service's form page (www.irs.gov/Forms-&-Pubs). While the readers' goal might be to file an annual tax return, they may need to obtain and download a form from the forms page, but they plan to fill out the tax return (a separate goal) later. Figure 4 illustrates an example of the relationship between the content interaction and the actual performance of the task studied.

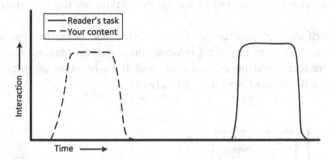

Fig. 4. Task and content interaction with a reading to learn to do *later* goal for accomplishing a task outside the website

The web usability goals for this reader goal include search-engine optimization and effectiveness, and term and vocabulary alignment. Depending on the nature of the content and the task, it might be necessary to assess the task and its performance as separate events. In this case, it would be necessary to include affordances to test the intermediate goal of learning the content before the task is attempted and consider using methods to collect and coordinate information about task completion. Learning, for example, could be measured through interactive quizzes in the content (such as through a game) but task completion would need to be measured in a way that is task appropriate. For example, a driver's license test preparation site could quiz the reader on the content read to determine the readers' learning and the content's effectiveness, and even provide feedback if desired. The task of passing the written driver's license test would occur later and be measured at the Department of Licensing. If possible, the two experiences could be related to evaluate the effectiveness of the test preparation and actual task completion. Asking the reader about satisfaction could also be done during and after the readers' content interaction, as long as the questions did not overly disturb the learning task.

Reading to Learn (to use Later or to Apply with Other Information). Reading to Learn to Use Later, without a particular or immediate task in mind, is similar to what Sticht described as *Reading to Learn* [18]. The critical distinction is that the reading task in the web is a subtask of the reader's ultimate goal of learning a new concept or skill. An example of a website that facilitates this type of reader goal, where the goals are accomplished after using the website or in conjunction with using other information, would be reading websites and books about design principles so as to use the information later when designing a website.

In a Reading to Learn to Use Later goal, as shown in Fig. 5, the reader reads information from many different locations, of which the content on the sponsoring organization's website might be only one information source. Unlike Reading to Be Reminded, the interaction with the content with this goal is more involved because the information they are reading is new and the reader might consult multiple sources to accumulate the information required to reach the learning goal. It is difficult to measure how well readers are accomplishing their ultimate learning goal when their interaction with the website may be one step of many and they might not use the information until much later.

The design of the web page could be modified to encourage or require readers to interact with the page so as to collect information about the readers' experience. For example, the content could include quizzes, and links or other affordances such as prompts to share the content with a social network.

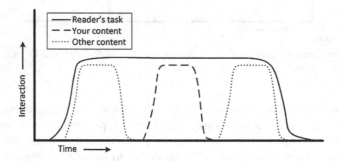

Fig. 5. Task and content interaction with a reading to learn to use later goal

3.2   Organization Goal Taxonomy

The previous section described five readers' goals, but organizations' goals for informational websites are also important and not always as clear or easy to measure. Halvorson and Rach [23] state that "content is more or less worthless unless it supports a key business objective and fulfills your users' needs."

To help organizations clarify their goals, we propose three goals for organizations that produce informational websites:

- Brand awareness
- Brand loyalty
- Cost reduction

We drew these goals from marketing literature and kept their "marketing" names to make them easier to relate to existing literature and metrics. Therefore, they will need some adaptation by organizations that do not have specific revenue-producing goals.

Measuring the influence of web content on the organization's goals requires a clear understanding of how the content contributes to the organizations' goals. Ittner and Larcker [24] note that 77 % of the companies they surveyed did not link their metrics to business performance. For the metrics discussed here to be meaningful, they must be linked to the organization's goals.

Brand Awareness. McGovern [25] says, "There is one word that describes all great Web brands: useful." This would seem to apply to commercial and non-commercial websites alike. Keller [26] describes two approaches to measuring customer-based brand equity:

1. "The 'indirect' approach attempts to assess potential sources of customer-based brand equity by measuring brand knowledge (i.e., brand awareness and brand image).
2. "The 'direct' approach attempts to measure customer-based brand equity more directly by assessing the impact of brand knowledge on consumer response to different elements of the firm's marketing program."

The methods to accomplish such measurements are typically survey based and take place outside the web experience. It is impossible to assess such measures accurately by asking or observing only the part of the market that comes to your website.

Measuring market-based goals requires some adaptation for products and brands that are not commerce-oriented. For example, the "market" for a government-sponsored website could be defined as those citizens who live within or interact with the government's jurisdiction. If there is no pre-defined market then, for an informational website, the market would consist of all the people who could benefit from the information. For the NASA website mentioned earlier, the market would include at least United States citizens; however, it is likely much larger than that. If, for example, a student in Germany wanted to research the NASA site, would that make him or her part of the market? If the market is defined as only U.S. citizens, then, the German student would not be included in the market. However, that does not mean he or she does not have something in common with the target market—in this case, an interest in NASA.

Tempting proxies for the market's awareness of a site are often measured by comparatively easy-to-collect website traffic and interactions, such as by counting page-views, click-throughs, engagement, interaction with content, and social media posts. Such metrics are important elements of an awareness metric, but they need to be considered in the context of the market as a whole. It is possible that a change in such metrics could simply reflect market shifts and not relate to the website or its content.

Brand Loyalty. Once the market is aware of the site, organizations might want to keep track of how likely first-time visitors are to return to the site and whether market awareness is being sustained. Some common metrics used to measure awareness are the Net Promoter Score and the Willingness to Search [27].

Reichfield [28] presented the Net Promoter Score as a way to determine brand loyalty by asking customers, "How likely is it that you would recommend our company to a friend colleague?" Reichfield [28] suggests this strongly indicates loyalty "because when customers recommend you, they're putting their reputations on the line." While the Net Promoter Score is a temptingly simple metric, Sauro [29] cautions that if it is used, it should be used with other metrics to provide the information required to explain it.

The Willingness to Search metric measures "the likelihood that customers will settle for a second choice product if their first choice is not available" [27]. In his commentary on the Net Promoter Score, Sauro [29] suggests Freed's word-of-mouth index [30] as a way to collect positive and negative aspects of the underlying sentiment. In any case, as Ittner and Larcker [24] observed, metrics should be carefully linked back to the financial goals of the business.

One non-market aspect of governmental websites is that there is usually only one per jurisdiction, which means there is often no alternative for the information provided by the site. However, a loyalty measure is still important, because visitors have the option to ignore an agency's website and also tell their friends to ignore it if it is not useful. The word-of-mouth index can alert the stakeholders of an informational website hosted by a government agency to the negative sentiment in their target market—even when there is no other source for the information.

Cost Reduction. Online content is an increasingly popular self-service technology and a way that organizations can reduce customer service costs [31]. When implemented well, online content can provide readers with information needed to accomplish tasks that would otherwise be more costly (e.g., call centers, live customer-service agents).

Tracking the cost savings offered by self-service content cannot, however, be done by monitoring content alone. To track the savings, the cost and usage of the alternatives to the content (e.g., call centers, customer support interactions) must be tracked against a baseline measured before introducing the self-service content. An exception to this, however, is in the reading to do here case where the self-service operations can be compared to the operations they replace.

4 Conclusion

Informational websites often have many stakeholders—readers and sponsoring organizations—with potentially different goals. That readers and organizations have different goals does not mean they must have competing goals. Identifying the relationship between the readers' tasks and the website's content can help guide the organization in authoring and designing the website content to fit the interaction model and can help organizations select which metrics will provide the most useful data. The taxonomies presented in this paper can help simplify and focus the discussion about these relationships within an organization as they plan, design, and author web content for informational websites in order to attract and retain the desired readers.

These taxonomies provide the authors of informational content that they will publish on informational websites with a means to model how readers will use their websites to accomplish their goals. They also help the stakeholders within an organization identify the goals that can be measured and tracked. These taxonomies are intended to be used in the context of existing audience and task-analysis studies—not to provide a substitute for them. These taxonomies provide a framework within which these studies and analyses can be applied to simplify and focus the discussion of the data they produce.

References

1. Schaupp, L.C., Fan, W., Belanger, F.: Determining success for website goals. In: HICCS 2006 Proceedings of the 39th Annual Hawaii International Conference on System Sciences, vol. 6, p. 107.2 (2006)
2. Rouet, J.F.: The Skills of Document Use: From Text Comprehension to Web-Based Learning, 1st edn. Lawrence Erlbaum Associates, Mahwah (2006)
3. Redish, J.: Letting Go of the Words: Writing Web Content that Works, 2nd edn. Morgan Kaufmann Elsevier, Waltham (2012)
4. Watson, R.: Incorporating usability into the API design process. In: Albers, M., Still, B. (eds.) Usability of Complex Information Systems: Evaluation of User Interaction. CRC Press, Boca Raton (2010)
5. International Organization for Standardization (ISO). Ergonomic Requirements for Office Work with Visual Display Terminals (VDTs) - part 11: Guidance on Usability (ISO/9241-11/1998). Geneva: International Organization for Standardization (1998)
6. Nielsen, J.: Usability Engineering. Academic Press, Cambridge (1993)
7. Quesenbery, W.: Balancing the 5Es of usability. Cut. IT J. **17**(2), 4–11 (2004)
8. Nielsen, J., Loranger, H.: Prioritizing Web usability. New Riders Publishing, Berkeley (2006)
9. Hertzum, M.: Images of usability. Int. J. Hum. Comput. Interact. **26**(6), 567–600 (2010)
10. Newman, W., Taylor, A.: Towards a methodology employing critical parameters to deliver performance improvements in interactive systems. In: Proceedings of IFIP TC.13 International Conference on Human–Computer Interaction, pp. 605–612. IOS Press, Amsterdam (1999)
11. Bevan, N.: Measuring usability as quality of use. Softw. Qual. J. **4**, 115–150 (1995)
12. Zhang, P., von Dran, G.M.: Satisfiers and dissatisfiers: a two-factor model for website design and evaluation. J. Am. Soc. Inf. Sci. **51**(14), 1253–1268 (2000)
13. Elling, S., Lentz, L., de Jong, M.: Website evaluation questionnaire: development of a research-based tool for evaluating informational websites. In: Wimmer, M.A., Scholl, J., Grönlund, Å. (eds.) EGOV. LNCS, vol. 4656, pp. 293–304. Springer, Heidelberg (2007)
14. Hornbaek, K.: Current practice in measuring usability: challenges to usability studies and research. Int. J. Hum. Comput. Stud. **64**, 79–102 (2006)
15. Google. (n.d.). Features – Google Analytics. http://www.google.com/analytics/features/. Accessed 31 January 2015
16. Dillman, D.A., Smyth, J.D., Christian, L.M.: Internet, mail, and mixed-mode surveys: the tailored design method, 3rd edn. Wiley & Sons Inc, Hoboken (2008)

17. Redish, J.C.: Reading to learn to do. IEEE Trans. Prof. Commun. **30**(4), 289–293 (1989)
18. Sticht, T.G., Fox, L.C., Hauke, R.N., Zapf, D.W.: The Role of Reading in the Navy. DTIC Document (1977)
19. Brandt, J., Guo, P.J., Lewenstein, J., Dontcheva, M., Klemmer, S.R.: Two studies of opportunistic programming: interleaving web foraging, learning, and writing code. In: Proceedings of the SIGCHI Conference on Human Factors in Computing Systems, ACM, pp. 1589–1598 (2009)
20. Google (n.d.). Bounce Rate - Analytics Help. https://support.google.com/analytics/answer/1009409?hl=en. Accessed 1 February 2015
21. Google (n.d.). Time on Page - Analytics Help. https://support.google.com/analytics/answer/1006924?hl=en. Accessed 1 February 2015
22. Tidwell, J.: Designing Interfaces, 2nd edn. O'Reilly Media, Sebastopol (2011)
23. Halvorson, K., Rach, M.: Content Strategy for the Web. New Riders Publishing, Berkeley (2012)
24. Ittner, C.D., Larcker, D.F.: Coming up short on nonfinancial performance measurement. Harv. Bus. Rev. **81**(11), 88–95 (2003)
25. McGovern, G.: Killer Web Content: Make the Sale, Deliver the Service, Build the Brand, 1st edn. A&C Black Trade, London (2006)
26. Keller, K.L.: Conceptualizing, measuring, and managing customer-based brand equity. J. Mark. **57**(1), 1–22 (1993)
27. Farris, P.W., Bendle, N.T., Pfeifer, P.E., Reibstein, D.J.: Marketing Metrics: The Definitive Guide to Measuring Marketing Performance. FT Press, Upper Saddle River (2010)
28. Reichheld, F.F.: The one number you need to grow. Harv. Bus. Rev. **81**, 46–55 (2003)
29. Sauro, J.: Should the Net Promoter Score Go? 5 Common Criticisms Examined (2014). http://www.measuringu.com/blog/nps-go.php. Accessed 8 February 2015
30. Freed, L.: Innovating Analytics: How the Next Generation of Net Promoter Can Increase Sales and Drive Business Results, 1st edn. Wiley & Sons Inc, Hoboken (2013)
31. Bitner, M.J., Ostrom, A.L., Meuter, M.L.: Implementing successful self-service technologies. Acad. Manag. Exec. **16**(4), 96–108 (2002)

Interaction Design

Designing Simulation-Based Training for Prehospital Emergency Care: Participation from a Participant Perspective

Beatrice Alenljung[1(✉)] and Hanna Maurin Söderholm[2]

[1] University of Skövde, Skövde, Sweden
beatrice.alenljung@his.se
[2] University of Borås, Borås, Sweden
hanna.maurin@hb.se

Abstract. Simulation-based training for prehospital emergency care is characterized by high degrees of complexity. Thorough knowledge of both the work and the setting is crucial and it is therefore important to involve both end-users and other stakeholders during the whole design process. This paper investigates a design process by focusing on how project participants experience the work process and participation of a multi-disciplinary, research-practitioner design team. This case study focuses on the work within a development project of a new prehospital emergency training facility. Open-ended interviews were conducted with the project participants halfway through the project. Strikingly, the results show that while there are problems and tensions that potentially could overturn the project, all participants express strong satisfaction with their participation in the project. This implies that the accumulated positive experiences are so strong that they overshadow tensions and problems that under other circumstances could have caused a project breakdown.

Keywords: User participation · Participatory design · Simulation-based training · Prehospital emergency care

1 Introduction

This paper investigates participants' experiences of participating in a multi-disciplinary, researcher-practitioner design project. The goal of the project was to design, develop and test a simulation-based training environment for prehospital emergency care.

Simulation-based approaches are important for training and testing critical tasks and situations that can be challenging to conduct in real emergencies [1], and hence very useful for pre-hospital care settings. Current training approaches have a number of limitations, and richer and more holistic approaches and simulation technologies are needed. This can be attained through a combination of different technologies and design solutions [2, 3]. The work within the project propose a richer model for simulation that, compared to current training, provides higher realism and the ability to train a wider range of situations, tasks, and processes in several different simulated physical environments.

© Springer International Publishing Switzerland 2015
M. Kurosu (Ed.): Human-Computer Interaction, Part I, HCII 2015, LNCS 9169, pp. 297–306, 2015.
DOI: 10.1007/978-3-319-20901-2_27

Technology design for healthcare settings is challenging. It is characterized by high degrees of complexity, and might include a wide range of use locations, stakeholder organizations, rules and regulations, healthcare personnel, tools and technologies. In prehospital work settings, a number of challenges are added, e.g., concrete factors such as time constraints, weather, portability requirements and communication infrastructure, but also to formal guidelines such as work protocols; security and safety aspects; different organizational and thus funding structures; and, the need for "hard evidence" in terms of improved patient outcomes [e.g. 4, 5]. This calls for multidisciplinary, holistic design and development approaches that take domain knowledge from multiple perspectives into account. Hence, it is important to involve end-users as well as other stakeholders during the whole technological development cycle.

The relationship between user participation and system success in terms of user satisfaction is strongest when the task and system complexities are high [6]. Users[1] can participate in a wide variety of way along several dimensions, e.g., as purely informants, full members of the project team, in parts of, or during the whole process [7]. One way of doing this is through participatory design (PD) [8].

The project presented in this paper applies the views of PD as stated by [9]: "every participant in a PD project is an expert in what they do, whose voice needs to be heard; that design ideas arise in collaboration with participants from diverse backgrounds; that PD practitioners prefer to spend time with users in their environment rather than 'test' them in laboratories" [9, p. 213]. Hence, user participation should take place in a way that gives high value to the project and the final product as well as makes everyone involved feel comfortable in the situation [7].

PD have been used since the 1980 s' [10], and also in prehospital care settings [11, 12]. While there is an extensive body of research on PD, few studies have explored how project members experience their participation as full active members of a PD project [13, 14]. This is one of the key issues, emphasized by [15] that need to be addressed by the research community. Thus, this paper aims to investigate how participants experience the work process and participation in a multi-disciplinary, research-practitioner design project in the context of designing simulation-based training for prehospital emergency care.

2   User Participation

User participation is defined as "a set of behaviors or activities performed by users in the system development process" [16, p. 149]. The importance of taking users' perspectives into consideration has been known for more than 30 years, and ever since Gould and Lewis [17] introduced the three fundamental principles of user-centered design, usability experts and others have struggled to address them, not least the principle "early focus on users and tasks" [17, p. 300]. Failing to understand the users has repeatedly been reported as a reason to failed system development projects [6, 7, 16, 18].

---

[1] In this paper, the term user includes end-users as well as other non-technical domain experts.

A widespread concept to address this is to let the users participate in the design process; user participation has been identified as one of the most important factors for system success [19]. Involving users is also important for other reasons, such as democratic empowerment that allows them to take active part in decision-making that influence them and their work, as well as competence development and learning [7, 20].

However, if not managed properly, user participation can negatively affect the development process, e.g., not achieving the intended objectives, becoming more difficult and less effective [6, 16, 19]. Wu and Marakas [21] investigated the impact of different aspects of user participation on perceived system implementation success. Aspects that influenced were, e.g., the users' perceived extent of participation, overall responsibility, top management support, user attitudes, system initiation, as well as congruence between user participation and user status in terms of functional expertise.

A movement that provides an approach for user participation is participatory design (PD) whose roots are participatory democracy [9], where cooperative design work is emphasized and users are viewed as co-designers [22, 23]. Olsson and Janson [24] have identified several values that are important to create a good atmosphere between users and designer: mutual respect; active participation on equal terms; common goal; common language; to listen; refrain from immediate implementation thinking; simple tools that reveal what work is about; and to document findings.

3 Research Setting

3.1 Project Initiation

The focus of this case study is on the work that was conducted in relation to the development of a new emergency training facility for a Prehospital Care Center (PCC) in western Sweden. In order to further develop their prehospital training, the PCC had acquired an advanced Laerdal patient simulator.[2] They wanted, however, to improve and develop the overall training approach, and the use of the patient simulator, so that the training better would reflect the full prehospital process and its complexity with respect to physical contexts and diversity in tasks, and they initiated the work to plan and build a new emergency training center.

Hence, the project initiative came from the practitioners at the PCC who contacted a group of informatics researchers at the local university. Together, they outlined an initial idea and set up the research project. The purpose of the facility is to enable advanced realistic simulations, covering the entire prehospital work process from call-out to delivery at the emergency care unit, including different work dimensions, e.g., medical treatment, transportation, communication and caretaking [2, 3].

They also invited experts in prehospital emergency care and in information science from another university. A joint project proposal was developed and partially funded through regional support, so that the project could start in January 2014.

---

[2] http://www.laerdal.com/gb/nav/207/Patient-Simulators.

3.2 Project Scope and Composition

The scope of the project was a joint effort to design, prototype, and test a holistic approach to training the entire care chain through rich simulation and serious games-components.

The project has an action design research approach [25] where all participating researchers and users are full members of the project group. Purposeful interventions are conducted in the users' organization, and an artefact is developed.

The project group consists of 15 members from two different universities, three academic fields, and users from (and related to) the PCC. The researchers include: informatics and information science researchers specialized in serious games, HCI/UXD, and, ICTs for emergency care; prehospital care researchers specialized in emergency care, pre-hospital training and simulation, and ICT for prehospital care. One of these had also been working in parallel as a paramedic for 15 years up until the project started. The participating users included paramedics, ambulance training officers; ambulance training administrators; an emergency physician; and a healthcare strategist. Thus, the users have been active participants during the whole process.

The authors of this paper (researchers in informatics and information science), are active participants in the project and therefore have personal and inside experience of it.

3.3 Work Process

The project started with field studies conducted by information science and informatics researchers in order to get a thorough understanding of the prehospital work process as well as the current practices of emergency training. This was followed by iterations of design and prototyping of simulation environments, tools and scenarios. All project members contributed to the evolving simulation-based training concept and prototype.

The project was led by an informatics researcher, with a collaborative, inclusive, PD inspired strategy. In the project, all experts (users as well as researchers) had influential power on areas within their own domain and/or specialization.

The work took place in several ways; during grand meetings with all project members, functional meetings between members working on different aspects, e.g., scenario building, and construction of the technical and physical parts of the prototype, as well as frequent communication via phone, email and Skype.

The first part of 2014 was devoted to conceptual and physical design iterations, including user testing and a small pilot study. The autumn of 2014 mainly focused on preparing for and conducting a pilot test, an experiment where the simulation environment was going to be evaluated by 24 paramedics. The research presented in this paper focuses on the process up until the experiment, that is, about half-way into the project.

4   Research Method

In order to investigate project participants' experiences of working in the project, open-ended interviews were conducted with 12 of the participants (total n = 15). Three project participants were omitted: one prehospital researcher could not be interviewed due to time constraint issues; and, the two paper authors (one informatics and one information science researcher).

A semi-structured interview guide was used. This approach helps in making certain that the basic parts of the interviews remain the same and reminds the interviewer of the main subject areas. A conversational interview style was established. The questions covered participants' perceptions of the project's direction and design, meeting culture, possibilities to influence, as well as general experiences of pros and cons of the project overall. Examples of questions were: If you were asked by an uninitiated to describe our project, how would you describe it? What is your viewpoint of the project goals? What is your opinion of the content of the meetings? What have you been able to influence so far? What have you not been able to influence so far, but that you wanted to?

All interviews were conducted at the participant's work place, and each lasted for about one hour. All interviews were recorded and subsequently transcribed. In the first stage of the data analysis the transcripts were coded in three high-level categories: a) expressions for that the project works (it was obvious during the interviews that everyone was very satisfied with the project so having a reverse category was not meaningful), (b) possible reasons for why the project works, and (c) problems or potential problems that the interviewees experienced or were worried about. All coded text segments was provided a condensed description. From the condensed data categories emerged, e.g., resources and time; roles, interpersonal relations; and, personal commitment. Further analysis was then made within each category participant group: (a) users, (b) prehospital care researcher, and (c) informatics researchers.

5   Results

The all-pervading theme is that all participants express strong satisfaction with the project so far. Some even stress that the project exceeds their expectations and their previous experiences of collaborative projects.

There are, however, also reports of problems and difficulties. These illustrate a continuous balance between intertwined experience-affecting aspects, primarily related to four main themes: (1) project organization and leadership; (2) interpersonal relationships and project vision; (3) lack of resources and support; and, (4) user-researcher collaboration.

5.1   Project Organization and Leadership

One of the themes that most clearly emerge from all participants' perspectives is their appreciation of how the project is organized. They felt that there is a clear and effective organization, reasonable meeting frequency, and an open, constructive and pleasant discussion climate. The users feel included in the dialogue, they feel that they both contribute and are being listened to.

All participants express that even though there are large differences in background, knowledge and competence; there is both an openness and willingness to understand each other and also to make an effort to explain things and be understood. Although the users find the academic and research-related aspects that now and then are discussed in the meetings are somewhat irrelevant, several of them consider the meeting discussions to have expanded their view on simulation-based training of prehospital emergency care and increased their understanding of its complexity and possibilities.

Participants in all categories express uncertainty about the formal overall goals of the project. Moreover, when asked to describe the project, they provide fairly different views of the project scope and its goals. Still, they consider everyone involved to be working in the same direction. The project leader acknowledges these differences; his strategy is to align the different goals and motivations for participating, and make them work together side-by-side.

Thus, in spite of both the inconsistencies and uncertainties concerning how the actual project goals are understood, and the differences in project members' backgrounds, the project is considered as running smoothly and is experienced as highly positive by all the participants.

5.2 Interpersonal Relationships and Project Vision

Participants' high engagement in the project was one of the most striking themes that emerged from the data. Across all participant categories expressions like "enjoyable", "interesting", "exciting", "motivating", "fun", "win-win", was used in relation to the different interview themes.

This seems to be strongly related to two factors. First, the interpersonal relationships between the individuals are reported to be very rewarding. The participants stress the joy of working together. They perceive each other as highly committed and easy to cooperate with. Second, the project vision is considered to be of high societal importance and all participants strongly believe in the new training concept. The potential benefits and usefulness of the new training approach are stressed; however, noteworthy is that the character of its importance and potential vary depending on participants' backgrounds. For instance, some emphasize the project's immediate relevance for improving the current training, while others stress more long-term potential for technology development or improvement of healthcare in a wider sense.

However, some participants, mostly in the informatics researcher category, think that their primary interest has been somewhat diminished due to limitations in technical resources. Still, they enjoy participating in the multi-disciplinary setting and find it worthwhile. In particular, the users and the informatics researchers express that they enjoy their collaboration and the mutual learning.

Thus, personal engagement and feelings of delight is salient, which can be interpreted as closely related the positive interpersonal relations and leading spirit of the project vision. Together, these seem to have significant weight in the balance between positive and negative overall experience of the project, not least considering the fact that there are a number of problematic aspects of the project, namely limitations in funding, time and resources.

5.3   Lack of Resources and Support

There are some intertwined problematic aspects that worry the participants; aspects that potentially could overturn or harm the project. These include: lack of financial resources; and, lack of explicit support for the long term goal, i.e., building a new emergency training facility for the PCC. To build such a center requires decisions from many levels; political, regional top management, and PCC management. Although there are many strong advocates that support the idea of a new emergency training facility, no final decisions are made at any level. This means that the future for a fully equipped training facility is unsecure, which is a source of worry for many of the participants.

Furthermore, the regional financial support that was awarded for the project (to support the design, prototype, and a pilot test of the suggested training concept) does neither allow funded project time for all participants, nor full coverage of all project-related costs. Thus, several members report that they had to "find" other ways to create possibilities to participate, i.e. by using their spare time, competence development time, and/or ask for funding from other sources to manage some of the project's expenses.

These fairly severe difficulties affect the participants negatively, but - interestingly enough - not to such an extent that they seem to have an effect on the permeating positive experience of the project. In spite of these problems, the participants find the collaboration rewarding, are highly committed, invest their own time, and strongly believe in the project vision and its potential societal benefits.

5.4   User-Researcher Collaboration

The collaboration between users and researchers is working satisfyingly according to the participants. However, there are indications of potential pitfalls that could undermine the feelings of satisfaction in the project.

There are signs of tensions in the user-researcher relations, e.g. the users express hesitation regarding some of the research-related activities in the project; the researchers emphasize scientific rigor and the users stress the importance of "getting things done" and taking a concrete form. The researchers need to publish the results appear a bit strange to the users. Nevertheless, in this project the users respect this need in spite of this "peculiarity", and the users found the academic perspective meaningful overall. For example, as expressed by one of the users; it feels empowering that academics are interested in our daily work and what we do.

Initially users found the lack of prehospital care knowledge among informatics researchers surprising. However, this tension vanished as the informatics researchers participated more in the daily activities at the ambulance center, engaged in meetings and design workshops, and thus acquired a better contextual understanding. After these initial problems, the users perceive the work with the informatics researchers as well-functioning and mutually beneficial. One of the users believes that the absence of a "gap" between them is because they are from diametrically different fields and thus already know that there are obvious differences between them - which make everyone extra careful to be clear, explain things and not assume healthcare or informatics-related expert knowledge.

There is however some tension between the users and the prehospital care researchers that seems to be stemming from them being from the same realm. Based on previous experiences, the users feel that healthcare researchers in general often use fancy language, and talk about their (the users') work in ways they do not recognize. There might also be a certain amount of competition in how training should be done, what does work, what the real current problems are, and how to improve training by new innovative approaches.

The prehospital researchers on the other hand, highly value the multi-professional project constitution and the different perspectives this includes, stating that all are dependent on each other's perspectives and competences. They are however also aware of the potential problems. In particular, one researcher who previously worked as an ambulance nurse acknowledges that the users might feel that there is too much of talk about research design and publications.

Nonetheless, regardless of the described tensions the positive overall experience of the project remains. A probable factor is the reported mutual dependence, with complementary competencies and little rivalry and prestige. Our interpretation is that these feelings are strong and to some extent compensate for or help to overcome differences and tensions.

6   Concluding Discussion

In this paper, we explore participants' experiences half-way into a project in which design, prototyping, and testing of a simulation-based training environment for prehospital emergency care has been conducted. The project is a joint multi-disciplinary, user-researcher effort, where the views of PD as stated by [9] have been applied. The aim of the study reported in this paper was to investigate users' experiences of their project participation in order to identify and understand what makes such a project be running well.

The results show that this is a much more complex pursuit than identifying a list of "success factors" or "best practices". Instead, there are several aspects, such as interpersonal relations, project leadership, and user-researcher collaboration that vary along a pros- and cons-dimension or axis, where pros can be viewed as reasons that evoke and increase positive feelings and cons can be seen as occasions that impose and amplify negative feelings. What seems important in order to achieve a positive overall participation experience is that the total pros and cons balance; the "sum" of pros outweighs cons that under other circumstances severely might harm the project.

However, many questions remain. Future studies should investigate and concretize the interplay between these aspects and dimensions, as well as the reasons and occasions that influence the participants' experiences in these types of projects. The next step for us is to conduct another round of interviews with the project participants to conclude the now (February 2015) finished project. In that study we intend to deepen and expand the investigation and our understanding of the findings reported in this paper.

References

1. Alklind Taylor, A.: Facilitation matters: A framework for instructor-led serious gaming. Doctoral Thesis, School of Informatics, University of Skövde, Sweden, Thesis No. 4. (2014)
2. Backlund, P., Heldal, I., Engström, H., Johannesson, M., Lebram, M.: Collaboration patterns in mixed reality environments for a new emergency training center. In: Modelling Symposium (EMS), 2013 European., p. 483–488. IEEE (2013)
3. Söderström, E., van Laere, J., Backlund, P., Maurin Söderholm, H.: Combining Work Process Models to Identify Training Needs in the Prehospital Care Process. In: Johansson, B., Andersson, B., Holmberg, N. (eds.) BIR 2014. LNBIP, vol. 194, pp. 375–389. Springer, Heidelberg (2014)
4. Söderholm, H.M., Sonnenwald, D.H.: Visioning future emergency healthcare collaboration: perspectives from large and small medical centers. J Assoc Inf Sci Technol 61(9), 1808–1823 (2010)
5. Sonnenwald, D.H., Söderholm, H.M., Welch, G.F., Cairns, B.A., Manning, J.E., Fuchs, H. Illuminating collaboration in emergency health care situations: paramedic-physician collaboration and 3D telepresence technology. Inform Res. 19(2) p. 618 (2014). http://InformationR.net/ir/19–2/paper618.html. Accessed 6 Oct. 2014
6. Lynch, T., Gregor, S.: User participation in decision support systems development: influencing system outcomes. Eur. J. Inform. Syst. 13, 286–301 (2004)
7. Kujala, S.: Effective user involvement in product development by improving the analysis of user needs. Behav. Inform. Technol. 28(6), 457–473 (2008)
8. Schuler, D., Namioka, A. (eds.): Participatory design Principles and practices. Erlbaum Associates, Hillsdale (1993)
9. Sanoff, H.: Editorial: Special issue on participatory design. Design Stud. 28, 213–215 (2007)
8. Bjerknes, G., Ehn, P., Kyng, M. (eds.): Computers and Democracy: A Scandinavian Challenge. Avebury, Aldershot (1987)
11. Kristensen, M., Kyng, M., Palen, L.: Participatory design in emergency medical service: designing for future practice. In: Proceedings of the SIGCHI Conference on Human Factors in Computing Systems, CHI 2006 pp. 161–170. Montréal, Québec, Canada. (2006)
12. Büscher, M., Mogensen, P. H.: Designing for material practices of coordinating emergency teamwork. In: Proceedings of the 4th International Conference on Information Systems for Crisis Response and Management (ISCRAM) (2007)
13. Bowen, S., McSeveny, K., Lockley, E., Wolstenholme, D., Cobb, M., Dearden, A.: How was it for you?experiences of participatory design in the UK health service. Co Design: International Journal of Co Creation in Design and the Arts 9(4), 230–246 (2013)
14. Bossen, C., Dindler, C., Iversen, O.S.: Impediments to user gains: Experiences from a critical participatory design project. In: Proceedings of PDC 2012, pp. 31–40. Roskilde, Denmark (2012)

15. Vines, J., Clarke R., Wright, P., Sejer Iversen, O., Wah Leong, T., McCarthy, J., Olivier, P.: Summary Report on CHI 2012 invited SIG: Participation and HCI: Why Involve People in Design? (2012). http://di.ncl.ac.uk/participation/wp-content/blogs.dir/20/files/2012/09/CHISIGReportFinal.pdf. Accessed 2 Feb 2015
16. Bano, M., Zowghi, D.: A systematic review on the relationship between user involvement and system success. Inform. Software Tech **58**, 148–169 (2015)
17. Gould, J.D., Lewis, C.: Designing for usability: key principles and what designers think. Commun. ACM **28**(3), 300–311 (1985)
18. Martikainen, S., Korpela, M., Tiihonen, T.: User participation in healthcare IT development: a developers' viewpoint in Finland. Int. J. Med. Inform. **83**, 189–200 (2014)
19. Subramanyam, R., Weisstein, F.L., Krishnan, M.S.: User participation in software developments projects. Commun. ACM **53**(3), 137–141 (2010)
20. Iivari, N.: "Constructing the users" in open source software development: an interpretative case study of user participation. Inform. Technol. People **22**(2), 132–156 (2009)
21. Wu, J.-T.B., Marakas, G.M.: The impact of operational user participation on perceived system implementation success: an empirical investigation. J. Comput. Inform. Syst. **46**(5), 127–140 (2006)
22. Iivari, N.: Participatory design in OSS development: interpretive case studies in company and community OSS development contexts. Behav. Inform. Technol. **30**(3), 309–323 (2011)
23. Khaled, R., Vasalou, A.: Bridging serious games and participatory design. International Journal of Child-Computer Interaction (2014) In Press
24. Olsson, E., Jansson, A.: Participatory design with train drivers – a process analysis. Interact. Comput. **17**, 147–166 (2005)
25. Sein, M.K., Henfridsson, O., Purao, S., Rossi, M., Lindgren, R.: Action design research. MIS Q. **35**(1), 37–56 (2011)

What About Document Folding? User Impressions and a Design Approach

Rodrigo Chamun, Angelina Ziesemer[✉], Isabel H. Manssour,
João B.S. de Oliveira, and Milene S. Silveira

Faculdade de Informática, PUCRS,
Avenida Ipiranga 6681, Prédio 32 – 90619-900
Porto Alegre, RS, Brazil
{rodrigo.chamun,angelina.ziesemer}@acad.pucrs.br
{isabel.manssour,joao.souza,milene.silveira}@pucrs.br

Abstract. Designing documents with folds is a difficult task with current desktop publishing software, and this subject is also hardly explored in the academic literature. Because the flat nature of the screen, document design is limited to a two dimensional space, demanding extra effort from designers to place the art with respect to the folds, sometimes forcing them to resort to paper prototyping. Results from interviews performed with design experts, helped us to understand the challenges and needs faced by them during the document creations. This paper presents an interactive visualization approach to compose foldable documents and to interact with the results without resorting to external means. We consider that a foldable document such as brochure is composed by panels joined at the edges and the content of each panel is designed separately. We describe our interactive approach and the results generated by a prototype we developed to support the composition of foldable documents.

Keywords: Document folding · User interfaces · Document layout

1 Introduction

There are many possibilities for creating documents with folds in the age of desktop publishing, and a large selection of software is available for this purpose. However, most software focuses on organizing content into a conventional sequence of pages rather than produce foldable documents composed by several smaller panels joined in arbitrary positions. This hampers the creation of documents that are meant to be folded, and compels the user to design the document before editing its content by, for example, measuring each part bounded by the folds and adding up the total area of the document. After the document size is set, the content is edited as a single page, even though it has logical divisions (cover, back, middle, back-cover, etc.). Systems like Scribus[1] offer features to add guides that will not appear on the final document separating the content

---

[1] http://www.scribus.net/.

© Springer International Publishing Switzerland 2015
M. Kurosu (Ed.): Human-Computer Interaction, Part I, HCII 2015, LNCS 9169, pp. 307–319, 2015.
DOI: 10.1007/978-3-319-20901-2_28

inside the document. This may help the user but adds nothing to the ease of changing the content of a single part later on. Moreover, due to the two dimensional nature of the screen it may be hard for the designers to understand the dynamics of the document and how the folds will behave, causing them to resort to techniques such as paper prototyping [5].

To understand the process of creating brochures, we performed a user study with design experts. They reported the routine of art creation related to foldable documents. Designer experts need to go through a variety of steps during the brochure creation process to achieve a good visualization and interaction before printing the final version of the document.

In this paper, we propose an interactive visualization approach for helping designers and eventual brochure creators to build, visualize and interact with foldable documents in a 3D environment. Users can create the document in two distinct stages: first, each brochure panel is designed separately; after this panels are assembled into one document. It gives users freedom to change the form of the document without worrying about its content and also they can validate the design by interacting with the document in a three dimensional view. A prototype was developed from the proposed approach to present the results regarding the visualization and interaction possibilities.

This paper is organized as follows: we start presenting the information gathered from the interviews with design experts and the existing solutions related to foldable documents. Next, we present details of the approach proposed to help users interact and visualize documents as brochures. Thereafter, we describe the prototype created and the results related to the possibilities of visualization and interaction with foldable documents.

2   Building Documents with Folds

There are many approaches related to document engineering centered in the document layout and content organization rather than the document shape and dynamics. From existing document design software such as InDesign[2], Photoshop[3] and CorelDraw[4], we see that they provide few features to support the design of foldable documents.

Generally, design experts adopt techniques such as paper prototyping to visualize the results of brochure creation, to see how it will be folded and also to interact with the document front-and-back sides, as the visualization that many tools offer is not enough to represent it. Paper prototyping [5] has been used to model a wide variety of design ideas and to help designers and users to interact with elements from an initial project.

Thus, to learn more about brochure creation and the designer's methods, we performed a user study as described in the next section.

---

[2] http://www.adobe.com/products/indesign.html.
[3] http://www.adobe.com/products/photoshop.html.
[4] http://www.corel.com/.

2.1   User Study

To gather information about designer needs during the brochure creation, we performed a set of interviews with 12 designers. The interviews follow a set of 12 questions from designer profile to experience with brochure creation.

From the participants, 7 were male and 5 female. The average time of experience in brochure creation reported by each participant is about 7 years, and 10 of them have a degree related to either Arts & Design or Marketing as we can see on Table 1.

Table 1. Information gathered about design experts during the interviews.

Participants	Degree	Experience (years)	Gender
P1	Marketing	8	F
P2	Engineering	15	M
P3	Marketing	10	M
P4	Art & design	6	F
P5	Marketing	1	M
P6	Marketing	5	M
P7	Art & design	14	M
P8	No degree	6	M
P9	Marketing	9	M
P10	Art & design	4	F
P11	Art & design	5	F
P12	Marketing	8	F

We asked each participant about the tools they use to design brochures and the most mentioned software were Illustrator (cited by 8), InDesign (cited by 7), followed by Photoshop and Corel Draw (used by 6 and 7 respectively). They clarified that they need a combination of software like Photoshop and others to create the art of panels and thereafter merge it using Illustrator, InDesign, etc. According to them, there are no standards for brochure creation and it depends essentially on designer habits or needs. We asked participants to described the steps to create a foldable document, focusing on the layout process:

P6: *"First we need to define the layout and the amount of pages it will have. We create the idea of the layout and we interact with it through a paper prototype to imagine the document composition and also to start thinking about the panels organization".*

Designers reported that they need to define the sequence of the foldable document to organize the pages and the content:

P4: *"We need to distribute the content along the panels and give it a logical sequence according to the layout we planed to create".*

P12: *"If we define the number of creases and there is not enough content to fill the pages, we need to create the document all over again".*

Most participants (10) comment that the brochure creation process is a hard and time consuming task. Also, participants said that one of the critical steps during brochure creation is related to the visualization of the layout structure and pagination of the front-and-back sides. To understand and visualize the sequences of the panels and how the pages will connect to each other, they usually print all brochure's faces and build a mockup, also known as paper prototype:

P6: *"For presenting to customers an idea or the work in progress, we usually take a photo from a mockup to show them the creases it will have and the document front-and-back sides".*

They commented about the connection among pages that some brochure layouts demands:

P2: *"The connection among the pages can be a critical stage in the brochure creation, because it demands time".*

P6: *"Sometimes the creases we create simply do not work because the amount of content we need to distribute among the pages is not enough. Also, there is no mirroring to visualize the back of each page".*

Yet, regarding the pages connection, participant *P12* add that: *"Once the connections among the pages change, it will increase the final product cost.*

Designers use paper prototyping as mockups for evaluating the final look of a brochure, its dynamics, to visualize its panels, pagination and the connection between its folds. This is a practice cited by all designers, because the tools they use do not have a simple approach to accomplish this task. The lack of visualization of the brochure front-and-back sides was the major complaint regarding the tools designer are used.

Paper prototypes are known by their low-fidelity to the final project and it can be frustrating for customers to imagine how a product will be when finalized. Furthermore, the project cost may increase quickly as the prototypes are printed over and over.

Therefore, the design of brochure documents, could benefit from 3D digital prototyping that can represent a document in high-fidelity [7] and also be fully interactive with panels and faces.

The data collected from the interviews helped us to understand the challenges faced by the designers during the brochure creation process. They also contributed to motivate the development of the proposed approach.

2.2 Existing Solutions

Little has been said about foldable documents in the literature: Chiu [2] proposed an approach to fold digital documents on multi-touch devices based on a focus-plus-context principle, in which the user folds the document to focus on a region they want to read. However, this approach is concerned only with document visualization and not with the design of foldable documents.

Also, Khalilbeigi et al. [4] perform experiments to explore interaction techniques for manipulating digital content with folds through a novel device concept that features double-sided displays. They found that mobile handheld devices have great potential to be explored in this field. However, they did not explore folding along different axes and they also used predefined hinges, limiting the paper configuration.

Straightforward solution is the use of templates. The design experts we interviewed do not usually take advantage of it, but it might be a fast way to create a document for the casual designer. Otherwise, the fact that the template is ready, waiting for content, may turn into a disadvantage if the user wants a personalized piece.

In the next section, we present our approach to build, visualize and interact with document with folds based on the results of the interviews reported in this section and the lack of related works with this goal.

3 Proposed Approach

The main ideas explained in this section may be divided in two parts. The first involves the concept of panels and explains how designers are used to build documents with folds. The second corresponds to a method to visualize and interact with the built document making full use of three dimensions. These two parts are described in the next subsections.

3.1 Working with Panels

In our approach, panels are page divisions that hold content in a document. When a sheet is folded in half, four panels are created, two at each side of the sheet, with the fold between them. When the paper is folded multiple times, some of the panels may overlap. Figure 1 illustrates panel overlapping in a tri-fold brochure. The dashed lines represent each fold in the paper and the middle panel is created from both left and right folds.

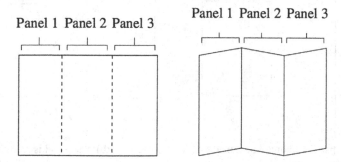

Fig. 1. A tri-fold brochure: dashed lines represent folds and the same document in perspective.

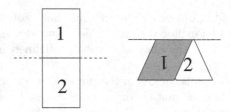

Fig. 2. Example of a horizontal fold.

Thus, the first part of our approach is an interactive method to shape the document. We assume that the panels are already designed and we provide an environment in which the document arrangement is a matter of dragging the panels around and connecting them.

Users select panels from a set of existing ones and drag them to an editing area. The creation of a fold corresponds to the action of joining two panels by their edges. As Fig. 2 illustrates, if the bottom of panel 1 is joined with the top of panel 2, they form a larger element and their common border is said to be a fold.

Either the front or the back faces of the panels will be facing each other when the new element is folded. The same idea applies if two panels are joined by their sides, but instead of a fold on the horizontal direction, a fold on the vertical direction will be formed. When two panels are joined they form a new panel that may be joined to other panels and to which other panels may be joined to. If panels have different sizes, the one that was dragged is resized to match the edge of the other panel, preserving its aspect ratio as shown in Fig. 3.

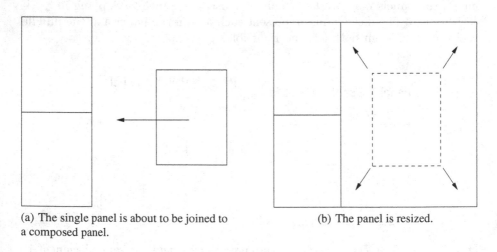

(a) The single panel is about to be joined to a composed panel.

(b) The panel is resized.

Fig. 3. Panels matching edges with different sizes.

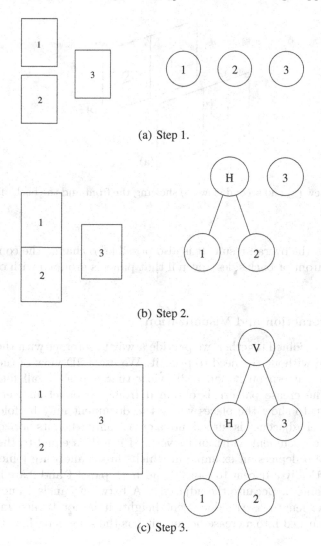

(a) Step 1.

(b) Step 2.

(c) Step 3.

Fig. 4. Steps to build a composed panel. On the left, how the composition is seen by the user, on the right how the composition is represented internally.

Fig. 4 shows step by step how Fig. 3(b) is created. In Fig. 4(a), there are three single panels, represented internally as three single nodes. On Fig. 4(b) panels 1 and 2 are joined, creating a horizontal fold. Their nodes, thus, share the same parent node (H) that represents the horizontal fold. Lastly, on Fig. 4(c), panel 3 is joined to the composed panel to create a vertical fold, thus, node 3 shares the same parent (V) as the horizontal fold node, which is a vertical fold node.

During the process, a second view shows the back of the document as if the document was held with its back facing a mirror, as in Figure 5. That view provides information on how the document will look when flipped and gives a

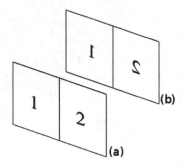

Fig. 5. First view (a) and second view (b) showing the front and the back of a document respectively.

better sense of the overall result. It is also possible to change the content of any panel (either front or back sides), even if that panel is grouped with other panels or groups.

3.2   3D Interaction and Visualization

Once panels are joined together, we provide a way to interact with the document for previewing without the need to print it. We use a 2D view of the document with a crease pattern on it and a 3D view that will show all folds that are performed. The crease pattern is obtained from the panel adjacencies and is used as a map to show the places where the document may be folded. In this context, a panel adjacency is turned into a crease only when its horizontal length is equal to the document width or its vertical length is equal to the document height. Figure 6 depicts an example in which three panels are joined together. Panel 1 is vertically adjacent to panel 2 and both panel 1 and 2 are horizontally adjacent to panel 3. Because the adjacency A between panels 1 and 2 does not have the same length as the document height, it is not turned into a crease whereas B is turned into a crease because it has the same length as the width of the document.

The creases are subject to restrictions depending on the current configuration of the 3D copy (that is how the document is currently folded). We define a crease as available when it is possible to fold the document through it and as unavailable when the action is impossible. Figure 7 illustrates a document being folded in half two times and how the crease pattern responds to the document configuration. First the vertical crease is folded, making the horizontal crease unavailable until its completion (frames 1 through 3). Then the horizontal crease is folded, making the vertical crease unavailable (frame 4). In this last case the vertical fold would still be unavailable even when the horizontal fold is completed because the former is blocked by the latter. A crease is said to be available only if all of its parts are collinear and it is not blocked by any other folded crease.

This document model resembles the work of Balkcom [1] on origami folding. The author models paper such that its creases are hinges and uncreased parts

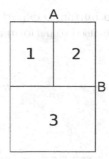

Fig. 6. The document may be folded through B but not through A.

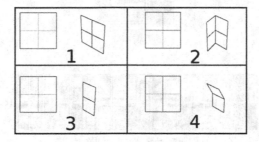

Fig. 7. A crease pattern and the document (1). When the vertical crease is half folded (2), the horizontal crease becomes unavailable. Once it is completed, the horizontal crease becomes available (3), so the paper may be folded horizontally, but when doing it, the vertical crease is blocked and turns unavailable (4). Crease status is shown as green when available and red when unavailable.

are rigid bodies. Comparing to our approach, panels adjacencies may be thought of as the hinges and the panels as the rigid bodies. Since our model simulates paper, it should also respect its properties such as upon on folding a paper, its distances should be preserved, and it should not intersect, although it is allowed to touch [3,6]. Due to the hard task of modeling paper (it remains an open problem [6]), our implementation is restricted to simple configurations on the folded document. Folding the document multiple times, specially where the document is already folded, is a limitation because it would require collision detection and resolution, techniques that would require extra computational complexity.

4   Prototype Description

We implemented a prototype in Java, using Processing[5] as the rendering engine. As shown in the Fig. 8 the prototype consists of a screen divided in two menus, one at the top, the other at the bottom, and a working area at the center.

---

[5] http://processing.org/.

The top menu in Fig. 8 (a) has a button to export the final work to a PDF file, and the bottom menu Fig. 8 (b) is used to perform actions that aid the document editing.

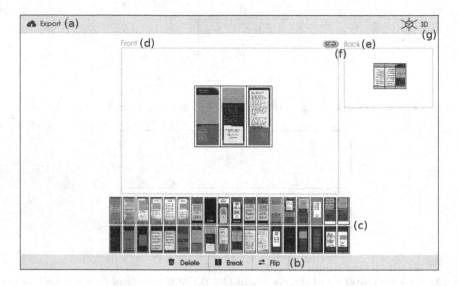

Fig. 8. Screenshot of the prototype.

The working area displays the panels used to build the final document Fig. 8 (c) and two other areas labeled as *front* Fig. 8 (d) and *back* Fig. 8 (e). The front area is where the document is built and is called *the editing area*. The back area is called *the mirror area* and shows how the content in the editing area would look like if it was held with its back facing a mirror. A cursor is shown over a page in this area if the mouse pointer is over the same page in the editing area. This gives a reference for users to quickly remember the back of the page in context. There is also a button (Fig. 8(f)) to flip the areas. When pressed, this button will rotate the editing and the mirror area revealing their backs, with the same effect of flipping a paper over a table. This allows the users to edit the document looking directly at its back while the front is shown in the mirror area. The 3D button (Fig. 8(g)) changes the view to the 3D perspective, where the users can visualize how the document will be and may interact with the document folding and unfolding it as they wish.

To start editing the document, users drag one panel from the list of panels (Figure 8(c)) to the editing area. Once there, panels are dragged around, joined by the edges or selected for flipping or removing. A fold is formed by dragging a panel close to another panel's edge, and once the edges are close enough, the panel being dragged snaps to the other one, automatically aligning and resizing if necessary and preserving its aspect ratio, becoming a compound element that can also be dragged, deleted, flipped and snapped. Users are also allowed to ungroup panels by selecting a group and clicking on the break button and to change the content of a panel at any moment – even if it is inside of a group – by releasing a panel with the new content over the panel with the content to be changed. The panels are never out of sight, if the user drags one panel too far from another, the editing area automatically zooms out to fit every panel within its bounds.

Once users want to manipulate the final product, they may select a group of panels and switch to the 3D mode by pressing the 3D button (Fig. 8 (g)). The users may interact with only one group of panels at a time, and the program will switch to the 3D mode only if a group is selected. The 3D mode is composed by two copies of the document, one is a flat version that holds the crease pattern as explained in Sect. 3 and the other is the 3D version that shows the folds the users perform on the document. The interaction is exclusively via the crease pattern, thus, every fold the users want to perform on the 3D copy must be issued from the crease pattern. As an example, Fig. 9 shows a configuration where every internal edge intersects with at least another edge. This means that the document can be folded one time horizontally, as the figure shows, and many times vertically. As one can expect from either figures, it should be possible to fold the document horizontally and then vertically or vice versa, however this is still a limitation of the prototype. This is, an implementation issue due to the problem of simulating paper digitally and not in the approach of joining panels to represent folds.

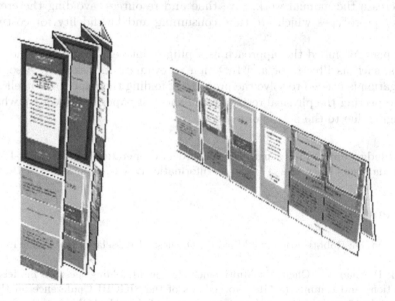

Fig. 9. Complex configuration folded vertically many times and horizontally.

5 Final Considerations

In this paper we presented a new interactive visualization approach for building documents with folds (a subject seldom discussed in the literature) that consists in dragging panels adjacent to each other to compose the document and then interact with it in a three dimensional view. The main difference between the works cited here and our approach is that we allow users to interact with the document by changing its content and exploring distinct types of folds avoiding the need of paper prototyping. This is a new method to interact with documents that are being designed and enhances its visualization during the development.

We conducted interviews with design experts and observed that paper prototyping is a technique widely used by them to visualize and interact with documents. However, this technique is labor intensive and time consuming when it is necessary to generate too many document versions. Thus, designers require approaches to ease the interaction and visualization of brochures. Based on their answers reported in such interviews, we proposed an approach to work with panels during the creation of foldable documents and a method to visualize and interact with the built document. Also, we developed a prototype that allows for users the panels visualization during the content organization process and interact with the document creases.

As next steps, we intend to present the results from a second phase of interviews with designer experts. We have presented to designers the developed prototype as a video to show the possibilities of interaction with the folds. They have agreed that it is helpful for visualization purposes and the 3D approach does can decrease the manual work, save time and resources, avoiding the creation of paper prototypes which are time consuming and low-fidelity for costumers visualization.

We plan to embed this approach as a plug-in into existing document design systems, such as Illustrator and InDesign to evaluate its usability. Also, more investigation is needed to solve the problem of folding the paper over itself many times respecting the physical restrictions a sheet of paper is subject to, which is challenging due to the nature of paper.

Acknowledgments. This paper was achieved in cooperation with Hewlett-Packard Brasil Ltda. using incentives of Brazilian Informatics Law (Law n. 8.2.48 of 1991).

References

1. Balkcom, D.: Robotic origami folding. Ph.D. thesis, Rensselaer Polytechnic Institute (2004)
2. Chiu, P., Liao, C., Chen, F.: Multi-touch document folding: gesture models, fold directions and symmetries. In: Proceedings of the SIGCHI Conference on Human Factors in Computing Systems. pp. 1591–1600. CHI 2011, ACM, New York (2011)
3. Demaine, E.D., Rourke, J. (eds.): A survey of folding and unfolding in computational geometry. In: Combinatorial and Computational Geometry, vol. 52, pp. 167–211. MIT press, Cambridge (2005)
4. Khalilbeigi, M., Lissermann, R., Kleine, W., Steimle, J.: Foldme: Interacting with double-sided foldable displays. In: Proceedings of the Sixth International Conference on Tangible, Embedded and Embodied Interaction. pp. 33–40. TEI 2012, ACM, New York (2012)

5. Lim, Y.K., Stolterman, E.: The anatomy of prototypes Prototypes as filters, prototypes as manifestations of design ideas. ACM Trans. Comput. Hum. Interact. **15**(2),
   7:1–7:27 (2008)
6. Rohmer, D., Cani, M.P., Hahmann, S., Thibert, B., et al.: Folded paper geometry
   from 2D pattern and 3D contour. In: Eurographics (short paper) (2011)
7. Rudd, J., Stern, K., Isensee, S.: Low vs. high-fidelity prototyping debate. Interactions **3**(1), 76–85 (1996)

Designing of a Natural Voice Assistants for Mobile Through User Centered Design Approach

Sanjay Ghosh and Jatin Pherwani(✉)

Samsung R&D Institute, Bangalore, India
{sanjay.ghosh, j.pherwani}@samsung.com

Abstract. With rapid advances in natural language generation (NLG), voice has now become an indispensable modality for interaction with smart phones. Most of the smart phone manufacturers have their Voice Assistant application designed with some form of personalization to enhance user experience. However, these designs are significantly different in terms of usage support, features, naturalness and personality of the voice assistant avatar or the character. Therefore the question remains that what is the kind of Voice Assistant that users would prefer. In this study we followed a User Centered Design approach for the design of a Voice Assistant from scratch. Our primary objective was to define the personality of a Voice Assistant Avatar and formulating a few design guidelines for natural dialogues and expressions for the same. The attempt was kept to design the voice assistant avatar with optimal natural or human like aspects and behavior. This paper provides a summary of our journey and details of the methodology used in realizing the design of a natural voice assistant. As research contribution, apart from the methodology we also share some of the guidelines and design decisions which may be very useful for related research.

Keywords: Voice assistant · Conversational agent · User centered design

1 Introduction

Within the human-computer interaction community there is a growing interest in agent or avatar-based user interfaces. Voice agents these days, come not only built within commercial smartphones but are also available as external applications which can be downloaded from many digital stores. A common characteristic seen amongst all these voice agents is the human like behavior and appearance they all exhibit. As voice based assistance in personal devices first came into picture, their behavior and characteristics were limited to fewer usage contexts than they are now. Voice assistance used to be more of a command and control agent [1]. The communication styles were also formal and structured, which gave the user an experience of interacting with an inanimate entity like a machine rather than a person. Presently, the behavior of the voice assistant is designed with an intention to be suitable in almost all contexts of usage. Moreover, it is possible to have informal and candid conversations with them as well. With

© Springer International Publishing Switzerland 2015
M. Kurosu (Ed.): Human-Computer Interaction, Part I, HCII 2015, LNCS 9169, pp. 320–331, 2015.
DOI: 10.1007/978-3-319-20901-2_29

modulations in language styles and speech parameters, creators try to impart quasi-human characteristics in new versions of voice assistant they come up with. It is imperative that as the voice user interfaces grow, the behavior of its avatar/agent will have to be way more flexible and adaptive. Creating a voice agent which is not only this dynamic but also so vast that it covers almost every usage context can be challenging. Through this paper we have tried to devise a methodology of designing a voice assistant with the end user being at the center stage. With an assertion being that, like designing any other user interface, the process of creating a voice assistant could also follow a user centered design approach. Contextual interviews, survey questionnaires and participatory design sessions were conducted to get an insight into the problem from user's point of view. Also these behaviors are communicative and conveyed to the user through spoken dialogues and non-verbal gestures. In this paper, we explore mainly the following research questions:

- Which personality attributes of a voice assistant are desired by the users and what kind of behavior is expected of it in different usage context?
- Which are the few analogous inferences from personal assistants in real life to help design a virtual voice assistant?
- What are the guidelines for natural behavior of a voice assistant in terms of language, non-verbal gestures and expressions?

The framework of our study stands on three main user centered activities which were performed to extract answers to our research questions. The results of all activities were then combined to form design guidelines for a voice assistant. While the three activities were independent of each other, each helps to formulate some aspect of the behavior of a voice assistant. In the first phase of our research, we studied personal assistants of many working individuals. Expected results from this study were to help understand the *communication style* of a personal assistant with their boss. Important inferences drawn from their behavior was a starting point in providing design guidelines to make a voice assistant natural and quasi-human. Now, personality is of importance to this exploration primarily because it influences the behavior of any voice assistant. In the second phase, we set ourselves out to explore the kind of *personality attributes* the user will prefer in different usage scenarios. A robot or voice avatar should be equipped with a consistent personality in order to help people form a conceptual model, which channels beliefs, desires, and intentions in a cohesive and consistent set of behaviors [2]. In addition, it can enhance the notion of a machine being a synthetic person rather than a computer. In the third phase, we study the *linguistic and speech and characteristics* of user created dialogue library for a voice assistant across different scenarios. Since language, speech and nonverbal cues like (gestures and expressions) are the main touch points of perceiving the behavior of any voice agent, user's direct perception regarding these were taken into account by a co-creation activity. Users were required to form the dialogues of a hypothetical voice assistant and describe the way it might be spoken by pointing out modulations in their speech. Therefore, by following various users centered design methods, we explored the design of a natural voice assistant (Fig. 1).

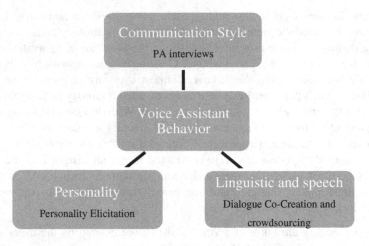

Fig. 1. Scope of study and methods used

2 Related Works

Several researches have been reported in the area of designing Voice Assistants or Conversational Assistants. Work by Ball et al. [3] describes the architecture for constructing an agent with speech and graphical interactions based on emotions and personality. Torrey et al. [4] proposed options for a robot's help-giving speech—using hedges or discourse markers, both of which can mitigate the commanding tone implied in direct statements of advice. Meerbeek et al. [5] described the design and evaluation of personality of a robotic TV assistant and the corresponding user's preference for control. It was observed that the users mostly preferred an extravert and friendly personality with low user control. Work by Heylighen et al. [6] points that for the formality of language and naturalness has a direct reflection of the personality and the work also proposes an empirical measure of formality. For instance linguistic use of nouns, adjectives, articles and prepositions are more frequent in formal styles; pronouns, adverbs, verbs and interjections are more frequent in informal styles. We borrowed this concept for the personality exploration of our Voice Assistant.

Therefore, earlier research reported in this area includes explorations of the personality for a robotic assistant for television [5], robot for giving advice [4], including emotions in a conversational agent [1, 3, 7]. Beyond the existing work in this area, our contributions lie in incorporating the user's perspective as an important element in formulating a personality for the voice avatar and creating dialogues library and expressions for the voice agents.

3 Personal Assistant Interviews

In the first phase of our research, with the intention of understanding the relationship and communication between a user and a voice assistant, we interviewed and observed human personal assistants. Our interview sessions were focused mainly to identify various personality traits of the assistants, understand how they handle various situations and observe explicit cues that are exhibited during a conversation between the bosses and his personal assistants. Seven participants were interviewed and observed for two hours at their work places. These set of participants were from three totally different geographies and culture, Indian, American and Korean, and also they had worked for bosses who were from various geographical origins. The recordings of these sessions were analyzed using affinity method and the emerging insights were categorized into social behavior and verbal or non-verbal expressions.

3.1 Assistant's Social Behavior

We formulate the social behavior of the assistants through our observations on three aspects:

- Emotional aspect, which includes mood adaptation, empathy and personal familiarity
- Functional aspect, which includes decision making, dependency, suggestion providing
- Functional aspect, which includes proactiveness and making interruptions

For assistant's mood adaptation to the mood of the boss, the statements from the assistants revealed that a moderate sensitivity to emotions is generally preferred. Assistants are fully aware of boss's mood but they try to maintain a neutral mood at all situations. When their boss is happy, the assistants showed slight happiness. When boss is sad, then assistants exhibit a neutral mood. We illustrated this aspect of mood adaptation by the assistants using the James Russell's Valence–Arousal circumplex chart [8] as shown in the Fig. 2. Assistant's mood space should be as congruent as possible for being a reactive companion but not an over-reactive one.

On our observations regarding interruptions, the assistants chose to interrupt only for matters that are more important as well as urgent than the ongoing task. Providing important and urgent information immediately is generally not considered as interruptions by the bosses. Assistants give active reminders/prompts only when the pre-defined schedules get disturbed. Assistants avoided all other interruptions coming from outside, they analyze and decide appropriate time and way to communicate. For communicating non important information, assistants prefer the time window between switching tasks.

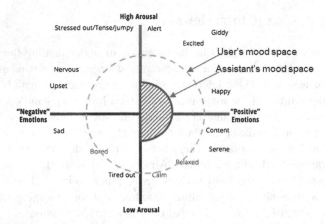

Fig. 2. Illustration of mood adaptation by the assistants on Valence–Arousal circumplex chart

3.2   Assistant's Verbal and Non-verbal Expressions

We observed the typical verbal and non-verbal expressions that the assistants follow and categorized then into following –

- Understanding non-verbal cues from others
- Use of non-verbal expression and gestures – including gaze aversion, head tilt and nod, facial expression
- Use of intonations – while listening and while speaking

On understanding other's non-verbal cues, assistants do that a lot to understand the condition of others, understand the level of other's satisfaction, infer the seriousness and priority of tasks, etc. Sometimes gaze is used as an input for the Voice assistant to trigger conversation and thus assistant must passively monitor the use non-verbal cues from users.

For non-verbal gestures as expression, observations were made at instants when the assistants were listening to some query or task, thinking or assimilating some information and when they were delivering some tasks. Table 1 summarized few common observations on these non-verbal expressions.

In terms of the speech constructs, assistants used intonations and discourse markers to provide feedback on its level of understanding while listening to others but these are not to be repeated very frequently. While speaking assistant provide feedback on its level of confidence on the response again through use of intonations and discourse markers. Also the speed of speaking must depend upon the kind or query, the content of the speech. We identified several examples of using intonations while assistant listening and speaking.

Table 1. Observations on non-verbal expression

State of voice assistant	Gaze aversion	Head tilt	Head nod
Listening (trying to understand)	Very less	Less (sideways/below)	No
Listening (query not understood)	No	High (sideways)	No
Listening (query moderately understood)	Less	No	Less
Listening (query well understood)	Med	No	Very high
Thinking	Very high	High (up)	No
Speaking generally	Less	Less	No
Speaking response	Very less	Very less	Less
Speaking instances	Very high	High (up)	No

4   Personality Elicitation

In the second phase of our study, the aim was to formulate an appropriate and user desirable personality for the voice assistant. A *personality* is defined as the collection of individual differences, dispositions, and temperaments that are observed to have some consistency across situations and time [9]. Big five theory has emerged from the consensus of several theories for describing personality as having different dimensions. The definition of voice assistant personality that we used in our exploration consist of 9 attributes considering various aspects of personality traits which we derive from various prior work including classical theory, the big five theory [10] as well as our insights from the earlier personal assistant interviews. Following are the set of considered 9 personality attributes -

- Dependable – how much the user can depend on it
- Controlling – how much does it control the user
- Engaging – how much does it keep the user engaged
- Adaptive – how much does it adapts to the user's circumstances
- Spontaneous – how quickly does it provide solutions to the user
- Inventive – how inventive are the solutions provided by it
- Empathetic – how much does it empathize with the user
- Expressive – how much does it expresses its thoughts to the user
- Similar – how congruent in personality is it to the user's own personality

Once we framed the set of personality attributes, we performed the Personality Elicitation session, a face to face survey discussion session with 30 participants to understand the importance and desirability of each of those attributes for a voice assistant. Our intent was to quantify, how much of each of these traits was desirable to a user. The questionnaire consisted of nine different hypothetical scenarios described in detail one relating to each of the personality attributes. Each scenario also presented counter situations of either of the extremes which may be due to either abundance or scarcity of the personality attribute in question. Five responses for each question were designed and given to a user with each response increasing in any one particular attribute. The users were asked to choose between the responses they would prefer in such a situation. For example, how would the user expect a voice agent to behave in a scenario where a meeting needs to be scheduled through voice input?

A sample scenario to evaluate the extent of *expressive* behavior that is preferred by the user is shown below. The scenario caters to a situation in which, a user is looking for navigation directions to an unfamiliar destination. The user would like to get directions all the way to his destination, in such a situation, how will the user expect a voice assistant to behave?

Response 1:   Straight 200 m, then take a left.
Response 2:   Speed up a bit to 200 m and then take a left turn.
Response 3:   Drive up to 200 m, take a hard left and enjoy the lakeside view while driving.
Response 4:   Keep going for 200 m followed by a hard left turn. Destination will be on your right, while you pass by the beautiful lake.
Response 5:   To reach your destination, drive up to 200 m and take a left for the busy west 81st street. You may wish to enjoy some good coffee at Monk's Café while it sits beside the beautiful lake.

The responses from voice assistant vary considerably from response 1 which is no-nonsense, straightforward but a bland answer. The excitement in voice assistant's response increases as we approach response number 5 also the information delivered is more and might be considered unnecessary at some point.

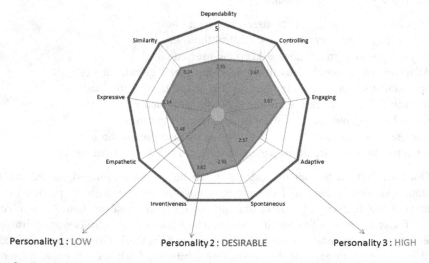

Fig. 3. Result from personality elicitation exercise showing three hypothetical personalities

The collected responses from all the participants were plotted on a spider graph to reflect the results. Two hypothetically extreme personalities were first plotted which would help compare the desired traits. The results on a glance show that a user prefers a moderate personality which neither extreme nor low on any of the nine attributes. Some interesting points being, users may not like a voice assistant to be over sympathetic; however the quality of inventiveness comes out to be a much desired one. Interestingly, this sort of preferred behavior is also consistent with the earlier findings from personal assistant interviews wherein, the assistant was expected to behave moderate and show emotions which were congruent to their bosses' mood (Fig. 3).

5 Crowdsourcing the Problem Through Co-creation

In the third and final stage of our study, desired behavior for the voice assistant was to be drawn on in terms of how they should display the use of linguistic and speech characteristics. This was done through a self-reporting method; as a part of framing the preferred responses from a voice assistant. We conducted crowdsourcing and co-creation sessions with 32 participants which included language enthusiasts and avid readers of literature in order to create natural dialogues for the voice assistant in various situations. The intent of this experiment was to extract the underlying common patterns in responses from the users. These patterns would be in terms of the language elements used, and distinguishable variations in speech characteristics. Since these linguistic cues are related to the personality of any individual [11], we can primarily use them to reflect the behavior of any voice agent. Discourse markers include repeated words, false starts, and fillers such as "uhm". Also observed is the use of phrases such as "like you know," "I mean," "well," "just," "like," and "yeah". These words operate at a pragmatic level; their meaning is derived not exclusively from their literal definition but from their use in context [4]. Use of hedges literally express uncertainty; they include qualifying types of language such as "I guess," "maybe," "probably," "I think," and "sort of." Use of interjections, formal/casual language, active/passive voice [4, 6] were few other linguistic characteristics we observed in the participants' responses. Additionally, a variety of subtle non-linguistic cues are used by individuals to communicate their emotional states such as, speech rate, voice type, pitch, loudness, pauses and stresses [8, 9]. Emotional valence is signaled by mean of the pitch contour and rhythm of speech. Dominant personalities might be expected to generate characteristic rhythms and amplitude of speech, as well as an assertive postures and gestures. Similarly, friendliness will typically be demonstrated through speech prosody [1].

The participants were given a set of user queries and corresponding responses from an existing voice assistant application covering various smartphone usage scenarios. The participants were asked to frame the response of the voice assistant as natural and in the way they would prefer to hear, with appropriate use of dialogue elements. The participants were allowed to frame these responses and also asked to add the spoken characteristics they would like the utterances to have. Participants could specify speech variables like pitch, speech rate and stress along with their language responses. The usage scenarios for the experiment were chosen such that different personality attributes of voice agent get reflected in the responses. The usage scenarios in mobile phones for which responses were collected were: Assistance during Navigation, Scheduling an event, Getting weather/sports information, doing a web search, playing music and general empathetic scenarios. A few patterns which came across as frequent i.e. more than 5 participants implied to the use of the kind of language or speech modulations were studied closely. Few of those insights on the linguistic and speech characteristics are mentioned here.

i. For less serious tasks, like entertainment or leisure tasks or for searches and general tasks, opinionating statements were used. This indicates that the user may not mind the voice assistant to suggest a choice or hold an opinion in contexts which don't have a serious consequence.

ii. Voice assistant in its response may use hedges when the information conveyed could have a certain degree of ambiguity. For instance, while telling about weather, the response were be framed with 'maybe cloudy' or 'looks like it would be sunny'.

iii. For tasks which require a greater involvement of the user and may have a risk involved, asking for confirmations was recommended. Interrogating statements with the purpose of confirmations were used in contexts like navigation, schedule management and online payments.

iv. The participants preferred to stress upon various instances of the voice assistant's replies. When asked, the reason for putting stress was to bring emphasis of the listeners to new information added by the voice assistant. For instance, Names, time values, location names and other nouns were stressed upon. Also if there was an action which maybe expected on users behalf was seen to be conveyed using stress in voice.

v. Interjections were required to be highly context specific. If a user query was followed by an interjection, the user gets an impression of his query being understood well. Only when the context of the user's query was perceived as a positive or pertaining to a task which involves low risks, would a voice assistant react with an excited interjection like "ahaan" or "wow!" However when the context is serious in nature, in general the use of interjections was lower in number.

As the next step, few of these raw dialogue generated by the participants in this co-creation session were then given to 6 animation artists and designers with the intent of generating the visuals of the gestural aspect of these communication. We were discovering various gestural cues like smiles, frowns, eyebrow shapes, head nods, head positions, body postures, etc. [14, 15]. Table 2 presents some of the visual responses from the participants and some of the analysis drawn from those in terms of guidelines for gestural expression.

Table 2. Visual responses from the participants and analysis on gestural expressions

	Voice Assistant Natural Response			
	Oh! What happened!	*I'm afraid Dr. Johnson is not at his clinic*	*but he is at the hospital*	*Should I make an appointment for you?*
Eyes	Very wide open	Dim	Slight gaze aversion (indicating elsewhere)	Wide open, Staring
Eyebrows	Raised	Raised, shrinked	Normal, straight	One pointing up other pointing down, stretched
Head position	Stable, forward	Slightly down	Moderate nodding, straight	Stable, straight
Expressions	Disappointment, sadness	Anxious, helplessness	Thinking	Concerned, showing sub-ordinance
Body gesture / Others	Dropped shoulders, slightly bent forward	Raised shoulders, raised hands	Finger pointing out	Bent knees, highly bent forward
Participant Responses				

6 Conclusions

The underlying goal of our study was to devise a methodology for deriving the appropriate behavior of a voice assistant avatar on mobile devices. Where many researchers have tried to formulate various methodologies for the same, ours was a user centered design approach. After carrying out the various activities with keeping user empathy in mind, we were able to come up with a few design directions for approaching the challenge of creating an avatar based voice assistant. Through the three phases of study, we identified few insights on the social behavior of the voice assistant, evolved the appropriate personality of the voice assistant as desired by the users and also formulated few guidelines for linguistic, speech as well as non-verbal expression constructs to be used by the voice assistant.

In summary, we identified that behavior of a voice assistant should be a moderate one, under various scenarios; the expression can vary up to only a certain range. User and assistant's mood space should be as congruent as possible for being a reactive companion but not an over-reactive one. The voice assistant is expected to be very proactive and must interrupt the user immediately if the matter is more urgent and important than current task. Voice Assistant must avoid all updates from outside and become a single accessible point for all updates at a later stage. Preferred time to give updates/notifications is when user is switching from an ongoing task to another. From the personality aspect we found that the overall results from the personality elicitation exercise was quite similar to the actual behavior exhibited by the human personal assistants in the workplace. Voice assistant was expected not to be over sympathetic; and inventiveness comes out to be a much desired one.

In the dialogue co-creation activities, a preference in the informality of language was primarily noted. From the responses of the participants in this activity we were able to formulate few guidelines to design natural responses for the voice assistant with use of various languages and linguistic constructs like hedges, discourse makers, intonations, pauses, stresses, etc. For instance, interjections should be used with newly introduced contexts, must immediately follow user's query and must be uttered with high speech rate. It should mostly be avoided for ongoing dialogue context. Pauses are expected before giving alternatives, suggestions or making any enquiry from the user. Speech Rate could be fast for commonly used statements, but slower while asking any user's decision or updating any information such as date, time, status, etc.

Finally, with all the design guidelines, dialogues and personality definitions evolved from our research we designed the prototype of the natural voice assistant avatar. Going forward, we plan to extend this work with participants from few other geographical origins to consider cultural sensitivity in the design. Next goal would also be to perform experimental evaluation of the voice assistant prototype with the users.

References

1. Breese, J., Ball, G.: Modeling emotional state and personality for conversational agents. Rapport technique MSR-TR-98-41, Microsoft research (1998)
2. Norman, D.: How might humans interact with robots. Keynote address to the DARPA-NSF Workshop on Human-Robot Interaction, San Luis Obispo, CA (2001)
3. Ball, G., Breese, J.: Emotion and personality in a conversational agent. In: Cassell, J., Sullivan, J., Prevost, S., Churchill, E. (eds.) Embodied Conversational Agents, pp. 189–219. MIT Press, Cambridge (2000)
4. Torrey, C., Fussell, S.R., Kiesler, S.: How a robot should give advice. In: 2013 8th ACM/IEEE International Conference on Human-Robot Interaction (HRI), pp. 275–282. IEEE (2013)
5. Meerbeek, B., Hoonhout, J., Bingley, P., Terken, J.: Investigating the relationship between the personality of a robotic TV assistant and the level of user control. In: The 15th IEEE International Symposium on Robot and Human Interactive Communication, ROMAN 2006, pp. 404–410. IEEE (2006)
6. Heylighen, F., Dewaele, J.-M.: Formality of language: definition, measurement and behavioral determinants. Interner Bericht, Center "Leo Apostel", Vrije Universiteit Brüssel (1999)
7. Becker, C., Kopp, S., Wachsmuth, I.: Why emotions should be integrated into conversational agents. In: Conversational Informatics: An Engineering Approach, pp. 49–68 (2007)
8. Russell, J.A.: A circumplex model of affect. J. Pers. Soc. Psychol. 39(6), 1161 (1980)
9. Dryer, D.C.: Getting personal with computers: how to design personalities for agents. Appl. Artif. Intell. 13(3), 273–295 (1999)
10. Costa, P.T., MacCrae, R.R.: Revised NEO Personality Inventory (NEO PI-R) and NEO Five-Factor Inventory (NEO FFI): Professional Manual. Psychological Assessment Resources (1992)
11. Pennebaker, J.W., King, L.A.: Linguistic styles: language use as an individual difference. J. Pers. Soc. Psychol. 77(6), 1296 (1999)

12. Cowie, R., Cornelius, R.R.: Describing the emotional states that are expressed in speech. Speech Commun. **40**(1), 5–32 (2003)
13. Brown, P.: Politeness: Some Universals in Language Usage, vol. 4. Cambridge University Press, Cambridge (1987)
14. Cassell, J., Vilhjálmsson, H.: Fully embodied conversational avatars: making communicative behaviors autonomous. Auton. Agent. Multi-Agent Syst. **2**(1), 45–64 (1999)
15. Ball, G., Breese, J.: Relating personality and behavior: posture and gestures. In: Paiva, Ana C.R. (ed.) IWAI 1999. LNCS, vol. 1814, pp. 196–203. Springer, Heidelberg (2000)

Comparative Analysis of Regular Grid Based Algorithms in the Design of Graphical Control Panels

Jerzy Grobelny and Rafał Michalski[✉]

Wrocław University of Technology, Wrocław, Poland
{jerzy.grobelny, rafal.michalski}@pwr.edu.pl
http://JerzyGrobelny.com, http://RafalMichalski.com

Abstract. The paper presents comparative investigation of the effectiveness of three algorithms used for optimizing control panel objects' arrangements. We examined two modified classical approaches involving changing of objects' pairs, that is CRAFT, and its simplified version as well as our implementation of the Simulated annealing concept. Their behavior was investigated in experimental simulation studies of two real-life problems: the truck control panel (small number of objects) and the control panel from a nuclear energy plant (big number of items). The statistical analysis of the obtained results showed the supremacy of the proposed version of the simulated annealing algorithm in both case studies.

Keywords: Display design · Control panels · Layout optimization · Ergonomics · CRAFT · Simulated annealing

1 Introduction

The interaction between a human and a machine is often conducted by means of a graphical interface including either physical or virtual panels with signaling and control components. The optimal layout of these panels lies within the scope of ergonomics and human-computer interactions. McCormick (1976) formulated general principles regarding interface components arrangements that lead to usable solutions. In his opinion the designer should take into account the following criteria: (a) the object's importance, (b) frequency of use, (c) sequences of using objects, and (d) objects' functional similarities. These general recommendations occurred to be quite troublesome in practical applications, therefore a number of tools have been proposed to support the design process. Among them there were attempts to apply formal models from the Facilities Layout Problems (FLP). Generally, classical FLP search for such an arrangement of n objects in n available places that minimizes the general cost which is proportional to distances between objects and depends on the number of transport operations between them. For extensive review see Kusiak and Heragu, 1987 as well as Singh and Sharma 2006. Two of the general panel design principles (c) and (d) may be analyzed in a similar way once the numerical specifications of objects' relationships are available. Wierwille (1981) proposed statistical methods that can be used for the

© Springer International Publishing Switzerland 2015
M. Kurosu (Ed.): Human-Computer Interaction, Part I, HCII 2015, LNCS 9169, pp. 332–339, 2015.
DOI: 10.1007/978-3-319-20901-2_30

operationalization of the principles (a) and (b). He named them a first order class models in contrast to rules (c) and (d) described as the second order ones. The first order class models concern relations between the operator and interface components while the second order principles deal with relations between objects.

Numerous optimization approaches in designing interfaces' layouts generally differ in (1) the way of objects' relationships operationalization, (2) included design criteria – the first and/or the second order (3) the way the size and shape of objects are represented. Bonney and Wiliams (1975) proposed a multicriteria and multistage model where objects' relationships were defined subjectively by a designer. Sargent et al. (1997) applied a classical CRAFT algorithm (Armour and Buffa, 1963) in their multistage method for a control panel operated by one person. They used the AHP technique (Saaty, 1980) for determining subjective links between objects including additionally relationships between objects and the operator. Their method also allows for modeling real dimensions of control panel components. Lin and Wu (2010) use similar to Sargent et al. (2007) modification of links data but add also the criterion of time needed to operate the panel based on the Fitts's law (1954). They employed the Branch and Bound algorithm for optimization which was proposed in the FLP area by Gavett and Plyter (1966).

Apart from classical algorithms there are also proposals based on artificial intelligence like genetic algorithms, ant colony or particle swarms. Hani et al. (2007), for instance, applied ant colony algorithm. A similar approach was presented by Shengyuan et al. (2013). In the former case links represented only the frequency of use while in the latter article the relationships reflected both the importance of objects and sequences of use. In both cases, shapes and sizes of components were not taken into account.

Despite multiple papers in this area it is difficult to find studies presenting comparisons of algorithms applied for searching optimal control panel or interface layouts. Thus, the main goal of this research is to compare the effectiveness of two relatively simple classical algorithms and our implementation of the simulated annealing concept. Their performance is examined in two, real-life examples. All algorithms operate on the regular grid and allow for modeling areas of individual components. Our approach, just like Sargent et al. (1997) and Lin and Wu (2010), includes both the first and the second order criteria.

2   Method

2.1   Applied Algorithms

For comparisons we used a classical version of the CRAFT algorithm originally presented by Buffa et al. (1964). The idea of this approach consists in making changes in objects locations by pairs as long as they improve the goal function value (GFV). The algorithm starts from the random objects' arrangements on a regular grid.

We also used a simpler than CRAFT algorithm also based on pairs swaps (Pairs). We just excluded the outer loop from CRAFT and, thus, the appropriate pairs' changes are stopped after only one run of the algorithm.

Our Simulated Annealing (SimAnn) algorithm was implemented according to the general idea described by Kirkpatrick et al. (1983). They recommended that in the first step of the algorithm one should accept worse solutions with the probability of 0.8. Starting from this assumption and preliminary estimation of the delta according to the procedure similar to Singh and Sharma (2008) we calculated Ti. The epoch length was set as a value proportional to the number of objects $k \times N$ such as in papers of Wilhelm and Ward (1987) or Heragu and Alfa (1992). The cooling scheme was specified as in Heragu and Alfa (1992), that is $T_j = r \times T_{j-1}$, where r = 0.9. The final temperature was determined by a number of predefined steps i as $T_f = 0.9^{(i-1)} \times T_i$. Parameter k and i were obtained by preliminary simulations for the examined case studies and amounted to $i = 100$ and $k = 5$. Finally, the T_f for the first and the second case study was set at 50 and 20000 respectively.

In all algorithms, there was a possibility of blocking specific objects in certain places of the regular grid.

2.2 Relationships Matrix Modifications

Two modifications of the relationships matrix were made in our approach. First, as it was proposed by Sargeant et al. (1997), we added the first order links (operator-objects) to the original matrix containing the second order relationships (object-object). The additional data represented assessments of all objects in relation to the most important or most frequently used item which is located in front of the operator.

Secondly, we added the possibility of including the areas occupied by individual components in conducted analyses. For this purpose, each object was modeled by the appropriate number of regular grid segments proportional to its real dimensions. One of the segments of a given object was set as the main one and all remaining were linked with it. Such an approach allowed for the inclusion of areas covered by objects but not their shapes.

2.3 Experimental Design

The presented above three algorithms along with described modifications were applied for the analysis of two real-life control panels considerably different in their complexity. The first project concerns truck driver informative panel layout. The solution to this problem was ordered by a company manufacturing such vehicles in Poland. The panel consisted of eight items: (1) Speedometer, (2) Tachometer, (3) Air pressure, (4) Oil pressure, (5) Water temperature, (6) Oil temperature, (7) Clock and Time of driving, (8) Diagnostic screen. It was assumed that the panel should be in the form of a digital, graphical display located at the center of the dashboard with all components arranged in one row. The sequences of objects' uses and their importances were determined by means of a questionnaire administered to 20 truck drivers. The drivers' opinions were expressed on five step scale. Since the speedometer was considered as the most important object (on the same scale), we added appropriate values to the relationships in the first row of the matrix. The final results rounded to the integer

Table 1. The relationships matrix including the first and the second order data for the truck panel layout case study.

Object	(1)	(2)	(3)	(4)	(5)	(6)	(7)	(8)
(1)	×	10	8	6	7	1	5	1
(2)	3	×	5	3	3	0	3	0
(3)	0	5	×	3	3	3	0	0
(4)	0	5	3	×	3	0	0	0
(5)	5	5	5	3	×	3	0	0
(6)	5	5	3	5	3	×	0	0
(7)	5	0	0	0	0	0	×	0
(8)	0	0	0	0	0	0	0	×

numbers are put together in Table 1. The shapes and sizes of the components were not defined so each segment of the regular grid represented one object.

The second example was taken from the paper of Sargent et al. (1997) and consisted of considerably bigger number of items than the first one. The original relationships data were modified by adding dummy objects to reflect the components sizes. Pilot tests showed that the links strengths between these additional items should be bigger than the biggest existing relationship value. We set it at the level of 500. Because the object 1 has the highest priority, its location was fixed in the center of the layout. The grid dimensions and the original null objects were the same as in the original work.

2.4 Simulation Procedure

In both cases the experimental simulation procedure was identical. We ran 100 times each of the three described earlier algorithms. Every iteration started from a random arrangement of segments. In the second case study the most important objects with the number 1 were placed in the center of the grid and blocked. In the truck panel case it was assumed that all objects are within a central visual field, so the most important component was not fixed. The goal function value was recorded in for every individual simulation.

3 Results

3.1 Truck Panel

The basic descriptive statistical data regarding the truck panel layout are demonstrated in Table 2.

Table 2. Basic descriptive statistics for the truck panel layout case study

Algorithm	Min	Max	Mean	[*]MSE	[**]SD
Pairs	266	279	271	0.474	4.74
CRAFT	266	279	269	0.342	3.42
SimAnn	266	266	266	×	×

[*] MSE – Mean Standard Error, [**] SD – Standard Deviation

As it can be observed, the best layout with the GFV = 266 could be obtained using any of the examined algorithms in 100 repetitions. The best performance was recorded for the SimAnn algorithm, where the best value was found in each iteration. The worst average GF values were registered for the simple Pairs procedure. Mean standard errors and standard deviations were smaller for the CRAFT than for the Pairs algorithm. The best layout configuration is illustrated in Fig. 1.

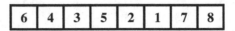

Fig. 1. The best layout for the truck panel layout case study (GFV = 266)

A standard one way Analysis of Variance showed that the differences in mean values for the algorithms are statistically significant at the level of 0.05. The ANOVA results are presented in Fig. 2.

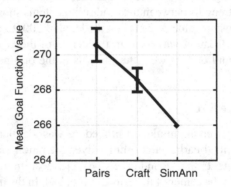

Fig. 2. Mean goal function values for the truck panel layout; $F_{(2, 297)} = 46$, $p < 0.00001$. Vertical bars denote 0.95 confidence intervals.

The Fischer LSD post hoc analysis revealed significant differences between all pairs of algorithms ($\alpha = 0.05$).

3.2 Nuclear Power Plant

Descriptive statistical data concerned with the second case study is presented in Table 3. Here again, the best average goal function values as well as the best solutions were obtained by means of the SimAnn algorithm. The worst mean values and solutions with minimal GFVs were observed for the Pairs algorithm. The Simulated annealing algorithm exhibited also the smallest values of standard deviation which may indicate that it provides consistently good solutions.

Table 3. Basic descriptive statistics for the nuclear energy plant control panel layout

Algorithm	Min	Max	Mean	*MSE	**SD
Pairs	59101	83294	68634	424	4240
CRAFT	54969	78585	67504	385	3852
SimAnn	51955	58137	54876	131	1314

* MSE – Mean Standard Error, ** SD – Standard Deviation

The best found solution for the nuclear plant control panel is shown in Fig. 3.

16	13	13	8	17	17	2	5	5	5	5	3	4	12	12	12	21	22	23	26
16	10	8	8	19	19	2	7	7	1	1	3	4	4	15	15	22	22	22	25
10	10	8	9	18	2	2	2	7	1	1	3	14	4	11	22	22	22	22	22
24	10	20	9	18	2	2	2	7	6	6	14	14	14	11	11	22	22	22	27

Fig. 3. Best layout obtained by simulated annealing algorithm for the nuclear energy plant control panel. GFV = 51 955.

For the comparison purpose we reproduced the original best objects' configuration obtained by the CRAFT algorithm in the work of Sargent et al. (1997). The result is given in Fig. 4.

25	21	19	19	20	12	12	5	5	5	5	6	6	4	4	11	15	15	22	23
16	16	9	9	8	8	12	7	7	1	1	2	4	4	11	11	22	22	22	22
26	18	18	8	8	10	10	7	7	1	1	2	2	3	14	14	22	22	22	22
27	17	17	13	13	10	10	2	2	2	2	2	3	3	14	14	22	22	22	24

Fig. 4. Original best layout for the nuclear power plant layout (Sargen et al., 2007). GFV = 69 484.

After inclusion of our relationships matrix modifications, the goal function for this solution amounted to GFV = 69 484 which is markedly worse than our best layout. Again, we apply the standard one way ANOVA which showed significant differences between average goal function values for the algorithms: $F(2, 297) = 507$, $p < 0.00001$. The results are illustrated in Fig. 5.

Also in this case the Fischer LSD post hoc analysis showed statistically meaningful ($\alpha = 0.05$) differences between all pairs of algorithms.

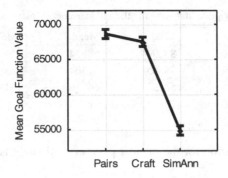

Fig. 5. Mean goal function values for the nuclear energy plant control panel layout; F(2, 297) = 507, p < 0.00001. Vertical bars denote 0.95 confidence intervals.

4   Discussion and Conclusions

In this research we analyzed two cases that differed considerably in terms of complexity. Despite that in both examples the applied approaches had similar properties. Firstly, the presented here modifications of the relationships' matrix enable, in a natural way, to include information about objects sizes in simple regular grid analyses. This way of preparing data allows for obtaining in a regular grid coherent objects structures without involving additional constrains. This concept probably offers greater flexibility of the generated solutions in relation to approaches that require imposing additional limitations. Perhaps thanks to this feature, all the best solutions in the second case study are better than the best solution obtained originally by means of the standard CRAFT with fixed locations of the same objects' segments. This outcome was observed regardless of the algorithm applied.

The second major result of the present study is concerned with the significant supremacy of the simulated annealing algorithm over the other investigated here. It seems that this type of metaheuristic suits the data structure of man-machine interface problems very well. It is especially true in big problems such as the nuclear power plant control panel. The benefits measured by the decrease both in the mean and minimal goal function values are meaningful in relation to the commonly applied in such problems CRAFT algorithm. In the second case study, the percentage gain amounted to 19 % for average goal function value and 5 % for the best solutions.

Some limitation of employing the simulated annealing algorithm is its efficiency. Though in this study we did not precisely recorded computation times, but we observed quite big differences between applied algorithms. Approximate times for the single simulation in the second case study equaled about 10 s for the simple pairs' changes, 2 min for CRAFT and, as much as 5 min for simulated annealing. Therefore, in case of bigger problems, repeating the simulated annealing or even CRAFT procedures may not be feasible. In such situation one may use the markedly faster pairs' changes algorithm. It provided the worst solutions but the difference in mean goal function values for the second case study in relation to classical CRAFT amounted barely 2 %.

Acknowledgments. The work was partially financially supported by the Polish National Science Center grant no. 2011/03/B/ST8/06238.

References

Bonney, H.M., Wiliams, R.W.: CAPABLE: a computer program to layout controls and panels. Ergonomics **20**, 297–316 (1977)

Buffa, E.S., Armour, G.C., Vollmann, T.E.: Allocating facilities with CRAFT. Harv. Bus. Rev. **42**(2), 136–158 (1964)

Cheng-Jhe, L., Changxu, W.: Improved link analysis method for user interface design– modified link table and optimisation-based algorithm. Behav. Inf. Technol. **29**(2), 199–216 (2010)

Gavett, J.W., Plyter, N.V.: The optimal assignment of facilities to locations by branch and bound. Oper. Res. **14**, 210–232 (1966)

Fitts, P.M.: The information capacity of the human motor system in controlling the amplitude of movement. J. Exp. Psychol. **49**, 389–391 (1954)

Hani, Y., Amodeo, L., Yalaoui, F., Chen, H.: Ant colony optimization for solving an industrial layout problem. Eur. J. Oper. Res. **183**(2), 633–642 (2007)

Heragu, S.S., Alfa, A.S.: Experimental analysis of simulated annealing based algorithms for the layout problem. Eur. J. Oper. Res. **57**(2), 190–202 (1992)

Kirkpatrick, S., Gelatt, C.D., Vecchi, M.P.: Optimization by simulated annealing. Sci. **220**(4598), 671–680 (1983)

Kusiak, A., Heragu, S.S.: The facility layout problem. Eur. J. Oper. Res. **29**(3), 229–251 (1987)

McCormick, E.J.: Human Factors in Engineering and Design. Mc Graw – Hill, New York (1976)

Saaty, T.L.: The Analytic Hierarchy Process. RWS Publications, Pittsburgh (1996)

Sargent, T.A., Kay, M.G., Sargent, R.G.: A methodology for optimally designing console panels for use by a single operator. Hum. Factors **39**(3), 389–409 (1997)

Shengyuan, Y., Chen, Y., Chen, W.: An intelligent algorithm method of element layout priority sequence on console's human machine interface. Adv. Mater. Res. **712–715**, 2441–2446 (2013)

Singh, S.P., Sharma, R.R.K.: A review of different approaches to the facility layout problems. Int. J. Adv. Manuf. Technol. **30**(5–6), 425–433 (2006)

Singh, S.P., Sharma, R.R.K.: Two-level modified simulated annealing based approach for solving facility layout problem. Int. J. Prod. Res. **46**(13), 3563–3582 (2008)

Wierwille, W.W.: Statistical techniques for instrument panel arrangement in Manned Systems Design, NATO Conference Series. Hum. Factors **17**, 201–218 (1981)

Towards Paperless Mobility Information in Public Transport

Stephan Hörold$^{(\boxtimes)}$, Cindy Mayas, and Heidi Krömker

Technische Universität Ilmenau, Ilmenau, Germany
{stephan.hoerold,cindy.mayas,
heidi.kroemker}@tu-ilmenau.de

Abstract. Following the integration of mobile applications into the mobility information system of public transport, public transport companies seek new opportunities to reduce paper-based information. A common example for these new opportunities is the so called 'paperless stop point'. This paper describes different expansion stages of public displays for mobility information at stop points, based on empirical evaluations with users and experts. Four stages are discussed, which range from static information screens to individual interactive displays. In addition, the widespread expectations of users and transport companies are described, which provide the base for the stage development, are described. As a result, this paper provides insight into typical challenges towards paperless mobility information at stop points in public transport.

Keywords: Public displays · Mobility information · Usability · Public transport

1 Introduction

Due to actual technological advances and new requirements, many transportation companies discuss new approaches in order to reach the passengers of public transport and fulfill their information needs [1]. While mobile applications are developed further and new functionalities are added continuously [2], other information systems are evaluated for optimizing potential as well.

Public transport already offers a wide range of information systems, from static, collective and stationary to dynamic, individual and mobile systems [3], which have been developed over the last decades and nowadays provide the information base for passengers. In the past, some of these systems have been modified and adapted to new requirements. Mobile tickets and e-ticketing have demonstrated the benefits and challenges of this adaption process [4].

However, with new mobile information systems and new technologies emerging, the contribution of traditional information systems to the mobility information system as a whole has to be questioned and a more drastic redesign has to be taken into account. One of these more traditional information systems is the paper-based information at stop points.

Enhancing the information quality and minimizing the costs e.g. for printing and manually updating the paper-based information, are two reasons for reducing the

© Springer International Publishing Switzerland 2015
M. Kurosu (Ed.): Human-Computer Interaction, Part I, HCII 2015, LNCS 9169, pp. 340–349, 2015.
DOI: 10.1007/978-3-319-20901-2_31

amount of paper-based information and for the development of paperless stop points in public transport.

Additional benefits of paperless stop points, based on the perspectives of transport companies, include e.g.:

- Actuality of information
- Readability of information
- Accessibility
- Multilingualism
- Consistency of information
- Additional information and functionality

On the other hand, the expected downsides are e.g.:

- Higher procurement and maintenance costs
- Hygiene issues
- Delays while waiting for other users to finish their interaction
- Higher repair costs caused by vandalism

Key elements of paperless stop points and stations involve the replacement of paper-based timetables, network plans, lists of transportation fees and maps of different content. While mobile applications already offer most of this information [5], the ownership of a smartphone, including the necessary public transport specific application, cannot be taken for granted.

At the moment, especially public screens and displays are used, to communicate real-time information on departures and to enhance the information quality [6]. Following this concept, it is only consequent to analyze further potential for transferring paper-based information to screens and displays. Due to the actual non-interactive and quite large presentation of paper-based information at stop points, the transfer raises several questions, regarding the user interface and the degree of interaction. This paper describes the different degrees of interactivity and the related typical challenges of public displays in public transport. The results are based on two usability evaluations as well as expert interviews, which are described in the following.

2 Method

The development of the user interface as well as the definition of the degree of interactivity, are primarily based on the goal of developing a product, which can be used with effectiveness, efficiency and satisfaction by different user groups [7]. The user-centered development process of the user interface consists of three concept stages and three evaluation stages and is based on preliminary consideration as shown in Table 1. These considerations integrate the requirements of public transport companies, the knowledge of experts and requirements of typical users of public transport and are based on the initial usage analysis of two test systems implemented in Cologne and Stuttgart in Germany [8].

In addition, the context of use [9] provides challenges for

- Optimizing usage times to grant more users access in a short time
- Selecting and enhancing suitable content
- Merging dynamic and static information

A list of company requirements and the results of the usage analysis of the test systems [8] provide the base for the development, including the following elements:

- Information needs of passengers at stop points in different categories
- Design ideas for the segmentation of the display, e.g. for menus and information
- Added value functions, which are not included within paper-based information

Table 1. Development and evaluation phases

Development	Method	Details
Preliminary considerations	Usage analysis	2 test systems
	Company requirements	Best-practice-Analysis
Basic concept		
Requirements	Expert workshop	9 experts
Fine concept		
Interactive Prototypes	Usability Evaluation 1	7 test users
Detailed concept		
Final Prototype	Expert Evaluation	3 expert interviews
	Usability Evaluation 2	16 test users
Final concept		

In a first step, these preliminary considerations are used to design two basic prototypes, in order to discuss the segmentation of the screen as well as the functionality with public transport and usability experts. As a result, one basic concept is chosen to refine the concept with users in the next step.

The second step is based on a fine concept, which is derived from the preliminary considerations, the basic concept and the expert workshop. The usability evaluation is performed as a lab-based usability evaluation with seven typical users from the future destination of the first implemented test system. The evaluation focuses on the following topics:

- Degree of interactivity
- Workflow for typical user goals
- Usability and functionality
- Design of icons

Based on this evaluation, a detailed concept with only one degree of interactivity and solutions for the identified usability problems are developed. The third evaluation phase with an equal test setting and a final prototype focusses on the topics:

- Fulfillment of information needs
- Different task completion strategies
- Usage times
- Usability and functionality

Both usability evaluations are supported by an eye-tracking evaluation, in order to provide additional information to the video and audio recording as well as the used questionnaires. An expert evaluation with representatives of disabled rights organizations, service employees of a local transportation company and a designer, completes this evaluation phase. Based on this final evaluation, the results are integrated into a final user interface design concept, which is transferred to all parts of the user interface and a detailed description of the concepts is derived.

3 Results

Public transport is characterized through different users, tasks and contexts [3] and therefore provides challenges for the development of nearly all information systems. Table 2 shows the different user groups within the first and second usability evaluation. For both usability tests, typical tasks along the journey were chosen, which are typically performed at stop points.

Table 2. User characteristics within the two evaluations

	Evaluation 1	Evaluation 2
Participants	7 users in one test group	16 users in three test groups
Usage of public transport	at least several times each month	Commuters
		Casual users
		Tourists
Age	22–62 years	17-63 years
Body height	1,60–1,93 m	1,63–1,93 m
	5,25–6,33 feet	5,35–6,33 feet
Special characteristics	–	One user with mobility impairments

3.1 Requirements and Expectations of Transport Companies

The expert workshop with representatives from five public transport companies revealed the following, partially opposing, requirements and expectations. After the workshop, these requirements and expectation were analyzed and three categories identified.

Content. The expectations reach from identical transfer of paper-based information to new information concepts, which are more similar to the content of mobile applications. In general, the experts agree that typical tasks at stop points have to be addressed. These tasks are e.g.:

- Journey planning
- Path finding
- Information about tickets

Therefore, the expectations towards the presentation of the content differ as well. Traditional presentations provide a high conformity with the user's expectations. Nevertheless, new concepts can support users with low knowledge of a system and of a place.

Functionality. The basic functionality that all experts agree upon is the distribution of the content through software systems, which easily provide access to the public display. As a result, more up-to-date information can be provided. From that point forward, three major notions can be identified:

- No additional functionality
- Adding functions to reduce usage times and to include real-time information
- Functionality concept which mainly provides individual information

All experts provided comprehensible reasons for these notions. The question, how mobile applications will shape the whole information system in the next years, is still open and the main source for the different notions.

Equipment and Environmental Aspects. At the moment, paper-based information at stop points takes up a lot of space. The used space can only be reduced, if some sort of functionality is added to navigate through the content. Thereby, the equipment is strongly connected to content and functionality. Companies favoring the identical transfer of paper-based information will need at least the same space as before. With new functionalities, the space can be reduced and the available space can be used for advertisement or something similar. In addition, the number of displays has to be defined, depending on passenger figures and usage times.

3.2   Requirements and Expectations of Users

The usability evaluations with typical users from public transport revealed a differentiated perspective on public displays and paperless information as well. Figure 1 shows the widespread expectations of users regarding the need for a replacement of paper-based information, individual journey planning and waiting times.

All users can see at least some benefits of public displays, e.g. regarding the actuality and accessibility of information. But their opinion on the degree of interactivity varies. Again, the different requirements and expectations are grouped in the three categories: content, functionality and equipment and environmental aspects.

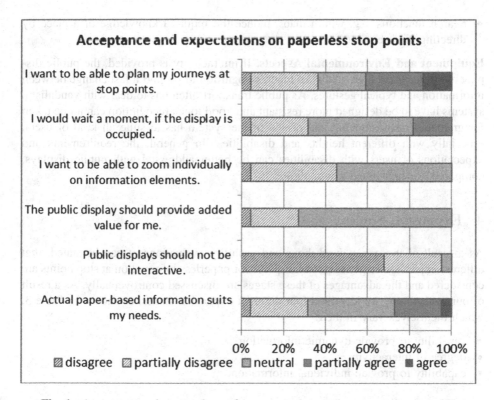

Fig. 1. Acceptance and expectations of users towards paperless stop points (n = 23)

Content. Users prefer a selection of paper-based information elements instead of a system providing all available paper-based information within an interactive system. This is mainly resulting from the already existing problem that users can hardly differentiate between the often very similar types of information elements, e.g. maps of different detail level.

The presentation of the content is important for the recognition of the system. For instance, timetables provide a well-known pattern for users. Therefore, the display is recognized even from a distance. Menus and icons support the recognition as well and signal interactivity. In contrast, advertisement reduces this recognition.

Functionality. Displays without any menus or dynamic elements are expected to provide less interactivity and functionality. However, even in this case users tested and searched for a zoom function. As soon as first dynamic or interactive functions are added, the expectation for more individual information rises.

Supporting functions are useful to ease the existing problems with paper-based information, e.g. complex maps and timetables. As a result, these support functions reduce the usage times and are very valid for an easy to use information system. Supporting functions are e.g.:

- Highlighting functions, e.g. in regard to the actual time, direct the users attention and minimize usage times

- Search functions, e.g. within maps, reduce the required knowledge of a place by directing the users attention

Equipment and Environmental Aspects. If interactivity is provided, the public display has to feature a high quality of touch recognition to support a fast change between information and typical gestures. As public transport often has to deal with vandalism, systems have to be designed more resistant and good touch recognition cannot be taken for granted. The positioning and design of the system has to suite all kind of users, especially with different heights and disabilities. In general, the requirements and expectations of users with disabilities can be better addressed with public displays, compared to paper-based information.

4   Expansion Stages

As a result of the expert workshops and usability evaluations, it can be stated, that different expansion stages of public displays for paperless information at stop points are considered and the advantages of these stages are discussed controversially. As a result of our evaluations, we identified four different expansion stages, as shown in Table 3, which themselves vary in their:

- capability to provide dynamic information,
- degree of interactivity,
- capability to provide individual information.

Table 3. Expansion stages of public displays in public transport

Stage		Dynamic information	Interactivity	Individualization
1	Static information	low	no	no
2	Dynamic Information	middle	no	no
3	Interactive Information	middle	yes	no
4	Interactive Individual Information	high	yes	yes

All stages provide different challenges about usage times, content and interface design. Nevertheless, they are based on the same goal, to support the user's tasks at stop points. **Static Information.** This stage provides similar information to the paper-based information and therefore is characterized by a comparable usability and usage time as well as an at least identical need for information space. For public transport companies, this stage provides a faster way to update the information e.g. on a monthly or daily basis. As a result, this stage provides at least more actual information than paper-based information, which results in better information for users.

Dynamic Information. As an extension of the static information, this stage provides more actual information by integrating support functions and real-time information. This aspect and the integration of disturbance and event information are the most valuable additions for users. Through these measurements, the usage times can be reduced compared to stage one. As an example, Fig. 2 shows the search duration for a

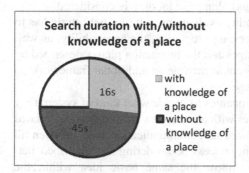 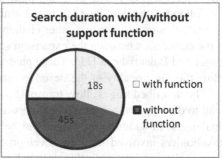

Fig. 2. Search duration with/without knowledge of a place and with/without support function

stop point on a map with knowledge of a place and without compared to the search duration with and without support function for users without knowledge of a place.

Interactive Information. One of the major disadvantages of the prior stages, the large screen size for parallel presentation of all information, is addressed in this stage by reducing the parallel information and introducing interactivity. As a result, not all the information is visible and the system can only be used by a single user, which may require more than one display at a stop point. Additionally, questions regarding the screen size, menu structure, usage times and overall usability have to be considered. This stage still focuses on the original paper-based information which can be supported with functions as mentioned in stage two and additional real-time information.

Interactive Individual Information. While stage one to three focus on collective information quite close to the original paper-based information, this stage focuses on individual information, based on basic public transport data. Therefore, stage four is able to fulfil the individual needs of different types of users and tasks with less need for specific knowledge of the system and of the place. An integration of real-time information as already known from mobile applications and websites in this stage is highly recommended.

5 Discussion

Our results show that compared to actual paper-based information at stop points, stage one can already provide sustainable benefit for the users, e.g. by providing more up-to-date information. The majority of test users welcome the development from paper-based information to public displays, but the expectations are widely spread. In addition, the question arises: whether a public display should provide the same functionality as a smartphone application, or if a combination can be found, which serves the different users' needs best. A public display could provide the collective and always available information while the mobile application carries the individual information.

Previous studies show [10], that a mix of different information systems enables the passengers to compare and recheck information, and therefore, provides security along the journey. This indicates that an answer to this question can only be found when the whole information system at a stop point and along the journey is considered.

Following the described lab-based usability evaluations, a future field study has to evaluate these questions and other challenges, e.g. regarding the accessibility, as well as the connection between the expansion stages and the interaction phases described by Vogel and Balakrishnan [11]. These phases could provide an additional framework, to refine the functionality of the described stages.

The described stages allow transport companies to decide what kind of system they want to develop and provide these companies with an overview of solutions and related challenges. In addition, the stages can be used as a communication base between all stakeholders involved into the development process. Considering the described heterogeneous expectations, this is vital to follow the same basic idea within the development.

Acknowledgements. This work was done in cooperation with the Association of German Transport Companies (VDV) and the German public transport companies: Kölner Verkehrsbetriebe (KVB), Rhein-Neckar-Verkehr Mannheim (RNV), Stuttgarter Straßenbahnen AG (SSB), Stadtwerke Bonn (SWB) und Verkehrsaktiengesellschaft Nürnberg (VAG). Additional results of the user interface design of paperless information at stop points in public transport are published within the VDV-Report 7036 [10].

References

1. Hörold, S., Mayas, C., Krömker, H.: Identifying the information needs of users in public transport. In: Stanton, N. (ed.) Advances in Human Aspects of Road and Rail Transportation, pp. 331–340. CRC Press, Boca Raton (2012)
2. Wirtz, S., Jakobs, E.-M.: Improving user experience for passenger information systems. prototypes and reference objects. IEEE Trans. Prof. Commun. **56**(2), 120–137 (2013). doi:10.1109/TPC.2013.2257211
3. Hörold, S., Mayas, C., Krömker, H.: User-oriented development of information systems in public transport. In: Anderson, M. (ed.) Contemporary Ergonomics and Human Factors 2013, pp. 160–167. CRC Press, Boca Raton (2013)
4. Payeras-Capellà, M.M., Mut-Puigserver, M., Ferrer-Gomila, J.-L., Castellà-Roca, J., Vives-Guasch, A.: Electronic ticketing: requirements and proposals related to transport. In: Navarro-Arribas, G., Torra, V. (eds.) Advanced Research in Data Privacy Studies in Computational Intelligence, vol. 567, pp. 285–301. Springer, Heidelberg (2015)
5. Hörold, S., Mayas, C., Krömker, H.: Passenger needs on mobile information systems – field evaluation in public transport. In: Stanton, N. (ed.) Advances in Human Aspects of Transportation: Part III, AHFE Conference, pp. 115–124. (2014)
6. Dziekan, K., Kottenhoff, K.: Dynamic at-stop real-time information displays for public transport: effects on customers. Transportation Research Part A: Policy and Practice **41**(6), 489–501 (2007). doi:10.1016/j.tra.2006.11.006. ISSN 0965-8564
7. ISO/IEC 25062:2006, Software Engineering – Software product Quality Requirements and Evaluation (SQuaRE) – Common Industry Format (CIF) for Usability Test Reports (2006)

8. VDV-Report 7029: Die Haltestelle der Zukunft. VDV, Cologne (2014)
9. Bevan, N.: Using the common industry format to document the context of use. In: Kurosu, M. (ed.) HCII/HCI 2013, Part I. LNCS, vol. 8004, pp. 281–289. Springer, Heidelberg (2013)
10. VDV-Report 7036: User Interface Design für die elektronische Aushanginformation. VDV, Cologne (2014)
11. Vogel, D., Balakrishnan, R.: Interactive public ambient displays: transitioning from implicit to explicit, public to personal, interaction with multiple users. In: Proceedings of the 17th annual ACM symposium on User interface software and technology (UIST 2004), pp. 137–146. ACM, New York (2004)

Study of Uninterruptible Duration Prediction Based on PC Operation

Hokuto Iga, Takahiro Tanaka, Kazuaki Aoki, and Kinya Fujita(⊠)

Graduate School, Tokyo University of Agriculture and Technology, 2-24-16
Nakacho, Koganei, Tokyo 184-8588, Japan
50014646103@st.tuat.ac.jp, kfujita@cc.tuat.ac.jp

Abstract. In order to manage interruptions adequately, the prediction of an office worker's uninterruptible duration is desired. We assumed three factors that may affect this uninterruptible duration: the type of work, the person's level of concentration, and the frequency with which the person is disturbed by others. For features related to the type of work, we adopted category of using application and determined the ratio of key-to-mouse usage. The rates of keystroke and mouse operation and the application-switching frequency were selected to reflect a person's concentration at work. A time of day was selected as an index which reflects the disturbance frequency. We then analyzed the relationship between these indices and the uninterruptible duration using 1200-h data. The results showed that, except for the time of day, a significant relationship exists between the uninterruptible duration and these indices. The combination of these indices appears promising for predicting the uninterruptible duration.

Keywords: Interruption · Prediction · Interruptibility · Uninterruptible duration · Work rhythm

1 Introduction

The frequency with which a person is interrupted while working has increased with the development of information systems. However, interruptions at inappropriate times may decrease a worker's productivity [1]. To address this concern, studies have been conducted to estimate user interruptibility and control of interruption timing. Estimating interruptibility has been attempted by assessing various worker conditions such as the worker's sitting position and the number of visitors received [2]; vital signals such as heart rate [3], pen usage, conversation status, and keystroke and mouse operation [4], and switching of applicationsoftware [5]. The combination of PC operation with the conversational status [6] or head motion [7] has also been examined as a means of improving the interruptibility estimation accuracy.

Furthermore, a remote awareness sharing system used in supporting the interruption judgment of a remote interrupter [8] and an automatic online communication mediating agent [9] have been developed. These systems allow an interrupter to recognize that a remote interruptee is not to be interrupted at the moment. However, these systems do not tell the interrupter how long he or she must wait until the interruptee can be

© Springer International Publishing Switzerland 2015
M. Kurosu (Ed.): Human-Computer Interaction, Part I, HCII 2015, LNCS 9169, pp. 350–359, 2015.
DOI: 10.1007/978-3-319-20901-2_32

interrupted. A solution for reconciling the conflicting needs of the interrupter and interruptee is to inform the interrupter of an expected waiting period. This method will allow the interrupter to perform work until the interruption time is reached, thus improving work efficiency. Simultaneously, this method prevents the interruptee from being interrupted while he or she is concentrating on the work. To achieve this, the prediction of interruptibility of a worker is required.

Several studies have been conducted on predicting future behavior of persons. For example, attempts to produce probabilistic predictions about a worker's return time to his or her office have been carried out on the basis of the personal history [10]. Additionally, modeling of work rhythm has been attempted [11]. However, predicting the duration in which a person cannot accept an interruption has not been studied. Therefore, this study examines the feasibility of predicting the uninterruptible duration of an office worker at a computer. Through experiments, this study assesses examined relationships between PC operation measures and the uninterruptible duration.

2 Prediction of Uninterruptible Duration

2.1 Duration of PC Work

Among studies on interruptibility estimation, methods employing PC-operation information have been found to be advantageous regarding the cost and implementation effort because they do not require setting up physical sensors in the work environment. Furthermore, prediction of uninterruptible duration, which a worker cannot accept an interruption, is desirable as mentioned in Sect. 1. Therefore, we defined the uninterruptible duration on the basis of the estimated interruptibility using PC-operation-based method [5]. The system estimates the "acceptable degree of interruption" at three levels: 1. Low, 2. Neither low nor high, and 3. High for every 500 ms. The system prioritizes application switching (AS) moments over continuous working period, because breakpoint of the work is more suitable for interruption [12]. However, the increase of interruptibility associated with AS ends in a few seconds [13]. Therefore, this study adopts an interruptibility estimation algorithm for the not application switching period (NAS), which is based on four PC-operation indices, as shown in Fig. 1. In this study, we defined the "uninterruptible duration" as a period in which

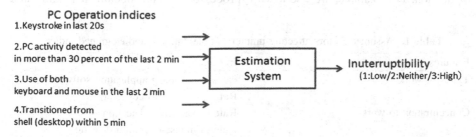

Fig. 1. Interruptibility estimation system

the average interruptibility score for 1 min is less than 2.5. The average score less than 2.5 represents that the estimated interruptibility was at most 2 for at least 30 s out of 1 min. Figure 2 illustrates the uninterruptible duration.

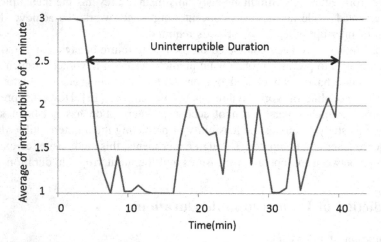

Fig. 2. Example of estimated interruptibility transition and definition of uninterruptible duration.

2.2 Measures of Uninterruptible Duration

Several factors are considered that affect the duration of work. We assumed three potential factors that affect the uninterruptible duration: the type of work, the worker's level of concentration, and the frequency of disturbance by others, as listed in Table 1.

Types of Work. Type of performing task might affect the uninterruptible duration. For example, Internet surfing will require less intellectual activity, then its uninterruptible duration to be short. In contrast, writing a document requires greater intellectual activity, we expect that uninterruptible duration will last longer. In addition, category of using application i.e., WEB browser, will have strong relationship with the task, i.e., Internet surfing. Thus, the types of work will be reflected on the category of using application software. Therefore, we have chosen the category of using application as a potential index of the uninterruptible duration.

Furthermore, uninterruptible durations vary even if a worker is using the same application. For example, we use a word processor for both document reading and

Table 1. Assumed factors affecting uninterruptible duration and examined indices

Features	Indices
Types of work	category of using application software
	Ratio of mouse-to-key usage
Concentration to work	Rate of keystroke detection
	Rate of mouse-operation detection
	Application switching frequency
Frequency of disturbance from others	Time of day

writing. Writing a document appears to require greater intellectual activity than reading a document. Moreover, document writing requires more keystrokes than does reading. Therefore, the ratio of mouse-to-key usage is considered as an index of uninterruptible duration.

Concentration at Work. If a worker loses concentration performing work because of internal factors such as fatigue, he or she will gradually lose focus on the task at hand. In addition, this lack of focus will induce a change in physical activity such as a decrease in the number of keystrokes. Therefore, measurements of the keystroke and mouse operation detection rates and application-switching frequency are assumed to predict the uninterruptible duration.

Frequency of Disturbance by Others. Disturbance by others is impossible to predict because it is an outside factor from a disturbed worker. However, the chance of disturbance, such as from visitors, will vary depending on time of day. Therefore, we hypothesized that a time of day has a relationship with the uninterruptible duration.

We then analyzed the relationship between the uninterruptible duration and the six selected indices, which are related to the previously mentioned three factors.

3 Analysis of Uninterruptible Duration

3.1 Analyzed Data

In order to analyze the relationship between the uninterruptible duration and PC operations, we recorded the PC operations of workers and automatically estimated the interruptibility levels as they worked. The experiment is shown in Fig. 3. We recruited four participants: two university students and two faculty members. The participants performed ordinary research and miscellaneous activities without any restriction on tasks to perform. The average recording time of PC operational record per day was approximately 10 h. The number of recorded days for a month varies with the participants from 10 to 20 days. The entire data set of PC operation consists of 1200-h. The individual recorded periods were three and two months for each student and each faculty member, respectively. The PC operation records include the system time, the estimated interruptibility, the name of application used primarily, and the keystroke and mouse usage. The activities observed most were: document writing, data analysis, programming, and internet surfing. Disturbances by others were occasionally observed.

The distribution of the recorded uninterruptible durations is shown in Fig. 4. Durations less than 3 min were excluded because predicting when these short tasks would end was unnecessary. In addition, we assumed that at least 3 min of PC-operation information is necessary for prediction. The number of uninterruptible durations exceeding 3 min was 1819. The average duration was 15.4 min. The most frequently observed duration was between 4 and 6 min. The number of observed uninterruptible durations exhibited a tendency to decrease with the duration. We also observed several long uninterruptible durations greater than 40 min. The application software primarily used by faculty members were web browsers and software development tools known as Visual Studio. Longer uninterruptible durations took place

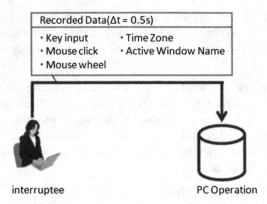

Fig. 3. Experimental system for collecting records for analysis

more frequency at night. The main application software used by students were web browsers and the Excel spreadsheet program. Students performed these activities primarily in the afternoon.

3.2 Method of Analysis

We clustered the uninterruptible durations on the basis of the six indices discussed in Sect. 2.2.

The using application software for each uninterruptible period is defined as the application whose total focus time is the longest among the used software. The applications used mostly were: Explorer, web browser, Acrobat Reader, Word, Excel, and Visual Studio.

The keystroke detection rate is determined on the basis of the proportion of the keystroke detection time during the uninterruptible duration. Here, the uninterruptible durations might be different among superficially similar activities such as writing business documents, user's manuals, and research manuscripts. Moreover, the differences in duration may be related to the keystroke detection rate. Therefore, we divided the keystroke detection rate into six percentage ranges: 0–5 %, 5–10 %, 10–15 %, 15–20 %, 20–30, and > 30 %.

The mouse-operation detection rate is defined as the proportion of mouse click or wheel usage time to the uninterruptible duration. We divided the mouse-operation detection rate into three percentage ranges: 0–5 %, 5–10 %, and > 10 %. We speculate that the uninterruptible duration of work having a high mouse-operation detection rate, such as when surfing the Internet, is shorter.

The rate of mouse usage is the proportion of the mouse-operation detection time to the keystroke detection time. We divided this rate into five ranges: 0–0.5, 0.5–1.0, 1.0–1.5, 1.5–2.0, > 2.0. A rate close to zero means that the worker is mainly using the keyboard. A value greater than one represents tasks mainly using mouse. We expect that tasks mainly using a mouse require less intellectual activity, and their uninterruptible durations are short.

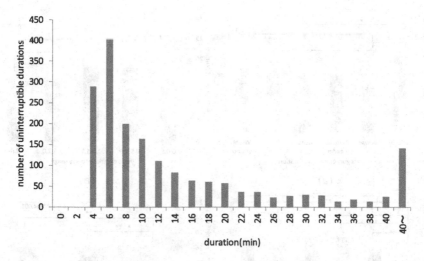

Fig. 4. Distribution of uninterruptible durations

The AS frequency is defined as the average switching frequency per minute. However, it is obviously difficult to work using application software, which is only focused on for few seconds. Furthermore, a previous study reported that it requires more than 2 s to start working after a task transition [13]. Therefore, we omitted applications, which are focused on for less than 2 s. The AS frequency was divided into four levels: 0–1, 1–2, 2–3, > 3. When the detected AS frequency is less than one, the worker is considered to be mainly using one software application. When the application-switching frequency exceeds three, it indicates that the worker is using multiple software applications for a task.

We defined a time of day as the time when the uninterruptible period starts, which is the time when the 1-min average interruptibility fell below 2.5. Because the frequency of interruption from other persons could be different in the morning, afternoon, and evening, we divided the time of day into four levels: before 12:00, 12:00–15:00, 15:00–18:00, and after 18:00. It is speculated that interruptions from others occur more often in the afternoon and less in the evening.

We calculated the above-mentions six indices for each detected uninterruptible duration, which represents a unit of concentrated work. Then, we calculated the average uninterruptible durations for each cluster of each index.

3.3 Results

Figure 5 shows the average uninterruptible durations for each cluster of the six indices. The dotted line represents the average value for all durations.

Category of using application. From the result, the uninterruptible durations were significantly different depending on the using application software. The uninterruptible duration was especially shorter when the interruptee was using a web browser. On the other hand, the duration became longer when the worker was mainly using Excel or

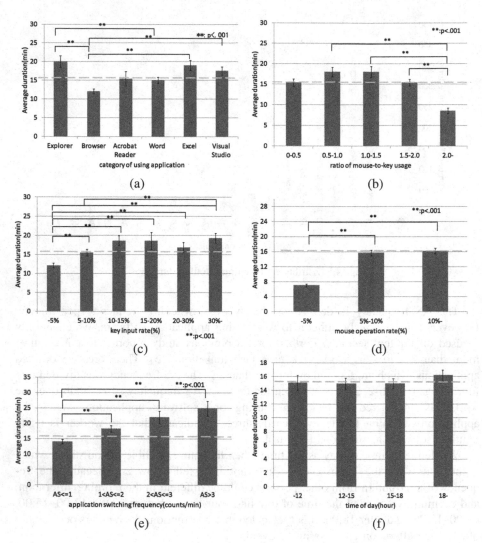

Fig. 5. Average uninterruptible durations for clusters of each feature: (a) category of using application, (b) ratio of mouse-to-key usage, (c) keystroke detection rate, (d) mouse-operation detection rate, (e) application-switching frequency, and (f) time of day.

Visual Studio. The longer lasting uninterruptible durations for the data analysis and programming suggest their larger task size in terms of intellectual activity requirements compared to web browsing.

Ratio of Mouse-to-Key Usage. Basically, a significant tendency is observed in which the uninterruptible durations decrease with the increase in the mouse-to-key usage ratio. This coincides with the expectation that PC operations using a mouse require less intellectual activity than text writing using a keyboard. Interestingly, it was also suggested that the uninterruptible duration was shorter when the time spent for mouse-operation was less than half for mouse operation.

Keystroke Detection Rate. As seen in Fig. 5(c), the uninterruptible duration tends to be longer when a worker is engaged in tasks requiring more keystrokes, as expected. Durations with a keystroke detection rate of less than 5 % were significantly shorter than the others.

Mouse Operation Detection Rate. The duration of work with a lower mouse-operation rate was short, similar to the keystroke detection rate. In particular, the average duration for work for a mouse-operation rate of 5 % or less was 7 min and significantly shorter than the other cases.

Application-Switching Frequency. In Fig. 5(e), an increase in the uninterruptible duration with the AS frequency is observed. It is speculated that the AS frequency reflects the degree of engagement of a worker in a task. It is also suggested that the durations for tasks less than or equal to an AS frequency of 1 min^{-1} are significantly shorter than the others.

Time of day. The uninterruptible durations during the evening were slightly longer than those during the day. This is in agreement with our assumption that there are fewer meetings and visitors in the evening, thereby making the uninterruptible durations longer. The durations in the morning were also slightly longer than those in the afternoon.

These results demonstrated that the average uninterruptible durations vary with the situation. The clusters based on the category of using application, the ratio of mouse-to-key usage (proportional to key usage), the keystroke detection rate, the mouse-operation detection rate, and the AS frequency exhibited significant relationships with the uninterruptible duration. These results suggest the possibility of predicting the uninterruptible duration by combining these indices.

4 Discussion

The average uninterruptible duration of all work was 15.4 min, as described in Sect. 3. The duration for editing a particular page in Wikipedia was 15 min [14] in the previous study. Therefore, the observed average uninterruptible duration in this study appears reasonable in terms of the continuous duration of a single task.

Additionally, we confirmed the variation in the uninterruptible duration with each index, as shown in Sect. 3. The observed differences almost fulfilled our expectation, such that the uninterruptible duration varies within the indices. However, the uninterruptible durations were longer, mainly when using Explorer, even though we expected the duration to be short. This is because an interruptee works using multiple files or applications through Explorer. Furthermore, the work duration when Word was mainly used was thought to be longer because the worker will concentrate on document writing. However, the average uninterruptible duration when a user was mainly using Word was less than the entire average of the uninterruptible duration. This result suggests that the interruptee uses Word for tasks requiring a higher intellectual load (e.g., writing manuscripts) and for tasks with a lower intellectual load (e.g., document viewing). For the ratio of mouse-to-key usage, we expected to confirm a longer duration when keystrokes are frequently detected. However, the durations when the ratio is within 0.5 to 1.5 (i.e., the key usage level and the mouse usage level were approximately the same) were the longest. We also considered that a ratio less than 0.5 includes data with little PC usage. For example, if a user had 10 keystrokes and two mouse clicks, it was categorized as a ratio less than 0.5, even though the uninterruptible duration is short.

In future studies, it is necessary to define and analyze the effects of other features such as combination of the currently used application. We consider that the inclusion of a secondary application in the analysis will provide more information on the nature of the work that the user is engaged in. For example, a user may use a web browser and editor at a same time while collecting information.

The prediction of the uninterruptible duration is also a future challenge. It is necessary to establish a mathematical prediction model of the uninterruptible duration based on the indices analyzed in this study. Modeling techniques in addition to ordinary multiple regression analysis, e.g., mathematical quantification theory class I, are needed to establish an adequate expression for a mathematical prediction.

5   Conclusion

In this study, we analyzed the relationship between the uninterruptible duration and six indices on the basis of 1200-h PC-operation data recorded from four participants. The indices—the category of using application, the keystroke detection rate, the mouse-operation detection rate, the ratio of mouse-to-key usage, and the AS frequency —demonstrated significant relationships with the uninterruptible duration. We also confirmed that the uninterruptible duration possibly depends on the time of day. The next step is to establish a prediction model for the uninterruptible duration on the basis of the discussed indices.

Acknowledgements. This work was partly supported by Kakenhi from JSPS, the fund for smart space technology toward a sustainable society from MEXT, and the fund for an ultrarealistic communication system from NICT.

References

1. Bailey, B.P., Joseph, A.K., John, V.C.: The effect of interruptions on task performance, annoyance, and anxiety in the user interface. Proc. INTERACT **1**, 593–601 (2001)
2. Hudson, S.E., Fogarty, J., Atkeson, C.G., Avrahami, D., Forlizzi, J., Kiesler, S., Lee, J.C., Yang, J.: Predicting human interruptibility with sensors: a wizard of oz feasibility study. In: Proceedings of SIGCHI, pp. 257–264 (2003)
3. Chen, D., Hart, J., Vertegaal, R.: Towards a physiological model of user interruptibility. Proc. INTERACT, Part **2**, 439–451 (2007)

4. Minakuchi, M., Takeuchi, T., Kuramoto, I., Shibuya, Y., Tsujino, Y.: An automatic estimation method for busyness at desktop. J. Hum. Interf. Soc. **6**(1), 69–74 (2004). (in Japanese)
5. Tanaka, T., Fujita, K.: Study of user interruptibility estimation based on focused application switching. In: Proceedings of CSCW, pp. 721–724 (2011)
6. Hashimoto, S., Tanaka, T., Aoki, K., Fujita, K.: improvement of interruptibility estimation during PC work by reflecting conversation status. IEICE Trans. Inf. Syst. **97**(12), 3171–3180 (2014)
7. Tanaka, T., Abe R., Aoki, K., Fujita, K.: Interruptibility estimation based on head motion and PC operation. Int. J. Hum.-Comput. Interact. (to appear)
8. Bjelica, M.Z., Nrazovac, B., Papp, I., Teslic, N.: Context-aware platform with user availability estimation and light-based announcement. IEEE Trans. Syst., Man, Cybern.: Syst. **43**, 1228–1239 (2013)
9. Tanaka, T., Fujita, K.: Interaction mediate agent based on user interruptibility estimation. In: Smith, M.J., Salvendy, G. (eds.) HCII 2011, Part I. LNCS, vol. 6771, pp. 152–160. Springer, Heidelberg (2011)
10. Yamagoe, K., Kuzuoka, H.: Developing of a meeting support system based on work rhythm. In: Proceedings of the Human Interface Symposium, pp. 741–744 (2003) (in Japanese)
11. Begole, J.B., Tang, J.C., Smith, R.B., Yankelovich, N.: Work rhythms: analyzing visualizations of awareness histories of distributed groups. In: Proceedings of CSCW, pp. 334–343 (2002)
12. Iqbal, S.T., Bailey, B.P.: Effects of intelligent notification management on users and their tasks. In: Proceedings of SIGCHI, pp. 93–102 (2008)
13. Tanaka, T., Fujita, K.: Discussion on duration of uninterruptiblity reduction at focused application-switching. J. Japan Soc. Fuzzy Theory Intell, Inform. **21**(5), 827–836 (2009). (in Japanese)
14. Geiger, R.S., Halfaker, A.: Using edit sessions to measure participation in wikipedia. In: Proc. CSCW, pp. 861–870 (2013)

Development of Tidy-up Promotion System by Anthropomorphication of Shared Space

Takayoshi Kitamura[1(✉)], Tiange Jin[2,3], Motoki Urayama[1],
Hirotake Ishii[1], and Hiroshi Shimoda[1]

[1] Graduate School of Energy Science, Kyoto University, Kyoto, Japan
{kitamura, tinange, uarayama, hirotake, shimoda}
@ei.energy.kyoto-u.ac.jp
[2] Faculty of Engineering, Kyoto University, Kyoto, Japan
[3] Graduate School of Engineering, The University of Tokyo,
Bunkyo, Tokyo, Japan

Abstract. Although it is important for our daily lives and works to keep things tidy and in order, it is difficult to always keep it especially in the shared space because it is unclear who has the responsibility. In this study, therefore, a method to persuade them to change their daily behaviors has been proposed from the concept of Ambient Intelligence. In order to realize the method, a system has been developed to encourage them to keep things tidy and in order by personifying the shared space. The personified system expresses its emotions in response to the degree of the disorder. The system consists of (1) a disorder estimation function from the captured image of the shared space by a camera, (2) an emotion creation function of the personified space by the transition of the disorder, and (3) an emotion expression function in appropriate timing. In addition, a case study had been conducted for 31 days to evaluate the system in a student room of a laboratory. As the result, the longer they stayed in the room, the more they watched the messages of the personified room, and improved their consciousness and habituation of keeping the room in order. However, the users who rarely stayed in the room did not improve the habituation.

Keywords: Ambient Intelligence · Persuasion · Nurturance · Anthropomorphism

1 Introduction

There are shared work spaces where we usually use for our daily work such as meeting rooms and work tables. However they are sometimes left disorderly because the responsibility to manage the shared work space is unclear. In this study, therefore, a tidy-up promotion system has been proposed as shown in Fig. 1 where a personified shared space joins the micro-blog community in which the users of the space join. And it submits the tweets which are corresponding to the emotions generated by the degree of disorder of the space. It aims that the tweets arouse the users' emotions to help the room (nursing desire [1]) and promotes their tidy-up behaviors. In addition in this study, the system was developed and evaluated through a month case study.

© Springer International Publishing Switzerland 2015
M. Kurosu (Ed.): Human-Computer Interaction, Part I, HCII 2015, LNCS 9169, pp. 360–369, 2015.
DOI: 10.1007/978-3-319-20901-2_33

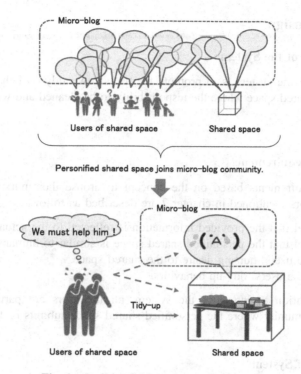

Fig. 1. Outline of tidy-up promotion system

2 Related Works

There are lots of research studies which utilize interaction with computers in order to persuade someone to do something. B.J Fogg summarizes them systematically by using a coined word 'captology' which means 'Computer as persuasive technologies' [2]. On the other hand, Ambient Intelligence (AmI) has been proposed which are intelligent agents embedded in the environment [3]. The captology based on the AmI has been also discussed. Here, Kaptein et al. indicate the following persuasion factors in order to promote their behavioral changes [4];

- They feel that the provided information is reflected to the actual state.
- They feel that the object which persuades is similar to humans.
- They feel that the persuasion is directly given to them.

In case of the shared space, however, it is difficult to realize the last factor because attribution of the responsibility is sometimes unclear.

The personified agents in micro-blog are called 'bot' and they are often used [5]. They have various mechanisms in order to be seen like human, but there is no work which promotes tidy-up behaviors based on arousal of nursing desire.

3 System Design

3.1 Objective of the System

The objective of the system is to promote the users' own tidy-up behaviors by personifying the shared space where the responsibility to be cleaned and well-arranged is unclear.

3.2 System Requirements

The system requirements based on the concept to arouse their nursing desire and persuading factors mentioned in chapter 2 are described as follows;

1. The users feel that the provided information is reflected to the actual state.
2. The users feel that the personified shared space is similar to humans.
3. It arouses the users' nursing desire to the shared space.
4. It improves the users' tidy-up behaviors.

As the precondition to introduce the system, all the users are participating to a micro-blog community where the personified shared space submits its tweets.

3.3 Outline of System

Figure 2 shows the process flow of the system. When detecting a user comes to the shared space, the degree of disorder is measured. Then the emotion of the shared space is generated by the current degree of disorder and its change from the time of the last submission to the micro-blog is calculated. If the time interval from the last submission is longer that a certain period, one of the prepared sentences corresponding to generated emotion is submitted.

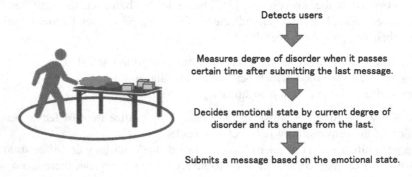

Detects users

↓

Measures degree of disorder when it passes certain time after submitting the last message.

↓

Decides emotional state by current degree of disorder and its change from the last.

↓

Submits a message based on the emotional state.

Fig. 2. Process flow of system

3.4   System Implementation

The system has been implemented as follows;

User Detection. In this study, the system employs an image processing method to detect the user because it is convenient to introduce the system into the practical work space using only ordinary camera. The human body detection method by HOG (Histograms of Oriented Gradients) feature values [6] of OpenCV [7] has been employed in the system.

Estimation of Degree of Disorder. Another image processing method has been employed to estimate the degree of disorder of the shared space. Actually a probabilistic Hough conversion has been employed which was proposed by Ishii [8]. This method extracts line segments from the captured image by probabilistic Hough conversion and the number of the extracted line segments is considered as the index of disorder. Most of artificial objects have rectilinear contours such as books and stationaries so that it becomes higher when there are lots of artificial objects in the shared space.

Generation of Emotional Messages. Table 1 shows examples of the emotional states and corresponding messages submitted to the micro-blog by the shared space. In this study, the degree of disorder is first measured by the number of the line segments ($Nseg$ (t)) and is classified into four categories which are 'Very ordered', 'Ordered', 'Disordered' and 'Very disordered'. Then the change of disorder degree from the last submission ($\Delta Nseg = Nseg(t) - Nseg(t-1)$) is calculated and classified into six categories. In other words, there are totally 24 states and they are corresponding to the emotions of the shared space as shown in Fig. 3.

As shown in Table 1 and Fig. 3 the emotional messages based on the left side of Fig. 3 express happiness and gratitude, while those on the right side express anger and sadness. The messages on the middle which have less change express moderate emotions. At u3 and t4 in Fig. 3, event information or question to the users are submitted in order not to bore them.

Message Submission to Micro-Blog. The typical micro-blogging service, Twitter [9], is employed in this study. The reason is because lots of people enjoy it so that it is easier to introduce this system into practical use. A PHP script, EasyBotter [5], is used to realize the mechanism to submit the messages into the timetable of Twitter. Plural messages which correspond to 24 emotional states were prepared in advance and they are submitted according to the degree of disorder of the shared space.

3.5   Information Presentation

The timeline of Twitter can be easily accessed by such as web browsers of PC and smartphones. In addition, a mini display which has 8-inch LCD is set around the shared space in order to make the users to easily notice the new message from the shared space

Table 1. 24 emotional states and examples to be submitted to micro-blog

State code	Emotion	Example message
T1	Delight	Oops! Cleared!! Surprized!! ＼(◎o◎)／
T2	Satisfied	Satisfied thanks to you. Thank you ♪ (*'o`)
T3	Easy, trust	This easy feeling... ('▽`) So good!!
T4	Optimistic	Welcome. I am pretty fine and calm. (＾ω＾)
T5	Anxious	It's clean, not too bad, but I feel uneasy... (＞＜)
T6	Uneasy	It's still OK... But I am expecting your tidy-up. •ω•
t1	Refreshing	∩(`•ω•´)∩ Wow! So beautiful! I feel refreshed!
t2	Gratitude	Thank you, thank you. (＾＾)
t3	Fine	OK! (•▽•) I'm fine.
t4	Interest in others	Today is meat day, isn't it? ＼(^o^)／
t5	Confused	What? You remain it? I'm confused. ('•ω•`)
t6	Depressed	Well, how am I going to be? I'm worrying. ('•ω•`)
u1	Recoverd	Oh! I can recover now.
u2	Calm down	Well, it's getting better. ε-('▽`*)
u3	Interest in others	Are you goint to your hometown in New Year vacation? (••)
u4	Impatient	Oops. Please help me! I can't stop to be impatient (;—□—) oops!
u5	Request	Please. m(＿＿)m Please clean up the table, please..
u6	Disappointed	Oh, I believed you... It's a pity. ('•ω•`)
U1	Reticent	('_゛)
U2	Lonely	It's untidy, isn't it? My mind is deserted. (>△<。)
U3	Sad	It was no use asking here. I want to cry. (';ω;`) umm.
U4	Dissatisfied	I'm dissatisfied now. Because anyone does nothing. (>△<。。)
U5	Angry	I'm sick! Help me right now! ＼()゛ε'()／
U6	Despair	("□")Wowwwwwwww, Oh, No!

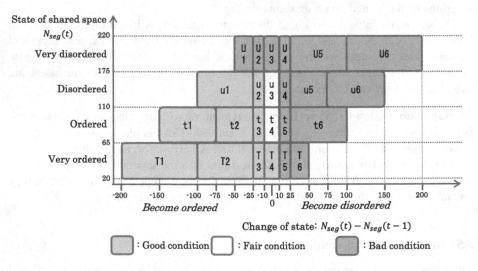

Fig. 3. Classification of generated emotional states

without active access to the timeline. Figure 4 shows a snapshot of the mini display. The timeline including the emotional messages by the shared space is displayed on the right, while the result of the image processing for the user detection and the measurement of disorder is on the left in order to realize one of the system requirements, 'the users feel that the provided information is reflected to the actual state.'

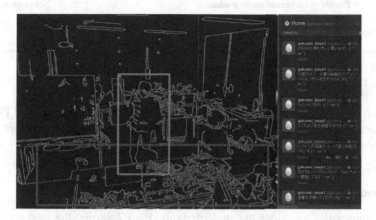

Fig. 4. A snapshot of mini display

4   Evaluation by Case Study

A case study was conducted in order to evaluate the proposed system. It confirmed whether the system requirements described in 3.2 are realized or not.

4.1   Place and Term

The case study was conducted in a student room of a laboratory of other university. The term was 31 days from December 22nd, 2013 to January 21st, 2014. It is because at least two weeks are necessary for the users to become accustomed to the new environment [10].

4.2   Participants

The participants are seven people who are P1 to P7 as shown in Table 2. P1 did not belong to the laboratory so that he didn't have his own desk in the room. However, he often comes there because of joint seminar. The frequencies of the space use and twitter

Table 2. Attributes of participants

Participant	Sex	Position	Frequency of shared table use (/day)	Frequency of accessing Twitter (/day)
P1	Male	1st year of master course	0	5
P2	Male	2nd year of master course	4	1
P3	Male	1st year of master course	10	Not registered
P4	Female	4th year of under graduate	4	Not registered
P5	Female	4th year of under graduate	2	11
P6	Male	Assistant professor	1	15
P7	Female	4th year of under graduate	5	15

submission in Table 2 express those before the case study. Although P3 and P4 didn't have the accounts of Twitter, they registered and got their own accounts before starting the case study.

4.3 Room Environment

Figure 5 shows the top view the student room. P2–P7 shows the desks which the participants P2–P7 occupies for their study, while table A, table B and a kitchen sink are their shared spaces. The table A was chosen to be the shared space in this case study because it has been frequently used for such as lunch and informal discussions.

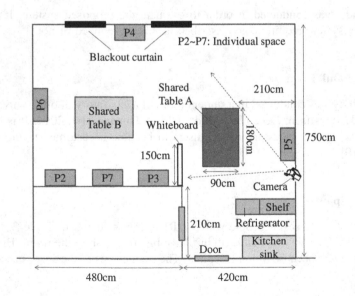

Fig. 5. Top view of student room

4.4   Procedure of Case Study

Figure 6 shows the schedule of the case study. As shown in the figure, the system had stopped from 12th day to 17th day because it was a New Year vacation so that few participants stayed at the room. Questionnaires and an interview were conducted along with the schedule in order to examine their subjective impressions to the system.

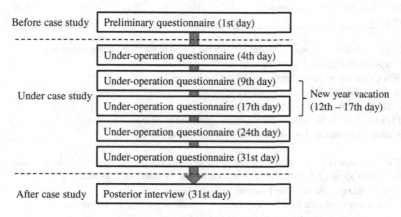

Fig. 6. Schedule of case study

4.5   Results

As shown in Fig. 7, there were long sojourn participants P2, P4, P5 and P7, and short sojourn participants P1, P3 and P6. The effectiveness of the system can be considered to be depending on the sojourn time at the room. They are, therefore, divided into two groups in the later analysis.

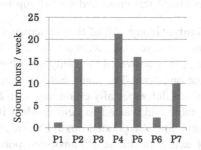

Fig. 7. Sojourn time of each participant

Evaluation by Short Sojourn Group. As shown in Table 3, P1 and P3 answered that their tidy-up behaviors were not promoted. Since they have not spent much time in the student room, they didn't have much chance to see the messages of the shared table. The reason why P3 answered 'No' for all the questions is that he rarely spent time

Table 3. Result of questionnaire and interview

Question	Short sojourn group			Long sojourn group			
	P1	P3	P6	P2	P4	P5	P7
The message fit the state of the shared table.	Fair	No	Fair	Yes	Fair	No	Fair
I felt the table is human like by the messages.	Fair	No	Fair	Yes	No	Yes	Yes
I felt familiarity to the table by the messages.	Yes	No	Yes	Yes	Yes	Yes	Fair
I felt desire to help the table by the messages.	Yes	No	Δ	Yes	Yes	Yes	Fair
My tidy-up behavior was promoted.	No	No	Yes	Yes	Yes	Yes	Fair
Opinion	C1	C3	C6	C2	C4	C5	C7

C1: It was difficult to see the relationship between the states of the table and the messages.
  It is better that he tweets even when no one is in the room.
  When using emoticons and net slang, I felt it like human.
C3: It may be possible that they don't tidy up when they are accustomed to the system.
  I felt uneasy because the camera always observed me.
C6: I felt familiarity to the table by the emoticons submitted to Twitter.
  Further operation may bore us. It needs some more things to cheer up.

C2: The consiousness of the table by introducing the systrem may depend on the individuals.
  In order to operate it further, it needs a method to hide the standard of disorder.
C4: I felt familiarity to the table but I couldn't see it like human.
  It is better to emphasize to be seen by someone in order to improve the tidy-up behaviors.
C5: I didn't understand whether the system worked well or not.
C7: The change of the emotion based on the change of disorder was too large.

because of his job hunting activity. He also mentioned that he sometimes felt uneasy for the camera installed in the room. Since P6 also belongs to other laboratory, his sojourn time was short. However he actively joined the events such as a year-end party and he was interested in the change of the messages depending on the change of the shared table state. He mentioned this promoted his tidy-up behaviors.

Evaluation by Long Sojourn Group. All of the participants in this group have been writing their theses during the case study term so that they have stayed long in the room. As shown in Table 3, they answered their tidy-up behaviors were promoted. P2 answered positive in all the questions. The main reason is that he felt the tweets of the shared table were like humans did, especially emoticons such as "(^ ^)" were effective. P4 felt familiarity to the table and wanted to help it when it suffered, however, she could not feel it like humans. She also pointed out that the messages of the shared table did not always reflect the actual situations. P5 answered positive in almost all of the questions, however, she sometimes felt the system didn't work well. P7 answered that he felt the space was like humans, however, he also mentioned that the change of the emotion based on the change of disorder was too large.

4.6   Discussion

As the results of the case study, the tidy-up behaviors of the participants who stayed longer were improved because they saw lots of messages by the shared space. However, only one participant answered positive in the question of "Did the tweets well fit the situation of the shared space?" so that one of the requirements, "1. The users feel that the provided information is reflected to the actual state" was not satisfied. As the message interactions between the participants and the shared table, some of them felt familiarity to the table and they indicated that the emoticons were effective for the familiarity. Further consideration is necessary to reveal how to create human-like messages which give human-like impressions. P3 mentioned that he felt uneasy to be observed by the camera. It is necessary to explain the system in advance and to obtain the consent of all the users when introducing it for practical use.

5   Conclusion

The authors have proposed a system which personifies a shared space and submits emotional messages into the timeline of micro-blog in order to improve the tidy-up behaviors of the users by arousing their nursing desire to help it. In addition, a case study had been conducted for 31 days to evaluate the system. As the results, 4 out of 7 participants answered they felt the nursing desire to help the space and 3 of them who had stayed long in the room also answered their tidy-up behaviors were improved. However, one of the system requirements, "the users feel that the provided information is reflected to the actual state", was not satisfied enough. It is necessary to consider the method to clearly present the mechanism of the system to introduce it for practical use.

Acknowledgement. This study was done through the help of professors and students of Kobe University. We sincerely appreciate their contribution.

References

1. Murray, H.A.: Explorations in Personality. Oxford University Press, Oxford (1938)
2. Fogg, B.J.: Persuasive Technology. Morgan Kaufmann, Stanford (2002)
3. Zelkha, E., Epstein, B., Birrell, S., Dodsworth, C.: From devices to "ambient intelligence". In: Digital Living Room Conference (1998)
4. Kaptein, A.M., et al.: Persuasion in ambient intelligence. J. Ambient Intell. Humanized Comput. **1**(1), 43–56 (2010)
5. Rutkin, A.: Twitter bots grow up. New Scientist **223**(2980), 20–21 (2014)
6. Dalal, N., Triggs, B.: Histograms of oriented gradients for human detection. In: Proceedings of IEEE Conference on Computer Vision and Pattern Recognition (CVPR), pp. 886–893 (2005)
7. OpenCV. http://opencv.org (Accessed on 1st December 2014)
8. Ishii, T.: Watching System for 'keeping things tidy and in order'. In: Proceedings of the 2011 IEICE General Conference (2011) (in Japanese)
9. Twitter. https://twitter.com (Accessed on 1st December 2014)
10. Sharma, R.S.: Who Will Cry When You Die?. Jaico Publishing House, India (2006)

E-Mail Delivery Mediation System Based on User Interruptibility

Yasumasa Kobayashi[1]([✉]), Takahiro Tanaka[2], Kazuaki Aoki[1],
and Kinya Fujita[1]

[1] Graduate School, Tokyo University of Agriculture and Technology,
2-24-16 Nakacho, Koganei, Tokyo 184-8588, Japan
50014646116@st.tuat.ac.jp, kfujita@cc.tuat.ac.jp
[2] Nagoya University, Furo-cho, Chikusa-ku, Nagoya 464-8601, Japan

Abstract. To eliminate the distraction caused by inappropriately timed e-mail delivery notification, we constructed a prototype e-mail delivery mediation system. The system was designed to mediate incoming e-mails based on user interruptibility, which is estimated from PC operational activities of the user. The system delivers e-mails at higher interruptibility times, especially at application switching moments, which are considered a substitute for task breakpoints in work which uses PC. A trial experiment with eight participants in an ordinary working environment was conducted. The experiment results suggested that e-mails were delivered at higher estimated interruptibility times and decreased feelings of hindrance regarding incoming e-mails. However, there were e-mail deliveries at low interruptibility moments even though participants were using the system. Therefore, further study must be conducted to improve the system and to conduct analysis on work efficiency.

Keywords: E-mail · Interruptibility · Interruption · Work efficiency

1 Introduction

Computer-mediated human-to-human communication in workplaces has become popular due to growth of computer technologies and the Internet. Such communication may facilitate smooth interaction between workers. However, there is a concern that computer system notifications not reflecting user states may decrease intellectual productivity [1]. For example, e-mail systems are considered a source of interruption even though they are well used in many workplaces [2]. In particular, increase of worker frustration is considered a major problem caused by frequent interruptions. Therefore, systems that adequately control user interruption are desired.

To address this issue, several studies have been conducted. Sharing awareness information among workers has been proposed to facilitate smooth communication. For example, myUnity shares awareness information, including recommended communication tools, selected by the interruptee [3]. This allows the sender to decide the appropriate time to interrupt a partner. A more automated system, MyVine, also bears mention [4]. MyVine automatically estimates and recommends communication tools

© Springer International Publishing Switzerland 2015
M. Kurosu (Ed.): Human-Computer Interaction, Part I, HCII 2015, LNCS 9169, pp. 370–380, 2015.
DOI: 10.1007/978-3-319-20901-2_34

based on location, PC operation status, and conversational status. These systems are proposed to facilitate smooth communication between employees, although workers still need to judge the timing and appropriateness of an interruption. Therefore, an automatic interruption mediation system is required.

In order to achieve automatic mediation via computer, the user's state must be estimated and reflected in the interruption timing. One of the indices of user state is called "User Interruptibility." It is the subjective extent to which a user can accept an interruption. Several methods are proposed to estimate user interruptibility. For example, keystroke-based estimation during PC operation [5] and sensor-based estimation [6] have been proposed. On the other hand, studies on multitasking suggest that interruption has a cognitive impact on an interruptee that it is reduced when the interruptee is interrupted at task breakpoints [7]. Therefore, user interruptibility estimation methods based on PC operational activities and application-switching, which is considered a task breakpoints in PC works, has been proposed [8–10]. Because that method uses no sensors, it has an advantage in terms of implementation effort in a real working environment. Therefore, this study is designed to mediate e-mail delivery based on the estimated user interruptibility based on PC operational activities and application-switching.

It is known that the interruption cost of e-mail is high. However, the automatic mediation of e-mail delivery with more acceptable timing has not yet been achieved. Therefore, we have developed a prototype incoming e-mail delivery mediation system (EDMS) based on the estimated user interruptibility to achieve more appropriate timing for e-mail delivery.

2 E-Mail Delivery Mediation System

2.1 System Requirements

In order to achieve appropriate mediation by the system, system requirements should be considered from receivers' and senders' points of view, in order to facilitate smooth communications between workers.

From a receiver's viewpoint, e-mail interruptions during busy working conditions (i.e. while the user's interruptibility is low) should be avoided so as not to disrupt the user. For example, interruptions should be delayed until a user reaches task breakpoints while the user is working on highly intellectual tasks. Additionally, the system should be used as extension of current e-mail systems in order to lower integration cost and to assure access to stored old e-mails.

From a sender's viewpoint, e-mails should not be delayed for an excessive time in order to smoothly communicate with their partner. Otherwise, overall performance of workers might decrease even though the receiver is not interrupted.

Therefore, the following requirements should be included in order to achieve an appropriate e-mail mediation system:

1. Defer e-mail when a user's interruptibility is low. This can be achieved by blocking e-mails while user interruptibility is low and allow e-mails to be delivered only when user interruptibility is high.
2. Low implementation cost of the system. This can be achieved by constructing the system as a program which is external to the mail server and e-mail clients.
3. Keep access to stored old e-mails. This can be achieved by constructing the system as a program compatible with current e-mail clients.
4. Prevent e-mails from being blocked for an excessive time. This can be achieved by increasing the chance of e-mail delivery depending on e-mail deferral time.

2.2   System Configuration

The configuration of the prototype system is shown in Fig. 1. The EDMS was implemented as a software application that functions between the mail client and the mail server, which supports POP over SSL. Therefore, EDMS is compatible with any existing e-mail client; this enables users to access old e-mails.

Essentially, the system relays commands from the client and responses from the server. Because e-mail delivery notification by mail clients depends on a received server response, the EDMS controls the notification timing by modifying the timing and content of the server response.

When the EDMS receives a response from the server notifying it of the existence of a new e-mail, the EDMS executes a notification determination algorithm (explained in Sect. 2.4) to determine the appropriateness of delivery timing based on estimated interruptibility.

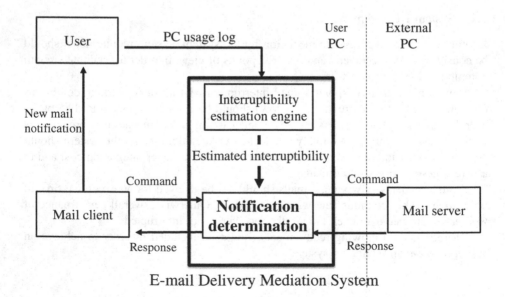

Fig. 1. System configuration

2.3 User Interruptibility Estimation Method

The EDMS estimates user interruptibility at three levels, i.e., "3: High," "2: Medium," and "1: Low". Estimation is based on the PC's operation activity levels at two different times: application switching (AS) moments and not application switching (NAS) periods. In both cases, the PC usage information, such as keystroke, mouse click, mouse wheel, active window name, process ID, window message, and the number of simultaneously open application windows, is used to estimate the interruptibility of a user. At AS moments, 19 indices are related to the degree of breakpoint, such as work discontinuity, application coupling, and indices that are related to the amount of PC operation activity, as shown in Table 1 [2]. For example, if the number of open windows decreases, the situation is considered to be the end of a task, which is estimated to show high interruptibility.

Table 1. Indices of interruptibility at AS moments

id	Group 1: Work Discontinuity
A	Increase of opened window.
B	Decrease of opened window.
C	Increase of opened window compared to ave. of last 2 min.
D	Decrease of opened window compared to ave. of last 2 min.
E	Window message (quit).
id	**Group 2: Application Coupling**
F	Window message (clipboard).
G	Parent-window to child-window transition.
H	Child-window to parent-window transition.
I	Reuse of the same application within 2 min.
J	Transition to the shell (Explorer).
K	Transition from the shell (Explorer).
L	Re-transition to the shell within 2 min.
M	Re-transition from the shell within 2 min.
N	Continuous use of one application over 2 min.
id	**Group 3: Physical Activity**
O	Continuous use of one application within 15 sec.
P	Typing activity within 20 sec before AS.
Q	Mouse activity within 20 sec before AS.
R	More than 10% operating time in last 2 min.
S	Use of both keyboard and mouse in last 2 min.

During NAS period, only the indices related to the amount of PC usage can be obtained, such as the keystroke usage, PC activity detection rate, a combination of keyboard and mouse usage, and transitions from the shell, as shown in Table 2 [3]. For example, if a user is working hard, then a higher amount of keyboard and mouse activity will be detected. This means the user's interruptibility will be estimated as low.

Table 2. Indices of interruptibility during NAS period

id	Effect of four indices on NAS interruptibility
T	Typing activity within 20 sec before
U	More than 30% operating time in last 2 min.
V	Use of both keyboard and mouse in last 2 min.
W	Re-transition from the shell within 5 min.

In addition, the estimated errors for exchanging high-interruptibility and low-interruptibility during AS and NAS were 22 % and 29 %, respectively, in an uncontrolled working environment. Because of the low chances of serious errors, such as incorrectly estimating low interruptibility as high, this method is considered capable of significantly reducing inappropriate interruptions during a low interruptibility state.

The advantage of the adopted estimation method is that it uses no sensors and can estimate interruptibility in real-time. Therefore, it is easily integrated into an actual working environment.

2.4   EDMS Algorithm and E-Mail Delivery Rules

The EDMS executes the following algorithm when it receives a response from the server notifying it of the existence of a new e-mail. Basically, the EDMS relays the server response to the client, with or without modification based on the user's estimated interruptibility.

1. EDMS holds the response from the server and waits for an increase in the estimated user interruptibility until the end of the automatic mail-checking period of the client (determination process). This waiting period allows the EDMS to send a response to the client at a suitable moment.
2. The EDMS transfers the actual server response to the client when the estimated interruptibility matches the delivery rules. If there is no match until the end of the new mail-checking period, the EDMS sends a modified response as if there were no incoming e-mail. Figure 2 (a) shows an example of mediated e-mail delivery, in which e-mail is blocked from the beginning of automatic e-mail checking until the user's estimated interruptibility reaches a high level. Figure 2 (b) shows an example

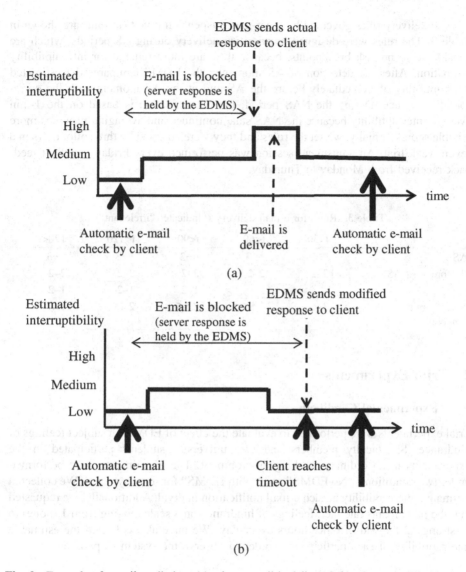

Fig. 2. Example of e-mail mediation: (a) when e-mail is delivered (b) when e-mail is blocked

in which an e-mail is blocked until the client reaches timeout because the user's estimated interruptibility did not reach a high level (notice that the determination process will occur at the beginning of the next automatic e-mail check by the client).

3. The EDMS checks for the existence of suspended e-mails and suspension time. If suspended e-mails exist, the rule is relaxed at 30-minute intervals so e-mails are not blocked for an excessive period, so as to facilitate smooth communication with the sender. If there are no suspended e-mails, the rules are initialized to be ready for new e-mail mediation.

The delivery rules governed by the e-mail suspension time t (in min) are shown in Table 3. The rules were designed to prioritize delivery during AS periods, which are considered to be task breakpoints, because they are more reliable for interruptibility estimation. After the detection of AS moments, the EDMS compares the estimated interruptibility of immediately before the AS and at the AS moment with the corresponding values. During the NAS period, the determination is based on the 1-min average interruptibility because the NAS state continues and averaging provides more reliable scores. Initially, we set the rules and they were adjusted by three pilot users in a seven-week trial. An adjustment session was performed every Friday to reflect feedback received from Monday to Thursday.

Table 3. Rules for e-mail delivery (*indicates "irrelevant")

	t<30	t<60	t<90	t<120	120<t
AS	*−3	*−3	*−3	*−3	*−3
(Before − At AS)	2–2	2–2	2–2	2–2	2–2
			1–2	1–2	1–2
NAS (1 min average)	3	2.5≤	2.5≤	2.1≤	1≤

3   Trial Experiments

3.1   Experimental Conditions

Trial experiments were performed to evaluate the effect of EDMS on subject feelings of hindrance. Six faculty members and two university students participated in the experiments in an ordinary working environment. The experiments were performed under two conditions: "No EDMS" and "With EDMS" for five days each. We collected estimated interruptibility at each e-mail notification interval. Additionally, we requested that the participants rate their feelings of hindrance on a scale ranging from 1 (none) to 7 (strong) at the end of office hours every day. We have also collected the estimated interruptibility of each participant in order to observe the system's operation.

3.2   Results

The estimated interruptibility at the moment of e-mail delivery is shown in Fig. 3. Data gathered while the participant was away from their keyboard was excluded. The average scores for without and with EDMS conditions were 2.24 and 2.50, respectively (t-test, $p < 0.05$). From the graph, it can be considered that the system successfully decreased inappropriate interruptions to a certain extent. Therefore, the system has operated successfully up to a certain level.

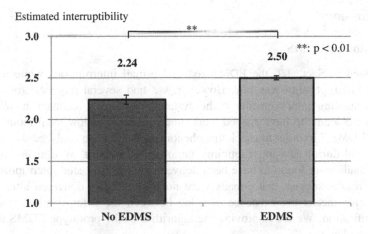

Fig. 3. The estimated interruptibility at the moment of e-mail delivery

We expected that mediation of incoming e-mails would decrease users' frustration. Therefore, we collected subjective feeling of hindrance, which were scored on a scale from 1 to 7 (1: no feeling of hindrance; 7: strong feeling of hindrance). As the result of mediation of incoming e-mails, feelings of hindrance decreased from 2.6 to 1.8 (t-test, $p < 0.05$), as shown in Fig. 4.

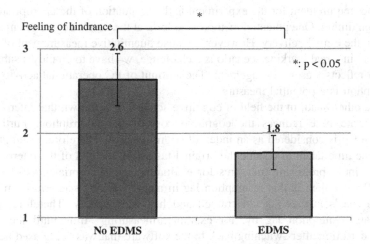

Fig. 4. Feeling of hindrance correlated to incoming e-mails

From these results, the EDMS may allow e-mail notifications to occur at more appropriate times and decrease user frustration.

4   Discussion

4.1   Prototype EDMS

As discussed in Sect. 3.2, the EDMS reduced e-mail interruptions while the user's estimated interruptibility was low. However, we had several requests from the participants regarding improvements to the system. One user's feedback mentions that "some e-mail seems to have arrived while interruptibility is low even though we are using the EDMS." In order to check this phenomenon, we have analyzed the amount of e-mail arrival during low-interruptibility periods. As a result, 34 e-mails out of 347 overall e-mails were found to have been delivered when estimated interruptibility was low. The results suggest that e-mails were not immediately delivered after determination, which means the existence of a lag between the determination process and actual notification. We are improving the algorithm of the prototype EDMS to reduce the response lag.

4.2   Evaluation Experiments

One concern regarding the conducted experiments is that we gave information about e-mail mediation condition to the participants. Therefore, cognitive bias in subjective hindrance scores is conceivable. To avoid this bias and obtain more reliable results, we need to conduct an experimental evaluation using a modified system, which randomly switches e-mail mediation mode.

Another requirement for the experiment is the evaluation of the appropriateness of interruption timing. One potential method is to look at the user's degree of engagement in a task at the e-mail delivery. However, because quantitative measurement of a user's engagement in a real working scenario is a challenge, we have to employ a substitutive index that reflects a user's engagement. The amount of PC operational activity at time of interruption is a potential measure.

On the other hand, in the field of cognitive science, it is known that interruption at an appropriate time reduces the cognitive cost of the interruption. Furthermore, resumption lag is considered as an index of cognitive cost. Therefore, resumption lag, which is the time taken to resume the original task from the end of the interruption, is one of the more promising measures for evaluating the appropriateness of an interruption. The problem is that resumption lag in a real working scenario is ambiguous because a user's task is not constrained and has wide variety. Therefore, we may approximate resumption lag by, for example, measuring "time until the first PC operation detection after switching back to the software that was being used before the e-mail interruption."

Furthermore, we can expect that receiving email at appropriate timing gives shorter response time. Because the user would switch to the email task after they have finished a subtask, a shorter response time would suggest that the user was at the breakpoint of a subtask. Therefore, response time, which is the time from notification until the user voluntarily switches to the mail client, may be addressed as another measure for evaluating the appropriateness of an interruption.

The final target of this study is to increase the work efficiency of users by avoiding inappropriate e-mail interruptions. However, overall work efficiency has not yet been evaluated. Furthermore, the examined environment and duration in this study is rather limited. Long-term experimental evaluation of work efficiency in a wider variety of working environments is needed.

Another concern of employing EMDS is that e-mail suspension may increase message-transmission delay in a working team. The overall team performance is based not only on e-mail receivers but also on senders. Therefore, analysis of the effect on e-mail senders and the entire team is also desired.

4.3 Limitations and Future Works

The current EDMS prototype does not reflect the importance or priority of e-mail on the delivery determination. Because the e-mail receiver may want to receive particular e-mails, such as e-mails warning of emergencies or e-mails from his/her superior, reflection of content and sender of e-mail in the delivery determination algorithm will also be addressed in future work.

5   Conclusions

We developed a prototype EDMS that allows the automatic mediation of e-mail delivery based on estimated interruptibility in order to provide e-mail notifications at appropriate times. Currently, the prototype EDMS is still improving the system response. The next step is an experimental evaluation in an actual working environment using the improved system.

Acknowledgements. This work was partly supported by KAKENHI from JSPS, funds for Smart Space Technology toward a Sustainable Society from MEXT, and funds for Ultra-realistic Communication Systems from NICT.

References

1. Barley, S.R., Meyerson, D.E., Grodal, S.: E-mail as a source and symbol of stress. Organ. Sci. **22**(4), 887–906 (2011)
2. Jackson, T., Dawson, R., Wilson, D.: The cost of email interruption. J. Syst. Inf. Technol. **5**(1), 81–92 (2001)
3. Wiese, J., Biehl, J.T., Turner, T., van Melle, W., Girgensohn, A.: Beyond yesterday's tomorrow: towards the design of awareness technologies for the contemporary worker. In: Proceedings of the 13th International Conference on Human Computer Interaction with Mobile Devices and Services, pp. 455–464. ACM (2011)
4. Fogarty, J., Lai, J., Christensen, J.: Presence versus availability: the design and evaluation of a context-aware communication client. Int. J. Hum. Comput. Stud. **61**(3), 299–317 (2004)

5. Minakuchi, M., Takeuchi, T., Kuramoto, I., Shibuya, Y., Tsujino, Y.: An automatic estimation method for busyness at deskwork. Trans. Hum. Interface Soc. **6**(1), 69–74 (2004). (in Japanese)
6. Fogarty, J., Hudson, S.E., Atkeson, C.G., Avrahami, D., Forlizzi, J., Kiesler, S., Yang, J.: Predicting human interruptibility with sensors. ACM Trans. Comput.-Hum. Interact. (TOCHI) **12**(1), 119–146 (2005)
7. Iqbal, S.T., Bailey, B.P.: Investigating the effectiveness of mental workload as a predictor of opportune moments for interruption. In: CHI 2005 Extended Abstracts on Human Factors in Computing Systems, pp. 1489–1492. ACM (2005)
8. Tanaka, T., Fujita, K.: Study of user interruptibility estimation based on focused application switching. In: Proceedings of the ACM 2011 Conference on Computer Supported Cooperative Work, pp. 721–724. ACM (2011)
9. Hashimoto, S., Tanaka, T., Fujita, K.: Improvement of interruptibility estimation during PC work by reflecting conversation status. IEICE Trans. Inf. Syst. **97**(12), 3171–3180 (2014)
10. Tanaka, T., Abe, R., Aoki, K., Fujita, K.: Interruptibility estimation based on head motion and PC operation. Int. J. Hum.-Comput. Interact. **31**(3), 167–179 (2015, to appear)

Workflow-Based Passenger Information for Public Transport

Cindy Mayas(✉), Stephan Hörold, and Heidi Krömker

Technische Universität Ilmenau, Ilmenau, Germany
{cindy.mayas, stephan.hoerold,
heidi.kroemker}@tu-ilmenau.de

Abstract. This paper presents a workflow-based concept of passenger information in public transport, in order to ensure a more intuitive and effective usage of mobile passenger information systems. The workflow-based navigation concept is derived from a pattern analysis and a field test of current mobile applications of passenger information, which mainly provide a function-based navigation. The results of a comparative usability test of workflow-based and function-based navigation concepts show, that workflow-based navigation can reduce the number of required tap actions in relation to function-based navigation concepts.

Keywords: Usability · Mobile applications · Workflow · Public transport

1 Introduction

Nowadays, passenger information systems not only include timetable and static trip information, but also real time and context specific information, for instance about interchanges, getting on and off the vehicle and disturbance information. Based on this information, most mobile applications provide a variety of functions [1]. Function calls within these applications are mainly available by menu and additional option buttons.

The resulting navigation process requires detailed foreknowledge of users about the system of public transport, for instance available functions of passenger information, labels, and situation specific benefits [2]. Especially, novices and occasional users of public transport are often not familiar with passenger information applications and their range of functionalities. Consequently, untrained users either require some time for exploring or never take advantage of the full range of functions. As a result, the usability of mobile passenger application systems in public transport is reduced for some user groups.

The objective of this paper is to increase the usability of mobile passenger applications, regarding the adequate access to functionalities. By replacing the function-based navigation by a workflow-based navigation, which is based on the context of the journey and the different means of transport, the access and the visualization of the functionalities are adapted to the relevant tasks and the relevant user needs along the journey [3].

© Springer International Publishing Switzerland 2015
M. Kurosu (Ed.): Human-Computer Interaction, Part I, HCII 2015, LNCS 9169, pp. 381–389, 2015.
DOI: 10.1007/978-3-319-20901-2_35

In particular, the complexity and diversity of information for travelers will increase, regarding the future of intermodal mobility, which combines public transport with individual transport and shared mobility services. Therefore, new strategies of integrated and holistic passenger information are required.

2 State of the Art

2.1 Best Practice: A Pattern Analysis of Mobile Applications

Based on the concept of Alexander [4], successful and established solutions for recurring challenges can be described as so called patterns for a specific area of application. While Alexander introduced the concept of pattern to the area of architecture, the pattern concept has been already adapted to other scientific areas, for instance software development [5], music and neuroscience [6], as well.

The design patterns, which are analyzed in this study, refer to the user interface of mobile applications for public transport, regarding the navigation functions and design. The revealed patterns give an overview of predominant navigation schemes within the development of mobile information systems in public transport. Although the design patterns do not describe rigid rules or regulations, limiting the development, design patterns are often applied by developers as tested and inspiring suggestions for solutions of interface design problems [7].

The analysis included 30 mobile applications for passenger information [8]. This variety of applications from different countries revealed the three following popular design concepts of navigating in mobile passenger applications:

- Bar navigation (cf. Fig. 1);
- Navigation on the main screen (cf. Fig. 2);
- Foldable navigation (cf. Fig. 3).

Bar navigation

Description of the pattern
The menu items are displayed as a bar-navigation-graph. This bar navigation is provided permanently and allows rapid switching between the functions. Selected sections are highlighted as the current position, in order to facilitate the orientation within the application.

Description of the problem
The items of the navigation bar have to be available for the users at all the screen of the application. These items have to be provided permanently and efficiently during the usage.

Example

Fig. 1. Pattern "bar navigation"

Navigation on the main screen

Description of the pattern
The menu items are displayed on a separate main screen. The application permanently includes one button to get back to this screen, in order to change the used function. The currently selected function has to be marked at an appropriate place on each screen additionally.

Description of the problem
Users have to be able to switch between different functional sections of the application.

Example

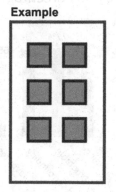

Fig. 2. Pattern "navigation on the main screen"

Foldable navigation

Description of the pattern
The menu items are not displayed permanently. The menu items are shown as a result of a defined action, for instance tapping at the right upper corner or sliding from the left margin. Subsequently, the menu bar is presented as an overlay of the current content.

Description of the problem
The menu items have to be easily available for the users, but they need to much space to be displayed permanently.

Example

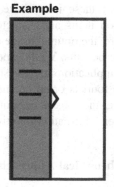

Fig. 3. Pattern "foldable navigation"

Next to these design patterns, the content of all analyzed navigation items is related to the same conceptual system, in which the names of the items always refer to a function or mobility specific content. The most common navigation items, which are used in more than 50 percent of the analyzed applications, are "planning", "departures/timetables", "favorites", and "position and surrounding". Furthermore "tickets", "messages" and "more functions" are used in more than 25 percent of the applications. A few applications also integrated the items "home", "options", "network maps" or other "services" into the navigation (cf. Fig. 4).

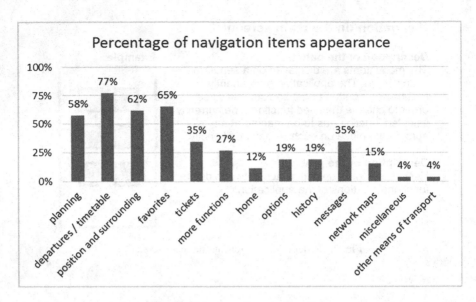

Fig. 4. Overview of navigation items

All of these items have in common, that the name and the distinction of the navigation items are characterized by the functions or content, which are included. Therefore, the optimal usage of the navigation requires foreknowledge of the functions and their benefits. While expert users have a lot of experience-based knowledge of the mobile applications and the structure of public transport, novice or occasional users, for instance tourists or ad hoc-users, cannot draw on that kind of knowledge. As a consequence, these users are not able to use all benefits of these mobile applications for passenger information intuitively.

2.2   Theoretical Approach: Information Needs Along the Journey

In contrast to the conceptual systems of the navigation items, the journeys of travelers consist of several recurring travel phases, for instance, trip planning, starting the journey, waiting for the vehicle, entering the vehicle and so on [9] (cf. Table 1). According to these travel phases, the information needs of the passengers vary [10] and the required kind of visualization differs correspondingly.

Table 1. Travel chain in public transport [10]

Phase	Preparation	Travel						
	Dealing with disturbances							
Step	1	2	3	4	5	6	7	8
	Planning the journey	Starting the journey	Waiting for the vehicle	Entering the vehicle	Travel with the vehicle	Transfer to another vehicle	Alighting from the vehicle	Heading towards the destination

The travel chain in public transport consist of different means of transportation, for instance busses, trams, or trains. Intermodal trips combine public, individual, or shared mobility services and consequently increase the complexity of the journey. The variety of means of transport implicates different information needs of the users and different information functions to fulfill them. For instance, the information need for travelling within a vehicle of public transport is characterized by the remaining travelling time and the destination station. In contrast, information on using a bike along the journey requires extra information on navigating in the streets.

3 Concept and Evaluation of the Workflow-Based Navigation

3.1 Design of the Workflow-Based Navigation

The increasing complexity of information requires a change to a more intuitive navigation in mobile applications for passenger information. The concept of workflow-based navigation [11] was especially developed for business applications and is orientated on the sequence of user tasks. The transfer of this concept allows an orientation for workflow-based navigation along the travel chain with specific user tasks, instead of the system's functions.

In order to reveal the required information and functions, according to the travel phases, a hierarchical task analysis (HTA) [12] of intermodal journeys with different mobility services was conducted. The HTA detailed the concept of a workflow-based navigation by assigning the relevant tasks. The necessity of parallel and sequential functions is systematically analyzed and ordered, in respect to the tasks of a journey. The results of the HTA revealed, that "trip preparation", "being on a trip section", and "changing between trip sections" are the most relevant stages of a trip with characteristic information needs. The task "handling disturbances" is considered as a subtask of all stages.

Finally, the relation between information and the stages of a trip is derived from a systematical analysis of the information needs along the journeys [10] and the results of a field study about the usage of mobile applications in public transport [13]. This field study of mobile applications for passenger information was conducted with 36 participants along a representative journey with one change of the vehicle. The number of intended function calls was gathered by analyzing the screencast of the smartphone and video data of a focus camera. Especially, the situation with functions switching within one task was analyzed, concerning the reasons of actions in a retrospective thinking aloud interview. Based on the results of this field study and a statistical analysis of intermodal travel behavior, the approach of the workflow-based navigation of mobile passenger information systems in public transport was developed.

3.2 Evaluation Method

The study compares the two conceptual navigation schemes function-based and workflow-based navigation in a usability test, which is conducted with users of mobile passenger information systems.

Test Method. The usability test [14] is based on a typical scenario in public transport. The scenario consists of a route planning task in combination with the first orientation tasks for travelling:

- Identifying the line, which has be chosen first;
- Identifying the destination station;
- Identifying the number of stop points to the destination station.

The interviewer accompanied each test session next to the test person, in order to answer questions and comments. The interactions with the mobile phone in each test session were video-taped and analyzed, in regard to the number and kind of user interactions. In order to ensure comparable results and reduce the learning effects, each user conducted the test either with the function-based or with the workflow-based navigation.

Test Persons. The test was conducted with 10 male test persons between the ages of 18 and 35 years of age. Every test person had medium knowledge of the public transport system and limited knowledge of the scenario place. All users were very experienced smartphone users.

Test Objects. For this study two functional prototypes of mobile applications for passenger information were developed. Due to a better comparability, both prototypes were designed according to the pattern of bar navigation (cf. Fig. 5). Thus, both navigation concepts were permanently present at the screen during all test tasks.

(1) *Function-based navigation.* The prototype with the function-based navigation includes the most popular navigation items "planning", "departures/timetables", and "favorites", which provide detailed information of a planned journey. In addition, "messages" of disturbances and a vehicle information function are included.
(2) *Workflow-based navigation.* The developed workflow-based navigation is orientated towards the stages of a trip, instead of the functions. The concept provides different levels of detail: a planning overview for the preparation, a journey overview, and detailed trip section views for the travel. The available information and functions are displayed at the according stages of the trip.

3.3   Evaluation Results

The user interactions were counted and documented in connection with the purpose and the kind of interaction, by the reference of the video material.

The first analysis criterion is the total number of user interactions. In contrast to the hypothesis, that a workflow-based navigation could decrease the total number of interactions, the results revealed only negligible differences for the mean value of the total number of interactions (cf. Table 2). But the single results of the test persons show a higher dispersion for the function-based navigation from a minimum of 7 interactions to a maximum of 12 interactions. Opposing these results, the workflow-based navigation shows a lower dispersion from 6 to 9 interactions.

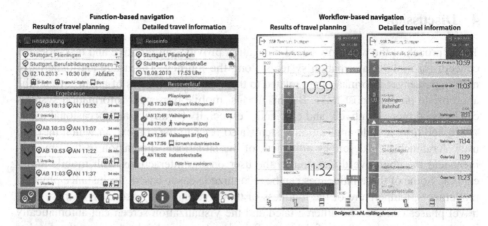

Fig. 5. Screenshots of the prototypes with function-based navigation (left) and workflow-based navigation (right).

Table 2. Number of interactions in comparison

	Total number of interactions	Number of tap actions	Number of swipe/slide actions
Functions-based navigation concept	$\bar{x} = 9$	$\bar{x} = 5.4$	$\bar{x} = 3.6$
	$\sigma = 1.9$	$\sigma = 1.34$	$\sigma = 0.89$
Workflow-based navigation concept	$\bar{x} = 8.4$	$\bar{x} = 3.2$	$\bar{x} = 5.2$
	$\sigma = 1.3$	$\sigma = 0.44$	$\sigma = 1.30$

$\bar{x}$ = mean; σ = standard deviation

The detailed analysis of the kind of interaction reveals more differences regarding the purpose and the actions. Both prototypes required the usage of tap actions, in order to reach the visualization screen for the next task, and swipe or slide actions, in order to compare the information of different trips or trip sections within one visualization screen. The mean value of the tap actions, which are the basic required actions to solve the tasks, are distinctively reduced from 5.4 tap actions in the function-based navigation to 3.2 tap actions in the workflow-based interactions, which nearly meets the minimum of three required tap interactions.

None of the interactions of the workflow-based navigation referred to the navigation bar, because all interaction steps could be clearly followed by interaction buttons in the visualization area, without returning to previous screens. The navigation buttons were highlighted, according to the next step of visualization, and were used as orientation by the users.

The lower number of tap interactions in the workflow-based navigation were equalized by the higher number of slide and swipe actions. Due to the vertical visualization of the trip results, the test persons used more slide actions to compare the results than for the horizontal visualization in the function-based navigation. Moreover, the lower mental workload to orientate and navigate between the functions in the workflow-based navigation might have encouraged the test persons to spend more time for comparing actions.

4 Discussion

The approach of the workflow-based navigation provides an intuitive and task-oriented concept for mobile information systems along the journey. The usage and benefits of mobile passenger information are related to the appropriate phases of a journey and the appropriate pre- and post-tasks. By this means, mobile passenger information systems can be used more intuitively and efficiently, especially by novice and occasional users.

In addition, mobile application systems also refer to the context, in which they are used. Krannich [15] describes influences of the situational dimension of the environment and the cognitive dimension of the user on the interactions with mobile applications. Some of these influences can be recognized sensor-based, for instance physical movements, temperature or the loudness of the environment. According to these data, travel phases can even be differentiated and the visualization screen can automatically be adapted to the workflow of the user. This development might decrease the number of required tap actions.

The revealed workflow-based navigation concept of mobile passenger information systems is validated in lab-based usability tests. As a next step, the results should also be validated in the field, using fully operative mobile applications as test objects, in order to compare the usage of function-based and workflow-based navigation, considering the different contextual influences of travelling. Further evaluation should also include individual mobility and shared mobility services, in order to evaluate the benefits of a seamless mobility information for integrated and intermodal journeys.

Acknowledgements. Part of this work was funded by the German Federal Ministry of Economy and Technology (BMWi) grant number 19P10003L within the project IP-KOM-ÖV and by the German Federal Ministry of Education and Reserach (BMBF) grant number 01FE14033 within the project Move@ÖV. Special thanks go out to the developers of the prototypes Markus Kniep and Christopher Schauer.

References

1. Wirtz, S., Jakobs, E.-M.: Improving user experience for passenger information systems. prototypes and reference objects. IEEE Trans. Prof. Commun. **56**(2), 120–137 (2013). doi:10.1109/TPC.2013.2257211
2. Mayas, C., Hörold, S., Krömker, H.: Meeting the challenges of individual passenger information with personas. In: Stanton, N.A. (ed.) Advances in Human Aspects of Road and Rail Transportation, pp. 822–831. CRC Press, Boca Raton (2012)
3. Hörold, S., Mayas, C., Krömker, H.: User-oriented development of information systems in public transport. In: Anderson, M. (ed.) Contemporary Ergonomics and Human Factors, pp. 160–167. CRC Press, Boca Raton (2013)
4. Alexander, C., Ishikawa, S., Silverstein, M.: A Pattern Language. Oxford University Press, New York (1977)
5. Gamma, E., Helm, R., Johnson, R., Vlissides, J.: Design Pattern-Elements of Reusable Object-Oriented Software. Addison-Wesley, Amsterdam (1994)

6. Gleininger, A., Vrachliotis, G.: Pattern, Ornament, Structure, and Behavior. Birkhäuser, Basel et al (2009)
7. Granlund, A., Lefreniere, D., Carr, D.A.: A pattern-supported approach to the user interface design process. In: Smith, M.J. (ed.) Usability Evaluation and Interface Design: Cognitive Engineering, Intelligent Agents and Virtual Reality. Lawrence Erlbaum Associates Publishers, Mahwah (2001)
8. VDV-Report 7035: Nutzerorientierte Gestaltungsprinzipien für mobile Fahrgastinformation. VDV, Cologne (2014)
9. Verband Deutscher Verkehrsrunternehmen: Telematics in Public Transport in Germany. Alba Fachverlag, Düsseldorf (2001)
10. Hörold, S., Mayas, C., Krömker, H.: Identifying the information needs of users in public transport. In: Stanton, N.A. (ed.) Advances in Human Aspect of Road and Rail Transportation, pp. 331–340. CRC Press, Boca Raton (2013)
11. Leymann, F., Roller, D.: Workflow-based applications. IBM Syst. J. 36(1), 102–123 (1997). doi:10.1147/sj.361.0102
12. Annett, J.: Hierarchical task analysis (HTA). In: Stanton, N., Hedge, A., Brookhuis, K., Salas, E., Hendrick, H. (eds.) Handbook of Human Factors and Ergonomics Method, pp. 33-1–33-7. CRC Press, Boca Raton (2005)
13. Hörold, S., Mayas, C., Krömker, H.: Passenger needs on mobile information Systems – Field evaluation in public transport. In: Stanton, N. A. (ed.) AHFE Conference Proceedings on Advances in Human Aspects of Transportation Part III, pp. 115–124 (2014)
14. Nielsen, J.: Usability Engineering. Academic Press, Boston et al (1993)
15. Krannich, D.: Mobile System Design – Herausforderungen, Anforderungen und Lösungsansätze für Design, Implementierung und Usability-Testing Mobiler Systeme. Books on Demand GmbH, Norderstedt (2010)

Concrete or Abstract User Interface?

Abbas Moallem[✉]

Charles W. Davidson College of Engineering, San Jose State University,
One Washington Square, San Jose, CA 95192-0085, USA
abbas.moallem@sjsu.edu

Abstract. This study investigates what kind of mental image a design triggers when a user views the user interface and whether that image would be matched with the image of the real object in the user's mind.

In this study, a standard scenario to design a remote control for lighting and temperature controls was given to 200 students completing an HCI course at graduate and undergraduate levels. The given scenario asked each student to provide a low fidelity prototype of a suggested design within a timeframe of 10 min. These prototypes were then classified and grouped into either concrete or abstract designs.

The results of these investigations show that a majority of participants perceive abstract representations for their design rather than concrete: a depiction of a real light switch to represent turning lights on and off.

Keywords: UI design · Paradigms · UI designer · Mental image

1 Introduction

User interaction with computers is now a constant in our lives, an active part of our daily routines. We are not only using computers to perform tasks but also for common instances working through remote Internet access to control devices such as home security devices, camera surveillance, and temperature light controls. All users, from young to old, count on user interfaces to work for them in helping them successfully complete their essential tasks. One of the issues that have been observed is how the interface should be designed so that it properly reflects how users want to view the devices they are remotely managing.

The question comes up as to what kind of mental image should the design trigger when a user views the user interface? The knowledge as to how this mental image matches the real concept of the user interface is key to creating a capable design.

A variety of researchers investigated mental images, imagery and perception and their effect on how we interact with our world. To mention a few examples, Norman suggests that people form internal representations or mental models of themselves and the objects with which they interact which create predictive and explanatory powers for understanding the interaction (Norman, 1983a) [1]. Gentner and Stevens (1983) [2] support the concept that mental models are based on the way people understand a specific knowledge domain. Johnson-Laird [3] believes that mental models play a

© Springer International Publishing Switzerland 2015
M. Kurosu (Ed.): Human-Computer Interaction, Part I, HCII 2015, LNCS 9169, pp. 390–395, 2015.
DOI: 10.1007/978-3-319-20901-2_36

central and unifying role in representing objects, states of affairs, sequences of events, the way the world is, and the social and psychological actions of daily life (p.397).

Many researchers are focused on how mental images differ among designers and users. Overall, two mental models are distinguished: a user's mental model, referring to what an end user believes about a system (Nielsen 2010) [4], and a designer's mental model, which refers to the conceptualization of what was invented by a designer. (Staggers and Norcio, 1993) [5]. Nielson believes that "What users believe they know about a UI strongly impacts how they use it. Mismatched mental models are common, especially with designs that try something new" (Nielson 2010). Several studies tend to investigate, understand and use mental representation to design interfaces that are based on users mental and propose formwork (X. Qian, Y. Yang & Yong Gong, 2011) [6].

Athaavankar's (1997) [7] study illustrates that a designer creates virtual models in his/her "mind's eye," then manipulates and alters them, and makes them behave according to his wishes during the development of his ideas.

This study tries to understand how the object type and designer representation affect the user interface of the devices that those interfaces control. To understand this we made the hypothesis that if the user interface were presenting the virtual image of the object that the UI controls, it would be easier for the user to manipulate or control through the UI versus an abstract representation by the user interface. For example, to turn a light on and off, it would be easier to click on a representation of lighting than checking a checkbox. Or to regulate temperature, it could be manipulating a virtual representation of a thermometer rather than entering or moving up and down a field.

2   Method

Over a period of one year (2014 and 2015), a design exercise was given to 200 graduate and undergraduate students who were taking an HCI class. The participants were a mixture of human factors and software engineering students. The students were at mid-level of the course and already had fundamental knowledge of HCI and user interface design. The exercise was given during class time, and students were given 10 min to provide a 1 page paper prototyping (low fidelity) of a design case with no other instruction besides what was written on the exercise description (Table 1).

After collecting the prototypes, they were classified into the following categories, Virtual and Abstract. The virtual were divided in two sub-categories: Concrete and Semi-Concrete (See Figs. 1, and 2).

3   Results

Charts 1 and 2 show the percentage of design types classified as Concrete, Semi Concrete and Abstract for the Light control and Temperature control.

The results show that 71 % of the participants who created a UI for light control had a more abstract meaning using a nonfigurative image of the object, 4 % Semi concrete (somehow visualizing the light) and only 25 % had a very concrete view of lighting to illustrate the on and off functions.

Table 1. Design exercise description

Design Exercise: A new service application offers people an online account where they are able to login and use a browser to view and remotely control one's home lighting and temperature. 6 Wi-Fi sensors are already installed on five lighting controls and one has been placed on the home temperature control device.
The requirements are:
• After logging in to the account through a browser (not needed for this exercise) the user should be able to see.
• Date and time
• 5 light switches and their status (i.e. on or off at the present time) with the ability to changed their status
• Home temperature at the present time with the ability to change the temperature
• Users: All home owners have different levels of computer knowledge
• Expectations: An extremely easy to use and robust system

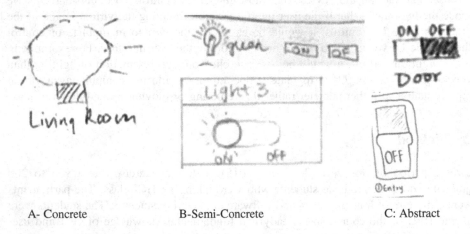

A- Concrete   B-Semi-Concrete   C: Abstract

Fig. 1. Classification of the design Categories for light control

For the temperature control group, the breakdown was 52 % abstract, 32 % semi-concrete and 16 % concrete.

4   Discussion

The results of this study suggest that the representations of the controls do not confirm our hypothesis that people tend to use a concrete representation of the object and its control. This is supported by the fact that 71 % in one case and 52 % in the second case were designing a user interface that was quite abstract.

This study just shows a trend but does not provide a fundamental answer or guideline as to what image would be better to create the right action and reliable representation in the mind of users. Factors such as the participants' background in

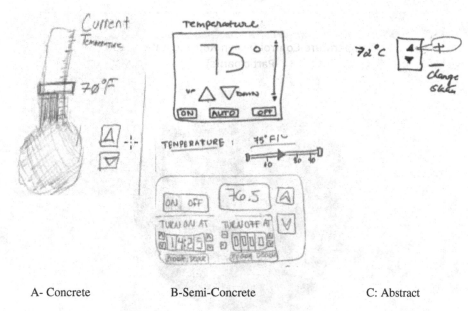

A- Concrete   B-Semi-Concrete   C: Abstract

Fig. 2. Classification of the design categories for temperature control

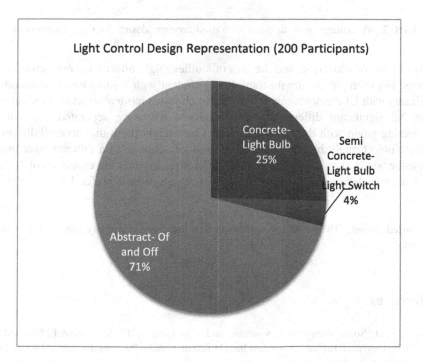

Chart. 1. Percentage of participants who used concrete design for light Control

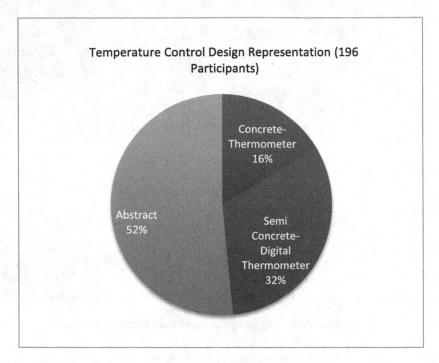

Chart. 2. Percentage of participants who used concrete design for temperature control

terms of level of education, and the area of studies might affect their respective design choices. For example one might think that a student with a software background and familiarity with UI elements might make them choose a more abstract choice, although when No significant differences were observed when we separated the software engineering group with the other discipline. Once might think that accessibility of the concrete object might be more accessible to older adults or to a different user profile.

Further study should investigate user preferences by showing examples of Abstract and Concrete designs and seeing what participants would prefer between the two choices.

Acknowledgement. Thanks all my students at San Jose State University who took part in this exercise.

References

1. Norman, D.: Some observation on mental model. In: Gentner, D., Stevens, A.L. (eds.) Mental Models. Lawrence Erlbaun Associate Inc., Hillsdale (1983). Psychology Press, 14 Jan 2014 - Psychology - p. 352
2. Gentner, D., Stevens, A.L.: Psychology Press, p. 352, 14 Jan 2014 (1983)
3. Johnson-Laird, P.N.: Mental Models. Harvard University Press, Cambridge (1983)

4. Nielson, J.: Mental Models, 18 October 2010.http://www.nngroup.com/articles/mental-models. Accessed 2 Feb 2015
5. Staggers, A., Norcio, A.F.: Mental models: concepts for human-computer interaction research. Int. J. Man-Mach. Stud. **38**(4), 587–605 (1993). http://userpages.umbc.edu/~norcio/papers/1993/Staggers-MM-IJMMS.pdf
6. Qian, X., Yang, Y., Gong, Y.: The art of metaphor: a method for interface design based on mental models, VRCAI 2011. In: Proceedings of the 10th International Conference on Virtual Reality Continuum and Its Applications in Industry (2011)
7. Athhavankar, U.A.: Mental imagery as design tool. Int. J. Cybern. Syst. **28**(1), 25–42 (1997)

Airway Cursor: A Pointing Technique Based on Direction of Mouse Movement Towards a Targets

Tomohiro Nakatsuji[✉], Keiko Yamamoto, Itaru Kuramoto, and Yoshihiro Tsujino

Kyoto Institute of Technology, Matsugasaki, Sakyo-ku, Kyoto 606-8585, Japan
`airway@hit.is.kit.ac.jp`

Abstract. In conventional pointing cursor environments, selecting a small object or an object that is at a distance from the cursor takes a considerable amount of time. To solve this problem, we propose a new pointing technique called "Airway Cursor." In the proposed technique, to select a target object, all users need to do is to specify the direction toward the target object. To specify the direction, the user simply moves the cursor a little toward the target object and then clicks. If there are multiple objects between the cursor and the target object, the user can select the target object by carrying out this operation on the intervening non-target objects until the target object is reached. This technique reduces the time to select an object by shortening the distance the mouse has to move.

1 Introduction

Pointing is one of the most common operations in graphical user interface (GUI) environments. Conventionally, to select a target object, the cursor first has to be moved to the exact position of the target object. Further, the selection area of the object is defined as the area on which a click is performed to select the object. Thus, in conventional pointing cursor environments, the selection area is the object itself. The time to select a target object follows Fitts' Law, defined in (1) and (2) [1,2]:

$$T_p = a + b \times ID, \tag{1}$$

$$ID = \log_2\left(\frac{A}{W} + 1\right), \tag{2}$$

where

- T_p is the average mouse movement time;
- ID is the difficulty of movement to select a target object;
- A is the distance between the current cursor position and the center of the target object;

© Springer International Publishing Switzerland 2015
M. Kurosu (Ed.): Human-Computer Interaction, Part I, HCII 2015, LNCS 9169, pp. 396–404, 2015.
DOI: 10.1007/978-3-319-20901-2_37

- W is the width of the target object; and
- a and b are empirically determined constants, which depend on the device and the user.

There are two known problems with the conventional pointing cursor technique: It takes a considerable amount of time to 1) select a small target object, and 2) select a target object that is at a distance from the current position of the cursor. In this paper, we focus on the latter issuue. This problem occurs when an user needs to move his/her mouse over a relatively long distance. Thus, to reduce the time taken, the distance the mouse moves to select the long-distance objects needs to be shortened. To solve the problem of selection of long-distance object, we propose a new pointing technique called "Airway Cursor." Airway Cursor improves pointing performance in the GUI by jumping to a desired target object from the current position of the cursor based on the direction of mouse movement; thereby, facilitating faster and easier selection. Using Airway Cursor, users can easily and quickly select a target object simply by moving their mouse slightly toward the target object.

2 Related Work

In conventional pointing cursor environments, the selection area is on the object; consequently, the cursor has to be moved to an arbitrary position on the object and clicked in order to select the object. From (1) and (2), T_p is reduced when the object increases in size. However, increases in the size of the object are accompanied by proportional increases in the object to screen ratio, which influence other objects, such as information displayed to the user, being difficult to arrange on the screen. This is especially problematic when there are many objects that need to be arranged.

Similarly, T_p can be reduced when the distance that the cursor needs to move is shortened. The distance from the cursor to objects can be shortened by reducing the size of the area over which the cursor needs to move (i.e., the screen). However, this means that the area in which all objects are arranged will get smaller. Consequently, all objects would have to become smaller. Thus, it is also difficult to shorten T_p.

There are two practical methods by which T_p can be reduced without the above disadvantages. The first method is to make mouse movement shorter than with the conventional pointing cursor. Bubble Cursor [3], Delphian Desktop [4], and Drop and Pop [5] are based on this idea.

With Bubble Cursor, users can select the object nearest to the cursor by clicking, even if the cursor is not on the object. This means that the effective size of the target object is expanded based on Voronoi diagram. Using this technique, enlarging the effective size of each target object can effectively reduce the distance to the target object, resulting in users being able to select target objects faster than with the conventional pointing cursor. However, with this technique, it is difficult to select a target object in areas that are densely packed with many prospective targets. This means that users cannot take full advantage of this technique in such the situation.

Delphian Desktop predicts the target object that users wish to select based on the direction and velocity of the mouse movement. After the prediction, the cursor jumps to the predicted target object. Thus, the cursor is moved faster to a faraway target object. However, the technique sometimes fails to predict the correct target object. In addition, in cases where the distance between a target object and the current position of the cursor is relatively short (less than 800 [px]), the method takes considerably more time than the conventional pointing cursor to select target objects.

The second method by which T_p can be reduced without the disadvantages is to decrease the rate of selection error, which occurs when the cursor passes through the selection area of a target object. Sticky Icon [6,7] and Birdlime Icon [8] are based on this technique. They can increase W in (1) and (2), but they also increase the user's cognitive load.

3 Airway Cursor

Airway Cursor aims to make mouse movement shorter than that of Bubble Cursor, and without the unreliable prediction of Delphian Desktop.

3.1 Overview

Airway Cursor has two modes: Airway mode and Point mode. In Airway mode, the entire screen is divided into two kinds of selection areas: a Focused area and Object areas. The Focused area is around the current position of the cursor, whereas an object area is determined for each object based on the bisector of each pair of objects (see Fig. 1). Users can select an object only by clicking the Focused or Object area that corresponds to that object. If a certain Object area is too small to click, then an object area is not created. Nevertheless, a farway object without its own object area can be selected by skipping on intermediate objects, as illustrated in Fig. 2, based on the division of areas that are refreshed at each object in the skipping activity. In Point mode, an object can be selected in the same manner as that of the conventional pointing cursor.

3.2 Assigning Selection Area

The method by which selection areas are assigned is illustrated in Fig. 3. In this figure, each number written in italic for each selection area indicates that the area is for the object with the corresponding number.

1. (a) **if** the cursor is on a certein object **then**
    i. the object under the cursor is labeled O_f.
    ii. A focused point is defined as the center of O_f.
    iii. A focused area is defined as a circular area whose center is the focused point. This area is the selection area of O_f.

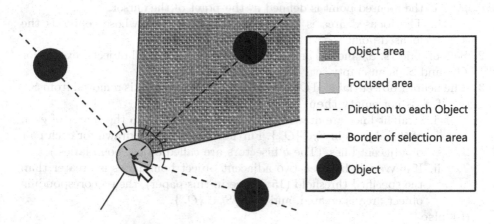

Fig. 1. Airway Cursor with object areas

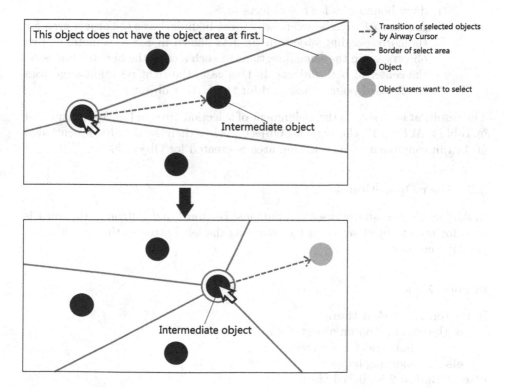

Fig. 2. The change of the object areas of Airway Cursor in a dense packing scenario

(b) **else**
    i. the focused point is defined as the point of the cursor.
    ii. The focused area is defined as a circular area whose center is the focused point.

2. Sets of objects, S_a and S_b, are defined. Initially, S_a has all objects, except for O_f, and S_b is an empty set.
3. The nearest object (labeled O_n) to the focused point in S_a is removed from S_a.
4. (a) **if** S_b is not empty **then**
    i. straight lines are drawn from the focused point to the center of each of the objects in $S_b \cup \{O_n\}$. Further, bisectors are drawn for each pair of adjacent lines. (These bisectors are called object boundaries.)
    ii. If any angle between two adjacent object boundaries is greater than the specified threshold (15 degree in this paper), then a coresponding object area is created, and $S_b = S_b \cup \{O_n\}$.
  (b) **else**
$$S_b = \{O_n\}.$$
5. (a) **if** S_a is not empty **then**
    Return to process 3.
  (b) **else**
    i. draw boundaries for the objects in S_b.
    ii. Assign each area between two object boundaries as the object area for the corresponding object in S_b. (As shown in Fig. 4, sometimes two objects are in the same direction. In such a case, the bisector line is on the center of both objects. In this case, the right selection area from the focused point is assigned for the farther object.)

The results at each step in the assignment of selection areas in Fig. 3 are displayed in Table 1. At Step 13, the angle for Object 5 is less than the threshold mentioned at 4.(a)ii; consequently, no selection area is created for Object 5.

3.3   User Operation

In Airway Cursor, an user uses two buttons: Button 1 and Button 2. Button 1 is used for target object selection (the same as the left button in the conventional pointing cursor).

In Point Mode:

if Button 1 is clicked **then**
    if the cursor is on an object **then**
        that object is selected.
    else   nothing happens.
else if Button 2 is clicked **then**
    a focused point is defined based on the cursor position (described in Sect. 3.2), and the mode is changed to Airway mode.

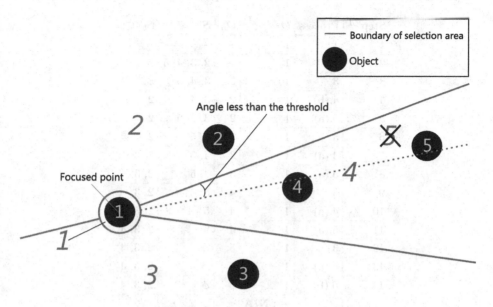

Fig. 3. Selection area assignment example

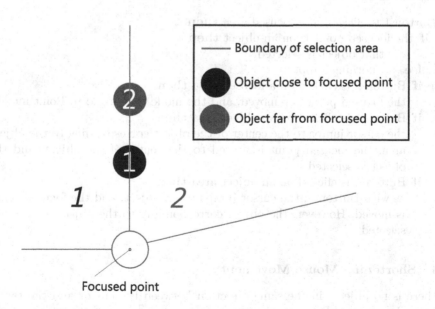

Fig. 4. Assigning object areas when two objects are in the same direction from the focused point

Table 1. Transition of object sets in the arrangement of selection areas in Fig. 3

Step #	Process	O_f	O_n	S_a	S_b
1	1	1	−	−	−
2	2	1	−	2, 3, 4, 5	ϕ
3	3	1	2	3, 4, 5	ϕ
4	4.(b)	1	2	3, 4, 5	2
5	5.(a)	1	2	3, 4, 5	2
6	3	1	3	4, 5	2
7	4.(a)	1	3	4, 5	2, 3
8	5.(a)	1	3	4, 5	2, 3
9	3	1	4	5	2, 3
10	4.(a)	1	4	5	2, 3, 4
11	5.(a)	1	4	5	2, 3, 4
12	3	1	5	ϕ	2, 3, 4
13	4.(a)	1	5	ϕ	2, 3, 4
14	5.(b)	1	5	ϕ	2, 3, 4
		− : N/A			

In Airway mode:

if Button 1 is clicked on a focused area **then**
    if the focused point is on an object **then**
           that object is selected.
    else   nothing happens.
else if Button 2 is clicked on a focused area **then**
        the focused point is removed, and the mode is changed to Point mode.
else if Button 1 is clicked on an object area **then**
        the cursor jumps to the center of the object corresponding to the object
        area, the focused point is moved to the center of the object, and the
        object is selected.
else if Button 2 is clicked on an object area **then**
        as with Button 1, the cursor jumps to an object, and the focused point
        is moved. However, the object corresponding to the object area is not
        selected.

3.4   Shortening Mouse Movement

If there is no objects in the same direction between the cursor and the target
object, the user needs only move the cursor the distance of the radius of the
focused area. On the other hand, if there are many objects in the same direction
between the cursor and the target object, the target object will not be assigned
an object area like the case for Object 5 in Fig. 3. In this case, the user needs

to select some intermediate objects. The distance between the cursor and the target object is represented by D_a in (3) below:

$$D_a = (N+1)D_c, \tag{3}$$

where

- N is the number of intermediate objects, and
- D_c is the radius of the focused area.

Initially, the cursor is on the focused area. If an object corresponding to the focused area is a target object, A in (2) is zero. In this situation, D_c can be suffiiciently small, because ID does not increase in any $W = D_c$. Consequently, even if N clicks are needed, D_a is sufficiently small that ID will not increase.

3.5 Influence of Multiple Clicks

Fitts' Law is assumed for the situation in which the user selects a target object via a single click. In the case where an intermediate object is utilized in selecting the target object by Airway Cursor, multiple clicks are needed, resulting in extra time being incurred. The extra time incurred by an aditional click is a in (1), which is mainly for recognizing the target object when using Airway Cursor to select a target object. The position of the target object remains unchanged during the selection process; consequently, the direction of each mouse movement between clicks can be easily predicted. This means that the constant a after the first click may be small. Therefore, the time for selecting a target object can be short, even when an user selects intermediate objects.

4 Conclusion

We proposed a new technique called "Airway Cursor" that reduces the distance the cursor needs to move to select a target object, regardless of how such objects are arranged. Consequently, users can select target objects quickly with Airway Cursor.

In future work, we plan to conduct experimental evaluations that compare the speed of Airway Cursor with other pointing techniques, specifically, Delphian Desktop and Bubble Cursor. The operation of Airway Cursor, Bubble Cursor, and Delphian Desktop is not familiar to most persons. Therefore, we anticipate that participants will need to practice with the three pointing techniques prior to the start of the actual evaluations.

References

1. Fitts, P.M.: The information capacity of the human motor system in controlling the amplitude of movement. J. Exp. Psychol. **47**(6), 381–391 (1954)
2. MacKenzie, I.S.: Fitts' law as a research and design tool in human-computer interaction. Hum. Comput. Interact. **7**(1), 91–139 (1992)
3. Grossman, T., Balakrishnan, R.: The bubbe cursor: enhancing target acquisition by dynamic resizing of the cursor's activation area. In: Proceedings of the SIGCHI Conference on Human Factors in Computing Systems, 281–290 (2005)
4. Asano, T., Sharlin, E., Kitamura, Y., Takashima, K., Kishino, F.: Predictive interaction using the delphian desktop. In: Proceedings of the 18th annual ACM symposium on User interface software and Technology, 133–141 (2005)
5. Collomb, M., Hascoet, M., Baudisch, P., Lee, B.: Improving drag-and-pop on wall-size display. In: Proceedings of Graphics Interface, 25–32 (2005)
6. Cockburn, A., Brock, P.: Human on-line response to visual and motor target expansion. In: Proceedings of Graphics Interface 2006, 81–87 (2006)
7. Mandryk, R.L., Gutwin, C.: Perceptibility and utility of sticky targets. In: Proceedings of Graphics Interface 2008, 65–72 (2008)
8. Tsukitani, T., Takashima, K., Asahi, M., Itoh, Y., Kitamura, Y., Kishino, F.: The birdlime icon: improving target acquisition by dynamically stretching target shape. In: Proceedings of the 22th Annual ACM Symposium on User Interface Software and Technology, 13–14 (2009)

Interactive Clinical Pedigree Visualization Using an Open Source Pedigree Drawing Engine

João Miguel Santos[1(✉)], Beatriz Sousa Santos[1,2],
and Leonor Teixeira[2,3]

[1] DETI/Department Electrónica, Telecomunicações e Informática,
Universidade de Aveiro, Aveiro, Portugal
{miguelsantos,bss}@ua.pt
[2] IEETA/Instituto de Engenharia Electrónica e Telemática,
Universidade de Aveiro, Aveiro, Portugal
[3] DEGEI/Department Economia, Gestão e Engenharia Industrial,
Universidade de Aveiro, Aveiro, Portugal
lteixeira@ua.pt

Abstract. Advances in Genetics have revealed that many diseases are related to genetic factors. In this context, family health histories play an increasingly important role in healthcare, aiding practitioners in the diagnosis, risk assessment and treatment of various conditions. The clinical pedigree, a graphic representation combining family structure and clinical information, is a well-accepted tool to represent family health histories. At present this tool remains underused, possibly due to the lack of pedigree management tools in health information systems. OntoFam addresses this problem by offering a clinical pedigree information system that can be integrated with current health information systems. This paper presents the method used to create OntoFam's interactive pedigree visualization by wrapping an existing open source pedigree drawing engine. The resulting environment allows practitioners to interactively view, create and manipulate pedigrees. This paper also describes the evaluation strategy that was developed to assess the system and includes its preliminary results.

Keywords: Family health history · Clinical family history · Pedigree · Health information system · Electronic health record · Ontofam · Hemophilia care

1 Introduction

The utility of Family Health Histories (FHHs) has been widely recognized, and is increasing as more and more diseases are linked to genetic factors [1, 2]. FHHs, also known as Clinical Family Histories, help practitioners in the diagnosis and risk assessment of patients and their family members in a cost-effective manner; provide insight as to the most adequate course of treatment for patients [2–4]; and enable the identification of at-risk individuals before diseases manifest, opening the possibility for counselling and preventive measures to delay, diminish or completely avoid diseases or symptoms [5].

© Springer International Publishing Switzerland 2015
M. Kurosu (Ed.): Human-Computer Interaction, Part I, HCII 2015, LNCS 9169, pp. 405–414, 2015.
DOI: 10.1007/978-3-319-20901-2_38

406   J.M. Santos et al.

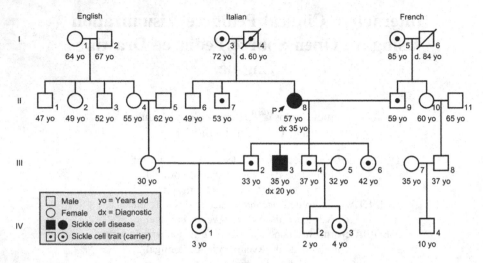

Fig. 1. Example pedigree in PSWG notation

There are several formats available to represent FHHs, both in text and graphical form [6–8]. The clinical pedigree, henceforward referred to as pedigree, is a broadly used graphical representation that combines genealogical and clinical information and offers a good balance of simplicity, expressivity and detail [4]. It is subject to standardization by the Pedigree Standardization Work Group (PSWG) that regularly issues recommendations regarding the use of symbols, annotations and layout of pedigrees [9, 10]. Figure 1 presents an example pedigree in PSWG notation, regarding a family with a history of sickle cell disease.

Several software packages allow the creation of such pedigrees [11–24], yet few integrate with existing Health Information Systems (HIS) or Electronic Health Records (EHR). Using different, disconnected tools for recording patient data and FHHs not only makes information less readily available, but also potentially results in out-of-date information and incoherent data. This problem is addressed by OntoFam [25], an ontology-based clinical pedigree information system that can be integrated with existing HIS.

During the conception of OntoFam, the team was confronted with the decision of whether to build or reuse a pedigree drawing engine (PDE) for the system's user interface. An investigation revealed that several open-source PDEs were available for reuse, though none inherently offered the desired degree of interactivity. In fact, most existing engines follow a "static" approach: they accept an input in a structured text format and output a graphic pedigree representation; any editing involves constructing a new input to obtain an updated pedigree. However, by wrapping an existing static PDE with additional functionality, it is possible to create an interactive visualization. This was the approach chosen for OntoFam.

This paper presents OntoFam's interactive pedigree visualization, which allows the dynamic creation and management of pedigrees. It reuses an existing static pedigree drawing engine and extends it to allow end users to directly manipulate patient information and family structure. Section 2 presents the method used to construct the visualization and Sect. 3 describes the evaluation strategies and presents the corresponding results. Section 4 concludes this paper.

2 Method

Madeline 2.0 Pedigree Drawing Engine [18] is the chosen PDE for the basis of OntoFam's pedigree visualization tool due to a unique combination of favorable characteristics:

- It generates pedigrees that conforms to most PSWG recommendations;
- It is able to correctly represent complex family structures that some other engines do not handle [26];
- It generates pedigrees in Scalable Vector Graphics (SVG), an XML (eXtensible Markup Language) based format that is rendered as vector graphics in modern browsers and is editable in external software, such as Inkscape, CorelDRAW or Adobe Illustrator;
- It is an open-source project, allowing aspects of the representation to be extended or fine-tuned, should the need arise;
- It is actively maintained (the most recent version is from mid-August, 2014).

In its current form, Madeline is a *"non-interactive program that is executed from a shell environment"* [27], that is, it is invoked through the command-line and accepts parameters to customize the output. Input data must be formatted in one of the several table-based formats allowed. Upon invocation, Madeline renders the corresponding pedigree onto a file in SVG format. Any changes to the rendered pedigree involve either editing the SVG in a compatible image editor or altering the input data and repeat the pedigree generation process.

A separate project that shares some of Madeline's authors, dubbed Madeline 2.0 Web Service, does allow pedigrees to be built interactively [28]. However, at present this service is closed-sourced, does not fully exploit Madeline's capabilities and requires direct manipulation of the inherent input data-table for relatively trivial tasks (such as identifying the proband, setting deceased states of specifying clinical conditions, among others).

OntoFam uses a different approach, in which the data-table input is completely hidden from the end user. The intent is to provide a user interface that is closer to practitioners' mindset, allowing data to be manipulated in a way that conforms to their needs and view-points, rather than those of the pedigree drawing engine.

The fact that Madeline uses SVGs was particularly relevant in the construction of OntoFam's visualization method. SVG is an XML language that uses elements to represent lines and shapes that, once rendered on a web browser, allows client-side script to interact with the elements and corresponding shapes. This enables end users to interact with pedigree elements and provides immediate solutions to the needs of selecting or activating represented individuals – client scripts react to the user action of clicking an individual by changing its visual aspect (i.e., changing the CSS style of the

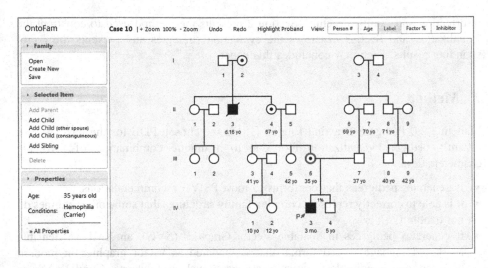

Fig. 2. OntoFam's user interface editing a 4-generation family pedigree

corresponding SVG element) and display a pop-up window with detailed patient information when an individual is double-clicked.

To add new individuals to the pedigree, menu options are provided to allow the insertion of relatives to a selected individual. For example, upon selecting an individual whose ancestry is not yet filled in, the interface will provide options to add the corresponding mother and father. Spouses, siblings and offspring can be added to individuals at any time. This "chained" insertion of individuals ensures that the family structure is always valid. Figure 2 presents OntoFam's user interface while editing a pedigree with 4 generations, and Fig. 3 exemplifies an individual's popup form, allowing its information to be viewed and edited.

OntoFam consists of a web application that uses single-page application (SPA) techniques to wrap Madeline's invocations and provide an interactive experience. Whenever the user requests the pedigree information to be changed, the following process occurs:

1. The user requests the addition, edition or deletion of an individual;
2. Client-side script validates the user action and sends the corresponding information to the web server;
3. OntoFam's family database is updated with the new information;
4. The current FHH is formatted according to Madeline's requirements;
5. Madeline is invoked and an SVG pedigree is generated;
6. The SVG is post-processed on the server;
7. The post-processed SVG is returned to the client and rendered on the browser, replacing the previous pedigree representation.

Step 6 is used to fine-tune visual aspects and overcome Madeline's limitations, such as the lack of individual and generation sequential numbering. The same effect could have been achieved by extending Madeline's source code, but the team found preferable to

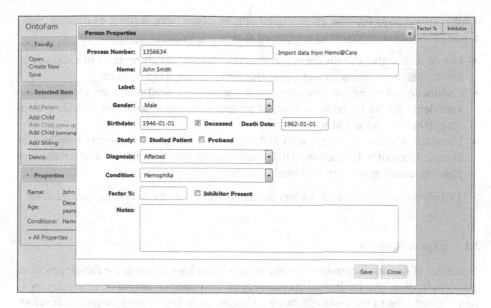

Fig. 3. Example popup form displaying the properties of an individual

use Madeline as-is and treat it as a "black-box". This illustrates a useful characteristic of SVGs: because they are XML documents, it is fairly easy to process and manipulate an existing graphic, unlike raster-based image formats.

Wrapping Madeline in this manner also allows OntoFam to replace its PDE with relative ease, should the need arise. Assuming the replacement engine produces comparable SVGs, the system changes will be limited to the translation of FHH information into the format accepted by the new engine.

Even though the process involves a number of steps, response times are adequate and users are not aware of delays caused by server roundtrips. The XMLHttpRequest (XHR) Application Programming Interface (API) is used in the background to exchange data with the server and, on step 7, user selections are preserved and scroll positions are maintained to ensure that, from the end user's point of view, the pedigree representation was "instantly" complemented with the new information.

3   Evaluation and Results

OntoFam is currently being integrated with an existing HIS for Hemophilia care – Hemo@Care [29]. Hemophilia is an X-linked congenital bleeding disorder, with an estimated frequency of 1 in 10,000 births [30]. Because Hemo@Care deals with a hereditary condition and is also developed in the University of Aveiro, it is an excellent candidate for integration with OntoFam. However, the fact that Hemophilia is a rare disease poses some challenges when it comes to evaluating the resulting system, namely the limited number of practitioners knowledgeable in Hemophilia care. Thus, it proved necessary to use evaluation strategies that could be applied with a limited number of participants. The chosen approach involves three distinct evaluation techniques, executed at different development stages:

- Use of an iterative development process, resorting to expert reviews to validate the most significant iterations and guide the forthcoming development;
- Conduction of user experience tests with (necessarily few) real users (practitioners knowledgeable in Hemophilia care) at project milestones, to assess overall system acceptance in real-world scenarios;
- Conduction of usability tests with non-expert users in greater numbers (students of Human-Computer Interaction [HCI] courses), to fine-tune the user interface and possibly detect generic (non-domain) usability problems.

Details and results of each technique are described in the following subsections.

3.1 Expert Reviews

A number of reasons determined the use of expert reviews to guide the development of the visualization. As previously mentioned, the number of available practitioners is very limited, due to the disease's rarity. Also, at early exploratory stages of development the user tasks are not always completely understood, hence controlled experiments with concrete tasks do not yet apply [31]. Finally, the team was interested in understanding what high-level cognitive tasks, such as decision-making and insight generation, are involved when using a pedigree management system in the context of Hemophilia care.

Two experts were involved in the periodic reviews: an HCI expert and a medical doctor with ample experience in Hemophilia care. The HCI expert relied on heuristic evaluation and personal experience to detect problems and validate design choices, while the medical doctor acted as a test user and, most importantly, enlightened the team regarding what low and high-level tasks were deemed necessary in her field. For example, it was revealed that women in reproductive age within a family with a history of Hemophilia should be educated about the possible implications in offspring, thus gender and age should be clearly represented in the visualization. The presence of inhibitors is also of great importance; therefore it should be visible on the pedigree. It was also learned that due to the X-linked nature of the disease, a pedigree can be used as a "map" to differentiate individuals that should be studied from those that can do without study (and thereby spare human and financial resources).

3.2 User Experience Tests

When expert reviews determined that the system was useable and feature-complete, the team proceeded to conduct user experience tests. The objectives of such tests include obtaining "*subjective feedback and opinions on the visualization tool*" [32] and assess the system adequacy in real-world scenarios. This is not a "final test", but rather an iterative process, where the results of a test session influence the next iterations of the development process and the design of the following test session.

Thus far, the team has conducted the first round of these tests. Two medical doctors knowledgeable in Hemophilia care were invited to participate, guided by three observers. After an open exploratory conversation, where the utility of pedigrees within the Hemophilia field was discussed, they were given a 10 min presentation on the system goals and functionality. They were then allowed to freely explore the system for another 10 min, where they created fictional test pedigrees. The team had prepared a set of introductory tasks to ensure familiarity with the system functionality; however, the participants found their way around the user interface with great ease and the observers were unanimous in deeming these tasks unnecessary.

The participants proceeded to the second set of tasks, which involved constructing a 4-generation pedigree with 26 individuals, similar to that represented on **Fig.** 2; analyzing existing pedigrees to detect individuals that should be studied and individuals that were unnecessarily studied; and analyzing an incorrect pedigree to detect errors, taking into account the known hereditary patterns of Hemophilia. Upon completing each task, participants were asked to rate its difficulty using a Likert-like scale. After performing all tasks, the participants were asked to answer a questionnaire to evaluate system quality and adequacy.

All tasks were correctly performed by both participants, with the exception of the pedigree construction. On this task, one of the participants confused the 4th generation branches and constructed an incorrect family structure. Nearing the end of the task the participant realized this problem but was told not to correct it, seeing as it was the system that was being evaluated, and not the user. This error suggests that functionality to indicate an individual's relation to the proband may be a useful addition to the user interface. Both users rated all tasks as easy or very easy, and all tasks were completed within the estimated completion time.

The answers to the questionnaire were very positive, with both participants agreeing that the system is adequate to represent FHHs related to Hemophilia care, and that they would both use the system and recommend it to colleagues (one participant mentioned that she would also like to use the system applied to the Thrombophilia field). When asked to rate the overall system on a scale of 1-10 (greater is better), one participant awarded an 8 and the other awarded a 9-10. No major problems with the system were found by the participants, though both provided suggestions for further development: the inclusion of molecular study information (on the patient data but not necessarily on the pedigree) and the possibility to represent adoptions (not completely necessary when dealing with hereditary diseases, but relevant nonetheless to get an holistic view of families with adopted members).

A second round of user experience tests is scheduled to occur shortly following the time of this writing, with participants distinct from those of the first round.

3.3   Usability Tests

Usability tests with a much larger number of participants are planned for the 1st semester of 2015. These will consist of controlled experiments performed by students of Human-Computer Interaction (HCI) courses in the University of Aveiro. Although these users are not domain experts, their familiarity with user interfaces and usability guidelines is likely to allow the detection of generic usability problems. User performance metrics, such as task completion time, error ratio and number of clicks, among others, may also help improve interface design.

4 Conclusions and Future Work

The method used to create OntoFam's interactive pedigree visualization by wrapping an existing pedigree drawing engine has proved successful. It hides the process of constantly feeding the PDE with new input to generate new output, and instead presents users with an environment where pedigrees can be directly manipulated. Even though the process involves server roundtrips and constant pedigree regenerations, the fact that these occur in the background and that the visual context is maintained (such as selection and scroll position) keeps users unaware of the actual complexity. In their view, the pedigree is instantly updated on the client browser whenever changes are made.

The results obtained in the concluded evaluation stages have been favorable, with comments and suggestions mostly pertaining to additional functionality rather than faulting the existing system. Results also suggest that practitioners already familiar with clinical pedigrees will have little or no trouble adapting to the visualization. Even though these are promising results, it must be noted that, thus far, the number of participants has been very limited and that broader evaluations should be performed. This will be the focus of forthcoming evaluation stages.

Acknowledgments. The authors would like to thank Dr.[a] Natália Martins, Dr.[a] Lúcia Borges and Dr.[a] Marina Costa for their collaboration and valuable suggestions and observations.

References

1. Kmiecik, T., Sanders, D.: Integration of Genetic and Familial Data into Electronic Medical Records and Healthcare Processes (2009). www.surgery.northwestern.edu/docs/KmiecikSandersArticle.pdf. Accessed 13 November 2012
2. Rich, E.C., Burke, W., Heaton, C.J., Haga, S., Pinsky, L., Short, M.P., Acheson, L.: Reconsidering the family history in primary care. J. Gen. Intern. Med. **19**, 273–280 (2004)
3. Morales, A., Cowan, J., Dagua, J., Hershberger, R.E.: Family history: an essential tool for cardiovascular genetic medicine. Congestive Heart Fail. (Greenwich, Conn.) **14**, 37–45 (2008)
4. Bennett, R.L.: The Practical Guide to the Genetic Family History, 2nd edn. Wiley, New York (2010)
5. Frezzo, T.M., Rubinstein, W.S., Dunham, D., Ormond, K.E.: The genetic family history as a risk assessment tool in internal medicine. Genet. Med. **5**, 84–91 (2003)
6. Butler, J.F.: The Family Diagram and Genogram: Comparisons and Contrasts. The American Journal of Family Therapy **36**, 169–180 (2008). 07 May 2008
7. Rempel, G.R., Neufeld, A., Kushner, K.E.: Interactive use of genograms and ecomaps in family caregiving research. J. Fam. Nurs. **13**, 403–419 (2007)

8. American College of Obstetricians and Gynecologists: Committee opinion no. 478: family history as a risk assessment tool. Obstet. Gynecol. **117**, 747–750 (2011)

9. Bennett, R.L., Steinhaus, K.A., Uhrich, S.B., O'Sullivan, C.K., Resta, R.G., Lochner-Doyle, D., Markel, D.S., Vincent, V., Hamanishi, J.: Recommendations for standardized human pedigree nomenclature. J. Genet. Couns. **4**, 267–279 (1995)

10. Bennett, R.L., French, K.S., Resta, R.G., Doyle, D.L.: Standardized human pedigree nomenclature: update and assessment of the recommendations of the national society of genetic counselors. J. Genet. Couns. **17**, 424–433 (2008)

11. Agarwala, R., Biesecker, L.G., Hopkins, K.A., Francomano, C.A., Schaffer, A.A.: Software for constructing and verifying pedigrees within large genealogies and an application to the old order Amish of Lancaster County. Genome Res. **8**, 211–221 (1998). 1 March 1998

12. Dudbridge, F., Carver, T., Williams, G.W.: Pelican: pedigree editor for linkage computer analysis. Bioinformatics **20**, 2327–2328 (2004). 22 September 2004

13. HaploPainter Team. HaploPainter Manual 1.0 (2012). http://haplopainter.sourceforge.net/HaploPainterManual_V1.0.pdf, 08 December 2012

14. He, M., Li, W.: PediDraw: a web-based tool for drawing a pedigree in genetic counseling. BMC Med. Genet. **8**, 31 (2007)

15. Hughes Risk Apps. Hughes Risk Apps User Guide (2009). http://www.hughesriskapps.com/Files/UserGuide-26x.aspx, 08 December 2012

16. Lee, W.J., Pollin, T.I., O'Connell, J.R., Agarwala, R., Schaffer, A.A.: PedHunter 2.0 and its usage to characterize the founder structure of the Old Order Amish of Lancaster County. BMC Med. Genet. **11**, 68 (2010)

17. Makinen, V.-P., Parkkonen, M., Wessman, M., Groop, P.-H., Kanninen, T., Kaski, K.: High-throughput pedigree drawing. Eur. J. Hum. Genet. **13**, 987–989 (2005)

18. Trager, E.H., Khanna, R., Marrs, A., Siden, L., Branham, K.E.H., Swaroop, A., Richards, J.E.: Madeline 2.0 PDE: a new program for local and web-based pedigree drawing. Bioinformatics **23**, 1854–1856 (2007). 15 July 2007

19. Brun-Samarcq, L., Gallina, S., Philippi, A., Demenais, F., Vaysseix, G., Barillot, E.: CoPE: a collaborative pedigree drawing environment. Bioinformatics **15**, 345–346 (1999). 1 April 1999

20. Cohn, W.F., Ropka, M.E., Pelletier, S.L., Barrett, J.R., Kinzie, M.B., Harrison, M.B., Liu, Z., Miesfeldt, S., Tucker, A.L., Worrall, B.B., Gibson, J., Mullins, I.M., Elward, K.S., Franko, J., Guterbock, T.M., Knaus, W.A.: Health Heritage ©, a web-based tool for the collection and assessment of family health history: initial user experience and analytic validity. Public Health Genomics **13**, 477–491 (2010)

21. Wong, L.: Visualization and manipulation of pedigree diagrams. Genome Inform Ser Workshop Genome Inform **11**, 63–72 (2000)

22. U.S. Department of Health & Human Services. My Family Health Portrait (2009). http://familyhistory.hhs.gov/. Accessed 12 September 2014

23. Zhao, J.H.: Pedigree-drawing with R and graphviz. Bioinformatics **22**, 1013–1014 (2006). Accessed 15 April 2006

24. Progeny Software, Progeny Clinical, version 8.0, (2011). http://www.progenygenetics.com/clinical/

25. Santos, J.M., Sousa Santos, B., Teixeira, L.: Using ontologies and semantic web technology on a clinical pedigree information system. In: Duffy, V.G. (ed.) DHM 2014. LNCS, vol. 8529, pp. 448–459. Springer, Heidelberg (2014)

26. Trager, E.H., Khanna, R., Marrs, A.: Comparison of Pedigree Drawing Programs (2011). http://eyegene.ophthy.med.umich.edu/madeline/comparisons/. Accessed 20 December 2014

27. Trager, E.H., Khanna, R., Marrs, A.: Madeline 2.0 Pedigree Drawing Engine Documentation (2011). http://eyegene.ophthy.med.umich.edu/madeline/documentation.php. Accessed 20 December 2014

28. Khanna, R., Trager, E.H.: Madeline 2.0 Public Web Service (2007). http://eyegene.ophthy.med.umich.edu/madeline/webservice.php. Accessed 1 October 2014

29. Saavedra, V., Teixeira, L., Ferreira, C., Sousa Santos, B.: A preliminary usability evaluation of Hemo@Care: a web-based application for managing clinical information in hemophilia care. In: Kurosu, M. (ed.) HCD 2009. LNCS, vol. 5619, pp. 785–794. Springer, Heidelberg (2009)

30. World Federation of Hemophilia. Guidelines for the Management of Hemophilia (2nd ed.) (2012). http://www.wfh.org/en/resources/wfh-treatment-guidelines

31. Tory, M., Moller, T.: Evaluating visualizations: do expert reviews work? IEEE Comput. Graph. Appl. **25**, 8–11 (2005)

32. Isenberg, T., Isenberg, P., Jian, C., Sedlmair, M., Moller, T.: A systematic review on the practice of evaluating visualization. IEEE Trans. Vis. Comput. Graph. **19**, 2818–2827 (2013)

User Requirements for Intermodal Mobility Applications and Acceptance of Operating Concepts

Ulrike Stopka[✉], René Pessier, and Katrin Fischer

Technische Universität Dresden, Dresden, Germany
ulrike.stopka@tu-dresden.de

Abstract. The mobility behavior of the European population has undergone significant changes in recent years. New services like bike, car and ridesharing are arising. The integrated use of different transport modes can be supported effectively by the features and services of sophisticated smartphones. This paper describes the methodology and research results concerning users' behavior, needs, and requests with regard to intermodal mobility applications.

Keywords: Intermodal mobility · Public transport · Mobility services · Mobile applications · User requirements · Preferences · Habit · Focus group · Operating concept

1 Motivation

Against the background of changing social values towards resource efficiency and environmental benefits today's mobility is less of a choice between different transport modes, but rather their intermodal integration during a trip. The advancing diversity of mobility services is combined by the users under very pragmatic aspects in order to get from A to B fast, reliably, conveniently and as cost effectively as possible. The resulting travel chains require a high level of information, routing, navigation, and guidance services including booking, smart ticketing and payment services, largely based on real-time data and reliable forecasts. This is supported by mobile applications.

As part of the research project "Dynamic Seamless Mobility Information" conducted by a consortium of different public transportation companies, service and IT companies as well as scientific institutions, the Technische Universität Dresden is investigating both the general user requirements for dynamic information services (step 1) and the operating concepts within the applications (step 2). In this article we present selected results of this research project.

© Springer International Publishing Switzerland 2015
M. Kurosu (Ed.): Human-Computer Interaction, Part I, HCII 2015, LNCS 9169, pp. 415–425, 2015.
DOI: 10.1007/978-3-319-20901-2_39

2   Status Quo of Mobility Application Development and Offered Services

Prevailing mobility applications already have a large number of features well established in terms of their technical feasibility. IT specialists are able to realize complex applications in the areas of information retrieval, route selection, favorite setting, navigation, travel companionship, alerts or ticket purchasing. However, the informational support of intermodal crosslinking as well as a seamless integration of different mobility services still has great potential. Figure 1 displays the result of a portfolio analysis of 35 mobility applications offered on the German market.

For the analysis, 22 functions were defined to characterize the information and service level of mobility applications along the travel chain. Following the approach of the Boston Consulting Group Portfolio Matrix [2], the vertical axis represents the degree of innovation and the horizontal axis displays the user satisfaction scores of each application. The innovation degree arose from the nature and scope of the different functions in combination with the number of highly innovative features. The user satisfaction scores were transferred from the application ratings found on the website of the iTunes App Store and Google Play Store respectively.

The result of the portfolio analysis shows that a variety of applications provides good functional core services but is improvable in terms of their innovation degree (cash cows). Far fewer applications (stars) offer very innovative features such as dynamic maps, augmented reality/3D function, voice navigation, proactive companion services, indoor routing, social network connections and crowdsourcing. Although some applications, such as Nokia HERE Transit, have a lot of innovative features, they are not able to convince the users with their performance (question marks) [1].

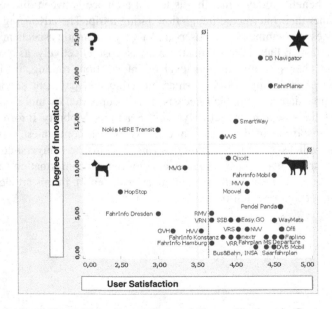

Fig. 1. Portfolio analysis of prevailing mobility applications in Germany [1]

Therefore, the aim of the research project "Dynamic Seamless Mobility Information" is to develop a highly innovative intermodal mobility application including trendsetting indoor navigation features in order to overcome the shortcomings of existing applications.

3 Identification of General User Requirements for Intermodal Mobility Applications

3.1 Methodology for User Requirement Identification

In order to investigate the general user requirements for intermodal mobility applications the empirical research based on two methodological approaches:

Qualitative Interviews. In focus group interviews, as a form of qualitative research [3], the participants were asked about their perceptions, opinions, needs, and attitudes towards using mobility applications in different pre-, on- and post-trip situations. Questions were asked in several interactive group settings encouraging participants to communicate freely with other group members.

The participants of the focus groups in Dresden and Frankfurt were selected specifically in accordance with relevant criteria. Prerequisite was the occasional or regular use of public transport. Furthermore, participants had already retrieved traffic information via stationary websites before, and possess a smartphone. In total, at least two subjects in each group had to be using mobility applications actively. In terms of socio-demographic characteristics, a balanced composition regarding age, sex, place of residence (urban, suburban and rural areas), employment status, stage of life, etc., was intended. People with mobility disabilities were explicitly included in each group.

The guideline supported focus group interviews covered four basic services: Routing & Navigation, Dynamic Trip Guidance, Social Media and Intermodal Crosslinking.

The objective of the qualitative focus group interviews was to analyze the user's preferences and requirements for intermodal applications, especially with regard to

- their information needs and their pre-, on- and post-trip information behavior,
- the capabilities and requirements for their own orientation and guidance,
- their attitude towards social networks and how social networks can be helpfully integrated in mobility applications,
- the circumstances under which the subjects are willing to change the transport means and how the mobility applications could provide incentives to turn towards previously unused services such as car sharing or bike sharing,
- to develop a typology of different user groups.

Quantitative Interviews. In order to prove the plausibility of findings from the focus group interviews a broader online market survey with a larger sample was conducted. The principal user preferences concerning intermodal mobility applications were investigated using a standardized questionnaire [4]. The survey was conducted in the area of the Rhine-Main Transport Association in the German state of Hesse in the period of March to April 2014. The composition of the sample is shown in Fig. 2.

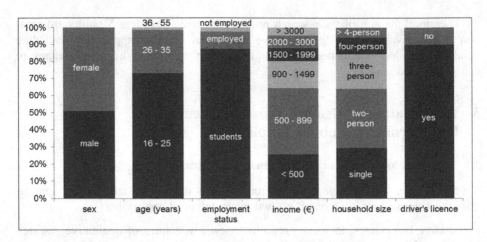

Fig. 2. Sample composition

The online questionnaire sent to 37,000 volunteers by e-mail accomplished a response rate of 5.3 % (i.e. 2000 fully completed questionnaires).

3.2 Selected Results of User Requirement Identification

The results of the qualitative and quantitative interviews described in Sect. 3.1 indicate:

- the **general user requirements** regarding the four basic services "Routing & Navigation", "Dynamic Trip Guidance", "Intermodal Crosslinking" and "Social Media"
- a **specific typology of user groups,** each of them in terms of their characteristics and user requirements for intermodal mobility applications internally homogeneous but clearly distinguishable from other groups externally.

General User Requirements. The following Table 1 summarizes the results of all focus groups as well as the online survey. It shows the most needed features and functions of mobility applications with reference to the four basic services. As an important result three user requirements could clearly be determined as the most needed and relevant ones across all phases of travel:

- automatic information about delays and disturbances of any kind
- calculation and display of alternative routes in case of disturbances
- automatic recognition of spontaneous target changes (or when entered manually) during the trip and recalculation of the route

User Typology. Based on the written and anonymized material of the focus group interviews a user typology was developed in four steps. Kelle's and Kluge's approach [5] served as methodological basis for the content analysis. As a result of this procedure four user types could be distinguished. They differ significantly from each other regarding the character traits "openness" and "level of structured behavior" (see Fig. 3).

The dimension "openness" includes a person's attitude towards recent technologies and the readiness to use or reject these. The dimension "level of structured behavior"

Table 1. Desired features and functions of basic services within mobility applications

Basic Service	Features	Functions
Routing & Navigation	route planning	• multimodal comparison of all transport modes with the possibility of intermodal linkage
	route planning and walking speed	• easy selection of walking speed "slow", "medium", "fast"; input of additional mobility restrictions such as luggage, bicycles, strollers etc. in order to calculate realistic transfer times • search options based on categories such as stations, POIs, addresses (auto-correction is must-have) • display of all available stops in the vicinity, not only the nearest
	details about stations, transfer hubs and whereabouts on the route	• to provide detailed information on station facilities such as ticket machines, lifts, stairs, restrooms, transfer spots, platforms, direction of travel etc. displayed by different symbols and signs
	indoor navigation	• to provide an overview about the complete building complex • navigation via images (also user-generated), landmarks, signs, and icons • use of augmented reality
	outdoor navigation	• in app-solutions desired (without using Google Maps) • synoptic view for related information (similar to Google Maps) • filter features for POI symbols, especially in case of augmented reality
Dynamic Trip Guidance	real-time data	• information about departure, scheduled and estimated time of arrival, delays, and disturbances in real-time • reliable information about assured connections
	storage of frequently traveled routes	• offline storage of the departure times for these routes • free choice whether information about disturbances are delivered via push or pull mode
	disturbance assistance	• reliable information about the cause and estimated duration of disturbances • planning of alternative routes • routing to the replacement station • information if the planned connection is at risk • automatic push message in case of deviation from schedule with respect to individual preferences
	inclusion of POIs in route calculation/rescheduling	• to take into account needed time for stopovers in the total routing • in case of delays, automatically finding and displaying alternative connections
Social Media	address transfer	• transferring start and destination addresses from social media (facebook, twitter, contact lists) • possibility of entering an address instead of a certain stop
	calendar	• link between the calendar and the mobility application to facilitate future trip planning • timely reminders • report of overlaps or disturbances on the planned route
	distrubance notifications via user networks	• relevance filter for notifications, only for important routes (routes with daily frequency, current route, interconnected route) • commuting features: Warning about disturbances on the daily route during the typical travel time causing tremendous delays • trouble notifications of users should be checked and verified by the transport operators
	complaints	• reporting complaints and irregularities (e. g. not working or damaged doors, windows, heating, air conditioners, ticket machines), gross dirt or lacking personnel services

Basic Service	Features	Functions
		• complaint forms allowing quick and easy information submission by predefined complaint categories • text editor to enter special incidents • quick response on complaints submitted
Intermodal Crosslinking	possible car and bike sharing services	• to provide notes for car/bike sharing services and appropriate information already during the initial setup of a mobility application • single sign-on for multiple service providers and offering "roaming" between different car and bike sharing providers
	taxi features	• display of different taxi providers • calculation of approximate price for selected trip • taxi request as an in-app solution
	ticketing	• ticket purchase on smartphones • to show the best ticket option • consideration of tariff zones and giving an alert when the valid tariff zone is left
	connection between public transport and use of private cars/ car sharing	• predictive journey time forecasting • display of P + R parking, including vacant capacities • calculation of additional time for searching parking space, transit times etc.
	choice and filter features	• display of available vehicles at car or bike sharing stations (vehicle type, state of charge, etc.) → car reservation and navigation to the station • reliable estimation of the route and arrival time should be given when shared vehicles are used on the route

describes the degree of personal planning needs, that is, whether a person acts more planned, structured and foresighted or rather spontaneously.

Subsequently, the main characteristics of the four user types are briefly described.

The Open-Minded Planner. The requirements of this user type are primarily aimed to his or her needs for structure. Those persons receive their needed security by planning. Statements such as "I'm not just going at random …" or "I always organize myself first before I leave…" are typical of this type of person. For the open-minded planner, the features and functions with regard to the basic service "routing and navigation" are most important, followed by the features of "dynamic travel guidance". His or her openness towards technical developments leaves a wide range for additional functions of mobility applications with a certain willingness to pay.

The Open and Flexible Type. This user type has the same enthusiasm for technology such as the open-minded planner, but requires much less structure and foresight. In extreme cases he or she is not even preparing for a journey. Statements like "and then I'll get from A to B somehow" are typical. He or she has much lower information needs and often makes spontaneous decisions. Therefore, the features and functions of "dynamic trip guidance" are most important for this person. The benefit for him or her using a mobility application is especially the retrieval of information, particularly in terms of real-time data. As a result, these users also have a great willingness to use sharing services (intermodal linkage), when access to these services is simple and straightforward.

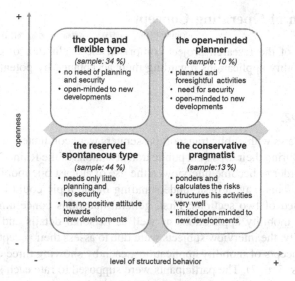

Fig. 3. User typology

The Conservative Pragmatist. Similar to the open-minded planner the decisions of this type are characterized by plans and structures. Information about the journey capabilities is searched at home on the Computer and frequently printed out for use while travelling. This type rarely falls back on smartphones or even mobility applications. The conservative pragmatist mostly uses his own vehicle and is only willing to switch to alternative transport means in case of incidents or unusual events. Then, car sharing options are taken into consideration as well as taxi features. These should be included in the application within the basic service "intermodal crosslinking".

The Reserved Spontaneous Type. This type has the lowest scores regarding the two dimensions "openness" and "level of structured behavior". In its spontaneity he or she is similar to the open-minded flexible type. In most cases, there is no time pressure and therefore no need to plan the routes carefully or to synchronize times. A typical statement is: "I always say, as long as the tracks are there, a train will come." Furthermore, trips on unfamiliar routes and in foreign cities are often taken by surprise. Towards recent technical developments this type is not very open-minded. This may even extend to a total refusal of smartphones and services. Thus, the reserved spontaneous type is the user group that can be associated least with a mobility application. The requirements are mainly related to obtain clear and easy accessible information. Additional functions and features seem rather daunting.

As Fig. 3 shows, the shares of the "open and flexible type" (34 %) and the "reserved spontaneous type" (44 %) are the highest within the sample. Therefore, the features and functions of mobility applications supporting particularly pre-, on-, and post-trip spontaneity as well as information retrieval (see Table 1) have the best performance measures and are needed most.

4 Evaluation of Operating Concepts

The second part of the research project comprised the evaluation of eight operating concepts for mobility applications regarding their acceptance by potential users.

4.1 Methodology

1,884 oral interviews with public transport passengers were conducted in November and December 2014 during their trips or at public transit stations of the Rhine-Main Transport Association. In order to become interviewee the use of at least one mobility application was prerequisite. This way, a basic understanding of the topic could be ensured. The interview consisted of two sections: First, general questions concerning the mobility behavior, use of mobility applications as well as personal details and attitudes were included. Secondly, the interview subjects were due to assess their acceptance regarding the operating concepts of mobility applications, each by showing three different screen designs (e.g. Figs. 5, 6, 7). The participants were supposed to rate each screenshot on a scale from 1 (poor operating concept) to 7 (good operating concept).

The following operating concepts had to be scored: Menu design, route search, route options overview, route details, social media, mode choice, indoor navigation and map display. Moreover, in-depth questions concerning different aspects of each concept were included.

In order to validate the user typology mentioned in Sect. 3.2 a cluster analysis was conducted. The dimensions "level of structured behavior" and "openness towards technologies" were determined by calculating the mean of five relating items. A two-step cluster analysis was applied comprising the Ward-Method in order to find the optimal number of clusters as well as the K-Means Cluster Analysis [6] for allocating the interviewees to the right clusters.

4.2 Results

The cluster analysis found evidence for four groups of participants. Figure 4 shows their size and position within the two dimensions. Table 2 gives an overview of characteristics describing the identified groups.

Especially cluster 4 is located slightly apart from the rest. This group mainly consists of participants at the age above 65 years who use public transit regularly. This cluster is neither very open-minded concerning technical innovations nor plans its trips intensively.

Table 2. Cluster characteristics

Cluster	Openness	Level of structuredness	Public transit use	Age
1	+	−	often	younger
2	+	+	*(no result)*	middle-aged
3	++	++	very often	*(no result)*
4	−−	−	occasional and regular	above 65 years

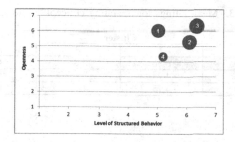

Fig. 4. Results of cluster analysis

Each of the eight operating concepts was analyzed separately. It has to be mentioned that the mean ratings are very close to each other. Therefore interpretation has to be done carefully. Generally, the existing operating concept from the Rhine-Main Transport Association was favored by the subjects. This effect must also be taken into account when assessing the results. Nevertheless, many differences reveal interesting preferences and attitudes. In the following, three selected operating concept evaluations will be presented

Operating Concept: Route Search. The results indicate the very classic operating concept for route searching is favored by the majority of interviewees (Fig. 5, screen 1). Especially frequent transit users, however, approve of the second screen which has a very modern design using only few buttons and additional options. Moreover, often used locations should be represented by shortcuts (e.g. photos) as seen in screen 3 (Fig. 5).

Operating Concept: Route Details. Generally, a design as seen on the second screen for displaying route details is barely accepted by the subjects. Tables seem to be a more appropriate format, especially for younger people. Further support regarding a better navigation than a simple route description is not desired (Table 4).

Cluster 4 rates screen 1 and 3 with very low values. Screen 2 however is favored by them. The higher average age in this group might cause a preference for less text.

Operating Concept: Indoor Navigation. Regarding indoor navigation, the most preferred solution uses augmented reality (Fig. 7, screen 1) in order to transfer the right instructions at the right time. Nevertheless, especially the elderly find written

Fig. 5. Screenshots: Route search (screen 1, 2, 3 from left to right)

Table 3. Mean ratings for operating concept "route search"

Mean Ratings	Cluster				Total Sample
	1	2	3	4	
Screen 1	6.30	6.30	6.34	4.98	5.79
Screen 2	4.55	4.94	3.07	3.13	4.90
Screen 3	4.76	4.75	4.72	4.90	4.56

Fig. 6. Screenshots: Route details (screen 1, 2, 3 from left to right)

Table 4. Mean ratings for operating concept "route details"

Mean Ratings	Cluster				Total Sample
	1	2	3	4	
Screen 1	6.32	6.42	6.16	3.11	5.62
Screen 2	4.71	4.75	4.81	4.67	4.78
Screen 3	4.74	4.64	4.64	3.07	5.41

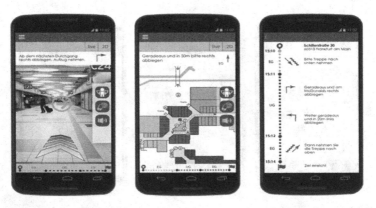

Fig. 7. Screenshots: Indoor navigation (screen 1, 2, 3 from left to right)

Table 5. Mean ratings for operating concept "indoor navigation"

Mean Ratings	Cluster				Total Sample
	1	2	3	4	
Screen 1	6,36	6,46	4,49	3,43	5,51
Screen 2	4,78	4,76	4,64	3,32	4,22
Screen 3	4,91	4,69	4,14	3,61	4,96

descriptions more helpful (Fig. 7, screen 3). Furthermore, intense public transit users have higher preferences for augmented reality than others (Table 5).

Cluster 3 and 4 gave low grades to all screenshots. Even though cluster 3 is open-minded concerning technical innovations, augmented reality elements could not convince these interviewees. On the contrary, the rather open-minded participants of cluster 1 and 2 show very high mean ratings for this operating concept.

5   Critical Assessment and Outlook

The investigation of detailed user requirements for mobile applications was very challenging. Every single user has specific requirements. Should these be implemented in one single application, it quickly becomes overloaded. Nevertheless, in order to successfully implement a "one design for all" approach the user requirements have to be balanced against each other. The developers should try to implement tailored packages of operating options for a few main user types.

Another problem was the identification of innovative future functionalities, as in most cases the subjects only had a limited knowledge and imagination. Therefore, it could be helpful to integrate research results from expert surveys.

References

1. Marsch, S.: DYNAMO: Analyse des Marktes für Mobilitätsapplikationen. Internal research paper, p. 62. Technische Universität Dresden, Dresden (2014)
2. Morrison, A., Wensley, R.: Boxing up or boxed in?: a short history of the boston consulting group share/growth matrix. J. Mark. Manage. **7**, 105–129 (1991)
3. Marshall, C., Rossman, G.B.: Designing Qualitative Research, 3rd edn. p. 115. Sage Publications, London (1999)
4. Thielsch, M.T., Weltzin, S.: Online-Umfragen und Online-Mitarbeiterbefragungen. In: Praxis der Wirtschaftspsychologie II: Themen und Fallbeispiele für Studium und Anwendung, pp. 109–217. MV Wissenschaft, Münster (2012)
5. Kelle, U., Kluge, S.: Vom Einzelfall zum Typus. Fallvergleich und Fallkontrastierung in der qualitativen Sozialforschung, pp. 91 et seqq. VS Verlag für Sozialwissenschaften, Wiesbaden (2010)
6. Arthur, D., Vassilvitskii, S.: k-means ++: The advantages of careful seeding. In: Proceedings of the Eighteenth Annual ACM-SIAM Symposium on Discrete Algorithms, pp. 1027–1035. Society for Industrial and Applied Mathematics (2007)

Reduce Complexity by Increasing Abstraction in Interactive Visual Components

Pedro M. Teixeira-Faria[1(✉)] and Javier Rodeiro Iglesias[2]

[1] School of Technology and Management,
Polytechnic Institute of Viana Do Castelo, Viana Do Castelo, Portugal
pfaria@estg.ipvc.pt
[2] School of Informatics Engineering, University of Vigo, Vigo, Spain
jrodeiro@uvigo.es

Abstract. The objective of this study is to introduce a method to abstract complex components in order to create a complete and functional user interface, simplifying the complexity process of user interface design. An example of a simple user interface of a game for younger children is explained and its visual states and transitions represented through a state diagram. However, the level of detail provided by simple components, to represent the user interface is very extensive, making lengthy the interface designing process. Thus, it was decided to increase the abstraction level by introducing a new complex component structure which, due to its encapsulation feature, allows to group components into other more complex components, but with more functionality. An abstraction process through grouping components by levels is detailed, with the intention of proving the validity of the *complex component* concept to simplify the creation of complete, free and functional user interfaces.

Keywords: Abstract interaction objects · Complex components · Visual interface representation

1 Introduction

In previous studies [8] an interactive visual user interface prototype was created, based in the direct manipulation interaction style. After the interface has been implemented it was considered that probably the implementation work could have been reduced if the system embraced a more abstract component concept. Much work in the field of interactive graphics involves describing an interface in terms of a collection of *interaction objects* [3, 6, 9]. An AIO represents a user interface object without any graphical representation and independent of any environment [10]. Usually, is understood as a conceptual representation of an interface object. A *concrete interaction object* (*CIO*) represents any visible and manageable user interface visual component that can be used to input/output information related to user's interactive task and are sometimes called *widgets* (*windows gadgets*). After analyzing the features of 3 AIOs available in the literature, it was considered the possibility to use *complex components* to create the same previous game interface. A detailed process to abstract *complex components* is used to verify the components assembling process, in order to increase the level of

© Springer International Publishing Switzerland 2015
M. Kurosu (Ed.): Human-Computer Interaction, Part I, HCII 2015, LNCS 9169, pp. 426–437, 2015.
DOI: 10.1007/978-3-319-20901-2_40

abstraction. The abstraction term is here introduced with the meaning of simplification, through component's encapsulation. In this way, it was considered to reduce the number of components necessary to use to design and to represent a user interface functionality, in spite of these components being more complex (with more functionality) as the abstraction level grows. Then, a user interface analysis is presented, considering the level of encapsulation (abstraction) introduced by complex components usage, considering the number of events, global transitions and visual states. Following, some conclusions related with the study are presented.

2 Defined Problem

The interactive visual user interface prototype previously created [8] consists of a simple game for younger children, containing visual elements representing sport balls and sport fields. It was possible to use a system to create the visual interface from an abstract representation which uses *simple components (SCs)*. After the 2D visual game interface had been specified using *SCs*, and a prototype be created, it was possible to verify and to conclude that the level of detail needed to specify visual interface components, using that system, is too deep and the specification becomes too complex for the size of actual direct manipulation interfaces, becoming impracticable the extensive use of it. Thus, it was decided to simplify the design process through seeking for a method to reduce the number of components needed to build a user interface.

3 Complex Components

The notion of *interaction object* do not need to be confined to graphics systems, because it represents a useful structure for thinking and reasoning about the behavior of interactive systems in general [3, 5]. In the interface designing process, it could be necessary the appropriate (AIOs) selection and four of them were analyzed: *interactor*, *abstract data view*, *virtual interaction object* and *complex component*. A concept of *interactor* has been introduced by [4, 6]. It is a component (object) in the description of an interactive system. The *interactors* do not indicate a specification language, but an adequate structure to model an interactive system. It appears as an algebraic conceptualization whose usefulness will be higher in the formal analysis of an interactive system. Some authors advocate the concept of dialog independence, where interactive systems are designed and implemented with the goal of providing a clear separation between the user interface and the application [1]. A user interface design concept which corresponds to that is the *Abstract Data View (ADV)* [2]. However, its specification is not considered in the context of a complete interface, focusing primarily on defining simple components with multiple states and the relationship between them. According with [9], in the context of user interface development, *interaction objects* play a key role for implementing the constructional and behavioral aspects of *interaction*. The author introduced the concept of *virtual interaction objects*, as synonymous of (AIOs). However, they are dependent of different interface toolkits supported by different platforms.

Thus, as none of the 3 previous analyzed AIOs supports components composition, it was decided to verify a new component structure [7] which supports that feature, among others related with supporting visual appearance and interaction: the *complex component*. Basically, a *CC* is a component composed of other components (simple/complex) which interact with each other through its *self events* (*SEs*) and *delegate events/actions* (*DEs/DAs*) working toward a common goal (e.g. a toolbar allows a user to select a specific tool to perform some task at a given time). *DEs* and *DAs* are together a union mechanism concept related with communication between *complex components*. *SEs* are encapsulated in a *complex component* and its internal functionality is responsible for triggering *DAs*, which will be responsible for triggering *DEs* that other *complex components* will receive. The detail of these internal *DAs* functionality is occluded from the interface designer who just needs to establish the connection between complex components through their *DEs*.

4 Detailed Process

In order to build the game interface previously indicated, 15 *simple components* were used. For each sport ball, three possible visual states have been created (*normal*, *selected* and *correct*) while in the case of the sport fields two visual states were created (*normal* and *correct*).

After creating all possible visual states of each component, it has been defined which components respond at which events (the balls and the sport fields in this case). It was decided to use the "*LeftClick*" event detection for the user interaction. The complete functionality of the game is represented by 20 states (nodes) and 48 transitions (arcs) between those states (Fig. 1). The initial state is represented by (*State 0*) and the final state is represented by (*State 19*). The connections (transitions) between the

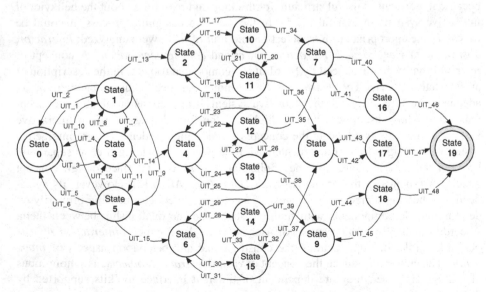

Fig. 1. State diagram representing the 48 game interface visual transitions

nodes (states) always have two parameters associated: the component of the original node and the event which triggers the visual state change. In order to simplify the state diagram understanding of this game interface example was decided to not include the information related with event identification, once the user event is always the same.

4.1 Complex Components: Level 0

The complexity to represent a user interface is given by the number of components and the number of events to consider, in order representing all the global visual states to be obtained, from visual transitions generated by user interaction with the interface components. Following, an analysis is made to the process (distributed over 4 levels) of creating the interface functionality using *complex components*. When considering the *complex component* concept we always need to establish an entrance level, on which will be defined the *simple components* to be used on a user interface and all the possible *visual transitions* between them. The *simple components* will be responsible for the interface visual aspect. In the case of the game previously described, at this level (*Level 0*) we will have 15 visual *simple components* and 12 possible visual transitions (Fig. 2) between them.

4.1.1 Simple Visual Components: Level 0

Each of the three balls can assume:

- (normal) visual state (SC_Ball_i_N, i = {1, 2, 3});
- (selected) visual state (SC_Ball_i_S, i = {1, 2, 3});
- (correct) visual state (SC_Ball_i_C, i = {1, 2, 3}).

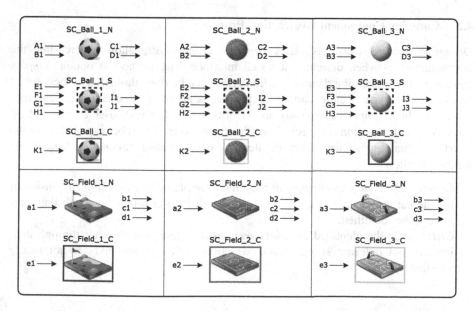

Fig. 2. 15 visual states and 12 visual transitions from *simple components*

Concerning the fields, they can assume:

- (normal) visual state (SC_Field_i_N, i = {1, 2, 3});
- (correct) visual state (SC_Field_i_C, i = {1, 2, 3}).

Throughout this paper the terms (*normal*, *selected* and *correct*) are used to identify the *complex components* visual states.

4.1.2   Visual Transitions: Level 0

The game functionality, previously described, indicates 4 distinct types of visual transitions that may occur between the referred 15 *simple components*:

- TB_1 – Pass the ball from the (normal) state to the (selected) state; (SC_Ball_i_N $\rightarrow$ SC_Ball_i_S, where i = {1, 2, 3});
- TB_2 – Pass the ball from the (selected) state to the (normal) state; (SC_Ball_i_S $\rightarrow$ SC_Ball_i_N, where i = {1, 2, 3});
- TB_3 – Pass the ball from the (selected) state to the (correct) state; (SC_Ball_i_S $\rightarrow$ SC_Ball_i_C, where i = {1, 2, 3});
- TF – Pass the field from the (normal) state to the (correct) state; (SC_Field_i_N $\rightarrow$ SC_Field_i_C, where i = {1, 2, 3}).

We consider a visual transition as a visual state change, triggered by an event (resulted from user interaction with the interface). According with the number of *simple components* and the game rules established, each of the 4 distinct visual transitions types may occur 3 times (3 visual transitions for each ball and 1 visual transition for each field). These transitions may occur triggered by events from the user or from the components itself.

4.2   Complex Component Abstraction Process

Designing hierarchically organized *complex components*, allows increasing the abstraction level when designing a visual interface. The method to obtain *complex components* by increasing their abstraction levels can be done through a process based on an iterative cycle. Before starting the process is necessary to establish an entrance level, in which *simple components* are identified together with user events and all possible visual transitions between them (those components will be responsible for the interface visual appearance). Then, the iterative cycle to abstract *complex components* follows 3 criteria:

- **Criterion 1**: a *complex component* must have *simple/complex components* inside of it (internal components) and the (*SEs*) in result of user interaction with the components be identified;
- **Criterion 2**: the identified *complex components* relate to each other through their input/output *delegate events/actions* which (or other conditions) are not totally satisfied;

– *Criterion 3*: with respect to new *complex component* creation conditions, if the interface is not fully functional and some of the *complex components* still have input/output (*DE/DA*) or other conditions not totally satisfied (e.g. still waiting for some preconditions to be accomplished), the abstraction level can be increased through grouping components.

On next level (*Level 1*) *simple components* will be grouped into *complex components*. Each ball can have 3 different visual representations and will be grouped in one *complex component*. Each field will be made of 2 different visual representations, which will also be grouped in one *complex component*. Following, 6 different *complex components* and their functionality will be verified.

4.3   Complex Components: Level 1

This second level corresponds to the first abstraction level of *complex components* creation: 6 *complex components* are created. Each ball CC_Ball_i, $i = \{1, 2, 3\}$ aggregates 3 *simple components* with their 2 user events and their 3 visual transitions and they can be represented as $CC\_Ball\_i = \{SC\_Ball\_i\_N, SC\_Ball\_i\_S, SC\_Ball\_i\_C\}$. The visual states of each ball *complex component* (CC_Ball_i) are directly related with the *simple components* that represent them. For this game, each visual state of a ball *complex component* is represented by a single *simple component* ($SC\_Ball\_i\_k$, $k = \{N, S, C\}$). The visual state of a ball *complex component* (CC_Ball_i) assumes the visual state of the *simple component* ($CC\_Ball\_i\_k$, where $i = \{1, 2, 3\}$ and $k = \{N, S, C\}$). The other three *complex components* are related with the fields: CC_Field_i, $i = \{1, 2, 3\}$. Each field aggregates 2 *simple components* ($CC\_Field\_i = \{SC\_Field\_i\_N, SC\_Field\_i\_C\}$) with its unique user event and his unique visual transition. Analogously to the balls, each field *complex component* (CC_Field_i) has two visual states ($CC\_Field\_i\_k$, where $i = \{1, 2, 3\}$ and $k = \{N, C\}$). At this first abstraction level, the 6 *complex components* are mutually independent. Each one has his visual states and accepts events which produce their transitions. Furthermore, initially there isn't any communication between those *complex components*.

4.3.1   Components User Interaction: Level 1

On (*Level 0*) 9 user events were considered, with which the user interacts in the game interface. At this present level (*Level 1*) creating the three ball *complex components* (CC_Ball_i, $i = \{1, 2, 3\}$) each of them reduces by one the number of user events to be considered. Six user events exist (*mouse click*) ($A'1$, $A'2$, $A'3$, $a1$, $a2$ and $a3$) (Fig. 3) which may be triggered over six different *complex components*. Exemplifying for the ($A'1$) event, this represents a mouse click on the (CC_Ball_1) *complex component* which is responsible for 2 visual transitions (TB_1 or TB_2). These two transitions are triggered by user interaction with the (*normal*) visual state or with the (*selected*) visual state, respectively. In the case of the fields, for each *complex component* only one visual state may receive user interaction (e.g. to click in (CC_Field_1) is equivalent to click in ($CC\_Field\_1\_N$) with ($a1$) user event). At the present level (*Level 1*) the user may trigger 6 user events over 6 *complex components*, reducing in 3 the number of user events to be managed.

### 4.3.2	Visual States and Transitions: Level 1

After 6 user events occurring over 6 *complex components* had been identified is important to detail the *self* and *delegate events* that proceed in result of user interaction with those *complex components* producing transitions between visual states. (Figure 3) represents components visual transitions (TB_1, TB_2, TB_3 and TF) that occur in result of *self* and *delegate events* (and *delegate actions*) possible to be triggered by user or by *complex components*. The interface functionality does not become complete, just using the 6 *complex components* (individually) and it is necessary to establish the missing links between *complex components*. The dashed arrows in gray represent *delegate events/actions* necessary to be enabled in order to the game interface become fully functional (each arrow corresponds to one *delegate action* triggered by a *complex component* and one *delegate event* received by another *complex component*). Each ball and each field receives a user event (*mouse click*). In the case of the balls, (TB_1) or (TB_2) transitions (represented by 6 black arrows) are triggered after user interaction ($A'1$, $A'2$ or $A'3$) which produces a *self event* over a ball.

For each ball, ($CC\_Ball\_i\_N$) visual state can change to ($CC\_Ball\_i\_S$) visual state, or the reverse, through (TB_1) or (TB_2) visual transitions, respectively. These transitions are triggered by user interaction ($A'i$) over a ball visual state ($CC\_Ball\_i\_k$, where $i = \{1, 2, 3\}$ and $k = \{N, S\}$) and can be represented by the function:

$$A'i = \begin{cases} TB\_1 \ if \ k = N \\ TB\_2 \ if \ k = S \end{cases} \tag{1}$$

In the case of the fields, at this moment, doesn't occur any visual transition triggered by user interaction. (TF) transitions still inactive because they depend on relations to be established between components, external to the fields. In the particular example of this game interface, at this level (*Level 1*) the functionality of each one of these 6 *complex components* doesn't allows yet triggering *delegate events* (not internally nor externally). Still considering the information provided by (Fig. 3) is verifiable that besides 6 user events ($A'1$, $A'2$, $A'3$, $a1$, $a2$ and $a3$) another 30 (15/15) *delegate events/actions* produce (TB_2 and TB_3) transitions (indicated over gray dashed arrows). (TF) transitions are triggered by ($a1$, $a2$ and $a3$) user events. Each ball receives 1 *user event* (corresponding to 2 *self events*), receives 5 *delegate events* and enables 2 *actions* in other components. In the case of the fields, each one receives 1 user event (corresponding to 1 *self event*), receives 0 *delegate events* and triggers 2 *actions* on other components.

### 4.3.3	Completing Visual Interface: Level 1

Until now, the analysis on creating the game visual interface using the 6 *complex components* (individually) demonstrates that the interface functionality is not complete because some transitions are only activated by *delegate events* triggered at a higher level of *complex component* abstraction or directly by the user interface designer, who

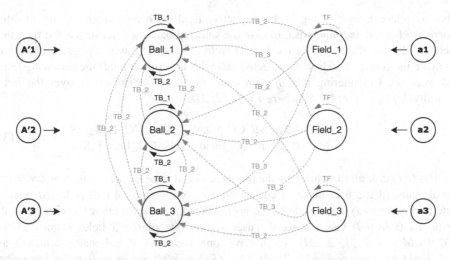

Fig. 3. Visual transitions of 6 *complex components* (*Level 1*)

has to manually establish the missing links between *complex components*. At this first *complex component* level, using 6 *complex components* without completing their functionality, some other invalid visual states and visual transitions could occur. Considering the game rules (in which only one ball can be selected at a time) and the possible user events over a ball, the following task was set: assuming that $A'j$ represents an user event (*mouse click*) over a Ball (*CC_Ball_j*, $j = \{1, 2, 3\}$) which can have one of the three possible visible states (*normal (N)*, *selected (S)* or *correct (C)*) identified as *CC_Ball_j_k*, where $k = \{N, S, C\}$ and $j = \{1, 2, 3\}$ a new (*BT*) task is defined, based on possible transitions:

$$BT(j, i) = \begin{cases} TB\_1 \ if \ k = N \wedge j = i \\ TB\_2 \ if \ k = S \wedge j = i \\ TB\_2 \ if \ k = S \wedge j \neq i \end{cases} \tag{2}$$

The (*BT*) task guarantees that just one ball can be selected at a time and allows changing (*CC_Ball_i*) visual states, according with game rules. When the user selects a ball (*CC_Ball_j*, $j = \{1, 2, 3\}$) that means (*BT*) task will verify the ball visual state, comparing it with all the balls visual state (*CC_Ball_i*, $i = \{1, 2, 3\}$):

- If the user clicks on a ball represented by CC_Ball_j and that is in (normal) state, the (BT) task executes a (TB_1) transition, which allows that ball to change his visual state from (normal) to (selected);
- If the user clicks on a ball and that already is in (selected) state the (BT) task executes a (TB_2) transition;
- For the other balls the (BT) task executes (*TB_2*) transitions for each ball that is in (*selected*) state.

The interface designer needs to establish relationships between the 3 *complex components* (balls) and the other 3 *complex components* (fields) and to ensure that: after a ball is selected, by clicking in the respective field, both components change to the (*correct*) visual state. Otherwise, in case the selected ball does not match the field the user has clicked, the ball is deselected. Therefore, according with the game objective (to make the correct match of the selected ball with the correct field) the following (*FT*) task was set. Considering that *aj* represents an event (*mouse click*) over the field identified by (*CC_Field_j_N, where j = {1, 2, 3}*):

$$FT(j, i) = \begin{cases} TF \wedge TB\_3 \; if \; \text{CC\_Field\_j\_N} \rightarrow \text{CC\_Ball\_i\_S} \\ TB\_2 \quad if \; \text{CC\_Field\_j\_N} \nrightarrow \text{CC\_Ball\_i\_S} \end{cases} \tag{3}$$

The (*FT*) task allows changing the interface visual state by activating new (*correct*) visual states (if the user makes a correct choice) or changing a ball (*selected*) visual state to the (*normal*) visual state (if the user makes an incorrect choice). After one ball be on its (*selected*) visual state, the user selects one of the 3 fields (*mouse click*) (*CC_Field_j, j = {1, 2, 3}*) which have one (*normal*) visual state identified as (*CC_Field_j_N, where j = {1, 2, 3}*). This (*FT*) task allows executing the following transitions:

- (*TB_3*) and (*TF*) transitions, if the field in which the user has clicked corresponds to the correct ball already selected (CC_Ball_i_S). That means, if the selected ball corresponds to the chosen field, both complex components (CC_Ball_i and CC_Field_j) change to the correct visual state (CC_Ball_i_C and CC_Field_j_C);
- (*TB_2*) transition, if there is no correct correspondence between the selected ball and the chosen field, which means that the ball on (*selected*) visual state changes to its (*normal*) visual state.

The correct connection will be validated by the (*FT*) task. The (*CC_Field_j*) (*TF*) transition results from a *self event* triggered by user interaction with one field. The (*CC_Ball_i*) (*TB_3*) transition is not directly related with user interaction, but is triggered by a *delegate event* received from the field correctly chosen by user. Both (*TF* and *TB_3*) transitions are simultaneously triggered and correspond both to the ball and the field final visual states (the *correct* states). Thus, the interface designer achieves the complete game interface functionality through establishment of missing connections between the 6 *complex components*. Following will be presented the interface representation considering the use of two *complex components*.

4.4 Complex Components: Level 2

At this abstraction level, 2 *complex components* are created (*CC_Balls* and *CC_Fields*). Each one aggregates 3 *complex components* defined in the previous level (*Level 1*): (*CC_Balls = {CC_Ball_i, i = 1, 2, 3}* and *CC_Fields = {CC_Field_i, i = 1, 2, 3}*). Each one (*CC_Balls*) and (*CC_Fields*) *complex component* acts as a container and represents examples of components with more than one visual state and more than one interaction. At this abstraction level is considered that the user may interact (*mouse click*) with 2 *complex components* representing the balls and the fields. Two user events exist (*mouse click*) (*A* and *a*) which may be triggered over the 2 *complex components* (*CC_Balls* and

CC_Fields). Therefore, at this level, a single user event acts on (*CC_Balls*) component which corresponds to click in one of the 3 interaction areas and whose action may trigger *self* or *delegate events*. The analogy is identical in the case of (*CC_Fields*). At this level, looking at the way *complex components* are structured, initially 2 new components exist, independent between each other (*CC_Balls* and *CC_Fields*). After the 2 *complex components* (*CC_Balls* and *CC_Fields*) have been created, the interface designer will verify that it can use them to complete the visual interface. For the interface functionality becomes complete (in order to obtain all the possible global visual transitions) it becomes necessary to make the connection between the 2 *complex components*, manually establishing the missed links between these 2 components, through their *delegate events/actions*. One possible way to complete this game interface could be using the rules established by (*FT*) task, previously defined, which establish the necessary links between balls and fields.

4.5 Complete Complex Component

After using the *complex component abstraction process* previously detailed, it was verified that is not possible to represent a complete and functional user interface through one *complex component* (has it could be the optimal result of this process). This happens because the final interface cannot fully respect the *Criterion 3* concerned with the *CC abstraction process*. Thus, the *final interface* is obtained through a *complete complex component* (*CCC*) which represents a complete visual object composed of related visual components, absolutely independent of any other interface components and in this case the complete game interface.

5 Reducing Complexity by Using Complex Components

In this section we intend to analyze the interface game representation process using two or six *complex components*. At (Level 1) above described, and considering the representation of six *complex components*, just the internal visual changes between states of each *complex component* are available. These visual changes result from transitions between the *normal*, the *selected* and the *correct* states. It is responsibility of the interface designer to complete the final representation of the game, establishing the missing links between the six *complex components*, through their *delegate events/actions*. At this level, the nine *self events* related to the six user events that can be triggered over the six *complex components* are already represented. It remains to establish the representation of 15 *delegate events* and the 15 (related) *delegate actions*, to the interface functionality becomes complete. To achieve that, the interface designer may implement the (*BT*) and the (*TF*) tasks which complete the missing functionality. In the second abstraction level, using two *complex components*, one of the interface functionality conditions, which requires that only one ball could be selected at a time, is already established. Therefore, the interface designer just needs to ensure proper connection between the balls and the fields. To achieve that, he must establish the representation of 9 *delegate events* and the 9 (related) *delegate actions*, in order to

Table 1. Using *simple components* versus *complex components*

number of	level 0	level 1	level 2
components	15 (SC)	6 (CC)	2 (CC)
visual states	20	20	20
global visual transitions	48	48	48
user events	9	6	6
self events	×	9	9
simple events	60	×	×
delegate events/actions	×	30	18
total events	60	36	24

complete the interface functionality. The interface designer can overcome this by implementing the (*TF*) task, which will complete the interface functionality.

In summary, comparing the representation of the game interface using six or using two *complex components* versus using *simple components*, it is verifiable that in both situations the complete functionality of the game is obtained, with the 20 visual states and the 48 possible transitions being represented. At (*Level 0*) above described, is necessary to create 60 single events, while considering the (*Level 1*) or (*Level 2*) of abstraction only 30 and 18 *delegate events/actions*, respectively, need to be established (Table 1). Also, a reduction on the number of user events necessary to be considered (less 3 user events) is obtained when comparing between using *simple components* and 6 or 2 *complex components*.

6 Conclusions

A test bed user interface was specified as a set of *SCs* [8] and as a set of *CCs* (as described in this paper). In both situations, the user understands the interface as a unique entity. Concerning the user interface specification, a simplification is observed when using the proposed *CCs* compared with the use of *SCs*. This simplification can be observed at:

- *Visual presentation*: the process of changing a *SC* is individually done. In the case of a *CC*, the visual state change process is encapsulated and internally done through the *SEs* available in the *CC*;
- *Component composition*: the possibility to group *SCs* into a *CC* and also to group *CCs* into other *CCs* allows to establish their positions with a single operation;
- *Component dialog*: the encapsulation provided by *CCs* allows to group components into other more *CCs*, but with more functionality. When a *CC* is used it will successively activate events, not only on the present *CC*, but also on the *CCs* contained in it. Therefore, there is a proliferation of events inherited from the *CCs* inside of it.

The apparent complexity perceived from the vast number of events involved is actually simplified by using *CCs*. Since the whole interaction process between *CCs* becomes totally transparent to the interface designer, the number of events that the interface designer has to control is reduced. This reduction is obtained as a consequence of the unneeded control of the interface designer over the *DAs* behaviour inside *CCs*. The designer just needs to verify the *SEs* (which arrive to the *CC*) and to identify the *DEs* in other *CCs*. From the interface abstraction analysis described in this paper, it was possible to verify that as the user interface abstraction increases through *CCs* encapsulation, more simplified becomes the user interface design, due to: (a) reduced number of needed components; and (b) simpler components to be used, due to the reduced number of events that the interface designer has to control.

Acknowledgments. This work was partially supported by:

(1) Grant SFRH/PROTEC/49496/2009 of MCTES – Ministério da Ciência, Tecnologia e Ensino Superior (Portugal).

(2) Project TIN2009-14103-C03-03 of Ministerio de Ciencia e Innovación (Spain)

(3) Project 10DPI305002PR of Xunta de Galicia (Spain).

References

1. Alencar, P., et al.: A Formal Approach to Design Pattern Definition & Application. University of Waterloo, Ontario (1995). http://citeseerx.ist.psu.edu/viewdoc/summary?doi= 10.1.1.51.5451
2. Alencar, P., Cowan, D., Lucena, C.: A logical theory of interfaces and objects. IEEE Trans. Software Eng. **28**(6), 548–575 (2002)
3. Carr, D.: Specification of interface interaction objects. In: CHI 1994 – ACM Conference on Human Factors in Computer Systems, pp. 372–378 (1994)
4. Duke, D., Harrison, M.: Abstract interaction objects. Comput. Graph. Forum **12**(3), 25–36 (1993)
5. Duke, D., Faconti, G., Harrison, M., Paternó, F.: Unifying views of interactors. In: Proceedings of the Workshop on Advanced Visual Interfaces, pp. 143–152, 1–4 June 1994
6. Faconti, G., Paternó, F.: An approach to the formal specification of the components of an interaction. In: Eurographics 1990, North-Holland, pp. 481–494 (1990)
7. Teixeira-Faria, P.M., Iglesias, J.R.: Complex components abstraction in graphical user interfaces. In: Jacko, J.A. (ed.) Human-Computer Interaction, Part I, HCII 2011. LNCS, vol. 6761, pp. 309–318. Springer, Heidelberg (2011)
8. Iglesias, J.R., Teixeira-Faria, P.M.: User interface representation using simple components. In: Jacko, J.A. (ed.) Human-Computer Interaction, Part I, HCII 2011. LNCS, vol. 6761, pp. 278–287. Springer, Heidelberg (2011)
9. Savidis, A.: Supporting virtual interaction objects with polymorphic platform bindings in a user interface programming language. In: International Workshop on Rapid Integration of Software Engineering Methods (RISE 2004), pp. 11–23. Springer Verlag, Luxembourg (2005)
10. Pinheiro da Silva, P.: User interface declarative models and development environments: a survey. In: Paternó, F. (ed.) DSV-IS 2000. LNCS, vol. 1946, pp. 207–226. Springer, Heidelberg (2001)

Graphical User Interface for Search of Mathematical Expressions with Regular Expressions

Takayuki Watabe[1](✉) and Yoshinori Miyazaki[2]

[1] Graduate School of Science and Technology, Shizuoka University,
Shizuoka, Japan
dgs13012@s.inf.shizuoka.ac.jp
[2] Graduate School of Informatics, Shizuoka University, Shizuoka, Japan
yoshi@inf.shizuoka.ac.jp

Abstract. This paper discusses a pattern-matching method with regular expressions for mathematical expressions on electronic documents. In ordinary regular expressions, a pattern is described as a string with meta-characters. However, strings are unsuitable for mathematical expressions because of their two-dimensional structure (e.g., fractions, superscripts, and subscripts). In addition, meta-characters for regular expressions are frequently used as normal characters, forcing users to type escape characters. Therefore, in this study, we propose a graphical user interface (GUI) to create patterns for mathematical expressions.

Keywords: Mathematical expressions · Pattern-matching · Regular expressions · GUI

1 Introduction

A mathematical expression used for describing mathematical concepts and models is a significant notation. Electronic documents, including web pages and e-books, often contain mathematical expressions and need to retrieve content. Search algorithms for natural language are partially adaptable to mathematical expressions because a mathematical expression consists of natural language characters. However, the layout of the characters in a mathematical expression is different from that in natural language; this suggests a need to develop search algorithms specifically for mathematical expressions.

Some studies on searching mathematical expressions have been conducted [1–3] typically in relation to search engines. Moreover, search algorithms can be used to highlight search results in a document or move to a page that comprises the results. In general, pattern-matching algorithms (string searching algorithms) are suitable for such applications. Previously, we proposed a search algorithm for mathematical expressions similar to a pattern-matching algorithm for natural language [4]. Using this algorithm, our search tool (MathRegExp) allows users to use regular expressions to describe patterns. Regular expressions can make patterns flexible using wildcards, Boolean *or*, the number of occurrences of character(s), etc. Although several studies have attempted

© Springer International Publishing Switzerland 2015
M. Kurosu (Ed.): Human-Computer Interaction, Part I, HCII 2015, LNCS 9169, pp. 438–447, 2015.
DOI: 10.1007/978-3-319-20901-2_41

to implement wildcards for searching mathematical expressions [5, 6], their functions and notations are different from those used in regular expressions. Our regular expressions for mathematical expressions are similar to the original regular expressions for plain texts.

In MathRegExp, a pattern is expressed as a string. However, using strings as the pattern has some problems. First, the two-dimensional layout of characters in mathematical expressions is represented one-dimensionally, preventing intuitive understanding of which expressions are to be matched to a pattern. Second, because meta-characters for regular expressions are frequently used as normal characters (e.g., "+", "(", and ")"), users must use escape characters, which are cumbersome and prone to mistakes. Because of these problems, novice users, including mathematics learners and liberal arts scholars, might find MathRegExp difficult to use. Therefore, in this study, we propose a graphical user interface (GUI) to create patterns for MathRegExp.

A GUI for describing mathematical expressions has been proposed previously [7]. Our GUI satisfies the further demand of the ability to input regular expressions for advanced and complex matching as well. Our GUI displays these as figures to solve the aforementioned problem of escaping meta-characters and provides users with two methods for inputting regular expressions.

2 Patterns

This section outlines the patterns of MathRegExp as strings to introduce its functions. Here, the proposed GUI internally generates patterns as strings. A pattern consists of characters, structures, and regular expressions, which will be discussed below.

2.1 Characters and Structures

Characters are represented in Unicode. Because Unicode contains categories for mathematical expressions, users can describe symbols appearing in various fields, including calculus, geometry, logic, and set theory.

We refer to the particular symbol layouts appearing in a mathematical expression as structures. A notation for a structure is the form \keyword{argument1}[{argument2} [{argument3}]] (where "[" and "]" indicate optionality). A keyword specifies a type of structure (e.g., fraction, superscript, or square root), and structures are allowed to be nested. For example, \frac{1}{\sqrt{2}} is acceptable for $\frac{1}{\sqrt{2}}$. Table 1 shows a list of structures.

The structures in Table 1 and characters in Unicode enable users to describe summation, definite integration, and maximum.

2.2 Regular Expressions

Regular expressions are divided into five categories, namely, wildcard, character class, quantification, Boolean *or*, and backreference.

Table 1. List of structures

Keyword	Description	Argument			Example
		1	2	3	
sub	subscript	subscript			$_1$
sup	superscript	superscript			^{2}
subsup	subscript and superscript	subscript	superscript		$^\infty_0$
under	underscript	base	underscript		$\lim_{n\to\infty}$
over	overscript	base	overscript		$\vec{a}$
underover	underscript and overscript	base	underscript	overscript	$\sum_{i=0}^{n}$
sqrt	square root	base			$\sqrt{x}$
root	radical with index	base	index		$\sqrt[3]{a}$
frac	fraction	numerator	denominator		$\frac{1}{2}$

A wildcard is represented as "." and matches an arbitrary character or arbitrary structure. For example, \frac{.}{2} matches $\frac{\sqrt{x}}{2}$.

A character class matches a character enclosed by "[" and "]". Therefore, [xyz] \sup{2} matches both x^2 and y^2. A negated character class matches a single character that is not contained between "[^" and "]". An abbreviated notation using "-" in character classes is acceptable: [0-9] matches an arbitrary single digit, and [^stx-z] matches any character other than "s", "t", "x", "y" and "z". Structures are unacceptable in character classes.

Quantification is described as "*", "+" and "?". "*" represents "zero or more of a preceding element," "+" matches "one or more of a preceding element," and "?" matches "zero or one of a preceding element." As an example, \sqrt{.+} matches $\sqrt{2a^2}$.

Boolean *or* is represented as "|". "|" separates alternatives, i.e., x|y matches both x and y individually.

A scope of quantification and Boolean *or* is specified by enclosing with "(" and ")". For example, (x\sub{.})+ matches x_1, x_2, x_3, etc., and (\sqrt{.}|.\sup {\frac{1}{2}}) matches $\sqrt{x}$ or $x^{\frac{1}{2}}$. In addition, a structure is assumed to be a character, hence the pattern \sqrt{.}+ is valid.

A backreference, notated as "\n" (*n* is a number), matches a mathematical expression identical with the expression matched with a part of a pattern enclosed by the nth parenthesis (i.e., "(" and ")"). For example, \frac{.+}{(.+)}-\frac {.+}{\1} matches the addition of two fractions with common denominators.

3 GUI

The method of creating patterns is similar to that of inputting ordinary text, namely, repeatedly inserting a character after a cursor. However, it might be necessary to create patterns with untypable characters, structures, or regular expressions.

3.1 GUI for Mathematical Expressions

Characters are input from the keyboard if they are typable. A palette is provided for inputting untypable characters, including Greek letters and mathematical symbols. Structure templates (i.e., empty structures) are displayed when the buttons are clicked. A double-lined rectangle indicates a structure argument, such as those in Fig. 1.

Users can position the cursor at the rectangle and input a pattern as an argument of the structure. The cursor is controlled by clicking or pressing arrow keys. When arrow keys are pressed, the cursor moves in the order of argument1, argument2, and argument3.

A structure is deleted by pressing the delete key after selecting the entire structure using rectangle selection or placing a cursor on one of the empty arguments (double-lined rectangles).

3.2 GUI for Regular Expressions

This chapter presents figures for regular expressions and methods of inputting and editing them.

3.2.1 Figures of Regular Expressions

Regular expressions are displayed on our GUI as figures rather than meta-characters. Table 2 shows the figures.

These figures represent the scope with a rectangle, allowing users to intuitively grasp the scope of mathematical expressions having two-dimensional structures. This representation also solves the problem that parentheses in regular expressions represented as strings have the double meaning of specifying scope and capturing backreferences. Here, the number of capturing (i.e., n of capturing in Table 2) is assigned as the order of inputting.

Quantification, Boolean *or*, and capturing are applied to a part of a mathematical expression. When multiple functions are applied to an identical part, merged figures are displayed. In a merged figure, "possibility of absence" (optionality) is represented as a broken-lined rectangle, "repetition" is three vertical lines following a rectangle,

Fig. 1. Templates of structures

Table 2. Figures of Regular Expressions

Description	Figure
Wildcard	
Character class	
Negated character class	
Quantification (+)	
Quantification (*)	
Quantification (?)	
Boolean *or*	
Capturing for backreference	*n*
Backreference	⟨*n*⟩

"Boolean *or*" is a spaced vertical line, and "capturing" is an appended number with a small rectangle. Figure 2 is an example of a merged figure representing $(x \mid y \mid z)*$.

3.2.2 Inputting Regular Expressions

A wildcard is inputted by clicking a button, similar to the inputting of untypable characters. The method for inputting a character class, a negated character class, or backreference is identical to that for inputting structures, namely, displaying a rounded rectangle (or a hexagon) and describing contents for character classes (or a reference number).

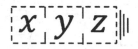

Fig. 2. Merged figure of $(x \mid y \mid z)*$

Our GUI provides two input methods for the functions with a scope (i.e., quantification, Boolean *or*, and capturing). The first method is identical to that for inputting structures, displaying a rectangle and describing a part of the pattern in the scope. The second is selecting a part of an already created pattern to specify the scope and assign the function.

We suppose that there are different procedures for creating patterns. Some users might decide to use regular expressions before creating a pattern, for example, a user inputs `\frac{. +}{()}\+\frac{. +}{\1}` as "addition of fractions with a common denominator" and then concretely describes the denominator. Others might add regular expressions to the pattern after describing a mathematical expression, for example, a user searches with a pattern such as `sinx` and then wishes to search trigonometric functions, searching again with `(sin|cos|tan)x`. Our GUI allows users to follow both the procedures by providing multiple input methods. The former users will employ the method for structures and the latter will use selecting and assigning method.

3.2.3 Editing Regular Expressions

Users edit wildcards such as characters, character classes, and capturing as structures.

When users edit regular expressions having scope, they must first select the scope. A scope is selected by clicking a rectangle or pressing right (left) cursor keys with the cursor just before (after) the rectangle. When a scope is selected, the cursor disappears and the selected rectangle blinks. The rectangle is blurred by clicking characters or structures in the pattern or pressing cursor keys, and the cursor appears at the appropriate position.

Types of editing regular expressions with a scope are divided into "assigning the function," "updating the scope," and "deleting the scope." Users assign a function using buttons. The buttons for quantification and backreferences behave as toggles. If a function is assigned to a scope, the button remains pressed. The button for Boolean *or* is used for adding alternatives. When the button is clicked, a spaced line is inserted in the rectangle, enabling the user to input a new alternative. Users can update a scope by dragging and resizing the selected rectangle. It is impossible for the scope of Boolean *or* to be updated because the function has multiple pattern parts. A scope is deleted by pressing the delete key with the selected scope. If a scope with Boolean *or* is deleted, the second to the last alternatives are also deleted.

3.3 Examples of Patterns

In Table 3, we show examples of patterns created using our GUI, the corresponding patterns as strings, and the matched mathematical expressions.

Table 3. Patterns and Matched Mathematical Expressions

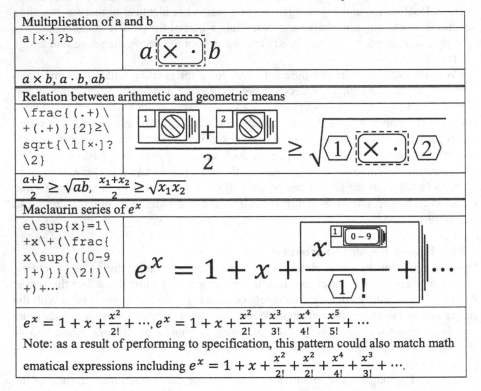

Multiplication of a and b	
`a[×·]?b`	$a\;\boxed{×\;\cdot}\;b$
$a \times b,\ a \cdot b,\ ab$	
Relation between arithmetic and geometric means	

`\frac{(.+)\`
`+(.+)}{2}≥\`
`sqrt{\1[×·]?`
`\2}`	

$\frac{a+b}{2} \geq \sqrt{ab},\ \frac{x_1+x_2}{2} \geq \sqrt{x_1 x_2}$	
Maclaurin series of e^x	

`e\sup{x}=1\`
`+x\+(\frac{`
`x\sup{([0-9`
`]+)}}{\2!}\`
`+)+···`	

$e^x = 1 + x + \frac{x^2}{2!} + \cdots, e^x = 1 + x + \frac{x^2}{2!} + \frac{x^3}{3!} + \frac{x^4}{4!} + \frac{x^5}{5!} + \cdots$	
Note: as a result of performing to specification, this pattern could also match mathematical expressions including $e^x = 1 + x + \frac{x^2}{2!} + \frac{x^2}{2!} + \frac{x^4}{4!} + \frac{x^3}{3!} + \cdots$.	

4 Implementation of Matching

This section explains how our matching algorithm is implemented. Highlighting matched parts of mathematical expressions in web pages, one application of our algorithm, including replacing, is detailed. Figure 3 is the conceptual diagram of the implementation.

We use the regular expressions library called Onigmo [8] internally. The library can describe recursive patterns in addition to ordinary functions of regular expressions. Recursion is indispensable to our manner of matching mathematical expressions because we use parentheses to represent structure (i.e., "{", and "}" in \keyword {content}). Correspondence of parentheses cannot be treated by ordinal regular expressions. For example, a pattern of \sqrt{. +}, which means "a square root including an arbitrary mathematical expression," matches \sqrt{x}\frac{1}{2} because . + in the pattern matches "x}\frac{1}{2." If the . + is revised to [^ {}] + , which means "repetition of a character unless {or }," to avoid this problem, then the pattern causes another problem that the pattern does not match the mathematical expression \sqrt{x\sup{2}}. A recursive pattern solves the problem. The details will be discussed later.

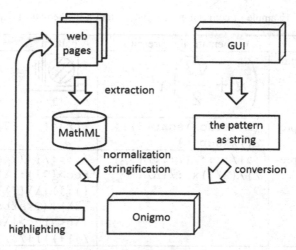

Fig. 3. Conceptual diagram

It is assumed that target mathematical expressions of our matching method are described in a format called MathML [9] Presentation Markup. This format is standard for describing mathematical expressions in electronic papers because it is recommended by W3C and can be used in HTML5. In MathML, a single mathematical expression can be described as various data. For example, two MathML data in Fig. 4 represent the identical mathematical expression: ab^2.

On the left-hand side in Fig. 4, a and b^2 are located on the same line. On the right-hand side, the superscript "2" is attached to ab. Such problems are found in several tags of MathML, which reduces the precision of the pattern-matching process. Therefore, we normalize MathML data to eliminate data variety before pattern-matching. Moreover, normalized data are stringified to a similar format for the patterns described in Sect. 2.

Patterns are created using the GUI, and the GUI generates patterns as strings following the aforementioned format. The patterns, however, are not interpreted appropriately as patterns with Onigmo, hence, they are converted before matching. An example of conversion is shown in Table 4.

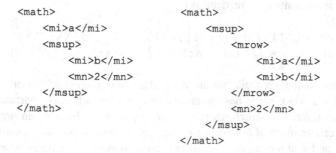

Fig. 4. Two kinds of data for ab^2

Table 4. Example of conversion of a pattern and a mathematical expression

	A mathematical expression	A pattern
Two-dimensional representation	$\left(a + \dfrac{\sqrt{3}}{2}\right) x^n$	
Stringified representation	`(a+\frac{\sqrt{3}}{2})x\sup{n}`	`\frac{.+}{2}`
Converted representation	`(a+/::::/{/:::/{3/}/}/{2/})x/:/{n/}`	`/::::/{((?<arb>(?<arbc>[^{}:/\\]|/(?![{}:])|\\{|\\}|\\:|\\\\)|(?<arbs>/:+(/{(\g<arbc>|\g<arbs>)*/})+)))+/}/{2/}`

The notable processes of the conversion are "replacing keyword," "setting scope," and "calling pattern recursively."

If keywords are retained in stringified mathematical expressions, normal characters in a pattern can match characters to represent keywords. For example, the pattern of a matches a in a keyword frac in a mathematical expression of \frac{1}{2}. To avoid this problem, we replace keywords with sequences of colons (:) and a colon as a normal character to \:.

In patterns for searching mathematical expressions, a structure behaves as a single character. Therefore, the pattern of \sqrt{2} + is acceptable. However, quantification (+) in this pattern plays the role of "one or more of a character of }" when it is interpreted as a pattern with Onigmo. In conversion, every structure is enclosed by parentheses for setting the appropriate scope.

The problem that \sqrt{. +} matches \sqrt{x}\frac{1}{2} is resolved by calling patterns recursively with two notations of Onigmo, (? < *name* >) and \g < *name* > . (? < *name* >) are used for naming a pattern enclosed by parenthesis as name, and \g < *name* > calls the named pattern. We replace wildcard as follows using these functions (indented for readability).

```
(? < arb>
(? < arbc > [^{}:/\\]|/(?![{}:])|\\{|\\}|\\:|\\\\)
|(? < arbs >/: + (/{(\g < arbc > |\g < arbs >)*/}) +)
)
```

The replacement represents "an arbitrary character (named arbc)" or "an arbitrary structure (named arbs)." arbc has the ability to match an arbitrary character including characters for describing structures (i.e., {, }, : , and /). In arbs, an argument of a structure is zero or more of arbc or arbs with \g < *name* > notations, namely, calling arbs in arbs, and making it possible to treat correspondence of parentheses for structures ({and}).

5   Conclusion

In this paper, we proposed a GUI to facilitate searching mathematical expressions based on a pattern-matching algorithm with regular expressions. Our GUI displays patterns two-dimensionally and reduces the number of escape characters, improving usability, especially for novice users, and preventing error or omission in patterns.

In the future, we aim to add an input method that does not require the use of a mouse. Some existing GUIs for mathematical expressions, including Microsoft Word and LyX, have an input method that enables users to input untypable characters by describing a backslash and a keyword and then pressing a space bar. We plan to expand this function to input not only untypable characters but also structures and regular expressions, allowing adept users to promptly create patterns.

Acknowledgement.   This work was supported by JSPS Grant-in-Aid for JSPS Fellows Grant Number 26-2758.

References

1. Yokoi, K., Aizawa, A.: An approach to similarity search for mathematical expressions Using MathML. In: 2nd Workshop Towards Digital Mathematics Library, pp. 27–35 (2009)
2. Miner, R., Munavalli, R.: An approach to mathematical search through query formulation and data normalization. In: Kauers, M., Kerber, M., Miner, R., Windsteiger, W. (eds.) MKM/CALCULEMUS 2007. LNCS (LNAI), vol. 4573, pp. 342–355. Springer, Heidelberg (2007)
3. Zanibbi, R., Yuan, B.: Keyword and Image-based retrieval of mathematical expressions. In: IS&T/SPIE Electronic Imaging, International Society for Optics and Photonics, vol. 7874 (2011)
4. Watabe, T., Miyazaki, Y.: Pattern matching algorithm for mathematical expressions with a regular expression. IPSJ J. Inf. Process. Soc. Jpan. 56(5), 1417–1427 (2015)
5. Miller, B.R., Youssef, A.: Technical aspects of the digital library of mathematical functions. Annals of Mathematics and Artificial Intelligence, Springer 38(1-3), 121–136 (2003)
6. Altamimi, M.E., Youssef, A.S.: Wildcards in math search, implementation issues. In: CAINE/ISCA, pp. 90–96 (2007)
7. Kovalchuk, A., Levitsky, V., Samolyuk, I., Yanchuk, V.: The formulator mathml editor project: user-friendly authoring of content markup documents. In: Autexier, S., Calmet, J., Delahaye, D., Ion, P.D., Rideau, L., Rioboo, R., Sexton, A.P. (eds.) AISC 2010. LNCS, vol. 6167, pp. 385–397. Springer, Heidelberg (2010)
8. Onigmo. https://github.com/k-takata/Onigmo
9. MathML. http://www.w3.org/TR/MathML/

Emotions in HCI

Understanding Visual Appeal and Quality Perceptions of Mobile Apps: An Emotional Perspective

Upasna Bhandari[1](✉), Tillman Neben[2], and Klarissa Chang[2]

[1] Department of Information Systems, School of Computing,
National University of Singapore, Singapore, Singapore
upasna.bhandari@u.nus.edu
[2] Chair of General Management and Information Systems,
University of Mannheim, Mannheim, Germany
neben@uni-mannheim.de, changtt@comp.nus.edu.sg

Abstract. In this study we look at user judgments like perceived quality and also visual appeal from an emotional perspective. This is important to examine since unlike existing studies that focus on the cognitive mechanism of first impression judgments, we use aesthetics framework forwarded by Lavie and Tractinsky, and Russells' circumplex model of emotions to examine the phenomenon. We also try to answer whether aesthetics lead to significant affective responses from users, which then trickle into quality perceptions and visual appeal, which are otherwise considered higher order judgments. Measurement of emotions has mostly been done through subjective evaluation e.g. self-report or survey. We use objective data (electro-dermal activity for arousal and facial electromyography for valence) in addition to subjective data to measure emotions. We design custom mobile app interfaces which users get exposed to achieve effective aesthetic manipulation.

Keywords: Mobile apps · Quality · Appeal · Emotions · Aesthetics · Neurois

1 Introduction

User judgments have primarily been studied from a perspective of usability and efficiency. An often-made assumption in these studies is that judgments are purely cognitive processes. However, research suggests how limited this cognition-centric paradigm is in explaining how judgments are formed [1]. In this study we explore how non-instrumental factors like emotions and aesthetics impact users' judgments in IT use. Specifically, we investigate how non-instrumental factors impact how users judge the overall visual appeal and the quality of an IT artifact. We establish linkages between emotional subcomponents (valence and arousal) and aesthetic subcomponents (classic and expressive) by building on the aesthetics model by [2] and the dimensional perspective of emotions [3].

© Springer International Publishing Switzerland 2015
M. Kurosu (Ed.): Human-Computer Interaction, Part I, HCII 2015, LNCS 9169, pp. 451–459, 2015.
DOI: 10.1007/978-3-319-20901-2_42

We posit that users' initial judgments when seeing an IT artifact for the first time are (a) dominantly driven by emotion and not cognition [4, 5], and (b) that the perception of an aesthetic design is a strong input factor to this process [2, 6, 7]. Visual aesthetics can shortcut user judgments concerning e.g. the software's quality. A clean and symmetric design may elicit a higher quality judgment, while a more creative aesthetic design can lead to a perception of higher quality as well. While classical aesthetics have been explored, expressive aesthetic remain underexplored. This is because the interfaces used for extant studies are designed following classical design guidelines, which do not elaborate on expressive aesthetics. It is important to see how these two subcomponents of visual aesthetics guidelines relate to quality perceptions.

Mobile applications (apps) are an interesting context for this study since initial adoption in case of mobile apps is high, but retention rate is extremely low. It has been reported that 26 % of people who download apps only use them once. Thus, users' first impression of the app is critically important. As Vilnai-Yavetz and Rafaeli pointed out, the switching costs for consumers are generally low [8]. While there are several studies that show that aesthetics are at the core of first impressions in website design, no such concrete evidence is available for mobile apps.

Our study addresses the following research questions:

RQ1: What is the impact of aesthetics on visual appeal and quality perception of mobile apps?

RQ2: What is the impact of emotions on visual appeal and quality perceptions of mobile apps?

RQ3: How do emotions affect the relationship between aesthetics and visual appeal and quality perceptions of mobile apps?

In existing studies emotions were most often measured based on self-rating scales. To overcome the subjectivity biases inherent to this approach we use peripheral physiological tools for recording objective body data [20]. We measure electro-dermal activity (EDA) for arousal and facial electromyography (fEMG) for emotional valence. Our stimuli are custom-designed interfaces of a mobile app that manipulates aesthetics.

2   Theoretical Background

2.1   The M-R Environmental Psychology Model

The environmental psychology model was proposed by [9] popularly known as the M-R model. The framework predicts that users respond to visual stimuli through the mediating effect of underlying emotions experienced when exposed to the stimuli. The underlying principle is that emotions mediate the relationship between stimuli from the environment and the behavior caused by it. In other words, the emotional response to the environmental stimuli is underlying how we chose to react to it. Different emotions will be generated by different stimuli, and this guides our subsequent behavior. Valence and arousal are the two main components of human emotions [3]. Together these two dimensions have been known to capture most of the variance in self-reported mood ratings. This framework helps us understanding the impact of aesthetics on user judgments via emotions [3].

Positive aesthetic responses cause positive interface evaluations [4, 5, 10] Thus the role of emotions in designing a holistic system that is functional and satisfies the pleasure of end users is extremely important. But in order to develop aesthetic design guidelines for eliciting certain emotional responses we require better understanding of what design generates certain emotional responses. Does design guided by symmetric principles (classical aesthetics) make users feel more positive, or does a design guided by originality (expressive aesthetics) excite them, which in turn leads to positive arousal. Since visual design is what users get exposed to initially, it is believed that the affective response to design is an important predictor of future interactions.

2.2 Quality Perceptions, Visual Appeal and Emotions

Perceived quality is a user judgment that can be predicted using measurements of emotions: an interface eliciting positive emotional response will lead to more positive quality perception. This is because while quality perceptions can be evaluated using instrumental factors like how efficiently the systems work; there are non-instrument quality perceptions as well. They are beyond task or whether they achieve desired goals or even if efficiency is achieved with the process. Rafaeli and Vilnai Yavetz attempted to link perceived quality with emotions [11]. They found strong support for emotion (valence and arousal) being linked to quality perceptions. This indicates that even though quality perceptions can be considered higher order evaluation, initial processing or visceral processing or type 1 system processing can predict them. The above-mentioned systems address the first affective response of the user after being exposed to the stimuli.

Visual appeal caters to the immediate processing that happens subconsciously when presented with stimuli. In general, positive experiences will be associated with higher visual appeal. In this regard, usability theory has long predicted the link between emotions and user judgments like visual appeal and attractiveness amongst others. Norman (2004) explains this in his model with the concept for visceral processing as well, visceral design is all about immediate emotional impact.

2.3 Perceived Visual Aesthetics and Emotions

Valence represents the pleasantness or unpleasantness dimension. Arousal represents the degree of activation associated with the emotion. The two dimensions capture most of the variance in self-reported mood ratings [12]. Theoretically, aesthetics consists of classical and expressive aesthetics. Classical aesthetics encapsulates all the dimensions that relate to visual clarity and symmetry. Expressive aesthetics encapsulates the dimensions that relates to the stimulation of creativity, such as fascinating design elements, originality, and visual sophistication.

Depending on the emotional responses to aesthetic parameters like classical or expressive users form judgment about the quality of the system. Theory of perception explains the idea that people conceive visual perception in its entirety, how the constituent elements work together and not what individual component stands for [13].

This implies that sum total is what influences user's perception about visual attributes. In other words, people tend to form integrative and compositional quality perceptions rather quickly since it is based on how visually the interfaces look, resulting in two interfaces with different visual compositions producing different quality perceptions. Users also have been found to rapidly judge the aesthetics of a webpage reliably within 50 ms [14]. However some studies that tried to replicate these effects failed so it cannot be said with utmost certainty.

3   Experiment Design

To test the research model, a 2*2 factorial within-subject design was conducted among twenty-one students at a major research university in Germany. We use a within-subject design because it allows to accounts for the brain's and body's idiosyncratic nature [15]. The independent variables are classical aesthetics (symmetry) and expressive aesthetics (originality). Valence and arousal are captured and analyzed as mediating variables. Visual appeal and quality perception are measured as dependent variables in this model. We focus on one dimension of classical (symmetry) and one dimension from expressive (originality) aesthetics scale. This is done to isolate and also have clear linkage between aesthetics and the emotional responses from users. We collect participants subjective as well as physiological responses. Below we explain our study design and discuss some results.

3.1   Independent Variables

Classical Aesthetics *(Symmetry)*: For inducing high and low levels of symmetry, we get support from model of classical aesthetics [2]. We took further guidelines from work by Park et al. to manipulate symmetry as one of the interface variations [16]. Symmetry is the mirroring of the visual composition across a vertical or horizontal pivot line [17]. The numeric value of symmetry is higher when objects of the same color and size are mirrored across vertical or horizontal axis [17]. We use these principles to arrive at interfaces with varying degrees of symmetry (Figs. 1, 2).

Expressive Aesthetics *(Originality)*: Support was found in design literature for originality being associated with custom-built shapes. Custom-built shapes add *originality* into the design. Taking inspiration from design literature we manipulate expressive aesthetics by using custom shapes instead of default square shape design (Table 1).

3.2   Mediating Variables

We use electrodermal activity (EDA) to measure arousal and use facial electromyography (fEMG) to measure valence. These are objective measures of galvanic skin conductance and facial muscle movements when users are exposed to the various interfaces. The reason why we use physiological measures of emotions is the bias induced with self-report measures of emotions. It has been argued that self-reported

Fig. 1. (a) Participant wearing EDA and EMG electrodes (b) Participant getting exposed to stimuli on mobile interface.

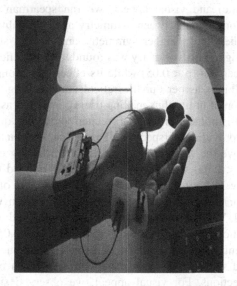

Fig. 2. (c) EDA electrodes on participants' palm

emotion measures are often not close to the actual emotion experienced, neurophysiological measures make it possible to have an effective and efficient measurement for arousal and valence when stimuli are presented for shorter duration.

Table 1. Group allocation for IVs: classical and expressive

Interface	Classical Aesthetics	Expressive Aesthetics
1	High	High
2	High	Low
3	Low	High
4	Low	Low

3.3 Dependent Variables

For perceived quality perception we used hedonic and pragmatic quality perception scale by Hassenzahl (AttracDiff 2, Hassenzahl 2004) [18]. Visual appeal was measured on a five-item 7 point Likert scale proposed by Lindgaard that accounted for 94 % of the visual appeal in the existing study [14].

4 Results

In order to explore the extent to which independent variables classic aesthetics (symmetry) and expressive aesthetics (originality) are correlated with quality perceptions (hedonic and pragmatic) and visual appeal, we ran spearman correlation test and observed significant correlation between symmetry and originality with visual appeal ($p < 0.05$). This implies that a higher symmetry and custom shapes induces better appeal of interface design. Also symmetry was found to be significantly correlated with pragmatic quality perception ($p < 0.05$) while its effect on hedonic quality perception was not significant. This is as per our theoretical underpinning. Symmetry has been known to induce motion of utility thus making users perceive it as something, which is pragmatic. However it is not significantly correlated to hedonic quality perception that looks at the pleasure providing perspective of interface. Originality was on the other hand was found to have the reverse effect. It was significantly correlated to hedonic quality perception ($p < 0.05$) while not significantly correlated to pragmatic quality perception. Originality is known to appeal to the activation of pleasure providing components of the interface and thus its significant correlation with hedonic quality perception is expected. Valence was significantly correlated with symmetry ($p < 0.05$) and arousal was significantly correlated with originality ($p < 0.05$) (Figs. 3, 4).

To see if dependent variables – quality perceptions (hedonic and pragmatic) and visual appeal – varied significantly between interfaces, we ran multiple comparisons with Bonferroni corrections. For visual appeal, we observed significant differences between interfaces:

1 (high classic/high expressive) and 2 (high classic/low expressive), ($p < 0.05$).
1 (high expressive/high classic) and 4 (low classic/low expressive), ($p < 0.05$).

No significant differences were obtained across interfaces for pragmatic quality perception however for hedonic quality perception there were significant differences between interfaces:

1 (high expressive/high classic) with 2 (high classic/low expressive), ($p < 0.05$) and 4 (high classic/low expressive), ($p < 0.05$).

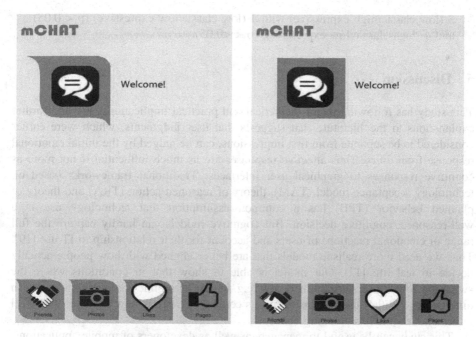

Fig. 3. Interfaces manipulated to obtain (a) High classical and high expressive aesthetics (b) High classical and low expressive aesthetics.

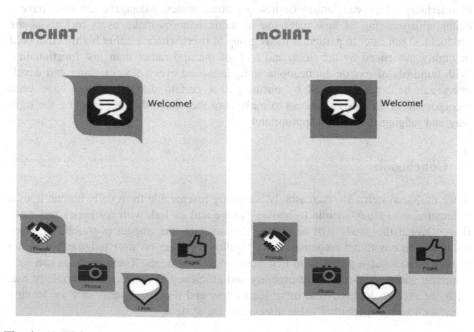

Fig. 4. (c) High expressive and low classical aesthetics (d) Low classical and low expressive aesthetics.

3 (low classic/high expressive) with 4 (low classic/low expressive) ($p < 0.05$) and 4 (high classic/low expressive), ($p < <0.05$).

5 Discussion

This study has following major theoretical and practical implications. We add further explanations to the literature that suggests that user judgments, which were earlier considered to be separate from first impressions, can be judged by the initial emotional response from users. Thus affective responses are as much influential if not more as cognitive responses to graphical user interfaces. Traditional frameworks based on technology acceptance model (TAM), theory of reasoned action (TRA) and theory of planned behavior (TPB) has a common assumption that technology use is a well-reasoned, cognitive decision. But cognitive models can hardly capture the full range of emotional reactions of users and account for their relationship to IT use [19]. Thus we need more realistic models that are better aligned with how people actually decide in real life [12]. Our model is able to show that in conditions where the switching cost of users is extremely low (e.g. in case of mobile applications), what can differentiate whether user adopts or rejects certain software is how it makes them feel rather than cognitively thinking about it.

This study can be useful to managers as well as developers of mobile applications. An improved understanding of design features (particular emphasis on aesthetics) and users' emotional responses to these aesthetic features can help in guiding development of interfaces which can induce desires emotional states. Managers can now have a better understanding of how particular aesthetic features make users feel about the product and can cater to particular focus group of users who are either highly emotional or highly influenced by the 'look and feel' of the app rather than just functionality. With hundreds of mobile applications being launched every day, manager and developers can be better prepared by ensuring that certain design features have been incorporated in the design process to make sure they have the users feeling the right way and judging the quality appropriately.

6 Conclusion

Since mobile systems are increasingly becoming inseparable from daily human lives it is imperative to study mobile technology usage and its link with aesthetics and emotions. Overall this study will be able to demonstrate that impact of mobile interface aesthetics on emotional responses has a "spillover" effect on user judgments that are usually considered separate from first impression judgments. These findings can substantially guide how we look at usability and efficiency in context of technology use. Also we need to look beyond these parameters and design systems that are leaving users with high experiential value after using the system.

References

1. Bhandari, U., Chang, K.: Role of Emotions and Aesthetics in ICT Usage for Underserved Communities: A NeuroIS Investigation (2014)
2. Lavie, T., Tractinsky, N.: Assessing dimensions of perceived visual aesthetics of web sites. Int. J. Hum Comput Stud. **60**(3), 269–298 (2004)
3. Russell, J.A.: Core affect and the psychological construction of emotion. Psychol. Rev. **110** (1), 145 (2003)
4. De Angeli, A., Sutcliffe, A., Hartmann, J.: Interaction, usability and aesthetics: what influences users' preferences? In: Proceedings of the 6th Conference on Designing Interactive Systems. ACM (2006)
5. Schenkman, B.N., Jönsson, F.U.: Aesthetics and preferences of web pages. Behav. Inf. Technol. **19**(5), 367–377 (2000)
6. Lindgaard, G.: Aesthetics, visual appeal, usability and user satisfaction: what do the user's eyes tell the user's brain? Aust. J. Emerg. Technol. Soc. **5**(1), 1–14 (2007)
7. Van der Heijden, H.: User acceptance of hedonic information systems. MIS Q. **28**(4), 695–704 (2004)
8. Vilnai-Yavetz, I., Rafaeli, A.: Aesthetics and professionalism of virtual servicescapes. J. Serv. Res. **8**(3), 245–259 (2006)
9. Mehrabian, A., Russell, J.A.: An Approach to Environmental Psychology. The MIT Press, Cambridge (1974)
10. Hartmann, J.: Assessing the attractiveness of interactive systems. In: CHI 2006 Extended Abstracts on Human Factors in Computing Systems. ACM (2006)
11. Rafaeli, A., Vilnai-Yavetz, I.: Instrumentality, aesthetics and symbolism of physical artifacts as triggers of emotion. Theor. Issues Ergon. Sci. **5**(1), 91–112 (2004)
12. Suri, G., Gross, J.J.: Emotion regulation and successful aging. Trends Cogn. Sci. **16**(8), 409–410 (2012)
13. Cupchik, G.C.: A critical reflection on Arnheim's Gestalt theory of aesthetics. Psychol. Aesthetics Creativity Arts **1**(1), 16 (2007)
14. Lindgaard, G., et al.: Attention web designers: you have 50 milliseconds to make a good first impression! Behav. Inf. Technol. **25**(2), 115–126 (2006)
15. Badcock, N.A., et al.: Validation of the emotiv EPOC® EEG gaming system for measuring research quality auditory ERPs. PeerJ **1**, e38 (2013)
16. Park, S.-E., Choi, D., Kim, J.: Visualizing e-brand personality: exploratory studies on visual attributes and e-brand personalities in Korea. Int. J. Hum. Comput. Interact. **19**(1), 7–34 (2005)
17. Ngo, D.C.L., Byrne, J.G.: Application of an aesthetic evaluation model to data entry screens. Comput. Hum. Behav. **17**(2), 149–185 (2001)
18. Hassenzahl, M.: The interplay of beauty, goodness, and usability in interactive products. Hum. Comput. Interact. **19**(4), 319–349 (2004)
19. Beaudry, A., Pinsonneault, A.: The other side of acceptance: studying the direct and indirect effects of emotions on information technology use. MIS Q. **34**(4), 689–710 (2010)
20. Dimoka, A., Pavlou, P.A., Davis, F.D.: Research commentary—NeuroIS: the potential of cognitive neuroscience for information systems research. Inf. Syst. Res. **22**(4), 687–702 (2011)

A Smartphone Application to Promote Affective Interaction and Mental Health

Maurizio Caon[1,2], Leonardo Angelini[1,2(✉)], Stefano Carrino[1,2], Omar Abou Khaled[1,2], and Elena Mugellini[1,2]

[1] HumanTech Institute, Bd de, Péroilles. 80, 1700 Fribourg, Switzerland
{maurizio.caon, leonardo.angelini, stefano.carrino, omar.aboukhaled, elena.mugellini}@hes-so.ch
[2] University of Applied Sciences and Arts Western Switzerland, Delémont, Switzerland

Abstract. In this paper, we describe a smartphone application that aims at motivating users to use facial expressions. This has a twofold goal: to reintroduce the use of facial expressions as nonverbal means in the computer-mediated communication of emotions and to provide the opportunity for self-reflection about the personal emotional states while fostering smiles in order to improve mental wellbeing. This paper provides a description of the developed prototype and reports the results of a first observation study conducted during an interactive event.

Keywords: Positive technology · Affective interaction · Computer mediated communication · Mental wellbeing · Facial expressions

1 Introduction and Background

The technological revolution thoroughly changed the way people communicate. There has been a shift from the physical to the virtual world and, nowadays, most of the human interaction is computer mediated. A consequence of this shift towards a more and more important role of the human-to-computer-to-human interaction (HCHI) is that all the nonverbal part of a normal face-to-face communication, such as paralanguage and kinesics, is totally missing. In particular, kinesics is the use of body motion communication such as facial expressions and gestures. The use of facial expressions is particularly important not only to convoy richer information in human communication but it also plays a crucial role in people's mental wellbeing. Indeed, in psychology, it is well known the principle that performing facial expressions directly influences our emotional state [11]. In fact, the James-Lange theory of emotion states that life experiences produce a direct physiological response via the human nervous system and the emotions occur as a consequence of these changes, rather than being the cause of them. In particular, Kleinke et al. conducted an experiment that produced interesting results confirming the aforementioned theory [13]. In fact, they found out that the test subjects reported an increased positive mood while performing positive facial expressions and a less positive experience while performing negative facial expressions.

© Springer International Publishing Switzerland 2015
M. Kurosu (Ed.): Human-Computer Interaction, Part I, HCII 2015, LNCS 9169, pp. 460–467, 2015.
DOI: 10.1007/978-3-319-20901-2_43

This was true even if the experiment participants were only mimicking these facial expressions. Moreover, the effects were enhanced when participants could see their reflection in a mirror. These findings become particularly relevant when associated to the benefits that smiling provide. In fact, smiling activates the release of neuropeptides that can help in fighting stress [18]. Moreover, smiling is also associated to the release of dopamine, endorphins and serotonin, which function as natural pain-reliever [15] and as anti-depressant [12].

In this paper, we present an application for smartphones that enables users to communicate in Social Awareness Streams (SAS) using facial expressions to share their emotional state. The main contribution of this work is twofold: (1) the introduction of kinesics in affective HCHI; (2) empowering users for the self-monitoring of their emotional states in order to support the expression of positive emotions. Through these two axes, the application allows augmenting the human expressivity for the communication of emotional states in CMC. This could also augment users' social skills in off-line interaction and, finally, their happiness. This interface has been implemented in a mobile environment because currently a big part of the population owns and uses the smartphone, which also provides ubiquitous interaction and continuous connection. Indeed, the smartphone can be considered a pervasive technology that deeply penetrated the current society and that, therefore, can effectively influence users' daily life.

The next section presents the related work; in the third section, the prototype interface is described in detail. The fourth section is dedicated to the observation study we conducted, while the last section presents the conclusion and future work.

2 Related Work

Positive technology aims at creating technologies that contribute to enhance happiness and psychological wellbeing. In [16], Riva et al. proposed a framework to classify positive technology according to their effect on three main features of personal experience:

- Hedonic: technologies used to induce positive and pleasant experiences;
- Eudaimonic: technologies used to support individuals in reaching engaging and self-actualizing experiences;
- Social/Interpersonal: technologies used to support and improve social integration and/or connectedness between individuals, groups, and organizations.

The smartphone application introduced in this paper integrates the Hedonic and Social/Interpersonal features. For this reason, we present the related works concerning these features and using facial expressions as main means of emotion communication.

2.1 Social/Interpersonal Feature

Facial expressions provide an important channel for emotional and social display and some works tried to introduce this nonverbal interaction in computer-mediated communication. For example, FAIM captures users' spontaneous facial expressions via a video and displays them as dynamic avatars in instant messaging software [7]. Similarly, Kuber and Wright developed an instant messaging application that recognized facial expressions through the Emotiv EPOC headset and displayed the users' emotional states with smileys [14]. This study showed that this approach improved affective interaction compared with normal text-based communication. Caon et al. used the same technology for the facial expression recognition but they applied this concept to the communication over the SASs and the feedback was displayed in the environment in a context-aware multimodal manner [4].

2.2 Hedonic Feature

The notion that inducing a person to perform a smile can make her happier encouraged some researchers to propose novel interfaces that aim at promoting smiles. For example, Tsujita and Rekimoto presented a variety of digital appliances, such as refrigerators, alarm clocks, mirrors et cetera that require the user to smile in order to function properly [20]. In [19], they described two field tests that they conducted with the refrigerator. This refrigerator integrated a camera to recognize and count the user's smiles, and only when the user smiled, the system facilitated opening the refrigerator door. These field tests showed that this system motivated users to smile more frequently, provided a tool for self-reflection and fostered communication in a couple. Hori et al. proposed a system composed of a smartphone and a wearable device, called communication pedometer, which applied the gamification approach to promote smiling during interpersonal communication [10]. The "Moodmeter" is a system that aimed at encouraging smiles in public spaces [9]. It was composed of a camera that recognized by-standers smiles and displayed it on a public display. This set up was replicated in many spots of the campus and it was possible to display a heat-map to show which spot was the "happiest". Another interesting work in this field is the mirror that manipulates the user facial expression [22]; the authors of this work demonstrated that it is possible to manipulate emotional states through feedback of deformed facial expressions in real time.

The smartphone application presented in this paper proposes an interface that enables users to use facial expressions to share emotional information. At the same time, like the work made by Tsujita and Rekimoto [20], aims at fostering smiles.

3 Prototype

The smartphone application presented in this paper has been designed to support the first and third features of the positive technology framework [16]. Indeed, it allows the user to use facial expressions to communicate her emotional state in SASs. Since this application aims at improving the computer-mediated interaction, it could also enhance the feeling of connectedness between the elements of a social group. At the same time, this application provides some feedback about the performed facial expressions and reminds the user to smile in order to induce positive emotions and increase happiness.

3.1   Interface for Affective Interaction

This part of the interface aims at enhancing the computer-mediated communication of emotions and can be classified in the Social/interpersonal feature of the framework of the positive technologies. The SASs, such as Twitter, do not allow a variety of different modalities and have also a limited number of characters per message; therefore, the expressivity of emotions in SASs is quite limited. We developed this app in order to provide ubiquitous sharing of emotions in SASs (i.e., Twitter) through text, images and emotions (Fig. 1(b)). This app induces the user to communicate her emotional state performing the associated facial expression using the front camera embedded in the smartphone. In particular, when a user wants to share a message in Twitter, she can open the app where she will find the interface to enter the text, to browse the pictures and, before sending the message, the app asks the user if she wants to share an emotion in this message. If she agrees, the app will show the view from the front camera in order to allow the user to focus on her face and on the emotion detected by the system, as depicted in Fig. 1(a). The algorithm for the user's facial expression recognition is able to recognize four different facial expressions associated to four emotions: smiling for happiness, frowning for sadness, scowling for anger, and winking for trust. The facial expression recognition has been implemented with the OpenCV library [1]. We used a supervised learning approach, where the user trains the system before the first utilization performing three times each expression. For the recognition phase, a similarity algorithm compares the ORB feature descriptors [17] for the mouth and eye regions. These regions are extracted using the Haar feature-based cascade classifiers proposed by Viola and Jones [21]. The app provides also an overview of the sent Tweets with the text, image and a smiley to represent the shared emotional state (Fig. 1(b)).

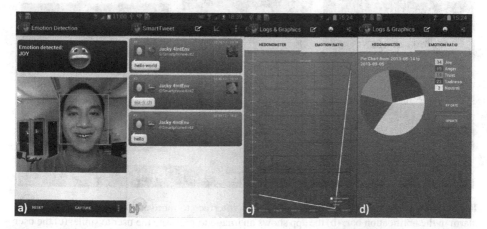

Fig. 1. Screenshots of the app (a) interface for emotion recognition; (b) overview of the sent Tweet with associated emotion; (c) the hedonometer; (d) the emotion pie chart.

The choice of giving to the user the opportunity of communicating her current emotional state using the facial expression aims at reintroducing the use of the kinesics typical of the nonverbal communication. In fact, the facial expressions and the gestures are very meaningful means of expression in the face-to-face communication and they add more information to the spoken sentences. In particular, affection not only allows experiencing a richer interaction but also helps to disambiguate meaning, facilitating a more effective communication [2].

3.2   Interface for Mental Wellbeing

This part of the interface aims at inducing positive emotions to increase the user's happiness and can be classified according to the hedonic feature of the positive technology framework. This application provides some statistics as feedback for user empowerment; indeed, they help users explore and understand information about themselves to support self-reflection and to identify opportunities for behavior change [6]. These statistics take into account the number of facial expressions performed during each day. Then, it is possible to show the number of smiles per day as a graph (Fig. 1(c)) and the percentage of all the performed facial expressions in a pie chart (Fig. 1(d)). Moreover, this application integrates a persuasive interface that solicits the user to smile when the smile counter detects a low level of happiness. In this case, the application triggers an alarm shown in the notification bar (Fig. 2(a)) and when the user acknowledges it, an interface showing funny or positive images coming from an RSS

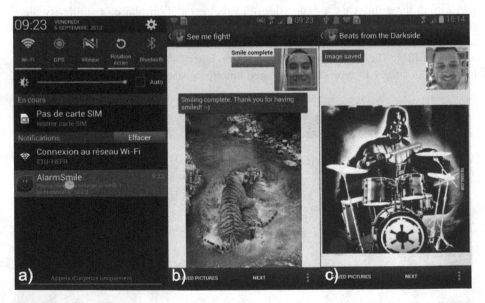

Fig. 2.   Three screenshots to show the persuasive interface to motivate the user to smile: (a) the alarm in the notification bar; (b) the app shows an image to motivate the user to smile; (c) the user can browse the RSS feed in every moment and the app saves in the smartphone the images that make the user to smile.

feed chosen by the user is displayed (Fig. 2(b)). In this screen, a progression bar shows how much the user should smile in order to accomplish this task. However, the user can access the RSS feed whenever she wants and when she smiles, the images are saved in the smartphone to allow the user to watch them again (Fig. 2(c)). This persuasive interface aims at inducing the user to smile in order to make her happier, as the works presented in [10] and [20]. In fact, as explained in Sect. 1, it is not important if the smile is unconscious or voluntary to increase positive mood, and the possibility to see the user's face smiling like in a mirror can even increase this effect. Indeed, as for the hedonic feature of positive technology, this interface aims at enhancing happiness. Moreover, this tool aims at supporting self-reflection to train the self-regulation of emotions, which also contributes to mental health [8].

4 Observation Study

We performed the observation study during a live demonstration held during the conference on Affective Computing and Intelligent Interaction (ACII 2013) at the International Conference Centre of Geneva in Switzerland on 4 September 2013. We set up a prototype composed of multiple input and output interfaces for the communication of emotional states [5]. In particular, the setup comprised two main input interfaces: a touch-enabled Smart TV using the Microsoft Kinect for the facial expression recognition and the Android smartphone running the application we developed. We conducted an observation study both on the field and with the recorded video; other findings were presented in [3]. Watching the video, we calculated the number of conference attendees involved in the interactive demonstration: 85 people stopped to watch the demo and 29 of them actually interacted with the prototype. The people attending the conference were of different ethnics, genders and ages; although all of them were interested in affective computing, there were researchers and practitioners with very heterogeneous backgrounds, providing a varied pool of subjects for our first public test. The testers generally demonstrated a large interest in the proposed prototype. In particular, the interaction through facial expressions was appreciated, even if considered too artificial. In fact, this kind of interaction implies that the user has to express her emotional state through voluntary facial expressions that in this case can be seen more as a gesture rather than an unconscious physiological reaction; for this reason, some participants suggested to integrate an automatic facial expression recognition that detects the unconscious expressions and to propose to the user to share the detected emotional status on the SAS. The interaction with the persuasive interface to motivate the user to smile provided the same result: the users felt of being "faking" a smile in order to save the images they liked. However, as explained in Sect. 1, mimicking positive facial expression is an effective means to increase the user's positive mood.

The most important research question we were trying to answer in this interactive event was to understand if performing facial expressions could be a problem in terms of user acceptability in a public context. In fact, using facial expressions to communicate with the mobile phone could be seen as awkward by the user, in particular in a social context like this event, where users were surrounded by a crowd that could be composed of friends, colleagues and strangers. The result after this first acceptability test is quite encouraging; indeed, nobody refused to perform facial expressions in front of the mobile phone for the communication of emotional states. This makes us think that in the current society, where "selfies" are a main trend invading the social networks, the use of a camera as means of communication is considered acceptable even in public spaces. We can consider these preliminary results encouraging, although we are aware that further tests are needed.

5 Conclusion and Future Work

In this paper, we presented a smartphone application integrating two features of positive technology: a Social/Interpersonal interface that aims at introducing a part of kinesics, i.e., facial expressions, in the computer-mediated communication of emotions. Moreover, this prototype takes advantage of the recorded emotions shared by the user in order to provide some statistics to enable self-reflection about the shared emotions; this aims at improving mental health and if the user did not smile enough during the day, a persuasive interface inspired by Tsujita and Rekimoto's work [19], motivates the user to smile.

As future work, we are integrating a gamification mechanism, like in Hori et al.'s work [10], to sustain user's engagement and to create an active community of people willing to improve their affective interaction and mental wellbeing.

Acknowledgments. We want to thank Alexandre Nussbaumer and Hoang-Linh Nguyen for their fundamental contribution to this work, which has been supported by Hasler Foundation in the framework of "Living in Smart Environments" project.

References

1. Bradski, G.: The opencv library. Doctor Dobbs J. **25**(11), 120–126 (2000)
2. Brave S, Nass C.: Emotion in human–computer interaction. In: The Human–Computer Interaction Handbook, pp. 81–93 (2003)
3. Caon, M., Angelini, L., Khaled, O.A., Lalanne, D., Yue, Y., Mugellini, E.: Affective interaction in smart environments. Procedia Comput. Sci. **32**, 1016–1021 (2014)
4. Caon, M., Angelini, L., Yue, Y., Khaled, O.A., Mugellini, E.: Context-aware multimodal sharing of emotions. In: Kurosu, Masaaki (ed.) HCII/HCI 2013, Part V. LNCS, vol. 8008, pp. 19–28. Springer, Heidelberg (2013)
5. Caon, M., Khaled, O.A., Mugellini, E., Lalanne, D., Angelini, L.: Ubiquitous interaction for computer mediated communication of emotions. In: Proceedings of ACII 2013, pp. 717–718 (2013)
6. Dey, A.: Persuasive technology or explorative technology? In: Berkovsky, S., Freyne, J. (eds.) PERSUASIVE 2013. LNCS, vol. 7822, p. 1. Springer, Heidelberg (2013)
7. El Kaliouby, R., Robinson, P.: FAIM: integrating automated facial affect analysis in instant messaging. In: Proceedings of IUI 2004, pp. 244–246. ACM (2004)
8. Gross, J.J., Muñoz, R.F.: Emotion regulation and mental health. Clin. Psychol. Sci. Pract. **2**(2), 151–164 (1995)

9. Hernandez, J., Hoque, M.E., Drevo, W., Picard, R.W.: Mood meter: counting smiles in the wild. In: Proceedings of UbiComp 2012, pp. 301–310. ACM (2012)
10. Hori, Y., Tokuda, Y., Miura, T., Hiyama, A., Hirose, M.: Communication pedometer: a discussion of gamified communication focused on frequency of smiles. In: Proceedings of AH 2013, pp. 206–212. ACM (2013)
11. James, W.: The Principles of Psychology, vol. 2. Dover Publications, New York (1950)
12. Karren, K.J., Smith, L., Gordon, K.J.: Mind/body health: The effects of attitudes, emotions, and relationships. Pearson Higher Ed (2013)
13. Kleinke, C.L., Peterson, T.R., Rutledge, T.R.: Effects of self-generated facial expressions on mood. J. Pers. Soc. Psychol. **74**, 272–279 (1998)
14. Kuber, R., Wright, F.P.: Augmenting the instant messaging experience through the use of brain-computer interface and gestural technologies. Int. J. Hum. Comput. Interact. **29**(3), 178–191 (2013)
15. Lane, R.D.: Neural correlates of conscious emotional experience. In: Cognitive neuroscience of emotion, pp. 345–370 (2000)
16. Riva, G., Banos, R.M., Botella, C., Wiederhold, B.K., Gaggioli, A.: Positive technology: using interactive technologies to promote positive functioning. Cyberpsychol. Behav. Soc. Netw. **15**(2), 69–77 (2012)
17. Rublee, E., Rabaud, V., Konolige, K., Bradski, G.: ORB: an efficient alternative to SIFT or SURF. In: Proceedings of ICCV 2011, pp. 2564–2571. IEEE (2011)
18. Seaward, B.: Managing Stress: Principles and Strategies for Health and Well-Being. Jones & Bartlett Publishers, Boston (2008)
19. Tsujita, H., Rekimoto, J.: Smiling makes us happier: enhancing positive mood and communication with smile-encouraging digital appliances. In: Proceedings of UbiComp 2011, pp. 1–10. ACM (2011)
20. Tsujita, H., Rekimoto, J.: Smile-encouraging digital appliances. IEEE Pervasive Comput. **12**(4), 5–7 (2013)
21. Viola, P., Jones, M.: Rapid object detection using a boosted cascade of simple features. In: Proceedings of CVPR 2001, vol. 1, pp. I-511–I-518. IEEE (2001)
22. Yoshida, S., Tanikawa, T., Sakurai, S., Hirose, M., Narumi, T.: Manipulation of an emotional experience by real-time deformed facial feedback. In: Proceedings of AH 2013, pp. 35–42. ACM (2013)

A Study on the Relationships Between Drivers' Emotions and Brain Signals

Songyi Chae[✉]

Human and Systems Engineering, UNIST,
100 Banyeon-ri, Eonyang-eup, Ulju-gun, Ulsan, Korea
robim0314@gmail.com

Abstract. In this study, the correlation between six basic emotions (happy, sad, angry, disgusted, scared, and neutral) and brain signals evoked by head-up display (HUD) images were found. 20 participants were exposed to 18 different HUD images in the laboratory and driving simulator-based settings. 16-channel electroencephalography (EEG) signals were obtained during exposure to each HUD image and were later used to calculate three EEG indices (EEG activity, concentration level and relaxation level). The participants reported their emotions induced by the observation of each HUD image on semantic differential scales with two bipolar adjectives (range: 1–7). Results showed that color was a key factor for determining the type of emotion evoked, whereas the amount of information provided determined the levels of brain activity in the central lobe. Neural activities in the temporal lobe showed a strong association with the concentration level. These findings between emotions and EEG signals can be used for designing a new type of DVI (driver-vehicle interface).

Keywords: Driver's emotion · Brain signal · Electroencephalography (EEG) · Driver-vehicle interface (DVI)

1 Introduction

Driving is a task which requires the simultaneous processing of various visual stimuli [1]. A head-up display (HUD) interface is a device which minimizes eye movement of a driver and provides the driver with important information, such as the speed, fuel gauge and navigation, at the front of the vehicle [2]. Thus, HUD enables a driver to concentrate on the road conditions ahead by eliminating reasons for disengaging their vision from infront of the steering wheel. The HUD image is easily recognized, even by first-time drivers [3], and generally enables drivers to feel safer while driving [4].

An extensive amount of research about HUD hardware design has been conducted, however the number of studies which concentrate on HUD image design is insufficient. Various aspects such as the reaction and performance rates corresponding to the provided information from HUD should be considered in HUD image design [1]. HUD image design must be suited to evoke positive emotions of the driver as they heavily impact driving performance and furthermore, the safety of both the driver and other vehicles. Therefore, this study investigates the electroencephalogram (EEG) signals and the emotions evoked by HUD images of the driver in prior research conducted by Smith in 2011 [5].

M. Kurosu (Ed.): Human-Computer Interaction, Part I, HCII 2015, LNCS 9169, pp. 468–476, 2015.
DOI: 10.1007/978-3-319-20901-2_44

In Smith's research, six pairs of emotion provoked by each of the 18 HUD images, were established by conducting a survey. This paper considers Smith's experiment as a foundation for HUD image design, hence uses existing HUD images to evaluate the emotions and EEG signals of drivers, therefore establishing a correlation between the two properties. Furthermore, the paper aims to develop a driver-vehicle interface (DVI) which investigates the elements of HUD image design that affect the emotions and EEG signals of drivers.

2 Method

2.1 Overview of Experiment

20 participants in both laboratory and driving-simulator based settings were exposed to visual stimuli in order to investigate the emotions and brain signals evoked by 18 HUD images (see Fig. 1) of various design elements including; content, amount of information, location, font, and color. 16 channels of EEG signals were measured while the participants observed each HUD image, in order to calculate the three EEG indices of; EEG activity, concentration level and relaxation level. Participants rated on scale of 1 to 7, the amount of emotion induced by the HUD images in regards to five pairs of antonyms and six individual emotive adjectives.

2.2 Participants

In this experiment, 20 participants with at least one year of driving experience were involved, consisting of 10 males and 10 females aged between 20 and 31 years of age. All participants did not have any auditory, physical or mental disorders.

2.3 Apparatus

The 18 HUD images used in the experiment are displayed in Fig. 1, while their characteristics are listed in Table 1. Each image was a different combination of 6 design elements including; form of main information, form of sub information, the amount of information, location, font, and color. Each design element had sub design level, where colour has 3 levels; orange, blue and green.

Poly G–A (Laxtha. Korea) equipment was used to investigate the brain waves of each participant and a sampling frequency of 256 Hz was used to produce EEG signals. The EEG electrodes used 16 channels according to the International 10–20 System of Electrode Placement and the attaching positions were Fp1, Fp2, F3, F4, F7, F8, C3, C4, T7, T8, P3, P4, P7, P8, O1, O2, as shown in Fig. 2.

2.4 Experimental Environment

Experiments were conducted under laboratory-based and driving simulator-based settings (see Fig. 3). In the laboratory, a basic experiment was conducted using the the

470   S. Chae

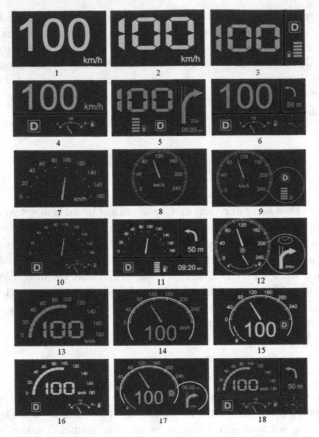

Fig. 1. 18 kinds of HUD images [5] (Smith, 2011) (Color figure online)

Table 1. Design factors of HUD images [5] (Smith, 2011)

Design elements		Sub design elements	
Main information form	Digital	Meter	Mixture
Sub information form	Digital	Meter	
Amount of information	1 item	3 items	5 items
	Speedometer	Speedometer	Speedometer
		Position of gear	Position of gear
		Fuel gauge	Fuel gauge
			Clock
			Navigation
Location	Left	Center	Right
Font	Arial	Electronic	
Color	Orange	Green	Blue

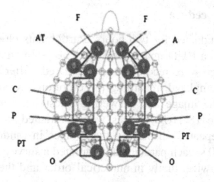

Fig. 2. Positions of EEG electrode attachments (Color figure online)

Geneva Affective PicturE Database (GAPED) in order to classify the possible emotions experienced by participants, before undertaking the HUD image experiment. The GAPED consists of six categories of visual emotion stimuli, each inducing an emotion of; scared, disgusted, angry, sad, neutral and happy. After the basic experiment, the 18 HUD images of 180 mm × 110 mm were displayed on a laptop.

Fig. 3. Laboratory (left) and driving simulator (right) environments

In the driving simulator-based experiment, the same HUD images were displayed on the right side of the center fascia.

The 16-channel EEG signals were measured while the participants observed the HUD images, in order to calculate the three EEG indices which measure the levels of EEG activity, concentration and relaxation of each participant. After observing each image, five pairs of antonyms and six individual emotive adjectives were rated on a scale of 1 to 7, corresponding to the amount of each emotion evoked by the images.

The five pairs of antonyms were; classic–modern, masculine–feminine, comfortable–insecure, soft–rough, certain–uncertain. For example, a score of 1 regarding 'masculine–feminine' means that the image articulated strong masculinity. Similarly, a score of 4 for 'comfortable–insecure' would suggest that the image conveyed neither a comfortable or insecure feeling to the participant, however the impression of the image was closer to being insecure. The six individual emotive adjectives were catagorized as; scared, disgusted, angry, sad, neutral and happy.

2.5   Experimental Procedure

The experiment was conducted for two hours. Participants closed their eyes for 30 s before being exposed to a HUD image for 30 s. The brain signals emitted during the observation of the image were recorded and evaluated. After the observation of the image, a survey was completed, regarding the emotions evoked by the image. This method of observing the image and answering questions regarding the image was repeated until all of the 18 HUD images were evaluated by each participant. The experiment was then repeated, displaying the images in random order. Again, after viewing the image for 30 s, each participant completed a survey until all of the 18 HUD images were evaluated twice, firstly in numerical order and then in a random order.

2.6   Data Analysis

The EEG signals corresponding to each emotion were evaluated after the experiment using the GAPED, which uses more drastic or explicit images as an effort to increase the availability of visual emotion stimuli. Noise in the recorded EEG signals was eliminated by pre-processing the data using frequencies in the range of 4 to 45 Hz, using a fast Fourier transform band pass filter. The three EEG analysis indicators of EEG activity, concentration and relaxation levels were considered. Alpha waves increased when at a comfortable state, and beta waves showed an increase at states of intentional activity, insecurity and tension. These characteristics were used to derive the following:

$$\text{EEG activity} = \text{Power Ratio of (Beta/Alpha)} \qquad ((1))$$

Theta waves decreased in the concentration state. The concentration level was defined by the SMR rhythm (12–15 Hz) which appeared during the unfocused attention state and the mid-beta rhythm (16–20 Hz) which appeared during the focused attention state:

$$\text{Concentration level} = \text{Power Ratio of (SMR + Mid} - \text{Beta)} /\text{Theta} \qquad ((2))$$

The relaxation level was observed at a relaxed state, and was calculated as the ratio of Alpha Power to High-Beta power.

$$\text{Relaxation level} = \text{Power Ratio of (Alpha/High} - \text{Beta)} \qquad ((3))$$

3   Results

3.1   Correlation Between Basic Emotions and EEG Signals

The mean values and standard deviation of the EEG analysis indices were obtained for each emotion and are represented by Table 2. The EEG signals were measured in microvolts (mV) however all values in Table 2 are represented as indices, therefore are unitless.

Table 2. Mean indices of EEG analysis for each basic emotion

	Scared	Disgusted	Sad	Angry	Neutral	Happy
EEG Activity	2.156 ± 0.902	1.938 ± 0.336	2.463 ± 1.037	1.366 ± 1.081	2.003 ± 0.801	2.380 ± 1.005
Concentration	0.486 ± 0.252	1.940 ± 0.922	0.413 ± 0.153	0.280 ± 0.220	0.452 ± 0.267	0.500 ± 0.276
Relaxation	1.913 ± 0.689	1.357 ± 0.172	1.708 ± 0.820	2.441 ± 0.585	1.576 ± 0.354	2.058 ± 0.653

According to the frequency range of the EEG signals which affect the emotions stimulated by the HUD images, delta (0–4 Hz), theta (0–4 Hz), alpha (8–13 Hz), beta (13–25 Hz), and gamma (25–30 Hz) waves were investigated, along with the levels of EEG activity, concentration and relaxation. The four primary elements were extracted by principal component analysis, using the VariMax rotation method which involved Kaiser normalization. The factor transform matrix is represented by Table 3 and the factors of rotation space was obtained (see Fig. 4).

Table 3. Factor transformation matrix of emotion and EEG analysis indices

	1	2	3	4
Happy	−.875			
Disgusted	.824			
Angry	.786			
Neutral	−.632			
Scared	.542			
EEG activity		−.943		
Alpha wave		.865		
Relaxation		.836		
Beta wave			.932	
Concentration			.902	
Sad				.922

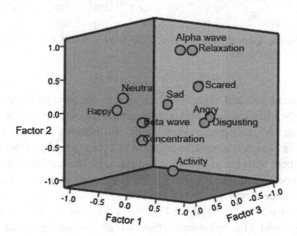

Fig. 4. Factors of emotion and EEG analysis indices

The principal component analysis graph shown by Fig. 4 represents each factor as an axis in three-dimensional space and illustrates the correlations between the alpha and beta waves; emotions and levels of EEG activity, concentration and relaxation; experienced by participants during the HUD image experiment. Factor 1 consists of happy and neutral emotions, substantial concentration levels and beta waves, hence group positive elements. Factor 2 shows the presence of significant alpha waves and relaxation levels and also, disgusted, sad and angry emotions, indicating a general provocation of anxious and negative emotions. Factor 3 showed a weak correlation between the EEG activity and indices and the emotions induced by HUD images.

3.2   Correlations Between HUD Images, Emotion and EEG Signals

Correlation analysis was performed to investigate the correlation between emotion and EEG analysis indices while participants were exposed to HUD images.

Pearson's correlation coefficients and the results of pairwise statistical significance were obtained and are shown in Table 4.

Table 4. Correlation coefficients of emotion and EEG analysis indices

	Activity	Concentration	Relaxation	Delta	Theta	Alpha	Beta	Gamma
Scared	$-.657^{**}$	.279	.020	$-.649^{**}$	$.517^{**}$	$.678^{**}$	$.446^{**}$	$-.379^{*}$
	.000	.100	.907	.000	.001	.000	.006	.023
Disgusted	$-.398^{*}$	.043	.315	$-.598^{**}$	.215	$.464^{**}$	$.568^{**}$	$-.023$
	.016	.803	.061	.000	.208	.004	.000	.893
Sad	$-.347^{*}$	.038	$.370^{*}$	$-.659^{**}$	.215	$.516^{**}$	$.605^{**}$	.029
	.038	.825	.026	.000	.207	.001	.000	.867
Angry	$-.510^{**}$	.214	.248	$-.657^{**}$	$.351^{*}$	$.579^{**}$	$.478^{**}$	$-.119$
	.001	.209	.145	.000	.036	.000	.003	.491
Neutral	$.510^{**}$	$-.184$	$-.231$	$.679^{**}$	$-.399^{*}$	$-.609^{**}$	$-.510^{**}$	.171
	.001	.283	.175	.000	.016	.000	.001	.320
Happy	$-.362^{*}$	.221	$.435^{**}$	$-.667^{**}$	.228	$.546^{**}$	$.574^{**}$	.026
	.030	.194	.008	.000	.180	.001	.000	.880

Note: **. Correlation coefficient significance level: 0.01 (both sides), *. Correlation coefficient significance level: 0.01 (both sides)

Scared, disgusted, sad and angry were relevant to negative emotions, and they were of lower levels when EEG activity and delta waves increased at the significance level of 0.01, however showed an increase when alpha and beta waves increased. For strong levels of happiness, which is a positive emotion, a strong correlation with the relaxation level, alpha and beta waves was shown when the significance level was 0.01. Neutral emotion was experienced predominantly by the participants when EEG activity increased and theta beta waves were of lower levels.

The EEG activity in each part of the brain was different, depending on the nature of each HUD image and Fig. 5 indicates that for all 18 images, participants showed activity in the left frontal lobe while being exposed to visual stimuli.

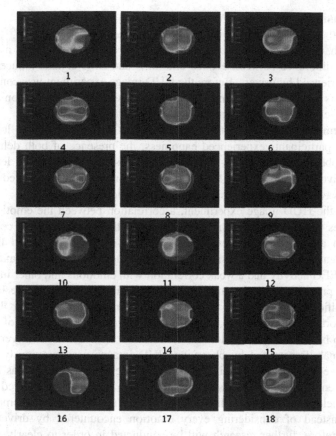

Fig. 5. EEG activity induced by each HUD image (Color figure online)

In the cases of the 4th, 15th, 7th and 18th HUD images, the parietal lobe was activated. One of the design elements of the image was the font, where Arial was used in every image except for the 18th image. Drivers experienced feelings of insecurity when the image was orange.

3.3   Comparison of Results of Prior and Current HUD Image Research

This study showed that emotions are induced by factors such as the amount and form of information provided, in which results of prior research were similar in a large percentage of cases. The results of the study showed a 80 % compliance with that of Smith's experiment for the antonym pair, 'modern–classic', 71 % for 'comfortable–insecure', and 100 % for 'certain–uncertainly', respectively. The emotions evoked by both the colour and location of information corresponded to the adjective pairs 'masculine–feminine' and 'soft–rough' both showed a 55 % in results of both studies, suggesting less compatibility between the current experiment and Smith's study.

4 Conclusion

This research was conducted as an effort to improve the interface of a vehicle by grasping the difference between evoked emotions and EEG signals induced by HUD images, experienced by drivers. Before the HUD image experiment was conducted, the activated parts of the brain depending on the different kinds of emotion felt by the participant, were identified through a basic experiment.

Neutral emotions showed theta and alpha waves in the frontal and left temporal lobes. When participants experienced happiness, the presence of both delta waves in the frontal lobe and alpha waves showed differences in both right and left temporal lobes. Negative emotions such as feeling disgusted, angry or sad, indicated differences in the beta waves between the frontal and temporal lobes.

Through the HUD image experiment, a correlation between the emotions evoked by the images was able to be found, by considering the beta waves and concentration levels which are affected by positive and neutral emotions. Also, in the case of increased negative emotions, the relation between alpha waves and relaxation levels were noted. EEG activity had a weak correlation with emotions and other indices. EEG activity was proportional to the amount of information provided by the HUD and it showed significant differences at the parietal and temporal lobes. After the interpretation of short-answer responses, the most effective design element of HUD was concluded to be color, as it had dominant effects on the emotion of drivers.

EEG signals transmitted by observing HUD images used previously in Smith's experiment were analysed according to design elements and emotions as first step to identify the emotions induced visual stimuli, which may be experienced by drivers inside a vehicle. The study was limited by the fact that only 6 basic emotions were evaluated, instead of considering every emotion encountered by drivers inside a vehicle. Therefore, further research will be conducted in order to clearly identify the difference in EEG signals depending on the emotions experienced by the participant, through undertaking more specific short-answer surveys and various analysis methods.

References

1. Yoo, H., Tsimhoni, O., Green, P.: The effect of HUD warning location on driver responses. In: International Transportation Systems World Congress, pp. 1–10 (1999)
2. Wierwille, W.W: Development of an initial model relating driver in-vehicle visual demands to accident rate. In: Third Annual Mid-Atlantic Human Factors Conference Proceedings, Virginia Polytechnic Institute and State University, Blacksburg, VA (1995)
3. Liu, Y.C.: Effect of using head-up display in automobile context on attention demand and driving performance. Displays 24, 157–165 (2003)
4. Tonnis, M., Lange, C., Klinker, G.: Visual longitudinal and lateral driving assistance in the head-up display of cars. In: Proceedings of the Sixth IEEE and ACM International Symposium on Mixed and Augmented Reality, Nara, Japan, pp. 128–131 (2007)
5. Smith, S., Fu, S.H.: The relationships between automobile head-up display presentation images and drivers' Kansei. Displays 32, 58–68 (2011)

Interactions in Affective Computing: Sharing a Haptic Experience Increases Calmness and Closeness

Norene Kelly[⊠]

Iowa State University, Ames, IA, USA
nbkelly@iastate.edu

Abstract. Our body representation and sense of self is constantly updated starting from the integration of different sensory inputs. Synchronous bodily stimulation has been used to manipulate sense of self, and can be applied to user experience design. This study manipulated multimodal stimulation to test factors potentially affecting mood and interpersonal closeness. The independent variables were: (1) the presence or absence of a haptic device (neck massager) on the participant; (2) the presentation of one of two videos, in which an actor expressed either energy or calmness while wearing the haptic device; and (3) the pre- and post-intervention time factor. The results showed a main effect for time for all dependent variables. A three-way interaction effect was evident for the measures of calmness and interpersonal closeness. The greatest reported increase in interpersonal closeness occurred in the haptic-energy video condition, an effect that was consistent with one of the study's hypotheses.

Keywords: Human computer interaction · Haptics · Affective computing · Mood · Interpersonal closeness · Embodied cognition · Social cognition · User experience · Therapeutic HCI · Multisensory integration · Self boundary

1 Introduction

As technology is increasingly a medium with which humans interact, the interface between the person and the machine is an increasingly salient interaction. Thus, it is possible to design technology with the intention of blurring this "boundary" (whether physically or conceptually) to augment user experience. The interface in human computer interaction (HCI) is commonly a computer screen, and in this study specifically featured a person—notable because other human beings and their bodily movements, which can be mapped onto our own bodies, are a distinctive and richly meaningful class of stimuli [1].

Given growing evidence that cognitive representations such as sense of self are not amodal but connected with our bodies, this experiment tested manipulations of the sensorimotor domain within a socially-situated HCI. Such research that advances theories of embodied and situated cognition (in which cognition is seen as taking place not only in the brain, but also in interaction with the world supported by the body) will be central for developments in HCI as well as in related fields such as artificial intelligence [2].

M. Kurosu (Ed.): Human-Computer Interaction, Part I, HCII 2015, LNCS 9169, pp. 477–488, 2015.
DOI: 10.1007/978-3-319-20901-2_45

1.1 Literature

Our body representation and sense of self is constantly updated starting from the integration of different sensory inputs [3, 4]. Sense of self begins with the body, but self is also one's psychological being (e.g., thoughts, feelings, attitudes), which in turn exists within a social matrix [5]. Conceptually, the self can be socially extended to other persons [6]. Relationships with loved ones are often described as a blurring of self-other boundaries; such merging can occur at both the conceptual and bodily level [7]. We use metaphors like "we are one" to convey our subjective experience of self in physical terms [8]. Our conceptual sense of self, then, is bound to our physicality and influenced by the sensorimotor domain, including bodily feedback [8, 9]. While one's body/self seems distinct from the world, this boundary is artificial [10]–an actuality that can be employed in user interface and interaction design.

Synchronous bodily *movement* has been used to manipulate conceptual self-boundaries. For example, in their study of synchrony and cooperation, [11] had participants walk in step in the experimental condition and walk normally in the control condition. They then asked the question: "How connected did you feel with the other participants during the walk?" Participants in the synchronous condition reported feeling more connected with their counterparts than those in the asynchronous condition.

Similarly, synchronous bodily sensation has been used to manipulate conceptual self-boundaries. Reference [7] brushed the cheek of study participants while participants watched the brushing applied to the face of a stranger shown in a video, in synchronous versus asynchronous conditions. The degree of self-other merging was determined by measuring participants' body sensations, their perception of face resemblance, their judgment of the inner state of the other, the closeness felt toward the other, and conformity behavior. The results showed that synchronous multisensory stimulation blurred self-other boundaries; participants exposed to synchronous stimulation showed more merging of self and other than participants exposed to asynchronous stimulation. The study concluded that multisensory integration can affect social perception and create a sense of self-other similarity [7]. Similar experiments have yielded this enfacement effect in the synchronous condition, which creates in the participant the sensations of being in front of a mirror [4].

The current study was based on such evidence that the ways we conceptualize, reason about, or visualize interpersonal experiences are influenced by the sensorimotor domain [8, 12]. The objective of this study was to take the metaphoric "overlap" that may arise between self and other and test it experimentally, and the significance is that the results can be applied to HCI. The evolution of technology toward adaptive systems that are capable of inferring emotion and incorporating multimodal interactions demands such research to provide a deeper understanding of the interplay of body and self, of emotion and social cognition.

1.2 Independent Variables and Hypotheses

The current experiment varied the conditions of the face-brushing experiment [7] by presenting versus not presenting a synchronous haptic experience (i.e., neck massager) between the participant and an actor (rather than synchronous versus asynchronous stimulation). The current study also included verbal content from the actor, which varied between two levels—energy and calm. For example, in the energizing video, the actor said the neck massager acted like coffee in making her energized, and in the calming video she said it acted like herbal tea to make her calm.

Hypothesis 1 predicted that the energy video would have an energizing effect and the calm video would have a calming effect in both the haptic and no haptic conditions. Hypothesis 1 further predicted that in the haptic conditions, these effects would be greater due to the synchronous haptic experience with the actor. In other words, the neck massager was intended to heighten similarity and familiarity, and was expected to aid in blurring the conceptual boundary between participant and actor in the haptic conditions. The synchronous haptic experience was hypothesized to convey "sameness" in both the tactile modality as well as the visual modality (in which it may be conceived as a shared morphology [13]), thus aiding in the transmission of the actor's mood via an emotional contagion [14].

Likewise, it was anticipated that the presence of the haptic device (the synchronous haptic experience) would result in participants perceiving a closer connection to the actor. Hypothesis 2 then predicted that participants in both the haptic-energy video and haptic-calm video conditions (as compared to those in the two no haptic conditions) would realize a pre-post gain in interpersonal closeness with the actor.

2 Methods

The study was a three-factor, between and within participants experiment. With regard to the two physiological measures, the study was a 2 (Haptic or No Haptic) × 2 (Energy Video or Calm Video) × 3 (Pre, Post 1, and Post 2 repeated measures) factorial design. With regard to the three self-report measures, the study was a 2 (Haptic or No Haptic) × 2 (Energy Video or Calm Video) × 2 (Pre and Post repeated measures) factorial design.

2.1 Dependent Variables

Based on the two hypotheses, two categories of dependent variables were of interest. One was the mood change (i.e., blurring of self-other boundary) from pre-video to post-video, which was expected to be affected by the actor's mood—more so in the haptic condition. Mood was measured by changes in heart rate and skin conductance, and subscales of [15] 's short mood scale. Reference [15] developed and evaluated the psychometric properties of this six-item scale based on the Multidimensional Mood Scale [16]. Two of the scale's three factors, Calmness and Energetic Arousal, were used in this study, as measured by four items. Reference [15] found reliability to be 0.90 for both Calmness and Energetic Arousal.

The second variable of interest was the self-other boundary as manifested in the participant's perception of interpersonal closeness to the actor. Participants responded to [7] 's version of [6] 's Inclusion of the Other in the Self Scale (IOS) scale (originally developed by [17]). The 7-point scale consists of a series of circles representing the self and the other person with different degrees of overlap. Reference [17] 's reliability check (test-retest) showed correlations between the original and the 2-week retesting as r = 0.83 overall and other measures supported the concurrent validity of the IOS Scale. Also to assess the self-other boundary, participants responded to the questions "How connected did you feel with the actor?", "How similar is the actor to yourself?", "How close do you feel to the actor," and "How much do you like the actor?", using a 9-point Likert scale. These questions were derived from [11] and [18], for which reliability was not reported. For this study, the interpersonal closeness measure (the sum of these four questions plus the IOS Scale) had a Cronbach's alpha of 0.87.

2.2 Apparatuses and Actor

The device used for haptic input was the Brookstone Shiatsu Neck and Shoulder Massager. Heart rate and skin conductance were measured with the FlexComp Infiniti Encoder. Video of the actor (an 18-year-old female college freshman) was recorded digitally on a Flip Video Camera and was viewed by participants on a 15-inch MacBook.

2.3 Participants

Healthy females between the ages of 18 and 30 were recruited via advertisements posted on campus and email invitations. Gender and age could be confounding factors, and therefore the study sought a somewhat homogenous sample of participants who resembled the actor in the video. Each participant read and signed consent documentation approved by the Institutional Review Board and received a $10 Caribou Coffee gift card for her participation.

Forty-eight women participated in the study. They ranged in age from 18 to 29, with a mean age of 21.29 (SD = 2.68). All were full-time students. About two-thirds (33) identified their race as White, whereas nine were Asian, two were Black or African American, and four offered multiple choices or left the question blank. About 90 % (44) were not Hispanic or Latino, whereas three were Hispanic or Latino, and one left the question blank.

Each of the 48 participants were randomly assigned to one of the four conditions, so that there were 12 participants in each condition. Related studies have used 10 to 18 participants per condition [4, 7, 11].

2.4 Procedure

A PC laptop contained the software (Biograph Infiniti Version 5.0.3 by Thought Technology Ltd.) used for the recording of physiological data. The accompanying hardware was FlexComp by Thought Technology Ltd., and consisted of the encoder, the SC-Flex/Pro sensor (for skin conductance), and the BVP-Flex/Pro sensor (for heart rate).

The investigator attached the skin conductance and BVP sensors to the non-dominant hand. Once the investigator began recording on the Biograph Infiniti, the participant responded to a brief demographic questionnaire and the Short Mood Scale. The investigator showed a still of the actor wearing the neck massager on the Mac-Book, and the participant responded to the interpersonal closeness measure. A rest period began, which took a total of 15 min from the start of the Biograph recording. The participant was offered a word search booklet to work on—a neutral activity to pass time.

About one minute prior to the start of the video (the 14-min. mark), the investigator placed the neck massager on the participant if she was assigned to the haptic condition. At the 15-min. mark, the investigator began the video on the MacBook—either calming or energizing, depending on the assignment. If the participant was in the neck massager condition, the investigator turned on the neck massager immediately after starting the video.

At the conclusion of the 3-min. video, the investigator turned off the neck massager (if applicable) and asked the participant to again respond to the Short Mood Scale. After showing the still of the actor wearing the neck massager on the MacBook, the participant again responded to the interpersonal closeness measure. The participant was then offered the word search booklet for the few remaining minutes of physiological data recording.

The period of physiological pre-data was defined as the five minutes prior to the start of the video. Two five-min. post-data periods were defined. Post 1 started one minute after the start of the video and Post 2 started at the conclusion of the video.

3 Results

A $2 \times 2 \times 3$ analysis of variance for the physiological dependent measures and a $2 \times 2 \times 2$ analysis of variance for the self-report dependent measures were computed, with repeated measures on the last factor. There was a significant main effect for time for all measures (Table 1), but no significant main effects for either haptic or video. Additionally, there were no significant effects for either Haptic $\times$ Time or Video $\times$ Time.

A three-way interaction effect was found for two measures. First, the calmness measure produced a three-way interaction effect, $F(1, 44) = 7.21$, $p = < .01$. A paired samples t-test revealed that one condition showed a significant pre-post increase: haptic-energy video ($p = < .05$). Second, there was a three-way interaction effect for interpersonal closeness, $F(1, 44) = 6.62$, $p = < .05$. A paired samples t-test revealed that two conditions showed a significant pre-post increase in interpersonal closeness: haptic-energy video and no haptic-calm video ($p = < .05$).

Therefore, Hypothesis 1 was not supported, but Hypothesis 2 was partially supported in that the haptic-energy video condition realized a significant pre-post gain in interpersonal closeness (14.33 ($SD = 5.37$) to 23.00 ($SD = 11.38$)) (Fig. 1).

Table 1. Changes of measures over time

Measure	Pre	Post 1	Post 2	F	η_p^2
Heart rate	78.11_a	75.97_b	76.95_c	8.00**	.15
	(12.54)	(11.93)	(11.90)		
	[74.38, 81.84]	[72.44, 70.50]	[73.42, 80.47]		
Skin conductance	4.57_a	5.71_b	5.79_b	60.85***	.58
	(4.81)	(5.14)	(5.21)		
	[3.15, 5.99]	[4.20, 7.23]	[4.25, 7.33]		
Calmness	8.40	–	9.29	6.037*	.12
	(2.92)		(2.67)		
	[7.57, 9.22]		[8.49, 10.09]		
Energetic arousal	7.77	–	6.77	8.82**	.17
	(2.18)		(2.47)		
	[7.15, 8.39]		[6.08, 7.46]		
Interpersonal closeness	16.46	–	19.96	9.53**	.18
	(6.07)		(8.63)		
	[14.69, 18.23]		[17.44, 22.48]		

Note. Below the means are standard deviations in parentheses and 95 % confidence intervals in brackets. Means with differing subscripts within rows are significantly different at the $p \leq .05$ based on Bonferroni adjustment for multiple comparisons.

*$p \leq .05$. **$p \leq .01$. ***$p \leq .001$.

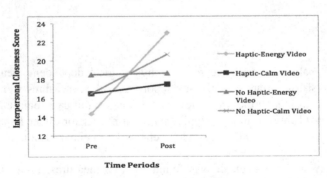

Fig. 1. Time × Haptic × Video interaction for interpersonal closeness measure

In summary, the results showed a main effect for time for all dependent variables: heart rate decreased, skin conductance increased, self-reported calmness increased, self-reported energetic arousal decreased, and self-reported interpersonal closeness to the actor increased. A three-way interaction effect was evident for the measures of calmness and interpersonal closeness. With regard to the primary hypotheses, there was a significant pre-post gain in interpersonal closeness for those participants who both shared the haptic experience *and* saw the video in which the actor conveyed energy. Interestingly, in this condition there was also a significant increase in participants' reporting a feeling of calmness.

4 Discussion

4.1 Heart Rate and Skin Conductance

Across conditions, there was a significant decrease in heart rate, which is in contrast to the hypothesis that heart rate would increase in the energy video conditions and decrease in the calm video conditions. Heart rate psychophysiology literature helps elucidate why heart rate decreased even in the presence of an actor showing energy.

A slowing of heart rate generally accompanies presentation of a novel stimulus [19]. Heart rate deceleration has been found to involve the mental intake of environmental stimuli or to accompany situations in which subjects "take in" perceptual materials; decreased heart rate has also been recorded during performance of a task as associated with increased sensitivity to stimulation [20].

In general, heart rate slows during intensive attention to stimuli [21]. However, if the external stimulus is a source of psychological stress, anxiety, or fear, heart rate will instead increase [21]. There is good support for the hypothesis that heart rate deceleration is associated with the orienting response and stimulus intake, and heart rate acceleration is associated with the defensive reaction and stimulus rejection [21]. In the present study, this hypothesis also appeared to be supported; neither of the videos, nor the haptic device, would generally be a cause of stress, anxiety, or fear, and therefore the decrease in heart rate can be interpreted as an orienting response and stimulus intake, and perhaps an indication of interest.

Across conditions, there was a significant increase in mean skin conductance, which is in contrast to the hypothesis that skin conductance would only increase in the energy video conditions and only decrease in the calm video conditions. The investigator's prediction that heart rate and skin conductance would rise and fall together was based on postulates of activation theory (e.g., [22]). However, criticisms of activation theory can be found in the principal of *stimulus-response specificity*, which states that specific stimulus contexts "...bring about certain patterns of responding, not just an increase or decrease in an unidimensional activation continuum... By definition, a stimulus-response specificity exists if a stimulus brings about a similar pattern of physiological responding among most subjects" [23, pp. 54, 65].

Directional fractionation is a special case of stimulus-response specificity which occurs when response directions are not uniform [24]. Therefore, for example, a person who is attentive to a potential threat will experience a decrease in heart rate and an increase in skin conductance. However, this particular physiological response does not necessarily imply stress, but is in fact an orienting response, which enhances our sensory processing while directing our attention to novel stimuli [23].

Therefore, the physiological response in this experiment was likely an orientation response to the presentation of the video, and this response was not affected by the haptic or video content factors.

4.2   Calmness and Energetic Arousal

Across conditions, there was a significant increase in self-reported calmness and decrease in self-reported energetic arousal. Additionally, there was a three-way interaction effect found for the calmness measure, for which further analysis revealed a significant effect in only one condition, haptic-energy video. These results are in contrast to the hypothesis that the two calm video conditions would increase calmness and that the two energy video conditions would increase energetic arousal.

First, why would calmness increase in the haptic-energy video condition? It is unusual that this effect did not also (or only) present in the haptic-calm video condition, and its absence may be due to insufficient power. Ideally a "control" condition of haptic-no video would have been implemented, but that was not feasible at the time of the study. Certainly, such neck massagers are marketed as relaxing (e.g., [25]), and although there is a dearth of experimental studies regarding their effects, the user generally has an expectation of relaxation or calming.

Second, why would energetic arousal decrease across conditions? One, this effect could be an artifact of the experimental procedure (i.e., the quiet room, generally low levels of stimulation, and the word search task during the measurement of baseline physiological measures). Two, the orienting response (as identified by the increase in skin conductance and decrease in heart rate) could have impacted self-reported mood. Specifically, participants may have been more aware of their heart rate decelerating rather than their skin conductance increasing. Heart rate is to some extent perceptible and breathing—the physiological process that most directly influences heart rate—can be voluntarily controlled; but voluntary control (or even awareness) of skin conductance is less likely [21, 26, 27]. Three, the experiment's video is similar to watching television, which "… appears to be a most potent means of providing relief from stress" [28, p. 107]. One reason for this is that television viewing likely disrupts "… rehearsal processes that would perpetuate states of elevated arousal associated with negative affective experiences" [28, p. 109]. Four, color that appeared in the video may have been a confounding factor. The actor wore a blue shirt and the background was blue-gray, and people tend to associate certain colors with certain emotional or arousal states. In two studies, [29] concluded that there was a systematic tendency for long-wavelength colors like red and orange to induce feelings of high arousal and for short-wavelength colors like violet and blue to induce feelings of low arousal. Similarly, [30] found that participants associated blue with the word group "calm, peaceful, serene."

4.3   Interpersonal Closeness

Across conditions there was an increase in interpersonal closeness as well as a three-way interaction effect, which revealed that two conditions showed a significant pre-post increase: haptic-energy video and no haptic-calm video. It was hypothesized that both haptic conditions would result in an increase in interpersonal closeness. Therefore, this hypothesis was partially supported by the increase in the haptic-energy video condition, which showed the largest mean increase. Although the mean increase in the no haptic-calm video condition was smaller, it was still significant. One potential issue is that of confounding variables—in this case, that participants' responses are likely in part influenced by the verbal content of the videos.

Another finding to examine is the increase in interpersonal closeness that was found in the haptic-energy video condition but not in the haptic-calm video condition. One possible reason for this is that energetic people may be perceived as more likeable, and likeability was part of the interpersonal closeness measure. For example, in a study of the personality traits of liked people, individuals who described themselves as "energetic/active" and "happy/joyful" were more liked in the sample of college freshman living in dormitories [31]. Certainly the actor in the energy video was more energetic and active than in the calm video, and it could also be argued that the energy video conveyed greater happiness and joy than the calm video.

Likewise, it is possible that the energy video engendered a more positive mood state than the calm video, thus resulting in a higher interpersonal closeness score. In a study of first-year college students, [32] hypothesized that positive emotions broaden people's feelings of self–other overlap in the beginning of a new relationship. They found that with new roommates, positive emotions predicted increased self–other overlap, which was measured with the Inclusion of Other in Self Scale [17] that was incorporated into the interpersonal closeness measure in the current study.

Additionally, various studies have found that mood can have a profound effect on information processing and judgments, as well as mimicry behaviors. For example, a correlation has been observed between mood and the non–conscious mimicry of a person on television; the more positive an individual's mood state, the more this individual mimicked the behavior of the person on the television [33].

5 Conclusion

The most notable finding of this study was the significant pre-post gain in interpersonal closeness in the haptic-energy video condition. The haptic effect found was as hypothesized, and possible reasons for the energetic condition interaction were suggested above. HCI applications that contain both haptic and interpersonal closeness factors would be wise to consider this effect and subject it to further testing.

With regard to the hypothesized (but unrealized) effect of the haptic factor blurring mood (i.e., increasing emotional contagion) between participant and actor, it is possible that the "experiential match" (the neck massager) between the actor and the participant was too subtle. The relevant literature emphasizes "action" (e.g., [1, 13]) and thus the passive haptic match between participant and actor (without movement) may not have been sufficient to invoke the hypothesized effects. On the other hand, mood was not a factor in the studies on synchronous stimulation and conceptual boundaries (e.g., [4, 7]) and therefore may not be susceptible to the manipulations performed in the present experiment.

This study was important in taking the metaphoric "overlap" between self and other and bringing it into the experimental realm. The study herein was based on theoretical evidence that this metaphor is grounded in the body (i.e., that sensorimotor inference informs concepts and social cognition) [8, 9, 12]. Additionally, these theories have been supported by studies that have demonstrated that simple body-based manipulations (e.g., of facial expression, posture, or movement) can causally influence the processing of emotional information [34] and that the cognitive phenomenon of self-other overlap can arise from a purely sensorial experience [7]. Future work must seek to understand the affective feedback loop between the user and the computer system; to design intelligent, adaptive systems, we need a deep comprehension not only of the computer system, but of the human system as well.

If an interaction designer seeks to increase users' feelings of interpersonal closeness to an actor, avatar, or virtual agent, synchronous haptic experience may prove useful. Important factors for exploration in future research include levels of immersion and levels of interaction. It may be that even in a low-immersion, low-interaction experience such as television viewing, a shared haptic experience can improve user experience. An example would be to use a football player's point of view for video while transmitting his heart rate to a user's smartwatch via haptic output, to more fully immerse the user in the player's experience.

In a similar example of HCI innovation, [35] described her students' development of a breathing sensor for users that mirrors the behavior of the user's character in the game. Synchronizing one's breath with the avatar's breath was necessary for game success, and [35] asserted that this type of experience is key to HCI design processes. "Without them we cannot create compelling and meaningful interactions in dialogue with our prospective users. But articulation of these experiences in academic texts is lacking—and sometimes very hard to capture… The dynamic gestalt of the interaction does not reveal itself to you until you experience it" [35, p. 10].

With regard to therapeutic applications, [36] summarized that touch is essential to our well-being, and that medical science is consequently developing therapies to incorporate haptics into the treatment of conditions such as autism spectrum, mood, anxiety and borderline disorders. They have prototyped a number of haptic devices that show promise in such treatments. While they did not explore the possibilities of pairing a haptic device with a computer mediation or video intervention (in a manner similar in the current study), that is certainly a possible avenue of investigation. If an increase in interpersonal closeness (or perhaps empathy) as well as calmness were goals of a given therapy, then synchronous haptic experience may be an appropriate piece of the interaction design of a novel HCI-based therapy.

Empirical findings such as those reported herein, coupled with advances in technology and user experience design, present new directions in blurring the boundary between the user and the interface. Such an embodied approach will likely prove valuable not only for refining human computer interaction, but for understanding the user as well.

Acknowledgments. The author thanks Dr. Stephen Gilbert for advising and supporting her Ph.D. studies, as well as Dr. Peter Martin, her advisor as she pursued her Masters (the source of this research). She is also grateful for the financial support provided by the Human Computer Interaction Graduate Program and the Department of Human Development and Family Studies at Iowa State University.

References

1. Semin, G.R., Cacioppo, J.T.: Grounding social cognition: synchronization, coordination, and co-regulation. In: Semin, G.R., Smith, E.R. (eds.) Embodied Grounding, pp. 119–147. Cambridge University Press, Cambridge (2008)
2. Garg, A.B.: Embodied cognition, human computer interaction, and application areas. Commun. Comput. Inf. Sci. **342**, 369–374 (2012)
3. Holmes, N.P., Spence, C.: The body schema and multisensory representation(s) of peripersonal space. Cogn. Process. **5**(2), 94–105 (2004)
4. Mazzurega, M., Pavani, F., Paladino, M.P., Schubert, T.W.: Self-other bodily merging in the context of synchronous but arbitrary-related multisensory inputs. Exp. Brain Res. **213**(2–3), 213–221 (2011)
5. Baumeister, R.F. (ed.): The Self in Social Psychology. Taylor & Francis, Psychology Press, Philadelphia (1999)
6. Schubert, T., Otten, S.: Overlap of self, ingroup and outgroup: pictorial measurement of self-categorization. Self Identity **4**, 353–376 (2002)
7. Paladino, M., Mazzurega, M., Pavani, F., Schubert, T.W.: Synchronous multisensory stimulation blurs self-other boundaries. Psychol. Sci. **21**(9), 1202–1207 (2010)
8. Lakoff, G., Johnson, M.: Philosophy in the Flesh: The Embodied Mind and Its Challenge to Western Thought. Basic Books, New York (1999)
9. Schubert, T.W., Koole, S.L.: The embodied self: making a fist enhances men's power-related self-conceptions. J. Exp. Soc. Psychol. **45**, 828–834 (2009)
10. Stoytchev, A.: Some basic principles of developmental robotics. IEEE Trans. Auton. Ment. Dev. **1**(2), 1–9 (2009)
11. Wiltermuth, S.S., Heath, C.: Synchrony and cooperation. Psychol. Sci. **20**(1), 1–5 (2009)
12. Semin, G.R., Smith, E.R.: Introducing embodied grounding. In: Semin, G.R., Smith, E.R. (eds.) Embodied Grounding, pp. 1–5. Cambridge University Press, Cambridge (2008)
13. Preston, S.D., de Waal, F.B.M.: Empathy: its ultimate and proximate bases. Behav. Brain Sci. **25**, 1–72 (2002)
14. Hatfield, E., Cacioppo, J.T., Rapson, R.L.: Emotional Contagion. Cambridge University Press, Cambridge (1994)
15. Wilhelm, P., Schoebi, D.: Assessing mood in daily life: structural validity, sensitivity to change, and reliability of a short-scale to measure three basic dimensions of mood. Eur. J. Psychol. Assess. **23**(4), 258–267 (2007)
16. Steyer, R., Schwenkmezger, P., Notz, P., Eid, M.: Der mehrdimensionale Befindlichkeitsfragebogen. Handanweisung [The Multidimensional Mood Questionnaire (MDMQ)]. Hogrefe, Göttingen (1997)
17. Aron, A., Aron, E.N., Smollan, D.: Inclusion of other in the self scale and the structure of interpersonal closeness. J. Pers. Soc. Psychol. **63**(4), 596–612 (1992)
18. Liviatan, I., Trope, Y., Liberman, N.: Interpersonal similarity as a social distance dimension: implications for perception of others' actions. J. Exp. Soc. Psychol. **44**, 1256–1269 (2008)
19. Lynn, R.: Attention, Arousal, and the Orientation Reaction. Pergamon, Oxford (1966)
20. Lacey, J.I., Kagan, J., Lacey, B.C., Moss, H.A.: The visceral level: situational determinants and behavioral correlates of autonomic response patterns. In: Knapp, P.H. (ed.) Expression of the Emotions in Man, pp. 161–196. International University Press, New York (1963)
21. Andreassi, J.L.: Psychophysiology: Human Behavior and Physiological Response. Lawrence Erlbaum Associates Inc., Mahwah (2000)
22. Cannon, W.B.: Bodily Changes in Pain, Hunger, Fear, and Rage. Appleton, New York (1915)

23. Stern, R.M., Ray, W.J., Quigley, K.S.: Psychophysiological Recording. Oxford University Press, New York (2001)
24. Lacey, J.I.: Somatic response patterning and stress: some revisions of activation theory. In: Appley, M.H., Trumbull, R. (eds.) Psychological Stress. Appleton Century Crofts, New York (1967)
25. Brookstone. http://www.brookstone.com/shiatsu-neck-and-shoulder-massager
26. Combatalade, D.C.: Basics of Heart Rate Variability Applied to Psychophysiology. Thought Technology Ltd., Montreal (2010)
27. Schachter, S.: The interaction of cognitive and physiological determinants of emotional state. In: Berkowitz, L. (ed.) Advances in Experimental Social Psychology, vol. 1, pp. 49–80. Academic Press, New York (1964)
28. Zillmann, D.: Television viewing and physiological arousal. In: Bryant, J., Zillmann, D. (eds.) Responding to the Screen: Reception and Reaction Processes, pp. 103–134. Lawrence Erlbaum, Hillsdale, NJ (1991)
29. Walters, J., Apter, M.J., Svebak, S.: Color preference, arousal, and the theory of psychological reversals. Motiv. Emot. 6(3), 193–215 (1982)
30. Wexner, L.B.: The degree to which colors (Hues) are associated with mood-tones. J. Appl. Psychol. 38(6), 432–435 (1954)
31. Wortman, J., Wood, D.: The personality traits of liked people. J. Res. Pers. 45, 519–528 (2011)
32. Waugh, C.E., Fredrickson, B.L.: Nice to know you: positive emotions, self-other overlap, and complex understanding in the formation of a new relationship. J. Posit. Psychol. 1(2), 93–106 (2006)
33. van Baaren, R.B., Fockenberg, D.A., Holland, R.W., Janssen, L., van Knippenberg, A.: The moody chameleon: the effect of mood on non-conscious mimcry. Soc. Cognit. 24(4), 426–437 (2006)
34. Winkielman, P., Niedenthal, P.M., Oberman, L.M.: Embodied perspective on emotion-cognition interactions. In: Pineda, J.A. (ed.) Mirror Neuron Systems, pp. 235–257. Humana Press, New York (2009)
35. Hook, A.: A cry for more tech at CHI! Interactions XIX.2, 10–11 (2012)
36. Vaucelle, C., Bonanni, L., Ishii, H.: Design of haptic interfaces for therapy. In: CHI 2009 Learning Challenges, pp. 467–470, Boston, MA, 6 April 2009

The Effect of Gamification on Emotions - The Potential of Facial Recognition in Work Environments

Oliver Korn[(⊠)], Sandra Boffo, and Albrecht Schmidt

University of Stuttgart, VIS, Stuttgart, Germany
{oliver.korn,albrecht.schmidt}@acm.org,
inf70415@stud.uni-stuttgart.de

Abstract. Gamification means using video game elements to improve user experience and user engagement in non-game services and applications. This article describes the effects when gamification is used in work contexts. Here we focus on industrial production. We describe how facial recognition can be employed to measure and quantify the effect of gamification on the users' emotions.

The quantitative results show that gamification significantly reduces both task completion time and error rate. However, the results concerning the effect on emotions are surprising. Without gamification there are not only more unhappy expressions (as to expect) but surprisingly also more happy expressions. Both findings are statistically highly significant.

We think that in redundant production work there are generally more (negative) emotions involved. When there is no gamification happy and unhappy balance each other. In contrast gamification seems to shift the spectrum of moods towards "relaxed". Especially for work environments such a calm attitude is a desirable effect on the users. Thus our findings support the use of gamification.

Keywords: Gamification · Assistive technology · Facial recognition · Affective computing · Computer-assisted instruction · Augmented reality · Human machine interaction

1 Introduction

Gamification is a delightful concept: it is a creditable idea to use "video game elements to improve user experience and user engagement in non-game services and applications" [3]. The link between emotions and motivation is important, especially in context of employee motivation: after all, increased engagement should have numerous benefits like improved performance and greater user satisfaction [10].

This article describes how gamification can be used in work contexts like industrial production. Since industrial production already involves processes with measurable physical outcomes (e.g. the number of parts produced per hour), gaming elements like scores and leaderboards could be implemented with comparatively little effort. Ideally

© Springer International Publishing Switzerland 2015
M. Kurosu (Ed.): Human-Computer Interaction, Part I, HCII 2015, LNCS 9169, pp. 489–499, 2015.
DOI: 10.1007/978-3-319-20901-2_46

the system should also be able to measure the effect that gamified work processes have on speed and quality.

However, if gamification is to succeed in such environments, a system employing it will need a back channel to determine if a specific intervention has increased or decreased a user's mood. A preferred approach to measuring the user's emotional state in work environments are facial expressions since they can be measured without physical contact to the worker.

2   State of the Art

The integration of gamification into business contexts has first been described by Reeves & Read [11]. However, they have been focusing on office contexts. A concept for the integration of gamification into production environments has first been described by Korn [6]. While this concept already included real-time feedback based on motion tracking, it lacked a feedback channel which allows monitoring the effects of gamification.

A more detailed model (Fig. 1) for implementing gamification in work environments was described in the context of context aware assistive systems (CAAS) two years later by Korn et al. [7].

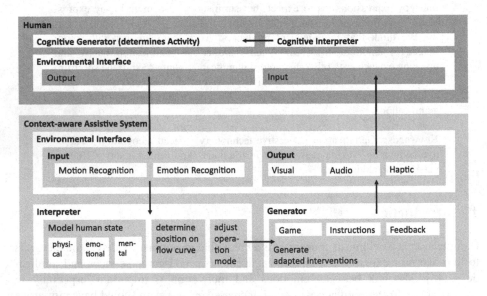

Fig. 1. CAAS-model by Korn et al.

This model also establishes the notion of a flow state as a desirable outcome of gamification. This is an emotional state in-between arousal and control where high skills and high demands converge – as described by Csíkszentmihályi in the late seventies [2].

However, in the context of this work the more important aspect is the integration of emotion recognition in the environmental interface. Within the CAAS-model emotion recognition is considered a pre-requisite for determining a user's current flow state and thus adapting the interventions generated by the system. A good example is the need to determine if a worker reduces work speed because of boredom or because of exhaustion. While boredom would require an energizing stimulus (or even an increase in production speed if the system allows for such adaptations), exhaustion would require just the opposite.

Some assistive systems in production environments already feature cameras for motion recognition [8]. Thus the preferred approach for measuring the user's emotional state is using these cameras to analyze the facial expressions. By using these cameras no additional system is required and also no physical contact to the worker – in contrast to sensors for galvanic skin response or most heart rate sensors.

In various studies Ekman showed that human emotions can be categorized into six basic categories: anger, sadness, happiness, surprise, disgust and fear [4, 5]. Each of these basic emotions is characterized by a typical facial expression caused by stretched or released facial muscles (Fig. 2).

Fig. 2. Basic emotions: surprise, sadness, happiness, contempt and anger.

A result of this research was the facial coding system (FACS). It focuses on special muscle groups around the mouth and the eyes. These are crucial in the activity of expressing emotions and thus are called "Action Units".

3 Implementation

For the purpose of the pioneering study, determining the states "happy" versus "not happy" was considered a sufficient granularity to measure the effects of gamification – other emotions like anger and fear or even disgust were considered as unlikely to appear (or at least to be shown) in a production work setting.

The emotion recognition system has to ensure a high performance because real-time evaluation is required. A feedback given a few seconds after the event is already considered a disturbance. To achieve performance in real-time, the image size of the captured faces has to be reduced. Also it is required to use simple methods of pattern recognition which can be computed fast.

3.1   Face Detection

At first the image region is reduced, since for analyzing facial expressions only the face is of interest. This minimizes the memory significantly. We implemented the Viola-Jones-Algorithm which uses three simple methods that can be computed fast.

The algorithm converts a grayscale input image into an integral image. Then it uses Haar-like features to detect faces. Haar-like features are rectangular patterns based on characteristic regions within a face like the region around the eyes or around the mouth. These characteristics are caused by variations of bright and dark parts as shown in Fig. 3.

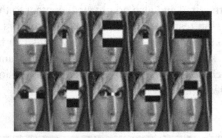

Fig. 3. Haar-like features.

3.2   Feature Extraction and Bag of Features

As mentioned before every emotion has characteristic features, i.e. characteristic feature points (key points). These key points were extracted from detected faces using the Speeded Up Robust Features algorithm (SURF) which is invariant towards scale and rotation [1]. Therefore it was considered to be well-suited for working processes where rotations and various illumination conditions are to be expected.

Similar to face detection it is based on the Haar-like features. The Fast-Hessian-Method is used to smooth the input image by convolution with Gaussian. Afterwards the algorithm detects key points. For every detected key point a feature vector with 64 entries is computed. Since every facial expression consists of various key points there are several 64D feature vectors for every emotion. Although every emotion causes numerous feature vectors based on unique key points, some of these points are "useless" as they do not describe an important point within the emotion. By using k-means clustering we created a "Bag of Features" for all important feature vectors of the emotions, i.e. their remarkable features. Thus similar key points were clustered and an emotion was recognized by its typical key points only.

3.3   Limitations of Facial Recognition

After the system was implemented we tested it both in the lab and in the wild. The emotional recognition (in our work-oriented scenario mainly the discrimination between happy and unhappy) was stable in the lab.

However, we found that in work environments the method is not reliable. The illumination changes quickly because of suboptimal lighting conditions in combination with the worker's movements. Although the SURF algorithm is supposedly invariant towards scale and rotation this caused problems: shadows on the face distort the expression and emotions were not recognized correctly. The changing illumination also increased latency. To counterbalance such effects and still avoid body-attached sensors, additional cameras and lighting would be required in work environments.

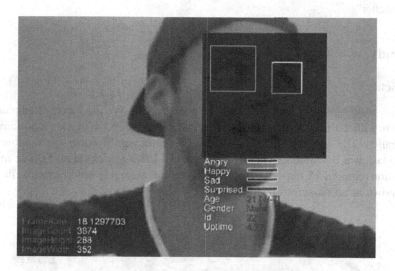

Fig. 4. Emotion detection based on SHORE.

To evaluate the effects of gamification in spite of the deficits of the facial detection system, the emotional states were identified in a "semi-automated" detection process:

1. The emotions were pre-classified by SHORE (Sophisticated High-speed Object Recognition Engine [9], Fig. 4).
2. The recognized emotions were re-assessed and fed into the system by human observers.

Technically this results in a Wizard-of-Oz study.

3.4   Gamification

While the focus of this work lies on the facial detection aspect, gamification is the underlying method which is being analyzed. When implementing gamification, we deliberately chose a simple and established approach:

- providing real-time multimodal feedback (audio and visual)
- displaying performance (required time and committed errors)
- using scores to increase motivation and establish flow

The gamification system allocates 10 points per step. Each mistake or slow step results in a score reduction of 10 points. Thus in the 15-step scenario the score was gradually reduced from a maximum of 150 points down to zero.

Reaching zero could either be a result of 15 mistakes or of 15 slow steps or a mixture of both. Although theoretically 15 slow and wrong steps would result in a negative score (here: −150) the score was capped at zero.

The probands received real-time feedback on both the time and the error rate. However, negative feedback was phrased positively to avoid demotivation, e.g. "you can do better".

4 Study

4.1 Setup

The study was conducted with ten probands age 19 to 38. We used a repeated measures approach with 10 task repetitions without gamification and 10 task repetitions with gamification. The sequence of tasks with and without gamification was randomized.

The task was assembling a model consisting of LEGO bricks (Fig. 5). The model's completion required 15 steps. As common in manual assembly environments, the steps were shown in an on-screen instruction.

Fig. 5. Lego model used in the study.

Each test subject completed a two-part questionnaire with an emotional self-evaluation. The first part was used before the assembly and the second part after the assembly. The questionnaire evaluated the effects recognized by the test persons.

Fig. 6. Setup in the assembly phase of the study.

During the assembly phase (Fig. 6) we measured the task completion time, the error rate and the emotions. The screen in front of the proband showed the instructions and (in the gamification part) the gamification elements.

The camera was placed in the center in front of the monitor and was re-adjusted for each proband to maximize the quality of the facial recognition.

4.2   Results

Several test persons were generally not comfortable with having to build the model several times. However, this was an intended effect which shows that repetitive work is not appreciated.

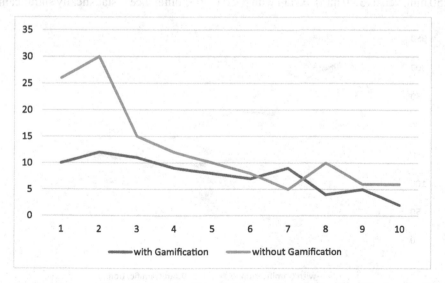

Fig. 7. Average number of errors in 10 repetitions with gamification (blue) and without gamification (red) (Color figure online).

When comparing the development of the error rate (Fig. 7), which is the most important business ratio in production environments, it is obvious that gamification decreases and equalizes the error rate. With p < 0.05 this difference is statistically significant.

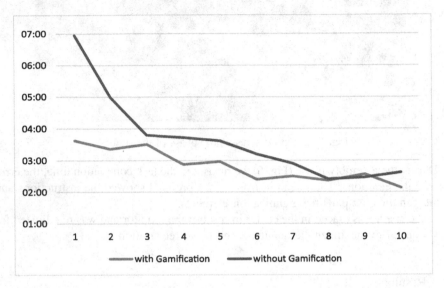

Fig. 8. Average task completion time in 10 repetitions with gamification (blue) and without gamification (red) (Color figure online).

The mean task completion time (Fig. 8) was 50 s lower with gamification than without (2:50 min. versus 3:40 min). Again with p < 0.05 this difference is statistically significant.

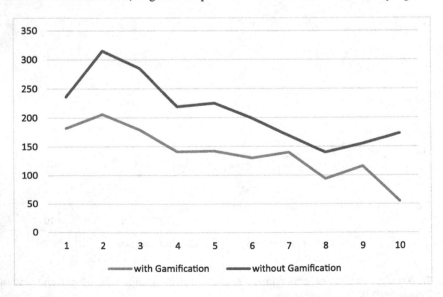

Fig. 9. Happy expressions with gamification (blue) and without gamification (red) (Color figure online).

When comparing the number of happy expressions (Fig. 9) the difference is striking: on average there are 138.5 expressions with gamification and 211.6 without. This finding contradicts intuition: we would expect more happy expressions with gamification. However, this counterintuitive finding is statistically highly significant ($p < 0.01$).

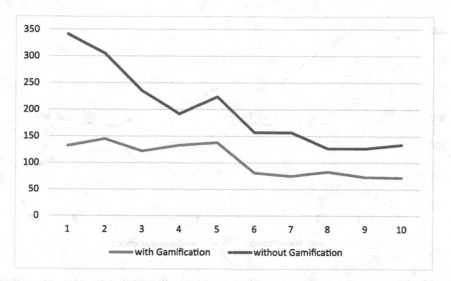

Fig. 10. Unhappy expressions with gamification (blue) and without gamification (red) (Color figure online).

The surprising result with regard to the happy expressions is counter-balanced when analyzing the unhappy expressions: on average there are 105.4 unhappy expressions with gamification and 199.9 unhappy expressions without gamification. This is what intuition would predict. Again, this finding is statistically highly significant ($p < 0.01$) (Fig. 10).

5   Discussion and Conclusion

Generally the test subjects stated that they felt the gamification elements very motivating. These assertions are confirmed by the quantitative results with respect to task completion time and error rate: gamification reduces both significantly.

The results regarding emotions are surprising. Without gamification there are not only more unhappy expressions (as to expect) but surprisingly also more happy expressions. Both findings are statistically highly significant. In our understanding, there are three potential explanations for this phenomenon:

1. the emotion detection method is not reliable: this is unlikely due to the additional human control
2. the participants deliberately or subconsciously conceal expressions of happiness in the gamification setup: this is possible but unlikely

3. when there is no gamification there are generally more emotions involved and
   happy and unhappy balance each other

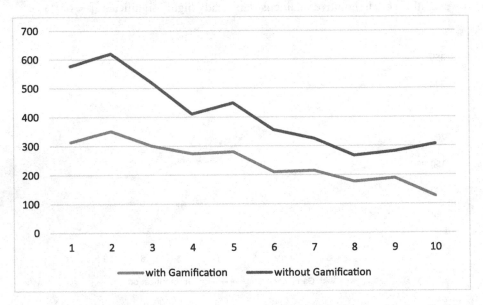

Fig. 11. Expressions of positive or negative emotions with gamification (blue) and without
gamification (red) (Color figure online).

We favor the third explanation. This hypothesis is supported by the fact that
obviously (Fig. 11) there are more emotions without gamification (highly significant
$p < 0.01$). As several probands have expressed their dislike for the repetitive task, a
psychological explanation of this phenomenon is the following: once there are stronger
emotions (here: disliking the task) they escalate and are displayed on both sides of the
spectrum.

In contrast gamification seems to shift the spectrum of moods towards "relaxed"
(i.e. no measurable expression). Especially for work environments such a calm attitude
is a desirable effect on the users. Thus our findings support the use of gamification.

6 Future Work

With only 10 probands this work can only be a first step into measuring the impact of
gamification on emotions in work environments. Still the findings are unexpected and
have to be validated by extensive studies with more test subjects. Also a more reliable
facial recognition is needed which (for this purpose) could be supported by
body-attached sensors.

References

1. Bay, H., Tuytelaars, T., Van Gool, L.: SURF: speeded up robust features. In: Leonardis, A., Bischof, H., Pinz, A. (eds.) ECCV 2006, Part I. LNCS, vol. 3951, pp. 404–417. Springer, Heidelberg (2006)
2. Csíkszentmihályi, M., Nakamura, J.: The concept of flow. In: Snyder, C.R., Lopez, S.J. (eds.) The Handbook of Positive Psychology, pp. 89–92. Oxford University Press, Oxford (2002)
3. Deterding, S., Sicart, M., Nacke, L., O'Hara, K., Dixon, D.: Gamification. using game-design elements in non-gaming contexts. In: Proceedings of the 2011 Annual Conference Extended Abstracts on Human Factors in Computing Systems, pp. 2425–2428. ACM (2011)
4. Donato, G., Bartlett, M.S., Hager, J.C., Ekman, P., Sejnowski, T.J.: Classifying facial actions. IEEE Trans. Pattern Anal. Mach. Intell. **21**(10), 974–989 (1999)
5. Ekman, P.: Facial expression and emotion. Am. Psychol. **48**(4), 384 (1993)
6. Korn, O.: Industrial playgrounds: how gamification helps to enrich work for elderly or impaired persons in production. In: Proceedings of the 4th ACM SIGCHI Symposium on Engineering Interactive Computing Systems, EICS 2012, pp. 313–316. ACM (2012)
7. Korn, O., Funk, M., Abele, S., Hörz, T., Schmidt, A.: Context-aware assistive systems at the workplace: analyzing the effects of projection and gamification. In: Proceedings of the 7th International Conference on Pervasive Technologies Related to Assistive Environments, PETRA 2014, pp. 38:1–38:8. ACM (2014)
8. Korn, O., Schmidt, A., Hörz, T.: Assistive systems in production environments: exploring motion recognition and gamification. In: Proceedings of the 5th International Conference on PErvasive Technologies Related to Assistive Environments, PETRA 2012, pp. 9:1–9:5. ACM (2012)
9. Küblbeck, C., Ernst, A.: Face detection and tracking in video sequences using the modifiedcensus transformation. Image Vis. Comput. **24**(6), 564–572 (2006)
10. McGonigal, J.: Reality is Broken: Why Games Make us Better and How they can Change the World. Penguin Books, New York (2011)
11. Reeves, B., Read, J.L.: Total Engagement: Using Games and Virtual Worlds to Change the Way People Work and Businesses Compete. Harvard Business Press, Boston (2009)

Towards the Evaluation of Emotional Interfaces

Damien Lockner[1,2(✉)] and Nathalie Bonnardel[1]

[1] Research Center in the Psychology of Cognition, Language and Emotion,
(PsyCLE, E.A.3273), Aix Marseille Université, Aix-En-Provence, France
{damien.lockner,nathalie.bonnardel}@univ-amu.fr
[2] Spicy Life, Toulon, France
damien.lockner@spicy.life

Abstract. The emotional design approach has become increasingly preponderant for the design teams. However, we observed that most of the efforts of the designers to elicit positive emotions are based on empirical and subjective approaches. This paper shares the state of our current research towards the proposal of heuristics for emotional and empathic interfaces. We focus on the actual design practices, and discuss methodologies to assess the emotions elicited by these design strategies.

Keywords: User experience design · Emotional design · Empathic design · Ergonomics

1 Introduction

1.1 From Usability to Emotional Design

During numerous years, ergonomic recommendations or « golden rules » [1, 2] have been put forwards, tending to focus on users' cognitive and perceptual-motor abilities. Ergonomists and designers have seeked for an ever-reduced cognitive load required by tasks and interactions. Thus, human-computer interaction is traditionally conceived and assessed through the restrictive scope of usability rather than based on what users feel when interacting with a system [3, 4].

Although this approach has led to an overall improvement of the interfaces ease-of-use, it is now being overstepped by design teams, as well as researchers. The « feeling » level has become a popular research topic in cognitive science and the science of design. New systems must also inject a little fun and pleasure into people's lives [1]. Thus, in addition to their functional characteristics, interactive systems must be regarded as conveying feelings through interfaces' design features. Pleasurable products would likely suggest security, confidence, pride, excitement and satisfaction, whereas displeasurable products would carry annoyance, anxiety, contempt and frustration [5].

Thus, the question of the feelings of users – preferentially associated to positive emotions - has become crucial for the interface project stakeholders.

© Springer International Publishing Switzerland 2015
M. Kurosu (Ed.): Human-Computer Interaction, Part I, HCII 2015, LNCS 9169, pp. 500–511, 2015.
DOI: 10.1007/978-3-319-20901-2_47

1.2   The Emotional Design, and the Designers

According to various design publications, many designers now seem to be aware of the emotional design issue. Friedman [6] manages a collection of web design books targeting an audience of designers. He underlines to his readers the crucial importance of an emotional approach towards design: "A strong, reliable emotional relationship between your clients and their audience could be the best thing that ever happens to your career." [6], this statement being supported by the various assets of an end-user positive emotion. Thus, in Friedman's books collections, and in several others, one may find a selection of websites, good examples of a 'surprising' or a 'delightful' experience. These publications are very representative of our question: Designers are today aware of the importance of emotional design; however, shared empiric solutions and case studies appear to be the only available resources to guide their works beyond the trial and error approach. It seems that the interface design stakeholders miss strong methodological tools and references to base their works on.

Ergonomic psychology could probably assist the designers in their tasks, helping them to define the emotions to elicit, and to target more accurately the design strategies leading to positive emotions. Designers would not be the only beneficiaries; also ergonomists in charge of interface assessments towards effective end-users needs, would identify more easily emotional design assets and improvements.

1.3   How to Design an Interface Emotionally? A State of Our Current Research

In this paper, we share the state of our current research towards the proposal of heuristics for empathic interfaces, targeting both designers and ergonomists communities.

As a first step of our research, we reviewed and pointed out several actual empirical practices and strategies used by interface designers to elicit a positive emotion.

As a second step, we present a methodological approach grounded into cognitive psychology, to assess those emotional design strategies. In addition, an emotional design process representation is proposed, in order to extract the design factors from the others that compose the global emotional experience of the user.

We conclude by introducing a potential third step, an alternative setup to assess emotional design interfaces in a more ecological environment.

2   Emotional Design and Interfaces: A Review of the Field Practice

2.1   Focus Group with Designers: From Emotions to Empathy

In order to establish a set of heuristics proposals, a first step in our research consists of identifying emotional design strategies by studying the nature of the actual empirical approaches used by designers. As a preliminary stage, a focus group was set up with three designers of complementary profiles, whose experience varied from four to eleven years: a user experience manager, a mobile product designer, and a user interface designer. The discussion was set up on an opened basis, framed by this initial question: "We are interested by the ways to elicit an emotion to the end-user through an interface. You may know or already use some specific strategies in order to elicit positive emotion. What would be those strategies?" Many aspects were evoked by the designers, presented here as a thematic synthesis.[1]

Primordial usability. Ergonomic requirements, such as Bastien's and Scapin's [3] lead to consistency, intuitiveness, and ease of learn. Those qualities participate to the feel of trust towards the application, and by extension, towards the brand or the under-lying product or service. Usability is also connected to the notion of 'robustness', understood as the actual effectiveness and efficiency, completed by the notion of 'perceived robustness', which addresses more graphic design strategies.

These usability requirements are crucial for the designers. Usability is not a strategy in itself; it is considered as a fundamental solid foundation without which emotional design cannot be built.

Error handling, and dialog. Beyond the notion of 'robustness' already evoked, the error message was considered as a good opportunity to engage a dialog with the user. Thus, it is an occasion to elicit an emotion. As one of the designers said: "We try to explain what happened in human terms. We suggest a way to solve the problem. If it is really not possible, then we apologize." This point underlines an important pattern: the designers try to get as close as possible to a natural human-to-human (friendly) relationship, rather than a usual disembodied human-to-computer interaction.

Identity. "The keyword is 'personalization' [...]. We create a relationship because people do not totally trust machines yet." In order to build a relationship similar to human behaviors, the user should be considered by the interface as a real identified person, rather than an impersonal iterated entity. Several ways are evoked by the designers: customized messages with the user's name, taking into account user's behaviors or geographic localization... Used in a proper way, these strategies may improve trust towards the application.

Identity does not only refer to the user, it also refers to the application. A strong and clear identity should also belong to the interface. The underlying design intention is to make the interface more human and less abstract: "They [the interface designers] talk to you [the interface user] as a human being. They talk to you nicely, normally, with their guts."

Targeted side content. Following the idea of a humanized interface, some content may be relevant, although they look surprising at first. The example of Balsamiq was evoked by the designers: Balsamiq is an application whose purpose is to design websites wireframes. In the help menu, you can find a link towards a cooking idea and its video recipe "What should I make for dinner?" [8]. This feature looks incongruous

---

[1] Detailed results are available in [4].

in a professional software. Beyond the first surprise, the intention of the software is to understand, sympathize with the user. The video recipe is accompanied with this little explanation: "We know how it is. It's 5 pm, and you've just had a glorious day of work, creating awesome wireframes for your next project. You are giddy with excitement, and cannot wait to see your designs in the hands of your sure-to-fall-in-love-with-it-immediately users. And then it hits you: crap, what should I make for dinner tonight? [...]."

Another more discreet example evoked by the designers is the little mention in the footer of each page of Vimeo [9]: "Made with ♥ in NYC." With this simple little sentence, Vimeo's designers become tangible humans, who feel love and passion towards their work, and who therefore hold high esteem to the end-users. As a consequence, the end-users return trust and sympathy towards the application.

Targeted audience. These last statements evoked by the interviewed designers share a common background: In order to apply a strong identity and tone to an application, the audience should be carefully defined and targeted. The designers explain that the most emotional the interface is, the most characterized the audience must be: "the most important stage is to understand who we are talking to, and to identify the right leverages, specific to that audience."

Gamification. Designers also mentioned game patterns as a way to engage the users more. Gamification is widely documented, so we chose not to develop it in this paper.

Conclusion: hedonomics and empathy. This focus group emphasized several emotional design patterns. Beyond the fundamental usability requirement, the notion of 'interface as a human' seems to emerge in order to elicit positive emotions. The more the user perceives the empathy of the [author/designer/interface], the more his/her use experience would be delightful. According to this hypothesis, several successive thresholds could be defined as we progress towards a positive emotion of the end-user:

1. The application is useful and effective.
2. The application's efficiency is optimal.
3. The communication strategy and the content are coherent and relevant towards the individual.
4. The end-user is aware of the existence of an author/designer: "These people made this for me."
5. The end-user is aware of the empathy of an author/designer: "These people understand me very well, they think about me, and want to please me."

We formulated these thresholds as a derivation from the works of Hancock, Pepe and Murphy [5] who proposed a 'hedonomic' pyramid, derived itself from Maslow's pyramid. We note that the highest the level of conception is, the more the underlying design strategies need to be targeted towards a specific audience. Most of the users may consider an application useful, but only some of them may perceive and respond to the author's empathy. Thus, emotional design strategies would only be applicable since the third level of this pyramid.

2.2   Designers' Returns of Experience: The Emotional Design Books

With the rising importance of the emotional approach in interface design, many technical publications, written by designers for designers, have appeared during these last years [7, 10–12]. These publications are mainly structured onto case reviews, with several commented examples. Therefore, this documentation constitutes a large resource in order to draw an overview of the actual design practices for emotional design. These publications gather many different approaches, which do not always refer strictly to positive emotion elicitation. Thus, persuasive design approaches were dismissed. Gamification would likely drive positive emotions as well, but was dismissed too, as it belongs to a different set of strategies.

Application personality. The notion of personality was evoked by several authors [10–12]. These authors note that users may behave and interact with an application or a product as if it was a real human being, even if those users are conscious that it is indeed an inanimate object [6, 13].

The design persona is a design technique whose goal is to define a consistent identity and personality to the application. If the application was a character, who would it be? How would it speak? What would be its values, and its way of mind? This technic provides a guideline to build an application identity, for a more humanized human-computer relationship [12]. Thus, building up an application personality compatible with the users' expectations would constitute a strong leverage on the user experience improvement; the user-interface relationship would be brought closer to a friendly relationship [14].

Çakmakli [14] thus proposes to get inspired by the traits characterizing a friend in order to design an emotional interface. She identifies a set of seven traits from a parallel with social psychology research on mate selection, which may be translated into design features:

- Attractiveness (sexy, cute, beautiful, graceful);
- Social status (lifestyle, social class, value system);
- Intelligence (smart, adaptive, intuitive, functions well);
- Trustworthiness (loyal, safe, trusting);
- Empathy (understanding, adaptive, communicative);
- Ambitious (innovative, forward thinking, aspiring, motivated);
- Exciting (good sense of humor, positively surprising, creative).

Çakmakli's categories [14] establish an interesting synthesis, as most of the strategies elicited by the designers in their publications may fit one of these traits. It also seems possible to bring some of these traits closer to the three emotional levels of Norman [15]: visceral, behavioral, or reflective.

2.3   Emotional Design Approach Mapping Diagram

The various sources that we compiled, based on a focus group and a design literature revue, led us to a mapping of the designers' strategies to the intended product design

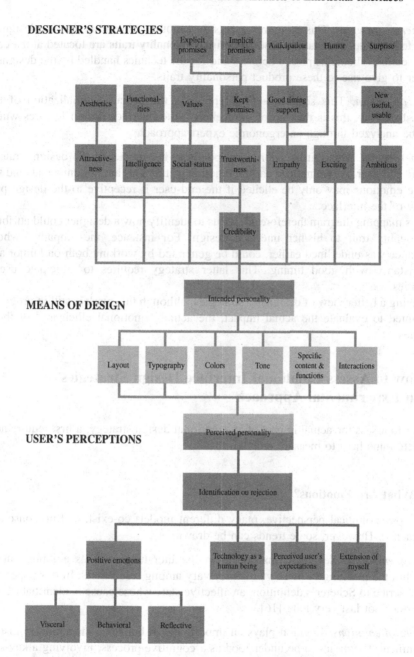

Fig. 1. Emotional Design Approach Mapping

personality. We therefore propose a diagram of our current understanding of the designers approach (see Fig. 1). The diagram is divided into three categories, which should be read from the top.

Designers' strategies. This group represents the emotional intention that the designers expect to build up. Çakmakli's product design personality traits are located at the core of this section. The items placed before stand for the technics handled by the designers in order to give rise to these product personality traits.

Means of design. This second section represents the actual materialization of the design. In a way, this is the "tip of the iceberg", the interface design features which could be analyzed through an ergonomic expert approach.

User perception. This third section corresponds to the impact of the design strategy onto the end-user. As we noticed earlier, emotional strategies are not universal, and the positive emotions may only be elicited if the end-user is receptive to the design personality of the interface.

This mapping diagram therefore allows us to identify how a designer could attribute a personality trait to his/her interface design. For instance, the empathy, whose importance was underlined earlier, could be generated by working both on humor and an assistance with good timing. This latter strategy requires to anticipate users' difficulties.

Having a better view of designers' strategies, although this work is still in progress, we wanted to evaluate the actual impact, the actual 'emotional efficiency' of those strategies.

3 How to Assess Emotional Interface Design Strategies? An Experimental Approach

In order to assess the actual impact of an emotional design strategy, a first requirement is to determine how to measure emotion.

3.1 What Are Emotions?

From a psychological perspective, many different models co-exist, and no consensus was reached. However, some trends can be drawn.

Defining emotions. Several terms appear in the literature, such as emotion, affect, mood, but the meaning of those words may vary among researchers. In this paper, we will subscribe to Scherer's definition: an affective state whose cause is identifiable, and which does not last very long [16].

The role of emotions. Emotion plays an import role in human's adaptation to his/her environment. Emotion can be understood as a cognitive process, involving a key-step of *appraisal*. Emotions is engaged in the evaluation of a stimulus, environmental or internal, in order to potentially prepare the body to an appropriate behavior.

In the context of design, according to a model proposed by Desmet [17], emotion is a result of an appraisal process based on individual factors and product features. Desmet also specifies that the product may drive thoughts, which become the effective source(s) of emotions. This can be related to Norman [15] who distinguishes three emotional levels of product interaction: a first "visceral" level standing for immediate and instinctive emotion, and two other levels connected to the perception of the interaction ("behavioral"), or to a more socio/intellectual assessment (the "reflective" level).

Characterizing emotions. Two main streams have emerged in order to characterize the different emotions: a dimensional perspective and a discrete perspective.

This latter discrete perspective considers emotions as a sum of categories, which can possibly be intersected or intensity-faded to get finer sub-categories. For instance, Plutchick [18] considers eight primary emotions (joy/sadness, trust/disgust, fear/anger, surprise/anticipation). These discrete models are quite popular, especially in the design field, because they are easily linkable to the 'folk psychology': most common vocabulary terms standing for different emotions are localized into discrete model schemes, making them easy to handle.

However, certain drawbacks were pinned on these discrete models. Emotions may be difficult to categorize [17]. A term-based categorization would imply to share a same cultural and language background. It would also imply to skip any inter-individual variation in the interpretation of the meanings of the terms. By definition, a discrete model limits the potential number of emotions, inducing biases. Therefore, other models co-exist, based on a dimensional perspective. Two dimensions emerge from most of the dimensional models: valence and arousal [19, 20]. Valence is a pleasure/displeasure scale, whereas activation corresponds to sleepiness/excitation. These scales define a circumplex space where it is possible to locate any 'folk-psychology' emotional term.

3.2 How to Measure Design-Driven Emotions During an Interface Use Experience?

The experience of interface use is quite specific: a long lasting experience during which emotions may change, and whose intensities may remain quite low. Therefore, a set of recording technics should be chosen accordingly. Moreover, having recorded the users' emotions would provide indicators of the overall emotional state of the users, whereas the impact of the emotional design may only partially contributes to this overall experience. Thus, two questions have to be addressed:

- Which set of recording technics should be chosen?
- How to extract the design-component from the other components constituting the emotional use experience?

Selecting assessment methods. Measuring emotions requires to associate emotional states with cognitive or physical changes. These changes may be readable through three components: physiological, behavioral and cognitive [21]. We therefore set up an experiment in order to assess a choice of specific emotional assessment methods [22].

Among the numerous available physiological methods, we turned towards electrodermal activity (EDA). This approach is based on the influence of activation on skin sweating. Electrodes are placed on two fingers of the participant to monitor these changes. EDA provides a constant monitoring during the use experience, and may therefore allow a mapping of the emotional state to the interface stimuli throughout the experience. The user cannot orientate the recording results, and some unconscious emotions may be detected. Our results confirmed that EDA is limited to the "activation" dimension of emotion. Therefore, it should only be used when the user actually interacts with the interface, whereas 'passive' reading and picture-viewing tasks would not lead to any readable data.

For the behavioral component, we turned towards the observation of changes on the user's face. This method is based on the facial action coding system (FACS) [23]. Noldus' Facereader [24] was developed in order to automate such analyses. Our results showed that a web interface does not provide enough emotional intensity to change users' face patterns. Therefore, finer technics, such as micro-electromyography (µEMG) would rather constitute better options.

The third cognitive component was set up through questionnaires. The principle is to record the user's subjective perception. Questionnaires being one-off, they do not allow a continuous monitoring, as we discarded any experience interruption. Two questionnaires were tested. The first one is the Geneva emotion wheel (GEW), which was developed following Scherer's emotional model [16]. A set of twenty emotion labels are arranged in a circle. Each label can be rated according to its intensity using a five points scale, from the center of the circle to its periphery. A free response area is also provided and the user may also indicate that no emotion was felt. A drawback of label-based questionnaires lies in the interpretation of the label meaning. Therefore, the second questionnaire we used is the self-assessment manikin (SAM) [25]. This questionnaire is composed of three scales, matching the three dimensions of the "valence arousal dominance" system. These scales make use of a pictures-based representation of emotional values, thus bypassing the terms-understanding issue. Our results showed that both scales were relevant for the assessment of short episodes. The SAM was notably easier to handle by the participants, although the third "dominance" scale was more difficult to understand.

Extracting the design-component from the emotional use experience. As evoked earlier, users' emotions are dependent on individual factors such as past experiences, culture, interests towards the task… User Interface design, from which designers are in charge, only constitutes one of the many variables influencing the overall emotional experience. We propose a diagram in order to represent the interactions between the components constituting the overall user emotion (Fig. 2).

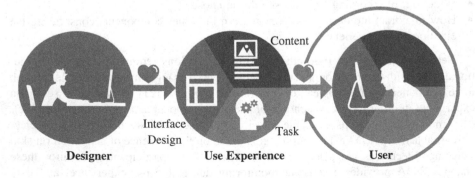

Fig. 2. Emotional design process

Two main components lead to the recorded overall emotion: the use experience (external stimulus), and the individual characteristics (internal stimulus, such as interests, expectations, past experiences). This scheme therefore matches Desmet's model [17]. However, Desmet's product component had to be enriched for the specific context of an interface use. We therefore identified three sub-components:

- The content stands for the textual and pictorial items communicated to the user. Those items are typically produced by redactors, who are distinct from the designers.
- The interface design stands for the layout and the presentation strategy of information and interaction. It directly refers to the means of design in the emotional design approach diagram (Fig. 1). Information design and interaction design may be distinguished as two sub-categories of the interface design.
- The task stands for the purpose actions supported by the interface (read, write, compare, organize, conceive...) Performing these tasks may affect the user's emotions.

One other component should also be taken into consideration:

- The specificities of the user at the moment of the interaction (internal stimulus), which include a variety of combined factors leading to the user's individuality (cultural profile, previous experiences, expertise, personality traits, mood, interests...). Some of these features being continuously affected by the use experience, the global processes should therefore be considered as continuous iterations.

Designers' emotional strategies only affect the interface design sub-component. To evaluate the emotional impact of a design strategy, its emotional value should be extracted from the overall emotional experience. An experiment was conducted to address this issue [26]. Two interfaces were provided to a set of users. These interfaces were designed for this experimental purpose and differed by a variety of design assets (layout proportions, colors, animations of the interactions and transitions...). The efficiency of both interfaces was similar, as well as the nature of the tasks: an article about a movie, spread upon four pages, with one title, one text, and one image per page.

The goal of the experiment was to measure the relative emotional impact difference between the two design strategies underlying these interfaces. Each participant used the two interfaces with a counter-balancing order to dismiss the individual specificities component. The two tasks being similar, it was also possible to dismiss the task component. The content component was assessed by isolating each content item, and by presenting them to the users during a previous phase. It was therefore possible to evaluate the emotional value of each content item, and to evaluate the global emotional values of the contents alone.[2] By substracting the contents value from the overall experience, we were therefore able to identify the relative emotional impact of the two different design options (see Fig. 3).

---

[2] Another experiment was conducted in order to appreciate more accurately the global emotional value of a web page contents according to the emotional value of each isolated piece of content. Results showed that low-valence content had more impact than neutral or high-valence content. The global emotional evaluation of a page content should therefore be balanced accordingly [4].

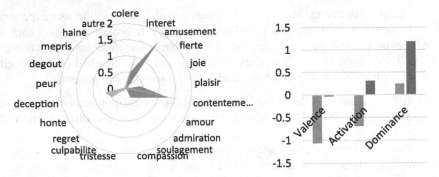

Fig. 3. Extract of the relative emotional impact of the interface design component for the two questionnaires GEW (left) and SAM (right), for design A (blue) and B (orange).

4   Conclusion from Experimental to Ecological Setup

The experimental setup presented in the previous section makes the evaluation of interface emotional design strategies possible. However, some of the designers' strategies are targeting longer terms behaviors. For instance, emotional design strategies intended to accompany a discovery phase may be different from the strategies maintaining the attractiveness on the longer run. Another experiment is therefore currently being performed to assess the efficiency of those longer term emotional strategies: a full scale website is deployed, with different variations matching the design strategies to be tested. Participants can use the application freely during two weeks. A set of indicators are logged by the program in order to track any evolutions in the used functions, which could be interpreted as a motivation shift, an expertise gain, or any behavioral pattern.

This establishes the current position of our research, and we hope this work will contribute to a better assessment of emotional interface design strategies, a required step towards the constitution of emotional design heuristics.

References

1. Norman, D.A.: The design of everyday things. Basic Books, New-York (2002)
2. Shneiderman, B., Pleasant, C.: Designing the User Interface: Strategies for Effective Human-Computer Interaction. Addison Wesley, Boston (2005)
3. Bastien, J.M.C., Scapin, D.: Ergonomic Criteria for the Evaluation of Human-Computer Interfaces. INRIA, France (1993)
4. Lockner, D.: Ph.D. thesis, directed by Bonnardel, N. Aix-Marseille University (2015 prev.)
5. Hancock, P.A., Pepe, A.A., Murphy, L.L.: Hedonomics: the power of positive and pleasurable ergonomics. Ergon. Des. **13**(1), 8–14 (2005)
6. Jordan, P.W.: Designing Pleasurable Products. Taylor and Francis, London (2000)
7. Friedman, V.: The current state of web design. Professional Web Design, vol. 2, pp. 6–70. Smashing Media GmbH, Freiburg (2012)
8. Balsamiq. http://balsamiq.com/dinner/

9. Vimeo. http://vimeo.com
10. Anderson, S.P.: Seductive Interaction Design. New Rider Press, Berkeley (2011)
11. Van Gorp, T., Adams, E.: Design for Emotion. Morgan Kaufmann, Waltham (2012)
12. Walter, A.: Designing for Emotions. A Book Apart, New York (2011)
13. Reeves, B., Naas, C.: The Media Equation: How People Treat Computers, Television and New Media like Real People and Places. Cambridge University Press, Cambridge (1998)
14. Çakmakli, A.: A good design = a good mate. In: 7th International Conference on Design & Emotion. Design & Emotion Society (2010)
15. Norman, D.A.: Emotional design: Why We Love (or Hate) Everyday Things. Basic Books, New York (2005)
16. Scherer, K.R.: What are emotions? And how can they be measured? Soc. Sci. Inf. **44**, 695–729 (2005)
17. Desmet, P.M.A.: A multilayered model of product emotions. Des. J. **6**, 4–13 (2003)
18. Plutchick, R.: A general psychoevolutionary theory of emotion. In: Plutchick, R., Kellerman, H. (eds.) Emotion: Theory, Research, and Experience: Vol. 1 Theories of Emotion. Academic Press, New York (1980)
19. Russell, J.A.: A circumplex model of affect. J. Pers. Soc. Psychol. **39**, 1161–1178 (1980)
20. Russell, J.A., Barrett, L.F.: Core affect, prototypical emotional episodes, and other things called emotion: dissecting the elephant. J. Pers. Soc. Psychol. **76**, 805–819 (1999)
21. Gil, S.: Comment mesurer les émotions en laboratoire ? Revue électronique de Psychologie Sociale **4**, 15–24 (2009)
22. Lockner, D., Bonnardel, N.: Emotion and Interface Design: How web design may elicit positive user affect? In: Proceedings of the 5th International Conference on KEER'2014 – Kansei Engineering & Emotion Research. Linköping University, Sweden (2014)
23. Ekman, P.: Universal facial expressions of emotion. Calif. Ment. Health Res. Digest **8**, 151–158 (1970)
24. Noldus. http://www.noldus.com
25. Bradley, M.M., Lang, P.J.: Measuring emotion: the self-assessment manikin and the semantic differential. J. Behav. Ther. Exp. Psychiatry **25**, 49–59 (2009)
26. Lockner, D., Bonnardel, N.: Emotion and Interface Design. In: Proceedings of the 5th International Conference on Applied Human Factors and Ergonomics. Jagiellonian University, Krakow, Poland (2014)

Analytical Steps for the Calibration of an Emotional Framework

Pre-test and Evaluation Procedures

Nicholas H. Müller[1(✉)] and Martina Truschzinski[2]

[1] Institute for Media Research, Chemnitz University of Technology,
Chemnitz, Germany
nicholas.mueller@phil.tu-chemnitz.de
[2] Chair of Automation Technology, Chemnitz University of Technology,
Chemnitz, Germany
martina.truschzinski@etit.tu-chemnitz.de

Abstract. The emotion model of the Smart Virtual Worker is the result of three years of interdisciplinary research. After successful implementation and pre-validation of the model and the surrounding simulation architecture, the model had to be calibrated by using real life working scenarios. The task of carrying differently weighed boxes over a 30 m distance was chosen as the foundation for the model. Subsequent fitting of the model led to a positive evaluation outcome which presented a mean 88 % fitting of the model's simulated emotional valence in relation to the observed real world behavior.

Keywords: Emotion framework · Work simulation · Workflow simulator · Emotional valence · Emotional model · Evaluation

1 Introduction

The 'Smart Virtual Worker' project has the goal to simulate work tasks in order to either help to improve existing workflows or by supporting the planning stages during the conceptualization of upcoming task sequences. This on one hand to improve the working conditions in general. But since in almost all the industrialized nations the workforce is ageing, companies will have to find ways of keeping their existing, highly skilled and qualified employees who might not be able to perform as well due to their age or medical conditions. Therefore, the SVW simulator is an easy to use software which is capable of replicating established workflows and to find alternative routes or task sequences. Although there are solutions which compute ergonomic parameters or environmental information, the emotional tendency of the workers is often overlooked. Therefore we implemented a dynamically adaptable emotion model (see Fig. 1), which

Nicholas H. Müller, Martina Truschzinski—This work has been funded by the European Union with the European Social Fund (ESF) and by the state of Saxony.

M. Kurosu (Ed.): Human-Computer Interaction, Part I, HCII 2015, LNCS 9169, pp. 512–519, 2015.
DOI: 10.1007/978-3-319-20901-2_48

is capable of differentiating between 27 distinct virtual worker types and attributes. Based on established psychological models [1–3] the computation is not based on fixed tables of corresponding emotions but allows for a unique and timely calculation of a psychological state [4]. Due to its modular programming, the emotion module itself is capable of working as a stand-alone version and is actively pursued as a way of enhancing human-robotic-interactions due to facilitating an emotional insight of a human's behavior for the robotic counterpart [5]. One of the main criticism regarding computational emotional architectures is the missing evaluation or at least real-world analysis of the computed data [6]. The presented paper describes our performed and ongoing process of analyzing and evaluating the model with real life counterparts.

2 The Emotion Model

Fitted into the overarching architecture of the Smart Virtual Worker Simulation, the emotion model itself is a standalone module, capable of operating, to the greatest possible extent, on its own. Within it carries a rudimentary virtual agent which is characterized by three individualizing variables: Constitution [C], Sensitivity [S] and Experience [E]. These three allow for 27 distinct agents to perform within the simulation. A low constitution, e.g. a much older simulated worker, might be able to perform very well still, due to a higher experience.

From left to right, the emotion model takes in the proposed body movement sequence by the motion generation module. This motion has itself already been evaluated by the ergonomic module which in turn rates it as being feasible, precarious or, in extreme circumstances, as alarming. These input variables are henceforth computed by the module, while incorporating the agent's characteristics (C, S and E), and three scales are adjusted. One for the sympathetic arousal (serving both as energy for the upcoming emotion and to facilitate an emotional transfer), another for the exhaustion and the emotional valence. As a result, the valence is either positive or negative which, together with the exhaustion factor, is handed over to the artificial intelligence, which, due to its reinforcement learning architecture, makes a decision about upcoming movements and task related actions of the simulated worker.

Over the course of last year two preliminary experiments ($N_1 = 2$, $N_2 = 6$) have been conducted leading up to an evaluation ($N_{eval} = 8$) in November of 2014. The goal of the first two experiments was twofold: First, to gather analytical data of subjects' heart-rate, endurance, speed and emotional state in order to calibrate the emotion module. And we conducted a second experiment to test the then calibrated module and to continually fine-tune its computational routines.

3 Pre-tests

For the analytical part, a two-day experimental setup has been developed. During day one, the test subjects were analyzed regarding their personal constitution and state of mind. This was done by having them answer a questionnaire to determine their experience in carrying heavy items, their usual workout routine, previous employments

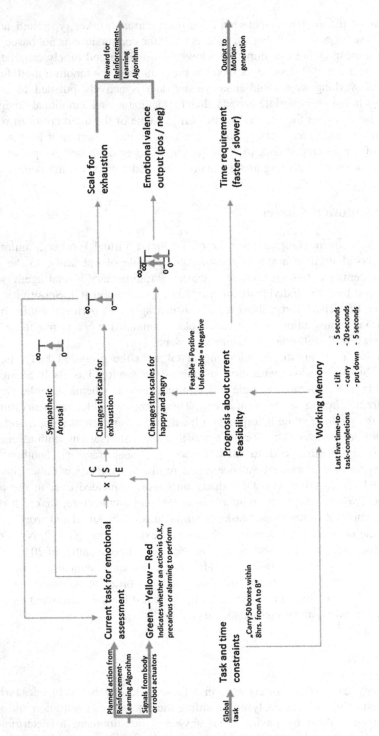

Fig. 1. The flow-chart of the SVW emotion module [4]

and questions about their assumed behavior during a hypothetical work related scenario. Afterwards, physiological measurements were gathered, namely running (starting with 100 m, followed by a five minute break, ending with running a 400 m round course) and lifting as well as continuously holding up a 5 kg weight as long as possible. Furthermore, their weight, height and further socio-demographic data was collected. During day two, the subjects had to carry differently weighed boxes (Experiment 1: 5 kg, 10 kg, 15 kg) over a distance of 30 m, regaining some strength by walking 30 m back without a box and continuously repeating these steps, until 10 boxes of each weight (30 boxes total) were carried across (see Fig. 2).

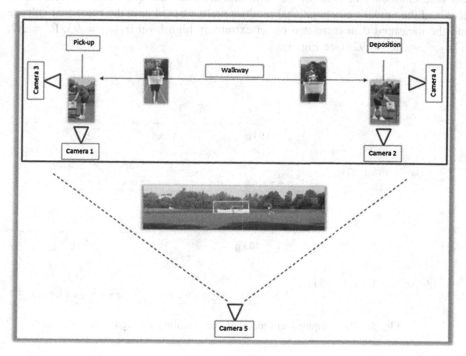

Fig. 2. The camera recording setup of the experiments

During the experiment, the multi-dimensional-mental-state-questionnaire (MDBF [10]) was used to determine the subject's emotional valence. Furthermore, their individually felt exhaustion was checked on a colored scale, ranging from green over yellow to red. In addition, their heart-rate, number of steps, speed and time was monitored electronically. To be able to check for specific emotionally stressful moments during the work task, and to be able to check for ergonomically critical movements, the whole experimental setup was recorded by five cameras. Two were monitoring the box pick-up and put-down spot from the side to check for precarious degrees between the upper and lower body. Two more were facing the subjects while they were carrying the boxes to their destination, which would allow for an analysis of their facial muscle activation, using the Facial Action Coding System by Eckman [7]. The fifth camera was used to record an overview of the experimental situation.

Afterwards, the data was analyzed and the individual test-subject's endurance-index [8] computed. Correlations between the heart-rate and the individual's exhaustion were calculated and presented a strong (r_{VPN1} = .5) and medium (r_{VPN2} = .37) coefficient. This allowed us to transfer the specific differences of the exhaustion scale during carrying and recuperation over into the exhaustion model of the virtual worker.

The individual's decisions were henceforth simulated within the SVW Framework and consequently matched to the observed biophysiological changes. In addition, the analyzed emotional valences of the multi-dimensional-state-questionnaire were calculated and the model's computational routines were adapted until the emotional valence and the measured data correlated on an extremely high level (r_{VPN1} = .93, R^2 = .87; r_{VPN2} = .96, R^2 = .92) (see Fig. 3).

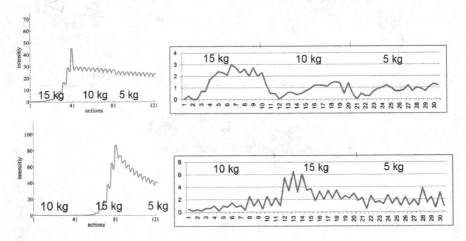

Fig. 3. The computed and reported strain while carrying the boxes

In order to validate these initial results we performed a second run of pre-tests (N = 6) with a change in the weight of the boxes. Since the first test showed only a marginal strain on the observed exhaustion when carrying 5 kg weighed boxes the available weights were now 10 kg, 15 kg and 20 kg. Otherwise the experimental setup remained the same with a two-day format. Due to this we were able to observe a much higher workload during the 20 kg episodes.

4 Evaluation of the Box Carrying

Based on the results from the pre-tests, the evaluation took place inside an empty factory building and the participants (N = 8) were compensated for their participation. The work space allowed for a distance of 20 m to carry the boxes from the pre-filled cupboards on the right side to the empty one on the left side. We used sand-filled plastic boxes which were weighed in differentiating increments, ranging from 10,2 kg up to 21,9 kg. Each cupboard held six boxes so 18 boxes had to be carried (see Fig. 4) back and the same 18 had to be returned (resulting in a total of 36 carried boxes, each weight twice).

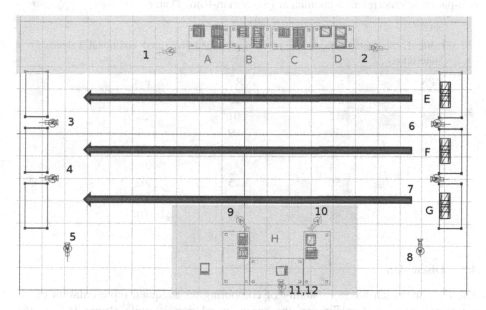

Fig. 4. The experimental setup of the evaluation with cameras

Due to the nature of the experiment the participants were tested sequentially. Each iteration began with an instruction of the participants, especially regarding their physical well-being. Afterwards the biophysiological equipment (Heart-Rate, Pedometer, Skin Conductance and EMG) was applied to individual parts of their body and initial calibrations of the equipment performed. Then they filled out the questionnaires already used during the pre-tests, allowing us to rate them regarding their constitution, sensitivity and experience of the upcoming work task.

Afterwards, they were led to the pre-filled cupboard. As in the pre-tests, they were free in choosing which weights of a cupboard to carry first, but that they would have to carry them from top left to bottom right and sort them back in their original order on the other side. Once a box has been placed there, they would have to walk back to the filled cupboard to fetch the next box. Before they would pick up one of the two boxes on the shelf, a confederate asked them to rate their exhaustion on the Borg-scale [9] and they would have to fill in the short MDBF Test [10] in order to assess their current level of emotional valence.

4.1   Results

Based on the measured Constitution, Sensitivity and Experience regarding carrying boxes as well as the individual choices which box and weight to carry first, the Smart Virtual Worker Simulation was run and computed corresponding emotional valences. Since a violation of normality was observed, the graphs were compared using the non-parametric correlation coefficient (Spearman-Rho) (Table 1).

Table 1. Spearman-Rho results of computed and measured emotional valence (*one-sided)

VPN	r_s	R^2	p < *
1	.50	.25	.01
2	.12	.01	.31
3	.30	.09	.11
4	.32	.10	.09
5	.64	.41	.001
6	.50	.25	.02
7	-,51	.26	.01
8	.58	.34	.01

4.2   Discussion

The data shows an 88 % capability of computing an adequate representation of the emotional valence. Furthermore, the mean correlation is quite strong ($r_m = .46$). Looking specifically at the data from participant seven, we see a negative correlated emotional valence, leading to the conclusion that there is something off regarding the computation of these specific physiological and psychological variables. The correlations of participants two, three and four are not significant but they still show a positive correlation between the measured and computed data streams. Furthermore, they show a low and two medium coefficients which is why in this specific context, the probability of error should be interpreted as a measure for the conformity of the measured and computed data rather than a rejection of the measurement alltogether.

5   General Discussion

Due to these steps, the calibrated emotion module is now capable of adequately predicting the emotional valence over the course of a specific work task. In combination with the results from the pre-test experiments and the evaluation, the emotion module is one of the first computed psychological models, which are not just working on a binary basis, but are positively evaluated against psychological empirical criteria. The next steps will be to match the existing computational routines to once more match the measured data as it was done during the pre-tests. Afterwards, to conduct other work sequences and to compare the model to those outcomes. Especially tasks with a much higher coordinative involvement with only low levels of strain, like putting together furniture, will become increasingly important for the continued refinement of the emotion model. Furthermore, besides looking for opportunities and applications as a robotic enhancement [11] we are currently exploring the practical applications of the emotion module without physical exhaustion due to performing heavy work, but psychological and cognitive fatigue. Therefore, beginning in 2015, the emotion module will be adapted to compute emotional valences during sitting but highly cognitive stressful tasks, as in air traffic controllers.

References

1. Zillmann, D.: Excitation transfer in communication-mediated aggressive behavior. J. Exp. Soc. Psychol. **7**, 419–434 (1971)
2. Zillmann, D.: Attribution of apparent arousal and proficiency of recovery from sympathetic activation affecting excitation transfer to aggressive behavior. J. Exp. Soc. Psychol. **10**, 503–515 (1974)
3. Zillmann, D.: Emotionspsychologische Grundlagen. In: Mangold, R., Vorderer, P., Bente, G. (eds.) Lehrbuch der Medienpsychologie, pp. 101–128. Hogrefe, Göttingen (2004)
4. Müller, N.H., Truschzinski, M.: An emotional framework for a real-life worker simulation. In: Kurosu, M. (ed.) HCI 2014, Part II. LNCS, vol. 8511, pp. 675–686. Springer, Heidelberg (2014)
5. Truschzinski, M., Müller, N.H., Dinkelbach, H.-U., Protzel, P., Hamker, F., Ohler, P.: Deducing human emotions by robots: computing basic non-verbal expressions of performed actions during a work task. In: ICIS 2014, Auckland (2014)
6. Marinier, R.P., Laird, J.E.: Computational Models of Emotion, pp. 166–167. SAGE Publications Inc., Thousand Oaks (2013)
7. Ekman, P.: Emotion in the Human Face. Cambridge University Press, New York (1982)
8. Saziorski, W.M., Aljeschinski, S.J., Jakunin, N.A.: Biomechanische Grundlagen der Ausdauer. Sportverlag, Berlin (1987)
9. CDC: Perceived Exertion (Borg Rating of Perceived Exertion Scale) (2011). http://www.cdc.gov/physicalactivity/everyone/measuring/exertion.html. Accessed on 3 February 2015
10. Steyer, R., Schwenkmezger, P., Notz, P., Eid, M.: Der Mehrdimensionale Befindlichkeitsfragebogen (MDBF). Handanweisung. Hogrefe, Göttingen (1997)
11. Truschzinski, M., Müller, N.H.: The emotion model of the smart virtual worker. Presented at the International Summer School on Social Human-Robot Interaction, Cambridge (U.K.), 26–30 August 2013

Automatic Interpretation of Negotiators' Affect and Involvement Based on Their Non-verbal Behavior

Zhaleh Semnani-Azad[1] and Elnaz Nouri[2](✉)

[1] Psychology Department, University of Waterloo, Waterloo, Canada
zsemnani@uwaterloo.ca
[2] Institute for Creative Technologies and Computer Science Department,
University of Southern California, Los Angeles, CA, USA
enouri@usc.edu

Abstract. Valid interpretation of the nonverbal behavior of the people involved in negotiations is important. Computational agents that are designed for negotiation benefit from the ability to interpret human nonverbal behavior for communicating more effectively and achieving their goals. In this paper, we demonstrate how the mode of involvement and relational affect of the negotiators involved in the interaction can be determined by several nonverbal behaviors such as that of the mouth, head, hand movements, posture and the facial expressions of the negotiators. We use machine learning to study involvement and affect in negotiation. Our results show that the prediction models built based on non-verbal cues can help identify the negotiator's attitudes and motivation in the interaction.

Keywords: Relational affect recognition · Involvement recognition · Negotiation · Nonverbal behavior interpretation

1 Introduction

Nonverbal communication plays a major role in the expression and perception of nonlinguistic messages that are exchanged between people during the negotiation [13]. Nonverbal messages in negotiation define the nature of the relationship between actors (e.g. [5]) provide a framework for interpreting communication (e.g. [7]) and guide decisions about subsequent manner in the interaction (e.g. [3]). Nonverbal messages also influence the negotiation outcomes [15] and how information is shared (e.g. [11, 19, 20]). Successful understanding of nonverbal messages can enhance the communication between the parties and facilitate reaching an integrative agreement. However understanding the meaning of nonverbal behavior of the negotiators can be a difficult task even for humans so if automatic models could be built for this purpose, not only computational agents that are designed for effective negotiation interactions would benefit from this ability but humans can also take advantage of it as well.

This paper describes the results of our attempt for automatic interpretation of the meaning and functions of the nonverbal cues in negotiation. We examine nonverbal

© Springer International Publishing Switzerland 2015
M. Kurosu (Ed.): Human-Computer Interaction, Part I, HCII 2015, LNCS 9169, pp. 520–529, 2015.
DOI: 10.1007/978-3-319-20901-2_49

cues in the interaction between two people when participants have different modes of relational affect (Positive, Negative) or level of involvement (Active, Passive). The dataset used in this paper consists of 180 individuals participating in negotiation. The negotiators were prompted to negotiate with different level of involvement and mode of relational affect by giving them different sets of instructions for approaching the negotiation (in terms of involvement and relational affect. This dataset thus provides a reliable rich test bed for us to train prediction models for interpretation of non-verbal messages in negotiation.

The communication literature has previously paid attention to nonverbal cues and different possible interpretations of the nonverbal features but machine learning techniques have not been used before to map non-verbal behavior features to the affect and involvement model [1] to our knowledge. We are assigning meaning to the non-verbal cues based on the "involvement-affect" model in order to interpret negotiators' high level goals. Our ultimate goal is to use our findings for development of computational agents that can engage in negotiation with people. In what follows we discuss how different features of the nonverbal behavior in negotiation help us recognize the involvement and relation affect automatically. We introduce "involvement-affect" model as the theoretical framework we used for interpretation of the nonverbal cues. We describe our dataset and features and discuss the result of our machine learning experiments. The paper also outlines the direction for future work.

2 Background

Communication literature has studied factors associated with the meaning of communicated messages in the interaction and has made effort to develop dimensions to represent them. We can refer to Osgood's semantic differential as an example which posits that meaning behind communicated messages can be grouped into three factors of responsiveness (ranging from "active" to "passive"), evaluation (ranging from "good" to "bad") and potency (ranging from "strong" to "weak") [17]. Research has shown that these factors are universal across cultures ([17, 21, 22]). Nonverbal behaviors such as body posture (hand movements and torso's position), facial expressions and vocal cues as well as hand-movements have been shown to reflect these dimensions of meaning ([8, 10]). These non-verbal cues can potentially facilitate the exchange of information in the negotiation if both the sender of the behavior and the observer share the meanings attached to the nonverbal cues [9].

"Involvement-Affect" Dimensional Model of Relational Messages. We use "involvement-affect" dimensional model of relational messages ([1, 18]) for our interpretation of the non-verbal cues in the negotiation. According to Prager's theorizing, nonverbal messages reflect two fundamental characteristics of a relationship: involvement and affect [1]. Various combinations of these produce various messages [1]. The involvement dimension captures the degree to which a person is engaged and involved, while the affect dimension reflects the extent to which a person experiences positive versus negative affect toward their counterpart. Nonverbal behaviors exhibited in conditions of high involvement are characterized as affiliative-intimate when accompanied with positive affect, and dominant-aggressive when amalgamated with negative affect. In contrast, nonverbal cues in conditions of low involvement combined with positive affect suggest social politeness, and avoidance-withdraw when accompanied by negative affect.

"Involvement-Affect" Model for Negotiations. The adaptation of the original "involvement-affect" model for negotiations proposes four negotiation approaches that convey a negotiator's attitudes, motivation [20]. This adaptation These four negotiation approaches are:

1. Passive negotiation involvement: the extent to which negotiators are uninvolved
2. Active negotiation involvement: the extent to which negotiators are involved
3. Negative relational affect: the extent to which negotiators dislike their counterpart
4. Positive relational affect: the extent to which negotiators like their counterpart

Figure 1 illustrates these 4 negotiation approaches along the original affect-involvement model. For example a dominant behavior in this model is interpreted as Negative Affect and High Involvement. A submissive behavior is interpreted as Positive Affect and Low Involvement. The data used for our work in this paper was collected based on the "Involvement-affect" Model for Negotiations.

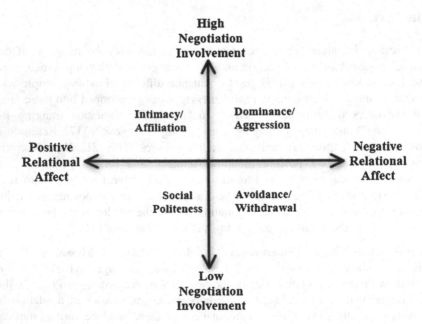

Fig. 1. Negotiation involvement-relational affect dimensions

3   Experimental Method

3.1   Dataset and Task

The dataset used consists of a total of 180 male students participating in a negotiation task. Only male participants were recruited because we did not want gender to influence the understanding of the nonverbal behavior. The negotiation task is an adapted 2-party version of the Towers Market negotiation simulation ([16, 24]) with two issues. The negotiations were videotaped. The negotiation scenario involved a baker and liquor storeowner negotiating their terms for sharing space in the Towers Market.

The manipulation for the modes of involvement and affect were incorporated in the role instructions. The manipulation reflected two levels of negotiation involvement: Active versus Passive and two levels of relational affect: Positive versus Negative. This resulted in over all four different sets of instructions to be provided to the participants (See Appendix A). The performance of the negotiators' and compliance to the instructions were tested and measured. In order to avoid negotiators' manipulated nonverbal expressions to influence one another, confederates were hired and trained blind to the hypotheses to act as counterparts to the study participants.[1]

3.2   Nonverbal Behavior Features

The coding scheme and description of nonverbal behaviors were adapted from prior research ([6, 12]). These nonverbal behaviors are multi modal and defined based on the vocal and visual features simultaneously. The behaviors of the negotiators were coded for mouth movement, posture, head movement, hand movement and facial expression. Table 1 lists the categories of the non-verbal behavioral features coded.

3.3   Annotation of the Dataset

We manually coded the data. Trained research assistants were used for this purpose. These categories were coded one at a time to reliably identify all the behaviors of interest. For example, all coders were first trained on the posture category (distinguishing whether the participants were leaning back, leaning forward, or maintaining a neutral posture.). After coding all sessions on posture, research assistants were trained on another behavioral category. Coders recorded their observations using the Noldus Observer, a computer-based coding system that captures both the frequency and duration of nonverbal cues [14]. The Noldus software uses the frequency and duration codes to compute a score indicating the percentage of time a negotiator spent exhibiting a particular nonverbal expression. These scores are what we used as the value for each of the features. So for each negotiation we had one value for each feature representing the overall percentage of that behavior in the interaction.

---

[1] The experimental design was done by Zhaleh Semnani-Azad and Dr Wendi Adair and is described in upcoming paper "Meaning and Function of Nonverbal Behavior in Negotiation: The Chinese and Canadian" which is in preparation for submission to the Journal of Organizational Behavior.

Table 1. Nonverbal behavior features

Categories	Nonverbal behaviors features
Mouth movement	Silence (Noticeable points when no one is saying anything)
	Verbal speech (Length and frequency of the person talking)
Head movement	Head down (Sagittal tilt forward)
	Head up
	Face side (Nose and Chin pointed away from partner)
	Face partner
	Shake
	Nod
	Rest head on arm
Hand movement	Hand gestures (Hand gestures and movements accompanying speech or in different positions)
	Palms down
	Palms up
	Hand in air
	Move hand speaking
	Move hands not speaking
	Hands on table
Facial expression	Open smile (Mouth open, lips not touching)
	Closed smile
	Smiling
	Non smiling
	Frown
Posture	Forward lean (Upper torso tilted forward, with back away from chair)
	Lean back (Posture leaning back in chair)
	Lean sideways
	Straight back (Rigid posture, back is not leaned against the chair)
	Move (Move the whole body during speech or silence)
Eyes	Eye contact speaking
	Eye contact listening
	No eye contact speaking
	No eye contact listening

4 Prediction Models

For our analysis, we left out the data corresponding to the negotiations that were missing some of the features and ended up with 138 data of negotiation that we used. We made two separate models one for determining the involvement: active versus passive and another one for determining the two levels of relational affect: positive versus negative.

4.1 Affect Prediction and Feature Selection

In this task we decide whether the negotiator has positive or negative affect. Accuracy of the prediction of the support vector machine (SVM) classifier with the polynomial kernel function (cache size 250007, exp = 1.0) is compared with Naïve Bayes classifier and two baseline prediction models: Majority baseline model which assigns the class of the most common observed class in the training dataset and the Random baseline that assigns the prediction label of "positive or negative" based on chance. These results are shown in Table 2. The SVM classifier performed significantly better than other models (P-value of the one way ANOVA on 10 fold accuracy < 0.05). Considering the size of our dataset, we decided to use the 10-fold cross validation paradigm for our prediction tasks.

Table 2. Comparison of the performance of prediction models for affect-involvement model

Model	Affect prediction accuracy	Involvement prediction accuracy
SVM	0.65	0.71
Naive Bayes	0.59	0.67
Majority baseline	0.52	0.51
Random baseline	0.50	0.50

Feature Selection for Affect Prediction with "Information Gain Attribute Evaluation" and "Ranker" search method (Threshold - 1.79) by using 10 fold cross-validation (stratified) showed that the following features were ranked the 6 most important features for this task: (move.hands.NOT.speaking, hand.in.air, verbal.speech, lean.back. eye.contact.speaking, forward.lean) SVM Attribute Evaluation algorithm's top 6 features are: (lean.back, move.hands.NOT.speaking, palms.down, open.smile, eye.contact. listening head.shake) These selections seem to resonate with the intuition that positive affect involves behavior such as: moving the hands around the body, or moving the body forward and keeping rapport with the other person by looking into their eyes ([2, 4, 23]).

4.2 Involvement Prediction and Feature Selection

In this task we decide whether the negotiator is highly involved in the negotiation or has low involvement in the task. The evaluation method for the model for prediction of involvement based on the non-verbal features was similar to the method used for affect. The results are presented in Table 2. Again the SVM classifier performed significantly better than the two major baseline (1-way ANOVA p-value and the Naïve Bayes classifier. The performance of SVM was on average better than the Naïve Bayes classifier but the differences were not statistically significant. Top features ranked by Information Gain Attribute Evaluation algorithm are: (non.smiling.mouth, open.smile, self.adaptors, lean.back) and with SVM Attribute Evaluation algorithm's (non.smiling. mouth, lean.back, palms.down, head.shake, move.hand.speaking, palms.up, straight. back). For both prediction tasks the SVM classifier outperforms the other models (for instance the Naïve Bayes). This can be due to the nature of the features that we are using in our model, which are a set of descriptive non-verbal features at this point. The analysis of the most useful features for both tasks implies that features corresponding to the mouth and hand movements are critical in determining both the affect and level of involvement.

5   Discussion

In this work we showed the non-verbal features can be used for understanding the motivation of the negotiators. Our results show that we can use these features for making such predictions and the SVM classifier seem to be an appropriate choice for making such models. The fact that for each nonverbal feature in the model we only used one value (score that captures how much this behavior was observed in the interaction) associated with the negotiation, might be keeping us from getting higher accuracy from our models. If these feature are calculated at different stages of each negotiation we can make more detailed analysis of the interactions. In that case CRF classifiers might be a better choice due to the sequential nature of the negotiation.

6   Future Work

The annotations of the non-verbal coded features in our dataset was done manually. It is possible to automatically extract these features. Since our goal is to use these models in computational agents we want the pipeline to be fully automatized. This is the initial step in our effort to use the learned models of behavior from this paper for online and automatic detection of the affect and involvement of the negotiator in a dynamic interaction. This would enable the computational agent to make decisions on the fly about what to do in the negotiation.

Appendix A: Negotiation Instructions[2]

Passive	Active
You own a highly successful wine business, Domaine Vintage Cellars OR traditional French bakery, Brown's Bakery. You inspected several equally desirable locations. You have many favorable alternatives and have several options. You are not too concerned about the final outcome of this negotiation since you have other attractive alternatives	You own a highly successful wine business, Domaine Vintage Cellars OR traditional French bakery, Brown's Bakery. You inspected several equally desirable locations. You do not have many favorable alternatives and have limited options. You are care a lot about the final outcome of this negotiation since there are no attractive alternatives
You are not very excited about the upcoming negotiation. It is not something you care much about, so it is hard for you to feel involved in the negotiation process. You are disinterested in the negotiation and are indifferent about the final outcome. In this negotiation, please remember that you are unexcited and do not feel very engaged or involved	You are very eager about the upcoming negotiation. It is something you are really into, so you feel extremely involved in the negotiation process. You are very lively, animated, and engaged and care a lot about the final outcome. In this negotiation, please remember that you are keen, interested, fascinated, and feel very involved
Positive	Negative
You own a highly successful wine business, Domaine Vintage Cellars OR traditional French bakery, Brown's Bakery. Your negotiating partner also owns a successful business. Other businessmen, who negotiated with your counterpart, reported a positive negotiation experience. They perceived the negotiation experience to be pleasant, cheerful, nice, and positive. You are very optimistic about the upcoming negotiation. You have a positive feeling about this and feel happy and merry. You are very cheerful and have a positive feeling. In this negotiation, please remember that you are nice, pleasant, favorable, and optimistic	You own a highly successful wine business, Domaine Vintage Cellars OR traditional French bakery, Brown's Bakery. Your negotiating partner also owns a successful business. Other businessmen, who negotiated with your counterpart, reported a negative negotiation experience. They perceived the negotiation experience to be unpleasant, and negative
	You are very pessimistic about the upcoming negotiation. You have a negative feeling about this and are unhappy and gloomy. You are very distrustful and have a bad feeling. In this negotiation, please remember that you are gloomy, unhappy, distrustful, and pessimistic

---

[2] These negotiation scenarios are prepared by Zhaleh Semnani-Azad and Dr Wendi Adair and are described in upcoming paper "Meaning and Function of Nonverbal Behavior in Negotiation: The Chinese and Canadian" which is in preparation for submission to the Journal of Organizational Behavior.

References

1. Anderson, P.A., Guerrero, L.K., Jones, S.M.: Nonverbal expressions of dominance and power in human relationships. In: The SAGE Handbook of Nonverbal Communication, pp. 259–278. SAGE Publications, Incorporated (2006)
2. Argyle, M., Dean, J.: Eye–contact, distance and affiliation. Sociometry **28**, 289–304 (1965)
3. Burgoon, J.K., Buller, D.B., Hale, J.L., Turck, M.A.: Relational messages associated with nonverbal behaviors. Hum. Commun. Res. **10**(3), 351–378 (1984)
4. Burgoon, J.K., Manusov, V., Mineo, P., Hale, J.L.: Effects of gaze on hiring, credibility, attraction and relational message interpretation. J. Nonverbal Behav. **9**, 133–146 (1985)
5. Carney, D.R., Cuddy, A.J., Yap, A.J.: Power posing brief nonverbal displays affect neuroendocrine levels and risk tolerance. Psychol. Sci. **21**(10), 1363–1368 (2010)
6. Coker, D.A., Burgoon, J.: The nature of conversational involvement and nonverbal encoding patterns. Hum. Commun. Res. **13**(4), 463–494 (1987)
7. Ekman, P., Friesen, W.V.: The repertoire of nonverbal behavior: categories, origins, usage, and coding. Semiotica **1**(1), 49–98 (1969)
8. Ekman, P., Friesen, W.V.: Constants across cultures in the face and emotion. J. Pers. Soc. Psychol. **17**(2), 124 (1971)
9. Ekman, P., Friesen, W.V.: A new pan–cultural facial expression of emotion. Motiv. Emot. **10**(2), 159–168 (1986)
10. Kudoh, T., Matsumoto, D.: Cross–cultural examination of the semantic dimensions of body postures. J. Pers. Soc. Psychol. **48**(6), 1440–1446 (1985)
11. Maddux, W.W., Mullen, E., Galinsky, A.D.: Chameleons bake bigger pies and take bigger pieces: strategic behavioral mimicry facilitates negotiation outcomes. J. Exp. Soc. Psychol. **44**(2), 461–468 (2008)
12. Manusov, V., Patterson, M.L. (eds.): The Sage Handbook of Nonverbal Communication. SAGE Publications, Incorporated (2006)
13. Mehrabian, A.: Nonverbal Communication. Aldine De Gruyter (2007)
14. Noldus, L.P.J.J., Trienes, R.J.H., Hendriksen, A.H.M., Jansen, H., Jansen, R.G.: The observer video–pro: new software for the collection, management, and presentation of time–structured data from videotapes and digital media files. Behav. Res. Meth. Instrum. Comput. **32**(1), 197–206 (3), 133–146 (2000)
15. Nouri, E., Park, S., Scherer, S., Gratch, J., Carnevale, P., Morency, L.P., Traum, D.R.: Prediction of strategy and outcome as negotiation unfolds by using basic verbal and behavioral features. In: 14th Annual Conference of the International Speech Communication Association (INTERSPEECH 2013), pp. 1458–1461. ISCA Archive, Lyon (2013)
16. Olekalns, M., Brett, J.M., Weingart, L.R.: Phases, transitions and interruptions: Modeling processes in multi–party negotiations. Int. J. Confl. Manage. **143**(3), 191–211 (2003)
17. Osgood, C.E., Suci, G.J.: Factor analysis of meaning. J. Exp. Psychol. **50**(5), 325 (1955)
18. Prager, K.J.: Intimacy in personal relationships. In: Hendrick, S., Hendrick, C. (eds.) Close Relationships, pp. 229–244. Sage, Thousand Oaks (2000)
19. Semnani-Azad, Z., Adair, W.L.: The display of dominant nonverbal cues in negotiation: the role of culture and gender. Int. Negot. **16**(3), 451–479 (2011)
20. Semnani–Azad, Z., Adair, W.L.: Watch Your Tone... Relational Paralinguistic Messages in Negotiation: The Case of East and West. Int. Stud. Manage. Organ. **43** (2013)
21. Tanaka, Y., Osgood, C.E.: Cross–culture, cross– concept, and cross–subject generality of affective meaning systems. J. Pers. Soc. Psychol. **56**, 143 (1965)
22. Triandis, H.C., Osgood, C.E.: A comparative factorial analysis of semantic structures in monolingual Greek and American college students. J. Abnorm. Psychol. **57**(2), 187 (1958)

23. Trout, D.L., Rosenfeld, H.M.: The effect of postural lean and body congruence on the judgment of psychotherapeutic rapport. J. Nonverbal Behav. **4**(3), 176–190 (1980)
24. Weingart, L.R., Bennett, R.J., Brett, J.M.: The impact of consideration of issues and motivational orientation on group negotiation process and outcome. J. Appl. Psychol. **78**(3), 504 (1993)

HCI and Natural Progression
of Context-Related Questions

Aggeliki Vlachostergiou[1]([✉]), George Caridakis[1,2],
Amaryllis Raouzaiou[1], and Stefanos Kollias[1]

[1] National Technical University of Athens, Iroon Polytexneiou 9,
15780 Zografou, Greece
{aggelikivl,gcari,araouz}@image.ntua.gr
[2] Department of Cultural Technology and Communication,
University of the Aegean, Lesvos, Greece
stefanos@cs.ntua.gr

Abstract. The ability of humans to effectively interact socially relies heavily on their awareness of the context the interaction takes place. In order for computer systems to accordingly possess the same ability, it is crucial they are also context-aware in terms of a formalization of context based on the W5+ framework aspects of Who, What, Why, Where, What and How. Research work presented in this paper contributes towards this goal by bridging the conceptual gap and exploiting semantics and cognitive and affective information of non verbal behavior and investigating whether and how this information could be incorporated in automatic analysis of affective behavior. A semantic concept extraction methodology is proposed and its application to indicative examples from the SEMAINE corpus is presented that validates the proposed approach.

Keywords: Human Computer Interaction · Affective Computing · Context awareness · Interaction context semantics extraction · SEMAINE

1 Introduction

One of the main challenges of recent years is to create more natural, sensitive and socially intelligent machines, that are not able only to communicate but also to understand social signals and make sense of the various social contextual settings [24]. Thus, besides communication through various channels and through verbal content (semantics), machines also need to be able to recognize, interpret, and process emotional information as humans. In human cognition, thinking and feeling are mutually present: emotions are often the product of our thoughts, as well as our reflections are often the product of our affective states. But, what does it mean to be socially intelligent when incorporating interaction context? So far, in natural conversations context awareness is defined as past visual information [10], general situational understanding [7], past verbal

---

G. Caridakis and A. Raouzaiou—These two authors contributed equally.

© Springer International Publishing Switzerland 2015
M. Kurosu (Ed.): Human-Computer Interaction, Part I, HCII 2015, LNCS 9169, pp. 530–541, 2015.
DOI: 10.1007/978-3-319-20901-2_50

information [13], cultural background [15], gender of the participants, knowledge of the general interaction setting in which an emotional phenomenon is taking place [4], discourse and social situations [2]. Accordingly, studies in intelligent Human-Computer interfaces (iHCI), which incorporate context, correspond to the following contextual aspects, known as W5+ formalization: Who you are with (e.g. dyadic/multiparty interactions [25]), What is communicated (e.g., (non)-linguistic message/conversational signal, and emotion), How the information is communicated (the person's affective cues), Why, i.e., in which context the information is passed on, Where the user is, What his current task is, How he/she feels (has his mood been polarized changing from negative to positive) and which (re)action should be taken to satisfy human's needs, goals and tasks [9].

Unfortunately, so far the efforts on human affective behavior understanding are usually context independent [12]. In light of these observations, understanding the process of a natural progression of context-related questions when people interact in a social environment could provide new insights into the mechanisms of their interaction context and affectivity. The "Who", "What", "Where" context-related questions have been mainly answered either separately or in groups of two or three using the information extracted from multimodal input streams [28]. Thus, as of date, no general W5+ formalizations exist, like the systems that answer to most of the "W" questions are founded on different psychological theories of emotion and they all fit specific purposes according to the goals of a particular research in various fields.

Recent research on progressing to the questions of "Why" and "How" has led to the emerging field of sentiment analysis [6,14,19], through mining opinions and sentiments from natural language, which involves a deep understanding of semantic rules proper of a language. Furthermore, the interpretation of cognitive and affective information associated with natural language and, hence, further inferring new knowledge and making decisions, in connection with one's social and emotional values and ideals, is of crucial importance. The problem when trying to emulate such cognitive and affective processes, is that while cognitive information is usually objective and unbiased, answering the "Why" context-related question through affective information is rather subjective and argumentative.

Under this view, our long-term goal is to understand whether and how context is incorporated in automatic analysis of human affective behavior and to propose a novel context-aware incorporation framework (Fig. 1) which (1): includes detection and extraction of semantic context concepts, (2): enriches better a number of Psychological Foundations with sentiment values and (3): enhances emotional models with context information and context concept representation in appraisal estimation, using publicly available on-line knowledge sources (OKS) in natural language processing [26]. As a first step in this work, we focus on bridging the gap at concept level by exploiting semantics cognitive and affective information, associated with the image verbal content (semantics), which for the needs of our research is the contextual interactional information between the user and the operator of the SEMAINE database [16], keeping fixed the "Where" context-related question. This context concept-based annotation method, that we are examining, allows the system to go beyond a mere syntactic analysis of the semantics associated with fixed window sizes[1]. In most of traditional annotation methods, emotions and contextual information are not always inferred by appraisals and thus contextual information about the causes of that emotion is not taken into account [8].

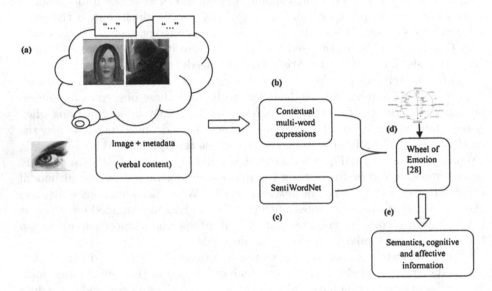

Fig. 1. System's Overview: **(a)** We discover semantic context concepts from verbal content (semantics) associated with SEMAINE dataset and **(b)** represent each one with multi-word expressions, enhanced with sentiment values **(c)**. A number of Psychological Foundations are enriched in terms of visuality **(d)**. We finally show that this proposed approach could show a clear connection between semantics, cognitive and affective information prediction **(e)**.

The structure of the paper is as follows: Sect. 2 discusses the challenges of existing emotion categorization models w.r.t. context concept semantic models; Sect. 3 details on the methodology that has been followed; Sect. 4 presents an analysis of the context-concept indicative examples generated from SEMAINE corpus; Sect. 5 discusses a number of suggestions to further enhance the framework's robustness and finally, Sect. 6 sets out conclusions and a description of future work.

2   Related Work

Emotions are complex states of feeling, resulting in physical and psychological reactions influencing both our thought and behavior. The study of emotions

---

[1] The window length corresponds to 16 conversational turns and is displayed on figures for future visualization purposes.

still remains an essential and open part of psychology. Of interest to Natural Language Processing (NLP) is being able to tell which emotion is expressed in the text. Predominantly, research on detecting emotions from text has focused on capturing emotion words based on three **emotion models**, i.e. categories of basic emotions, emotion dimensions and cognitive-appraisal categories, particularly the componential model [5,12].

Unlike the categorical and dimensional approaches, recently, increasingly attention has been dedicated to another set of psychological models, referred to as componential models of emotion, which are based on the appraisal theory and might be more appropriate for developing context-aware frameworks [18]. However, how to use the appraisal approach for automatic analysis of affect is an open research problem. In the componential models of emotion, various ways of linking automatic emotion analysis and appraisal models of emotion are proposed. This link aims to enable the addition of contextual information into automatic emotion analyzers, and enrich their interpretation capability in terms of a more sensitive and richer representation.

However, these emotional models have some limitations. Categorical approaches usually fail to describe the complex range of emotions that can occur in daily communication. Furthermore, the dimensional space neither allows to compare affect words according to their reciprocal distance, nor models the fact that two or more emotions might be experienced at the same time.

Particularly, a number of 2D-dimensional approaches are mainly used to **visualize Psychological Foundations**. An early example is Russell's circumplex model [21], which uses the dimensions of arousal and valence to plot 150 affective labels. Similarly, Whissell considers emotions as a continuous 2D space with evaluation and activation as dimensions [27]. Another bi-dimensional model is Plutchik's wheel of emotions [20], according to which emotions are adaptive as they are based on evolutionary principles, even though we conceive emotions as feeling states. These feeling states are part of a process involving both cognition and behavior and containing several feedback loops. Eventually, all such approaches work at word level, so they are unable to grasp the affective valence of multiple-word concepts.

However, since the above models currently focus on the objective inference of affective information when associated with natural language opinions, appraisal-based emotions are not taken into account. Nevertheless, in view of their suitability to context modeling, emphasis should be given on emotional models based on cognitive appraisal, which characterize emotional states in terms of detailed evaluation of emotions acquisition and especially implicit methods. For an extended overview on modeling affect, the reader is referred to [5,12].

Semantic context concepts. For a more applicable semantic context concept model, rather than a theoretical one such as the componential model, research has been focused on mining opinions and sentiments from natural language. This is challenging, as it requires a deep understanding of the explicit and implicit and semantic language rules, struggling with NLP's unresolved problems such as negation handling, named-entity recognition, word-sense disambiguation, etc. Concept-based approaches [23] aim to grasp the conceptual and affective information associated with natural language opinions. Additionally, concept-based approaches can analyze multi-word expressions that don't explicitly convey emotion, but are related to concepts doing so. For example, instead of gathering isolated opinions about a whole "event" (e.g. birthday party), users are generally more interested in comparing different events according to their specific set of semantically related concepts, e.g. "cake", "surprised friend", or "gift" (which can be considered as contextual information for improving search results), associated with a set of affectively related concepts, e.g. "celebration" or "special occasion". This taken-for-granted information referring to obvious things people normally know and usually leave uncommented, is necessary to properly deconstruct natural language text into sentiments. For example, the concept "small room" should be appraised as negative for a hotel review and "small queue" as positive for a post office, or the concept "go read the book" as positive for a book review but negative for a movie review.

3   Methodology

3.1   Corpus for Semantic Context Concepts Extraction

The model here is confronted with the SEMAINE corpus [16]. This corpus comprises manually-transcribed sessions where a human user interacts with a human operator acting the role of a virtual agent. These interactions are based on a scenario involving four agent characters: Poppy: happy and outgoing, Prudence: sensible and level-headed, Spike: angry and confrontational and Obadiah: depressive and gloomy. Agent's utterances are constrained by a script, however, some deviations to the script occur in the database.

3.2   Pre-processing

The pre-processing submodule firstly interprets all the affective valence indicators usually contained in the verbal content of transcriptions, such as special punctuation, complete upper-case words, exclamation words and negations. Handling negation is an important concern in such scenario, as it can reverse the meaning of the examined sentence. Secondly, it converts text to lower-case and, after lemmatizing it, splits the sentence into single clauses according to grammatical conjunctions and punctuation.

These n-grams are not used blindly as fixed word patterns but exploited as reference for the module, in order to extract multiple-word concepts from information-rich sentences. So, differently from other shallow parsers, the module can recognize complex concepts also when irregular verbs are used or when these are interspersed with adjective and adverbs, for example, the concept "buy easter present" in the sentence "I bought a lot of very nice Easter presents".

3.3 Semantic Context Concept Parser

The aim of the semantic parser is to break sentences into clauses and, hence, decon-struct such clauses into concepts. This deconstruction uses lexicons which are based on sequences of lexemes that represent multiple-word concepts extracted from Con-ceptNet, WordNet [17] and other linguistic resources.

Under this view, the Stanford Parser[2] has been used according to Python NLTK[3]; a general assumption during clause separation is that, if a piece of text contains a preposition or subordinating conjunction, the words preceding these function or are interpreted not as events but as objects. Secondly, dependency structure elements are processed by means of Stanford Lemmatizer for each sentence. Each potential noun chunk associated with individual verb chunks is paired with the stemmed verb in order to detect multi-word expressions of the form "verb plus object". The pos-based bigram algorithm extracts concepts, but in order to capture event concepts, matches between the object concepts and the normalized verb chunks are searched. It is important to build the dependency tree before lemmatization as swapping the two steps result in several imprecisions caused by the lower grammatical accuracy of lemmatized sentences. Each verb and its associated noun phrase are considered in turn, and of more concepts is extracted from these.

3.4 Opinion and Sentiment Lexicon

Current approaches to concept-level sentiment analysis mainly leverage on exist-ing affective knowledge bases such as ANEW [3], WordNet-Affect [22] and SentiWordNet [11]. However, for the needs of our current work, we use the Sen-tiWordNet, which is a concept-level opinion lexicon and contains multi-word expressions labeled by their polarity scores.

4   Research Findings

In this section, we present an analysis of context-concept indicative and repre-sentative but not exhaustive examples generated from SEMAINE coprus [16]. Additionally, we provide a list of the main research findings observed during the analysis.

The first example is extracted from **Session 70 for Prudence**, focusing to phrases [16–32] and [48–64]. During this interactional context, the discussion revolves round the context-related question: What is discussed? referring to the topic "holidays" and the topic "trip" in phrases [50–64]. The user is not inter-ested in the topic of "work" and thus says that the topic is boring. Throughout this interaction, both the operator and user have the same subjective opinions, as both of them repeat several times the words "excessive" and "absurd" refer-ring to the "trip" topic.

---

[2] http://nlp.stanford.edu:8080/parser/.
[3] http://nltk.org.

19 - Prudence: "And have you considered where you might go for holidays?"
20 - User: "(Looks around in thought). Ah yeah. I'm thinking about going to Australia."
...
56 - User: "(Nods smiling). That is absolutely absurd. I concur. (Looks around smiling). But it was... fantastic fun. Eh... four guys doing a road trip from Houston to New Orleans as well. Emm... Obviously myself included. (Licks lips). An... A lot of eating, a lot of drinking, a lot of not talking about research. It was fantastic."
57 - Prudence: "Well it sounds like it was an... excessive trip."
58 - User: "Very excessive."

The second example refer to **Spike operator role in Session 73**. Studying the phases 56–73, it is observed that the user is empathized by the operator. Multi-word expressions such as "that's a lot" and "piss me off" are highlighted. The user tells that he is often mistaken for an American, whereas he is Canadian and shows that he has been annoyed by this confusion. Taking into consideration that Spike's role is to make user angry, these expressions are employed as a way to reinforce user's annoyance.

56 - User: "Hmm... The world doesn't really think highly of Americans."
57 - Spike: "Yeah... But Canadians are just the same aren't they?"
...
72 - User: "That's a lot. (Smiles, nods)."
73 - Spike: "That would piss me off."

In Session 72, the Obadiah role, we identified a number of appraisal expressions. This finding is aligned with Obadiah's affective style. In this role, the operator expresses attitudes about life and about the user, which triggers short-distance repetitions. This is presented in phases [37–38] and [41–42], in which affect related words such as "happy", "feeling", "sad", "bored" and "interested" are highly repeated.

37 - Obadiah: "Life is hard sometimes."
38 - User: "(Nods). Life can suck sometimes. I agree."
...
41 - Obadiah: "Yeah. But you can't be cheery all the time."
42 - User: "(Shakes head). Oh God I'm not cheery (laughs).[...]"

Finally, **in Session 71, Poppy** in phases [24–32] due to her happy and outgoing operator character seems to be aligned with the user's sentences, providing feedback such as "hmh", or "yeah", but without repeating user's words.

24 - User: "Yeah it's... very fast. Very... high contact which I... tend to like. Emm... Haven't done it in a while so (smiling and wide eyed) I guess that makes me a bit sad."

25 - Poppy: "Ah..."
26 - User: "Emm... Yeah."

"What" is discussed: identifying the topic. Due to the fact that in SEMAINE corpus, in which only the user is a teller, the former occupies the 65,5 % of the total speech duration, hence, the speech activity is not equally distributed between the user and the operator. Additionally, in a more depth analysis, this phenomenon is also observed while computing the percentage of user's speech for all sessions corresponding to a specific operator's role. The speech activity percentages vary from 60,6 % for Obadiah (minimum) to 70,4 % for Prudence (maximum). However, that could be partially explained taken into account the role of personalities of the four agents (played by human operators). For example, Prudence is even-tempered sensible, making the user to talk more, while Obadiah's depressive mood may lead the user to talk less. On the contrary, as far as the role of Poppy, in the session 26, the happy operator asks to the user, "where is the best wake you ever had?". The user's answers "in a tent in kiliman- jaro". Here, the agent's question opens a new topic without completely defining it. It is the user's answer which chooses the new topic, but after following the indications given by the agent's questions.

"Why" and "How" he/she feels - context related questions: identifying the affective style and the sentiments of operators and users. Apart from the context interactional topic, the user's and operator's lexical and affec- tive style as well as the operator's role depend also on the type of the corpus. On the whole, it is expected that the specific vocabulary that is used corresponds to the 5 min interaction and to a restrained vocabulary specific to the **opera- tor's** role and to its linguistic style respectively. Examining the most frequent words used by the depressive Obadiah ("miserable", "suffering", "disappointed") and by Poppy ("excellent", "cool", "exciting", "happiness") is observed that it is possible to extract information for the affective style of each operator role. On the whole, with regard to the operator's identity, the expressions of affect are more numerous, excepting for the Prudence sessions. This is probably, due to the Prudence's personality that the operators have to play: a sensible and level-headed person who expresses appraisals about the user's behavior and asks the user to express attitudes about specific things. Furthermore, for the role of Spike, we found that the most frequent words used (Table 1), such as "fool" and "annoyed", incorporated a more offensive affective style, probably due to the fact that when the operator playing Spike is offending the user, the former sometimes repeats operator's words.

On the other hand, for SEMAINE **users**, the most frequent words corre- spond to different topics and users lexical opinions or topics of their corpus, are defined by specific adverbs and include words such as "weekend", "holiday", that are indicative of the discussed topic. Consequently, the user's sentiments are in accordance to the type of agent played by the operator. As expected, Poppy and Prudence sessions express affective information with negative sentiments. Finally, the distribution is more balanced concerning Spike.

Table 1. Top ranked words (score > 0.025) in SEMAINE coprus

word	score	operator role	word	score	user
miserable	0.02561	Obadiah	bloody	0.03224	2
excellent	0.02579	Prudence	beautiful	0.09622	9
fool	0.03250	Spike	shipped	0.02506	11
annoyed	0.03123	Spike	hang	0.02506	11
excellent	0.03417	Poppy	language	0.03233	12
aha	0.03379	Poppy	room	0.04196	16

5   Discussion

Gradually, the new multi-disciplinary area that lies at the crossroads between Affective Computing, Human-Computer Interaction (HCI), social sciences, linguistics, psychology and context awareness is distinguishing itself as a separate field. It is thus possible to better recognize, interpret and process opinions and sentiments, incorporate contextual information and finally to understand the related ethical issues about the nature of mind and the creation of emotional machines. For applications in fields such as real-time HCI and big social data analysis [1], deep natural language understanding is not strictly required: a sense of the semantics associated with text and some extra information (affect) associated with such semantics are often sufficient to quickly perform tasks such as emotion recognition and cognitive and affective information detection.

We have illustrated a method for extracting context concept aspects from SEMAINE corpus interaction. The proposed framework only leverages on any taken-for-granted information. By allowing sentiments to flow from multi-word concept to multi-word concept, we could possibly achieve a better understanding of the contextual role of each concept within the sentence.

As far as the selection of the corpus is concerned, on which the experiments will be performed every time, the new trend is the collection of data in real time through new sources of opinion mining and sentiment analysis which abound. Webcams installed in smartphones, touchpads, or other devices let users post opinions in an audio or audiovisual format rather than in text. Aside from converting spoken language to written text for analysis, the audiovisual format provides an opportunity to mine opinions and sentiment. Many new areas might be useful in opinion mining, such as facial expression, body movement. Affect analysis, a related field, addresses the use of linguistic, acoustic and (potentially) video information. This field focuses on a broader set of emotions or the estimation of continuous emotion primitives; for example, valence can be related to sentiment.

Furthermore, as far as the presence and the position of the multi-word concepts in the text unit, further examination is necessary, as typically bi-grams and tri-grams, are often taken into account as useful features. Some methods also rely on the distance between terms. Part-of-speech (POS) information (nouns, adjectives, adverbs, verbs, etc.) is also commonly exploited in general textual analysis as a basic form of word sense disambiguation. Certain adjectives, in particular, have been proved to be good indicators of sentiment and sometimes have been used to guide feature selection for sentiment classification. In other works, the detection of sentiments was performed through selected phrases, which were chosen via a number of pre-specified POS patterns, most including an adjective or an adverb. However, such approaches and their performance are strictly bound to the considered domain of application and to the related topics.

Finally, most of the literature on sentiment analysis has focused on text written in English and, consequently, most resources developed, e.g., sentiment lexicons, are in English. Adapting such resources to other languages should be seriously considered as the choice of words and their intended meaning are personally, contextually, culturally and socially dependent and differ on the level of the different expertise and purposes of tagging users, resulting many times in tags that use various levels of abstraction to describe a resource.

6   Conclusions

Technology has the potential to investigate how to tackle the issues of context awareness of Human-Computer analysis and to progress towards real-world affect analysis. In this work, we attempted to automatically detect semantic concepts, and broad the scope of affect analysis both quantitatively (identify and describe more (non)-emotional states) and qualitatively (enrich the contextual information content by establishing links with contextual appraisal determinants, cognitive and affective information). We would like to emphasize that our findings are clearly preliminary with inevitable limitations. Probably the main limitation is the absence of a more appropriate corpus.

Our future research work will concentrate on further refinement of the existing corpora w.r.t. their productivity and reproducibility. These indicative but not exhaustive results provide the insight of the effectiveness of our proposed framework for the automatic recognition of spontaneous affective states in a human-agent interaction scenario based on nonverbal behavior and contextual information and provides additionally an important contribution to research on affect recognition "in the wild". Future work, will involve exploration of re-evaluation of objective words in SentiWordNet by assessing the sentimental relevance of such words and their associated sentiment sentences. In addition, work will be undertaken exploring the proposed method in a fully unsupervised method, depending only on the accuracy of the context-concept parser and the sentiments, rather than training the SEMAINE corpus, along with using an enhanced set of rules and opinion lexicon.

Acknowledgements. This research has been co-financed by the European Union (European Social Fund ESF) and Greek national funds through the Operational Program "Education and Lifelong Learning" of the National Strategic Reference Framework (NSRF) - Research Funding Program: Thales. Investing in knowledge society through the European Social Fund.

References

1. Akerkar, R.: Big Data Computing. CRC Press, New York (2013)
2. Bock, R., Wendemuth, A., Gluge, S., Siegert, I.: Annotation and classification of changes of involvement in group conversation. In: Proceedings of the Humaine Association Conference on Affective Computing and Intelligent Interaction, pp. 803–808. IEEE (2013)
3. Bradley, M.M., Lang, P.J.: Affective norms for english words (anew): instruction manual and affective ratings. Technical report C-1, The Center for Research in Psychophysiology, University of Florida (1999)
4. Brown, P.J., Bovey, J.D., Chen, X.: Context-aware applications: from the laboratory to the marketplace. Pers. Commun. 4(5), 58–64 (1997)
5. Calvo, R.A., D'Mello, S.: Affect detection: an interdisciplinary review of models, methods, and their applications. IEEE Trans. Affect. Comput. 1(1), 18–37 (2010)
6. Cambria, E., Hussain, A., Havasi, C., Eckl, C.: SenticSpace: visualizing opinions and sentiments in a multi-dimensional vector space. In: Setchi, R., Jordanov, I., Howlett, R.J., Jain, L.C. (eds.) KES 2010, Part IV. LNCS, vol. 6279, pp. 385–393. Springer, Heidelberg (2010)
7. Carroll, J.M., Russell, J.A.: Do facial expressions signal specific emotions? judging emotion from the face in context. J. Pers. Soc. Psychol. 70(2), 205 (1996)
8. Castellano, G., Caridakis, G., Camurri, A., Karpouzis, K., Volpe, G., Kollias, S.: Body gesture and facial expression analysis for automatic affect recognition. In: Scherer, K.R., Bänziger, T., Roesch, E.B. (eds.) Blueprint for Affective Computing: A Sourcebook, pp. 245–255. Oxford University Press, New York (2010)
9. Duric, Z., Gray, W.D., Heishman, R., Li, F., Rosenfeld, A., Schoelles, M.J., Schunn, C., Wechsler, H.: Integrating perceptual and cognitive modeling for adaptive and intelligent human-computer interaction. Proc. IEEE 90(7), 1272–1289 (2002)
10. El Kaliouby, R., Robinson, P., Keates, S.: Temporal context and the recognition of emotion from facial expression. In: Proceedings of the HCI International Conference, pp. 631–635. American Psychological Association (2003)
11. Esuli, A., Sebastiani, F.: Sentiwordnet: a publicly available lexical resource for opinion mining. In: Proceedings of the 5th Conference on Language Resources and Evaluation, LREC 2006, vol. 6, pp. 417–422 (2006)
12. Gunes, H., Schuller, B.: Categorical and dimensional affect analysis in continuous input: current trends and future directions. Image Vis. Comput. 31(2), 120–136 (2013)
13. Knudsen, H.R., Muzekari, L.H.: The effects of verbal statements of context on facial expressions of emotion. J. Nonverbal Behav. 7(4), 202–212 (1983)
14. Liu, B.: Sentiment analysis and opinion mining. Synth. Lect. Hum. Lang. Technol. 5(1), 1–167 (2012)
15. Masuda, T., Ellsworth, P.C., Mesquita, B., Leu, J., Tanida, S., Van de Veerdonk, E.: Placing the face in context: cultural differences in the perception of facial emotion. J. Pers. Soc. Psychol. 94(3), 365 (2008)
16. McKeown, G., Valstar, M., Cowie, R., Pantic, M., Schroder, M.: The semaine database: annotated multimodal records of emotionally colored conversations between a person and a limited agent. IEEE Trans. Affect. Comput. 3(1), 5–17 (2012)
17. Miller, G.A.: Wordnet: a lexical database for english. Commun. ACM 38(11), 39–41 (1995)
18. Mortillaro, M., Meuleman, B., Scherer, K.R.: Advocating a componential appraisal model to guide emotion recognition. Int. J. Synth. Emot. (IJSE) 3(1), 18–32 (2012)

19. Pang, B., Lee, L.: Opinion mining and sentiment analysis. Found. Trends Inform. Retrieval **2**(1–2), 1–135 (2008)
20. Plutchik, R.: The nature of emotions human emotions have deep evolutionary roots, a fact that may explain their complexity and provide tools for clinical practice. Am. Sci. **89**(4), 344–350 (2001)
21. Russell, J.A.: Affective space is bipolar. J. Pers. Soc. Psychol. **37**(3), 345 (1979)
22. Strapparava, C., Valitutti, A., et al.: Wordnet affect: an affective extension of wordnet. In: LREC, vol. 4, pp. 1083–1086 (2004)
23. Tsai, A.C.R., Wu, C.E., Tsai, R.T.H., Hsu, J.Y., et al.: Building a concept-level sentiment dictionary based on commonsense knowledge. IEEE Intell. Syst. **28**(2), 22–30 (2013)
24. Vinciarelli, A., Pantic, M., Bourlard, H.: Social signal processing: survey of an emerging domain. Image Vis. Comput. **27**, 1743–1759 (2009)
25. Vlachostergiou, A., Caridakis, G., Kollias, S.: Context in affective multiparty and multimodal interaction: why, which, how and where? In: Workshop on Understanding and Modeling Multiparty, Multimodal Interactions (UMMMI 2014), pp. 3–8 (2014)
26. Vlachostergiou, A., Caridakis, G., Kollias, S.: Investigating context awareness of affective computing systems: a critical approach. In: 6th International Conference on Intelligence Human Computer Interaction (IHCI 2014) (2014)
27. Whissell, C.: The dictionary of affect in language. Emot. Theory, Res. Experience **4**, 113–131, 94 (1989)
28. Zeng, Z., Pantic, M., Roisman, G.I., Huang, T.S.: A survey of affect recognition methods: audio, visual, and spontaneous expressions. IEEE Trans. Pattern Anal. Mach. Intell. **31**(1), 39–58 (2009)

Emotional Engagement for Human-Computer Interaction in Exhibition Design

Mengting Zhang[✉], Cees de Bont, and Wenhua Li

School of Design, The Hong Kong Polytechnic University, Hong Kong, China
{mickey.mengting.zhang,vivian.lee8686}@gmail.com,
Cees.debont@polyu.edu.hk

Abstract. Research of human-computer interaction in exhibition design previously focuses more on how technologies could be used to create splendid effect or impressive experience [1], rather than to interwoven technology with metaphoric, intuitive and narrative content. While in socio-cultural exhibition, the communication of meaning and knowledge itself is more emphasized. Besides, emotional engagement, which could evoke memory, feelings and cognition, could be an important method for HCI in exhibition design. However, less study has explored this area. In this article, the potentials of emotional engagement for HCI in exhibition design are outlined through a project in Shek Kip Mei district in Hong Kong. The project have three stages: documentation, abstraction and conceptualization. It represents one possible flow that could generate emotional engagement from the socio-cultural contents for visitors. The experience gained from this project could facilitate designers, planners, museum curators and academic researchers in creating emotional engaged exhibition.

Keywords: Emotion trigger · Interaction design in exhibition

1 Introduction

1.1 Human Side of HCI

Human-computer interaction concerns the communication between human and machine. Therefore it "draws supporting knowledge on both sides. On the machine side, techniques in computer graphics, operating systems, programming languages, and development environments are relevant. On the human side, communication theory, graphic and industrial design disciplines, linguistics, social sciences, cognitive psychology, and human performance are relevant. And, of course, human aspects such as emotions and feelings become relevant as well" [2]. However, the main stream HCI before emphasizes more on the machine side relating to science, technology and engineering. It is till recent decade, more focus shifts to human side, including design based on user behavior, context of using, socio-cultural factors, as well as experience [3]. HCI design is further identified in "multiple levels simultaneously - as technological artifacts, social facts, and cultural narratives" [4].

© Springer International Publishing Switzerland 2015
M. Kurosu (Ed.): Human-Computer Interaction, Part I, HCII 2015, LNCS 9169, pp. 542–549, 2015.
DOI: 10.1007/978-3-319-20901-2_51

1.2 HCI for Exhibition Design

The shift of HCI from machine side to human side has also affected exhibition and museum design. HCI is no longer only recognized as advanced technological means, which brings fancy eye-catching effects without actual meaning. It is applied in the development of narrative, emotional and educational contents, which could facilitate more complex learning process. As learning is a dynamic process of acquiring information, knowledge and skills, HCI enables actively and socially engagement in knowledge building than passively reception [5]. Information and knowledge could be visualized, documented and communicated through exploration and interaction by various means, such as touch, vision, sound and smell [6, 7]. This process could be explained explicitly by Perry (1993)'s theory: physical engagement with exhibits ("hands-on"), intellectual engagement ("minds-on"), emotional engagement (affective reactions), and social engagement (e.g., discussion among visitors) [8]. Among all of the types of engagement, this paper mainly focuses on emotional engagement.

1.3 Emotional Engagement of HCI

Emotion is difficult to articulate and study as a result of its "context, volatile and ephemeral" attributes [9]. Emotional responses occur as a result of our reptilian and mammalian brains' quickly function. It is called immediate "impressions and associations" [10]. Therefore, human is able to perceive and react to the overall virtual environments that they are situated, while specifically response to single sound, image, emoticons, and word simultaneously [10]. Since emotions, such as pleasure and fun have become important research topics within HCI fields [11], designers put more efforts in embedding emotional and metaphoric content with real objects, interface, and systems through combination of visual, audio, and physical experience [12]. By observing and experiment, designers understand how users build intuitive knowledge of the world by interacting with daily objects via watching, touching, playing, recognizing or perceiving and how they attach emotions and sensations to them [2]. Therefore, designers can create contents, which line up experience with emotional response more naturally and intuitively. One of the methods that used to evoke emotions is metaphor, as feelings are hard to interpret in words [2]. Metaphors could influence its users by tapping "into cultural, historic and emotional knowledge that we humans have built up in the course of our lives" [2]. Rokeby (1997) stated the effect of metaphor as it "borrows cliché's from the culture but then reflects them back and reinforces them [13]. Hence, metaphors could be generated from socio-cultural knowledge that users are familiar with and the familiarity may trigger intense emotional response. This paper describes the process that how we uses local contents of Shek Kip Mei in Hong Kong to create metaphors in HCI for exhibition design, which encourage emotional engagement of visitors.

1.4   Shek Kip Mei Project

Shek Kip Mei (SKM) is a district in Hong Kong, where the first public housing programme was launched for the resettlement of refugees. The project is located in the first and only survival building of the programme in the region of SKM. It aims to recreate socio-cultural scenario in an exhibition that illustrates the daily life, living environment, tradition and the close bond of inhabitants around this unique spatial morphology. It also provides an insight to the social, economic, and cultural condition of Hong Kong from 1950s to1970s. The SKM project lasts for about one year from briefing to the opening. Multidisciplinary parties collaborate for it, including scholars, inhabitants, government officers, social organizations, designers, and IT specialists, etc.

2   Methods

In Mignonneau and Sommerer (2005)'s study, they identified a few questions that should be asked before creating emotional, intuitive and metaphoric interaction experience. These questions serve as important clues for the SKM project. The main purpose of the exhibition is for education, commemoration and heritage preservation. It allows non-trained visitors of different ages, social backgrounds and cultural knowledge to access with ease (Table 1).

Table 1. Clues for SKM exhibition design

Questions [2]	Clues
1. Which emotion or sensation do I want to convey?	Reminiscence, memorable, optimistic, hopeful
2. What do I want the user to feel when experiencing this system?	Interesting, natural, intuitive, enlighten, happy
3. What is the cultural and historic background of the user?	Hong Kong resident and international travelers
4. What is the emotional and metaphoric knowledge already available to the user?	The socio-cultural status of SKM
5. What kind of object or interface can convey this desired emotion or sensation?	Touch screen, projector, sensor, audio, video, and image
6. Which interface would feel most natural and most intuitive to the user?	Gesture Control, static display

The design process could be divided into three stages, including documentation of information and knowledge, abstraction of representative elements, and conceptualization of metaphoric scenario. The three stages are illustrated with a diagram below (Fig. 1).

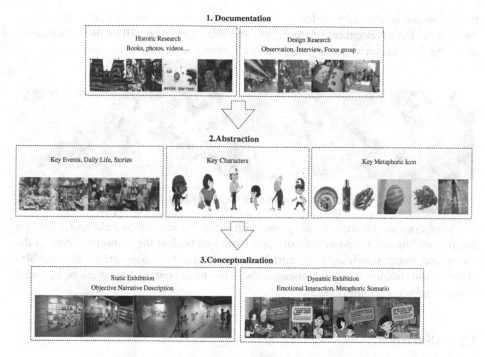

Fig. 1. Stages of emotional engagement HCI design

2.1   Documentation

As the aim of the project is to design emotional engagement between visitors and SKM socio-cultural heritage, the content requires certain level of accuracy and clarity to reflect the history. Therefore, at the beginning of the project, large amount of time is spent on the organization of various sources of data and information. Books, photos, videos, and documentaries relevant to SKM are collected and reviewed (Fig. 2).

Fig. 2. Historic research

New information is generated from observation, interview and focus group with the help of Housing Authority, the Hong Kong government department and local inhabitants, social organizations and scholars. Researchers pay six visits to SKM to observe local environment, architectural features, and daily life of inhabitants. Their findings are captured by photos, videos, and memos, which are analyzed in data form.

Interviews are conducted with local inhabitants to generate personal perspective about the history, the development of the region and life experience. All of the information, data, and facts acquired are organized and classified according to categories.

Fig. 3. Interview, observation and focus group of local participants

After documentation, a focus group with sixty participants is held to review the documented materials and give feedbacks. Participants clear the ambiguity, correct the errors and share new insights to enrich the contents. The focus group also enables different stakeholders to reach consensus about the main content that would be included in the exhibition design (Fig. 3).

2.2   Abstraction

In abstraction stage, the documented materials are further consolidated as key events, important figures, high frequent daily activities, and stories (Fig. 4). Together they form a chain in timeline, which reflect the significant changes in the socio-cultural life of the region.

Fig. 4. Events, daily life and stories

Among all of the stories and important events, several symbolic characters and metaphoric icons are abstracted. The characteristics include a firefighter, a housewife, a girl, an engineer, an old lady, and a traveler (Fig. 5). The metaphoric icons include iron frog, plastic flower, thermos bottle, washbowl, plastic ball, and jump house games, etc. (Fig. 6). These symbolic characters and metaphoric icons are abstracted as a result of highly relevance with key events and activities happen in 1950s–1970s. For instance, the firefighter appears in the storyline of the major fire in 1952, which led to the introduction of the first public housing programme in Hong Kong. While as most of SKM families live in a poor condition, housewives bear the burden of bred children as well as make money simultaneously. Therefore homemade plastic flower by housewives is very popular at that time. Many young children help their mother to make plastic flower, while they also enjoy outdoor games, such as jump house. A large portion of visitors may share similar memories, which could be recalled by the characters, icons, stories, and scenarios. This synergy could evoke emotional connection between visitor and the exhibits, also among visitors themselves. It arouses their empathy for the hard life, and inspire them with the persistency and optimisticism of inhabitants to conquer difficulty. If visitors do not know any background information about the exhibition, they may be curious about who and what they are. Both types of emotional engagement would reinforce the visiting experience.

Fig. 5. Key characters

Fig. 6. Key metaphoric icons

2.3 Conceptualization

At the stage of conceptualization, two forms of exhibition are discussed and confirmed: static exhibition and dynamic exhibition. The materials abstracted from the second stage are classified again in line with their nature to match with the two types of exhibition. The objective facts, figures, events are elaborated in static exhibition by narrative description, heritage artifact demonstration, video and photo display, full size realization and installation of living situation (Fig. 7). For instance, the timeline presents the development of SKM district since 1950s till now. The concrete pipe which is recycled from site are resituated in the exhibition to play documentary. The underline metaphor is that children before used concrete pipe as their playground for hide and seek. While the subjective stories, symbolic characters, and metaphoric icons are interwoven into the dynamic HCI exhibition (Fig. 8). Projector, sensors and touchscreens are applied to create an immersive environment and emotional experience for visitors. Based on the characters and icons abstracted at the second stages, several stories, activities are created to represent the daily life in SKM. For instance, how neighbors help each other in hard time, etc.

Fig. 7. Static exhibition

Fig. 8. Dynamic exhibition

3 Discussion

The SKM project attracts thousands of Hong Kong residents, travelers, and students to visit each year after its opening. Many middle aged and elder visitors reflect that the exhibition contents conveyed accurate, resourceful and meaningful information and knowledge, which is educational and memorable. The HCI design is very popular among young people, as it is interesting, attractive and thought-provoking. Young children cherish the better life they have today. The design process that this paper presents includes three stages: documentation, abstraction, and conceptualization. The process could also be applied in other socio-cultural HCI design project.

References

1. Dirk, V.L., Christian, H., Jonathan, O.: Interaction and interactivities: collaboration and participation with computer-base exhibits. Public Underst. Sci. **14**(1), 91–101 (2005)
2. Laurent, M., Christa, S.: Designing emotional, metaphoric, natural and intuitive interfaces for interactive art, edutainment and mobile communications. Comput. Graph. **29**, 837–851 (2005)
3. Buxton, W.: Less is more (more or less): some thoughts on the design of computers and the future. In: Denning, P. (ed.) The Invisible Future: The Seamless Integration of Technology in Everyday Life. McGraw Hill, New York (2001)
4. Boehner, K., DePaula, R., Dourish, P., Sengers, P.: Affect: from information to interaction. In: Proceedings of the 4th Decennial Conference on Critical Computing, pp. 59–68. ACM, Aarhus (2005)
5. Hooper-greenhill, E., Moussouri, T.: Researching Learning in Museums and Galleries: A Bibliographic Review. RCMG, Leicester (2002)
6. Kristin, K., Eva, M., Carmen, Z., Stephan, S., Friedrich, W.H.: Computer support for knowledge communication in science exhibitions: novel perspectives from research on collaborative learning. Edu. Res. Rev. **4**, 196–209 (2009)
7. Shamsidar, A., Mohamed, Y.A., Mohd, Z.T., Mawar, M.: Museum exhibition design: communication of meaning and the shaping of knowledge. Procedia – Soc. Behav. Sci. **153**, 254–265 (2014)
8. Perry, D.: Designing exhibits that motivate. In: Borun, M., Grinell, S., McNamara, P., Serrell, B. (eds.) What Research Says About Learning in Science Museums, vol. 2, pp. 25–29. Association of Science-Technology Centers (ASTC), Washington, DC (1993)
9. Hassenzahl, M.: Emotions can be quite ephemeral; we cannot design them. Interactions **11**, 46–48 (2004)
10. Trevor, V., Edie, A.: Design for Emotion. Morgan Kaufman, Massachusetts (2012)
11. Monk, A., Hassenzahl, M., Blythe, M., Reed, D.: Funology: designing enjoyment. SIGCHI Bull.: Suppl. Interactions, 11 (2002)
12. Dinkla, S.: Pioniere interaktiver Kunst von 1970 bis heute: Hatje Cantz Ostfildern (1997)
13. Rokeby, D.: Constructing experience. In: Dodsworth, C. (ed.) Digital Illusions. Addison-Wesley, New York (1997)

Author Index

Printed in the United States
By Bookmasters